PEARSON BACCALAUREATE

Economics

DAVID FINAMORE

SERIES EDITOR: CHRISTIAN BRYAN

Supporting every learner across the IB continuum

essentials

Published by Pearson Education Limited,
Edinburgh Gate, Harlow, Essex, CM20 2JE.

www.pearsonglobalschools.com

Text © Pearson Education Limited 2014

Edited by Fern Labram, Abi Saffrey and Claire Annals
Proofread by Claire Annals and Sarah Lustig
Typeset and project managed by Cambridge Publishing Management Limited

The right of David Finamore to be identified as author of this work has been asserted by him in accordance with the Copyright, Designs and Patents Act 1988.

First published 2014

20 19 18 17

IMP 10 9 8 7 6 5 4 3 2

British Library Cataloguing in Publication Data
A catalogue record for this book is available from the British Library

ISBN 978 1 447 95037 0
eBook only ISBN 978 1 447 95038 7

Printed in Slovakia by Neografia

Acknowledgements
The authors and publisher would like to thank Ellen Vriniotis of ACS Athens, Rizma Rizwan of City and Islington College, Ellen Dittmar of Western Academy of Beijing, Susanna Joachim of Nymphenburger Schulen, Kania Grazyna of 33 Liceum IMM Kopernika, Sami Sorvali of Kannas School, Diane Howlett of Szczecin International School, Brian Hull of AIS Kuwait, Jacques Weber of British International School of Jeddah, Adrianna Anderson of International Community School, and Michael Ashleman of Wellington, for their invaluable help in the development of this series by piloting the concept material.

With thanks to the EAL reviewer Baljit Nijjar and the subject specialist Graham Mallard, for their helpful and constructive advice that greatly improved the clarity and accuracy of the text.

The author and publisher would like to thank the following individuals and organisations for permission to reproduce their data and illustrations:

Figures
Figure on page 253 copyright © World Family Organization, http://www.worldfamilyorganization.org; Figure on page 259 adapted from http://hdr.undp.org/sites/default/files/Country-Profiles/PAK.pdf, United Nations with permission; Figure on page 259 adapted from http://hdr.undp.org/sites/default/files/reports/14/hdr2013_en_complete.pdf, United Nations with permission.

Inside front cover: **Shutterstock.com:** Dmitry Lobanov

Tables
Table on page 113 adapted from http://www.bea.gov/, Source: U.S. Bureau of Economic Analysis; Table on page 188 adapted from http:www.imf.org/external/pubs/ft/fandd/basics/target.html, IMF; Table on page 256 adapted from https://www.cia.gov/library/publications/the-world-factbook/ IMF; Table on page 257 adapted from http://hdr.undp.org/sites/default/files/reports/14/hdr2013_en_ complete.pdf, United Nations with permission; Table on page 257 adapted from United Nations Human Development Report 2011, United Nations with permission; Table on page 258 adapted from http://www.tradingeconomics.com/pakistan/gdp, www.tradingeconomics.com with permission; Table on page 274 adapted from http://www.oecd.org/dac/stats/documentupload/MLI.JPG,© OECD, 2011/12; Table on page 274 adapted from http://www.oecd.org/dac/stats/documentupload/BGD.JPG, © OECD

Every effort has been made to trace the copyright holders and we apologise in advance for any unintentional omissions. We would be pleased to insert the appropriate acknowledgment in any subsequent edition of this publication.

Websites
Pearson Education Limited is not responsible for the content of any external internet sites. It is essential for tutors to preview each website before using it in class so as to ensure that the URL is still accurate, relevant and appropriate. We suggest that tutors bookmark useful websites and consider enabling students to access them through the school/college intranet.

The assessment criteria, level descriptors, learning outcomes and command terms have been reproduced from IBO documents. Our thanks go to the International Baccalaureate Organization for permission to reproduce its intellectual copyright.

The material has been developed independently by the publisher and the content is in no way connected with or endorsed by the International Baccalaureate (IB). International Baccalaureate® is a registered trademark of the International Baccalaureate Organization.

Dedications
To Rosemary, Emma and Chloe

Contents

Introduction

Welcome to your Essentials Guide to Economics. This book has been designed to solve the key problems of many Diploma students:

- relating material you have been taught to the syllabus goals and outcomes
- remembering it from one lesson to the next
- recalling it months later in an exam situation
- demonstrating your understanding of it in an exam situation within a strict time limit.

Who should use Essentials Guides?

Essentials Guides have been carefully designed with all IB (International Baccalaureate) students in mind as they serve as highly effective summaries and revision guides.

However, they have also been created with the particular interests in mind of IB **students whose first language is not English**, and who would like further support. As a result, the content in all Essentials Guides has been edited by an EAL (English as an additional language) expert to make sure that the language used is clear and accessible, key terms are explained, and essential vocabulary is defined and reinforced.

Key features of an Essentials Guide

Reduced content: Essentials guides are not intended to be comprehensive textbooks – they contain the essential information you need to understand and respond to each Learning Outcome (LO) published in the IB subject guide. This allows you to understand, review, and revise material quickly and still be confident you are meeting the essential aims of the syllabus. The content is precise and to the point. We have reduced the number of words as much as possible to ensure everything you read has a clear meaning, is clearly related to the LO, and will help you in an exam.

Format and approach: The content of the book is organized according to the Learning Outcomes (LOs). Each LO is looked at separately, which allows you to use the book as a first-text, or a revision guide, or as a way to help you understand material you have been given from other sources. The content is explained as clearly as possible, and you can be sure the information relates directly to the LOs.

Sub-headings: The pages are organized using logical sub-headings to help you understand the most important points of the LO. This organization also provides you with a guide on what an effective exam answer might look like. The sub-headings can be used to help you during revision, as a planning model before you start writing your answer, or for the actual answer to help you focus the examiner on how you are addressing the question.

Model sentences: These summarize key concepts so that you gain a clearer understanding of them. They are examples of the sort of sentences you could use in an exam. Set out below are a few examples:

> Model sentence: **If MR > MC increasing output increases profit, if MC > MR reducing output increases profit therefore profit is maximized where MR = MC.**

> Model sentence: **A change in a non-price determinant of demand or supply causes the market to be in disequilibrium at the original equilibrium price. Price must change in order to eliminate the excess demand or excess supply and continues to change until the market clears at the new equilibrium price and equilibrium quantity.**

> Model sentence: **In the long-run firms enter the industry when economic profit is positive and some existing firms exit when economic profit is negative thereby altering market supply until P = ATC and restoring the long-run position under perfect competition where only normal profit is made.**

Trouble shooters: These are step-by-step guides aimed at helping you to answer a question or complete a calculation. Two examples are set out below:

Explain how market failure is caused by imperfect information – a step-by-step guide

Trouble shooter

When suppliers have negative information about a good that is not shared with the consumers **marginal private benefit** will be greater than **marginal social benefit**.

The **market equilibrium** is socially inefficient because marginal social cost is greater than **marginal social benefit** meaning that the cost of the **resources** used to produce the next unit is greater than the benefit society gains from the **consumption** of it.

There is a **misallocation of resources**: too many resources are allocated to the production of the good so price and output are too high.

When consumers have all the information **demand** falls and **market failure** caused by asymmetric information is corrected.

Consumers now have all the information and place a lower value on the consumption of the next unit. Price, output and consumption fall. Fewer resources are now allocated to the production of the good.

The **social optimum equilibrium** is achieved where MSB = MSC.

Calculations of AP and MP – a step-by-step guide

Trouble shooter

Add the first worker. Quantity of workers changes from 0 to 1 and output changes from 0 to 4:
AP = TP/V = 4/1 = 4
MP = ΔTP/ΔV = (4 – 0)/(1 – 0) = 4/1 = 4 units

Add the next worker. Quantity of workers changes from 1 to 2 and output increases from 4 to 9 units:
AP = TP/V = 9/2= 4.5 units
MP = ΔTP/ΔV = (9 – 4)/(2 – 1) = 5/1 = 5 units

Add the next worker. Quantity of workers changes from 2 to 3. Output changes from 9 to 15 units:
AP = TP/V = 15/3 = 5 units
MP = ΔTP/ΔV = (15 – 9)/(3 – 2) = 6/1 = 6 units

Add one more worker. Quantity of workers changes from 3 to 4. Output changes from 15 to 20 units:
AP = TP/V = 20/4 = 5 units
MP = ΔTP/ΔV = (20 – 15)/(5 – 4) = 5/1 = 5 units

Vocabulary and synonym boxes: These are included to help identify and support your understanding of subject-specific and difficult words. These useful words and phrases are colour-coded in the margins. We have avoided using a highly academic tone, which is often found in many textbooks, in order to make the text more accessible to students whose first language is not English. However, at the same time we have ensured that the complexity of the content is at the level required by successful Diploma students, and so the key subject-specific vocabulary needed is highlighted in a separate box.

Glossary

assembly line an arrangement of workers and machines in a factory along which the good being made passes from one operation to the next until the good is completed

elite a group of people with a high level of power/influence because they have money/knowledge/skills

Internal Assessment section: This is intended to help you gain excellent marks for your IAs. It contains advice on choosing an article and writing your first draft. There is also a detailed explanation on how to gain maximum marks under each of the IB assessment criteria that includes examples of economic analysis and evaluation to show you what the examiners are looking for.

Extended Essay section: This contains lots of advice on how to complete your EE successfully. You will find advice on choosing an essay title and on how to present your essay in a formal and academic way. There is a detailed explanation of how to gain maximum marks for each of the IB assessment criteria. There is also advice on how to write an email requesting help from an outside source, how to reference books and articles, and how to write up your bibliography.

In the accompanying eBook you will find a complete digital version of the book. There are also links to spoken audio files of the model sentences and vocabulary terms and definitions, to help with comprehension and pronunciation. In addition, all the vocabulary lists are located together as downloadable files.

Above all, we hope this book helps you to understand, consolidate, and revise your course content more easily than ever, helping you to achieve the highest possible result in your exams.

David Finamore

How to use your enhanced eBook

Jump to any page

Switch from single- to double-page view

Highlight parts of the text

Create notes

Search the whole book

Zoom

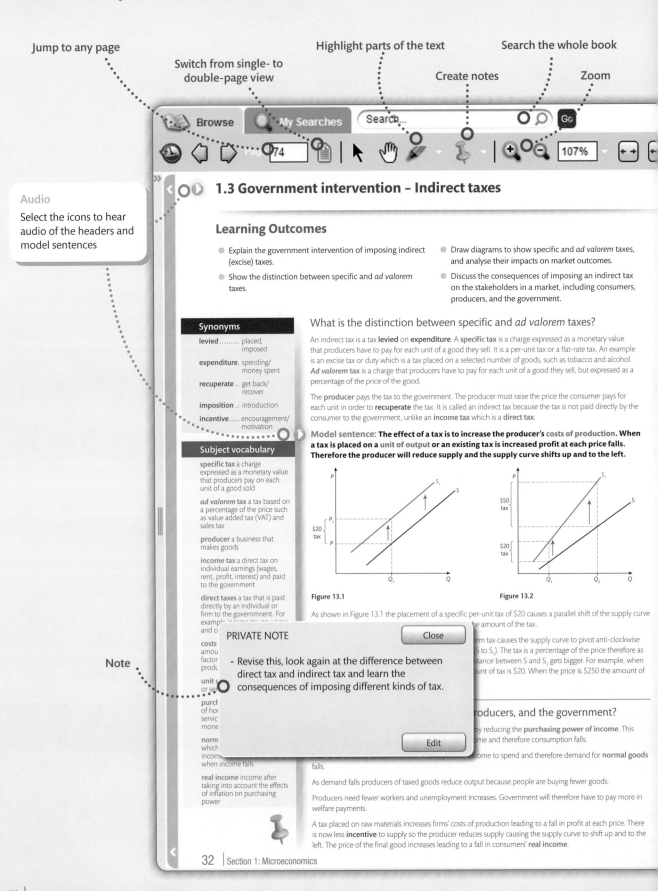

Audio

Select the icons to hear audio of the headers and model sentences

Browse | **My Searches** | Search... | Go

Page 74 | 107%

1.3 Government intervention – Indirect taxes

Learning Outcomes

- Explain the government intervention of imposing indirect (excise) taxes.
- Show the distinction between specific and *ad valorem* taxes.

- Draw diagrams to show specific and *ad valorem* taxes, and analyse their impacts on market outcomes.
- Discuss the consequences of imposing an indirect tax on the stakeholders in a market, including consumers, producers, and the government.

Synonyms

levied .... placed, imposed

expenditure. spending/ money spent

recuperate .. get back/ recover

imposition .. introduction

incentive..... encouragement/ motivation

Subject vocabulary

specific tax a charge expressed as a monetary value that producers pay on each unit of a good sold

ad valorem tax a tax based on a percentage of the price such as value added tax (VAT) and sales tax

producer a business that makes goods

income tax a direct tax on individual earnings (wages, rent, profit, interest) and paid to the government

direct taxes a tax that is paid directly by an individual or firm to the governmnent. For example income tax on wages and c

costs amou factor produ

unit or se

purch of hov servic mone

norm which income when income falls

real income income after taking into account the effects of inflation on purchasing power

What is the distinction between specific and *ad valorem* taxes?

An indirect tax is a tax **levied** on **expenditure**. A **specific tax** is a charge expressed as a monetary value that producers have to pay for each unit of a good they sell. It is a per-unit tax or a flat-rate tax. An example is an excise tax or duty which is a tax placed on a selected number of goods, such as tobacco and alcohol. *Ad valorem* **tax** is a charge that producers have to pay for each unit of a good they sell, but expressed as a percentage of the price of the good.

The **producer** pays the tax to the government. The producer must raise the price the consumer pays for each unit in order to **recuperate** the tax. It is called an indirect tax because the tax is not paid directly by the consumer to the government, unlike an **income tax** which is a **direct tax**.

Model sentence: The effect of a tax is to increase the producer's costs of production. When a tax is placed on a unit of output or an existing tax is increased profit at each price falls. Therefore the producer will reduce supply and the supply curve shifts up and to the left.

Figure 13.1

Figure 13.2

As shown in Figure 13.1 the placement of a specific per-unit tax of $20 causes a parallel shift of the supply curve e the amount of the tax.

em tax causes the supply curve to pivot anti-clockwise S to S₁). The tax is a percentage of the price therefore as stance between S and S₁ gets bigger. For example, when unt of tax is $20. When the price is $250 the amount of

PRIVATE NOTE | Close

- Revise this, look again at the difference between direct tax and indirect tax and learn the consequences of imposing different kinds of tax.

Edit

Note

roducers, and the government?

by reducing the **purchasing power of income**. This me and therefore consumption falls.

ome to spend and therefore demand for **normal goods** falls.

As demand falls producers of taxed goods reduce output because people are buying fewer goods.

Producers need fewer workers and unemployment increases. Government will therefore have to pay more in welfare payments.

A tax placed on raw materials increases firms' costs of production leading to a fall in profit at each price. There is now less **incentive** to supply so the producer reduces supply causing the supply curve to shift up and to the left. The price of the final good increases leading to a fall in consumers' **real income**.

32 | Section 1: Microeconomics

See the definitions of key terms in the glossary

Switch to whiteboard view

Create a bookmark

The increase in costs leads to a fall in international competitiveness. The higher price causes consumers to substitute **imported goods** for domestically produced goods.

The imposition of tax can lead to **inflation**. The disadvantages of inflation are discussed in detail on pages 149–50.

Model sentence: When a tax is levied on a normal good demand falls due to higher prices, producers reduce output, and unemployment in the industry increases. A tax on raw materials increases firms' costs of production, price therefore rises and the firm becomes less internationally competitive leading to higher unemployment in exporting industries.

The government must raise **tax revenue** to pay for the provision of goods and services that would be underconsumed and undersupplied if left to the **free market**. (This will be discussed later in the chapter on market failure.) A tax generates revenue for the government that it can use to provide things such as **infrastructure**, healthcare, education, the armed forces, and **welfare payments**.

There are many effects of a tax on the economy and these will be discussed further in later units.

Test your understanding of this unit by answering the following questions

- Distinguish between a direct tax and an indirect tax.
- Using diagrams to illustrate your answer, explain the difference between a specific tax and an *ad valorem* tax.
- Discuss the effect the imposition of a tax has on a consumer.

Subject vocabulary

imported goods goods sold into a country from another country

inflation an increase in the general level of prices of goods/services in an economy over a given time period, usually a year

tax revenue the income the government receives through the levying and collection of taxes

free market a market where the forces of demand and supply are allowed to operate without any forms of intervention

welfare payment a payment made by the government to someone, usually because the person is unemployed or earns a low income

Glossary

infrastructure the basic structure/systems of a country (e.g. roads/railways)

Definitions with audio
Click on highlighted terms to see the definition and hear the audio.

Learning Outcomes

- Explain, using diagrams, how the **incidence** of indirect taxes on consumers and firms differs, depending on the **price elasticity of demand** and on the **price elasticity of supply**. (HL)

- Plot demand and supply curves for a product from **linear functions** and then illustrate and/or calculate the effects of the imposition of a specific tax on the market (on price, quantity, consumer expenditure, producer revenue, government revenue, consumer surplus, and producer surplus). (HL)

What are the effects on price and quantity of the imposition of a specific tax (HL) – a step-by-step guide

Trouble shooter (see Figure 14.1 and Figure 14.2)

The tax causes the supply curve to shift up and to the left by the amount of the tax (from S to S_{tax}) because the tax rate is given by the vertical distance between the original and new supply curves.

The firm wants to make consumers pay all the tax by setting price at P_2.

However at P_2 quantity supplied > quantity demanded. To eliminate the **excess supply** price must fall from P_2 to P_{tax}.

Price increases from P_e to P_{tax} and quantity falls from Q_e to Q_{tax}.

Synonyms

incidence ....occurence/frequency

Subject vocabulary

price elasticity of demand (PED) a measure of how quantity demanded responds to a change in price in percentage terms

price elasticity of supply (PES) a measure of how quantity supplied responds to a change in price in percentage terms

linear function an equation, the graph of which is a straight line

excess supply occurs when quantity supplied is greater than quantity demanded

Vocabulary lists
Select the icons at the back of the book to see complete vocabulary lists

1.1 Competitive markets: Demand and supply

Learning Outcomes

- Outline the meaning of the term market.
- Explain the negative causal relationship between price and quantity demanded.
- Describe the relationship between an individual consumer's demand and market demand.
- Explain that a demand curve represents the relationship between the price and the quantity demanded of a product, *ceteris paribus*.
- Draw a demand curve.

- Explain how factors including changes in income (in the cases of normal and inferior goods), preferences, prices of related goods (in the cases of substitutes and complements), and demographic changes may change demand.
- Distinguish between movements along the demand curve and shifts of the demand curve.
- Draw diagrams to show the difference between movements along the demand curve and shifts of the demand curve.

What is a market?

A market is where buyers and sellers meet in order to exchange money for **goods** and **services**. They do not always meet **in person**. Goods can be bought by **consumers** and sold by **suppliers** at on line markets such as Amazon and eBay. The amount of money a consumer pays the supplier in exchange for a good is called the price. There are markets for the **factors of production**. For example there is a market for labour (workers). Labour is needed by producers to make goods. The producers are the buyers of labour and individual people are the sellers of their own labour.

Why is there a negative causal relationship between price and quantity demanded?

Quantity demanded is the amount of a good that consumers are willing and able to buy at a given price over a given period of time. This means that consumers must not only want the good but also have enough money to be able to buy it and that the amount demanded is measured over a specific period of time such as a day, a week, or a year. When consumers are willing and able to buy the good **demand** is called 'effective demand'.

The law of demand states that as price falls quantity demanded increases and as price increases quantity demanded falls. There is a negative or inverse relationship between price and quantity demanded.

There are two effects on quantity demanded of a change in price that explain the negative relationship: the **income effect** and the **substitution effect**.

What is the income effect?

As price falls the quantity of the good that can be bought with the same **income** increases. Therefore as price falls quantity demanded increases. As price increases the quantity of the good that can be bought with the same income falls. Therefore as price increases quantity demanded falls.

What is the substitution effect?

A substitute is a good that can be used in place of another good. As the price of a good falls it becomes relatively cheaper than the substitute good causing some consumers to buy the good in place of the substitute. As the price of a good rises it becomes relatively more expensive than the substitute good causing some consumers to buy the substitute good in place of the good. A change in price therefore leads to a change in quantity demanded.

Model sentence: There is a negative relationship between price and quantity demanded because of the income and substitution effects on quantity demanded of a change in price. The income and substitution effects explain the law of demand.

What is the difference between individual consumer demand and market demand?

The **demand schedule** is a table that shows the relationship between price and quantity demanded. Table 1.1 shows the quantity demanded by 4 individual consumers over a range of different prices. The last column shows the **market demand** which is the **sum** of the individual consumer's demand.

Price $	Consumer 'a'		Consumer 'b'		Consumer 'c'		Consumer 'd'		Market demand
10	50	+	100	+	80	+	150	=	380
15	40	+	90	+	70	+	120	=	320
20	30	+	80	+	60	+	110	=	280

Table 1.1

Subject vocabulary

demand schedule a table showing the quantity demanded over a range of prices – the information from which can be used to plot a demand curve

market demand the sum of the demand of the individual consumers in the market

determinants of demand factors that affect quantity demanded at each price

demand curve a graph that shows the relationship between price and quantity demanded

Synonyms

sum.................total

isolate ....separate

Why does the demand curve represent the relationship between price and quantity demanded, *ceteris paribus*?

Price of potato chips (P)/$	Quantity of potato chips demanded per week (Q)
2.50	5
2.00	10
1.50	15
1.00	20
0.50	25

Table 1.2 *Demand schedule: potato chips*

The demand schedule (Table 1.2) shows quantity demanded at each price. Price is a **determinant of demand**. A change in price causes a change in quantity demanded.

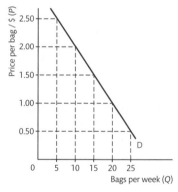

Figure 1.1

The **demand curve** is drawn using the information found on the demand schedule. The points are plotted on a graph. Price on the vertical axis and quantity demanded on the horizontal. The demand curve shows the relationship between price and quantity demanded, *ceteris paribus*. This Latin phrase means 'all other things being equal' or 'all other things being held constant'.

Why does a change in price cause a movement along the demand curve?

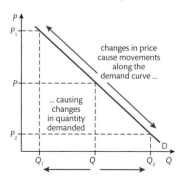

Figure 1.2

A change in the price of the good itself leads to a change in quantity demanded and causes a movement along the demand curve. An increase in price leads to a fall in quantity demanded and a movement up and along the demand curve. A fall in price leads to an increase in quantity demanded and a movement down and along the demand curve. Only a change in price causes a movement along the demand curve.

Model sentence: ***Ceteris paribus* means all other things being held constant. All determinants of demand other than price are held constant in order to isolate the effect on quantity demanded of a change in price.**

What are the non-price determinants of demand and how do they affect demand for a good and cause a shift of the demand curve?

Subject vocabulary

normal goods goods for which demand increases when income increases, and falls when income falls

inferior goods goods for which demand falls as income increases

complements goods that are used together

Glossary

steepness the height-size of the angle-gradient

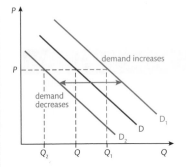

Figure 1.3

Income

Demand for **normal goods** increases as income increases. The demand curve shifts up and to the right to show more is demanded at every price. Demand for **inferior goods** falls as income increases. The demand curve shifts down and to the left to show less is demanded at every price. Examples of normal goods are holidays and eating out. Examples of inferior goods might be second-hand cars and less expensive cuts of meat. Each consumer reacts differently to a change in income. What is an 'inferior good' for one person may not be for another.

Preferences/tastes/fashion

As a good becomes more fashionable demand increases. The demand curve shifts up and to the right to show that quantity demanded increases at every price. As it becomes less fashionable demand falls. The demand curve shifts down and to the left to show that less is demanded at every price.

The price of related goods

Substitutes are goods that can be used in place of another good. An increase in the price of beef leads to an increase in quantity demanded of lamb at every price and the demand curve for lamb shifts up and to the right.

Complements are goods that are used together. When the price of games consoles falls quantity demanded rises. More games consoles are sold. Demand for video games to use with the games consoles increases. More video games are demanded at every price. To show this the demand curve for video games shifts up and to the right.

Demographic changes

These are changes to the characteristics of the population, such as size and age structure. When the population increases quantity demanded for most goods increases at every price and the demand curve shifts up and to the right.

Model sentence: Only a change in the price of a good itself causes a movement along the demand curve illustrating a change in quantity demanded. A change in any other determinant of demand causes a shift of the demand curve illustrating a change in quantity demanded at every price.

Test your understanding of this unit by answering the following questions

- What is a market?
- Explain why a change in price leads to a change in quantity demanded.
- Why do economists use the phrase *ceteris paribus*?
- Distinguish between a movement along the demand curve and a shift of the demand curve.

Learning Outcomes

- Explain a demand function (equation) of the form $Qd = a - bP$. (HL)

- Plot a demand curve from a linear function (e.g. $Qd = 60 - 5P$). (HL)

- Identify the slope of the demand curve as the slope of the demand function $Qd = a - bP$, that is ^-b (the coefficient of P). (HL)

- Outline how a change in 'b' affects the **steepness** of the demand curve. (HL)

- Outline why, if the 'a' term changes, there will be a shift of the demand curve. (HL)

Explain how to plot a demand curve from a linear function and explain the cause of a change in the slope and a shift of the demand curve (HL)

A **linear function** is an equation that states how a **variable** is determined, the graph of which is a straight line. The **demand function** Qd = a – bP states how **quantity demanded** of a good is determined by the price of the good. 'Qd' is quantity demanded, 'a' is quantity demanded when price is zero. The **coefficient** 'b' determines the responsiveness of quantity demanded to a change in price and sets the slope of the **demand curve**, 'b' is negative in a demand function reflecting the fact that there is an **inverse relationship** between quantity demanded and price. As price increases quantity demanded decreases. 'P' is price. The demand function provides the information needed to plot a demand curve.

Calculate quantity demanded from a demand function – a step-by-step guide (HL)

Trouble shooter

This is how to calculate quantity demanded when price is €4 using the demand function
Qd = 60 – 5P (5P means 5 multiplied by price)

Qd = 60 – (5 × P)   (I have put 5 × P in brackets because I have to do this calculation first.)

Qd = 60 – (5 × 4)   Simplify by multiplying 5 by 4

Qd = 60 – 20   Simplify by subtracting 20 from 60

Qd = 40

When price is €4 quantity demanded is 40 units.

A **demand schedule** is a table that shows the relationship between price and quantity demanded.

The calculations of quantity demanded at a range of prices using the demand function Qd = 60 – 5P are in the demand schedule Table 2.1.

Price €	Qd = 60 – 5P	Quantity demanded
0	Qd = 60 – (5 × 0) = 60 – 0 = 60	60
1	Qd = 60 – (5 × 1) = 60 – 5 = 55	55
2	Qd = 60 – (5 × 2) = 60 – 10 = 50	50
3	Qd = 60 – (5 × 3) = 60 – 15 = 45	45
4	Qd = 60 – (5 × 4) = 60 – 20 = 40	40
5	Qd = 60 – (5 × 5) = 60 – 25 = 35	35
6	Qd = 60 – (5 × 6) = 60 – 30 = 30	30
7	Qd = 60 – (5 × 7) = 60 – 35 = 25	25
8	Qd = 60 – (5 × 8) = 60 – 40 = 20	20
9	Qd = 60 – (5 × 9) = 60 – 45 = 15	15
10	Qd = 60 – (5 × 10) = 60 – 50 = 10	10
11	Qd = 60 – (5 × 11) = 60 – 55 = 5	5
12	Qd = 60 – (5 × 12) = 60 – 60 = 0	0

Table 2.1

Price €	Qd = 60 – 10P	Quantity demanded
0	Qd = 60 – (10 × 0) = 60 – 0 = 60	60
1	Qd = 60 – (10 × 1) = 60 – 10 = 50	50
2	Qd = 60 – (10 × 2) = 60 – 20 = 40	40
3	Qd = 60 – (10 × 3) = 60 – 30 = 30	30
4	Qd = 60 – (10 × 4) = 60 – 40 = 20	20
5	Qd = 60 – (10 × 5) = 60 – 50 = 10	10
6	Qd = 60 – (10 × 6) = 60 – 60 = 0	0

Table 2.2

linear function an equation; the graph of which is a straight line

variable a value that can change

demand function an equation that shows how quantity demanded of a good is determined by the price of the good

quantity demanded the amount of a good consumers are willing and able to buy at a given price over a given period of time

coefficient a number used to multiply a variable by

demand curve a graph that shows the relationship between price and quantity demanded

inverse relationship a change in the value of one variable leads to an opposite change in direction in the value of the other variable. For example an increase in price leads to a fall in quantity demanded.

demand schedule a table showing the quantity demanded over a range of prices – the information from which can be used to plot a demand curve

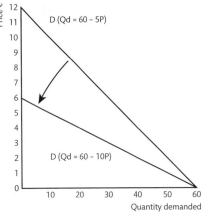

Figure 2.1

Now change the value of 'b' from 5 to 10 and calculate the quantity demanded using the function Qd = 60 – 10P. These calculations are in the demand schedule Table 2.2. When 'b' = 5 quantity demanded falls by 5 units as price increases by €1. When 'b' = 10 quantity demanded falls by 10 units as price increases by €1. The higher the value of 'b' the more responsive quantity demanded is to a change in price.

The information from Tables 2.1 and 2.2 (page 5) is plotted to give the **demand curves** in Figure 2.1.

continued from page 7

Subject vocabulary

demand curve a graph that shows the relationship between price and quantity demanded

demand the amount of a good that consumers are willing and able to buy at each price

To illustrate the fact that quantity demanded is more responsive to a change in price when the value of 'b' is larger the demand curve rotates anti-clockwise from where the demand curves meet and becomes less steep.

Model sentence: A change in the value of 'b' changes the responsiveness of quantity demanded to a change in price and causes the slope of the demand curve to change.

How to shift the demand curve (HL)

Price €	Qd = 50 – 5P	Quantity demanded
0	Qd = 50 – (5 × 0) = 50 – 0 = 50	50
1	Qd = 50 – (5 × 1) = 50 – 5 = 45	45
2	Qd = 50 – (5 × 2) = 50 – 10 = 40	40
3	Qd = 50 – (5 × 3) = 50 – 15 = 35	35
4	Qd = 50 – (5 × 4) = 50 – 20 = 30	30
5	Qd = 50 – (5 × 5) = 50 – 25 = 25	25
6	Qd = 50 – (5 × 6) = 50 – 30 = 20	20
7	Qd = 50 – (5 × 7) = 50 – 35 = 15	15
8	Qd = 50 – (5 × 8) = 50 – 40 = 10	10
9	Qd = 50 – (5 × 9) = 50 – 45 = 5	5
10	Qd = 50 – (5 × 10) = 50 – 50 = 0	0

Table 2.3

The value of 'a' in the demand function Qd = 60 – 5P changes from 60 to 50. The calculations of quantity demanded for the new demand function Qd = 50 – 5P are shown in the demand schedule Table 2.3.

The changes in quantity demanded caused by the change in the value of 'a' can be seen by comparing the information in Tables 2.1 and 2.3.

When the value of 'a' falls from 60 to 50 **demand** falls. Quantity demanded at every price is reduced by 10 units.

Subject vocabulary

continued from page 7

supply curve a graph that shows the relationship between price and quantity supplied

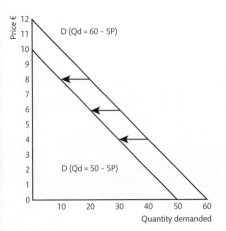

Figure 2.2

The demand curve shifts down and to the left in Figure 2.2 to illustrate the fall in demand.

Model sentence: A change in the value of 'a' causes a change in demand. An increase in the value of 'a' increases the quantity demanded at every price and the demand curve shifts up and to the right. A decrease in the value of 'a' causes a fall in quantity demanded at every price and the demand curve shifts down and to the left.

Synonyms

firm...... business/producer/supplier

sum...... total

Learning Outcomes

● Explain the positive causal relationship between price and quantity supplied.

● Describe the relationship between an individual producer's supply and market supply.

● Explain that a supply curve represents the relationship between the price and the quantity supplied of a product, *ceteris paribus*.

● Draw a supply curve.

● Explain how factors including changes in costs of factors of production (land, labour, capital, and entrepreneurship), technology, price of related goods, expectations, indirect taxes and subsidies, and the number of firms in the market can change supply.

● Distinguish between movements along the supply curve and shifts of the supply curve.

● Construct diagrams to show the difference between movements along the supply curve and shifts of the supply curve.

What is the relationship between an individual producer's supply and market supply?

Tubs of vanilla ice-cream supplied per week				
Price £	Firm 1	Firm 2	Firm 3	Firm 4	Market supply
2	2000	500	3000	1500	7000
3	3000	1000	4000	3000	11000
4	4000	1500	5000	4500	15000
5	5000	2000	6000	6000	19000
6	6000	2500	7000	7500	23000

Table 3.1

The **supply schedule** Table 3.1 shows **quantity supplied** by the 4 individual **firms** at each given price. The **sum** of the individual firms' **supply** is the **market supply**.

Subject vocabulary

supply schedule a table showing the quantity supplied over a range of prices – the information from which can be used to plot a supply curve

quantity supplied the amount of a good that firms are willing and able to produce at a given price over a given period of time

supply the amount of a good that a firm is willing and able to produce at each price

market supply the sum of the supply of the individual firms in the industry

law of supply states that there is a positive causal relationship between price and quantity supplied. As price rises quantity supplied rises.

positive causal relationship a change in the value of one variable causes the value of the other variable to change in the same direction. For example an increase in price causes an increase in quantity supplied.

ceteris paribus Latin phrase meaning 'all other things being equal' or 'all other things being held constant'

resources the inputs into the production process, the factors of production

production the act of making goods and services

continued on page 6

Explain the positive causal relationship between price and quantity supplied

The **law of supply** states that there is a **positive causal relationship** between price and quantity supplied. As price rises quantity supplied rises.. A change in price causes quantity supplied to change in the same direction. As price increases quantity supplied increases and as price falls quantity supplied falls. This is because a firm's main objective is to maximize profit. As price increases, *ceteris paribus*, profit increases therefore firms increase quantity supplied by switching **resources** away from the **production** of other goods so that they can produce more of the good that earns greater profit. As price falls profit falls *ceteris paribus* and firms reduce quantity supplied.

Model sentence: It is profit that motivates firms to produce goods. When profit earned from the sale of a good increases the firm increases quantity supplied and when profit falls it reduces quantity supplied.

Explain that a supply curve represents the relationship between the price and the quantity supplied of a product, *ceteris paribus*, and distinguish between a movement along and a shift of the supply curve

A change in the price of a good causes a movement along its **supply curve** (see Figure 3.1a on page 8). As the price of a good falls, *ceteris paribus*, profit falls. Resources are switched away from the production of the good causing a fall in quantity supplied and a movement down and along the supply curve. As price rises a firm increases quantity supplied causing a movement up and along the supply curve.

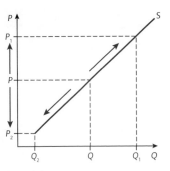

Figure 3.1a

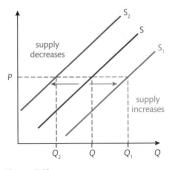

Figure 3.1b

What are the non-price determinants of supply and why do they cause a shift of the supply curve?

A change in any **determinant of supply** other than price leads to a change in the quantity supplied at each price and a shift of the supply curve. The non-price determinants of supply are explained here.

As the price of **factors of production** increase the **costs of production** increase and profit at each price decreases. A firm will reduce the **quantity supplied** at each price. The supply curve shifts to the left (Figure 3.1b). As costs of production decrease profit at each price increases and a firm will increase the quantity supplied at each price, causing the supply curve to shift to the right (Figure 3.1b).

Productivity is the quantity of **output** per unit of **input**. **Productivity** increases if fewer inputs are used to produce a given quantity of goods. As fewer **resources** are used, costs of production decrease and more profit is made. At each price more profit is made on each unit sold. The firm will increase the quantity supplied at each price causing the supply curve to shift down and to the right. Productivity decreases if more inputs are used to produce a given quantity of goods. Costs of production rise and profit falls. The firm reduces the quantity supplied at each price causing the supply curve to shift up and to the left.

A change in the price of a **related good** will lead to change in supply of the alternative good. A farmer can grow wheat and corn. They are **substitutes in production**. If the price of corn increases it becomes more profitable to produce. Higher profits on corn act as an **incentive** for the farmer to take factors of production away from the production of wheat and use them to produce more corn instead. There are two effects of doing this: the quantity supplied of corn increases as price rises and there is a movement up and along the supply curve for corn, and the quantity supplied of wheat decreases at each price and the supply curve for wheat shifts up and to the left.

The climate and natural disasters affect supply. The quantity supplied of grapes will decrease at each price if growing conditions are not suitable or if there is a disease of the crop. The supply curve shifts up and to the left.

As profits earned in an **industry** increase new firms will move into the industry attracted by the high profits. The number of firms producing the good increases, leading to an increase in the quantity supplied to the **market** at each price and the **market supply** curve shifts down and to the right.

An indirect tax, such as value added tax (VAT) and duty, is a tax placed on goods and services. The tax in effect increases the costs of production. As costs of production increase, profit at each price decreases and the firm will reduce the quantity supplied at each price and the supply curve shifts up and to the left.

A subsidy is a payment made by the government to a firm. The aim is to reduce price and increase **consumption** and supply. A subsidy in effect decreases costs of production. Profit at each price increases and the firm will increase the quantity supplied at each price. The supply curve shifts down and to the right.

Model sentence: A change in the price of a good leads to a change in quantity supplied of the good and a movement along its supply curve. A change in any other determinant of supply leads to a change in supply of the good and a shift of its supply curve.

Test your understanding of this unit by answering the following questions

- Explain why a change in price leads to a change in quantity supplied.
- Explain how a change in a non-price determinant of supply affects the amount of a good a firm wishes to produce.
- Distinguish between a movement along the supply curve and a shift of the supply curve.

Learning Outcomes

- Explain a supply function (equation) of the form Qs = c + dP. (HL)

- Plot a supply curve from a linear function (e.g. Qs = −30 + 20P). (HL)

- Identify the slope of the supply curve as the slope of the supply function Qs = c + dP, that is d. (HL)

- Outline how a change in 'd' affects the steepness of the supply curve. (HL)

- Outline why, if the 'c' term changes, there will be a shift of the supply curve. (HL)

Explain the meaning of a supply function, plot a supply curve from a linear function and explain how a change in 'd' affects the steepness of the supply curve (HL)

The **supply function** Qs = c + dP is an equation that shows the relationship between price and quantity supplied. 'Qs' is quantity supplied, 'c' is quantity supplied when price = 0, the **coefficient** 'd' determines the **slope** of the **supply curve** and 'P' is price. The supply function Qs = c + dP is a **linear function** therefore the supply curve will be a straight line. dP is positive because as the price of a good rises, the quantity supplied also rises.

Calculate quantity supplied from a supply function (HL) – a step-by-step guide

Trouble shooter

How to work out quantity supplied when price is €4 using the supply function
Qs = −30 + 20P (20P means 20 multiplied by price)

Qs = −30 + (20 × P)	(I have put 20 × P in brackets because I have to do this calculation first)
Qs = −30 + (20 × 4)	Simplify by multiplying 20 by 4
Qs = −30 + 80	Simplify by adding 80 to −30
Qs = 50	

When price is €4 quantity supplied is 50 units.

The calculations of quantity supplied of cups of coffee per day in a cafe at a range of prices using the supply function Qs = −30 + 20P are shown in the **supply schedule** Table 4.1.

Price €	Qs = ⁻30 + 20P	Quantity supplied
0	Qs = −30 + (20 × 0) = −30 + 0 = −30	−30
1	Qs = −30 + (20 × 1) = −30 + 20 = −10	−10
2	Qs = −30 + (20 × 2) = −30 + 40 = 10	10
3	Qs = −30 + (20 × 3) = −30 + 60 = 30	30
4	Qs = −30 + (20 × 4) = −30 + 80 = 50	50
5	Qs = −30 + (20 × 5) = −30 + 100 = 70	70
6	Qs = −30 + (20 × 6) = −30 + 120 = 90	90

Table 4.1

The value of 'd' in the supply function Qs = −30 + 20P changes from 20 to 30. The new supply function Qs = −30 + 30P is now used to calculate quantity supplied. The calculations are shown in the supply schedule Table 4.2. The effects of this change on quantity supplied can be seen by looking at Tables 4.1 and 4.2. When 'd' = 20 quantity supplied increases by 20 units as price increases by €1. When 'd' = 30 quantity supplied increases by 30 units as price increases by €1. The higher the value of 'd' the more responsive quantity supplied is to a change in price.

Subject vocabulary

supply function equation that shows how quantity supplied of a good is determined by the price of the good

coefficient a number used to multiply a variable by

supply curve a graph that shows the relationship between price and quantity supplied

supply schedule a table showing the quantity supplied over a range of prices – the information from which can be used to plot a supply curve

linear function an equation; the graph of which is a straight line

Glossary

slope the angle/gradient of the curve

Price €	Qs = $^-$30 + 30P	Quantity supplied
0	Qs = –30 + (30 × 0) = –30 + 0 = –30	–30
1	Qs = –30 + (30 × 1) = –30 + 30 = 0	0
2	Qs = –30 + (30 × 2) = –30 + 60 = 30	30
3	Qs = –30 + (30 × 3) = –30 + 90 = 60	60
4	Qs = –30 + (30 × 4) = –30 + 120 = 90	90
5	Qs = –30 + (30 × 5) = –30 + 150 = 120	120
6	Qs = –30 + (30 × 6) = –30 + 180 = 150	150

Table 4.2

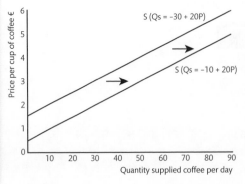

Figure 4.1

The information from the supply schedules in Tables 4.1 and 4.2 is plotted on a graph to give the supply curves in Figure 4.1. Quantity supplied is not plotted when it is negative so the first point plotted is where quantity supplied is zero.

To illustrate that quantity supplied is more responsive to a change in price the supply curve rotates clockwise from where they meet and the slope of the supply curve becomes less steep.

Model sentence: A change in the value of 'd' changes the responsiveness of quantity supplied to a change in price and causes the slope of the supply curve to change.

Subject vocabulary

supply the amount of a good that a firm is willing and able to produce at each price

Outline why a change in the value of 'c' shifts the supply curve (HL)

Price €	Qs = $^-$10 + 20P	Quantity supplied
0	Qs = –10 + (20 × 0) = –10 + 0 = –10	–10
1	Qs = –10 + (20 × 1) = –10 + 20 = 10	10
2	Qs = –10 + (20 × 2) = –10 + 40 = 30	30
3	Qs = –10 + (20 × 3) = –10 + 60 = 50	50
4	Qs = –10 + (20 × 4) = –10 + 80 = 70	70
5	Qs = –10 + (20 × 5) = –10 + 100 = 90	90
6	Qs = –10 + (20 × 6) = –10 + 120 = 110	110

Table 4.3

The value of 'c' in the original supply function Qs = –30 + 20P changes from –30 to –10. The calculations of quantity supplied from the new supply function Qs = –10 + 20P are shown in Table 4.3.

Subject vocabulary

continued from page 11

excess supply occurs when quantity supplied is greater than quantity demanded

surplus occurs when quantity supplied is greater than quantity demanded, another term for excess supply

market clears when quantity demanded equals quantity supplied and there is no surplus or shortage

equilibrium price the price at which the quantity consumers are willing and able to buy is equal to the quantity firms are willing and able to produce

excess demand occurs when quantity demanded is greater than quantity supplied

shortage when quantity demanded is greater than quantity supplied (another term for excess demand)

Figure 4.2

The quantities supplied at each price when 'c' = –30 and when 'c' = –10 are shown in Tables 4.1 and 4.3. As the value of 'c' increases by 20 from –30 to –10 the quantity supplied at each price increases by 20 units. The information from the supply schedules is plotted on a graph Figure 4.2. The supply curve shifts down and to the right to illustrate the increase in **supply**.

Model sentence: A change in the value of 'c' causes a change in the quantity supplied at each price. An increase in the value of 'c' causes an increase in quantity supplied at each price and the supply curve shifts down and to the right. A decrease in the value of 'c' causes a decrease in quantity supplied at each price and the supply curve shifts up and to the left.

Synonyms

eliminate ... remove/get rid of

Glossary

interact affect each other/act together

Learning Outcomes

- Explain, using diagrams, how demand and supply **interact** to produce **market equilibrium**.

- Analyse, using diagrams, and with references to excess demand or excess supply, how changes in the determinants of demand and/or supply result in a new market equilibrium.

- Calculate the equilibrium price and equilibrium quantity from linear demand and supply functions (HL only).

- Plot demand and supply curves from **linear functions**, and identify the equilibrium price and equilibrium quantity (HL only).

- State the quantity of excess demand or excess supply in the previous diagram (HL only).

Explain how demand and supply interact to produce market equilibrium

Table 5.1 is a **demand and supply schedule** for copper, a metal bought by firms. It is used in the **production** of many goods.

World supply and demand for Copper		
Price $ per ton	Qs (million)	Qd (million)
4000	12	18
5000	13	17
6000	14	16
7000	15	15
8000	16	14
9000	17	13

Table 5.1

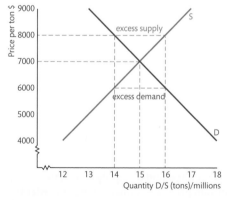

Figure 5.1

The market is in equilibrium at a price of $7000 per ton where **quantity demanded = quantity supplied**. At prices other than $7000 quantity demanded does not equal quantity supplied and the market is in **disequilibrium**. The **demand curve** and supply curve for copper are plotted in Figure 5.1.

At $8000 quantity supplied = 16m tons and quantity demanded = 14m tons, an **excess supply** of 2m tons. Producers of copper must lower prices to **eliminate** the **surplus**. As price falls quantity demanded increases, causing a movement down and along the demand curve, and quantity supplied decreases causing a movement down and along the supply curve. Price continues to fall until the surplus is eliminated and the **market clears** at the **equilibrium price**.

At $6000 quantity supplied = 14m tons and quantity demanded = 16m tons, an **excess demand** of 2m tons. When there is a **shortage** producers know they can get a higher price. As price increases quantity demanded decreases, causing a movement up and along the demand curve, and quantity supplied increases causing a

Subject vocabulary

market equilibrium occurs when the quantity demanded of goods produced in an industry equals the amount of goods firms in the industry are willing to supply

linear function an equation, the graph of which is a straight line

demand schedule a table showing the quantity demanded over a range of prices – information that can be used to plot a demand curve

supply schedule a table showing the quantity supplied over a range of prices - the information can be used to plot a supply curve

production the act of making goods and services

quantity demanded the amount of a good consumers are willing and able to buy at a given price over a given period of time

quantity supplied the amount of a good that firms are willing and able to produce at a given price over a given period of time

disequilibrium occurs in a market where the quantity supplied does not equal the quantity demanded at the actual price

demand curve a graph that shows the relationship between price and quantity demanded

continued on page 10

movement up and along the supply curve. Price continues to increase until the equilibrium price is reached and the market clears.

Model sentence: When a market is in disequilibrium and there is excess demand or supply of the good the price must change in order to eliminate the excess. As price changes it leads to a change in quantity demanded and supplied and price continues to change until quantity demanded equals quantity supplied and the market clears.

Analyse how changes in non-price determinants of demand/supply cause an excess in the market and lead to a new equilibrium price

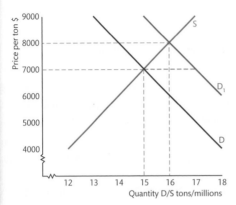

Figure 5.2

Copper is used in the production of many goods. **Demand** for copper is a **derived demand**. As incomes (a **determinant of demand**) increase demand for **normal goods** increases causing an increase in demand for copper. The demand curve shifts up and to the right as shown in Figure 5.2.

At $7000 quantity supplied remains at 15m tons but quantity demanded increases to 17m. There is a shortage and **producers** know that they can get a higher price. As price increases quantity supplied increases causing a movement up and along the supply curve S and quantity demanded falls causing a movement up and along the demand curve D_1. Price increases until the market clears at the new equilibrium price of $8000 per ton and the new **equilibrium quantity** of 16m tons.

The producers of copper have bought more technologically advanced **capital** leading to greater **productivity**. Cost per ton falls and more **profit** is now made on the sale of a ton of copper. The producers increase **supply** and the supply curve shifts down and to the right as shown in Figure 5.3.

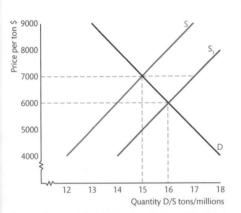

Figure 5.3

At the price of $7000 quantity demanded remains at 15m tons but quantity supplied increases to 17m. In order to sell the surplus price must fall. As price falls quantity supplied decreases causing a movement down and along the supply curve S_1 and quantity demanded rises causing a movement down and along the demand curve D. Price falls until the market clears at the new equilibrium price of $6000 per ton and the new equilibrium quantity of 16m tons.

Model sentence: A change in a non-price determinant of demand or supply causes the market to be in disequilibrium at the original equilibrium price. Price must change in order to eliminate the excess demand or excess supply and continues to change until the market clears at the new equilibrium price and equilibrium quantity.

Calculate the equilibrium price and quantity from linear functions (HL)

Below is set out the calculations of the equilibrium price and equilibrium quantity demanded and supplied of **widgets** from the **demand function** Qd = a − bP = Qd = 100 − 10P and the supply function Qs = c + dP = Qs = −20 + 20P.

At equilibrium quantity demanded = quantity supplied.

Therefore at equilibrium $100 - 10P = -20 + 20P$ simplify by adding 20 to both sides of the equation.
$20 + 100 - 10P = 20 - 20 + 20P$
$120 - 10P = 20P$ simplify by adding 10P to both sides
$120 - 10P + 10P = 20P + 10P$
$120 = 30P$ simplify by dividing both sides by 30
$120/30 = 30P/30$
$4 = P$. Equilibrium price = $4.

How to work out the equilibrium quantity.
Put 4 in the place of P in the demand function $Qd = 100 - 10P$.
$Qd = 100 - (10 \times 4)$. I have put 10×4 in brackets because I have to do this calculation first.
$Qd = 100 - 40$
$Qd = 60$ units

The equilibrium quantity can be worked out using the supply function by putting 4 in the place of P in the supply function $Qs = -20 + 20P$.
$Qs = -20 + (20 \times 4)$
$Qs = -20 + 80$
$Qs = 60$ units

The equilibrium price of widgets, given these supply and demand functions, is $4 and the equilibrium quantity demanded and supplied is 60 units.

Calculate excess supply and the new equilibrium price using demand and supply functions (HL)

Costs of production are a **determinant of supply**. When costs of production increase, profit made on each unit sold falls and the firm reduces supply. The increase in the costs of production causes a change in the value of 'c' (the quantity supplied when price is zero), in the supply function $Qs = c + dP$. Assume that the supply function changes from $Qs = -20 + 20P$ to $Qs = -50 + 20P$. Determinants of demand have not changed so the demand function remains $Qd = 100 - 10P$.

The original **equilibrium price** is $4. Quantity demanded at $4 is 60 units. To calculate quantity supplied at $4 put 4 in the place of P in the new supply function $Qs = -50 + 20P$.
$Qs = -50 + (20 \times 4)$ simplify by multiplying 20 by 4
$Qs = -50 + 80$
$Qs = 30$ units

At the price of $4 quantity demanded = 60 and quantity supplied = 30. There is **excess demand** of 30 units (60 – 30) at the original equilibrium price. The firm knows it can get a higher price. Price rises in order to eliminate the **shortage**.

Calculate the new equilibrium price – a step-by-step guide

Trouble shooter

At equilibrium quantity demanded = quantity supplied therefore at equilibrium
$100 - 10P = -50 + 20P$

$100 - 10P = -50 + 20P$ simplify by adding 50 to both sides of the equation

$50 + 100 - 10P = 50 - 50 + 20P$

$150 - 10P = 20P$ simplify by adding 10P to both sides

$150 - 10P + 10P = 20P + 10P$

$150 = 30P$ simplify by dividing both sides by 30

$150/30 = 30P/30$

$5 = P$

The new equilibrium price = $5. To find the new equilibrium quantity put 5 in the place of P in the demand function Qd = 100 – 10P.

Qd = 100 – (10 × 5) simplify by multiplying 10 by 5

Qd = 100 – 50

Qd = 50 units

Put 5 in the place of P in the supply function Qs = –50 + 20P.

Qs = –50 + (20 × 5) simplify by multiplying 20 by 5

Qs = –50 + 100

Qs = 50 units. The new equilibrium price is $5 and equilibrium quantity is 50 units.

Table 5.2 shows the calculations of quantity demanded and quantity supplied of widgets for the demand function and the two supply functions. The original equilibrium and the equilibrium after the change in the determinant of supply are highlighted. The decrease in the value of 'c' causes a fall in the quantity supplied at each price of 30 units.

Price $	Qd = 100 – 10P	Qd	Qs = – 20 + 20P	Qs	Qs = – 50 + 20P	Q
0	Qd = 100 – (10 × 0) = 100 – 0	100	Qs = –20 + (20 × 0) = –20 + 0	–20	Qs = –50 + (20 × 0) = –50 + 0	–50
1	Qd = 100 – (10 × 1) = 100 – 10	90	Qs = –20 + (20 × 1) = –20 + 20	0	Qs = –50 + (20 × 1) = –50 + 20	–30
2	Qd = 100 – (10 × 2) = 100 – 20	80	Qs = –20 + (20 × 2) = –20 + 40	20	Qs = –50 + (20 × 2) = –50 + 40	–10
3	Qd = 100 – (10 × 3) = 100 – 30	70	Qs = –20 + (20 × 3) = –20 + 60	40	Qs = –50 + (20 × 3) = –50 + 60	10
4	Qd = 100 – (10 × 4) = 100 – 40	60	Qs = –20 + (20 × 4) = –20 + 80	60	Qs = –50 + (20 × 4) = –50 + 80	30
5	Qd = 100 – (10 × 5) = 100 – 50	50	Qs = –20 + (20 × 5) = –20 +100	80	Qs = –50 + (20 × 5) = –50 + 100	50
6	Qd = 100 – (10 × 6) = 100 – 60	40	Qs = –20 + (20 × 6) = –20 +120	100	Qs = –50 + (20 × 6) = –50 + 120	70

Table 5.2

Plot demand and supply curves from the linear functions and identify the excess, the equilibrium price, and equilibrium quantity (HL)

Subject vocabulary

demand curve a graph that shows the relationship between price and quantity demanded

supply curve a graph that shows the relationship between price and quantity supplied

market clears when quantity demanded equals quantity supplied and there is no surplus or shortage

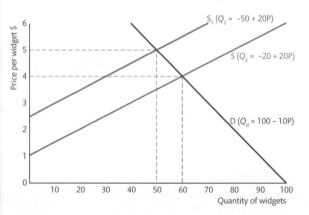

Figure 5.4

The **demand curve** and **supply curve** shown in Figure 5.4 are plotted from the information in Table 5.2. The change in the value of 'c' causes a shift of the supply curve up and to the left. At the original equilibrium price of $4 there is now excess demand of 30 units. Price increases to eliminate the excess until the **market clears** at the new equilibrium price of $5 and new equilibrium quantity of 50 units.

Test your understanding of this unit by answering the following questions

- Using a diagram to illustrate your answer and with reference to a determinant of supply, explain the effect on equilibrium price and quantity of an increase in the supply of strawberries.
- Calculate equilibrium price and quantity from the demand function Qd = 1000 – 100P and the supply function Qs = –200 + 200P.
  The value of 'c' in the supply function falls to –500. Calculate the excess at the original equilibrium price and find the new equilibrium price and quantity.

Learning Outcomes

- Explain why scarcity **necessitates** choices that answer the 'what to produce?' question.

- Explain why choice results in an opportunity cost.

- Explain, using diagrams, that price has a signalling function and an incentive function, which result in a **reallocation** of resources when prices change as a result of a change in demand or supply conditions.

Why does scarcity mean that firms must make choices about what to produce and why does a choice result in an opportunity cost?

Resources are **scarce**. If a **firm** uses its resources to produce a good it cannot use them to produce a different good. The firm must choose what good to produce. Economists assume that a firm chooses to produce the good that earns the highest profit. (In reality firms have many objectives and maximizing profit is not always the primary objective. Alternative objectives will be discussed in a later unit.) In order to earn this profit the firm must **forgo** the profit it would have earned from producing a different good. The **opportunity cost** of doing something is the next best alternative forgone, therefore the opportunity cost of producing the good making the highest profit is the profit that would have been made from using the scarce resources to produce the good that earns the next highest profit.

Explain the rationing, signalling, and incentive function of price and explain how changes in price lead to a reallocation of resources

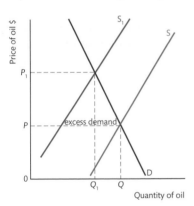

Figure 6.1

When **supply** of a resource such as oil (Figure 6.1) decreases, the supply curve **shifts** up and to the left from S to S₁ causing excess demand at equilibrium price P. Price increases to reflect the increasing scarcity of the good and as price rises the shortage is **eliminated**. The increase in price sends a **signal** to buyers to **ration** their use of the resource. **Quantity demanded** falls leading to a movement up and along the demand curve D and the resource is **conserved**. As the resource becomes scarcer the supply curve shifts further up and to the left and the excess demand becomes greater. Price must increase even further in order to eliminate the excess leading to greater rationing and conservation of the resource.

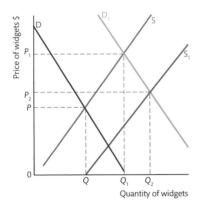

Figure 6.2

An **incentive** is something that motivates a producer or consumer to change behaviour. Figure 6.2 shows the demand and supply diagram for the market for widgets. Demand increases and the demand curve shifts up and to the right from D to D₁. Price increases to in order to eliminate the excess demand at the equilibrium price P. As price increases, *ceteris paribus*, profit increases acting as an incentive for firms in the **industry** to **allocate** more resources to the production of the good in order to increase **quantity supplied**. This leads to a movement up and along the supply curve S.

Increasing prices act as an incentive for consumers to reduce **consumption** leading to a movement up and along the new demand curve D₁. The market clears where quantity demanded equals quantity supplied at the new equilibrium price P₁ and new **equilibrium quantity** Q₁.

Firms outside the industry will be encouraged by the higher profits to reallocate resources to the production of widgets and enter the market. This causes the **market supply curve** to shift down and to the right from S to S₁.

Glossary

necessitates makes something necessary

conserved saved/used more sparingly

Synonyms

reallocation . redistribution

scarce .... limited/finite

firm .... business producer/supplier

forgo .... sacrifice/give up

shifts .... moves

eliminate .. remove/get rid of

signal .... sign/message

ration .... limit/restrict

incentive ... encouragement/ motivation

allocate ..... distribute

consumption . use

Subject vocabulary

resources the inputs into the production process, the factors of production

opportunity cost the next best alternative forgone

supply the amount of a good that a firm is willing and able to produce at each price

quantity demanded the amount of a good consumers are willing and able to buy at a given price over a given period of time

industry a group of firms that produce the same or similar goods or services

quantity supplied the amount of a good that firms are willing and able to produce at a given price over a given period of time

equilibrium quantity the output that results when quantity demanded is equal to quantity supplied

market supply curve a curve that shows the total of the quantity supplied at each price by all firms in the market

excess supply occurs when quantity supplied is greater than quantity demanded

consumer sovereignty occurs when firms allocate resources to the production of goods in accordance with the wants of consumers

ceteris paribus Latin phrase meaning 'all other things being equal' or 'all other things being held constant'

There is **excess supply** in the market at P_1. Price falls to eliminate the excess. A fall in price leads to a fall in profit, thereby reducing the incentive to make the good, leading to a fall in quantity supplied and a movement down and along the supply curve S_1. The fall in price sends a signal to consumers to increase quantity demanded, leading to a movement down and along the demand curve D_1. The market clears at the new equilibrium price P_2 and equilibrium quantity Q_2.

A change in the pattern of consumer demand causes excess demand or excess supply of goods produced by firms in different industries. Prices change to reflect the excesses in the markets, signalling to producers the change in consumer preferences. The change in profit caused by the change in prices provides the incentive for firms to alter the amount of resources allocated to the production of each good. In this way the factors of production are allocated to the production of goods in accordance with the wants of the consumer. This is **consumer sovereignty**. What is produced is determined by the wants of the consumer.

Model sentence: An increase in demand for a good causes a shortage of the good and price rises to eliminate it. The increase in price sends a signal to firms that consumers want more of the good. As price rises, *ceteris paribus*, profit earned on the sale of each unit of output rises thereby providing a greater incentive for firms to allocate more resources to the production of the good in order to increase quantity supplied.

Model sentence: A price increase sends a signal to consumers to use less of the good or leave the market altogether in order to ration their scarce income. Therefore quantity demanded falls. The higher price provides the incentive for the consumers to alter their behaviour and buy less of the good.

Learning Outcomes

- Explain the **concept** of consumer surplus.
- Identify consumer surplus on a demand and supply diagram.
- Explain the concept of producer surplus.
- Identify producer surplus on a demand and supply diagram.

- Explain that the best allocation of resources from society's point of view is at the **competitive market equilibrium**, where social (community) surplus (consumer surplus and producer surplus) is maximized.

Subject vocabulary

competitive market equilibrium it is the level of output and price at which market demand is equal to market supply

consumer surplus the difference between the price a consumer is willing and able to pay and the price the consumer actually pays

producer surplus the difference between the price a firm is willing to accept for a unit of output and the price the consumer actually pays

consumer welfare a measure of the benefit obtained from the consumption of goods

unit of output a single good or service produced by a firm

What are consumer and producer surplus?

A consumer buys a cup of coffee. The price on the menu is $3. The consumer is willing to pay as much as $4 but actually pays $3. The difference between the price the consumer is willing to pay and the price the consumer actually pays is called **consumer surplus**. The individual's consumer surplus is $1 ($4 − $3 = $1). The owner of the cafe might be willing to take $2 for a cup of coffee but actually gets $3. The difference between the actual price received and the price the seller is willing to take is called **producer surplus**. The producer surplus is $1 ($3 − $2 = $1).

What is the relationship between price, consumer surplus, and consumer welfare?

Consumer surplus is the additional benefit gained by the consumer from paying a price which is below the price the consumer is willing to pay. As price falls, *ceteris paribus*, the difference between the price the consumer is willing to pay and the price actually paid gets bigger, resulting in an increase in consumer surplus and therefore an increase in benefit. **Consumer welfare** is a measure of the benefit obtained from the **consumption** of a good. Therefore a fall in price and the following increase in consumer surplus represent a consumer welfare gain.

What is the relationship between price, producer surplus, and producer welfare?

Benefit gained for a producer is determined by the amount of profit earned from the sale of each **unit of output**. As price increases, *ceteris paribus*, profit increases and therefore the **firm**'s benefit increases. Producer surplus is the additional benefit gained from receiving a price which is above the price the firm is willing to take. As price increases, *ceteris paribus*, the difference between the price the firm is willing to take and the actual price received gets bigger leading to an increase in producer surplus and therefore an increase in benefit. **Producer welfare** is a measure of the benefit gained by a firm from the sale of goods. Therefore an increase in price and the following rise in producer surplus represent a producer welfare gain.

Model sentence: A change in price leads to a change in the difference between the price a consumer is willing to pay and the price actually paid, and in the difference between the price producers are willing to take and the price actually received, therefore as price changes consumer and producer surplus changes.

What are market consumer and market producer surplus?

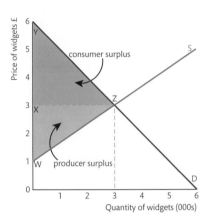

Figure 7.1

Figure 7.1 is a demand and supply diagram for a **widget**. The **equilibrium price** is £3 and the **equilibrium quantity** is 3000 units. We can read from the demand curve that at £4 consumers are willing to buy 2000 units. At £5 quantity demanded is 1000 units. Consumers are willing to pay more for the 3000 units than they actually pay. This is the market consumer surplus which is the additional benefit gained by all the consumers in the market. This represents their welfare gain. The consumer surplus is the area above equilibrium price and below the demand curve labelled X, Y, Z.

It can be read from the supply curve that some of the firms in the market are willing to supply widgets at prices below the equilibrium price of £3. At £1.50 firms are willing to supply 750 units per week. At £2.50 **quantity supplied** is 2250 units. Firms in the **industry** are willing to supply the 3000 units for less money than they actually receive. This is the producer surplus which is the additional benefit gained by the firms and represents the firms' welfare gain. Producer surplus is the area below the equilibrium price and above the supply curve labelled W, X, Z.

Why is society's welfare maximized at equilibrium point and why are resources allocated efficiently when markets are in equilibrium?

A competitive market is one that has lots of buyers and lots of firms. There are too many firms for them to **collude** and agree a price or output for the industry and, with so many firms and buyers, no buyer or firm acting on their own is big enough to influence total **market demand** or **market supply** and is therefore not able to affect **market price**.

Consumer surplus is the additional benefit gained by the buyer from paying a lower price than that which the consumer is prepared to pay. Therefore consumer benefit is **maximized** when consumer surplus is maximized.

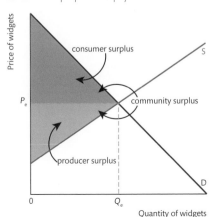

Figure 7.2

Producer surplus is the additional benefit gained by a firm from receiving a higher price than that which it is willing to take. Therefore producer benefit is maximized when producer surplus is maximized.

Community or **social surplus** is the **sum** of the additional benefit consumers and producers receive at a given price. Therefore society's benefit is maximized when the sum of consumer and producer surplus is maximized. **Welfare** is a measure of benefit therefore society's welfare is maximized when social surplus is maximized.

When the market is in **equilibrium** the sum of consumer surplus and producer surplus is maximized. Therefore society's welfare is maximized when the market is in equilibrium. The firms must **allocate** a specific quantity of **resources** to the **production** of this good in order to produce output at Q_e. This is the point of **allocative efficiency**. It is the best or optimal allocation of resources from the point of view of society because welfare is maximized at the equilibrium point Q_e P_e.

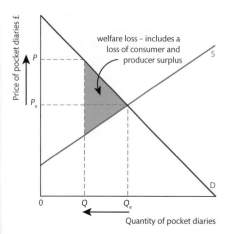

Figure 7.3

When there are only a few firms in the industry they are able to collude. The firms can agree to set a higher price in order to increase producer surplus. We can see in Figure 7.3 that as price increases from P_e to P, quantity demanded falls from Q_e to Q. The industry reduces output from Q_e to Q. Fewer resources are now allocated to the production of this good. At P the market is in **disequilibrium**. Quantity demanded does not equal quantity supplied. The community or social surplus is now smaller. The loss of social surplus is represented by the shaded area in the diagram. There is a loss of welfare when price is above equilibrium price. It is allocatively inefficient. More resources need to be allocated to the production of this good in order to maximize social surplus and society's welfare.

Model sentence: An efficient allocation of resources occurs when the market is in equilibrium and social surplus is maximized.

Test your understanding of this unit by answering the following questions

- Using a diagram to illustrate your answer, explain what happens to consumer surplus when price increases.
- Using a diagram to illustrate your answer, explain what happens to producer surplus when price falls.
- Explain why there is a welfare loss when price is greater than equilibrium price.
- Explain why allocative efficiency occurs at equilibrium point in a competitive market.

1.2 Elasticity: Price elasticity of demand (PED)

Learning Outcomes

- Explain the concept of price elasticity of demand, understanding that it involves responsiveness of quantity demanded to a change in price, along a given demand curve.

- Calculate PED using the following equation: PED = percentage change in quantity demanded / percentage change in price.

- State that the PED value is treated as if it were positive although its mathematical value is usually negative.

- Explain using diagrams and PED values, the concepts of price elastic demand, price inelastic demand, unit elastic demand, and perfectly inelastic demand.

- Explain the determinants of PED, including the number and closeness of substitutes, the degree of necessity, time, and the proportion of income spent on the good.

What is price elasticity of demand and how is it calculated?

Price elasticity of demand (PED) measures the responsiveness of quantity demanded for a good to a change in its price.

It is calculated using the formula $PED = \dfrac{\text{percentage change in quantity demanded}}{\text{percentage change in price}} = \dfrac{\%\Delta Qd}{\%\Delta P}$

Δ is the Greek letter delta. It is used in mathematics and means 'change in'.

This formula is used when the changes are given in percentages.

Calculation of PED using the formula $PED = \dfrac{\%\Delta Qd}{\%\Delta P}$ – a step-by-step guide

Trouble shooter

Price falls by 6% leading to an increase in quantity demanded of 9%.

I will enter the percentage changes into the formula:

$PED = \dfrac{9}{-6}$ simplify by dividing 9 by −6
($\%\Delta P$ is negative because price has decreased)

PED = −1.5 (PED is negative because a positive number divided by a negative number gives a negative number)

When the changes are in raw values we use the formula:

$PED = \dfrac{\Delta Qd/Qd}{\Delta P/P}$ ($\Delta Qd/Qd$ means ΔQd divided by Qd)
($\Delta P/P$ means ΔP divided by P)

ΔQd is the change in quantity demanded, Qd is the original quantity demanded, ΔP is the change in price and P is the original price.

Calculation of PED using the formula $PED = \dfrac{\Delta Qd/Qd}{\Delta P/P}$ $\Delta Qd/Qd$ – a step-by-step guide

Trouble shooter

Price increases from $3 to $9 causing quantity demanded to fall from 12,000 units to 4000 units.

ΔQd = −8,000 units (¡ is negative because quantity demanded falls).

Original Qd = 12, 000 units, ΔP = $3 to $9 = $6 (it is positive because price has increased) and Original price = $3.

Now the calculations are added into the formula:

$PED = \dfrac{-8000/12000}{6/3}$ simplify by dividing −8000 by 12,000 and by dividing 6 by 3

$PED = \dfrac{-0.67}{2}$ Simplify by dividing −0.67 by 2

PED = −0.34 (PED is negative because a negative number divided by a positive number gives a negative number)

price elasticity of demand (PED) a measure of how quantity demanded responds to a change in price in percentage terms

quantity demanded the amount of a good consumers are willing and able to buy at a given price over a given period of time

How to calculate an unknown value when all the other values are known – a step-by-step guide

Trouble shooter

Calculation of the change in quantity demanded caused by a change in price when the original price, the change in price, the original quantity demanded, and the value of PED are known.

P = $4, new price = $6, original quantity demanded = 120 units, and PED = −0.5

The figures are entered into the formula PED = $\frac{\Delta Qd/Qd}{\Delta P/P}$

−0.5 = $\frac{\Delta Qd/120}{2/4}$ simplify by dividing 2 by 4

−0.5 = $\frac{\Delta Qd/120}{0.5}$ simplify by multiplying both sides of the equation by 0.5

−0.25 = ΔQd/120 simplify by multiplying both sides of the equation by 120

−30 = ΔQd

New quantity demanded = original Qd − ΔQd

120 − 30 = 90

An increase in price from $4 to $6 causes quantity demanded to fall from 120 units to 90 units.

Why is the value of PED negative?

A price increase is a positive change and it causes quantity demanded to fall which is a negative change and as price falls (negative change) quantity demanded rises (positive change). So price and quantity demanded have an **inverse relationship** reflecting the **law of demand**. In order to work out PED the percentage change in quantity demanded is divided by the percentage change in price. When one value is positive the other value is negative. A negative number divided by a positive number gives a negative number (minus divided by plus is minus) and a positive divided by a negative gives a negative (plus divided by minus is minus). As the value of PED is always negative economists often ignore the minus sign.

Explain using diagrams and PED values, the concepts of price elastic demand, price inelastic demand, unit elastic demand, and perfectly inelastic demand

Figure 8.1a and 8.1b show **demand curves** for two different goods served during one week at a cafe.

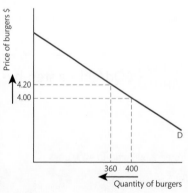

Figure 8.1a

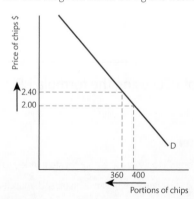

Figure 8.1b

In Figure 8.1a an increase in price of 5% causes quantity demanded to fall by 10%: PED = −10/5 = (−) 2. The %ΔQd > %ΔP so the **absolute value** of PED is greater than 1 (ignoring the minus sign) and demand is **price elastic**. In Figure 8.1b a price rise of 20% causes quantity demanded to fall by 10%. PED = −10/20 = 0.5 (ignoring the minus sign). The %ΔQd < %ΔP so the absolute value of PED is less than 1 and demand is **price inelastic**. When %ΔQd = %ΔP the absolute value of PED is equal to 1 and demand is **price unit elastic**.

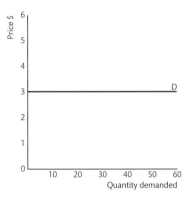

In Figure 8.2 at a price of $3 quantity demanded has no end. It is infinite. As price changes, quantity demanded falls from infinity to zero. To reflect this the demand curve is horizontal at price. As price changes, the change in quantity demanded is infinite. Any number divided by or into infinity equals infinity. A 5% increase in price for example causes quantity demanded to fall from infinity to zero.

$$PED = \frac{\%\Delta Qd}{\%\Delta P} \quad PED = \frac{\infty}{5} = \infty \ (\infty \text{ means infinity}).$$

Demand is **perfectly elastic** with respect to price.

Figure 8.2

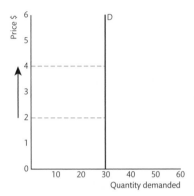

In Figure 8.3 a change in price causes no change in quantity demanded. The change in quantity demanded = 0. Quantity demanded is 30 units at all prices. To reflect this the demand curve is vertical at 30 units. Any number divided by or into 0 equals 0. Price increases from $2 to $4. This is a 100% increase causing quantity demanded to change by 0. To reflect this the demand curve is vertical at 30 units.

$$PED = \frac{\%\Delta Qd}{\%\Delta P} = \frac{0}{100} = 0.$$

Demand is **perfectly inelastic** with respect to price.

Figure 8.3

Model sentence: The value of PED is determined by the relative size of the percentage change in price and quantity demanded: when the percentage change in quantity demanded is greater than the percentage change in price, PED has an absolute value greater than 1 and demand is price elastic and when the percentage change in quantity demanded is less than the percentage change in price, PED has an absolute value less than 1 and demand is price inelastic.

Explain how PED is determined

Quantity demanded of a good is more responsive to a change in its price when there are lots of close **substitutes** available for consumers to buy instead of the good. Demand is more price elastic.

If a good is a **necessity** (e.g. oil) quantity demanded is less responsive to a change in its price and demand is more price inelastic. Demand for luxury goods is more price elastic than for necessities because **consumption** of luxury goods is not essential.

If a good is **addictive** (e.g. tobacco) it is more difficult to reduce consumption following an increase in price. Therefore demand is more price inelastic.

It is difficult for consumers to immediately change patterns of consumption. It takes time to find suitable substitutes and to ration use of a good following an increase in price. Over a short period of time demand is more price inelastic but becomes less price inelastic over time, as consumers are able to find substitutes and reduce consumption further.

The price of some goods is very low. **Expenditure** on them makes up a very small **proportion** of a consumer's income so that even after a large increase in price there is little or no change in quantity demanded. If the price of a box of matches increases by 15% the change in quantity demanded would be much less than 15%, therefore demand is price inelastic.

Model sentence: The more close substitutes there are available on the market the easier it is for consumers to switch expenditure and buy an alternative good, therefore demand for a good with many close substitutes will be more price elastic.

Learning Outcomes

- Calculate PED between two **designated** points on a demand curve using the PED equation.
- Explain why PED varies along a straight line demand curve and is not represented by the slope of the demand curve.
- Examine the role of PED for firms in making decisions regarding price changes and their effect on total revenue.
- Explain why PED for many primary goods is relatively low and the PED for manufactured goods is relatively high.
- Examine the significance of PED for government in relation to indirect taxes.

Calculate and explain PED along a straight line demand curve (see Figure 9.1a/b)

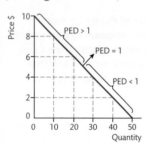

Figure 9.1a

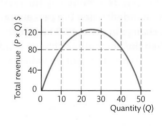

Figure 9.1b

As price increases from $2 to $4 **quantity demanded** falls from 40 to 30 units. (See pages 19–21 for a detailed explanation of how to calculate PED.)

$\text{PED} = \dfrac{\Delta Qd/Qd}{\Delta P/P} = \dfrac{-10/40}{2/2} = \dfrac{-0.25}{1} = (-)\,0.25$. PED < 1 so demand is **price inelastic**. Remember when stating the value of PED that the minus sign is ignored – it is treated as a positive.

Revenue = price × quantity. When price is $2 revenue = $2 × 40 = $80.

When price is $4 revenue = $4 × 30 = $120, an increase of $40. As price rises from $2 to $4 revenue increases by $40. As price falls from $4 to $2 revenue falls from $120 to $80, a fall of $40.

Therefore when demand is price inelastic an increase in price leads to an increase in revenue and a fall in price leads to a fall in revenue because the percentage change in price is greater than the percentage change in quantity demanded.

As price increases from $6 to $8 quantity demanded falls from 20 to 10 units.

$\text{PED} = \dfrac{-10/20}{2/6} = \dfrac{-0.5}{0.33} -10/20 = -0.5 = (-)\,1.51$. PED > 1 so demand is **price elastic**.

When price is $6 revenue = $6 × 20 = $120. When price is $8 revenue = $8 × 10 = $80, a fall of $40. As price rises from $6 to $8 revenue falls from $120 to $80, a decrease of $40. As price falls from $8 to $6 revenue increases from $80 to $120, a rise of $40.

Therefore, when demand is price elastic an increase in price leads to a fall in revenue and a fall in price leads to an increase in revenue, because the percentage change in quantity demanded is greater than the percentage change in price.

The **slope** remains constant moving along a straight line **demand curve**. The measure of the slope of the demand curve is in absolute terms. For example, a price increase of $2 from $2 to $4 causes a fall in quantity demanded from 40 to 30 units and a price increase of $2 from $6 to $8 causes a fall in quantity demanded from 20 to 10 units. In both cases price changes by $2 causing quantity demanded to change by 10 units. PED, on the other hand, measures the relationship between a percentage change in price and a percentage change in quantity demanded. It is measured in relative terms. A change in price or quantity when price or quantity is low results in a relatively large percentage change. A change in price or quantity when price or quantity is high results in a relatively small percentage change. For example, a price increase of $2 from $2 to $4 is a 100% increase in price whereas a price increase of $2 from $6 to $8 is only a 33.33% increase in price, even though the actual price in both cases changes by the same amount.

Explain the relationship between PED and total revenue (see Figure 9.1a/b)

At first, as price increases from zero the percentage change in price > the percentage change in quantity demanded. Demand is price inelastic, therefore revenue increases as price rises. As price continues to rise it causes a movement up and along the demand curve. Price elasticity of demand becomes less price inelastic, because the difference between the rate at which price and quantity demanded changes begins to fall. While the percentage change in price is greater than that of quantity demanded, revenue will continue to rise as price increases, but at a **diminishing** rate. This means that, as price increases, the addition to total revenue is positive, but the increase in total revenue is less than the increase gained by the previous increase in price. When the percentage change in price = the percentage change in quantity demanded, total revenue is **maximized**. The value of PED = 1 and demand is **unit price elastic**. This occurs halfway along the straight line demand curve at a price of $5 and a quantity of 25 units.

As price increases above $5 the percentage change in quantity demanded > the percentage change in price, therefore revenue begins to fall. As price continues to rise, PED becomes more elastic. Total revenue falls at an increasing rate until price is $10 and quantity demanded is 0 and there is no revenue.

Revenue maximization

If a firm's **output** and price is at a point on the demand curve where PED is inelastic the firm can increase revenue by increasing price and reducing output. If output and price is at a point where PED is elastic the firm can increase revenue by lowering price and increasing output. Therefore, in order to maximize revenue, a firm sets output or price where PED = 1 and demand is unit price elastic.

Model sentence: When the absolute value of PED is less than 1 increasing price causes revenue to rise and when the absolute value of PED is more than 1 reducing price causes revenue to rise, therefore revenue is maximized when the absolute value of PED = 1.

Examine the role of PED for firms in making decisions regarding price changes and their effect on total revenue

A firm launching a new good wants to maximize revenue over the life of the good. The firm will try to get individual consumers to pay the most they are willing to pay. In other words the firm tries to steal as much **consumer surplus** as possible. Initially the firm charges a high price and a quantity of units are sold to less price-sensitive consumers who are willing and able to pay the high price. When **demand** of these consumers has been met and sales begin to fall the firm lowers price at a point on the demand curve where PED is inelastic, more consumers enter the **market** to buy the good, and revenue increases. Over time the firm continues to lower the price in order to increase quantity demanded and increase revenue. This **pricing strategy** is called skimming the market and is particularly used by firms producing new technological goods. In **industries** where there are firms producing **branded goods** a new firm might reduce the price of its new good in order to gain **market share**. As brand awareness rises and the good is established in the market, PED becomes more inelastic and the firm can raise the price and increase revenue.

Why is PED for primary goods lower than the PED for manufactured goods?

Primary goods such as wheat have fewer **substitutes** than **manufactured goods**. Primary goods are more likely to be **necessities**. Manufactured goods are often **luxuries**. In countries where incomes are relatively high consumers spend a lower proportion of income on primary goods and a higher proportion on manufactured

23

goods. Therefore quantity demanded of primary goods is less sensitive to a change in price than quantity demanded of manufactured goods. Therefore the value of PED is likely to be lower and demand less price elastic for primary goods than for manufactured goods.

Examine the significance of PED for government in relation to indirect taxes

An indirect tax is a tax imposed on producers by the government. It is a tax placed on a good or service. Examples include **duties** on cigarettes, alcohol, fuel, and value added tax (VAT).

When a government increases the duty on a good, the price of the good increases leading to a fall in quantity demanded. If demand is highly price elastic the rate of change in quantity demanded > the rate of change in price and a duty that raises price will cause a large decrease in sales increasing **unemployment** in the **industry**. The government places taxes on goods that are more price inelastic because the fall in quantity of goods bought is not as great, therefore there are not as many job losses and the **tax revenue** (tax per unit × quantity sold) collected by the government from the sale of the goods will be greater.

Test your understanding of this unit by answering the following questions

- Explain why revenue is maximized when the absolute value of PED = 1. Use a diagram to illustrate your answer.
- Explain why PED is lower for primary goods than for manufactured goods.

Learning Outcomes

- Outline the **concept** of **cross-price elasticity of demand**, understanding that it involves **responsiveness** of demand for one good (and hence a **shifting** demand curve) to a change in the price of another good.

- Calculate XED using the following equation XED = $\dfrac{\text{percentage change in quantity demanded of good x}}{\text{percentage change in price of good y}}$

- Show that substitute goods have a positive value of XED and **complementary goods** have a negative value of XED.

- Explain that the (absolute) value of XED depends on the closeness of the relationship between two goods.

- Examine the **implications** of XED for businesses if prices of substitutes or complements change.

Calculation of XED

XED measures the responsiveness of demand for one good to a change in the price of another good.

It is calculated using the formula XED = $\dfrac{\text{percentage change in quantity demanded of good x}}{\text{percentage change in price of good y}}$

How does the price of one substitute affect the demand for the other? – a step-by-step guide

Trouble shooter

Goods 'X' and 'Y' are substitutes: one good can be used in place of the other. As the price of good 'Y' increases it becomes **relatively** more expensive than good 'X'. Some consumers buy good 'X' in place of good 'Y'. This leads to a fall in **quantity demanded** for good 'Y' (a movement up and along the **demand curve**) and an increase in demand for good 'X' (a shift up and to the right of the demand curve).

As the price of good 'Y' falls it becomes relatively cheaper than good 'X'. Some consumers buy good 'Y' in place of good 'X' leading to an increase in quantity demanded for good Y (a movement down and along the demand curve) and a fall in demand for good × (a shift down and to the left of the demand curve).

Model sentence: In the case of two substitutes an increase in the price of one leads to a fall in quantity demanded of that good (a movement up and along its demand curve) and an increase in demand for the other good (a shift up and to the right of its demand curve).

Calculate XED and explain why it is always positive in the case of substitutes

There are two **barber** shops in the high street, John's and Sam's. John increases the price of a haircut from £20 to £25. Some customers go to Sam's instead of John's. Quantity demanded of haircuts at John's falls and demand for haircuts at Sam's increases from 100 a week to 150.

How to calculate XED from the information above – a step-by-step guide

Trouble shooter

Use the formula $XED = \dfrac{\Delta QdX/QdX}{\Delta PY/PY}$

ΔQdX is the change in quantity demanded for service X, Qd is the original quantity demanded for service X, ΔPY is the change in price of service Y, and P is the original price of service Y.

$XED = \dfrac{50/100}{5/20}$ simplify by dividing 50 by 100 and 5 by 20

$XED = \dfrac{0.5}{0.25}$ simplify by dividing 0.5 by 0.25

$XED = 2$

There is a **positive correlation** between the price of one good and the demand for another when the goods are substitutes. An increase in price of one good causes an increase in demand for the other. A positive divided by a positive equals a positive.

If John reduces the price some customers have their haircut at John's instead of Sam's leading to an increase in quantity demanded at John's and a fall in demand at Sam's. The fall in price of one service leads to a fall in demand for the other. A negative divided by a negative equals a positive. Therefore the value of XED for substitutes is always positive.

The services are close substitutes: one can easily be **consumed** in place of the other. The demand for one service is very sensitive to a change in the price of the other.

The greater the similarity between two goods the more responsive demand for one good is to a change in the price of the other and the higher the value of XED.

How does the XED of substitutes affect businesses?

It is useful for a firm to know the effect on demand for their good when a **rival business** changes its price and the effect on demand for a rival's good when it changes price. This knowledge helps firms develop a **pricing strategy** that increases **revenue** and **profit**.

How does the price of one complementary good affect the demand for the other? – a step-by-step guide

Trouble shooter

Goods 'X' and 'Y' are complements: they are used together. As the price of good 'Y' falls quantity demanded increases (a movement down and along its demand curve). As more of good 'Y' is sold demand for good 'X' which is used with good 'Y' increases (a shift up and to the right of the demand curve).

As the price of good 'Y' increases quantity demanded falls (a movement up and along its demand curve). As less of good 'Y' is sold demand for good 'X' decreases (a shift down and to the left of the demand curve).

Model sentence: In the case of complementary goods an increase in the price of one good leads to a fall in quantity demanded of that good (a movement up and along its demand curve) and a fall in demand for the other good (a shift to the left of its demand curve).

Calculate XED and explain why it is always negative in the case of complements

The price of using mobile phones falls and quantity demanded increases, leading to a movement down and along the demand curve. As more phones are sold the demand for 'apps' (applications) increases causing the demand curve for apps to shift up and to the right.

The price of mobile phones falls by 10% and this leads to a 25% increase in quantity demanded of 'apps'.

$$XED = \frac{\%\Delta QdX}{\%\Delta PY} = \frac{25\%}{-10\%} = -2.5$$

Let's say the price of using mobile phones increases by 10% leading to a 25% fall in quantity demanded of 'apps'.

$$XED = \frac{-25\%}{10\%} = -2.5$$

The value of XED is always negative in the case of complements because of the **inverse relationship** between the price of one good and the demand of the other. A positive divided by a negative equals a negative. A negative divided by a positive equals a negative.

Lots of people use 'apps' on their mobile phones, therefore the number of phones sold has a large impact on the demand for 'apps'. Demand for 'apps' is highly responsive to changes in the price of mobile phones. The stronger the relationship between the two complementary goods the higher the negative value of XED.

How does the XED of complements affect businesses?

Trips to the cinema and confectionery and fizzy drinks are strong complements. The profit on the sale of confectionery and drinks at the cinema is very high. The owner knows how much on average each customer spends on these items. Reducing the price of cinema tickets to attract more customers will lead to an increase in demand for confectionery and drinks. It is possible that this pricing strategy might increase profits overall.

Unrelated goods

Goods are unrelated when an increase in the price of one good does not affect the demand for the other.

Test your understanding of this unit by answering the following questions

- Explain why the value of XED is positive in the case of substitutes.
- Calculate the XED when price of one good falls from $9 to $6 causing quantity demanded for the other good to increase from 120,000 units to 200,000 units. Comment on the relationship between the two goods.
- 'As the price of petrol increases demand for more fuel-efficient cars will increase'. Using the concept of cross-price elasticity of demand, comment on the validity of this comment.

Subject vocabulary

inverse relationship a change in the value of one variable leads to an opposite change in direction in the value of the other variable

unrelated goods goods that are not linked in their use

Synonyms

concept(s)........ idea(s)/ theory/ies

shifting............ moving

Learning Outcomes

- Outline the **concept** of income elasticity of demand, understanding that it involves responsiveness of demand (and hence a **shifting** demand curve) to a change in income.

- Calculate YED using the following equation
$$YED = \frac{\text{percentage change in quantity demanded}}{\text{percentage change in income}}$$

- Show that normal goods have a positive value of YED and inferior goods have a negative value of YED. Distinguish, with reference to YED, between necessity (income inelastic) goods and luxury (income elastic) goods.

- Examine the implications for producers and for the economy of a relatively low YED for primary goods, a relatively higher YED for manufactured goods, and an even higher YED for services.

How does a change in income affect demand in the case of normal goods?

Income elasticity of demand measures the **responsiveness** of **quantity demanded** to a change in **income**.

It is calculated by using the formula YED = $\dfrac{\text{percentage change in quantity demanded}}{\text{percentage change in income}}$

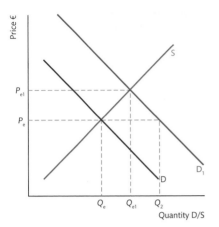

As income increases, **demand** for flights increases, leading to a shift up and to the right of the **demand curve** and **excess demand** (Q_2-Q_e) at the **equilibrium price** P_e. Price increases to **eliminate** the excess. As price rises there is a movement up and along the **supply curve** and up and along the new demand curve D_1. Price rises until quantity demanded = **quantity supplied** at P_{e1}. An increase in income causes price to rise from P_e to P_{e1} and quantity demanded and supplied to increase from Q_e to Q_{e1}. A fall in income leads to a shift down and to the left of the demand curve and a fall in equilibrium price and quantity demanded and supplied.

Figure 11.1

Calculate YED – a step-by-step guide

Trouble shooter

A consumer's income increases from $30,000 to $40,000 leading to an increase in quantity demanded from 120 to 160 units. The formula used to calculate YED when not given the changes in percentage terms is

$$YED = \frac{\Delta Qd/Qd}{\Delta Y/Y}$$

ΔQd is the change in quantity demanded, Qd is the original quantity demanded, ΔY is the change in income, and Y is the original income.

$YED = \dfrac{40/120}{10\,000/30\,000}$ simplify by dividing 40 by 120 and 10 000 by 30 000

$YED = \dfrac{0.33}{0.33}$

$YED = 1$

The proportional change in quantity demanded (0.33) = the proportional change in income (0.33) YED = 1 and demand is income unit elastic.

There is a **positive correlation** between income and quantity demanded for **normal goods** (income and quantity demanded change in the same direction). Therefore the value of YED for a normal good is positive: a positive number divided by a positive number gives a positive number and a negative divided by a negative gives a positive.

What is the difference between normal goods that are necessities and those that are luxuries?

When the proportional change in quantity demanded < the proportional change in income YED is less than 1. This means that quantity demanded is relatively insensitive to changes in income. Demand is **income inelastic** and goods are described as **necessities**. For example, a fall of 3% in income leads to a 0.6% fall in the quantity of bread demanded.

$YED = \dfrac{\%\Delta Qd}{\%\Delta Y} = \dfrac{-0.6}{-3} = 0.2$ YED is positive and less than 1, therefore bread is a necessity.

income elastic demand for a good is income elastic when the value of income elasticity of demand is greater than 1

luxuries when income changes demand for a luxury good changes at a greater rate. Demand is relatively sensitive to changes in income.

inferior goods goods for which demand falls as income increases

negative correlation a relationship between two variables such that they move in the opposite direction

market where buyers and sellers meet to exchange money for goods and services

manufactured goods goods produced from raw materials

output the quantity of goods produced by a firm, industry or economy

capital (goods) manufactured goods that are used in the production of other goods

primary good a good that has not been processed and is in a raw state (e.g. fruit/wheat)

direct taxes a tax that is paid directly by an individual or firm to the governmnent. For example income tax on wages and company profits.

disposable income household income after direct taxation has been deducted

industry a group of firms that produce the same or similar goods or services

When the proportional change in quantity demanded > the proportional change in income YED is greater than 1. This means that quantity demanded is highly responsive to changes in income. Demand is **income elastic** and goods are described as **luxuries**.

For example, incomes increase by 4% leading to a 6% increase in the quantity of taxi journeys demanded.

$$YED = \frac{\%\Delta Qd}{\%\Delta Y} = \frac{6}{4} = 1.5 \qquad YED > 1, \text{ therefore a taxi journey is a luxury service.}$$

Model sentence: As quantity demanded becomes more responsive to changes in income, demand becomes more income elastic and the positive value of YED increases.

Explain how a change in income affects demand in the case of inferior goods

In the case of inferior goods, as income increases demand falls, leading to a shift down and to the left of the demand curve and a fall in quantity demanded. As income falls demand increases, leading to a shift up and to the right of the demand curve and an increase in quantity demanded. YED is negative for an **inferior good** because there is a **negative correlation** between income and quantity demanded (income and quantity demanded change in opposite directions). A positive divided by a negative gives a negative and a negative divided by a positive gives a negative.

Calculation of YED

An increase in national income of 3% leads to a 1% fall in the quantity of bus journeys demanded.

$$YED = \frac{\%\Delta Qd}{\%\Delta Y} = \frac{-1}{3} = -0.33$$

YED is negative, therefore a bus journey is an inferior service.

Explain the factors that affect YED

Consumers react differently to changes in their income because the amount of benefit gained from the **consumption** of a good varies from person to person. Goods that are luxuries to some are necessities to others.

If already on a very high income an increase in income might lead to no changes in the consumption of goods. In this case YED would be 0. (A number divided into zero = zero.)

Chicken is a luxury good in China. As incomes increase, quantity demanded increases at a greater rate. As incomes continue to increase, the value of YED for chicken will begin to fall. In time chicken might become income inelastic.

YED changes over the life of a good. Demand for mobile phones when first brought to **market** was income elastic. They were luxury goods. As price has fallen over time demand has become less income elastic. For many the good is no longer a luxury. Some models have become inferior goods. But in poorer countries demand will still be income elastic.

YED depends upon how the good is described. For example, demand for bread in general is income inelastic and a necessity, but demand for specialist bread, such as organic raisin and walnut bread, is income elastic and a luxury.

Explain how YED affects government and producers

A business can predict what will happen to demand when income changes if it knows the YED. When incomes are expected to increase firms producing luxury **manufactured goods**, such as iPads, and services, such as foreign holidays, will have to make plans if the firm wants to increase **output** in order to meet the higher levels of demand. The firm will need to employ and train more workers and buy new **capital**. When incomes are expected to fall the same firms would have to consider reducing the size of the work force and the size of production. The firm might also consider producing an inferior good. Firms can reduce the risk of business failure by producing a range of goods with different YED values.

Why is demand for primary goods income inelastic?

The demand for many **primary goods** is income inelastic. That is, the proportional change in income is greater than the proportional change in quantity demanded so the value of YED <1. As incomes rise the demand for many primary goods such as tea, coffee, and sugar increases, but by a proportionately smaller amount. If income rose by 30% the percentage change in quantity demanded of sugar or tea would be much smaller.

YED and tax

Direct tax is a tax on income. It is called a direct tax because it goes directly from the payer of the tax to the government. Increasing tax reduces consumers' **disposable income** and causes a fall in demand for necessities and luxury goods and an increase in demand for inferior goods. This will have an impact on employment in those **industries** producing goods that have high positive and high negative YEDs.

Test your understanding of this unit by answering the following questions

- Organic bread has a YED of 4 and basic white bread has a YED of 0.1. Incomes are expected to increase by 5% next year. Calculate the percentage increase in quantity demanded for both types of bread.
- Discuss the **implications** of the expected increase in income for the bread-making industry.

Synonyms

implications .... effects/outcomes

responsiveness ... reaction/sensitivity

Learning Outcomes

- Explain the concept of price elasticity of supply, understanding that it involves responsiveness of quantity supplied to a change in price along a given supply curve.

- Calculate PES using the following equation
  $$PES = \frac{percentage\ change\ in\ quantity\ supplied}{percentage\ change\ in\ price}$$

- Explain, using diagrams and PES values, the concepts of elastic supply, inelastic supply, unit elastic supply, **perfectly elastic supply**, and **perfectly inelastic supply**.

- Explain the determinants of PES, including time, mobility of factors of production, unused capacity, and ability to store stocks.

- Explain why the PES for primary goods is relatively low and the PES for manufactured goods is relatively high.

Why is there a positive correlation between price and quantity supplied?

As price increases, *ceteris paribus*, profit increases. Assuming that firms are profit maximizers they will allocate more **resources** to the production of the good that is now more profitable in order to increase **output**. As price rises output rises. When price falls profit falls and firms reduce output as it is now less profitable. **Price elasticity of supply** (PES) measures the **responsiveness** of quantity supplied to a change in price and is calculated using the formula $PES = \dfrac{percentage\ change\ in\ quantity\ supplied}{percentage\ change\ in\ price}$

Calculations of PES – a step-by-step guide

Trouble shooter

Price increases from $8 to $10 leading to an increase in quantity supplied from 8000 units to 9000 units. The formula used to calculate PES when the changes are in raw values is $PES = \dfrac{\Delta Qs/Qs}{\Delta P/P}$

ΔQs is the change in quantity supplied, Qs is the original quantity supplied, ΔP is the change in price, and P is the original price.

$PES = \dfrac{1000/8000}{2/8}$ simplify by dividing 1000 by 8000 and 2 by 8

$PES = \dfrac{0.125}{0.25}$ simplify by dividing 0.125 by 0.25

$PES = 0.5$

The proportional change in quantity supplied (0.125) < the proportional change in price (0.25) therefore PES < 1 and supply is **price inelastic**.

Subject vocabulary

perfectly elastic supply at a particular price quantity supplied is infinite but falls to nothing as price changes. The absolute value of PES is equal to infinity.

perfectly inelastic supply quantity supplied does not change as price changes. PES equals zero.

ceteris paribus Latin phrase meaning 'all other things being equal' or 'all other things being held constant'

resources the inputs into the production process, the factors of production

output the quantity of goods produced by a firm, industry or economy

price elasticity of supply (PES) a measure of how quantity supplied responds to a change in price in percentage terms

price inelastic the percentage change in quantity demanded/supplied < the percentage change in price

Subject vocabulary

supply curve a graph that shows the relationship between price and quantity supplied

demand curve a graph that shows the relationship between price and quantity demanded

demand the amount of a good that consumers are willing and able to buy at each price

perfectly inelastic supply quantity supplied does not change as price changes. PES equals zero.

price unit elastic the percentage change in quantity demanded / supplied = the percentage change in price. PED/PES = 1

perfectly elastic supply at a particular price quantity supplied is infinite but falls to nothing as price changes. The absolute value of PES is equal to infinity.

factors of production the inputs into the production process (land, labour, capital and entrepreneurship)

output the quantity of goods produced by a firm, industry or economy

short run a period of time when at least one factor is variable and the others are fixed

capital (goods) manufactured goods that are used in the production of other goods

Glossary

slope the angle/gradient of the curve

When the changes are in percentage terms use the formula $PES = \dfrac{\%\Delta Qs}{\%\Delta P}$

Price falls by 2% leading to a fall in quantity supplied of 3%. $PES = \dfrac{\%\Delta Qs}{\%\Delta P} = \dfrac{-3}{-2} = 1.5$

The percentage change in quantity supplied (–3%) > the percentage change in price (–2%) therefore PES > 1 and supply is price elastic.

There is a positive **correlation** between quantity supplied and price (they change in the same direction), therefore PES is positive (a positive divided by a positive gives a positive and a negative divided by a negative gives a positive).

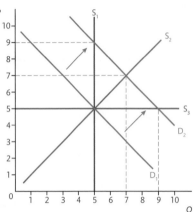

Figure 12.1 shows a demand and supply diagram with 3 **supply curves** each representing different values of PES. The **demand curve shifts** up and to the right from D_1 to D_2. The rate of change in price and quantity supplied caused by an increase in **demand** varies depending on the initial price and quantity supplied and the **slope** of the supply curve. Keeping the initial price and quantity supplied unchanged, as S_1 rotates clockwise the slope becomes less steep. The proportional change in price caused by the same increase in demand falls and the proportional change in quantity supplied rises.

Figure 12.1

Supply curve 1

Demand increases and the demand curve shifts up and to the right from D_1 to D_2. Price increases from $5 to $9 leading to no change in quantity supplied. Quantity supplied stays at 5 units.

$YED = \dfrac{\Delta Qs/Qs}{\Delta P/P} = \dfrac{0/5}{4/5} = \dfrac{0}{0.8} = 0$ (0 divided by any number = 0)

PES = 0, supply is **perfectly inelastic** with respect to price.

Supply curve 2

The demand curve shifts up and to the right. Price increases from $5 to $7 leading to an increase in quantity supplied from 5 units to 7 units.

$PES = \dfrac{\Delta Qs/Qs}{\Delta P/P} = \dfrac{2/5}{2/5} = \dfrac{0.4}{0.4} = 1$ PES = 1, supply is **price unit elastic**.

Supply curve 3

Demand curve shifts up and to the right. Price does not change but quantity supplied increases from 5 units to 9 units.

$PES = \dfrac{\Delta Qs/Qs}{\Delta P/P} = \dfrac{4/5}{\infty} = \dfrac{0.8}{\infty} = \infty$ (any number divided by infinity = ∞) PES = ∞.

Supply is **perfectly elastic** with respect to price.

Model sentence: The less responsive quantity supplied is to a change in price the lower the value of PES and the more price inelastic the supply.

Factors that determine how responsive quantity supplied is to a change in price

Time

In the very **short run** (the time period immediately after a price increase) the **factors of production** are fixed and a firm cannot increase **output** so supply is perfectly inelastic with respect to price. In the short run the quantity of labour is variable (changeable) but the quantities of capital and land are fixed (unchangeable). The firm can only increase output by adding more labour to existing **capital** so supply is price inelastic. Output can be increased by a relatively small amount by only adding labour. In the **long run** the quantities of all factors are variable, therefore the firm can employ more labour and buy more capital in order increase output even more so supply becomes more **price elastic**. Over time quantity supplied becomes more responsive to a change in price. The value of PES increases, supply becomes more price elastic and the slope of the supply curve becomes less steep.

For **primary goods** quantity supplied is less responsive to changes in price. For example, a farmer decides which crops to grow a long time before the goods come to market. It takes a long time to move **resources** away from the production of one crop to the production of another. It is not possible to change the quantity supplied in the short term therefore supply of agricultural goods is more price inelastic. Manufactured goods are likely to be more price elastic than agricultural goods because it is easier for firms producing manufactured goods to reallocate their factors to different production processes and thereby increase output.

Capacity

When a firm is operating at full **capacity** (all the firm's labour and capital is being used) it is difficult to increase output. Supply is more **price inelastic**. A firm is able to increase output if it has **spare** capacity. The greater the amount of capital and labour not being used by the firm the more responsive quantity supplied is to an increase in price so supply is more price elastic.

Stocks

Quantity supplied can be increased when the firm is able to hold lots of stock. These are goods held in storage. Goods can be released onto the market very quickly, therefore supply is more price elastic.

Availability and mobility of resources

In order to increase output a firm must get more resources. In a period of high economic activity **unemployment** is very low. Workers are in **short supply**. **Raw materials** might not be available. When resources needed for the production of a good are in short supply, quantity supplied of that good is less responsive to increases in its price and supply is more price inelastic. When there is a slowdown in economic activity **demand** for resources is lower. More are available for firms to use. Quantity supplied can be increased more easily so supply is more price elastic.

There is a greater supply of **unskilled labour** than **skilled**. It is easier for firms that use unskilled labour to increase the size of the workforce in order to increase output, so supply is more price elastic. When specialized capital and skilled labour are needed, factors are less mobile. A firm will not be able to employ factors quickly in order to increase output so supply is more price inelastic.

Model sentence: When the factors used in the production of a good are easily available, firms in an industry can quickly employ them in order to increase output in response to an increase in price and therefore supply is more price elastic.

Test your understanding of this unit by answering the following questions

- Price of corn increases by 10% leading to an increase in quantity supplied of 1%. Comment on the value of PES.
- Explain why PES becomes more elastic over time.
- Explain why PES is likely to be more inelastic during high levels of economic activity.

1.3 Government intervention – Indirect taxes

Learning Outcomes

- Explain the government intervention of imposing indirect (excise) taxes.
- Show the distinction between specific and *ad valorem* taxes.
- Draw diagrams to show specific and *ad valorem* taxes, and analyse their impacts on market outcomes.
- Discuss the consequences of imposing an indirect tax on the stakeholders in a market, including consumers, producers, and the government.

Synonyms

levied .... placed, imposed

expenditure. spending/ money spent

recuperate .. get back/ recover

imposition .. introduction

incentive ..... encouragement/ motivation

Subject vocabulary

specific tax a charge expressed as a monetary value that producers pay on each unit of a good sold

ad valorem tax a tax based on a percentage of the price such as value added tax (VAT) and sales tax

producer a business that makes goods

income tax a direct tax on individual earnings (wages, rent, profit, interest) and paid to the government

direct taxes a tax that is paid directly by an individual or firm to the governmnent. For example income tax on wages and company profits.

costs of production the amount the firm pays for the factors of production used to produce goods or services

unit of output a single good or service produced by a firm

purchasing power a measure of how many goods and services a given amount of money can buy

normal goods goods for which demand increases when income increases, and falls when income falls

real income income after taking into account the effects of inflation on purchasing power

What is the distinction between specific and *ad valorem* taxes?

An indirect tax is a tax **levied** on **expenditure**. A **specific tax** is a charge expressed as a monetary value that producers have to pay for each unit of a good they sell. It is a per-unit tax or a flat-rate tax. An example is an excise tax or duty which is a tax placed on a selected number of goods, such as tobacco and alcohol. *Ad valorem* **tax** is a charge that producers have to pay for each unit of a good they sell, but expressed as a percentage of the price of the good.

The **producer** pays the tax to the government. The producer must raise the price the consumer pays for each unit in order to **recuperate** the tax. It is called an indirect tax because the tax is not paid directly by the consumer to the government, unlike an **income tax** which is a **direct tax**.

Model sentence: The effect of a tax is to increase the producer's costs of production. When a tax is placed on a unit of output or an existing tax is increased profit at each price falls. Therefore the producer will reduce supply and the supply curve shifts up and to the left.

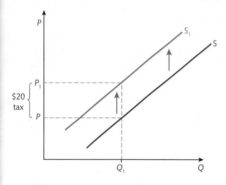

Figure 13.1

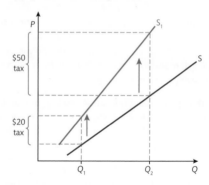

Figure 13.2

As shown in Figure 13.1 the placement of a specific per-unit tax of $20 causes a parallel shift of the supply curve up and to the left (S to S$_1$) at each level of output by the amount of the tax.

As shown in Figure 13.2 the **imposition** of an *ad valorem* tax causes the supply curve to pivot anti-clockwise around the quantity supplied when price equals zero (S to S$_1$). The tax is a percentage of the price therefore as price increases the amount of tax increases and the distance between S and S$_1$ gets bigger. For example, when the rate of a sales tax is 20% and price is $100 the amount of tax is $20. When the price is $250 the amount of tax is $50.

How does a tax affect consumers, producers, and the government?

A tax increases the price consumers have to pay thereby reducing the **purchasing power of income**. This means fewer goods can be bought with the same income and therefore consumption falls.

After a tax is levied consumers have less disposable income to spend and therefore demand for **normal goods** falls.

As demand falls producers of taxed goods reduce output because people are buying fewer goods.

Producers need fewer workers and unemployment increases. Government will therefore have to pay more in welfare payments.

A tax placed on raw materials increases firms' costs of production leading to a fall in profit at each price. There is now less **incentive** to supply so the producer reduces supply causing the supply curve to shift up and to the left. The price of the final good increases leading to a fall in consumers' **real income**.

The increase in costs leads to a fall in international competitiveness. The higher price causes consumers to substitute **imported goods** for domestically produced goods.

The imposition of tax can lead to **inflation**. The disadvantages of inflation are discussed in detail on pages 149–50.

Model sentence: When a tax is levied on a normal good demand falls due to higher prices, producers reduce output, and unemployment in the industry increases. A tax on raw materials increases firms' costs of production, price therefore rises and the firm becomes less internationally competitive leading to higher unemployment in exporting industries.

The government must raise **tax revenue** to pay for the provision of goods and services that would be underconsumed and undersupplied if left to the **free market**. (This will be discussed later in the chapter on market failure.) A tax generates revenue for the government that it can use to provide things such as **infrastructure**, healthcare, education, the armed forces, and **welfare payments**.

There are many effects of a tax on the economy and these will be discussed further in later units.

Test your understanding of this unit by answering the following questions

- Distinguish between a direct tax and an indirect tax.
- Using diagrams to illustrate your answer, explain the difference between a specific tax and an *ad valorem* tax.
- Discuss the effect the imposition of a tax has on a consumer.

Subject vocabulary

imported goods goods sold into a country from another country

inflation an increase in the general level of prices of goods/services in an economy over a given time period, usually a year

tax revenue the income the government receives through the levying and collection of taxes

free market a market where the forces of demand and supply are allowed to operate without any forms of intervention

welfare payment a payment made by the government to someone, usually because the person is unemployed or earns a low income

Glossary

infrastructure the basic structure/systems of a country (e.g. roads/railways)

Learning Outcomes

- Explain, using diagrams, how the **incidence** of indirect taxes on consumers and firms differs, depending on the **price elasticity of demand** and on the **price elasticity of supply**. (HL)

- Plot demand and supply curves for a product from **linear functions** and then illustrate and/or calculate the effects of the imposition of a specific tax on the market (on price, quantity, consumer expenditure, producer revenue, government revenue, consumer surplus, and producer surplus). (HL)

What are the effects on price and quantity of the imposition of a specific tax (HL) – a step-by-step guide

Trouble shooter (see Figure 14.1 and Figure 14.2)

The tax causes the supply curve to shift up and to the left by the amount of the tax (from S to S_{tax}) because the tax rate is given by the vertical distance between the original and new supply curves.

The firm wants to make consumers pay all the tax by setting price at P_2.

However at P_2 quantity supplied > quantity demanded. To eliminate the **excess supply** price must fall from P_2 to P_{tax}.

Price increases from P_e to P_{tax} and quantity falls from Q_e to Q_{tax}.

Synonyms

incidence .... occurence/frequency

Subject vocabulary

price elasticity of demand (PED) a measure of how quantity demanded responds to a change in price in percentage terms

price elasticity of supply (PES) a measure of how quantity supplied responds to a change in price in percentage terms

linear function an equation, the graph of which is a straight line

excess supply occurs when quantity supplied is greater than quantity demanded

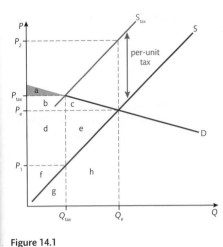

Figure 14.1

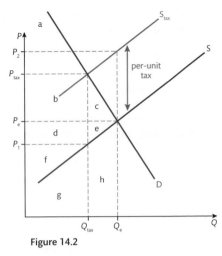

Figure 14.2

Model sentence: The producer wants to pass on all of a tax imposed on a good to the consumers to pay, but increasing the price by the full amount of the tax causes excess supply at that price and therefore price must fall in order to eliminate the excess.

The incidence of tax (HL) – a step-by-step guide (see Figures 14.1 and 14.2)

Trouble shooter

Total expenditure = $P_{tax} \times Q_{tax}$, areas b, d, f, and g.

Tax per-unit is $P_{tax} - P_1$.

Total **tax revenue** = $(P_{tax} - P_1) \times Q_{tax}$, area b + d

Amount of tax paid by the consumers = $(P_{tax} - P_e) \times Q_{tax}$, area b

Amount of tax paid by the producer = $(P_{tax} - P_1 \times Q_{tax}$, area d

Amount of **producer revenue** kept by the producer = $P_1 \times Q_{tax}$, area f + g

What is the effect of the imposition of a specific tax on consumer and producer surplus (HL) – a step-by-step guide

Trouble shooter

Consumer surplus is the difference between the price consumers are willing to pay and the price actually paid. It is the area above **market price** and below the **demand curve**:

Consumer surplus before tax: area a + b + c

After a tax is added the price increases from P_e to P_{tax}.

Consumer surplus after tax: area a

Loss of consumer surplus: area b + c

Producer surplus is the difference between the price the firm is willing to take and the actual price received. It is the area below the market price and above the supply curve.

Producer surplus before tax: area d + e + f

After tax the amount the firm receives falls from P_e to P_1.

Producer surplus after tax: area f

Loss of producer surplus: area d + e

Welfare loss caused by a tax (HL) – a step-by-step guide

Trouble shooter

Loss of consumer surplus: area b + c

b is not lost by society because it is tax revenue which now benefits the government.

c was a benefit to consumers and is lost completely.

Loss of producer surplus: area d + e

d is not lost by society because it is tax revenue.

e was a benefit to the producer and is lost completely.

c and e is the deadweight **welfare loss** of the tax.

What are the effects of PED and PES on the incidence of tax? (HL)

In Figure 14.1 the value of **PED** > the value of **PES**. **Demand** is more **price elastic** than **supply**. Quantity demanded is relatively more **responsive** to a change in price than quantity supplied. Producers are not able to pass on a large amount of the tax to the consumers because quantity demanded would fall too much. The producer must pay most of the tax therefore d > b.

In Figure 14.2 the value of PES > the value of PED. PED is less price elastic than supply. Quantity demanded is relatively less responsive to a change in price than quantity supplied, therefore producers are able to pass on most of the tax therefore b > d.

When demand is more **price inelastic**, *ceteris paribus*, tax revenue is greater because as price increases consumers continue to buy the good in similar quantities. Tax is paid on a larger number of goods than when demand is more price elastic.

Model sentence: The incidence of tax is determined by the price elasticity of supply and demand. When supply is more price elastic than demand most of the tax is paid by the consumer. If demand is more price elastic than supply producers will pay most of the tax.

Show the effect of a tax using linear functions (HL)

See pages 5–6 and 9–10 to find out how to plot the demand and supply curves from the functions Qd = 2000 – 200P and Qs = –400 + 400P for prices from $0 to $6.

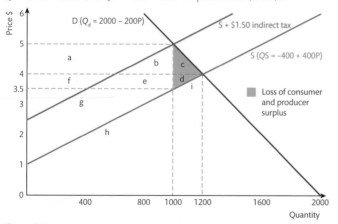

Figure 14.3

The **equilibrium price** is $4 and quantity is 1200 units. A **per-unit tax** of $1.50 is imposed in effect increasing the firm's **costs of production**. Less profit is now made at each price so the firm reduces supply causing the supply curve to shift up and to the left by the amount of the tax. There is a **parallel shift** up and to the left of the supply curve from S to S + $1.50 as seen in Figure 14.3.

Equilibrium price increases from $4 to $5 and quantity falls from 1200 to 1000 units.

Tax revenue is = tax per unit × quantity = $1.50 × 1000 = $1500. It is the area a + b + e + f.

Tax paid by consumers is area a + b. Price has risen by $1 therefore consumers are paying $1 of the $1.50 per-unit tax. The total amount of tax that consumers pay = $1 × 1000 = $1000.

Tax paid by the producer is area f + e. Consumers pay $1 of the $1.50 tax therefore the producer must pay $0.50 per unit. The amount of tax the producer pays = $0.50 × 1000 = $500.

Subject vocabulary

welfare loss the sum of the loss of consumer and producer surplus caused by market or government failure

price elasticity of demand (PED) a measure of how quantity demanded responds to a change in price in percentage terms

price elasticity of supply (PES) a measure of how quantity supplied responds to a change in price in percentage terms

demand the amount of a good that consumers are willing and able to buy at each price

price elastic the percentage change in quantity demanded/supplied > the percentage change in price

supply the amount of a good that a firm is willing and able to produce at each price

price inelastic the percentage change in quantity demanded/supplied < the percentage change in price

ceteris paribus Latin phrase meaning 'all other things being equal' or 'all other things being held constant'

incidence of tax the amount of a tax that is paid by the consumers and the amount paid by the producer

equilibrium price the price at which the quantity consumers are willing and able to buy is equal to the quantity firms are willing and able to produce

per-unit tax a set charge on each particular unit of a good that is sold

costs of production the amount the firm pays for the factors of production used to produce goods or services

parallel shift a change in the location of a curve (demand or supply, for example) after which the new curve is the same distance from the original curve at every point

Synonyms

responsive .... reactive/sensitive

Subject vocabulary

social surplus the sum of consumer surplus and producer surplus

consumer welfare a measure of the benefit obtained from the consumption of goods

producer welfare measure of the benefit gained by a firm from the sale of goods

equilibrium quantity the output that results when quantity demanded is equal to quantity supplied

output the quantity of goods produced by a firm, industry or economy

costs of production the amount the firm pays for the factors of production used to produce goods or services

supply the amount of a good that a firm is willing and able to produce at each price

supply curve a graph that shows the relationship between price and quantity supplied

excess supply occurs when quantity supplied is greater than quantity demanded

quantity traded the number of goods bought and sold

Original consumer **expenditure** (price × quantity) is $4 × 1200 = $4800. This is area e + d + f + g + h + i. Expenditure after tax is represented by the area a +b + f + e + g + h.

Consumer surplus is the area above price and below the demand curve. After the increase in price the consumer loses area a + b + c of consumer surplus.

Area a + b = $1 × 1000 = $1000

The area of the triangle c = ½ × the base × the height = 0.5 × 200 = $100

Loss of consumer surplus = $1000 + $100 = $1100

Original producer revenue (price × quantity) is $4 × 1200 = $4800. This is area e + d + f + g + h + i. The revenue after tax, area g + h, is $3.5 × 1000 = $3500, a decrease of $1300.

Producer surplus is the area below price and above the supply curve. After the tax the producers lose area f + e + d of producer surplus.

Area f + e = 0.5 × 1000 = $500

The area of the triangle d = ½ × the base × the height = 0.25 × 200 = $50

Loss of producer surplus = $500 + $50 = $550

Total loss of **social surplus** = loss of consumer surplus + loss of producer surplus = $1100 + $550 = $1650. Not all of this amount is lost completely because $1500 of it goes to the government and is used to buy goods and services. The welfare loss caused by the tax = $1650 – $1500 = $150. This is area c + d.

Consumers pay most of the tax because demand is more price inelastic than supply at $4 therefore producers can pass on the majority of the tax to consumers.

Consumer welfare loss is greater than the **producer's welfare** loss. The increase in price paid by the consumer is greater than the decrease in price received by the producer.

Test your understanding of this unit by answering the following questions

- Explain what determines the incidence of tax.
- Using the functions Qd = 1600 – 200P and Qs = –200 + 200P plot the demand and supply curves for prices from $0 to $6. A per-unit tax of $1 is imposed. Draw the new supply curve. Show the new equilibrium price and **equilibrium quantity**. Calculate the tax revenue, the amount of tax paid by the producer and the consumer, the change in expenditure and producer revenue, and illustrate the welfare loss.

Learning Outcomes

- Explain the government intervention of providing subsidies and describe examples of subsidies.
- Draw a diagram to show a subsidy and analyze the **impacts** of a subsidy on market outcomes.
- Discuss the **consequences** of providing a subsidy on the stakeholders in a market, including consumers, producers, and the government.

- Plot demand and supply curves for a product from linear functions and then illustrate and/or calculate the effects of the provision of a subsidy on the market (on price, quantity, consumer expenditure, producer revenue, government expenditure, consumer surplus, and producer surplus). (HL)

impacts........... effects

consequences.. results/
outcomes

firm.......... business/
producer/supplier

incentive... encouragement/
motivation

eliminate .. remove/get rid of

Subsidies are payments made by government to **firms**, per unit of **output**. A subsidy reduces **costs of production** increasing profit per unit at every price. This provides an **incentive** for firms to increase **supply**. The **supply curve** shifts down and to the right by the amount of the subsidy because the vertical distance between the original supply curve and the new supply curve represents the unit value of the subsidy. Price falls from P_e to P_{sub} in order to **eliminate** the **excess supply** and **quantity traded** increases from Q_e to Q_{sub}.

What are the effects of a subsidy on producer revenue and consumer and government expenditure? (see Figure 15.1) – a step-by-step guide

Trouble shooter

$P_1 - P_{sub}$ is the size of the subsidy on each unit.

Government expenditure on the subsidy = $(P_1 - P_{sub}) \times Q_{sub}$ (area b + c + d + e + f + g + h).

Supply curve shifts down and to the right from S to S_{sub}.

Price falls from P_e to P_{sub}.

Quantity traded increases from Q_e to Q_{sub}.

Consumer expenditure before subsidy = $P_e \times Q_e$ (area e + f + i + j + l).

And after subsidy = $P_{sub} \times Q_{sub}$ (area i + j + k + l + m).

Producer revenue before subsidy = $P_e \times Q_e$ (area e + f + i + j + l).

And after subsidy = $P_1 \times Q_{sub}$ (area b + c + d + e + f + g + h + i + j + k + l + m).

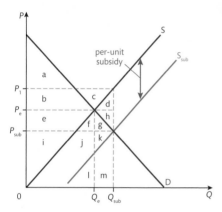

Model sentence: A subsidy lowers the price consumers pay causing quantity demanded and consumer surplus to rise. A subsidy increases the price producers receive and increases the output sold therefore producer revenue and producer surplus increases.

Figure 15.1

Subject vocabulary

government expenditure spending by a government in a specified period of time on such things as transport infrastructure, welfare payments, national defense, education, and health services which is financed by tax revenue and borrowing

consumer expenditure the money paid by consumers in exchange for goods

producer revenue the income a firm receives from consumers in exchange for goods (revenue = price × quantity sold)

consumer surplus the difference between the price a consumer is willing and able to pay and the price the consumer actually pays

producer surplus the difference between the price a firm is willing to accept for a unit of output and the price the consumer actually pays

welfare the benefit gained from consuming and producing goods

quantity demanded the amount of a good consumers are willing and able to buy at a given price over a given period of time

domestic firm a firm that produces its output in the home country

Glossary

society a group of individuals involved with each other in some way. In economics it often refers to the three main stakeholders, the consumers, the producers, and government

Synonyms

agricultural...... farming

What are the welfare effects of a subsidy?

	Before subsidy	After subsidy	Change in welfare
Consumer surplus (CS)	a + b	a + b + e + f + g	e + f + g
Producer surplus (PS)	e + i	b + c + e + i	b + c

Table 15.1

The subsidy benefits consumers and producers. Consumers buy more at a lower price. This is an increase in CS. Producers sell more at a higher price. This is an increase in PS. To get the additional **welfare** the government must pay the subsidy. The subsidy = $(P_1 - P_{sub}) \times Q_{sub}$. This is area b + c + d + e + f + g + h. To work out the effect on **society**'s welfare we subtract the costs from the benefits.

The gains in welfare (PS + CS) = b + c + e + f + g

Minus cost of subsidy   = $\underline{b + c + d + e + f + g + h}$

Total welfare   = –(d + h)

The cost to society is greater than the benefits. Area d + h represents the welfare loss caused by the subsidy.

Should governments provide subsidies?

Governments give subsidies in order to lower price and increase **quantity demanded** of goods and services such as education and training that may benefit consumers and society. They do this to protect **domestic firms** and industries from cheaper imports to maintain sales and save domestic jobs, and to make sure a good such as a basic **agricultural** good is supplied by producers in the quantities needed. The welfare of the producers of the subsidized agricultural good also increases because they sell more goods at a higher price.

Subject vocabulary

opportunity cost the next best alternative forgone

investment the addition to capital stock

surplus occurs when quantity supplied is greater than quantity demanded, another term for excess supply

resources the inputs into the production process, the factors of production

disposable income household income after direct taxation has been deducted

wants goods and services that people desire

consumer welfare a measure of the benefit obtained from the consumption of goods

demand curve a graph that shows the relationship between price and quantity demanded

supply curve a graph that shows the relationship between price and quantity supplied

linear function an equation, the graph of which is a straight line

demand schedule a table showing the quantity demanded over a range of prices – information that can be used to plot a demand curve

supply schedule a table showing the quantity supplied over a range of prices – the information can be used to plot a supply curve

equilibrium price the price at which the quantity consumers are willing and able to buy is equal to the quantity firms are willing and able to produce

equilibrium quantity the output that results when quantity demanded is equal to quantity supplied

Synonyms

scarce............ limited/finite

Glossary

infrastructure the basic structure/systems of a country (e.g. roads/railways)

There is a welfare loss and an **opportunity cost** of a subsidy. If the government spends money subsidizing an industry it is not able to spend it on something else such as **investment** in **infrastructure** that would bring benefits to society.

A subsidy encourages industries to increase supply. Goods can be over produced causing a **surplus** that cannot be sold and must be thrown away. This is a waste of the world's **scarce resources**. This happens in the agricultural industry for some goods after subsidies are given to farmers.

The government might increase taxes to pay for the subsidy. Consumers' **disposable income** falls and they can buy fewer goods and satisfy fewer **wants** leading to a fall in **consumer welfare**.

Test your understanding of this unit by answering the following question

- Using a demand and supply diagram explain the effects on welfare caused by a subsidy.

Explain the effect of a subsidy using linear functions (HL)

See pages 5–10 to find out how to calculate prices and quantities and how to plot **demand curves** and **supply curves** from **linear functions**.

Price $	Qd = 30 – 4P	Qd	Qs = 6 +2P	Qs
1	30–(4x1)=30–4=26	26	6+(2x1)=6+2=8	8
2	30–(4x2)=30–8=22	22	6+(2x2)=6+4=10	10
3	30–(4x3)=30–12=18	18	6+(2x3)=6+6=12	12
4	30–(4x4)=30–16=14	14	6+(2x4)=6+8=14	14
5	30–(4x5)=30–20=10	10	6+(2x5)=6+10=16	16
6	30–(4x6)=30–24=6	6	6+(2x6)=6+12=18	18

Set out in Table 15.2 is the **demand and supply schedule** for the functions $Qd = 30 – 4P$ and $Qs = 6 + 2P$.

The demand and supply curves are plotted from the information on the demand and supply schedule as seen in Figure 15.2.

Table 15.2

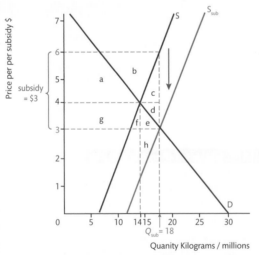

Figure 15.2

Now add a $3 subsidy per unit. Producers get $3 more per kilo than the consumers pay. The new linear supply function is:

$Qs = 6 + 2(P+3)$ Simplify by multiplying 2 by (P+3)

$Qs = 6 + 2P + 6$

$Qs = 12 + 2P$

Calculate the **equilibrium price and quantity** and plot the new supply curve using the linear functions $Qd = 30 – 4P$ and $Qs = 12 + 2P$.

At equilibrium price Qd = Qs therefore $30 – 4P = 12 + 2P$

$30 – 4P = 12 + 2P$ Simplify by adding 4P to both sides

$30 = 12 + 6P$ Simplify by subtracting 12 from both sides

$18 = 6P$ Simplify by dividing both sides by 6

$3 = P$

Put 3 in place of P in the linear function $Qd = 30 – 4P$

$Qd = 30 – (4 \times 3)$

$Qd = 30 – 12$

$Qd = 18$

Set out below in Table 15.2 is the supply schedule for the supply function Qs = 12 + 2P.

The new supply curve can now be plotted using the information from the supply schedule Table 15.3. The new supply curve S$_{sub}$ is shown in Figure 15.2.

Price $	Qs = 12 + 2P	Quantity supplied
1	12 + (2 × 1) = 12 + 2 = 14	14
2	12 + (2 × 2) = 12 + 4 = 16	16
3	12 + (2 × 3) = 12 + 6 = 18	18
4	12 + (2 × 4) = 12 + 8 = 20	20
5	12 + (2 × 5) = 12 + 10 = 22	22
6	12 + (2 × 6) = 12 + 12 = 24	24

Table 15.3

Calculate the addition to producer surplus (PS) due to a subsidy (HL) – a step-by-step guide

Trouble shooter

Producers receive an additional $3 per unit sold after the subsidy.

The additional PS is the area below the new price of $6 (the new equilibrium price + the subsidy per unit) and above the supply curve S.

It is represented by the area a + b.

To work out a + b calculate a + b + c and then subtract c.

Calculation of the area a + b + c

(6 − 4) × 18 = 2 × 18 = 36

Calculation of the triangle c

The area of a triangle is ½ × the base × the height

The base = 4 and the height = 2

The area of c = 0.5 × 4 × 2 = 2 × 2 = 4

Change in PS = 36 − 4 = $32 million

Calculate the addition to consumer surplus (CS) due to a subsidy (HL) – a step-by-step guide

Trouble shooter

Price paid falls from $4 to $3 after the subsidy.

The additional CS is the area under the demand curve, above the new equilibrium price $3 and below the original equilibrium price $4.

It is represented by the area e + f + g.

To work out e + f + g calculate d + e + f + g, and then subtract d.

Calculation of the area d + e + f + g

(4 − 3) × 18 = 1 × 18 = 18

Calculation of the triangle d

The area of a triangle is ½ × the base × the height

The base = 4 and the height = 1

The area of d = 0.5 × 4 × 1 = 2 × 1 = 2

Change in CS = 18 − 2 = $16 million

Subject vocabulary

underground parallel markets an illegal market in goods or currencies that operates along side the legal market

non-price rationing mechanisms methods such as ration cards, waiting lists, and queuing that are used to ration goods and services to eliminate the excess demand when price is not allowed to rise

price ceiling the maximum legally allowable price set by government

market price the price determined by the interaction of demand and supply in a competitive market

Calculate the effect of a subsidy on society's welfare (HL) – a step-by-step guide

Trouble shooter

Welfare benefits = additional PS + additional CS = 32+ 16 = $48 million

Cost of the subsidy is the subsidy per unit multiplied by the number of units sold $3 × 18 = $54 million

Benefit – cost = 48 – 54 = –6

Overall welfare loss is $6 million (area c + d)

Model sentence: A subsidy raises the price producers receive and lowers the price consumers pay, therefore consumer and producer surplus both increase leading to a gain in consumer and producer welfare. The cost to society of a subsidy is the subsidy per unit multiplied by the quantity sold which is paid by the tax payers. The costs outweigh the benefits, therefore the provision of a subsidy causes a welfare loss overall.

Test your understanding of this unit by answering the following questions

- Calculate the equilibrium price and quantity, and plot the demand and supply curves using the linear functions Qd = 21 – 2P and Qs = –3 + 4P.
- Calculate the new equilibrium price and quantity after a subsidy of $1 is placed on the good. Plot the new supply curve. Show and calculate the additional consumer and producer surplus and the welfare loss.

Learning Outcomes

- Explain why governments impose price ceilings and describe examples of price ceilings, including food price controls and rent controls.

- Draw a diagram to show a price ceiling and analyze the **impacts** of a price ceiling on market outcomes.

- Examine the possible **consequences** of a price ceiling, including shortages, inefficient resource allocation, welfare impacts, **underground parallel markets**, and **non-price rationing mechanisms**.

- Discuss the consequences of imposing a price ceiling on the stakeholders in a market, including consumers, producers, and the government.

- Calculate possible effects from the price ceiling diagram, including the resulting shortage and the change in consumer expenditure (which is equal to the change in firm revenue). (HL)

Subject vocabulary

quantity demanded the amount of a good consumers are willing and able to buy at a given price over a given period of time

quantity supplied the amount of a good that firms are willing and able to produce at a given price over a given period of time

market clears when quantity demanded equals quantity supplied and there is no surplus or shortage

Glossary

legally allowed by law

What are the effects of a price ceiling?

A **price ceiling** is set by the government. It is the maximum **legally** allowable price and its purpose is to reduce the good's **market price**.

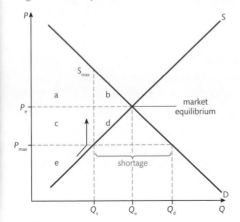

Figure 16.1

In Figure 16.1, at the equilibrium price P_e **quantity demanded = quantity supplied** and the **market clears**. A maximum price P_{max} is set and price falls causing a movement down along the demand curve. Quantity demanded increases from Q_e to Q_d. At P_{max} less profit is earned so firms reduce quantity supplied. There is a movement down and along the supply curve and quantity supplied falls from Q_e to Q_s. At P_{max} quantity demanded is greater than quantity supplied. The shortage is Q_s to Q_d. In a free market the price would increase in order to **ration** the good and **eliminate** the shortage. As this cannot happen the good must be rationed in some other way.

The government can introduce **ration cards** that limit the amount each person can buy. Waiting lists and queues will form to ration use.

There are consumers willing and able to pay a higher price. There is an **incentive** for suppliers to act illegally and supply the good at prices above P_{max} in an informal or black market. If this occurs then the supply curve is not vertical at P_{max} but continues to slope upwards.

Welfare loss

When the market is in equilibrium the **sum** of **consumer and producer surplus** is maximized. Therefore society's total surplus and **welfare** is maximized at P_e. The area representing total welfare is a + b + c + d + e. After a price ceiling is set price cannot rise above P_{max} therefore quantity supplied does not rise above Q_s. If no goods are supplied illegally on the black market at prices above P_{max} the supply curve is vertical at P_{max}. Total welfare is now area a + c + e. Area b + d is the welfare loss.

In order to maximize society's welfare the price ceiling must be removed. Price will then rise and firms allocate more **factors of production** to the good in order to increase output and continue to do so until the shortage is eliminated and the market is in equilibrium. The firms must allocate a specific quantity of factors to the production of this good in order to produce output at Q_e. This is the point of allocative efficiency. It is the best or optimal **allocation** of **resources** from the point of view of society because welfare is maximized (the sum of C_s and P_s is maximized) at the equilibrium point $P_e Q_e$ (see pages 16–18 on allocative efficiency).

Why does the government set a maximum price?

For example, a government introduces rent controls in a city so that more people are able to afford to pay the rent and live and work there. In New York City rents on some properties are controlled. This is a benefit to those people who find a place to rent because they pay a rent below the market price. However, the maximum price can create a shortage of rented accommodation as the lower rent discourages quantity supplied.

A maximum price for a **staple food** such as bread reduces the price so more people can afford to buy the good. However, the effect of this government action leads to a fall in consumption of the good not an increase. Those who get the good at the maximum price are better off because they pay less for it but those who are unable to buy the good are worse off.

What action can the government take to increase consumption?

A **subsidy** placed on a good increases **profit** at each price and firms increase **supply**. If the correct amount of subsidy per unit is provided it will cause a parallel shift of the supply curve down and to the right so that quantity demanded equals quantity supplied at the maximum price and the shortage is eliminated. The subsidy increases consumption from Q_s to Q_d.

The government can produce the good increasing supply and thereby eliminating the **excess demand**. For example, the government could increase the supply of bread. Additional supply equal to the shortage causes a parallel shift of the supply curve to the right. Quantity demanded equals quantity supplied at the maximum price and the shortage is eliminated. Government supply of bread increases consumption from Q_s to Q_d.

Instead of increasing supply in order to increase consumption the government could encourage consumption by increasing demand. Advertising, for example, would increase demand causing the demand curve to shift up and to the right and quantity consumed would rise.

There are **opportunity costs** of all the government actions. Government revenue spent on subsidies or advertising, for example, cannot be spent on alternative goods and services.

Model sentence: The imposition of a price ceiling causes price to fall below the free market equilibrium price. At the lower price, quantity demanded increases and quantity supplied falls leading to a shortage of the good and a decrease in the amount of the good consumed.

Test your understanding of this unit by answering the following question

- Discuss the effects of the imposition of a maximum price in a market of your choice.

Glossary

ration card a card/voucher issued by a government to let the holder get goods that are in short supply

Synonyms

impacts...........effects

consequences..results/ outcomes

ration .... allowing people to have only a fixed amount of something when there is a shortage

eliminate .... remove/get rid of

incentive..... encouragement/ motivation

sum............ total

allocation.... distribution

imposition .. introduction

Subject vocabulary

consumer surplus the difference between the price a consumer is willing and able to pay and the price the consumer actually pays

producer surplus the difference between the price a firm is willing to accept for a unit of output and the price the consumer actually pays

welfare the benefit gained from consuming and producing goods

factors of production the inputs into the production process (land, labour, capital and entrepreneurship)

resources the inputs into the production process, the factors of production

staple food a food that is eaten by lots of people, particularly those on a relatively low income

subsidy payments made by government to firms per unit of output

profit the difference between total revenue and total cost

supply the amount of a good that a firm is willing and able to produce at each price

excess demand occurs when quantity demanded is greater than quantity supplied

opportunity cost the next best alternative forgone

Calculate the effects of a price ceiling (HL)

Before government intervention

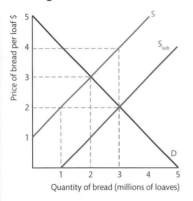

Figure 16.2

In Figure 16.2 equilibrium price is $3 and quantity is 2 million. At $3 quantity demanded = quantity supplied and the market clears.

Total **consumer expenditure** and **producer revenue** = price × quantity = $3 × 2 million = $6 million.

After intervention

A price ceiling of $2 is set. At $2 quantity demanded = 3 million and quantity supplied = 1 million.

The maximum price causes excess demand of 2 million (3 million − 1 million = 2 million).

Total consumer **expenditure** and producer revenue = price × quantity sold = $2 × 1 million = $2 million.

The fall in consumer expenditure and producer revenue caused by the price ceiling = $6 million − $2 million = $4 million.

Eliminating the shortage

The government could impose a per-unit subsidy. Quantity demanded at the maximum price is 3 million. To eliminate the shortage of 2 million, quantity supplied must increase to 3 million. As can be seen in Figure 16.2 the price needs to rise to $4 in order to provide the incentive for firms to increase quantity supplied to 3 million. The per-unit subsidy necessary to eliminate the excess demand is the distance between the supply curves S and S_{sub} which is $2. The total subsidy needed is the per-unit amount multiplied by the number of units to be subsidized = $2 × 3 million = $6 million.

Learning Outcomes

- Explain why governments **impose price floors**, describe examples of price floors, including price support for **agricultural** products and minimum wages.

- Draw a diagram of a price floor and analyse the impacts of a price floor on market outcomes.

- Examine the possible consequences of a price floor, including surpluses and government measures to **dispose** of the surpluses, inefficient resource **allocation**, and welfare impacts.

- Discuss the consequences of imposing a price floor on the stakeholders in a market, including consumers, producers, and the government.

- Calculate possible effects from the price floor diagram, including the resulting surplus, the change in consumer expenditure, the change in producer revenue, and government expenditure to **purchase** the surplus. (HL)

What are the effects of a price floor on stakeholders and why do governments impose them?

A price floor set by the government is the minimum price a **firm** receives for a unit of **output**. The price is not allowed to fall below the minimum price. The purpose of a price floor is to increase market price.

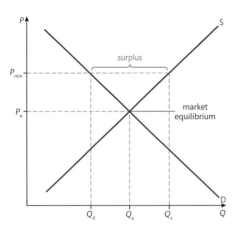

Figure 17.1

In Figure 17.1, the equilibrium price P_e quantity demanded = quantity supplied and the market clears. A minimum price P_{min} is set. It is above equilibrium price. At this higher price quantity demanded falls from Q_e to Q_d. At P_{min} more profit is earned so firms increase quantity supplied and it rises from Q_e to Q_s. Quantity supplied > quantity demanded. The **surplus** is Q_d to Q_s. In a free market the price would fall in order to eliminate the **excess supply** but this is not possible when a price floor is imposed.

After the minimum price is set the market is in **disequilibrium**. Encouraged by a higher price firms increase the **factors** allocated to the production of the good in order to increase quantity supplied from Q_e to Q_s. However, the value consumers place on the consumption of Q_s of output, as measured by the price they are prepared to pay for it, is far below P_{min}, which is the price producers need to receive if they are to produce that amount. Consumers therefore will not buy all the output at that price. At P_{min} consumers are only prepared to buy output up to Q_d, therefore there is a surplus of Q_d to Q_s. If the surplus is thrown away all the factors used to produce those goods are wasted. They could have been used to produce alternative goods that consumers would buy. Therefore a minimum price leads to an inefficient use of **scarce** factors as more wants could have been satisfied if those factors had been used to produce alternative goods.

Governments set a minimum price on some foods such as corn and wheat in order to guarantee output and to protect farmers' incomes. The price floor acts as an incentive for farmers to use their **resources** to produce the particular good. Consumers now pay a higher price and their **real incomes** and consumer surplus falls. Farmers benefit because **producer revenue** increases and they are more certain how much **income** they will earn in the future. The amount of the increase in revenue depends on how the government deals with the surplus.

What measures can government take to dispose of the surplus?

Increasing demand

The government increases demand by buying the excess supply ($Q_s - Q_d$). The demand curve shifts up and to the right until a new equilibrium is reached at P_{min} and Q_s.

Government expenditure = $P_{min} \times (Q_s - Q_d)$ and consumer expenditure = $P_{min} \times Q_d$.

Total producer revenue = $P_{min} \times (Q_s - Q_d) + P_{min} \times Q_d = P_{min} \times Q_s$.

$P_{min} \times Q_s$ is the producer revenue after the minimum price is set and this is greater than $P_e \times Q_e$ which is the producer revenue in the industry before price controls are introduced.

This is a relatively large increase in producer revenue and income but it has cost the government $P_{min} \times (Q_s - Q_d)$. There is an **opportunity cost** to this government expenditure. The money used to buy the surplus cannot be used to **invest** in other areas such as education.

The surplus bought by the government can be sold back to farmers as animal feed or exported at very low prices. The price the government pays the producers for the surplus is greater than the price received from selling it.

The government could simply throw away the surplus. This means that all the resources used to produce the good are wasted.

Reducing supply

The government pays farmers not to use their land to produce the good. This reduces supply and the **supply curve** shifts up and to the left. A new equilibrium can be reached at P_{min} Q_d if enough land is taken out of use to eliminate the excess supply. Quantity demanded = quantity supplied and the market clears but it has cost the government the amount it must pay farmers not to produce. There is an opportunity cost to this government expenditure and to do nothing with the land is a waste of scarce resources. Producer revenue increases because farmers get a higher price from the consumer and they get money from the government.

How does PED and PES affect the size of the surplus?

The size of the surplus and the size of the increase in **expenditure** and producer revenue depend on the difference between the equilibrium price and the floor price and the **price elasticity of demand** and **price elasticity of supply**. Look at Figure 17.1. If **supply** becomes more **price elastic**, quantity supplied at the minimum price rises and the surplus increases (you can see this by rotating the supply curve clockwise so that it is less **steep**). If supply becomes more **price inelastic**, quantity supplied at the minimum price falls and the surplus decreases. If demand becomes more inelastic and the demand curve becomes steeper, quantity demanded at the price floor increases and the surplus falls. When the surplus gets bigger government expenditure needed to buy it increases.

What are the effects of a minimum wage?

Governments set a **minimum wage**, which is an example of a price floor, to ensure workers can satisfy their basic needs. People supply their labour and firms demand labour. As **wage** rises so does the incentive to

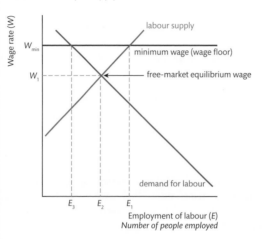

work, therefore the quantity of labour supplied rises, but as the cost of employing a worker rises quantity demanded falls. E_2 is the number employed at the equilibrium wage W_1. Quantity demanded = quantity supplied. There is no unemployment. All the people who want to work at wage W_1 can get work and firms can hire all the workers they require. A minimum wage is set above the equilibrium at W_{min}. The number wanting to work increases from E_2 to E_1 and quantity demanded falls from E_2 to E_3. The excess from E_1 to E_3 are unemployed. Overall the number of people working falls from E_2 to E_3 but total unemployment is greater because more people are now looking for work at the higher minimum wage.

Figure 17.2

There is a **trade-off** between higher wages and employment. Those who are employed are better off but this is at the cost of higher unemployment. This type of unemployment is called **classical or real-wage unemployment**. It occurs when wages are above the market clearing level leading to an excess supply of labour.

Calculate the effects of a minimum price (HL)

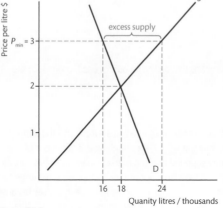

Equilibrium price for a litre of milk is $2 and equilibrium quantity is 18 000 litres. A minimum price of $3 per litre is set by the government. Quantity supplied increases to 24 000 litres and quantity demanded falls to 16 000 litres leading to a surplus of 8000 litres.

Consumer expenditure (price × quantity) before the minimum price is set = $2 × 18 000 = $36,000. After the price floor is imposed expenditure = $3 × 16 000 = $48,000, an increase of $12,000. Consumers pay a higher price per unit and **consumer surplus** falls.

Figure 17.3

If the government does not **intervene** in the market, producer revenue will be difficult to work out exactly. Producers try to sell the first 16 000 litres at $3 per litre = $3 × 16 000 = $48,000. Producers will then sell the surplus at prices below $3 per litre.

If the government reduces supply by paying farmers not to produce milk, total producer revenue will be $48,000 plus the payments from the government.

If the government increases demand by buying the surplus (8000 litres) then producer revenue is the sum of consumer expenditure and the government expenditure on the surplus.

Consumer expenditure   = $3 × 16 000 = $48,000

Government expenditure = $3 × 8000 = $24,000

Total producer revenue = $3 × 24 000 = $72,000

Synonyms

intervene .... get involved

1.4 Market failure – The meaning and types of market failure

Learning Outcomes

- Analyze the **concept** of market failure as a failure of the market to achieve allocative efficiency, resulting in an over-allocation of resources (overprovision of a good) or an under-allocation of resources (under-provision of a good).

- Describe the concepts of marginal private benefits (MPB), marginal social benefits (MSB), marginal private costs (MPC), and marginal social costs (MSC).

- Describe the meaning of externalities as the failure of the market to achieve a social optimum where MSB = MSC.

Subject vocabulary

factors of production the inputs into the production process (land, labour, capital and entrepreneurship)

allocative efficiency the best or optimal allocation of resources from society's point of view. It occurs when the market is in equilibrium and social surplus is maximized (where $P = MC$).

marginal cost the change in total cost resulting from a change in output of one unit

resources the inputs into the production process, the factors of production

equilibrium a market is in equilibrium where the quantity supplied is equal to the quantity demanded

producer surplus the difference between the price a firm is willing to accept for a unit of output and the price the consumer actually pays

free market a market where the forces of demand and supply are allowed to operate without any forms of intervention

surplus occurs when quantity supplied is greater than quantity demanded, another term for excess supply

shortage when quantity demanded is greater than quantity supplied (another term for excess demand)

benefit the satisfaction gained from the consumption of a good

marginal benefit is the additional benefit received by a person from the consumption of an additional unit of output

What is market failure?

Markets fail when **factors of production** are not allocated efficiently. **Allocative efficiency** occurs when price, which is the value consumers in society place on the **consumption** of the marginal unit of output, is equal to the **marginal cost**, which is the value of the **resources** used to produce the additional unit. An allocatively efficient outcome occurs when the market is in **equilibrium** where the sum of consumer and **producer surplus**, which is called community surplus, is maximized. Therefore a **free market** fails when there is a **surplus** or **shortage**. Either too many factors are allocated to the production of the good, leading to over provision of the good (surplus) or not enough factors are allocated to the production of the good, leading to under provision of the good (shortage). When price, the value consumers in society place on the benefit gained from the next unit consumed, does not equal marginal cost community surplus is not maximized and the market fails.

Why is the marginal benefit curve the demand curve?

Price is a reflection of the value consumers place on the consumption of the marginal or additional unit. Consumers gain a **benefit** or utility from the consumption of the additional unit of a good consumed and price is a measure of the benefit gained. As consumers consume more of a good the additional or **marginal benefit** gained falls. This is the **law of diminishing marginal utility**. Therefore the value the consumers place on the additional unit, which is the price, also falls. So as quantity consumed increases the price the consumers are prepared to pay falls. If consumers are to buy more of a good the price must fall to reflect the fall in the benefit gained from the consumption of it. The **demand curve** is a reflection of the price consumers are willing to pay for an additional unit of a good, which itself is a reflection of the additional or marginal benefit gained from the consumption of the next unit. The demand curve is therefore derived from the marginal benefit curve which shows the relationship between the benefit gained and quantity consumed.

What is the difference between marginal private benefits and marginal social benefits? – a step-by-step guide

Trouble shooter

The benefit gained by the consumer from the consumption of a good is called private benefit.

The benefit gained from the consumption of an additional unit of the good is called **marginal private benefit**.

The consumption of some goods has a **spillover effect** on third parties. People outside of the market benefit from the good being consumed despite not paying for the good or consuming it.

These are additional benefits gained by society. The benefits gained by third parties are called **external benefits** or **positive externalities** because they are benefits that go to people who are external to or outside the market.

Marginal external benefit is the benefit gained by third parties from the consumption of an additional unit of the good.

Marginal social benefit is the benefit society gains from the consumption of the additional unit. It is the sum of marginal private benefit and marginal external benefit

Model sentence: Marginal private benefits plus marginal external benefits equals marginal social benefit. The difference between MPB and MSB is MEB.

An example of a good that has positive externalities associated with its consumption is healthcare. If people are healthier it benefits others. Disease is less likely to spread and workers will be more productive at work helping the economy to grow. Education is another example. When consumed third parties benefit. Society needs a well-educated workforce to remain competitive. Society benefits from having doctors and engineers.

What is the difference between marginal private costs and marginal social costs? – a step-by-step guide

Trouble shooter

Firms incur costs when producing goods and services. For example firms pay rent and wages.

These costs are called **private costs**.

Firms also create costs that must be paid for by third parties.

These costs are called external costs or negative externalities. For example, costs of pollution.

They are costs created by the firm when producing goods but are paid for by society, often the taxpayer.

The true cost of production includes both private costs and external costs.

Marginal social cost is the cost to society of producing the additional unit of output. This is the sum of marginal private costs and marginal external costs.

Model sentence: Marginal private costs plus marginal external costs equal marginal social costs. The difference between MPC and MSC is MEC.

For example, a factory leaks harmful emissions into the atmosphere causing health problems to those living in the area. There are costs associated with this, such as the loss of earnings through illness of individuals affected and the cost, perhaps to the tax-payer, of treating the illnesses. The damage to the environment creates costs for future generations to pay.

Explain why externalities cause the market to fail to achieve a social optimum where MSB = MSC

In order to increase the **quantity supplied**, firms in an **industry** must allocate more resources to the production of the good. Therefore as quantity supplied increases, costs of the resources used to make the good increase. Marginal cost is the addition to **total cost** from increasing output by one unit. Marginal cost rises as output rises because of **diminishing returns to the variable factor**. For example, in the **short run** the quantity of labour is variable and the quantity of capital is fixed. A firm adds an additional worker (the marginal worker) to a fixed quantity of capital in order to increase supply of the good. As the firm continues to add labour to the fixed quantity of capital the addition to total output created by employing an extra worker falls. Therefore marginal cost, which is the addition to total cost of producing the next unit of output increases. Therefore as supply increases marginal cost increases. The supply curve therefore represents the marginal cost curve.

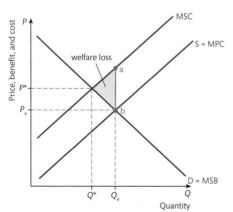

Consumers do not consider the marginal external benefits when deciding how much of a good to consume. They only consider marginal private benefits. Firms do not take into account the marginal external costs when setting output. They only consider the marginal private costs. Below is an explanation of the effects on a market when external costs exist.

Figure 18.1. *a to b represents the external costs*

Subject vocabulary

law of diminishing marginal utility a theory stating that the amount of satisfaction gained from the consumption of a good falls as more of the good is consumed

demand curve a graph that shows the relationship between price and quantity demanded

marginal private benefit the additional private benefit generated by the consumption or production of an additional unit of output

spillover effect externalities caused by the production or consumption of a good that affects people who are not directly involved in its production or consumption

external benefit occurs when the production or consumption of a good causes a benefit to third parties

positive externalities occur when the production or consumption of a good causes benefits to third parties. The existence of positive externalities means that social benefit is greater than private benefit.

marginal external benefit the additional positive externalities generated by the consumption or production of an additional unit of a good or service

marginal social benefit marginal social benefit = marginal private benefit + marginal external benefit. It is the additional social benefit generated by the consumption or production of an additional unit of output.

private costs the cost incurred by firms or consumers from their own production or consumption of a good

quantity supplied the amount of a good that firms are willing and able to produce at a given price over a given period of time

industry a group of firms that produce the same or similar goods or services

total cost the sum of total fixed cost and total variable cost

diminishing marginal returns to a variable factor as more of a variable factor is added to a quantity of fixed factors the product of each additional unit of the variable factor will, at some point, begin to fall

short run a period of time when at least one factor is variable and the others are fixed

In Figure 18.1 the market is in equilibrium at P_e, Q_e. If the firm had to pay all costs associated with the production of Q_e of goods, including the external costs, the price of P_e would not be enough to cover the costs. If the firm had to pay the social costs the firm would make a loss at P_e. The only reason it can make a **profit** at P_e is because it does not have to pay the external costs.

At Q_e MSC is greater than price. That is, the value of the resources used by society to produce the additional unit is greater than the value society places on the consumption of it. This is an allocatively inefficient outcome as far as society is concerned.

Social optimum price and level of output is achieved at P^* Q^*, where MSB = MSC. This is, as far as society is concerned, an allocatively efficient outcome: Price = MSC. The value society places on the additional unit of output consumed is equal to the value of society's resources used to produce it.

At output between Q^* and Q_e MSC exceeds MSB. Costs to society of this output are greater than the benefit society gains. This is a welfare loss and the whole area of welfare loss where MSC > MSB is shown in Figure 18.1.

Model sentence: When external costs exist the good will be under priced, over produced, and over consumed. Left to the free market too many factors will be allocated to the production of the good.

Test your understanding of this unit by answering the following questions

- Explain the difference between private benefits and costs and external benefits and costs.
- Explain why negative externalities cause allocative inefficiency in free markets.

Learning Outcomes

- Explain, using diagrams and examples, the **concepts** of negative externalities of production and **consumption**, and the welfare loss associated with the production or consumption of a good or service.

- Explain that demerit goods are goods whose consumption creates external costs.

- Evaluate, using diagrams, the use of policy responses, including market-based policies (taxation and tradable permits), and government **regulations**, to the problem of negative externalities of production and consumption.

- Explain, using diagrams and examples, the concepts of positive externalities of production and consumption, and the welfare loss associated with the production or consumption of a good or service.

- Explain that merit goods are goods whose consumption creates external benefits.

- Evaluate, using diagrams, the use of government responses, including subsidies, legislation, and advertising to influence behaviour, and direct provision of goods and services.

Explain, using diagrams, why negative externalities of production cause welfare loss

Model sentence: Private costs are the costs created by the firm when producing goods that are paid for by the firm (e.g. wages, rent, and the cost of raw materials). Negative externalities or external costs are created by the firm but the firm does not pay the cost (e.g. costs associated with health problems and environmental damage caused by the harmful emissions from a factory).

The external costs are paid for by **third parties**, not the firm. Third parties are external to the market. They are not involved as producers or consumers yet must pay a cost.

Social costs are the sum of private and external costs (PC + EC = SC). **Marginal private cost** is the addition to total cost from producing the next unit. **Marginal external cost** is the addition to total external cost from producing the next unit. Added together they equal **marginal social cost** (MPC + MEC = MSC). Therefore when negative externalities occur the marginal social cost curve is above the marginal private cost curve.

In this example it is assumed that there are no external benefits associated with the production of the good, only external costs. Therefore MSB = MPB. The **profit**-maximizing firm does not take into account the external costs when making decisions about the level of output. So the firm sets output at Q_e where MPC = MSB. Note that the firm is not producing at the **social optimum level of output** where marginal social cost equals marginal social benefit. Factors are misallocated. Too many factors are allocated to the production of the good.

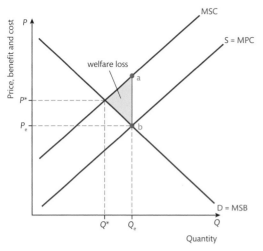

Figure 19.1

Output is too high and price is too low. Between Q_e and Q^* MSC > MSB. The value of the resources used by society to produce the additional unit (MSC) is greater than the benefit gained from the consumption of it (MSB). On all these units of output between Q_e and Q^* there is a **welfare loss**. Total welfare loss is shown by the shaded area in Figure 19.1.

Explain, using diagrams, why negative externalities of consumption cause welfare loss

Model sentence: Consumers gain a private benefit from the consumption of goods. There are some goods that when consumed create external costs or negative externalities that third parties must pay.

The consumption of alcohol leads to violence, vandalism, accidents, and absenteeism from work and long-term health problems. The consumption of tobacco and other drugs create external costs, such as health problems caused by passive smoking and **burglaries** committed to fund the purchase of drugs. The use of cars creates external costs such as air pollution and noise pollution, as well as the cost to society of dealing with car accidents. The external costs of the consumption of fatty foods include the cost to society of provision of healthcare associated with obesity.

Model sentence: Goods that create negative externalities in consumption are called demerit goods.

The consumer does not consider the external costs when deciding how much of the good to consume. Only the marginal private costs and the **marginal private benefits** are taken into account. The consumer will consume up to the point where marginal private cost equals marginal private benefit. That is where the cost to the consumer of the additional unit, which is mainly the price paid, is equal to the value of the benefit gained from the consumption of the additional unit. **Private optimum level of consumption** is at Q_e and price P_e shown in Figure 19.2. However, the benefit gained by the consumer is greater than the benefit enjoyed by society as a whole. Therefore the **marginal social benefit** is less than marginal private benefit and the marginal social benefit curve is below the marginal private benefit curve as shown in Figure 19.2.

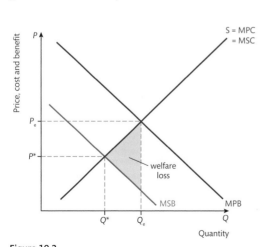

Figure 19.2

An explanation of welfare loss – a step-by-step guide

Trouble shooter (See Figure 19.2 on page 49)

At the private optimum level of consumption Q_e marginal social cost exceeds marginal social benefit.

This means the cost to society from the consumption of the next unit of the good is greater than the benefit society gains from the consumption of it.

Social optimum level of consumption is at Q^* where MSC = MSB.

For all consumption between Q^* and Q_e MSC > MSB.

On each of these units consumed there is a welfare loss. The total welfare loss is the shaded area shown in Figure 19.2.

If all the consumers took into account the external costs they would place a lower value on the consumption of the additional unit and the demand for the good would fall.

Evaluate, using diagrams, government policies aimed at reducing the negative externalities of production

Taxation

A firm aims to maximize profit and only takes into account private costs, setting output at Q_e and at price P_e as shown in Figure 19.3. In order to reduce the welfare loss caused by the marginal social costs being greater than marginal social benefits at the equilibrium Q_e P_e, the government can place a tax on the good thereby increasing the private costs causing the MPC curve to shift up and to the left.

If the tax set by government is equal to the marginal external cost at the social optimum level of output Q^* then marginal private cost rises so that marginal private cost + tax equals marginal social cost. The firm sets output at the social optimum level where MPC + tax = MSB thereby removing the welfare loss. In effect the government, through taxation, tries to make the private optimum level of output the same as the social optimum level of output where MSC = MSB.

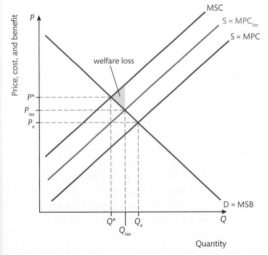

Figure 19.3

External costs, such as the cost to society of pollution, are difficult to assess. Costs might be undervalued therefore the government, acting on inaccurate information, places a tax that is less than the external costs. Private costs are increased and the MPC curve shifts up and to the left to S = MPC$_{tax}$. However, the private optimum level of output is still greater than the social optimum. The tax has reduced welfare loss but is not enough to correct **market failure** completely. At P_{tax}, Q_{tax} MSC is still greater than MSB leading to the welfare loss shown in the shaded area in Figure 19.3.

Model sentence: A tax makes the 'polluter pay'. It internalizes the externality. This means that the costs that were paid by third parties are now paid by consumers and producers who are in the market.

A tax reduces and can even eliminate welfare loss, if the value of the tax is sufficient to increase private costs so that MPC equals MSC at the social optimum level of output where MSC = MSB. An **allocatively efficient** outcome is achieved at P^* Q^* as shown in Figure 19.3.

The tax increases price. This can lead to a fall in international competitiveness, especially if foreign firms are not taxed in the same way. Jobs can be lost in exporting industries. As price increases **real income** falls and **consumer welfare** might actually fall.

Legislation and regulation

The government can pass laws that force firms to reduce output, thereby reducing the external costs. This is very difficult to achieve. Firstly the government must evaluate the external costs correctly if the enforced level of output in the industry is to correct market failure. Secondly it cannot trust firms to stick to the social optimum level of output, particularly if high profits are being made. Therefore the government has to use **resources** to monitor the industry and **enforce** the regulations. The **opportunity cost** of such action has to be taken into account. The resources are not available to use elsewhere. It is possible that the cost of enforcing and monitoring is greater than the external costs. This is an example of **government failure**.

Firms by law could be made to buy new, more technologically advanced, capital designed to reduce harmful emissions. This has two effects. It reduces the harmful emissions that cause the negative externalities associated with pollution and it increases firms' marginal private costs, thereby reducing the private optimum level of output in the industry.

A complete **ban** is likely to lead to government failure. Again the policy has to be enforced. It would also lead to an increase in costs associated with a rise in unemployment as jobs are lost, and all consumer and producer surplus gained at the social optimum price and output will be lost resulting in a loss of social welfare.

Tradable permits

Tradable permits are issued to firms in an **industry** giving them the legal right to **emit** pollution up to a specified limit. A firm can either use the permits or sell them to another firm on the tradable permit market which then transfers the right to pollute. The government decides on the amount of pollution allowed to be emitted by an industry and then issues permits to the firms. If a firm has used up its allowance it can buy permits from other firms. The system provides an **incentive** for firms to invest in **cleaner technology**, thereby reducing pollution levels below the allowed amount and enabling them to sell the unused permits. If the cost of installing the new technologically improved capital is less than the price received from the sale of the permit then the firm benefits. As the supply of permits on the market falls and the government reduces the supply of permits the price rises and the incentive to reduce the level of pollution through **investment** in new capital increases. Through this market-based solution the industry is encouraged to reduce their levels of pollution to the desired amount, thereby reducing the negative externalities and correcting market failure.

The system requires monitoring and enforcing which uses up **scarce** resources and the government still has the problem of assessing the level of pollution allowed by the industry that ensures the social optimum level of output and the correction of market failure.

An example of a 'cap and trade' system was the Kyoto Protocol – an international agreement to reduce pollution from greenhouse gases which came into force in 2005. Each of the 170 or so countries that signed the **treaty** agreed to reduce the levels of greenhouse gases. Countries which do not achieve their targets are fined and those developed countries that exceed their permitted level are able to buy permits from less developed countries which have more generous allowances to pollute.

Evaluate, using diagrams, government policies aimed at reducing the negative externalities of consumption

The effect of an indirect tax – a step-by-step guide

Trouble shooter (See Figure 19.4 on page 52)

An indirect tax placed on a good is a way of internalizing the externality.

The aim is to make the producers and consumers in the market pay the external costs associated with the consumption of the good rather than third parties who are external to the market.

A per-unit indirect tax increases marginal social costs by the amount of tax and the MSC curve shifts up to the left from MSC to MSC_{tax}.

Private optimum level of consumption = social optimum level of consumption where MSC = MSB.

Subject vocabulary

resources the inputs into the production process, the factors of production

opportunity cost the next best alternative forgone

government failure occurs when government intervention, designed to correct market failure, causes a more inefficient allocation of resources than would be the case if government had not intervened

tradable permits an allowance issued by the government that allows a firm to emit pollution up to a specified limit. There is a market for permits where firms who have reached their limit can buy permits from firms who have not used up their allowance

industry a group of firms that produce the same or similar goods or services

clean technology/ies a term used to describe technologically advanced capital that reduces waste, harmful emissions, and allows for the use of fewer non-renewable resources when used in the production process

investment the addition to capital stock

Glossary

enforce make people obey rules/laws

ban official order stopping something from being used/done

treaty(ies) formal written agreement(s) between countries/governments

Synonyms

emit .... release/produce

incentive ..... encouragement/motivation

scarce .... limited/finite

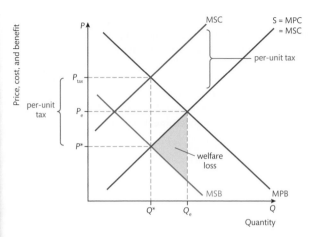

The consumer pays a higher price at P_{tax} and consumption falls to the social optimum level Q^* thereby reducing the external costs associated with the consumption of the good. The government gains **tax revenue** which can be used, for example, to fund negative advertising campaigns that will reduce the perceived private benefit of the good and reduce demand for the good causing the MPB curve to shift down and to the left.

Figure 19.4

Governments use this method, amongst others, to reduce the external costs associated with the use of tobacco and alcohol. Demand for these goods is relatively **price inelastic** because they are habit forming, therefore even a relatively high per-unit tax may not reduce consumption to the social optimum level. Also even if the government set a high tax many consumers would seek to buy the good in an illegal market or **black market** where no tax is paid to the government. Therefore consumption falls by much less than the desired amount and the external costs remain high. At the same time the government receives much less tax revenue. This is an example of government failure. This occurs when government intervention leads to a more inefficient outcome than would occur without that intervention.

A tax increases the price the consumer pays thereby reducing the **purchasing power** of income. **Consumer surplus** is reduced and welfare is lost. Consumers earning relatively low incomes will be affected the most.

Banning the good

Prohibition of alcohol in the USA between 1920 and 1933 made the production and transportation of alcohol illegal. It opened up a huge illegal market. Tax revenue previously raised by the government fell to zero while consumption continued. Banning alcohol created high costs associated with the attempts to enforce the law and gave rise to much criminal activity involved in supplying for the demand. Many scarce resources were used to prevent production and consumption and the policy failed to control the external costs. Indeed it is likely that the negative externalities associated with the consumption of alcohol increased. Another example of government failure.

Banning smoking in public spaces and buildings has had some success in reducing consumption and governments continue to regulate in this area with some governments considering making smoking in private cars and in homes illegal, although this will be difficult and costly to enforce.

Negative advertising and education

In many schools students are taught about the dangers of alcohol and tobacco consumption. Governments fund advertising in the media and on the products aimed at reducing the perceived private benefit of consumption and raising awareness of the external costs associated with consumption, such as passive smoking. This reduces **demand** for the good causing the MPB curve to shift down and to the left. There is an opportunity cost of government intervention as the resources used cannot be put to alternative uses.

Model sentence: Left to the free market demerit goods are over consumed because consumers do not take into account the external costs. At the private optimum level of consumption MSC > MSB. Government must intervene to reduce consumption so that it falls to the social optimum level where MSB = MSC thereby maximizing society's welfare.

Explain, using diagrams, why positive externalities of production cause welfare loss

Positive externalities or external benefits occur when benefits from the production of a good are enjoyed by third parties who are external to the market. Society enjoys benefits that are created by firms producing certain goods. When a firm trains its workforce it incurs a private costs but when a worker leaves to join another firm that firm enjoys the benefit of the trained workers without incurring the private cost associated with training.

Firms in the paper industry plant trees regularly. Softwoods such as fir, spruce, and pine are used. They grow relatively quickly. Society benefits from the environmental advantages associated with trees but does not pay a private cost. Firms move into areas and pay local taxes. These taxes can be used by local government to make improvement to public spaces in the area. Again others outside of the market have benefited without incurring a cost. The firm producing enjoys private benefits but there are external benefits created by the firm that are enjoyed by third parties who do not pay a private cost.

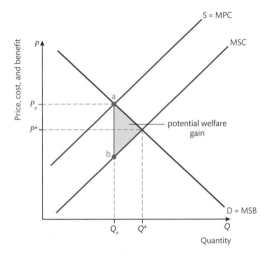

Figure 19.5

The marginal private cost incurred by the firm is greater than the marginal social cost. The firm chooses to set output at the private optimal level Q_e where MPC = MSB (when MSB = MPB) as shown in Figure 19.5. At Q_e marginal social benefit exceeds marginal social cost, an **allocatively inefficient** outcome because at Q_e the benefit to society gained from the next unit produced is greater that the value of the resources used to produce it. Q_e to Q^* shows an area of output where MSB > MSC. It is the shaded area in Figure 19.5 showing the potential welfare gains of increased production. At Q^* marginal social benefit equals marginal social cost. That is, the benefit to society gained from the production of the next unit is equal to the value of the resources used in the production of it. P^* Q^* is the **social optimum equilibrium**.

P_e Q_e is an allocatively inefficient equilibrium. Price is too high and output is too low. The free market fails because not enough resources are allocated to the production of the good.

Subject vocabulary

allocative efficiency the best or optimal allocation of resources from society's point of view. It occurs when the market is in equilibrium and social surplus is maximized (where P = MC).

social optimum equilibrium occurs in a market where the benefit society receives from the consumption of the next unit is equal to the cost incurred by society of the next unit (MSB = MSC)

merit good a good/service that the government believes will be under consumed if left to the free market. Consumption of a merit good may generate positive externalities, therefore the social benefit of consumption is greater than the private benefit. Individuals do not take into account the positive externalities when deciding the amount to consume, therefore the good is underprovided and under consumed.

Explain, using diagrams, why positive externalities of consumption cause welfare loss

Consumers gain a private benefit from the consumption of a good. The addition to total benefit from the consumption of an additional unit is called the marginal private benefit. The consumption of some goods creates external benefits or positive externalities. These are benefits enjoyed by third parties. People who are external to the market. Marginal private benefit plus marginal external benefit equals marginal social benefit. The private consumption of healthcare creates positive externalities. Society benefits because the spread of disease can be reduced and workers who are healthier are more productive helping the economy to grow. There are external benefits associated with the consumption of education. A literate workforce is relatively more productive. Society benefits from having engineers, scientists, doctors, and so on. Private consumption of education not only benefits the consumer but also benefits third parties. Goods that create external benefits are called **merit goods**.

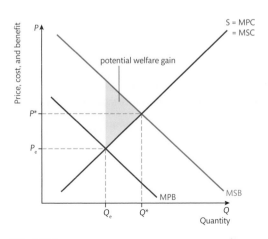

Figure 19.6

In Figure 19.6 it is assumed that there are no external costs therefore MSC = MPC.

An explanation of welfare gain – a step-by-step guide (see Figure 19.6 on page 53)

Trouble shooter

Private optimum equilibrium is at $P_e Q_e$ where marginal private benefit equals marginal social cost.

At this level of consumption marginal social benefit, which is marginal private benefit + marginal external benefit, exceeds marginal social cost.

This means the benefit society gains from the consumption of the next unit is greater than the cost to society of the next unit.

The shaded area shows the potential welfare gain available to society if consumption increases from Q_e to Q^*.

At the social optimum equilibrium, $P^* Q^*$, MSB = MSC.

This means the benefit gained by society from the consumption of the next unit equals the cost to society of the next unit.

Q_e is an allocatively inefficient level of consumption. Consumption is too low. The free market fails because not enough resources are allocated to the production of the good.

Model sentence: Left to the free market merit goods are under consumed. Consumers do not take into account the external benefits. At the private optimum level of consumption MSB > MSC. Government must intervene to increase consumption so that it rises to the social optimum level where MSB = MSC thereby maximizing society's welfare.

Evaluate, using diagrams, government policies aimed at increasing the production and consumption of merit goods and goods that create positive externalities in production

Discuss how a per-unit subsidy paid might correct market failure caused by positive externalities in production

MSB > MSC at the private optimum level of output chosen by the firm. On all output between Q_e and Q^*, the social optimum level of output, MSB > MSC therefore there is a potential welfare gain available on each unit of output from Q_e to Q^*. Total possible welfare gain is represented by the area a, b, c shown in Figure 19.7. A subsidy, a payment made by the government to a firm, provides an incentive for the firm to increase output. In

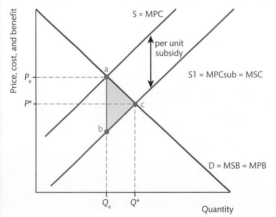

effect the per-unit subsidy reduces the firm's costs of production per unit and increases profit per unit at each price. The firm increases **supply** and the supply curve shifts down and to the right. The vertical distance between S = MPC and S_1 = MPCsub = MSC is the value of the subsidy per unit. The firm increases output form Q_e to Q^* and society gains all the potential welfare. The social optimum equilibrium is where MSB = MSC. That is where the benefit society gains from the consumption of the next unit equals the cost of the resources used to produce it. The effect of the subsidy is to reduce price and increase production and consumption.

Figure 19.7

It is difficult to assess the value of the external benefits associated with the production of a good. Therefore the subsidy may not be enough to correct **market failure** and ensure **allocative efficiency** or indeed the subsidy might lead to overproduction and consumption of the good. There is a significant opportunity cost associated with subsidies. The total cost of the subsidy equals the subsidy per-unit multiplied by the social optimum level of output. Subsidies come from the tax payer and are paid from government tax revenue. The resources used are then unavailable to use in the provision of other community goods and services. There are further opportunity costs. The tax levied to subsidize firms leaves households with less **disposable income**. Consumers are not able to use that money to gain benefit from the consumption of more goods and firms' welfare is affected because of the fall in **producer revenue**.

Direct provision by the government

The government could produce the good that has **positive externalities** associated with its production. For example, the government could provide training for workers through government-run institutions. Governments in countries with relatively free markets are often reluctant to become involved in the production of goods. They believe an efficient outcome is more likely if left to the markets. Governments recognize that they do not have the management expertise and other skills required for successful intervention. Also if losses are incurred the tax payer will have to fund them. Governments are very wary of the possible losses and the huge **opportunity costs** associated with direct provision.

Discuss how a per-unit subsidy paid might correct market failure caused by positive externalities in consumption

Education and health care are often subsidized by governments. At the free market level of consumption Q_e **marginal social benefit** is greater than **marginal social cost** leading to a loss of welfare. Left to the free market there will be a **misallocation of resources**. There will be an inefficient allocation of resources, the good would be under consumed and society would not enjoy enough of the external benefits available from the private consumption of the goods. A subsidy shifts the MPC curve down and to the right from S = MSC to S_{sub}. This lowers the price and increases consumption. Price falls from P_e to P_{sub} and consumption increases from Q_e to Q^*, which is the social optimum level where MSB = MSC, leading to an increase in welfare.

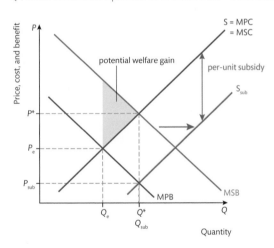

Figure 19.8

There is a large opportunity cost associated with subsidies. The tax revenue used to subsidize the industry cannot be used to provide other community goods. The government needs to have enough tax revenue to be able to raise consumption in this way. Less developed countries with relatively low income and therefore low tax revenue find subsidizing such **merit goods** very difficult. In such countries society is unable to enjoy the external benefits created by the consumption of education and healthcare.

The government can promote the consumption of merit goods through education and advertizing. The government can attempt to raise the perceived private benefit thereby increasing demand for the good. The MPB curve shifts up and to the right so that MPB = MSB. The social optimum level of consumption is achieved at Q^* where MSB = MSC. This strategy is not likely to see success in the short term and again there is an opportunity cost.

The external benefits for the economy from the consumption of education and healthcare are very large; therefore some governments provide it free at the point of use. The services are provided entirely through government expenditure. In other countries they are provided by a combination of the state, private firms, and charities.

Test your understanding of this unit by answering the following questions

- Discuss, using diagrams, policies the government could adopt to correct market failure caused by negative externalities in consumption and production.
- Discuss, using diagrams, policies the government could adopt to correct market failure caused by positive externalities in consumption and production.

Learning Outcomes

- Using the **concepts** of rivalry and excludability, and providing examples, distinguish between public goods (non-rivalrous and non-excludable) and private goods (rivalrous and excludable).
- Explain, with reference to the free-rider problem, how the lack of public goods indicates market failure.
- Discuss the implications of the direct provision of public goods by government.

Synonyms

concept(s) ......idea(s)/ theory/ies

consumption ..use

diminish ....become smaller

incentive ..... encouragement/ motivation

Subject vocabulary

free market a market where the forces of demand and supply are allowed to operate without any forms of intervention

non-rivalrous describes a good whereby consumption of it by one person does not reduce the amount available to others

non-excludable describes a good whereby it is impossible to stop people benefiting from the consumption of it once it has been supplied

quasi-public goods goods that share some of the characteristics of public goods but are not fully non-excludable and non-rivalrous. A road is an example. Most roads are free at the point of use but it is possible to make people pay through tolls and when traffic is heavy the amount available to others to use does begin to diminish so there can be rivalry in consumption.

social optimum level of output the level of production or consumption where marginal social benefit is equal to marginal social cost

Glossary

national defence the systems that a country uses to defend itself against attack

flood barrier a structure that stops/slows down the overflow of water

flood defences structures put into place to protect dry areas from water

Distinguish between public goods and private goods

Public goods are goods that would not be supplied if left to the **free market**. Public goods would not be supplied because they share two characteristics: the goods are **non-rivalrous** and **non-excludable**.

Model sentence: A good is non-rivalrous when consumption by one person does not diminish the amount of the good available for others. A good is non-excludable when once supplied it is impossible to stop people gaining a benefit from the consumption of it.

A private good is both rivalrous and excludable. Consumption of the good by one person does diminish the amount available for others thereby stopping others from consuming it. Once it is supplied it is possible to stop people gaining the benefits from the consumption of it.

A chocolate bar is a private good. It is rivalrous and excludable. After the chocolate has been consumed by one person it is no longer available for consumption by others and once supplied it is possible to stop a person consuming it. Simply put, if a person does not pay for the bar of chocolate he/she cannot enjoy the benefit gained from its consumption.

National defence is a pure public good. It is entirely non-rivalrous and non-excludable. One citizen enjoying the benefits of national security, for example, does not diminish the amount available for others to enjoy and once provided by the government it is impossible to stop people enjoying the benefits it provides. The **flood barrier** across the River Thames in London is another example. Consumption by one does not reduce the amount of benefits in terms of safety and protection of property available for others and once provided it is not possible to exclude people from enjoying the benefits it brings.

Some goods, such as roads, are non-rivalrous and non-excludable to some extent. These goods are called **quasi-public goods**. At quiet times one person driving on a motorway does not, in any meaningful sense, diminish the amount of the motorway available for others to enjoy although at busy times the next person using the motorway does start to cause congestion and the amount of space available for others starts to diminish. Also it is possible to stop people enjoying the benefit gained from driving on the road by installing barriers. Only if a consumer pays the toll can they use the road. Nevertheless, the cost of road construction is extremely high and therefore a motorway would not be built without at least some government expenditure.

Explain why the free-rider problem leads to market failure and why the government intervenes

Why does the market fail if left to the free market? A step-by-step guide

Trouble shooter

There are benefits gained by society from the consumption of national defence and **flood defences** as well as costs to society of providing the goods.

The social optimum level of output and consumption is where marginal social benefit equals marginal social cost.

However, because of the free-rider problem, left to the free market there will be no output.

This means that for all output between zero and the **social optimum level** marginal social benefit is greater than marginal social cost.

This means that the benefit to consumers in society from the consumption of the additional unit is greater than the cost to producers in society of the resources used to supply it.

The free-rider problem leads to a misallocation of resources. No resources in a free market would be allocated to the supply of the public good leading to a loss of welfare.

The government must supply the good, using **tax revenue**, up to the social optimum level in order to maximize society's welfare thereby correcting **market failure**. Evaluating the benefits and costs is not easy and often open to debate. For example, should the government install nuclear weapons and if so how many and of what size? The benefits of nuclear deterrence is greatly disputed and the costs are enormous. The politicians must balance the benefits and the costs and decide the amount and type of weapons necessary to maximize society's welfare. There are **opportunity costs** associated with expenditure on public goods. Resources are limited and if spent on national defence they are not available to provide other pure public goods, quasi-public goods or merit goods.

Model sentence: If people cannot be excluded from enjoying the benefits of a good they have no incentive to pay for it. They would 'free ride', enjoying the benefits without incurring a cost. If consumers do not pay there is no profit available so it will not be supplied.

Test your understanding of this unit by answering the following questions

- Distinguish between pure public goods and merit goods.
- Explain why the free-rider problem leads to market failure.

Subject vocabulary

tax revenue the income the government receives through the levying and collection of taxes

market failure when resources are not allocated or used efficiently

opportunity cost the next best alternative forgone

cap and trade scheme a system whereby a limit or cap is placed on certain types of emissions. Producers are able to sell or trade their unused allowances to producers that have gone over their limit.

Learning Outcomes

- Describe, using examples, common access resources.

- Describe sustainability.

- Explain that the lack of a pricing mechanism for common access resources means that these goods may be overused/depleted/degraded as a result of activities of producers and consumers who do not pay for the resources that they use, and that this poses a threat to sustainability.

- Explain, using negative externality diagrams, that economic activity requiring the use of fossil fuels to satisfy demand poses a threat to sustainability.

- Explain that the existence of poverty in economically less-developed countries creates negative externalities through over-**exploitation** of land for agriculture, and that this poses a threat to sustainability.

- Evaluate, using diagrams, possible government responses to threats to sustainability, including legislation, carbon taxes, **cap and trade schemes**, and funding for clean technologies.

- Explain, using examples, that government responses to threats to sustainability are limited by the global nature of the problems and the lack of ownership of common access resources, and that effective responses require international cooperation.

Explain the term 'the tragedy of the commons' and 'sustainability'

There are many differing views amongst economists on the meaning of the term 'sustainability'. Generally it is agreed that sustainability is about using the world's existing resources today to satisfy our present needs in a way that does not stop others in the future satisfying their needs.

The tragedy of the commons is a theory about the overuse of resources. It refers to the **depletion** of resources that are held in common (available for everybody to use). Continued, uncontrolled exploitation of a resource is unsustainable because it will be overused and therefore will not be available for others in society to use in the future. The situation arises when individuals or firms cannot be excluded from gaining private benefit from the **consumption** of the resource.

For example, when parts of the ocean are held in common fishermen cannot be stopped from taking their **trawlers** into the area to fish. The fishermen gain a private benefit and therefore have an **incentive** to carry on catching fish despite the fact that over exploitation of this resource will eventually lead to the stocks of fish available falling to very low levels or might lead to the extinction of a particular species, thereby reducing the amount available for others to enjoy in the future. Any future private benefit will be limited and welfare will be lost.

Glossary

exploitation making use of something to gain maximum profit from it

depletion reduction in amount

trawlers type of fishing boat

Synonyms

consumption..use

incentive..... encouragement/ motivation

Explain why a resource that has no price might not be sustainable

Unsustainable use of a resource occurs when it is free, and open to all to exploit. Uncontrolled access leads to over exploitation, leaving very little for others to use and it eventually might run out completely. When a price is not charged for the direct use of a resource the resource is not rationed (see pages 15–16 for a detailed explanation of the rationing function of price). In markets, generally when price rises for a resource consumers **ration** their use of it, and as the resource becomes scarcer and as supply falls, the price increases leading to a greater fall in consumption. In this way **scarce** resources are **conserved**.

Model sentence: When there is no price there is no incentive to ration use of the resource thereby leading to its depletion. This is not sustainable because the resource will run out and there will be little if any left for future generations to enjoy.

Explain, using negative externality diagrams, why the use of fossil fuels poses a threat to sustainability

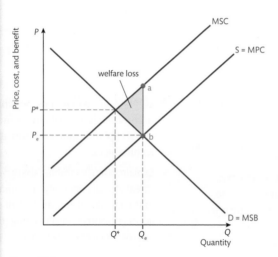

Figure 21.1

As fossil fuels such as coal, oil, and natural gas are burnt they **emit** harmful greenhouse gases into the atmosphere. There are **external costs** or **negative externalities** caused by these **emissions** such as damage to people's health from breathing the polluted air and damage to rivers, forests, and farming land from **acid rain**. Most scientists argue that the burning of fossil fuels is a major cause of global warming, the external costs of which may be very high. Future generations may have to pay the external costs of production. For example, if climate change causes the sea level to rise, the **flood barrier** across the Thames in London may need to be replaced. In this case the third parties are the future generations of taxpayers who will have to pay for its construction.

Suppose an **industry** burns coal as a source of energy. The industry pays the private cost which is the price of the coal. The burning of coal creates external costs that are not paid for by the firm but are paid by third parties. The social optimum level of output is where **marginal social cost = marginal social benefit** at Q*. However, the industry sets output where MPC = MSB at Q_e where the MSC > MSB. This causes **welfare loss** on all units from Q_e to Q*. There is a misallocation of resources. Price is too low and output is too high. The government must **intervene** in order to correct market failure.

Driving cars causes negative externalities from the burning of petrol. Cars emit harmful gases that pollute the air creating **respiratory** problems as well as contributing to global warming. **Marginal private benefit** is greater than marginal social benefit. This reflects the fact that the private benefit gained from the use of cars is greater than the benefit gained by society. The individual car user sets consumption at Q_e where MPB = MPC. The social optimum level of output is at Q* where MSB = MSC. As seen in Figure 21.2 on all output between Q_e and Q* MSC > MSB causing a welfare loss on all these units. Total welfare loss is the shaded area. There is a misallocation of resources when left to the free market. Consumption is too high. In order to reduce the negative externalities associated with car use and correct market failure the government must intervene.

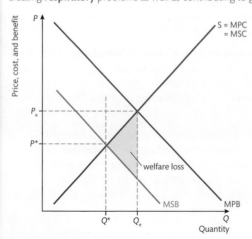

Figure 21.2

The burning of fossil fuels in huge quantities today reduces the amount available for others in the future, thereby affecting the ability of future generations to satisfy needs and wants. Also the external costs associated with the burning of fossil fuels will be paid by future generations thereby reducing the amount of income they will have available to satisfy needs and wants. It can be argued that the world's scarce resources are being used today to satisfy the growing needs of the current population in a way that diminishes the ability of future generations to satisfy their needs. Therefore it is unsustainable.

Explain why negative externalities created by the over-exploitation of land for agricultural output particularly affect less-developed countries

People in LDCs are relatively poor. They often rely entirely on the production of **primary goods** and agricultural goods for their incomes. The world price of such goods tends to fall over time as new methods of production are employed that increase output from the land such as new fertilizers and capital equipment. As supply increases, price falls. Capital in LDC is often relatively less technologically advanced as low incomes mean farmers are not able to buy expensive capital. Nor are farmers able to buy fertilizers. Therefore **productivity** is lower. As world price falls over time and the agricultural industry becomes relatively less productive incomes become difficult to maintain. Farmers over-use the land trying to maximize output in the short term. Land is never left fallow (unused). When land is continuously used to grow crops year on year, the soil cannot retain the nutrients and moisture in the longer term, therefore the quality and productivity of the land falls overtime. Over exploitation of the land creates external costs, such as long-term soil **degradation**. Future generations will find it increasingly difficult to earn an income from farming the land.

Evaluate, using diagrams, possible government responses to threats to sustainability and explain the need for international agreement

Extension of property rights

Model sentence: A resource held in common is overused because nobody owns it and therefore no price is charged or cost incurred to use it.

This is unsustainable in the long term. A river that is not owned by any person or group is at risk of being polluted by firms' harmful emissions. If ownership is given to a water company, for example, each time a firm polluted the river, it could be charged or fined, thereby increasing the firms' **private costs** and affecting output decisions.

Government could give people the right to **sue** firms if air pollution leads to health problems, thereby increasing the producers' marginal private costs and reducing private optimum level of output, resulting in fewer external costs. Extending property rights internalizes the externality: negative externalities are brought back into the **market mechanism**.

Cattle can **graze** on common land for free. Therefore the land is over exploited and in the long term the soil will be degraded. If ownership of the land was passed to the farmers in the area it would give them greater incentive to consider the benefits gained from use of the land over the longer term rather than just in the short term.

Subsidizing clean technologies

The burning of fossil fuels creates lots of external costs so governments around the world want to increase the use of renewable sources of energy such as wind power, solar power, hydropower, and biofuels as a way of reducing the negative externalities associated with the consumption of fossil fuels. Many countries have signed **treaties**, agreeing to cut emissions of harmful gases and are fined if they do not achieve the agreed targets. Governments can encourage the development, production, and use of such renewable energy through the provision of a **subsidy**. (See pages 36–38 for a full explanation of the effects of a subsidy and a diagram illustrating the effects).

Subsidies given to the solar and wind power industries in effect reduce **costs of production** causing firms to increase **supply**. The price consumers pay falls and quantity consumed increases. Firms gain greater **revenue** as they receive the price paid by the consumer plus the subsidy per unit sold.

As revenue and profit rise in the solar and wind power industries resources are reallocated. More resources are used in the development and production of renewable energy while fewer are used in the fossil fuel industry thereby reducing negative externalities.

There are some external costs associated with renewable energy. Wind farms are an **eyesore** to some and create noise pollution. There is evidence that the value of houses near wind farms have been negatively affected. Some scientists are concerned that renewable energy creation is relatively inefficient and that supply

Subject vocabulary

primary good a good that has not been processed and is in a raw state (e.g. fruit/wheat)

productivity the quantity of output per unit of input

private costs the cost incurred by firms or consumers from their own production or consumption of a good

market mechanism the process by which consumers and producers, acting in their own interest in a free market, determine the market price and quantity of a good and therefore the quantity of resources allocated to the production of the good

subsidy payment made by government to firms per unit of output

costs of production the amount the firm pays for the factors of production used to produce goods or services

supply the amount of a good that a firm is willing and able to produce at each price

revenue the income a firm receives from consumers in exchange for goods (revenue = price × quantity sold)

Glossary

degradation becoming worse in condition

sue make a legal claim for harm done

graze feed on grass

treaty(ies) formal written agreement(s) between countries/governments

eyesore something that is very ugly

of energy from such sources will never be able to meet the world's growing demand. This would lead to market failure in the goods markets as the ability of industries to produce output is restricted through lack of energy.

Cap and trade schemes

Such schemes use **market forces** to correct **market failure** caused by **negative externalities** (see page 51 for a full explanation of how the use of tradable permits can correct market failure). The government issues permits to firms in the industry giving them permission to pollute up to a specified amount for which the firm pays a price. In effect the holder of permits has the property rights and can sell them. The sum of the firms' allowable levels of pollution is the total amount of pollution allowed in the industry.

If a firm uses up its allowance to pollute it can buy permits from those firms who have not used up theirs. There is a **market** for the permits. There is a fixed **supply** of permits and if **demand** increases for the **output** of the industry some firms may wish to buy more permits in order to increase output. Therefore the price of permits will increase and some firms will now consider **investing** in cleaner production methods rather than buying permits. Over time the government can restrict the supply of newly issued permits in order to increase the price of the permits on the market. This in turn increases the incentive for firms to invest in new cleaner **capital** that reduces levels of harmful emissions, thereby reducing the **external costs** and correcting market failure.

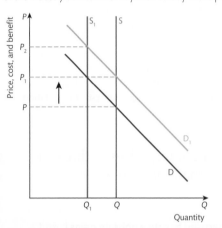

Figure 21.3

Supply is **perfectly inelastic** with respect to price. Supply is fixed. Increases in demand for permits results in an increase in price from P to P_1 as shown in Figure 21.3. The government can reduce supply of new permits and the supply curve shifts to the left causing price to rise from P_1 to P_2.

This method is seen as an efficient way in which to reduce emissions. Those firms where the cost of replacing capital is less than the price of permits will replace their capital and sell their permits. Those firms who find it more costly to cut down on levels of pollution emitted will buy permits instead. Over time, because of falling supply and perhaps increasing demand, the price of permits increases providing greater incentive for the remaining firms to buy the new capital. In this way, through the use of market forces, the external costs created by an industry can be massively reduced.

Scarce resources must be used by the government to monitor the schemes to ensure all firms are polluting within the allowed amount. Those that over pollute are heavily fined. There is a major **opportunity cost** of such schemes because the spent resources are not available for the government to use elsewhere. The next best alternative is **forgone**.

Carbon taxes

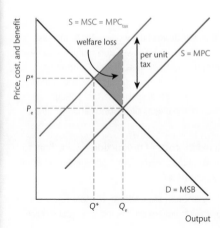

Figure 21.4

A carbon tax is a charge set by government on the use of fossil fuels. The amount of the tax is dependent on the amount of carbon that is released when the fuel is burned. The higher the amount of carbon, the greater the external costs therefore the higher the tax must be to correct market failure. Figure 21.4 shows the effect of a tax. At the private optimum level of output, Q_e, MSC > MSB leading to a welfare loss, shown as the shaded area. The tax increases marginal private costs so that MPC_{tax} = MSC at the **social optimum level of output**. The firm reduces output from Q_e to Q^* where MSC = MSB which is the social optimum level. The market outcome is that price rises and quantity falls thereby reducing the negative externalities brought about by the burning of the fossil fuel.

Because the tax makes using fossil fuels more expensive, it encourages producers and consumers to reduce consumption by rationing their use of it and they have an incentive to use fuels with less carbon emissions.

Subject vocabulary

market forces the forces of demand and supply that interact in a competitive market and determine equilibrium price

market failure when resources are not allocated or used optimally

negative externalities occur when the production or consumption of a good creates costs that must be paid by third parties. The existence of negative externalities means that social cost is greater than private cost.

market where buyers and sellers meet to exchange money for goods and services

supply the amount of a good that a firm is willing and able to produce at each price

demand the amount of a good that consumers are willing and able to buy at each price

output the quantity of goods produced by a firm, industry or economy

invest to buy capital goods and services

capital (goods) manufactured goods that are used in the production of other goods

external cost occurs when the production or consumption of a good creates a cost that must be paid by third parties

perfectly inelastic supply quantity supplied does not change as price changes. PES equals zero.

opportunity cost the next best alternative forgone

social optimum level of output the level of production or consumption where marginal social benefit is equal to marginal social cost

Synonyms

forgone .... sacrificed/ given up

The international perspective

The impact of any government policy response implemented to correct market failure caused by negative externalities is going to be very limited if only a few governments support and enforce such policies. **Economic growth** increases harmful emissions because often old technologies are used in production. In China, for example, where output has increased dramatically in the last few decades there has been a huge increase in harmful emissions offsetting reductions made elsewhere. Some scientists argue that pollution is causing the world's climate to change and this will create far-reaching external costs. Therefore they call for an international response to the problem.

Subject vocabulary

economic growth an increase in real GDP

Test your understanding of this unit by answering the following questions

- Explain why a resource that is held in common may be overused.
- Explain how subsidies might be used to correct market failure caused by the use of fossil fuels.
- Explain how the extension of property rights can internalize the externalities caused by over exploitation of resources.
- Evaluate the use of a tradable permits scheme as a method to reduce the global level of harmful emissions.

Learning Outcomes

- Explain, using examples, that market failure may occur when one party in an economic transaction (either the buyer or the seller) possesses more information than the other party. (HL)
- Evaluate possible government responses, including **legislation**, **regulation**, and provision of information. (HL)

- Explain how monopoly power can create a welfare loss and is therefore a type of market failure. (HL)
- Discuss possible government responses, including legislation, regulation, **nationalization**, and **trade liberalization**. (HL)

Explain why imperfect information leads to market failure (HL)

A market is a place where buyers and sellers come together to exchange goods and services for money. **Asymmetric information** occurs in a market when a buyer and a seller do not share all information. One party in the transaction has access to information that the other party does not thereby gaining an advantage. More often than not it is the seller who has information regarding the good that is not shared with the buyer. For example, a second-hand car dealer knows that there is a fault with a car. The seller does not inform the buyer of this fact. The buyer places a greater value on the **benefit** gained from owning the car than he would if he had perfect knowledge. Therefore the buyer is prepared to pay a higher price than he would if in possession of all the information. The second-hand car market fails because of asymmetric information.

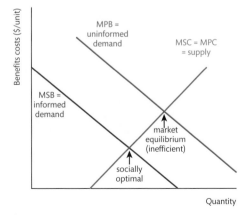

Figure 22.1

Glossary

legislation law/set of laws

Synonyms

regulation(s) ..... law(s)/rule(s)

Subject vocabulary

nationalization the process by which a government takes ownership of a private firm or industry

trade liberalization the removal of, or reduction, in the international barriers to trade, such as tariffs and quotas

asymmetric information a situation in which one person in a market has more information than the other person

benefit the satisfaction gained from the consumption of a good

Subject vocabulary

marginal private benefit is the additional private benefit generated by the consumption or production of an additional unit of output

market equilibrium occurs when the quantity demanded of goods produced in an industry equals the amount of goods firms in the industry are willing to supply

resources the inputs into the production process, the factors of production

misallocation of resources occurs when the allocation of resources leads to welfare loss and therefore a reallocation of resources could increase society's welfare

market failure when resources are not allocated or used optimally

social optimum equilibrium occurs in a market where the benefit society receives from the consumption of the next unit is equal to the cost incurred by society of the next unit (MSB = MSC)

insider trading the practice of profiting from trading in shares through having information that is not available to others in the market

public limited companies a form of business organization in which shares are offered for sale to the general public. Shareholders own the business and receive a share of the profits. Liability is limited to the amount paid for the shares.

share a unit of ownership of a company's capital. The owner is entitled to a proportion of the company's profit.

merger the joining together of two or more companies to make one larger company

Synonyms

consumption .... use

manipulate .... influence/
control

Glossary

exaggerating making something sound better than it really is

Explain how market failure is caused by imperfect information (HL) – a step-by-step guide (see Figure 22.1 on page 61)

Trouble shooter

When suppliers have negative information about a good that is not shared with the consumers **marginal private benefit** will be greater than marginal social benefit.

The **market equilibrium** is socially inefficient because marginal social cost is greater than marginal social benefit meaning that the cost of the **resources** used to produce the next unit is greater than the benefit society gains from the **consumption** of it.

There is a **misallocation of resources**: too many resources are allocated to the production of the good; price and output are too high.

When consumers have all the information demand falls and **market failure** caused by asymmetric information is corrected.

Consumers now have all the information and place a lower value on the consumption of the next unit. Price, output and consumption fall. Fewer resources are now allocated to the production of the good.

The **social optimum equilibrium** is achieved where MSB = MSC.

Model sentence: If consumers do not have all the information regarding a good they will over value the benefit gained from the consumption of it and will therefore be prepared to pay a higher price.

Explain how market failure caused by asymmetric information might be corrected (HL)

In order to correct market failure and reduce the welfare loss caused by imperfect information the government must intervene in the market and provide the full information regarding goods and services.

Firms attempt to **manipulate** consumer demand through advertising and marketing, often **exaggerating** the benefits available from use of the good. Consumers then believe there to be a greater private benefit than there actually is. This leads to market failure and welfare loss as previously explained. It is very difficult for the government to intervene effectively in the case of marketing. It is illegal for firms to make false claims about their goods, but there is a very fine line between exaggerating benefits and lying about the benefits. Nevertheless, in many countries governments have legislated in this area to try to protect consumers from inaccurate and misleading information.

There are laws against **insider trading** in the stock market. This occurs when an individual or group of individuals are in possession of information regarding a **public limited company** that is not shared with the rest of the market. For example, when two companies merge it is likely that the value of a **share** will increase. If some people know about the **merger** before it is known by the market then they can make enormous capital gains from buying the shares at a relatively low price and then selling after the increase in price brought about by the increase in demand for shares once the information has been made available to the market. Governments have made insider trading illegal and the penalties relatively tough.

Estate agents sell houses on behalf of the owners in return for a small percentage of the selling price. Agents may have information regarding a house that would, if known by the market, reduce demand and selling price of the property. The agent might not share the information because of the incentive of a higher price and therefore a higher fee.

It is very difficult for the government to intervene and correct market failure. When the information is known by only a few people then the government is unlikely to know about it. Asymmetric information has to be identified and then it must be proved that a person had the information and acted to benefit from it before he or she can be punished.

The government can, through advertising and education, increase the amount of information available for consumers. Warnings concerning questionable business practice can be issued thereby allowing the consumer to make a correct assessment of the true benefit gains from consumption. For example, consumers made aware of the risks of certain financial investments are able to make a decision about whether or not to invest based on better and unbiased information.

Explain how monopoly power can create a welfare loss (HL) (see pages 85–93 for a detailed explanation of the consequences of monopoly power)

A firm that is the sole supplier of a good has **monopoly power**. The firm is the industry and therefore can control price or **quantity supplied**. The firm reduces output in order to increase price thereby increasing **producer revenue** and profit. Increasing price reduces **consumer surplus** and increases **producer surplus** and creates a loss of society's welfare. The monopolist's **market power** is used to increase producer surplus (PS) at the expense of consumer surplus (CS).

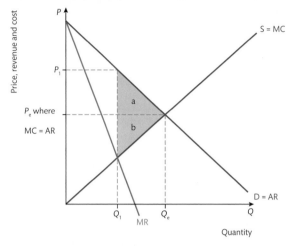

Figure 22.2

Free market equilibrium is at $P_e Q_e$ as shown in Figure 22.2. This is where MC = AR. CS and PS are maximized therefore community surplus, which is the sum of CS and PS, is maximized. When community surplus is maximized social welfare is maximized. $P_e Q_e$ is the social optimum equilibrium. This equilibrium is only achieved when there is no intervention in the market and when no firm has the power to affect industry supply or price.

The **monopolist** reduces output to Q_1. Price rises to P_1. At $P_1 Q_1$, P > MC. This means the value consumers in society place on the consumption of the additional unit is greater than the cost of the **resources** used to produce it. There is a welfare loss to society on all output from Q_1 to Q_e. This is represented in the diagram by the shaded area a, the loss of CS, and area b, the loss of PS. The sum of the two losses is the welfare loss caused by the restriction of output and the increase in price.

Not enough resources are allocated to the production of the good. Monopoly power causes welfare loss and the market to fail.

Discuss possible government responses to monopoly power (HL)

The government can intervene to try to correct market failure by making markets more competitive. The government can reduce barriers to entry, for example, by granting licences to more airlines allowing them to compete on specific routes. State monopolies could be opened up to competition. Greater competition will drive down prices and increase consumption thereby reducing welfare loss.

Industries become more concentrated after mergers. Governments, through for example the **monopolies commission**, sometimes do not allow mergers to take place thereby retaining a greater degree of competition in the market and therefore ensuring lower prices and greater consumption.

Competition laws make certain practices illegal, such as the formation of **cartels**. In **oligopolistic markets** it is possible for firms to **collude** and set a higher price in order to increase profit. Such laws could be strengthened, monitored, and penalties increased to reduce this behaviour.

Government agencies, such as Ofwat in the UK – which was set up to monitor providers of water and sewage services – can work to limit **abuse** of market power. Agencies, for example, have the power to limit the extent of any price increase in the industry thereby minimizing any welfare loss.

Test your understanding of this unit by answering the following questions

- Explain why asymmetric information leads to welfare loss. Illustrate your answer with a diagram.
- Explain how a monopolist causes welfare loss. Illustrate your answer with a diagram.
- Using examples and a diagram, explain how market failure caused by monopoly power might be corrected.

Subject vocabulary

monopoly power the degree of control a firm has over the setting of price

quantity supplied the amount of a good that firms are willing and able to produce at a given price over a given period of time

producer revenue the income a firm receives from consumers in exchange for goods (revenue = price × quantity sold)

consumer surplus the difference between the price a consumer is willing and able to pay and the price the consumer actually pays

producer surplus the difference between the price a firm is willing to accept for a unit of output and the price the consumer actually pays

market power the ability of a firm to change the market price of a good or service

free market equilibrium a free market is in equilibrium where the quantity supplied is equal to the quantity demanded

monopolist a firm that dominates an industry

resources the inputs into the production process, the factors of production

monopolies commission a public body that investigates mergers and other matters regarding competition law in the UK

cartel a collection of firms that agree to work together to maximize their joint profit

oligopolistic market describes a market that is controlled by a small number of firms

collude to act together with others to achieve a common goal, such as raising prices/maximizing profile

Glossary

abuse misuse/the wrong use

1.5 Theory of the firm and market structures – production and costs (HL)

Learning Outcomes

- Distinguish between the short run and long run in the context of production.
- Define total product, average product, and marginal product and construct diagrams to show their relationship.
- Explain the law of diminishing returns.
- Calculate total, average, and marginal product from a set of data and/or diagrams.

Distinguish between the short run and the long run in the context of production

In the **short run** the quantity of at least one **factor of production** is fixed and in the **long run** all factors are variable. In the short run a car producer might be able to increase **output** by employing more workers but be unable to increase the amount of **capital**. A farmer might be able to increase the amount of capital and labour but not be able to increase the amount of land needed to grow more output. It takes time to increase **productive capacity**. For example, the car **manufacturer** must order the capital from the manufacturer. Capital is **specialized** and can take a long time to make. After the firm has received the machines it can add the **variable factor** labour to the higher level of capital in order to increase output. When the firm wants to raise the level of capital again it must go through this process.

Define total product, average product, and marginal product and construct diagrams to show their relationship

Total product (TP) is the number of units of output produced in a given period of time. **Average product** (AP) is the quantity of total output produced per unit of the variable factor while holding all other factors constant. AP is calculated by dividing total product by the quantity of the variable factor used. AP = TP/V where TP is total product and V is the quantity of the variable factor. **Marginal product** (MP) is the change in total output brought about by adding one more unit of the variable factor.

Labour	TP	AP	MP
0	0		
			4
1	4	4	
			5
2	9	4.5	
			6
3	15	5	
			5
4	20	5	
			4
5	24	4.8	
			2
6	26	4.33	
			0
7	26	3.7	
			-2
8	24	3	

Table 23.1

The quantity of labour is variable and the quantity of capital is fixed. Table 23.1 shows the effect on TP, AP, and MP of employing one more worker in a small **workshop**. Add the first worker to the capital and **production** can begin. The MP is the gain in output resulting from employing the additional worker. For example, the MP of worker 1 is 4 units and the MP of worker 4 is 5 units. MP appears between each change in the number of workers because it shows the change in output as we move from one quantity of workers to the next.

Calculations of AP and MP – a step-by-step guide

Trouble shooter

Add the first worker. Quantity of workers changes from 0 to 1 and output changes from 0 to 4:

$AP = TP/V = 4/1 = 4$

$MP = \Delta TP/\Delta V = (4 - 0)/(1 - 0) = 4/1 = 4$

Add the next worker. Quantity of workers changes from 1 to 2 and output increases from 4 to 9 units:

$AP = TP/V = 9/2 = 4.5$ units

$MP = \Delta TP/\Delta V = (9 - 4)/(2 - 1) = 5/1 = 5$

Add the next worker. Quantity of workers changes from 2 to 3. Output changes from 9 to 15 units:

$AP = TP/V = 15/3 = 5$ units

$MP = \Delta TP/\Delta V = (15 - 9)/(3 - 2) = 6/1 = 6$ units

Add one more worker. Quantity of workers changes from 3 to 4. Output changes from 15 to 20 units:

$AP = TP/V = 20/4 = 5$ units

$MP = \Delta TP/\Delta V = (20 - 15)/(5 - 4) = 5/1 = 5$ units

What is the law of diminishing returns to a factor?

The law states that as more units of the variable factor are added to a given quantity of the fixed factor the additional output gained from each additional unit of the variable factor employed will at some point begin to fall. At first as additional workers are added output rises at an increasing rate as can be seen in the calculations shown above. From 0 to 3 workers the increase in output from employing the next worker is greater than the increase in output from employing the previous worker. MP is increasing as each worker is added. This is increasing marginal returns to a factor. The additional output gained from adding the fourth worker is less than the gain from adding the third worker. As more workers are added output continues to increase but at a diminishing rate. This is the law of diminishing marginal returns to a factor. Adding the eighth worker causes output to fall from 26 to 24 units: $MP = -2$.

The information in Table 23.1 is plotted on to the graph Figure 23.1.

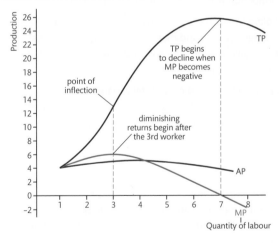

Figure 23.1

Why do AP and MP rise and then fall?

When 1 worker is employed in the workshop she has to do all of the work: collecting the **raw materials**, operating the machine, repairing the equipment, cleaning up, and so on. Add another worker whose job is to collect the raw materials and the first worker can spend more time operating the machine producing output. Add another to specialize in cleaning and even more time can be spent on production. Each worker specializes in doing one job and they become quick and good at it. Look at Table 23.1. Average product or output per worker increases from 0 to 3 workers. **Labour productivity** is rising. As more workers are added the workshop becomes overcrowded. Workers get in each other's way. Diminishing marginal returns to a factor set in at 3 workers. This is the **point of inflection** on the diagram and where the MP curve is at its highest point. Output is still increasing as workers are added but at a diminishing rate.

drag(s) .... pull(s)

firm........... business/
producer/
supplier

scarce........ limited/finite

sum........... total

incur .... experience/
encounter

MP becomes negative after the seventh worker. Adding the eighth worker reduces output. The TP curve begins to slope downwards at this point and the MP curve dips under the horizontal axis.

If the addition to output from the next worker (MP) is greater than the average output per head (AP), employing the next worker will increase the average and productivity increases. If the addition to output (MP) is less than the average output per head (AP) employing the next worker will **drag** down the average and productivity falls. Therefore AP = MP at AP's highest point.

Trouble shooter

To help you understand the relationship between AP and MP think about the following situation. A footballer has played 10 games and has scored 10 goals. The average number of goals per game = total number of goals/quantity of games = 10/10 = 1 goal. He plays the eleventh game and scores 4 goals. The addition to the total number of goals scored is 4 and this is greater than the average of 1 goal per game. Therefore the average will increase: (10 + 4) 14 goals/(10 + 1) 11 games = 1.27 goals per game. Work out what happens to the average if he scores 1 goal in the next game. Now work out the average when he scores zero goals in the next game.

Test your understanding of this unit by answering the following questions

- Using a diagram to illustrate your answer, explain the relationship between total product, average product, and marginal product.

Learning Outcomes

- Explain the meaning of economic costs as the opportunity cost of all resources employed by the firm (including entrepreneurship).

- Distinguish between explicit costs and implicit costs as the two components of economic costs.

- Explain the distinction between the short run and the long run, with reference to fixed costs and variable costs.

- Distinguish between total costs, marginal costs, and average costs.

- Draw diagrams illustrating the relationship between marginal costs and average costs, and explain the connection with production in the short run.

- Explain the relationship between the product curves (average product and marginal product) and the cost curves (average variable cost and marginal cost), with reference to the law of diminishing returns.

- Calculate total fixed costs, total variable costs, total costs, average fixed costs, average variable costs, average total costs, and marginal costs from a set of data and/or diagrams.

fixed cost a business cost that does not change as the quantity of goods or services the business produces changes, such as rent

economic cost of production the sum of explicit costs and implicit costs

opportunity cost the next best alternative forgone

resources the inputs into the production process, the factors of production

explicit costs payments made by firms for inputs such as wages, rent and payments for raw materials

implicit costs the opportunity cost of using resources which are self-owned and not purchased

Explain the meaning of economic cost

Model sentence: The economic cost of production is the opportunity cost of production. If a firm is using its scarce resources to make a good it then cannot use them to make the next best alternative. The opportunity cost is the value that would have been gained had the resources been used to produce the next best alternative.

Economic costs of production are the **sum** of **explicit costs** and **implicit costs**. The distinction between the costs is best explained using an example.

Distinguish between explicit and implicit costs – a step-by-step guide

Trouble shooter

Maria is an **entrepreneur** who opened a restaurant. In order to do this she gave up a job paying €60,000 per year and used €20,000 from her **savings** to pay the **start-up costs**.

The business or **accounting costs** included rent, wages, **raw materials**, gas, and electricity. The sum of these costs in the first year was €100,000. Economists call accounting costs explicit costs and these are the market value of the resources bought by the entrepreneur from other individuals and firms. For example, there is a market for property and the value of the rent (an explicit cost) is determined by **the forces of demand and supply** in this market.

Maria's calculation of her costs differed from the accountant's. She gave up her time to become an entrepreneur and to work in her restaurant. Time that she could use to earn €60,000. Therefore the next best use of her time is valued at €60,000. She spent €20,000 of her own savings that could earn 5% **interest**. The next best use of the €20,000 savings is valued at €1000.

These are the hidden costs which economists call implicit costs. Maria's time and savings are her own resources. She did not pay somebody for them. Their value is given by their opportunity cost which is the amount that her self-owned resources could earn if put to the next best alternative use.

Maria's accounting costs = €100,000

Her economic costs = explicit costs + implicit costs = €100,000 + €61,000 = €161,000.

Explain the distinction between the short run and the long run, with reference to fixed costs and variable costs

In the **short run** the quantity of at least one **factor of production** into the production process is fixed. In the **long run** the quantities of all factors are variable. Fixed factors give rise to fixed costs and variable factors give rise to **variable costs**.

Total fixed costs (TFC) are the sum of the costs that do not change as **output** changes. In the short run the costs are **incurred** even if output is zero. Rent is a fixed cost. The rent is the same no matter how many units are produced and must be paid even if the firm stops producing.

Total variable costs (TVC) are the sum of the costs that change as output changes. To increase output the firm needs to buy more raw materials and pay for more workers therefore variable costs rise. These costs are only incurred when the firm is producing goods.

Total cost (TC) = Total fixed cost + Total variable cost

Output	TFC	TVC	TC	AFC	AVC	ATC	MC
0	100	0	100				
1	100	100	200	100	100	200	100
2	100	180	280	50	90	140	80
3	100	230	330	33.33	76.67	110	50
4	100	260	360	25	65	90	30
5	100	280	380	20	56	76	20
6	100	290	390	16.67	48.33	65	10
7	100	325	425	14.29	46.43	60.7	35
8	100	400	500	12.5	50	62.5	75
9	100	510	610	11.11	56.67	67.78	110
10	100	650	750	10	65	75	140

Average total cost = Total cost/output: ATC = TC/Q

Average fixed cost = Total fixed cost/output: AFC = TFC/Q

Average variable cost = Total variable cost/output: AVC = TVC/Q

Marginal cost = the change in total cost brought about by the production of an additional unit of output.

Table 24.1

Table 24.1 shows calculations for all types of costs from 0 to 10 units of output.

Subject vocabulary

entrepreneur an individual who, in pursuit of profit, brings together the other factors of production in order to produce a good or service

savings income that is not spent

start-up costs expenses linked to setting up a new business before it starts producing and selling goods or services

accounting cost the value of resources bought from individuals or firms (explicit costs)

raw material the basic material from which a good is made

forces of demand and supply changes in the determinants of demand and supply in a market that affect the market price and the allocation of resources

interest the price paid for the use of borrowed money/ the money earned from bank deposits

short run a period of time when at least one factor is variable and the others are fixed

factors of production the inputs into the production process (land, labour, capital and entrepreneurship)

long run a conceptual moment in time when all factors are variable

variable costs costs that change as the level of output changes

total fixed cost the sum of the costs that do not change as output changes

output the quantity of goods produced by a firm, industry or economy

total variable cost the sum of the costs that change as output changes

total cost the sum of total fixed cost and total variable cost

average total cost equal to total cost divided by quantity of output

average fixed cost equal to total fixed cost divided by quantity of output

average variable cost equal to total variable cost divided by quantity of output

marginal cost the change in total cost resulting from a change in output of one unit

Why does the AFC curve slope downwards? (see table 24.1 on page 67)

TFC = $100 at all levels of output because fixed costs do not change as output changes.

AFC is the fixed cost per unit of output.

AFC = TFC/Q: At 1 unit of output AFC = 100/1 = $100 and at 10 units AFC = 100/10 = $10.

TFC does not change with output therefore as output increases AFC falls.

As shown in Figure 24.1 the AFC curve falls as output increases.

Why is the average variable cost curve U-shaped?

TVC is the sum of the costs that change with output. As output rises TVC rises. AVC is the variable cost per unit of output.

Here are some calculations of AVC (AVC = TVC/Q): at 1 unit AVC = 100/1 = $100. At 7 units AVC = 325/7 = $46.43. At 10 units AVC = 650/10 = $65.

As output increases between 1 and 7 units AVC falls from $100 to $46.43. Between 7 and 10 units AVC rises from $46.43 to $65. In the short run the firm adds variable factors of production to the fixed factor in order to increase output. To begin with, when workers are added **average product** rises at an increasing rate. Output per worker increases because the rate of change in output is greater than the rate of change in the number of workers. AP rises at an increasing rate because as more workers are added they can specialize in doing one job and they become quick and very good at performing that one task. Therefore the rate at which output increases is greater than the rate at which the cost of the **variable factor** increases. AVC = TVC/Q, so if Q increases at a greater rate than total variable costs AVC falls. This occurs because eventually, as more workers are added to the fixed quantity of capital **diminishing average returns** set in and average product falls. At some point, as more and more workers are added to a fixed quantity of capital, the additional output produced by the next worker falls below the additional output produced by the addition of the previous worker. This occurs because the work-place becomes overcrowded and workers begin to get in each other's way. Therefore the rate at which the cost of the variable factor increases is greater than the rate at which output increases. The output per worker falls resulting in an increase in the cost per unit of output. As shown in Figure 24.1 the AVC curve initially falls as output increases but begins to rise when diminishing returns to the variable factor set in.

Why is the average total cost curve U-shaped?

ATC is the total cost per unit of output. ATC = AFC + AVC. ATC, like AVC, initially falls as output increases and eventually begins to rise. As output increases from 1 to 7 units ATC falls and then begins to rise. AVC is included in ATC so ATC falls and then eventually rises for the reasons already explained. In Figure 24.1 the ATC curve like the AVC curve is U-shaped. At first as output increases falling AFC has a major impact on ATC dragging it down but as output continues to rise the rate at which AFC falls begins to diminish so its effect on ATC lessens. However as output continues to increase, eventually diminishing returns to labour set in and AVC begins to rise. As AFC falls at a diminishing rate and AVC begin to rise at some point as output increases ATC will begin to rise.

Why is the marginal cost curve U-shaped?

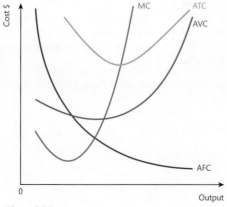

Figure 24.1

Marginal cost is the change in total cost resulting from a change in output of one unit. Here are some calculations: between 0 and 1 output changes 1 unit and TC increases from 100 to 200, a change of $100. MC = 100/1 = $100 and so between 5 and 6 units MC = 10/1 = $10 and between 6 and 7 units MC = 35/1 = $35.

Initially when workers are added **marginal product** increases. This means that the addition to output from adding the next worker is greater than the extra output gained from adding the previous worker. The rate of change in output gained from adding one more worker continues to increase therefore the additional cost of the next unit produced falls. Therefore the firm is experiencing increasing **marginal returns to the variable factor**. At some point as more and more workers are added to the fixed capital **diminishing marginal returns to the variable factor** set in. Marginal product begins to fall: the additional output gained from adding another worker is less than the additional output gained from adding the previous worker. The additional cost per unit of output therefore begins to rise. In Figure 24.1 the MC curve, like the ATC and AVC curves, is U-shaped.

Figure 24.1 shows the relationship between the average cost curves and marginal cost curve in the short run when at least one factor is fixed.

As output increases AFC falls. ATC = AFC + AVC. Therefore the difference between ATC and AVC is AFC. AFC falls as output increases and the difference between ATC and AVC gets smaller. So as output increases the distance between the two curves gets smaller.

Why does MC = ATC at the lowest average cost per unit?

If the addition to total cost from the production of one more unit (MC) is greater than the total average cost then producing that unit will increase ATC. If the addition to total costs is less than the average total cost then producing the unit will reduce ATC.

Model sentence: When marginal cost is less than average total cost increasing output lowers average total cost and when marginal cost is greater than average total cost increasing output increases average total cost. Therefore marginal cost per unit of output equals total average cost per unit at the lowest possible total average cost per unit. This means that the marginal cost curve cuts the average total cost curve at the average total cost curve's lowest point.

Test your understanding of this unit by answering the following questions

- Distinguish between explicit costs and implicit costs.
- Explain why the average variable cost curve is U-shaped.

Learning Outcomes

- Distinguish between increasing returns to scale, decreasing returns to scale, and constant returns to scale.
- Outline the relationship between short-run average costs and long-run average costs.
- Using a diagram, explain the reason for the shape of the long-run average total cost curve.
- Describe factors giving rise to economies of scale, including specialization, efficiency, marketing, and indivisibilities.
- Describe factors giving rise to diseconomies of scale, including problems of coordination and communication.

What is the relationship between short-run average costs and long-run average costs?

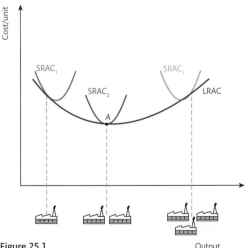

Figure 25.1

In the **long run** the quantities of all **factors of production** that the firm can use are variable. The firm can change the number of factories and capital. Workers are added to capital that is variable not fixed therefore the law of diminishing returns to a factor cannot be applied in the long-run.

Production in the long-run consists of a series of **short-run** periods of production where workers are added to a fixed quantity of factors. In the example in Figure 25.1 workers are added to the first factory containing a fixed quantity of capital. At first workers' **productivity** increases but at some point it begins to decrease therefore SRAC per unit falls and then rises resulting in the U-shaped short-run average cost curve SRAC$_1$. The firm can increase **output** by adding more workers but as productivity starts to fall SRAC begin to rise. If the firm wants to increase output and raise productivity thereby continuing to bring down average costs per unit it must increase the quantity of fixed factors, which it can do in the long-run. The firm opens a second factory and workers are now added to a greater quantity of fixed factors. Productivity at first increases but eventually decreases giving rise to $SRAC_2$. Average cost per unit has fallen and is at the lowest point on the SRAC curve as a result of increasing the quantity of fixed factors. After the third factory is opened workers are added to a greater quantity of fixed factors giving rise to $SRAC_3$. Average-cost per unit has risen. Increasing output beyond point A leads to an increase in average costs per unit. At first average cost per unit in the long-run falls as workers are added to increasing quantities of fixed factors but at some level of output average cost per unit begins to rise as the number of fixed factors is increased.

The long-run average cost curve is a **tangential** to the short-run average cost curves. Note that as long-run average costs are falling the point of tangency is where short-run average costs are also falling and as long-run average costs increase the point of tangency is where short-run average costs are also increasing. LRAC curve is tangent to SRAC curve at SRAC curve's lowest point only when output is produced at lowest average cost possible, which is the lowest point on the LRAC curve.

Why do average costs per unit fall and then rise in the long run?

As the firm increases the quantity of fixed factors and increases output it gains **economies of scale** until the LRAC curve turns upwards. These are the cost advantages of **large-scale production** that are not available to smaller firms.

Monetary economies of scale occur when firms are able to reduce the price paid for **resources**. The reductions in costs are because of the power the large firm has in the market place. It produces lots of goods and therefore buys lots of **raw materials** in bulk and can **negotiate** a lower price with the supplier reducing the cost of their raw materials. A large firm employs lots of workers. It may be the biggest employer in an area. As a very big buyer of labour it is able to push down wages, thereby reducing labour costs. Cost savings enjoyed by firms who are able to buy resources in very large quantities are called marketing economies of scale.

Financial economies of scale are enjoyed by large firms because banks are more likely to lend to large firms and lend at a lower interest rate. This is because large firms have larger **revenues** and more **assets**, therefore the risk of defaulting on the loan is less than it is for smaller firms. Banks compete with each other for the firm's business. This pushes down the interest rate thereby reducing the cost of **loan repayments**. Real-economies of scale occur when reductions in cost are brought about by increases in productivity gains from large scale production. **Specialization** and the division of labour occurs the most when goods are mass produced. The production process is broken down into a large number of smaller separate tasks on an **assembly line**. Each worker performs one particular task all the time. By specializing in only one task the worker becomes very quick at performing it. Specialization and division of labour greatly increases output per worker thereby reducing average cost per unit. Managerial economies of scale are enjoyed by large firms because they are able to hire the best and most efficient workers in all areas of the business. A good tax accountant, for example, can reduce the firm's tax liability thereby reducing costs.

A big firm earns large **producer revenues** and can afford the high cost of the most technologically advanced large-scale capital. Using it can massively increase **output per head** and reduce average cost per unit. This type of capital is indivisible. The cost of it is the same no matter how many goods are produced. It is only profitable to buy this capital if it can be used a lot of the time. The cost can then be spread over a very large number of units. Small firms with lower output cannot use this type of capital because average cost per unit would be far too high.

A small firm is not able to run a national advertising campaign because of the high cost of doing so. A large firm is able to spread the cost over a large number of units, thereby massively reducing the average cost per unit of advertising. A large firm can afford to run an international marketing campaign. The cost of making a TV commercial is the same no matter how many people see it and the more people that see it the lower the cost per potential customer.

However, firms must be careful. If **demand** falls the firm must reduce output and stop using all the large-scale capital. The cost of the capital will be spread over fewer units of output and average cost per unit will increase. This will reduce profits. Also some capital is highly **specialized** and if demand falls for the good the capital cannot be used to produce alternative goods that are in demand. This means it will have little resale value.

Model sentence: Monetary economies of scale occur when large firms use their market power to negotiate lower prices with their suppliers of resources, thereby reducing average costs per unit. Real economies occur when firms are able to use resources more efficiently, thereby increasing productivity and reducing average costs per unit.

As a firm continues to grow it experiences **diseconomies of scale** and long-run average costs begin to rise. A large firm finds it more difficult to respond to changes in the market. It will have a complex management structure. The firm will experience communication problems and instructions from management can be misunderstood, sometimes deliberately as some managers in the organization may well have different objectives. The large organization has to employ more workers who are not directly involved in the production of goods. This increases the number of workers but not output, resulting in a fall in **productivity** and an increase in average cost per unit. Workers who work on the shop floor and who specialize doing the same task all the time will be bored and demotivated. The firm is likely to see a rise in **absenteeism** and a fall in output per head giving rise to increases in average costs. As a firm grows in size and the production process becomes more unwieldy it becomes more difficult for managers to coordinate resources effectively , including supervision and organization of the workers. It's difficult to make sure all workers are trying to achieve the set goals of the firm as the workforce gets bigger. These problems lead to a fall in productivity and a rise in long-run average costs.

What is the difference between increasing returns to scale, decreasing returns to scale, and constant returns to scale?

Returns to scale

In order to increase output the firm increases factors of production. The firm experiences **increasing returns to scale** when the rate of change in factors leads to a greater rate of change in outputs. When a 10% increase in factors leads to a 30% rise in output average cost per unit falls. Increasing returns are made possible because

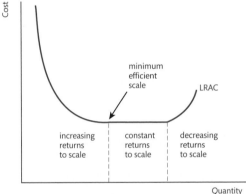

Figure 25.2

of the economies of scale enjoyed by firms that are expanding output. At some point the economies are **exhausted** and **constant returns to scale** are experienced where the rate of change in factors is equal to the rate of change in output. Average costs per unit remain the same. As output increases further the firm experiences diseconomies of scale causing **decreasing returns to scale** where the rate of change in factors is now greater than the rate of change in output. Average cost per unit increases. The minimum efficient scale of production is the lowest level of output where average cost is at its lowest.

Test your understanding of this unit by answering the following questions

- Explain why the long-run average cost curve is U-shaped.
- Explain the relationship between short-run average costs and long-run average costs.
- Explain why decreasing returns to scale will eventually set in as a firm grows.

Learning Outcomes

- Distinguish between total revenue, average revenue, and marginal revenue.

- Illustrate, using diagrams, the relationship between total revenue, average revenue, and marginal revenue.

- Calculate total revenue, average revenue, and marginal revenue from a set of data and/or diagrams.

Explain the distinction between total, average, and marginal revenue

Revenue is the **income** a firm receives from the sale of its goods in a given period of time. **Total revenue** (TR) is calculated by multiplying the price of the product it sells by quantity sold: TR = P × Q. **Average revenue** (AR) is revenue per unit of output and is calculated by dividing total revenue by quantity sold: AR = TR/Q. **Marginal revenue** (MR) is the addition to total revenue gained from the sale of the next unit of output and it is calculated by dividing the change in total revenue by the change in output: MR = ΔTR/ΔQ.

What is the relationship between average revenue (AR) and price?

AR = TR/Q and TR = P × Q. Replace TR with P × Q in the formula AR = TR/Q and we get AR = P × Q/Q. Divide Q by Q and we get AR = P. If the producer sells all the units it makes at the same price then average revenue is equal to that price.

Explain the effects on different revenues when the market is perfectly competitive

Subject vocabulary

industry a group of firms that produce the same or similar goods or services

output the quantity of goods produced by a firm, industry or economy

market supply the sum of the supply of the individual firms in the industry

market price the price determined by the interaction of demand and supply in a competitive market

demand curve a graph that shows the relationship between price and quantity demanded

perfectly price elastic at a particular price quantity demanded is infinite but falls to nothing as price changes. The absolute value of PED is equal to infinity.

quantity demanded the amount of a good consumers are willing and able to buy at a given price over a given period of time

Price ($)	Output	TR ($)	AR ($)	MR ($)
10	0	0		
				10
10	1	10	10	
				10
10	2	20	10	
				10
10	3	30	10	
				10
10	4	40	10	
				10
10	5	50	10	
				10
10	6	60	10	

Table 26.1

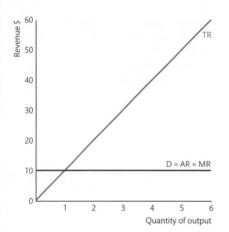

Figure 26.1

In a perfectly competitive market (we will cover perfect competition in detail later) the firm is very small and one of very many in the **industry** all selling identical goods. The firm's **output** cannot affect the **market supply** and so the firm cannot affect price but it is able to sell all that it can produce at the **market price**. The firm's **demand curve** is **perfectly price elastic** (PED = ∞) at market price because **quantity demanded** falls to zero when the firm increases price. This happens because consumers will stop buying from the firm and buy identical goods at a lower price from one of its competitors (for a full explanation of perfectly elastic demand see pages 20–21).

See Table 26.1 and Figure 26.1. Assume market price is $10. The firm sells each extra unit of output at the same price therefore an increase in output of 1 unit leads to a change in total revenue of $10: MR = ΔTR/ΔQ = 10/1 = $10. AR = P therefore AR = $10. TR increases at a constant rate as output increases resulting in the straight-lined TR curve.

Table 26.1 shows the information regarding revenues in a perfectly competitive market over a range of output when price = $10. MR relates to a change in the level of output so appears midpoint between output levels. The information has been plotted onto the graph Figure 26.1.

Explain the effects on revenues for firms that face a downward-sloping demand curve

In reality the firm must lower price in order to increase quantity sold (see Table 26.2). As price falls output increases. AR = P therefore AR falls as output increases. This can be seen in Figure 26.2 where the revenue curves have been plotted.

Price ($)	Output	TR ($)	AR ($)	MR ($)
450	0	0		
				400
400	1	400	400	
				300
350	2	700	350	
				200
300	3	900	300	
				100
250	4	1000	250	
				0
200	5	1000	200	
				−100
150	6	900	150	
				−200
100	7	700	100	
				−300
50	8	400	50	

Table 26.2

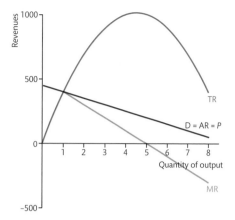

Figure 26.2

Note that MR changes in steps of 100 and AR changes in steps of 50. MR falls at twice the rate of AR.

Model sentence: The slope of the MR curve is twice as steep as the slope of the AR curve because in order to increase units sold the firm must lower the price on all units and not just on the next unit. The firm forgoes revenue on previous units in order to gain revenue on the additional unit sold.

A calculation of an increase in TR as output increases – a step-by-step guide (see Table 26.2)

Trouble shooter

When price = $300 quantity sold = 3 units: TR = $300 × 3 = $900

The firm lowers price from 300 to 250 and quantity sold rises to 4 units.

When price = $250 quantity sold = 4 units: TR = $250 × 4 = $1000

TR increases by $100.

Why does TR rise?

Each of the first 3 units could have been sold for $300 but are now sold for $250.

Revenue **forgone** on the first 3 units = (300 – 250) × 3 = 50 × 3 = $150

Revenue gained on the extra unit sold = $250

Overall gain = 250 – 150 = $100. This is the MR.

MR = ΔTR/ΔQ = 100/1 = $100

Increasing output from 3 to 4 units leads to an increase in total revenue.

What is the relationship between MR and TR?

As price continues to fall in order to increase sales the revenue gained from selling one more unit decreases and the loss in revenue from the units that could have been sold at a higher price increases. Therefore, marginal revenue, which is the addition to total revenue from the sale of the next unit, falls as price falls and output sold increases. Eventually MR becomes negative. This happens when the revenue gained from selling the next unit is less than the loss in revenue from the units that could have been sold at a higher price. When MR becomes negative total revenue starts to fall.

Look at Figure 26.2. As price falls and output sold increases MR is positive but falling. Therefore TR increases but at a diminishing rate. TR is maximized when MR = 0. When MR becomes negative it **drags** down TR.

Subject vocabulary

profit maximization where the difference between total revenue and total costs is as big as possible

economic profit the difference between total revenue (price × quantity sold) and economic costs (explicit costs + implicit costs)

total revenue price × quantity sold

explicit cost payments made by firms for inputs such as wages, rent, and payments for raw materials

implicit cost the opportunity cost of using resources which are self-owned and not purchased

accounting cost the value of resources bought from individuals or firms (explicit costs)

purchased resources an input into the production process that is bought by the firm or the entrepreneur from an individual or another firm

raw material the basic material from which a good is made

Trouble shooter

When price = $200 quantity sold = 5 units: TR = 200 × 5 = $1000.

The firm lowers price to $150 and quantity sold rises to 6 units: TR = 150 × 6 = $900.

TR decreases from $1000 to $900, a fall of $100.

Why does TR fall?

Each of the first 5 units could have been sold for $200 but are now sold for $150.

Revenue forgone on the first 5 units = (200 – 150) × 5 = 50 × 5 = $250

Revenue gained on the extra unit sold = $150

An overall loss of $100 (150 – 250). This is the MR.

$MR = \Delta TR/\Delta Q = -100/1 = -\$100$.

Increasing output from 5 to 6 units leads to fall in total revenue.

Test your understanding of this unit by answering the following questions

- Explain why total revenue is maximized when marginal revenue = 0.
- Explain why AR = P.
- Explain the relationship between marginal revenue and total revenue.

Learning Outcomes

- Describe economic profit as the case where total revenue exceeds economic cost.

- Describe normal profit as the amount of revenue needed to cover the costs of employing self-owned resources (implicit costs, including entrepreneurship) or the amount of revenue needed to just keep the firm in business.

- Explain that economic profit is profit over and above normal profit, and that the firm earns normal profit when economic profit is zero.

- Explain why a firm will continue to operate even when it earns zero economic profit.

- Explain the meaning of loss as negative economic profit arising when total revenue is less than total cost.

- Calculate different profit levels from a set of data and/or diagrams.

- Explain the goal of **profit maximization** where the difference between total revenue and total cost is maximized or where marginal revenue equals marginal cost.

Subject vocabulary

opportunity cost the next best alternative forgone

self-owned resource an input into the production process that is owned by the firm or entrepreneur, such as time. It is an implicit cost of production the value of which is its opportunity cost.

entrepreneur an individual who, in pursuit of profit, brings together the other factors of production in order to produce a good or service

continued on page 75

What is economic profit?

Economic profit is the difference between **total revenue** (TR = P × Q) and economic costs (explicit + implicit costs).

Therefore economic profit = (P × Q) – **explicit costs** – **implicit costs**.

The meanings of explicit and implicit costs are discussed in detail on pages 66–7. Explicit costs are the **accounting costs**. They are the costs of the **purchased resources** such as **raw materials**. Implicit costs are the **opportunity costs** of the **self-owned resources** such as the time of the **entrepreneur**.

A firm makes an economic profit when total revenue is greater than economic costs (when (P × Q) > explicit costs + implicit costs). If economic costs are greater than total revenue the firm earns negative economic profit (a loss). In this situation the firm's **resources** earn less economic profit than they could earn if used to produce the next-best alternative. The firm will consider doing something else with its resources. The entrepreneur might consider saving on the costs involved in operating the business by leaving the industry.

Why does a firm continue to operate when economic profit is zero?

Economists subtract explicit costs and implicit costs from total revenue to work out economic profit. So if a profit is made all costs are covered including the opportunity costs of the self-owned resources. When economic profit is zero (TR = economic costs) the entrepreneur continues to run the business because the purchased resources and the self-owned resources are earning profit that is equal to that which could be earned if the resources were put to the next best alternative use. When economic profit is zero there is no incentive for the entrepreneur to reallocate the resources to the production of a different good.

What is the distinction between normal and abnormal profit?

Model sentence: An economic profit of zero is called normal profit. It occurs when revenue = the explicit costs + implicit costs. An economic profit that is greater than zero is called abnormal or supernormal profit.

Abnormal profit is earned when total revenue is greater than the economic costs. Firms aim to earn as much profit as possible. However, in competitive markets where lots of firms make similar goods there is much price competition and abnormal profits tend to be driven down towards normal profit.

What is the difference between economic profit and accounting profit?

Accountants do not consider implicit costs when calculating profit. **Accounting profit** = total revenue – explicit costs (the cost of the purchased resources). No account is taken of the opportunity costs of the self-owned resources. Accounting profit is greater than economic profit. (Whenever the word 'profit' is mentioned from now onwards it refers to 'economic profit' unless stated otherwise.)

Output	TR ($)	MR ($)	TC ($)	MC ($)	Profit ($)
1	500		1000		−500
		500		200	
2	1000		1200		−200
		500		300	
3	1500		1500		0
		500		400	
4	2000		1900		100
		500		500	
5	2500		2400		100
		500		600	
6	3000		3000		0
		500		700	
7	3500		3700		−200

Table 27.1

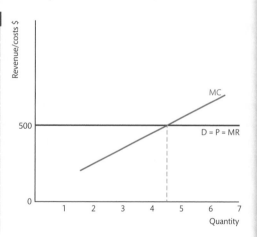

Figure 27.1

Subject vocabulary

resources the inputs into the production process, the factors of production

normal profit occurs when economic profit is equal to zero, i.e., when the difference between total revenue and total costs (explicit and implicit costs) equals zero

abnormal/supernormal profit occurs when economic profit is greater than zero, i.e., when total revenue is greater than total cost (explicit and implicit costs)

accounting profit the difference between total revenue and the explicit costs (costs of the purchased resources)

perfectly elastic demand at a particular price quantity demanded is infinite but falls to nothing as price changes. The absolute value of PED is equal to infinity.

marginal revenue the additional revenue generated from the sale of the additional unit of output produced

output the quantity of goods produced by a firm, industry or economy

marginal cost the change in total cost resulting from a change in output of one unit

Glossary

intersect cut across or through

In the example set out in Table 27.1 the firm is in a very competitive industry. It faces a **perfectly elastic demand** curve with respect to price and can sell all it can make at the market price of $500. Total revenue = P × Q. Each time an extra unit is sold total revenue increases by the price. **Marginal revenue** (MR) = ΔTR/ΔQ = 500/1 = $500 so price = MR. Total cost = explicit + implicit costs. Marginal cost (MC) = ΔTC/ΔQ and these are given. Profit = TR – TC.

Profit is maximized when the difference between TR and TC is maximized. This is between 4 and 5 units of **output**. At this level of output MR = $500 and MC = $500 so we know that profit is maximized at the level of output where marginal revenue = **marginal cost**. The information on MR and MC has been plotted on to the graph in Figure 27.1. The profit, maximizing level of output is where the marginal cost curve and the marginal revenue curve **intersect**. The firm's objective is to maximize profit and therefore it sets output where MR = MC.

Subject vocabulary

Why the profit-maximizing level of output is where MR = MC – a step-by-step guide

Trouble shooter

If the addition to total revenue the firm receives from selling the next unit (MR) is greater than the addition to the total cost of producing it (MC) then producing and selling the next unit adds to profit. If the addition to total cost of producing the next unit (MC) is greater than the addition to total revenue then producing the next unit reduces profit. Therefore the firm maximizes profit by producing at the level of output where MR = MC.

In Table 27.1 when the firm increases output from 2 to 3 units the MR = $500 and the MC = $300. MR > MC. Producing the unit adds $200 to profit (500–300). When output is increased from 5 to 6 units MR = $500 and MC = 600. MC > MR so producing this unit reduces profit by $100.

Model sentence: If MR > MC increasing output increases profit, if MC > MR reducing output increases profit therefore profit is maximized where MR = MC.

Test your understanding of this unit by answering the following questions

- Distinguish between normal and abnormal profit.
- Explain why profit is maximized where MR = MC.
- Explain why a firm will continue to operate even when it earns zero economic profit.

Learning Outcomes

- Describe, using examples, the assumed characteristics of perfect competition: a large number of firms; a homogeneous product; freedom of entry and exit; perfect information; perfect resource mobility.

- Explain, using a diagram, the shape of the perfectly competitive firm's average revenue and marginal revenue curves, indicating that the assumptions of perfect competition imply that each firm is a price taker.

- Explain, using a diagram, that the perfectly competitive firm's **average revenue** and marginal revenue curves are derived from market equilibrium for the industry.

- Explain, using diagrams, that it is possible for a perfectly competitive firm to make economic profit (supernormal profit), normal profit, or **negative economic profit** in the **short run** based on the marginal cost and marginal revenue profit maximization rule.

- Explain, using a diagram, why, in the **long run**, a perfectly competitive firm will make normal profit.

- Explain, using a diagram, how a perfectly competitive market will move from short-run equilibrium to long-run equilibrium.

Subject vocabulary

Perfect competition is an **economic model** used to predict outcomes of economic occurrences in highly competitive industries. The characteristics or features of this type of **market** are very precise and taken as a whole the characteristics are not shared by industries in the real world. It is a model that can be used to judge the competitiveness of actual industries. The assumed characteristics have consequences.

Describe the characteristics of perfect competition and their effects – a step-by-step guide (the characteristics are are in bold italics)

Trouble shooter

There are many firms and buyers in the market: no buyer or firm is big enough to be able to influence **market demand** or market supply and thereby influence market price. Firms and buyers are price takers. They take the price that is determined by **market forces**. Firms cannot get together and agree a price or output level because there are too many of them.

The firms in the industry produce homogeneous goods: there is no **marketing** or **branding**. The goods are **perfect substitutes**. The buyers in the market therefore have no preference as to which firm they buy from.

Firms and buyers have perfect knowledge: buyers and firms know the prices charged by every firm in the market and entrepreneurs know the profits being made in that particular industry and in other perfectly competitive industries. If a firm sets a price higher than the market price all buyers will know that they can pay a lower price for an identical good. Remember economists assume that consumers aim to maximize **benefit** with their **income** and therefore will buy the good at the lowest price. **Quantity demanded** for the firm with the higher price falls to zero.

The industry has no barriers to entry or to exit: existing firms in an industry cannot stop new firms entering and existing firms can exit the industry and go to another.

All the factors of production are perfectly mobile: factors can be put to an alternative use instantly therefore profit from the use of the factors can be immediately maximized. Entrepreneurs know the profits being made in that particular industry and in other perfectly competitive industries, there are no barriers to entry and factors are perfectly mobile, therefore firms simply move into markets where profit is highest. The implicit **assumption** is that firms aim to maximize profit.

Describe marginal revenue (MR) and average revenue (AR) under perfect competition

Market supply and market demand under perfect competition obey the **law of demand** and the **law of supply**.

Price is determined by the **forces of demand and supply** in the industry. There are so many firms that no individual firm's output can influence market supply and so cannot affect market price. The firm takes the market price. The industry demand and supply diagram is shown in Figure 28.1a.

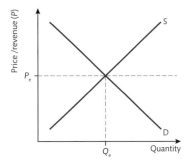

Figure 28.1a

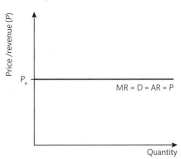

Figure 28.1b

The **equilibrium price** Pe is taken by the firm in the industry. The firm is able to sell all its **output** at Pe. Firms produce homogeneous goods and buyers have perfect knowledge so know all prices in the industry. If the firm increases price all buyers simply buy an identical good from another supplier and the quantity demanded from the firm falls to zero. Therefore **price elasticity of demand** is infinity and the **demand curve** is perfectly elastic with respect to price (see pages 19–21 for a detailed explanation of PED).

A reminder of why average revenue = price:
TR = P × Q, AR = TR/Q, substitute TR for P × Q, AR = P × Q/Q, divide Q by Q, AR = P.

Assume Pe = $10. The firm sells each extra unit of output at the same price therefore an increase in output of 1 unit leads to a change in total revenue of $10: $MR = \Delta TR/\Delta Q = 10/1 = \$10 = P = AR$.

Price, marginal revenue, and average revenue remain constant as the output of the firm is increased. Therefore when plotted on a graph they are represented by a horizontal line as seen in Figure 28.1b: price = demand = marginal revenue = average revenue.

Distinguish between profit in the short run and in the long run under perfect competition

In the short run firms cannot change the amounts of the fixed factors they employ, new firms cannot enter the industry and existing firms are not able to exit. Therefore price in the short run is determined by consumer demand and the supply of the existing firms in the industry.

Subject vocabulary

benefit the satisfaction gained from the consumption of a good

income the payment received by the factors of production (e.g. wages paid to labour, rent paid to the owners of land)

quantity demanded the amount of a good consumers are willing and able to buy at a given price over a given period of time

barriers to entry factors that prevent/make difficult the entry of new firms into an industry or market

factors of production the inputs into the production process (land, labour, capital and entrepreneurship)

law of demand states that there is a negative causal relationship between price and quantity demanded. As price rises quantity demanded falls.

law of supply states that there is a positive causal relationship between price and quantity supplied. As price rises quantity supplied rises.

forces of demand and supply changes in the determinants of demand and supply in a market that affect the market price and the allocation of resources

equilibrium price the price at which the quantity consumers are willing and able to buy is equal to the quantity firms are willing and able to produce

output the quantity of goods produced by a firm, industry or economy

price elasticity of demand (PED) a measure of how quantity demanded responds to a change in price in percentage terms

demand curve a graph that shows the relationship between price and quantity demanded

Glossary

marketing advertising and promotion

assumption(s) something thought/believed to be true but without proof

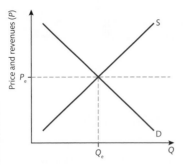

Figure 28.2a

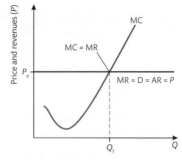

Figure 28.2b

As shown in Figure 28.2b the firm's **marginal cost** curve has been included. Profit is maximized where MR = MC so the firm sets output at Q_f where the firm's MC curve **intersects** its MR curve (see page 76 for a detailed explanation of the profit maximizing rule).

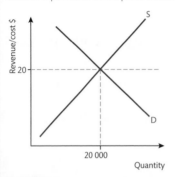

Figure 28.3a

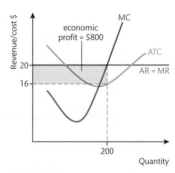

Figure 28.3b

Figure 28.3a shows a market in equilibrium in the **short run**. The firm takes the market price $20. The firm's ATC curve has been included in Figure 28.3b. It is U-shaped and intersects the firm's MC curve at ATC's lowest point (see pages 68–9 for a detailed explanation of the shape of the ATC and its relationship with MC).

The firm maximizes profit by setting output at 200 units where MR = MC. **Normal profit** is earned when **economic profit** = zero. This occurs when revenue or price per unit (AR) equals total cost per unit (ATC). At this point the firm's **explicit costs** and **implicit costs** are just covered (see pages 74–5 for a detailed discussion on profit).

Economic profit greater than zero is called **abnormal profit**. In Figure 28.3b price = $20 and the average total cost (ATC) = $16. Price > ATC therefore the firm is more than covering the explicit and implicit costs, earning **positive economic profit** or abnormal profit of $4 on each unit sold. Total abnormal profit, represented by the shaded area = (P – ATC) × quantity = ($20 – $16) × 200 units = $4 × 200 = $800.

In the **long run** firms can change the amount of their factors of production and new firms can enter the market. Existing firms earning positive economic profit increase the amount of fixed factors employed and new firms, attracted by the abnormal profits, enter the industry causing the market supply curve to shift to the right as shown in Figure 28.4a. (Remember firms have perfect knowledge so they know the size of profits in the industry, all their factors are perfectly mobile and there are no barriers to entry.)

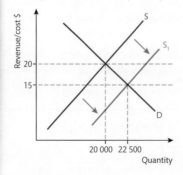

Figure 28.4a

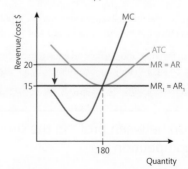

Figure 28.4b

To **eliminate** the **excess supply** at $20 the price falls. The **market clears** at $15. The firm takes the new equilibrium price. Price and marginal revenue fall from $20 to $15. The profit-maximizing level of output falls from 200 units to 180 units. The firm's **market share** is smaller because more firms are now in the industry.

At an output of 180 units price = ATC. The firm now earns normal profit. In the short run the firm can earn abnormal profit but in the long run price and profit are driven down through increased market supply. Abnormal or positive economic profit can only be earned in the short run.

Synonyms

eliminate .... remove/ get rid of

Subject vocabulary

excess supply occurs when quantity supplied is greater than quantity demanded

market clears when quantity demanded equals quantity supplied and there is no surplus or shortage

market share the proportion of the market supply of a good or service that is controlled by a firm

supply curve a graph that shows the relationship between price and quantity supplied

negative economic profit occurs when total cost (explicit cost + implicit cost) is greater than total revenue

Negative economic profit in the short run and long run under perfect competition

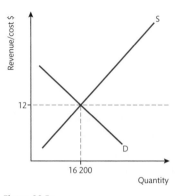

Figure 28.5a

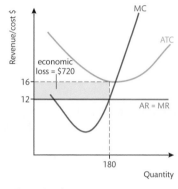

Figure 28.5b

The market price is $12 as shown in Figure 28.5a.

The firm sets output at 180 units where MR = MC. Price = $12 and ATC = $16.

ATC > P therefore the firm is not covering its explicit and implicit cost. Economic profit is negative so a loss per unit is made. Total economic loss, represented by the shaded area = (P – ATC) × quantity = ($12 – $16) × 180 units = –$4 × 180 = –$720.

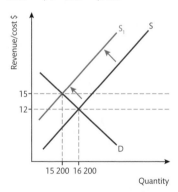

Figure 28.6a

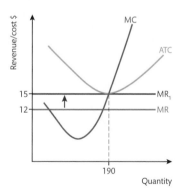

Figure 28.6b

In the long run some firms leave the market to try to earn at least normal profit in another industry. As firms leave market supply falls and the **supply curve** shifts to the left from S to S$_1$ as shown in Figure 28.6a. Equilibrium price, the price the firm takes, rises to $16 and the firm's market share rises to 190. Price now equals ATC so economic profit = 0. In the long run **negative economic profit** is eliminated and normal profits are earned.

The long-run equilibrium under perfect competition is where P = AR = MR = ATC = MC.

Model sentence: In the long run firms enter the industry when economic profit is positive and some existing firms exit when economic profit is negative thereby altering market supply until P = ATC and restoring the long-run position under perfect competition where only normal profit is made.

Subject vocabulary

marginal cost the change in total cost resulting from a change in output of one unit

price the amount of money a consumer pays a producer in exchange for a good

Glossary

shut down stop operating

assumption(s) something thought/believed to be true but without proof

exceed(s) are/is greater than

Why does the marginal cost curve act as the firm's supply curve?

If the price the firm receives from the sale of the next unit produced is less than the **marginal cost** (the cost of producing that next unit) the firm would make a loss on that extra unit and will therefore not supply it. The firm must receive a price that is at least equal to the marginal cost if it is to supply an extra unit. The marginal cost curve therefore shows the minimum price the firm must be paid if it is to supply an additional unit of output. The supply curve and the marginal cost curve both show the quantity of goods a firm or an industry is willing to supply at each price therefore they are the same: S = MC.

Test your understanding of this unit by answering the following questions

● Using diagrams to illustrate your answer, explain why under perfect competition a firm's economic profit equals zero in the long run.

Learning Outcomes

● Distinguish between the short-run **shut-down price** and the break-even price.

● Explain, using a diagram, when a loss-making firm would shut down in the short run.

● Explain, using a diagram, when a loss-making firm would shut down and exit the market in the long run.

● Calculate the short-run shutdown price and the breakeven price from a set of data.

Subject vocabulary

perfect competition a theoretical market structure which has the required characteristics that ensures no buyer or seller has the power to be able to influence market price

industry a group of firms that produce the same or similar goods or services

profit/economic profit the difference between total revenue (price × quantity sold) and economic costs (explicit costs + implicit costs)

output the quantity of goods produced by a firm, industry or economy

total fixed cost the sum of the costs that do not change as output changes

average total cost is equal to total cost divided by quantity of output

total revenue price × quantity sold

explicit cost payments made by firms for inputs such as wages, rent, and payments for raw materials

implicit cost the opportunity cost of using resources which are self-owned and not purchased

Explain when a loss-making firm would shut down in the short run

Under **perfect competition** when a firm is making a loss it might choose to leave the **industry**. Some firms may decide to stay if they believe price will soon increase so that P = ATC once again and normal profit is restored. Set out below is an explanation of the shut-down rule. It is based on the **assumption** that a firm's objective is to maximize **profit** or minimize loss. A loss can be described as a negative profit. Therefore, in effect, minimizing loss is the same as maximizing profit. In the short run the quantity of at least one of the factors is fixed and the others are variable. Therefore even when the firm is not producing any **output** it must pay the costs related to the fixed factors. These are the **total fixed costs** and they are the minimum cost the firm must pay in the short run. Therefore if the firm stops producing the loss will be only the fixed costs. The loss will increase if the firm continues to produce when the price per unit is less than the average variable cost at all levels of output.

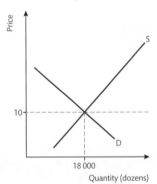

Figure 29.1a

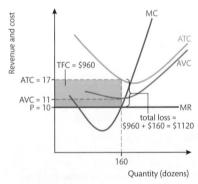

Figure 29.1b

As shown in Figures 29.1a and b, the market price of $10 taken by the firm is determined in the market. The average variable cost curve has been included on the diagram. It can be seen that at all levels of output **average total cost** and average variable cost **exceed** price. To maximize profit or minimize loss the firm sets output where MR = MC (see trouble shooter on page 76 for a detailed explanation of profit-maximization point). At an output of 160 units ATC = $17 and AVC = $11.

Calculation of total loss made by the firm when it continues to produce

Economic profit = **total revenue** (P × Q) − total cost (**explicit costs** + **implicit costs**) (ATC × Q)

Economic profit = $10 × 160 − $17 × 160 = $1600 − $2720 = −$1120 (represented by the two shaded areas in Figure 29.1b)

Calculation of the loss made when the firm shuts down in the short run

The minimum cost the firm must pay in the short run are the fixed costs. This is the cost incurred at zero output. To calculate this cost AFC must be isolated.

ATC = AFC + AVC   subtract AVC from both sides
ATC − AVC = AFC
AFC = $17 − $11 = $6
TFC = AFC × Q = $6 × 160 = $960
Total revenue and total variable cost if the firm shuts down = 0
Profit = TR − TC = 0 − $960 = −$960 (represented by the larger of the shaded areas)

Calculation of the additional loss caused by the firm continuing to produce

TVC = AVC × q
TVC = $11 × 160 = $1760
TR = p × q = $10 × 160 = $1600
Loss caused by the production of the 160 units = TR − TVC = $1600 − $1760 = $160 (represented by the smaller of the shaded areas)

Why does the firm shut down when average variable cost is greater than the price?

The variable cost per unit is greater than price at all levels of output. Therefore every time the firm makes a unit of output it adds to the loss. As can be seen in the calculation above the firm can reduce total loss by $160 if it stops producing, limiting the loss to $960 which is the total fixed costs. The goal of the firm is to maximize profit or to minimize loss therefore in this position the firm shuts down in the short run.

Model sentence: A firm shuts down production in the short run when the loss from stopping production is less than the loss from producing at any level of output; that is when average variable cost at any level of output is greater than price.

If price = **average variable cost** then total revenue = **total variable cost**. The firm is just covering the variable costs. The firm's loss is only the fixed costs. In this position the firm might continue to produce in the short run. By doing so it continues to serve its customers and employ its workers and will be able to benefit if the market price increases.

If price is greater than AVC then TR > TVC. Each unit of output can make a contribution to covering some of the fixed costs. The firm will continue to produce because it makes less of a loss than it would if it closed down.

Explain why a firm would leave the market in the long run

A firm cannot continue to make a loss **indefinitely**. In the **long run** all factors are variable so the firm can develop strategies designed to reduce average total cost so it is covered by the price. For example, the firm can increase the scale of production, opening new factories and increasing the amount of capital. By doing so the firm experiences **economies of scale** and average total cost might fall enough so that it equals price. (See pages 69, 70 and 71 for a detailed explanation of costs in the long run.)

When price = average total cost, all costs, which include explicit costs and implicit costs are covered. This means that the **purchased resources** and the **self-owned resources** will be earning at least as much as they could if put to use producing the next best alternative. When price = ATC **economic profit** is zero and the firm is earning **normal profit** (see pages 74–5 for a detailed explanation of economic profit). In this situation the firm has no **incentive** to leave the industry. If price is less than ATC the firm is not covering its costs including the **opportunity cost** and therefore will exit the industry. The **break-even price** is the price required to keep the firm in the industry in the long run. It is the price that is equal to the average total cost.

Model sentence: When average total cost is greater than price the firm earns negative economic profit. It can increase profit by reallocating its factors. So if price does not cover average total cost in the long run the firm will shut down.

The rules that profit-maximizing firms follow – a step-by-step guide

Trouble shooter

In the short run: the firm should only produce output if the price it receives is greater than the average variable cost.

In the long run: the firm should only produce output if it earns at least a normal profit. In other words if price is equal to or greater than average total cost.

In the short and long run: the firm should set the level of output where marginal revenue is equal to marginal cost if it has made the decision to continue production.

Test your understanding of this unit by answering the following questions

- Explain, using a diagram, when a loss-making firm would shut down in the short run.
- Explain, using a diagram, when a loss-making firm would shut down and exit the market in the long run.
- Using the following information calculate the economic profit or loss: P = $20, MC = $16, ATC = $22, AVC= $18, quantity = 50 units. (MC, ATC, and AVC include both explicit and implicit costs).

Subject vocabulary

short run a period of time in which the quantity of at least one factor is fixed

Learning Outcomes

- Explain the meaning of the term allocative efficiency.
- Explain that the condition for allocative efficiency is P = MC.
- Explain, using a diagram, why a perfectly competitive market leads to allocative efficiency in both the **short run** and the **long run**.
- Explain the meaning of the term productive/technical efficiency.

- Explain that the condition for **productive efficiency** is that production takes place at minimum average total cost.
- Explain, using a diagram, why a perfectly competitive firm will be productively efficient in the long run, though not necessarily in the short run.

Subject vocabulary

long run a conceptual moment in time when all factors are variable

productive efficiency occurs when a given quantity of output is produced at the minimum total cost per unit of output

output the quantity of goods produced by a firm, industry or economy

benefit the satisfaction gained from the consumption of a good

marginal cost the change in total cost resulting from a change in output of one unit

resources the inputs into the production process, the factors of production

Explain why the condition necessary for allocative efficiency is P = MC

As shown in Figure 30.1 the price of butter is $6000 per tonne. This means that consumers in society place a maximum value of $6000 on the next tonne of butter consumed. The price consumers in society are willing to pay for the additional **output** is a reflection of the **benefit** consumers receive from the consumption of it. When output is at Q_1 the **marginal cost** is $8000. This means the price or value of the **resources** used to produce the additional tonne of butter is greater than the value consumers in society place on the consumption of it. In other words price is less than marginal cost. In order to enjoy the benefit of consuming the additional output valued at $6000 society must use resources valued at $8000. By using the resources valued at $8000 to produce the additional tonne of butter consumers in society **forgo** the benefit they would have enjoyed from the consumption of the alternative goods that could have been produced with the resources. In this situation the welfare of consumers can be increased if the resources used to produce the additional tonne of butter are **reallocated** and used to produce alternative goods.

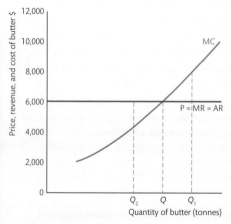

Figure 30.1

Synonyms

forgo .... sacrifice/give up

reallocate(d) ... redistribute(d)

When output is at Q_2 price is $6000 and marginal cost is $4500. This means that the value society places on the consumption of the additional tonne of butter is greater than the value of the resources used to produce it. In other words price is greater than marginal cost. In this situation society's welfare can be increased if resources used to produce other goods are reallocated and used to produce more butter instead.

When output is at Q price is $6000 and marginal cost is $6000. This means that the value society places on the additional tonne of butter equals the value of the resources used to produce it. In other words price equals marginal cost. Allocative efficiency is realized when the value society places on the additional tonne of butter is equal to the value of the resources used to produce it (P = MC). This means the value society places on the additional tonne is equal to the value of the next best alternative use of the resources, which is the **opportunity cost** of the production of the additional tonne of butter.

Maximization of society's welfare and allocative efficiency

Model sentence: When P < MC the value society places on the consumption of the additional unit is less than the value of the resources used to produce it therefore society's welfare can be increased by reallocating resources away from the production of the good to the production of alternatives in order to reduce output.

Model sentence: When P > MC the value society places on the consumption of the additional unit is greater than the value of the resources used to produce it therefore welfare can be increased by reallocating resources away from the production of other goods to the production of the good in order to increase output.

Model sentence: When P = MC the value society places on the consumption of the additional unit is equal to the value of the resources used to produce it, therefore society's welfare cannot be increased by the reallocation of resources and allocative efficiency is realized.

Allocative efficiency occurs when price = marginal cost. Society's welfare is maximized. Any reallocation of resources will reduce society's welfare.

Explain why a perfectly competitive market leads to allocative efficiency in both the short run and the long run – a step-by-step guide (see pages 76–9 for a full explanation of short run and long-run equilibrium under perfect competition)

Trouble shooter

The objective of all firms, in the short and long run, is to maximize profit.

Therefore they set output where MR = MC (see page 76 for an explanation of profit maximization).

Under **perfect competition** the firm's **marginal revenue** is equal to price.

Therefore at profit-maximizing level of output price = marginal revenue = marginal cost.

Therefore allocative efficiency is achieved under perfect competition in the short run and the long run.

Model sentence: The equalization of price and marginal cost, which is the condition necessary for an efficient allocation of society's resources, is the direct result of the profit maximizing behaviour of price-taking firms under perfect competition where the firms' marginal revenue is equal to price.

Distinguish between productive efficiency and technical efficiency

A firm is being productively efficient when it is combining factors in such a way as to produce output at the lowest possible **average total cost**. Technical efficiency occurs when the output from a given quantity of labour and capital is maximized. If a firm is technically efficient it cannot produce more output without increasing the quantity of labour and/or capital.

perfect competition a theoretical market structure which has the required characteristics that ensures no buyer or seller has the power to be able to influence market price

positive economic profit occurs when the difference between total revenue and total costs (explicit and implicit costs) is greater than zero

allocative efficiency the best or optimal allocation of resources from society's point of view. It occurs when the market is in equilibrium and social surplus is maximized (where P = MC).

abnormal/supernormal profit occurs when economic profit is greater than zero, i.e., when total revenue is greater than total cost (explicit and implicit costs)

industry a group of firms that produce the same or similar goods or services

supply the amount of a good that a firm is willing and able to produce at each price

market supply the sum of the supply of the individual firms in the industry

equilibrium price the price at which the quantity consumers are willing and able to buy is equal to the quantity firms are willing and able to produce

market price the price determined by the interaction of demand and supply in a competitive market

normal profit occurs when economic profit is equal to zero, i.e., when the difference between total revenue and total costs (explicit and implicit costs) equals zero

break even occurs when a firm makes normal profit. All costs, explicit and implicit, are just covered.

Productive efficiency in the short run and the long run

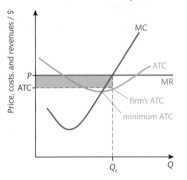

Figure 30.2

Figure 30.2 shows the position of a firm under **perfect competition** in the short run. Price is greater than ATC therefore the firm is earning **positive economic profit**. The firm sets output at Q_f where MR = MC, the condition necessary to maximize profit. P = MC which is the condition necessary to achieve **allocative efficiency**. However, ATC is higher than the minimum. The firm is able to survive in business despite producing at higher than necessary ATC because it is earning **abnormal profit**.

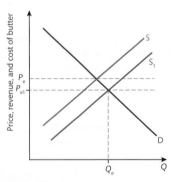

Figure 30.3a   **Figure 30.3b**

In the long run, attracted by the abnormal profit, new firms enter the **industry** and **supply** increases. As shown in Figure 30.3a the **market supply** curve shifts to the right from S to S_1 and **equilibrium price** falls from P_e to P_{e1}. The firm takes the **market price** so the price the firm receives falls from P to P_1 until price equals average total cost and **normal profit** is earned.

More firms are now in the industry, increasing competition and driving price and profit down. In order to earn at least normal profit and **break even** the firm must reduce average total costs. Profit is now maximized at a lower level of output so the firm reduces output to where MR = MC. The long-run equilibrium, P = MR = ATC = MC, is restored.

The outcomes of the long-run equilibrium P = AR = MR = ATC = MC under perfect competition – a step-by-step guide

Trouble shooter

MR = MC therefore the firm is maximizing profit.

P (AR) = MC therefore allocative efficiency is achieved.

MC = ATC therefore productive efficiency is achieved (remember MC intersects ATC at ATC's lowest point).

P (AR) = ATC therefore normal profits are earned and the firm breaks even.

Test your understanding of this unit by answering the following questions

- Using a diagram to illustrate your answer, explain how productive efficiency is achieved in the long run under perfect competition.
- Why does reducing output when price is less than marginal cost increase society's welfare?
- Explain why under perfect competition allocative efficiency is achieved in both the short run and the long run.

Learning Outcomes

- Describe, using examples, the assumed characteristics of a monopoly: a single or **dominant** firm in the market; no close substitutes; significant barriers to entry.

- Describe, using examples, barriers to entry, including economies of scale, branding, and legal barriers.

- Explain that the average revenue curve for a monopolist is the market demand curve, which will be downward sloping.

- Explain, using a diagram, the relationship between demand, average revenue, and marginal revenue in a monopoly.

- Explain why a monopolist will never choose to operate on the inelastic **portion** of its average revenue curve.

Under perfect competition firms have no **market power**. There are very many firms that make up the industry all making **homogeneous goods** so consumers can choose from which firm they buy. They cannot influence **market supply** and are unable to affect the price. Firms are price takers. There are no **barriers to entry** to the industry so new firms can enter when positive economic profits are earned, increasing market supply and driving down price and profit. The assumed characteristics of perfect competition have consequences and this is true for all **market structures** including monopoly.

Describe the consequences of the assumed characteristics of monopoly – a step-by-step guide

Trouble shooter

The firm is the industry in the case of a pure monopoly (the term 'monopoly' is also used to describe an industry that has one dominant firm).

The firm is the single seller in the market.

It is the only firm producing the good, therefore there are no close substitutes available for consumers to buy.

The firm therefore has the **monopoly power** to set the price of the good, and because of this the **monopolist** is called a price maker.

If abnormal profits are made at the set price the monopolist is able to protect them because there are many and high barriers to entry into the industry.

Potential new firms attracted by the high profits available will find it difficult, if not impossible, to enter the industry.

The monopolist therefore holds onto its market power to control price and can continue to earn abnormal profit, not only in the short run but also in the long run.

Barriers to entry

Without the barriers to entry a monopolist would not be able to maintain its power to set price and earn abnormal profit. Firms in the industry can put up artificial barriers that stop competitors entering the industry. Other barriers – called natural barriers – exist because of the high costs new firms must pay in order to compete against large firms and the fact that the large firms can produce at relatively low average cost.

Natural barriers

The monopolist enjoys **economies of scale** (see pages 69–71 for a detailed explanation of economies of scale). These are the cost advantages of producing on a large scale. A potential new entrant is likely to be comparatively small and will not enjoy the same economies of scale as the incumbent therefore its **average total cost** will be higher and it will not be able to compete. The firm will not be able to make a normal profit at the established price because its average total cost will be higher than the price. Potential new entrants know that they will struggle to compete with the incumbent so do not enter the industry. **Start-up costs** are very high. To enter such an industry requires a lot of money, much of which could be lost if the business fails. Capital is often specialized and expensive and gaining market share will require a major international **marketing**

sunk costs a cost that has already been incurred by a firm and cannot be recovered

resources the inputs into the production process, the factors of production

raw material the basic material from which a good is made

predatory pricing occurs when a firm sets a price that is so low other firms in the industry are unable to compete and therefore leave the market

positive economic profit occurs when the difference between total revenue and total costs (explicit and implicit costs) is greater than zero

demand curve a graph that shows the relationship between price and quantity demanded

average revenue revenue per unit of output (= total revenue/ output)

Synonyms

significant .... major/large

scarce .... limited/finite

extracted .... removed

grip .... hold

Glossary

mines deep holes in the ground used for removing coal, gold, etc.

government franchise the right, sometimes exclusive, to produce a good or service officially granted a firm by a government

patent a government license that gives the holder exclusive rights to a process, design, or new invention for a designated period of time. It gives a firm the right to stop another firm from making, using or selling that which has been granted a patent.

campaign. This is an example of a **sunk cost** – a cost that cannot be recovered by the firm when it exits the industry. Achieving and maintaining brand recognition is costly and in order to remain competitive once in the industry the firm will need to spend lots of money on research and development (R&D). This acts as a **significant** barrier to entry into the pharmaceutical industry for example, where high start-up costs and sunk costs increase the risk of business failure. Firms are simply not prepared to take the risk, leaving the incumbent as the sole supplier.

If the incumbents control important **scarce resources** it acts as a barrier to entry. If potential entrants are unable to obtain a resource required for production they cannot enter the industry. For example, if the monopolist owns the **mines** from which the **raw material** required in the production process is **extracted** the resource will be unavailable to other potential producers.

Artificial barriers

A monopolist may have large reserves of profit to be able to fight any immediate competition. It could buy out a rival firm. This business strategy is called predatory acquisition. The monopolist could set its price below the new firm's average total cost leaving the new firm unable to make a profit and eventually driving it out of the industry. This strategy is called **predatory pricing**. The monopolist can keep its price low in one market for relatively long periods of time if it is operating in a number of markets because it can use profit earned in one market to enable it to make losses in the other caused by its predatory pricing strategy. This is called cross-subsidization.

The monopolist can run a very costly marketing and advertising campaign in order to strengthen its brand and its **grip** on market share. These actions are deliberately taken by the incumbent to drive new firms out of the industry and to discourage potential entrants.

Legal barriers

There are legal barriers to entry. A **government franchise** gives the recipient firm the exclusive right to sell a good or service. For example, a train company might have the legal right to be the sole provider of a service on a particular route. A **patent** gives the holder the exclusive right to make a good. No other firm can legally produce and sell the good. For example a drug company obtains a patent on a new drug. The company is the sole supplier of the drug. Other firms are not legally allowed to make the drug.

Model sentence: New firms are attracted to markets that are making positive economic profit but are unable to enter and compete when there are high barriers to entry. Therefore the monopolist is able to maintain its power to set price and earn abnormal profit in the long run.

Why does the monopolist face a downward-sloping demand curve?

There is one firm in a monopoly. The firm is the industry. Therefore the firm's **demand curve** is the market demand curve. Consumers place a different value on the next unit consumed. Some are prepared to pay a higher price for an additional unit than others. Some consumers will only buy an additional unit when price is reduced reflecting the value they place on the additional unit. If the monopolist wishes to increase quantity sold it must reduce price and to reflect this the demand curve slopes downwards.

Model sentence: In a perfectly competitive market the firm faces a perfectly elastic demand curve as it is able to sell all its output at the market price but the monopolist's demand curve is the market demand curve and it slopes downwards. This means the monopolist must reduce price in order to increase output sold.

Describe the relationship between average revenue, marginal revenue, total revenue, and price (see pages 71–3 for a detailed explanation of the revenues (AR, MR, TR) for firms facing a downward-sloping demand curve)

Consumers buy the additional unit only if the monopolist reduces price. As previously discussed P = AR. When price falls **average revenue** falls. When price falls quantity demanded increases, therefore as AR falls quantity demanded increases. This means that the average revenue curve reflects the same information as the demand curve therefore the AR curve is also referred to as the demand curve.

It is assumed that the firm charges the same price on all units sold therefore the firm can only gain the revenue from the sale of the next unit if it reduces the price on all previous units.

Quantity of output (Q)	Price (P) = average revenue (AR)	Total revenue (TR)	Marginal revenue (MR)
0	450	0	–
1	400	400	400
2	350	700	300
3	300	900	200
4	250	1000	100
5	200	1000	0
6	150	900	–100
7	100	700	–200
8	50	400	–300

Table 31.1

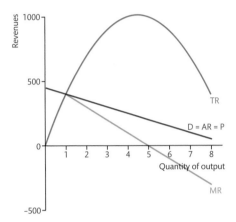

Figure 31.1

As price continues to fall and **output** increases the firm **forgoes** increasingly more revenue from the sale of the previous units while the revenue from the sale of each additional unit decreases. **Marginal revenue**, which is the change in **total revenue** from selling the next unit, therefore falls as price falls as shown in Table 31.1. If the revenue generated from the sale of the next unit is greater than the loss in revenue from the previous units marginal revenue will be positive, so producing and selling the next unit will add to total revenue. As shown in the table, reducing price in order to sell the next unit when marginal revenue is positive leads to a rise in total revenue. Marginal revenue (the change in total revenue from the sale of the next unit) becomes negative when the revenue gained from selling the next unit is less than the loss in revenue from the sale of the previous units that could have been sold at a higher price. If the change in total revenue from the sale of the next unit is negative then total revenue will fall if that unit is produced and sold. As shown in the table when marginal revenue becomes negative total revenue starts to fall. In Figure 31.2 when the marginal revenue curve becomes negative at just over 5 units the total revenue curve starts to fall. Therefore total revenue is maximized when marginal revenue = 0.

Why does a monopolist choose to operate on the elastic portion of its demand curve? (see pages 22–3 for a detailed explanation of PED, revenue, and elasticity along a demand curve)

Total revenue is maximized where marginal revenue = 0. As shown in Figure 31.2. if the firm reduces or increases output below or above 5 units total revenue falls. This is because **price elasticity of demand** (PED) varies over a range of prices along a downward-sloping, linear demand curve. Why would the monopolist not consider increasing output beyond 5 units? PED is inelastic along this section of the average revenue or demand curve.

Output (Q)	Price (P)/$	Total revenue (TR = P × Q)/$	Marginal revenue (MR = ΔTR/ΔQ)/$	Average revenue (AR = TR/Q)/$
0	–			
1	10	10	10	10
2	9	18	8	9
3	8	24	6	8
4	7	28	4	7
5	6	30	2	6
6	5	30	0	5
7	4	28	–2	4
8	3	24	–4	3
9	2	18	–6	2
10	1	10	–8	1

Table 31.2

quantity demanded the amount of a good consumers are willing and able to buy at a given price over a given period of time

short run a period of time when at least one factor is variable and the others are fixed

output the quantity of goods produced by a firm, industry or economy

average variable cost is equal to total variable cost divided by quantity of output

long run a conceptual moment in time when all factors are variable

normal profit occurs when economic profit is equal to zero, i.e., when the difference between total revenue and total costs (explicit and implicit costs) equals zero

average total cost is equal to total cost divided by quantity of output

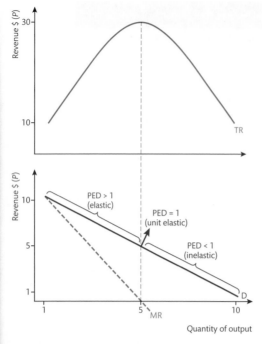

Figure 31.2

As shown In Table 31.2, reducing price from $5 to $4 causes quantity demanded to rise from 6 to 7.

$$PED = \frac{\Delta Qd/Qd}{\Delta P/P} = \frac{1/6}{-1/5} = \frac{0.166}{0.20} = (-)\,0.83$$

PED < 1 therefore demand is price inelastic. The rate of change in the fall in price is greater than the rate of change in the increase in **quantity demanded**. Total revenue = price × quantity therefore when PED is inelastic a fall in price will lead to a fall in total revenue.

The revenue gained from the sale of the next unit in this case is $4. The monopolist now only gets $4 for the 6 previous units, which is $24, when it used to get $5 for the 6 units, which is $30. This is a loss in revenue of $6. By reducing price the monopolist gains $4 from the sale of the additional unit but loses $6 because it has to sell the previous units at a lower price. Therefore total revenue falls by $2 ($4 – $6). The monopolist is assumed to be self-interested and therefore it will not reduce price in order to increase output when marginal revenue is negative and PED is inelastic, because to do so reduces the monopolist's total revenue. The monopolist will produce where MR is positive and this is along the section of the demand curve that is price elastic.

Test your understanding of this unit by answering the following questions

- Explain why a monopolist's demand curve slopes downwards.
- Distinguish between natural barriers to entry and artificial barriers to entry.
- Using a diagram to illustrate your answer explain the shape of a monopolist's marginal revenue curve.
- Explain the relationship between price elasticity of demand and marginal revenue.

Learning Outcomes

- Explain, using a diagram, the short- and long-run equilibrium output and pricing decision of a profit-maximizing (loss-minimizing) monopolist, identifying the firm's economic profit (or losses).

- Explain the role of barriers to entry in permitting the firm to earn economic profit.

- Explain, using a diagram, the output and pricing decision of a revenue-maximizing monopoly firm.

- Compare and contrast, using a diagram, the equilibrium positions of a profit-maximizing monopoly firm and a revenue-maximizing monopoly firm.

- Calculate from a set of data and/or diagrams the revenue-maximizing level of output.

Like all firms it is assumed that the monopolist aims to maximize profit and follows the golden rules for profit maximization set out below.

Profit maximization is the objective of all firms in all industries

In the **short run**: The firm should only produce **output** if the price it receives is greater than the **average variable cost**.

In the **long run**: The firm should only produce output if it earns at least a **normal profit**. In other words if price is equal to or greater than **average total cost**.

In the short and long run: The firm should set the level of output where **marginal revenue** is equal to **marginal cost** if it has made the decision to continue production.

Profit and loss in the short run

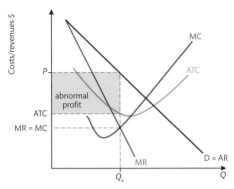

Figure 32.1

The **monopolist** sets output at the level where marginal revenue equals marginal cost in order to maximize profit (see pages 74–6 for a detailed explanation of profit maximization). As shown in Figure 32.1 profit-maximizing level of output is Qe and the price consumers are willing to pay for this quantity, marked P on the diagram, is determined by the demand curve. When output is set at Qe price is greater than average total cost therefore the monopolist earns **positive economic profit** or **abnormal profit** on each unit sold. The total abnormal profit earned is calculated by subtracting average total cost from price and multiplying by the quantity sold: $(P - ATC) \times Q$.

Abnormal profit is represented by the shaded area (see pages 74–6 for a detailed explanation of abnormal profit). **Barriers to entry** is an assumed characteristic of monopoly (see pages 85–6 for a full explanation of barriers to entry) and they prevent new firms entering the **industry** to compete for the abnormal profit therefore the monopolist is able to earn positive economic profits in the long run.

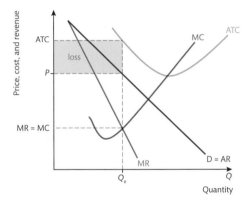

Figure 32.2

Figure 32.2 shows the monopolist making a loss. At the profit-maximizing level of output where marginal revenue equals marginal cost average total cost is greater than price. A loss is made on each unit sold. The total loss is the difference between ATC and price multiplied by quantity: $(ATC - P) \times Q$. Total loss is represented by the shaded area. The monopolist will continue to produce in the short run so long as the price it receives for a unit of output is greater than average variable cost because the firm is making at least some contribution to covering **fixed costs**. In the long run the monopolist will **shut down** production if at least a normal profit cannot be earned (see pages 80–82 for a full explanation of shut-down decisions).

Model sentence: A monopolist maximizes profit by setting output where marginal revenue equals marginal cost. If price is greater than average total cost at this level of output the firm can earn positive economic profit in the long run because the high barriers to entry prevent new firms from competing and driving prices and profit down.

Distinguish between profit maximizing and revenue-maximizing – a step-by-step guide (see Figure 32.3 on page 90)

Trouble shooter

Marginal revenue is the addition to **total revenue** from producing and selling the next unit.

Therefore when marginal revenue is positive (up to Q_{revmax}) producing and selling the next unit will add to total revenue.

Beyond Q_{revmax} marginal revenue is negative therefore producing and selling output will reduce total revenue.

In order to maximize revenue the firm sets output where marginal revenue equals zero, Q_{revmax} on Figure 32.3, at price P_{revmax}. At this point total revenue is at its highest.

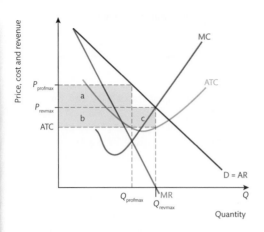

In order to maximize profit the monopolist sets output at $Q_{profmax}$ where marginal revenue equals marginal cost. This is below revenue-maximizing level of output. Profit-maximizing price is greater than revenue maximizing price. The profit-maximizing firm produces less and charges more than if its objective is to maximize revenue. When profit maximizing the firm earns abnormal profit of $(P_{profmax} - ATC) \times Q_{profmax}$ which is represented by the areas a + b. By reducing price and increasing quantity sold to maximize revenue, the monopolist earns abnormal profit of $(P_{revmax} - ATC) \times Q_{revmax}$ which is represented by area b + c. $(P_{revmax} - ATC) \times Q_{revmax} < (P_{profmax} - ATC) \times Q_{profmax}$. The firm gains area c of profit but forgoes the larger area a, therefore profit falls.

Figure 32.3

Test your understanding of this unit by answering the following questions

- Using a diagram to illustrate your answer, explain why a monopolist can earn abnormal profit in the long run.
- Using a diagram to illustrate your answer distinguish between a profit maximizing monopolist and a revenue maximizing monopolist.

Synonyms

firm...... business/producer/supplier

Learning Outcomes

- With reference to economies of scale, and using examples, explain the meaning of the term 'natural monopoly'.

- Draw a diagram illustrating a natural monopoly.

- Explain, using diagrams, why the profit-maximizing choices of a monopoly **firm** lead to allocative inefficiency (welfare loss) and productive inefficiency.

- Explain why, despite inefficiencies, a monopoly may be considered desirable for a variety of reasons, including

the ability to finance research and development (R&D) from economic profits, the need to innovate to maintain economic profit, and the possibility of economies of scale.

- Draw diagrams and use them to compare and contrast a monopoly market with a perfectly competitive market, with reference to factors including efficiency, price and output, research and development (R&D), and economies of scale.

Subject vocabulary

continued from page 91

long run a conceptual moment in time when all factors are variable

consumer surplus the difference between the price a consumer is willing and able to pay and the price the consumer actually pays

producer surplus the difference between the price a firm is willing to accept for a unit of output and the price the consumer actually pays

real income income after taking into account the effects of inflation on purchasing power

Why is a monopoly sometimes necessary if wants are to be satisfied?

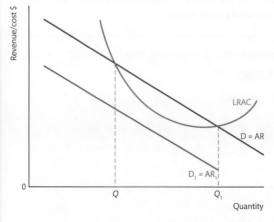

Figure 33.1

The case of natural monopoly

In some industries the **total fixed costs** are very high. They represent a high proportion of the firm's **total costs**. Fixed costs do not change with output therefore the **average fixed cost**, that is fixed cost per unit, is very high at low levels of output and falls as output rises. Only when the monopolist controls all of the market, leading to very high levels of output, can the high fixed costs be covered by revenue (price × quantity). **Long-run average costs** fall because the firm has all the market and can enjoy all the available **economies of scale** (see pages 69–71 for a full explanation of economies of scale).

The demand curve and average revenue curve D = AR represents **demand** when the firm has 100% **market share**. Between output Q and Q_1 price is greater than long-run average cost therefore the monopolist earns positive economic profits. When another firm or firms enter the market the incumbent firm's demand falls at each price and the demand curve shifts to the left to $D_1 = AR_1$. There is no level of output where price is equal to or greater than average cost, therefore at any level of output the firm makes a loss. It can be assumed other firms will face similar **cost structures** and they too would not be able to make normal profit in the end. Therefore, all firms would **shut down** production and the good or service would not be supplied leading to **significant welfare loss**. Natural monopolies tend to exist in industries where there are very high infrastructure costs such as gas and electricity suppliers and water and sewage services. The cost for each of the firms of laying the pipes over the same vast areas, and of maintenance, means that the competing firms would not be able to cover the enormous fixed cost of the infrastructure and would not, because of their size, enjoy all economies of scale. This is why in many countries state monopolies were created to provide these services.

Compare output and price under perfect competition and under monopoly

In perfectly competitive markets firms have no **market power**. They are unable to influence **market price** or output. The forces of **market demand** and **market supply** determine industry equilibrium price and output. Firms are price takers. If price is greater than average total cost the firm earns positive economic profit on each unit sold but only in the short run. Firms have perfect knowledge of profits earned in the industry and in other perfectly competitive industries, **factors of production** are perfectly mobile and there are no **barriers to entry** preventing new firms from competing for the high profit. Therefore, new firms enter the industry increasing market supply causing a fall in price and driving profit down to normal. The degree of competition determines price and output.

A monopolist on the other hand is the industry. The firm has market power. It can set price or output and can earn positive economic profit in the long run because, unlike in perfect competition, new firms are not able to enter the industry and compete. Therefore, market supply does not increase and price and profit are not driven down leaving the monopolist earning abnormal profit in the **long run**.

Model sentence: Price and profit are lower and output is higher under perfect competition than under monopoly because in perfectly competitive markets there are no barriers to entry so new firms can enter the industry to compete for the high profits thereby increasing market supply and driving price and profit down.

Compare welfare and efficiency under perfect competition and under monopoly

Consumers pay a higher price and consume fewer goods under monopoly than under perfect competition. The monopolist is able to reduce **consumer surplus** and increase **producer surplus** thereby reducing consumer welfare and increasing producer welfare. As price is higher, **real incomes** fall. The consumer can buy fewer goods and satisfy fewer wants with the same income thereby reducing the consumer's welfare.

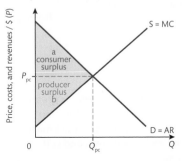

Figure 33.2a

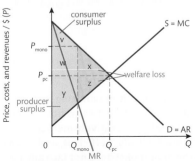

Figure 33.2b

free market a market where the forces of demand and supply are allowed to operate without any forms of intervention

price elastic the percentage change in quantity demanded/ supplied > the percentage change in price

demand curve a graph that shows the relationship between price and quantity demanded

marginal revenue the additional revenue generated from the sale of the additional unit of output produced

marginal cost the change in total cost resulting from a change in output of one unit

profit the difference between total revenue (price × quantity sold) and economic costs (explicit costs + implicit costs)

allocative efficiency the best or optimal allocation of resources from society's point of view. It occurs when the market is in equilibrium and social surplus is maximized (where P = MC).

resources the inputs into the production process, the factors of production

productive efficiency occurs when a given quantity of output is produced at the minimum total cost per unit of output

abnormal/supernormal profit occurs when economic profit is greater than zero, i.e., when total revenue is greater than total cost (explicit and implicit costs)

X-inefficient a lack of technical and productive efficiency that exists in large firms

perfect competition a theoretical market structure which has the required characteristics that ensures no buyer or seller has the power to be able to influence market price

Glossary

steeper has a higher/bigger angle/gradient

Synonyms

consumption ... use

reallocate(d) .... redistribute(d)

Figure 33.2a shows equilibrium in the market under prefect competition. Price and output are determined solely by the forces of demand and supply in a **free market**. Figure 33.2b shows price and output in the market under monopoly where the firm is the industry and price and output are determined by the monopolist. It is assumed that the sum of the costs incurred by the firms in a perfectly competitive industry are equal to the costs incurred in the industry if it were controlled by a monopolist.

The monopolist faces a downward-sloping demand curve unlike the firm under perfect competion which faces a **perfectly elastic demand curve**. (Figure 33.2a shows a downward-sloping demand curve because it is the demand curve for industry not the firm.) The slope of the monopolist's **marginal revenue** curve is **steeper** than its demand curve and lies below it (see pages 71–3 for a detailed explanation of the relationship between the demand curve and the marginal revenue curve). In Figure 33.2b the monopolist sets output at Qmono where marginal revenue equals **marginal cost** in order to maximize **profit**. Note that Qmono, which is output under monopoly is lower than Qpc which is output under perfect competition and the price under monopoly, Pmono, is higher than Ppc which is price under perfect competition.

Area a represents consumer surplus in a free market under perfect competition and this falls to area v under monopoly as price is higher. Area b is producer surplus in the free market and rises to area w + y under monopoly. Area × + z is the welfare loss caused by monopoly power. Area × is the loss of consumer surplus and area, is the loss of producer surplus. Area y + w is the area representing producer surplus under monopoly. Note that the monopolist loses area z but gains area y. y + w > y + z, therefore producer surplus increases. This is why the monopolist uses its market power to reduce output.

Model sentence: The monopolist has market power and therefore can increase price by reducing output in order to earn abnormal profit leading to an increase in producer surplus at the expense of consumer surplus.

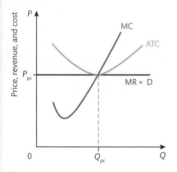 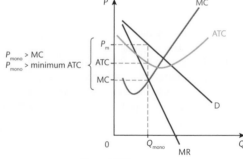

Figure 33.3a **Figure 33.3b**

Figure 33.3a shows the firm's long-run equilibrium position under perfect competition. Note that price equals marginal cost at profit-maximizing level of output. This is the condition for **allocative efficiency** (see pages 82–4 for a full explanation of the efficiencies). Under monopoly in Figure 33.3b price is greater than marginal cost at profit-maximizing level of output and therefore is not allocatively efficient. The price, which is the value consumers in society place on the **consumption** of the additional unit, is greater than the marginal cost, which is the value of the resources used to produce it. Therefore the welfare of the consumers in society can be increased by **reallocating resources** away from the production of other goods to the production of the good in order to increase output and reduce price until price equals marginal cost.

Productive efficiency is achieved when a unit of output is produced at lowest possible average cost. Note under perfect competition at Q_{pc} average total cost equals marginal cost. This is the condition for productive efficiency because marginal cost equals ATC at ATC's lowest point. Under monopoly ATC is greater than marginal cost. The firm is not minimizing its ATC therefore it is productively inefficient. The monopolist is able to survive in business despite being productively inefficient because the firm is earning **abnormal profit**. Technical efficiency occurs when the output from a given quantity of labour and capital is maximized. If a firm is able to increase output with a given quantity of labour and capital then it is technically inefficient. **X-inefficiency** occurs when technical efficiency is not achieved. Under **perfect competition**, a firm that does not use the resources it owns efficiently will make a loss and not survive in the long run. It is not essential for a monopolist to use the resources it owns efficiently because the lack of competition and abnormal profit ensures the monopolist can remain in business. The incentive to be technically efficient is not so great for the monopolist.

Model sentence: At the profit-maximizing level of output of a monopolist, price is greater than average total cost, therefore it earns positive economic profit; price is greater than marginal cost therefore it is allocatively inefficient; average total cost is greater than marginal cost therefore it is productively inefficient, and it can be technically inefficient and still survive because the monopolist does not face any competition.

Explain why the existence of monopoly power is not always against the interest of the consumer

There are lots of firms that have monopoly power, such as Apple and Sony. These firms enjoy **substantial economies of scale** (see pages 69–71 for a full explanation of economies of scale). Given that such a firm produces at very high levels of output their long-run average cost is very much lower than if the firm were operating in a perfectly competitive market producing comparatively very low levels of output. In Figure 33.4 the initial profit-maximizing level of output for the monopolist is Q_m leading to price P_m whereas under perfect competition the industry output is Q_{pc} and price is P_{pc}. Output is higher and price is lower than under monopoly. This is the generally accepted view. However, if the monopolist enjoys huge economies of scale average costs fall and the marginal cost curve shifts to the right. Q_{mi} is now the monopolist's profit-maximizing level of output where MR = MCl. P_{mi} is below P_{pc} and Q_{mi} is greater than Q_{pc}. Therefore it can be argued that it is possible for consumer welfare to be **enhanced** by the existence of monopoly.

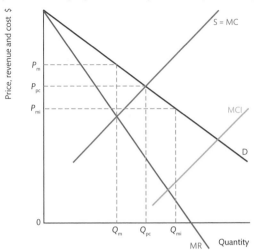

Figure 33.4

The firm with monopoly power earns **positive economic profit** not available to a firm in the long run under perfect competition. Money is available for research and development and therefore the monopolist is able to innovate and bring to market many new goods, far more than would be developed and brought to market under perfect competition. New goods create new wants that can be satisfied, potentially increasing **consumer welfare**. Monopolists supply large markets and enjoy huge economies of scale. Average costs are therefore relatively low making the industry internationally competitive, leading to an increase in the sale of exports and greater employment in the industry.

Test your understanding of this unit by answering the following questions

- Is monopoly bad for the consumer?
- Compare and contrast efficiencies under perfect competition and monopoly.

Synonyms

substantial ...... large

enhanced .... improved/made better

characteristics .. features

Subject vocabulary

economies of scale the cost advantages gained by a firm from increasing the scale of its production. Average cost falls in the long run as the size of a firm's operation increases.

positive economic profit occurs when the difference between total revenue and total costs (explicit and implicit costs) is greater than zero

consumer welfare a measure of the benefit obtained from the consumption of goods

---

Learning Outcomes

- Describe, using examples, the assumed **characteristics** of monopolistic competition: a large number of firms; differentiated products; absence of barriers to entry and exit.

- Explain that product differentiation leads to a small degree of monopoly power and therefore to a negatively sloping demand curve for the product.

- Explain, using a diagram, the short-run equilibrium output and pricing decisions of a profit-maximizing (loss-minimizing) firm in monopolistic competition, identifying the firm's economic profit (or loss).

- Explain, using diagrams, why in the long run a firm in monopolistic competition will make normal profit.

- Distinguish between price competition and non-price competition.

- Describe examples of non-price competition, including advertising, packaging, product development, and quality of service.

- Explain, using a diagram, why neither allocative efficiency nor productive efficiency are achieved by monopolistically competitive firms.

- Compare and contrast, using diagrams, monopolistic competition with perfect competition, and monopolistic competition with monopoly, with reference to factors including short-run, long-run, market power, allocative and productive efficiency, number of producers, economies of scale, ease of entry and exit, size of firms, and product differentiation.

market structure the structure is determined by the characteristics of a market and it is the characteristics that affect the level of competition, prices and profit

benefit the satisfaction gained from the consumption of a good

industry a group of firms that produce the same or similar goods or services

collude to act together with others to achieve a common goal, such as raising prices/maximizing profile

differentiated goods substitute goods that in some way have been made distinct, often through branding

barriers to entry factors that prevent/make difficult the entry of new firms into an industry or market

market share the proportion of the market supply of a good or service that is controlled by a firm

branding the process of creating a distinct logo, name, and image for a good in order to make it different from other goods in the market

quantity demanded the amount of a good consumers are willing and able to buy at a given price over a given period of time

price elasticity of demand (PED) a measure of how quantity demanded responds to a change in price in percentage terms

negative sloping a downward-sloping line that represents the negative relationship between the two variables

marginal unit the next or the additional unit of output produced or consumed

What are the assumed characteristics of monopolistic competition?

The **implicit** assumptions in all **market structures** are that the firms' objective is to maximize profit and consumers aim to maximize **benefit**. The assumptions of monopolistic competition are very similar to those of perfect competition. There is only one major difference. In perfect competition all goods are homogeneous (identical) whereas in monopolistic competition firms produce goods that are heterogeneous or differentiated (varied/not the same). As in all market structures the assumed characteristics have consequences. They affect the behaviour of consumers and firms, and ultimately affect the levels of profit and efficiency.

Describe the effects of the assumed characteristics of monopolistic competition – a step-by-step guide (the characteristics are in bold italics)

Trouble shooter

There are many firms and buyers in the market: the actions of individual consumers or firms have little if any effect on the **industry** as a whole. There are many firms so it is not possible for them to **collude**.

The firms in the industry produce differentiated goods: the consumer can tell the difference between the goods. The goods are substitutes but consumers may prefer one good over another. This gives the firm some price setting power.

The industry has very low barriers to entry or to exit: existing firms in an industry cannot stop new firms entering the industry, and existing firms can leave one industry and use their resources to produce goods in another industry very easily.

Examples of monopolistically competitive industries include beauty salons, hairdressers, clothes retail outlets, restaurants, car repair shops, painting and decorating, plumbers, and electricians. Note that these industries tend to contain a large number of small firms and have comparatively low and few barriers to entry. All firms in monopolistic competition try in some way to differentiate themselves from the competition in order to gain enough **market share** to maximize profit.

Why do firms under monopolistic competition face a downward-sloping demand curve?

The goods produced by the firms in the industry are differentiated for example by **branding**, quality, packaging, design, style, and colour. Some consumers may prefer a good produced by a particular firm, for example people are very loyal if they have received good customer and after-sales service. Whatever the reason, if a consumer believes that he/she gains comparatively greater benefit from the consumption of a good from a particular firm he/she will value it more highly than the substitute goods and will be prepared to pay a higher price. A firm can raise price and **quantity demanded** does not fall to zero as it would under perfect competition where **price elasticity of demand** = infinity and the firm faces a horizontal demand curve. The firm in monopolistic competition faces a downward, **negatively sloping** demand curve indicating that the firm has some market power and can affect price. Where there are many close substitutes available PED is more elastic and the **slope** of the demand curve is less **steep**. The PED of successfully branded goods, for example, will be less elastic and the slope of the demand curve steeper because in the eyes of the consumers the branded good is perceived to be different from and better than the substitutes. Consumers value it more.

The firm is after all the sole supplier of its good. It has some price-setting ability but still faces lots of competition from firms selling substitutes. It is this that gives this market structure its name: monopolistic competition.

Model sentence: The greater the benefit the consumer enjoys from the consumption of the marginal unit the greater the value the consumer places on that unit and therefore the greater the price the consumer will be prepared to pay for it. If the firm can, through differentiating the good, increase the benefit the consumer enjoys from the consumption of the marginal unit it can charge a higher price.

Why do firms in monopolistic competition only make abnormal profit in the short run?

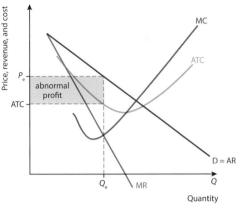

Figure 34.1 *Short-run position*

Firms face a downward-sloping demand curve therefore the **average revenue curve** slopes downwards. The **marginal revenue curve** is twice as steep as the average revenue curve (see pages 71–3 for a full explanation of the relationship between average revenue and marginal revenue). Each firm aims to maximize profit so price is set to give the quantity demanded that matches the level of **output** where marginal revenue equals marginal cost (see pages 74–6 for a full explanation of profit maximizing point).

Figure 34.1 shows the **short-run** position for a firm in monopolistic competition. At profit-maximizing level of output where MR = MC the price is greater than **average total costs**, therefore the firm earns **positive economic profit** or abnormal profit on each unit sold. Total abnormal profit = $(P_e – ATC) \times Q_e$ and is represented in the diagram by the rectangle labelled abnormal profit (see pages 74–6 for a full explanation of economic profit).

Explain how abnormal profit is driven down to normal profit in the long run – a step-by-step guide

Trouble shooter

Firms and potential **entrepreneurs** have very good knowledge so they know that abnormal profits are being earned.

There are few and low **barriers to entry** and **factors of production** are mobile so new firms can easily enter the industry in order to compete for the **abnormal profit**.

The market share of each firm falls as new firms enter the industry. Therefore, **demand** falls and the demand curve shifts down and to the left.

New firms continue to enter until each firm's demand curve has shifted far enough to the left that their demand curves are just touching the average total cost curve at profit-maximizing level of output as shown in Figure 34.2.

At profit-maximizing level of output, where MR = MC, price = ATC. Each firm in the industry is now earning normal profit.

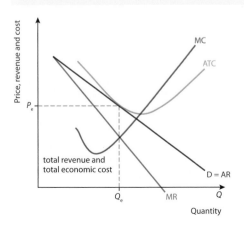

Figure 34.2

Model sentence: In the long-run under monopolistic competition each firms' total revenue (price × output) equals their total economic costs (ATC × output). Zero economic profit is earned by each firm because revenue is only just covering all costs including the cost of the purchased resources (explicit costs) and the opportunity cost of the self-owned resources (implicit costs).

Note the area representing total revenue (price × quantity) is the same size as the area representing total economic costs (ATC × quantity).

Subject vocabulary

average revenue curve a curve which represents the average revenue over a range of output (= total revenue/output). It is the same as the demand curve.

marginal revenue curve a curve which represents the marginal revenue over a range of output

output the quantity of goods produced by a firm, industry or economy

short run a period of time when at least one factor is variable and the others are fixed

average total cost is equal to total cost divided by quantity of output

positive economic profit occurs when the difference between total revenue and total costs (explicit and implicit costs) is greater than zero

entrepreneur an individual who, in pursuit of profit, brings together the other factors of production in order to produce a good or service

barriers to entry factors that prevent/make difficult the entry of new firms into an industry or market

factors of production the inputs into the production process (land, labour, capital and entrepreneurship)

abnormal/supernormal profit occurs when economic profit is greater than zero, i.e., when total revenue is greater than total cost (explicit and implicit costs)

demand the amount of a good that consumers are willing and able to buy at each price

total economic costs the cost of all the resources used by a firm in the production of a quantity of goods or services. It is the sum of explicit and implicit costs

zero economic profit occurs when the difference between total revenue and total costs (explicit and implicit costs) equals zero. It is the same as normal profit.

allocatively inefficient a market is allocatively inefficient when it is in disequilibrium, where price does not equal marginal cost leading to a suboptimal allocation of resources from society's point of view

productively inefficient describes a firm that is not producing goods at the lowest aveage cost

marginal cost the change in total cost resulting from a change in output of one unit

social welfare the sum of consumer and producer welfare. Social welfare is maximised where price equals marginal cost leading to an optimum allocation of resources from society's point of view

resources the inputs into the production process, the factors of production

positive economic profit occurs when the difference between total revenue and total costs (explicit and implicit costs) is greater than zero

long run a conceptual moment in time when all factors are variable

abnormal/supernormal profit occurs when economic profit is greater than zero, i.e., when total revenue is greater than total cost (explicit and implicit costs)

normal profits occurs when economic profit is equal to zero, i.e., when the difference between total revenue and total costs (explicit and implicit costs) equals zero

monopoly power the degree of control a firm has over the setting of price

marginal revenue the additional revenue generated from the sale of the additional unit of output produced

average revenue revenue per unit of output (= total revenue/output)

Why are firms in a monopolistically competitive market inefficient?

Monopolistically competitive firms are **allocatively inefficient** and **productively inefficient** in the short and the long run. At the profit-maximizing level of output price is greater than **marginal cost**. In other words the value consumers in society place on the consumption of the additional unit is greater than the value of the resources used to produce it. Therefore it is allocatively inefficient. **Social welfare** can be increased by **allocating** more **resources** to the production of the good, thereby increasing output and lowering price until the value consumers in society place on the consumption of the additional unit is equal to the value of the resources used to produce it, that is where price or average revenue = marginal cost (the point where AR = MC is shown in Figure 34.3).

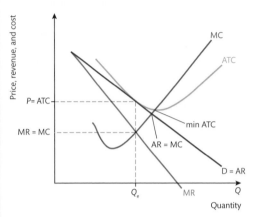

Figure 34.3

Productive efficiency is achieved when a unit of output is produced at lowest possible average total cost. Marginal cost cuts average total cost at average total cost's lowest point (as shown in Figure 34.3) therefore the condition for productive efficiency is MC = ATC at profit-maximizing level of output. However in monopolistic competition, indeed in all market structures other than perfect competion, ATC > MC when MR = MC, therefore a monopolistically competitive firm is productively inefficient.

Distinguish between monopolistic competition and other market structures

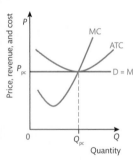

Figure 34.4a

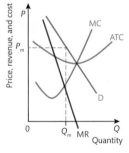

Figure 34.4b

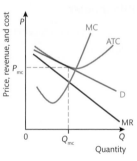

Figure 34.4c

All diagrams represent long-run equilibrium positions: a perfect competition, b monopoly, c monopolistic competition.

Positive economic profit can only be earned in the **long run** when barriers to entry prevent new firms entering the industry. This happens under monopoly whereas under perfect competition new firms, attracted by the **abnormal profit**, enter the industry as there are no barriers to entry. Industry supply increases reducing market price. The price the firm takes falls until price equals ATC and **normal profits** are once again earned. Under monopolistic competition there are very low barriers to entry so new firms enter the industry to compete for the abnormal profits. With more firms in the industry each firm's market share falls leading to a fall in demand. The demand curve of the existing firms shifts down and to the left. New firms continue to enter the industry until each firm's demand curve has shifted far enough to the left that their demand curves are just touching the average total cost curve at profit maximizing level of output. AR = ATC therefore only normal profit is earned.

The condition for allocative efficiency is P = MC. A firm with any amount of **monopoly power** faces a downward-sloping average revenue curve. **Marginal revenue** falls at a faster rate than **average revenue** (AR is equivalent to price) therefore marginal revenue is less than price at all levels of output other than zero (see pages 90–93 for a full explanation of efficiency under monopoly). This means that at any profit-maximizing level of output, where marginal revenue equals marginal cost, price is greater than marginal cost. Under perfect competition the firm faces a horizontal average revenue curve. Price equals marginal revenue so when the firm sets output where MR = MC price equals marginal cost and allocative efficiency is achieved (see pages 82–4 for a full explanation of allocative efficiency when demand is perfectly elastic).

Model sentence: In all market structures, other than perfect competition, the firm faces a downward-sloping demand curve so price is greater than marginal cost when profits are maximized. Therefore all imperfectly competitive markets are allocatively inefficient.

Neither monopoly nor monopolistic competition is productively efficient. Output is restricted in order to gain higher profit so the firm fails to produce at the lowest possible average total cost. Note on Figure 34.4b and c that when MR = MC output is not at the lowest point on the ATC curve, whereas under perfect competition, shown in Figure 34.4a, the firm is producing at the lowest point on the ATC curve and is therefore productively efficient. The monopolist faces no competition and earns abnormal profit in the long run so its incentive to use its resources in the most efficient way is diminished leading to **technical inefficiency**. When firms are in competitive markets they must use their resources to produce the maximum possible output otherwise they will not survive.

A monopolist, unlike firms under perfect and monopolistic competition, might enjoy massive **economies of scale** and therefore can reduce average total costs in the long run. As argued in pages 90–93, the existence of monopoly power is not always against the interest of the consumer. It is possible that average total cost and price could be lower under monoply than in more competitive markets and the higher profits earned in the long run by the monopolist might lead to lots of R&D so more new goods will come onto the market creating new wants that consumers can satisfy thereby increasing **consumer welfare**.

In a perfectly competitive world consumers have no choice. All goods in all industries are the same, while the monopolist has no incentive to differentiate output. Under monopolistic competition there is both price and **non-price competition**. Firms must consider the pricing strategies of its competitors when setting price and differentiate their goods in order to gain and maintain **market share**. This gives the consumer a choice between a variety of similar goods in all industries.

Distinguish between price competition and non-price competition

Goods produced by the firms in a monopolistically competitive industry are substitutes. A firm lowers price to try to get consumers to switch expenditure and buy their good rather than a rival firm's good and to bring new consumers into the market. When setting price firms consider the prices charged by other firms in the industry.

Firms also take part in non-price competition through, for example, promotions and advertising, 'style' of packaging, colour, quality of customer and after-sales service, quality of the product, and loyalty cards. Advertising is a very important way in which firms differentiate their goods. A firm's advertising campaign has two main purposes: to increase demand causing the demand curve to shift down and to the right thereby increasing revenue (price × quantity) and profit, and to make demand more **price inelastic** causing the demand curve to become steeper (demand curve rotates clockwise). The firm then might be able to increase total revenue by raising price because quantity demanded is now less responsive to changes in price (see pages 22–4 for a full explanation of the relationship between PED and revenue).

Test your understanding of this unit by answering the following questions

- Using diagrams to illustrate your answer, explain why abnormal profit cannot be earned in the long run under monopolistic competition.
- Compare and contrast allocative efficiency and productive efficiency under monopolistic competition and perfect competition.
- Explain why competitively monopolistic firms differentiate their goods.

Subject vocabulary

imperfectly competitive market a market that is not perfectly competitive, therefore producers or consumers have a degree of market power, allowing some control over price

technical inefficiency occurs when the given inputs into the production process are not combined in such a way as to maximize output

economies of scale the cost advantages gained by a firm from increasing the scale of its production. Average cost falls in the long run as the size of a firm's operation increases.

consumer welfare a measure of the benefit obtained from the consumption of goods

non-price competition a strategy whereby one firm makes its good or service different from those produced by other firms in the industry in order to gain market share

market share the proportion of the market supply of a good or service that is controlled by a firm

price inelastic the percentage change in quantity demanded/supplied < the percentage change in price

Glossary

dilemma difficult choice

Learning Outcomes

- Describe, using examples, the assumed characteristics of an oligopoly: the dominance of the industry by a small number of firms; the importance of interdependence; differentiated or homogeneous products; high barriers to entry.

- Explain why interdependence is responsible for the **dilemma** faced by oligopolistic firms – whether to compete or to collude.

- Explain how a concentration ratio may be used to identify an oligopoly.

Subject vocabulary

market structure the structure is determined by the characteristics of a market and it is the characteristics that affect the level of competition, prices, and profit

benefit the satisfaction gained from the consumption of a good

economic profit the difference between total revenue (price × quantity sold) and economic costs (explicit costs + implicit costs)

productive efficiency occurs when a given quantity of output is produced at the minimum total cost per unit of output

homogeneous goods goods that are exactly the same

differentiated goods substitute goods that in some way have been made distinct, often through branding

barriers to entry factors that prevent/make difficult the entry of new firms into an industry or market

niche market a relatively small specialized market within a much bigger market. For example, there is a mass market for chocolate but within this market there is a niche market for luxury chocolate.

long-run average cost the cost per unit of output when all factors are variable

interdependent firms are interdependent when each firm is affected by the decisions of the other firms and will react to the decisions of other firms. This is a characteristic of oligopoly.

collude to act together with others to achieve a common goal, such as raising prices/maximizing profile

market price the price determined by the interaction of demand and supply in a competitive market

Glossary

assumption(s) something thought/believed to be true but without proof

Synonyms

characteristics... features

significant .... major/large

rivals .... competitors

What are the implicit assumptions?

The implicit **assumptions** in all **market structures** are that the firms' objective is to maximize profit and consumers aim to maximize **benefit**. As in all market structures the assumed **characteristics** have consequences, affecting the behaviour of firms and consumers, **economic profits** that can be earned, and each firm's allocative efficiency and **productive efficiency**.

Describe the assumed characteristics of oligopoly and explain their effects – a step-by-step guide

Trouble shooter

A few large firms dominate the market producing **homogeneous goods** or **differentiated goods** in an industry with high **barriers to entry**. There might be lots of firms in the industry but most of them will have a relatively small proportion of market share often serving **niche markets**. The few large firms in the industry serve a mass market producing goods in very high quantities. The firms therefore experience **significant** economies of scale allowing them to produce at relatively low **long-run average costs**.

As there are only a few firms dominating the market selling homogeneous goods (such as steel, copper, wheat, and milk) or differentiated substitutes (such as cars, fizzy drinks, washing powder, and shampoo) they are **interdependent**. This means the decisions on price and differentiation (often achieved through branding) by one firm affect the other firms in the industry and will cause the other firms to react. Firms in the industry take into account how **rivals** might react before taking decisions. For example, if a firm increases price the firm knows other firms will react. How the firm thinks the others will react affects its decision. When one supermarket introduced 24-hour opening in the larger stores it knew this decision would cause its rivals to react.

As there are only a few firms in the industry selling homogeneous goods or differentiated substitutes it is possible for them to **collude** and set price or industry output in order to increase profit. Abnormal profits would attract the attention of potential rivals but it is difficult for new firms to enter the industry to compete for the high profits because of the high barriers to entry. Therefore firms in an oligopolistic industry can earn abnormal profit in the long run.

Explain why interdependence is responsible for the dilemma faced by oligopolistic firms – whether to compete or to collude

Under perfect competition there are lots of small firms in the industry. Each firm's output represents a very small proportion of total industry supply therefore each firm is unable to influence industry supply and therefore cannot, by increasing supply or decreasing supply, affect **market price**. The firms are independent. A decision by one firm does not affect other firms in the industry. Also there are so many firms in a perfectly competitive market it is not possible for them to collude and set price. This is not the case under oligopoly where collusion is practical because there are only a few firms. Also firms are interdependent. A decision made by one firm impacts on rivals and the other firms react to the decision.

Model sentence: Under oligopoly each firm's decisions relating to output, price, and differentiation are dependent upon the corresponding decisions made by the rival firms. Also there are only a few firms in the industry so it is possible for them to collude in order to set industry supply or market price. It is interdependency that gives rise to the two main theories of oligopoly: collusive oligopoly, a market where firms do not compete and non-collusive oligopoly, a market where firms do compete.

Explain how a concentration ratio may be used to identify an oligopoly

An industry dominated by two firms is called a **duopoly**. An oligopolistic industry might be dominated by three firms or more. The **concentration ratio** is the measure of the percentage market share in an industry held by the largest firms. Working out the concentration ratio of an industry is one way to establish its competitiveness. It is used to judge the market structure.

A concentration ratio is expressed in the form: CRx where × represents the number of firms that control a percentage of total market share. CR4 = 80% means that the four firms with the largest market share together produce 80% of the total output of the industry. If two firms merge the market becomes more concentrated with a new ratio CR3 = 80%. CR4 = 90% means that four firms together produce 90% of an industry's supply. This signifies a very highly concentrated market where the firms have a high degree of market power. Although it is possible that one of the four firms has 80% of total market share and the rest is split between the other three largest firms. In this situation the dominant firm has a very high degree of **monopoly power** and the market structure is more monopolistic than oligopolistic.

CR5 = 5% means that the five firms with the largest market share together produce only 5% of total industry output signifying that they have no market power and that the industry is very competitive.

The five-firm concentration ratio for the dupermarket industry in the UK is about 87% signifying that the industry is oligopolistic, whereas furniture manufacturing has a five-firm concentration ratio of 4% signifying it is a competitive market and not oligopolistic.

Test your understanding of this unit by answering the following questions

- Explain how a concentration ratio can determine the competitiveness of an industry.
- Explain why firms in oligopolistic markets are interdependent.

Subject vocabulary

duopoly a type of oligopoly where there are only two sellers. The term is also used to describe a market that is dominated by two sellers or two firms.

concentration ratio the proportion of market share controlled by a specified number of firms

monopoly power the degree of control a firm has over the setting of price

strategic interdependence a characteristic of oligopoly is the interdependence of firms. Each firm is affected by the decisions of the other firms and will react to the decisions of other firms. Strategic interdependence means that firms under oligopoly take this into account when making business decisions.

Learning Outcomes

- Explain how game theory (the simple prisoner's **dilemma**) can illustrate **strategic interdependence** and the options available to oligopolies.

- Explain the term 'collusion', give examples, and state that it is usually (in most countries) illegal.

- Explain the term 'cartel'.

- Explain that the primary goal of a cartel is to limit competition between member firms and to maximize joint profits as if the firms were collectively a monopoly.

- Explain the incentive of cartel members to cheat.

- Analyse the conditions that make cartel structures difficult to maintain.

- Describe the term 'tacit collusion', including reference to price leadership by a dominant firm.

Explain how game theory (the simple prisoner's dilemma) can illustrate strategic interdependence and the options available to oligopolies

Two criminals have been arrested for their part in a robbery. They are locked up in separate cells and are unable to communicate with each other. The police believe that the evidence against the two men may not be strong enough to gain a **conviction** at **trial** but the **prisoners** do not know this. The police want them at least to spend some time in prison so they present to each prisoner the same set of **plea bargains** as follows:

If both prisoner × and prisoner Y **confess**, the offer from the **prosecutor** is 4 years in jail.

If prisoner × confesses but prisoner Y denies having been involved in the robbery then × will be **released** and prisoner Y will go to jail for 12 years.

Table 36.1

If prisoner Y confesses but prisoner × denies having been involved in the robbery then Y will be released and prisoner × will go to jail for 12 years.

If prisoner × and prisoner Y both deny involvement in the robbery each will serve just 2 years in prison.

The information above is shown in Table 36.1

Glossary

dilemma difficult choice

conviction court decision that someone is guilty of a crime

trial looking at evidence in a court to see if someone is guilty of a crime

prisoner(s) person/people in jail

plea bargain(s) agreeing to say something in court which shortens your jail time

confess admit to doing something wrong

prosecutor court lawyer trying to prove someone is guilty of a crime

charge(s) police statement(s) saying someone may be guilty of a crime

Synonyms

released .... freed

If both prisoners deny the **charges** each will serve a relatively short sentence of 2 years in prison. If both confess each will serve 4 years. If prisoner × denies any involvement and prisoner Y confesses prisoner × will serve the maximum 12 years and Y will be released and the same is true the other way around. The risk for the prisoners

Subject vocabulary

oligopolistic market describes a market that is controlled by a small number of firms

industry a group of firms that produce the same or similar goods or services

duopoly a type of oligopoly where there are only two sellers. The term is also used to describe a market that is dominated by two sellers or two firms.

profit the difference between total revenue (price × quantity sold) and economic costs (explicit costs + implicit costs)

supply the amount of a good that a firm is willing and able to produce at each price

monopolist a firm that dominates an industry

cartel a collection of firms that agree to work together to maximize their joint profit

output the quantity of goods produced by an economy, firm, or number of firms

marginal revenue the additional revenue generated from the sale of the additional unit of output produced

marginal cost the change in total cost resulting from a change in output of one unit

productively inefficient describes a firm that is not producing goods at the lowest average cost

of denying the charge is very high. The risk of a long prison sentence is likely to **deter** each prisoner from denying involvement in the crime. So when the prisoners are unable to cooperate the most likely outcome is for them both to confess and serve the 4 years thereby avoiding the worst possible outcome: 12 years in prison. Therefore when prisoners do not cooperate they avoid the worst outcome but they do not achieve the best outcome possible which is two years in prison. The best outcome is possible only if they cooperate. Instead of confessing they would agree to deny any involvement in the crime and serve just 2 years in prison. Therefore the best outcome for the prisoners is achieved through cooperation.

Firms in an **oligopolistic market** must decide whether to compete or cooperate with their rivals on price. Each of the firms in the **industry** are selling close substitutes. Set out below is a version of the prisoner's dilemma game but this time set in the context of a **duopoly**.

Currently both firms set price at $12 and are earning **profits** of $13 million. Both firms are considering changing the price of their good but without colluding. Each firm knows that if they change the price it will cause the other firm to react in some way.

Firm Y can lower price or leave it at $12. Firm Y knows that firm × has the same two options. If firm Y leaves the price at $12 and firm × lowers its price to $10 then firm Y's profit will fall from $13 million to $5 million whilst firm X's profits increase to $15 million as lots of customers buy from firm × instead of firm Y. If firm × leaves the price at $12 and firm Y lowers its price to $10 then X's profit falls to $5 million while Y's increases to $15 million as lots of customers buy Y's goods instead of X's. If firm Y lowers price to $10 and firm × does the same then profit for both firms falls from $13 million to $9 million. The worst possible outcome for firm Y is if it holds price at $12 and firm × lowers its price to $10. This is true the other way around. Therefore in order to avoid the worst possible outcome each firm will lower price leading to a fall in profit from $13 million to $9 million. Non-cooperation has not resulted in the best possible outcome for the two firms. If the firms collude they could agree to maintain price at $12 and thereby achieve the best possible outcome: profit of $13 million for both firms. This information is shown in Table 36.2.

Table 36.2

What is collusion and what is the primary objective of a cartel?

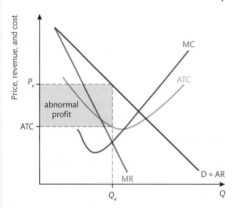

Figure 36.1

Collusion is an agreement between rival firms not to compete in order to raise price and to maximize joint profit. Collusion between firms can be formal and explicit. This means that firms have officially agreed to pursue strategies that are beneficial to them, although in most countries such agreements have been made illegal in order to protect consumer interest. Rivals will try to come to an agreement on a price that maximizes profit in the industry or may collectively agree to restrict the **supply** of the goods produced in the industry in order to maximize profits. Rivals might agree to not compete for market share with each other in particular parts of the country leaving each firm a **monopolist** in their own region of the country. A **cartel** is a group of firms which have entered into such agreements.

If the cartel includes all the firms in the industry it then has the power to decide on the level of **output** of the industry or set the price, just like a monopolist. Output, Q_e, is set at profit-maximizing point where **marginal revenue** = **marginal cost** giving price at P_e as seen in Figure 36.1. Price is greater than average total cost so abnormal profit of P_e – ATC is earned on each unit sold. Total abnormal profit is $(P_e – ATC) × Q_e$, the shaded area in Figure 36.1. A collusive oligopoly, like a monopoly, is **productively inefficient** because it does not produce at lowest possible ATC and it is allocatively inefficient as price is greater than marginal cost.

Model sentence: Firms collude to avoid the consequences of competition: lower prices and lower profit. By cooperating, firms are able to agree on industry output and price and thereby maximize profit.

Explain the incentive of cartel members to cheat and why they are unstable

In most countries cartels are illegal and members of an illegal cartel are likely to cheat. The price they agree is set high and profit earned is **abnormal**. If each firm has agreed to limit supply to an agreed **quota** it is very tempting for each of them to break the agreement and increase output in order to enjoy even greater profits. Also firms will not trust each other to keep their promise and the belief that other firms will in time break the agreement is often enough incentive for a firm to increase supply. This problem of trust is made worse the more firms there are in the cartel. Also the greater the number of firms the greater the difficulty of coming to agreements and **enforcing** each firm's quota.

The quota the firm has agreed to may not be at the firm's profit-maximizing level of output. If marginal revenue exceeds marginal cost at the firm's agreed level of output then the firm is likely to cheat and break the agreement by increasing output until marginal revenue equals marginal cost and profits are maximized thereby increasing total industry output.

Abnormal profits earned in the industry will attract new entrants and as long as some are able to overcome the barriers to entry, they will enter the industry thereby increasing industry output. Profits for firms in the industry will fall as they are now shared amongst more firms.

Model sentence: In a cartel where abnormal profit is being earned it is very tempting for a firm to increase supply to earn more profit. However, as the firm's output increases it causes industry output to increase beyond the industry's profit-maximizing level of output.

Describe the term 'tacit collusion', including reference to price leadership by a dominant firm

Collusion is illegal in many countries including the USA, and members of the European Union. Therefore firms in oligopolistic markets are more likely to engage in **non-collusive** activity or **tacit collusion** to avoid the disadvantages of competing.

Price leadership is a form of tacit collusion. The dominant firm in the oligopoly sets the price and the other firms follow the price. An example of this can be seen in the independent schools market in the UK. When the dominant school increases school fees the other schools increase their own. They will usually increase their fees so that price **differentials** are maintained. This is not something that has been formally agreed between the schools. It is an example of a hidden or tacit agreement. In this way schools do not compete directly on price.

Test your understanding of this unit by answering the following questions

- Explain why cartels are unstable.
- Explain the term 'price leadership'.
- Explain why firms in a cartel are tempted to cheat.
- What is the difference between formal collusion and tacit collusion?
- Why are firms in an oligopolistic industry tempted to collude?

Subject vocabulary

abnormal/supernormal profit occurs when economic profit is greater than zero, i.e., when total revenue is greater than total cost (explicit and implicit costs)

quota a physical limit placed on the number of goods that can be traded or produced

non-collusive describes a market where firms do not act together with others in order to achieve a common goal

tacit collusion a situation in which two or more firms in an oligopolistic market agree on a business strategy, without the agreement being explicit: it usually takes the form of price leadership

price leadership when firms follow the price set by the dominant firm in the industry

price rigidities the idea that prices can respond very slowly to changes in demand and supply therefore it can take a long time before a surplus or shortage is eliminated

Glossary

enforcing making people obey rules/laws

Synonyms

differentials.... differences

Learning Outcomes

- Explain that the behaviour of firms in a non-collusive oligopoly is strategic in order to take account of possible actions by rivals.

- Explain, using a diagram, the existence of **price rigidities**, with reference to the kinked-demand curve.

- Explain why non-price competition is common in oligopolistic markets, with reference to the risk of price wars.

- Describe, using examples, types of non-price competition.

Explain that the behaviour of firms in a non-collusive oligopoly is strategic in order to take account of possible actions by rivals

Firms in oligopolistic markets are interdependent. Each firm in the industry knows that any decision it makes will affect other firms and that other firms will react. So each firm will take into account the possible reactions

Subject vocabulary

pricing strategy a plan made and used by a firm with the aim of increasing revenue and profits through the setting of price

kinked-demand curve a kink or bend in the demand curve that is the result of firms reducing price in response to a competitor reducing price and keeping prices constant in response to a competitor increasing price

quantity demanded the amount of a good consumers are willing and able to buy at a given price over a given period of time

demand curve a graph that shows the relationship between price and quantity demanded

price elastic the percentage change in quantity demanded/supplied > the percentage change in price

market share the proportion of the market supply of a good or service that is controlled by a firm.

revenue the income a firm receives from consumers in exchange for goods (revenue = price × quantity sold)

price inelastic the percentage change in quantity demanded/supplied < the percentage change in price

price war when firms in the same industry progressively cut prices in an attempt to increase their market share

profit the difference between total revenue (price × quantity sold) and economic costs (explicit costs + implicit costs)

productivity the quantity of output per unit of input

average total cost equal to total cost divided by quantity of output

benefit the satisfaction gained from the consumption of a good

demand the amount of a good that consumers are willing and able to buy at each price

of the other firms before deciding what action to take. One model that examines the **dilemma** faced by firms when considering **pricing strategies** is the **kinked-demand curve theory**. This theory assumes that if a firm reduces price the other firms will do the same and reduce their prices and that if a firm increases price the others will react by holding their prices constant.

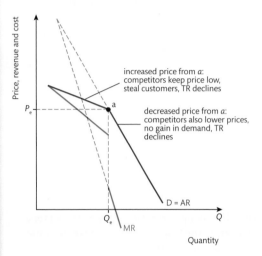

These **assumptions** result in the oligopolistic firm's demand curve being kinked as shown in Figure 37.1. A firm thinks about increasing price above P_e. Before it does this it must consider the possible reactions of the other firms. If the other firms keep their original price then **quantity demanded** might fall a lot as consumers stop buying from the firm and buy from the other firms instead. The percentage fall in quantity demanded will be greater than the percentage increase in price so the **demand curve** above P is relatively **price elastic**. If the firm increases price it will lose lots of its **market share** to the other firms and **revenue** will fall. This outcome is a possibility and the firm does not want to take the chance of losing revenue and market share so decides not to increase price.

Figure 37.1

The firm considers reducing price but thinks that the other firms will match the price reduction for fear of losing market share. Therefore if the firm reduced price quantity demanded would rise as new consumers enter the market attracted by the lower price but it would not gain any new customers from other firms as all firms have reduced price. Therefore if the firm lowered price the percentage change in price would be greater than the percentage change in quantity demanded and so the demand curve below P_e is relatively **price inelastic**. If the firm reduces price it will lose revenue. The firm does not want to take the chance of this happening so decides not to reduce price. Also the firms do not want to get involved in a **price war** where firms continue to cut price in response to the reductions in price of the rival firms. If this happens then all firms will see a fall in **profit**.

Model sentence: A firm believes that if it changes price revenue and profit will fall because of the reactions of other firms. Therefore the firm does not change price. This applies to all the firms in the oligopolistic market so price in the market remains stable.

As the firms decide not to compete on price they must consider other ways to compete.

Describe types of non-price competition

As firms cannot increase market share, revenue, and profit through changes in price they try to do so in different ways. Firms try to increase **productivity** and reduce **average total cost** in order to raise profit. Firms will invest heavily in strengthening the brand. Firms try to **differentiate** their brand through advertising, trying to convince buyers in the market that the good will give them greater **benefit** than the substitutes. The firm not only wants to increase **demand** but also aims to make demand more price inelastic. They may focus on quality of product or after-sales service, packaging, and design. Non-budget airlines compete with each other on the quality of service and inflight meals for example. Independent schools compete on what they offer students such as music, art, and sport facilities and many compete on the results students achieve. Supermarkets compete on loyalty cards, opening times, and the range of products available in the store including non-food items such as clothes and electrical goods, and services such as dry cleaning.

Test your understanding of this unit by answering the following question

- Explain price stability in a non-collusive oligopolistic market.

Learning Outcomes

● Describe price discrimination as the practice of charging different prices to different consumer groups for the same product, where the price difference is not justified by differences in cost.

● Explain that price discrimination may only take place if all of the following conditions exist: the firm must possess some degree of market power; there must be groups of consumers with differing price elasticities of demand for the product; the firm must be able to separate groups to ensure that no resale of the product occurs.

● Draw a diagram to illustrate how a firm maximizes profit in third-degree price discrimination, explaining why the higher price is set in the market with the relatively more inelastic demand.

What is price discrimination?

Firms that charge different prices for the same or similar goods or services are practising **price discrimination**. A monopolist is the sole supplier of a good or service and has the **market power** to charge different prices to different types of customers. Examples include gas and electricity suppliers charging different prices to businesses and households and train companies charging a lower price for young people or a lower price for a journey at off-peak times. The cost of production of the goods and services sold is the same whether sold at a lower or higher price. Price charged is not related to the cost per unit. A firm price discriminates because doing so increases **total revenue** and profit.

What are the conditions necessary for price discrimination to exist? – a step-by-step guide

Trouble shooter

The **price elasticity of demand** for the good or service must vary from one type of customer to the next or one market to the next.

PED varies because the **quantity demanded** of a good or service by some consumers is more sensitive to changes in price than it is for other consumers.

The firm must have a degree of **monopoly power**. Price discrimination therefore could not take place under **perfect competition** where firms take the market price.

The firm must be able to separate customers or markets in some way and prevent customers from buying and then subsequently selling the goods or services to different customers or across different markets. For example, it must be possible for a rail company to stop a young person from buying a low-priced train ticket and then selling it to an older person at a higher price thereby making a monetary gain.

There are three degrees of price discrimination. First-degree price discrimination occurs when the firm charges the maximum price each buyer in the market is willing to pay for a quantity of goods. Second-degree price discrimination or 'excess capacity pricing' occurs when a firm sells its spare capacity at a lower price than the price originally charged. For example, a hotel that has lots of rooms unfilled might reduce price in order to increase sales of rooms. An airline might offer 'last-minute deals' to try to sell unsold seats.

Model sentence: Third-degree discrimination can occur when different types of customers or different markets have different price elasticities of demand but only if the customers or markets can be seperarated to prevent resale of the good.

Using a diagram to illustrate your answer explain how a firm maximizes profit in third-degree price discrimination

Consumers or markets that have relatively low elasticities of demand, when demand is **price inelastic**, are relatively insensitive to changes in price and therefore firms will set a higher price. For example, quantity demanded of a certain make of car may be less responsive to a change in price in the UK than in Italy. The car manufacturer will then set a higher price for the car in the UK than in Italy as long as the market can be separated to prevent resale.

Commuters are charged different prices for rail journeys at different times because the train companies make assumptions about the type of consumer that travels at certain times. If travelling in the mornings and evenings at certain times it is assumed that customers are travelling to and from work. The train companies know that the journey is essential and that there are often few if any suitable substitutes available. Therefore demand will be relatively **price inelastic**. Those travelling for leisure purposes, who can travel in the middle of the day, have more suitable substitutes available and the journey is not a necessity therefore demand is relatively **price elastic**. Price charged varies depending on the elasticity of demand of the customers. Those with relatively price inelastic demand will be prepared to pay a higher price.

Airlines charge a much higher price for 'business class' than for a standard fare. This has little to do with the extra space given to business class travellers and the complementary drinks and higher quality meals. It has much more to do with the fact that often the firm that employs the traveller pays for the ticket and demand is relatively more price inelastic for firms than for individuals. This explains why flying is often more expensive during the week than at weekends. Airlines assume those flying during the week are business travellers.

If a customer needs to travel on that day a higher price will be charged than if the flight was booked in advance because there is a higher degree of urgency to travel and no or few substitutes are available. Therefore demand is relatively more price inelastic.

Another example is phone companies charging a higher price to businesses than to households for phone calls. The cost to the telephone company is the same in each case but because price elasticity of demand differs in the two markets a different price is charged.

Firms assume that old people and young people such as students are likely to have relatively low incomes and are very sensitive to changes in price. Businesses such as cinemas, restaurants, and hairdressers often charge a lower price to these type of customers.

Firms take advantage of the fact that elasticies vary to maximize **revenue** and **profit**. In Figure 38.1a and b the **marginal revenue** curves are drawn for each distinct market. Figure 38.1a shows the MR curve for market A and b for market B. The marginal revenue in markets A and B are added together to give the whole market's marginal revenue curve shown in Figure 38.1c. In market A demand is relatively more price inelastic than in market B therefore the **slope** of the **demand curve** in market A is steeper than the demand curve in market B. The MR curve is twice as **steep** as the demand curve (see pages 71–73 for a detailed explanation of the slope of the MR curve). It is assumed that the firm aims to maximize profit and will therefore set output in the market as a whole where marginal revenue equals **marginal cost** as shown in Figure 38.1c. The marginal cost is transferred across to the two distinct markets A and B as shown by the broken line. In each market output is set where MR = MC and the price required so that quantity demanded is equal to the profit-maximizing level of output is read from the demand curve in each market. (See pages 74–76 for a detailed explanation of profit maximizing point.)

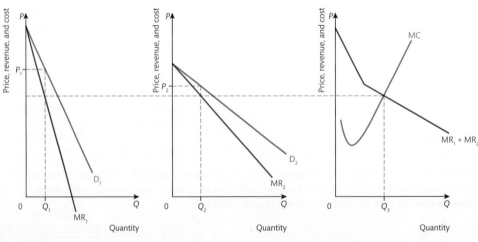

| Figure 38.1a | Figure 38.1b | Figure 38.1c |

Output in the the relatively more price inelastic market A is restricted to Q_1 and price is set at P_1. Price is higher and output is lower in market A than in the relatively more price elastic market B. This is a reflection of the different price elasticities of demand. Price is higher in market A because quantity demanded is less responsive to changes in price than in market B. Market A can bear a higher price.

The market is **allocatively inefficient** because price is greater than marginal cost in both markets. The value the consumer places on the consumption of the next unit of output, which is the price, is greater than the value of the resources used to produce the unit, which is the marginal cost, therefore society's welfare would be increased if more **factors of production** were allocated to the production of the good. (See pages 82–4 for a detailed explanation of allocative efficiency).

It is possible that by price discriminating total industry output increases therefore the good or service is bought by more consumers. Price discrimination can benefit some comsumers. At the lower price some consumers may be able to enter the market and gain benefit from the consumption of the good whereas if the price is set for the whole market it might be too high for those particular consumers. In this way there is a **welfare gain** for those particular consumers. However, many consumers will pay a price greater than a price set for the whole market. The firm captures their **consumer surplus** and welfare is lost (see pages 16–18 for a detailed explanation of consumer surplus and welfare).

Test your understanding of this unit by answering the following questions

- Using a diagram to illustrate your answer, explain how a firm maximizes profit in third-degree price discrimination.
- Explain the conditions necessary for price discrimination to occur.
- Explain how some consumers can benefit from price discrimination.

Subject vocabulary

factors of production the inputs into the production process (land/labour/capital/entrepreneurship)

welfare gain an increase in consumer or producer surplus

consumer surplus the difference between the price a consumer is willing and able to pay and the price the consumer actually pays

corporate social responsibility a concept whereby companies when making decisions consider the impact of their actions on society and the environment

Learning Objective

- Describe alternative goals of firms, including revenue maximization, growth maximization, satisficing, and **corporate social responsibility**.

Explain the difference in market outcomes if a firm pursues revenue maximization rather than profit maximization

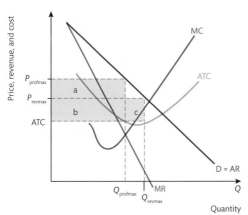

Figure 39.1

The theory of the firm rests upon the **assumption** that firms aim to maximize profit. In reality firms have many competing objectives, some of which conflict with the goal of profit maximization. One measure of how well a firm is performing is the amount of **producer revenue** made. Some managers might receive bonus payments if sales increase so they have an **incentive** to maximize revenue and not profit. (See pages 74–76 for a detailed explanation of marginal revenue, marginal cost, and profit maximization.)

Glossary

assumption(s) something thought/believed to be true but without proof

Subject vocabulary

producer revenue the income a firm receives from consumers in exchange for goods (revenue = price × quantity sold)

total revenue price × quantity sold

Synonyms

incentive.... encouragement/motivation

Revenue maximization – a step-by-step guide (see Figure 39.1)

Trouble shooter

Marginal revenue is the addition to **total revenue** from producing and selling the next unit.

Therefore when marginal revenue is positive (up to Q_{revmax}) producing and selling the next unit will add to total revenue.

Beyond Q_{revmax} marginal revenue is negative therefore producing and selling output will reduce total revenue.

In order to maximize revenue the firm sets output where marginal revenue equals zero, Q_{revmax} on Figure 39.1, and charge P_{revmax}. At this point total revenue is at its highest.

monopolist a firm that dominates an industry

abnormal/supernormal profit occurs when economic profit is greater than zero, i.e., when total revenue is greater than total cost (explicit and implicit costs)

pricing strategy a plan made and used by a firm with the aim of increasing revenue and profits through the setting of price

quantity demanded the amount of a good consumers are willing and able to buy at a given price over a given period of time

market share the proportion of the market supply of a good or service that is controlled by a firm

price elasticity of demand (PED) a measure of how quantity demanded responds to a change in price in percentage terms

price inelastic the percentage change in quantity demanded/supplied < the percentage change in price

sole trader a type of business that is owned and controlled by one person

public limited companies a form of business organization in which shares are offered for sale to the general public. Shareholders own the business and receive a share of the profits. Liability is limited to the amount paid for the shares.

shareholders individuals or institutions that own at least one share in a company. They are the owners of the company and are therefore entitled to a share of the profits.

divorce of ownership from control a situation that occurs in large companies where the owners, who are the shareholders, do not make the business decisions

In order to maximize profit the **monopolist** sets output at $Q_{profmax}$ where marginal revenue equals marginal cost. This is below revenue maximizing level of output. Profit maximizing price is greater than revenue-maximizing price. The profit-maximizing firm produces less and charges more than if its objective is to maximize revenue. When profit maximizing the firm earns **abnormal profit** of $(P_{profmax} - ATC) \times Q_{profmax}$ which is represented by the areas a + b. By reducing price and increasing quantity sold to maximize revenue, the monopolist earns abnormal profit of $(P_{revmax} - ATC) - Q_{revmax}$ which is represented by area b + c. $(P_{revmax} - ATC) \times Q_{revmax} < (P_{profmax} - ATC) \times Q_{profmax}$. The firm gains area c of profit but **forgoes** the larger area and therefore profit falls.

Model sentence: When marginal revenue is positive producing and selling the marginal unit of output will add to total revenue. However, if the marginal cost of the additional output is greater than the marginal revenue then producing the marginal unit will lead to a fall in profit.

Why might a firm try to maximize growth rather than profit?

Growth is measured in a number of ways: quantity of goods sold, total producer revenue and size of market share. It is quite possible for a firm to follow a **pricing strategy** that in the short run leads to a fall in profit but in the long run might see profit rise. For example, a firm reduces price in order to increase **quantity demanded** and to get a foothold in the market and increase **market share**. Once the brand is established and **price elasticity of demand** is relatively more **price inelastic** the firm puts up price increasing both producer revenue and profit.

What is satisficing?

Satisficing is a combination of two words: satisfy and suffice. A **sole trader**, such as a **plumber** or a restaurant owner, not only owns the business but works in it and controls the decision making. **Public limited companies** are owned by **shareholders**. Shareholders do not work in the business, they do not control decision making. They simply take a share of the profits. The control of the business is separated from ownership. This is called the **divorce of ownership from control**. It is likely that shareholders want to maximize profit because this will benefit them, but the many employees may not share this aim. Sales managers, for example, may be paid bonus payments if they hit a sales target, therefore they will benefit if they maximize sales revenue even if an increase in output and sales reduces profit. Middle and senior management are often most interested in developing their careers and may well **pursue** policies that do not increase profit. These people know that they have to keep an eye on profit and earn enough to keep the shareholders happy but as long as this occurs they can keep their jobs while at the same time pursuing their own interests. Doing this is called satisficing: doing just enough to satisfy all stakeholders including the owners.

Why do large firms consider their responsibility to society when making decisions?

Many large firms are concerned about their brand image. If a firm treats its workers badly or harms the environment, for example, it will gain a bad reputation and damage the image of the brand which will have a negative impact on sales and profit in the long run. Also by being seen to do good works, such as funding community projects, donating large sums to charities, and using environmentally friendly methods of production the firm can gain a good reputation and strengthen the brand image. It is true that decision makers in the firm may want to do such things because of ethical considerations and that doing so will reduce profits in the short run. However, by strengthening the brand producer revenue and profit may well increase in the long run and it is more likely that this is the main consideration when making such decisions.

Test your understanding of this unit by answering the following question

- Discuss alternatives to profit maximization.

2.1 Economic activity – The level of overall economic activity

Learning Outcomes

- Describe, using a diagram, the circular flow of income between households and firms in a closed economy with no government.

- Identify the four factors of production and their respective payments (rent, wages, interest, and profit) and explain that these constitute the income flow in the model.

- Outline that the income flow is numerically equivalent to the expenditure flow and the value of output flow.

- Describe, using a diagram, the circular flow of income in an open economy with government and financial markets, referring to leakages/withdrawals (savings, taxes, and import expenditure), and injections (investment, government expenditure, and export revenue).

- Explain how the size of the circular flow will change depending on the relative size of injections and leakages.

Describe the circular flow of income model for a closed economy

A country has a closed economy when it does not trade with other countries.

The model is a simplified representation of how **income** moves through the economy. There are two sectors in this model: households and firms. Government, banks, and international trade are not included at this stage.

Model sentence: Households own all the factors of production. Firms hire the factors from households in order to produce goods and services. Using the payments for the factors of production, households buy the goods and services from the firms.

This information is set out in Figure 40.1, a simple model of the circular flow of income in a closed economy.

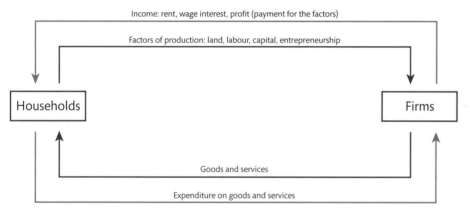

Figure 40.1

The flow of income – a step-by-step guide

Trouble shooter

1. Households own all the factors. The firms hire them from households in order to produce goods.

2. Payments for the factors flow from firms to the households. The goods and services are sold to the households.

3. The households buy the goods and services from the firms using the income received for the use of the factors.

The model shows **resources** flowing from households to firms and goods and services flowing from firms, to households. These are called real flows. In order to **facilitate** the exchange of resources for goods and services a society needs money. Money flows from the firms to the households as payment for the use of the factors of production and money flows from the households to the firms as payment for the goods and services.

Subject vocabulary

land this factor includes not only the physical land, which is usually a fixed resource, but also the natural resources obtained from the land and sea, some of which are renewable, such as timber

labour the people available to work with capital and land in order to produce output

capital manufactured goods that are used in the production of other goods

entrepreneurship the process of bringing together factors of production in order to produce goods or services with the aim of making a profit

public good a good that is non-excludable and non-rival. Once provided it is not possible to stop people benefitting from the consumption of it and therefore people free ride - they do not pay. The good will not be supplied left to the free market because no firm would be able to make a profit. Also, consumption of the good by one person does not diminish the amount available for others to consume.

merit good a good/service that the government believes will be under consumed left to the free market. Consumption of a merit good may generate positive externalities, therefore the social benefit of consumption is greater than the private benefit. Individuals do not take into account the positive externalities when deciding the amount to consume, therefore the good is underprovided and under consumed.

tax revenue the income the government receives through the levying and collection of taxes

interest the price paid for the use of borrowed money/ the money earned from bank deposits

interest rate the percentage amount charged by a lender for money borrowed

Glossary

national defence the systems that a country uses to defend itself against attack

Synonyms

proportion .... amount

Identify the four factors of production and their respective payments

The four factors of production are **land**, **labour**, **capital**, and **entrepreneurship**. Rent is the payment made for the use of land and includes payment for the use of the natural resources taken from the land. Wage is the payment for the use of labour. Interest is the payment for the use of capital and profit is the reward for enterprise and risk taking. These are the four components of income: rent, wage, interest, and profit.

Model sentence: There are four components of income paid by firms to households. Rent paid for the use of land, wage for labour, interest for capital, and profit for enterprise.

The flow of income in the model – a step-by-step guide (see Figure 40.1)

Trouble shooter

Money complements real flows.

Money acts as a means of exchange: Factors are exchanged for money and goods are exchanged for money.

This money earned by the factors and paid by the firms is collectively called income.

Income flows from firms to household as payments made for the use of the factors of production.

The income earned by households flows back to firms as payment for the goods produced using the factors.

Incomes flow between firms and households in this way continuously.

Outline that the income flow is numerically equivalent to the expenditure flow and the value of output flow

In this simple model no income leaks out of the circular flow. Therefore the income paid by firms to households for use of the factors is equal to the amount of income spent by households in exchange for the goods and services the firms produce. Therefore the monetary value of the goods and services flowing from firms to households is equal to the flow of households' expenditure on them.

Model sentence: The income earned by the factors of production = the expenditure on the goods and services = the value of the goods and services.

Describe, using a diagram, the circular flow of income in an open economy

A country has an open economy when it trades with other countries. Elements need to be added to the circular flow in order to make it more representative of real economies.

Households do not spend all income earned on goods produced domestically. Some income is spent on imports and goes to firms abroad. Some income is taxed and goes to the government. Some income can be saved and this goes to banks and other financial institutions such as pension providers.

These income flows are called leakages or withdrawals from the circular flow and are shown in Figure 40.2 as imports, savings, and taxes.

The government taxes income and spends it on, for example, **public goods** such as **national defence** and **merit goods** such as education and health. The expenditure of government **tax revenue** is an injection into the circular flow and it goes to firms in exchange for the goods and services and in turn the money goes to households as income paid for the use of the factors needed to make them.

Firms borrow money from banks in order to buy **capital** goods. This investment is funded by borrowed money. Some households save a **proportion** of income at banks for which the banks pay **interest**. The banks then lend the money to firms for which the firms pay interest. The **interest rate** on borrowing is greater than the rate for savings. In this way banks make a profit. Investment, which is the addition to capital stock, is an injection into the circular flow. The money goes to firms who produce capital goods and services. In turn the money goes to the households as income.

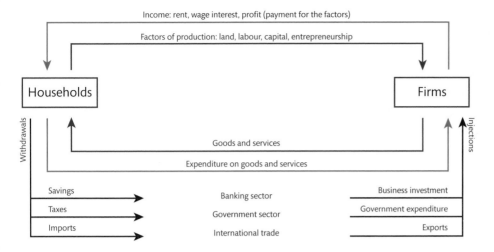

Figure 40.2

Many **domestic firms** sell their goods and services abroad, exporting goods to foreign buyers all over the world. Consumers in the rest of the world buy the goods and the money flows to the domestic firms. It is an injection into the circular flow. It is a flow of money coming from abroad to the domestic firms and in turn the money flows to households as payment for the factors.

Model sentence: Tax on income leaks out of the circular flow so that government expenditure can be injected into the circular flow, income saved leaks out so that investment can be injected in and income spent on imports leaks out while income spent on exports is injected in.

Explain how the size of the circular flow will change

The leakages and injections into the circular flow are not always equal. Often **government expenditure**, an injection, exceeds tax revenue, a leakage. When this happens the government is running a **budget deficit**. The government must borrow the difference from the financial markets. The **accumulation** of budget deficits is called the **national debt**: the total amount the government owes. Households save a certain proportion of their income but firms might be borrowing less for investment than the amount saved, therefore in this case the leakage exceeds the injection. The amount of income spent on imports might be greater than the income spent by foreigners on **exports**. This leads to a **current account deficit**: a situation where expenditure on imports > expenditure on exports. More money is flowing out of the circular flow than is flowing in with respect to international trade. When leakages > injections, the amount of income flowing round the circular flow falls and when injections > leakages, the amount increases.

The government can act to correct an imbalance between leakages and injections. Reducing the interest rate on loans for investment will increase investment. However, in most countries it is the central bank that controls the interest rate not the government.

Cuts in government expenditure will reduce the budget deficit and the government's borrowing requirements. Government can increase tax rates so that tax revenue equals government expenditure. Subsidies given to exporting industries will increase the demand for and expenditure on exports thereby reducing the current account deficit.

Test your understanding of this unit by answering the following questions

- State the four factors of production along with their respective payments.
- Describe, using a diagram, how factors and money move between firms and households in the circular flow of income model for a closed economy.
- Explain, using a diagram, why income = expenditure = value of goods and services.
- Describe, using a diagram, the circular flow of income in an open economy with leakages and injections.

Learning Outcomes

- Distinguish between gross domestic product (GDP) and gross national product (GNP)/**gross national income (GNI)** as measures of economic activity.

- Distinguish between the nominal value of GDP and GNP/GNI and the real value of GDP and GNP/GNI.

- Distinguish between total GDP and GNP/GNI and per capita GDP and GNP/GNI.

- Examine the output method, the income method, and the expenditure method when measuring national income.

- Evaluate the use of national income statistics, including their use for making comparisons over time, their use for making comparisons between countries, and their use for making conclusions about standards of living.

- Explain the meaning and significance of 'green GDP', a measure of GDP that accounts for environmental destruction.

How is gross domestic product (GDP) measured?

There are three ways GDP is calculated:

The output method

This is the sum of the **monetary value** added to the **inputs** in the production process by all the firms in the economy in a given year. The costs of the inputs or **resources** used in the production process are subtracted from the sales **revenue** (price × quantity sold) in order to calculate the monetary value added by the firm. This means that the inputs are not double counted.

The income method

This is a measure of the sum of all income earned by households in a given year. It is the sum of all payments made by firms to households for the use of the **factors of production**. Total income is the sum of rent, wages, interest, and profit.

The expenditure method

This is a measure of the monetary value of total spending on goods and services in a given year.

Model sentence: Total expenditure is the sum of household expenditure on domestically produced goods (C), expenditure by firms on capital goods which is investment (I), expenditure by government (G), and expenditure on exports by foreigners minus expenditure on imports (X–M).

As explained earlier; the income earned by the factors of production = the expenditure on the goods and services = the value of the goods and services. Although the monetary value of a country's output can be measured in these three ways the value will be the same in each case.

The following are acceptable definitions of **gross domestic product**. GDP is the monetary value at **market price** of all **final goods** and services produced in a country in a given year. It can also be defined as the sum of all expenditure in a country in a given year. This can be expressed algebraically as GDP = C + I + G + (X–M).

Distinguish between gross domestic product (GDP) and gross national product (GNP)/gross national income (GNI)

GDP is a measure of the value of all final goods and services produced in a country in a given year. No account is taken of the ownership of the factors of production. As long as the goods and services are produced in the country the value of them is included in GDP. However, there are many firms producing output in a country that are owned by foreigners. For example, the Australian bank Macquarie operates in the UK. The value of its output is included in the GDP of the UK but is not included in Australia's GDP. The profits earned by the bank are included in the UK's GDP but not in Australia's GDP.

GNP/GNI includes the income generated by a country's factors wherever in the world the country's factors are located. So the profit earned by Macquarie in the UK is included in Australia's GNP/GNI. The income earned on overseas **assets** is called property income from abroad.

GNP/GNI is a measure of income that is earned based on the ownership of the factors. In order to calculate GNP income paid to foreign factors (such as profit made by the foreign firms) is subtracted from GDP. Then the income earned by domestically owned factors operating in foreign countries is added. The difference between them is called net property income from abroad. Therefore GNP/GNI = GDP + net property income from abroad.

Many developing countries try to encourage **foreign direct investment** to raise GDP. In such a country where many foreign firms own **productive capacity** its GDP is greater than GNP. Income earned is included in the GDP but often does not stay in the country. Some of the income flows back abroad. For example, profits flow out of the country to the firms' country of origin and foreign workers often send wages back home. This again is a loss of income. Because the income is not spent in the country it does not contribute to economic growth.

What is net national product?

Capital does not last forever. The capital stock of a country is continuously losing its value and must at some point be replaced. This occurs because of 'wear and tear': damage caused to the capital through use. The loss in value of the capital stock is called depreciation and the expenditure to replace it is called capital consumption. This capital is replaced. This **investment** does not add to the productive capacity of the country although it is included in GNP. So growth of GNP year on year is at least in part because firms have been replacing capital therefore GNP is not an accurate measure of actual increases in productive capacity. To get a more accurate indicator of the economy's current performance and its potential performance the expenditure on replacement capital, which is called capital consumption, is not included in the calculation of net national product. NNP = GNP – capital consumption. Another way of stating it is NNP = GNP – depreciation.

Distinguish between nominal GDP and real GDP

Calculation of GDP is achieved through the addition of the stated price of all final goods produced in a country in a given year. GDP which measures the value of output in current prices is called **nominal GDP**. Increases in GDP year on year can come about partly because prices increase. In other words increases in GDP can occur because of **inflation** rather than an increase in economic performance. Nominal GDP will overstate any increase in the value of output.

To obtain an accurate indicator of the actual value of the output from one time period to another the effects of inflation must be taken into account. Nominal GDP is adjusted to take into account the effects of inflation on the value of output in order to value output at constant prices. **Real GDP** = nominal GDP adjusted for inflation.

Model sentence: The word real placed in front of a variable, such as GDP and interest rate, means that the effect of inflation on its true value has been taken into account thereby allowing a valid comparison of the variable over time.

What is GDP per capita (per head)?

GDP per capita is GDP divided by the population of the country. This is a useful statistic because it is a more realistic indicator of economic performance and the **standard of living** of people living in the country. Total income earned in 2012 in Brazil was $2,500,000 million. The same income was earned in the UK. On these figures alone it is impossible to make a judgement concerning standards of living. The two countries may have generated the same total income but the population of Brazil is greater than the UK's. Income per capita in Brazil in 2012 was $12,000 whereas in the UK it was $39,000.

Evaluate the use of national income statistics

What is the purpose of the statistics?

One of the key macroeconomic objectives of a government is economic growth. GDP is an indicator of growth. The government needs the statistics year on year to assess the effectiveness of their economic policies. If GDP rises it is evidence of growth. If GDP falls or 'flat lines' the government may decide to change economic policy. Also, in a democracy, the people use information on GDP when considering voting intentions. This is because GDP is considered to be an indicator of the standard of living. Investment by firms in productive capacity is

hidden economy part of the economy where illegal and untaxed trade occurs

productivity the quantity of output per unit of input

output the quantity of goods produced by a firm, industry or economy

external cost occurs when the production or consumption of a good creates a cost that must be paid by third parties

negative externalities occur when the production or consumption of a good creates costs that must be paid by third parties. The existence of negative externalities means that social cost is greater than private cost.

third parties people who are not directly involved in a transaction but are nevertheless affected by the transaction. People who are external to the market.

green GDP green GDP equals GDP minus the negative externalities of production

nominal value the value expressed in monetary terms, not adjusted for inflation

real value the nominal or numerical value adjusted to take into account the effect of inflation

always a risk. GDP is an indicator of future levels of demand. If economists predict growth in GDP it increases business confidence and firms are more likely to invest. There are, however, matters that should be taken into account when drawing conclusions based upon GDP statistics.

Income distribution

GDP per capita is a better indicator than GDP of standards of living in a country. However, this statistic does not take into account the distribution of income. Income in all countries is distributed unequally. In many countries there is a small minority that earns the majority of the total income. Therefore average income per head is not a reliable indicator of the overall well-being of the population.

Accuracy

The task of gathering the information needed to calculate GDP is complex. To obtain highly accurate figures on the value of all final goods produced in a year is difficult. In advanced countries the statistics are likely to be more accurate because the systems used to work out GDP and GNP are well established and have been **refined** over many years. Nevertheless, the accuracy of national statistics cannot be taken for granted.

The hidden economy

Informal markets or black markets exist in all countries. Some economic transactions are not recorded. Jobs are done for 'cash in hand'. An electrician accepts cash for rewiring a house and does not declare his earning to the tax officials in order to avoid paying tax. Some firms pay workers cash in hand in order to avoid taxes associated with the employment of workers. The higher the taxes the greater the incentive to avoid paying them. Illegal transactions are not recorded. Examples include the black market for tobacco and other drugs. In less developed countries agricultural goods produced go unrecorded as the output is consumed by those who grow it. All the above occurs in the '**hidden economy**'. Black markets are usually bigger in developing countries. Governments have less control over markets therefore the informal sector accounts for a relatively higher proportion of GDP than in developed countries.

The GDP of a country is **understated** and the extent to which it is depends in part on the size of the hidden economy. However, the value of the goods and services produced and consumed in the hidden economy varies considerably between countries making comparisons of national statistics across countries less valid.

Voluntary work for charities and other organizations is not recorded and yet such activity has a major impact on the well-being of many in society. Housework and bringing up children are essential activities for a successful economy, but are not included in the statistics.

Negative externalities

Increases in GDP are a reflection of increasing **productivity** and output. When more firms produce more **output** there are increases in the **external costs** associated with production such as noise and air pollution and traffic congestion. Such **negative externalities** have a damaging effect on **third parties**. For example, health problems are caused by the poor quality of the air in urban and industrial areas and climate change could be accelerated by rapid increases in economic activity. The relatively unregulated building of factories can have a negative impact on the landscape. Economic activity impacts on the quality of life for many living now and for future generations. These negative consequences should be taken into account when examining the impact of increasing GDP on the standard of living and welfare of the population.

Explain the meaning and significance of 'green GDP'

Negative externalities are created in production. The calculation of **green GDP** takes into account the external costs such as environmental **degradation** noise, air, and water pollution, the costs of clearing up and dealing with industrial waste, and assessing the costs of climate change.

Green GDP = Actual GDP – the external costs of production

The task of evaluating the external costs is a huge one. The extent of environmental damage is difficult to assess and of course any value placed on external costs associated with climate change is controversial and highly debatable.

Test your understanding of this unit by answering the following questions

- Distinguish between GDP and GNP.
- Distinguish between the **nominal value** of GDP and the **real value** of GDP.
- Describe the output, the income, and the expenditure methods of measuring national income.
- Discuss the usefulness of GDP as a measure of economic well-being.

Learning Outcomes

- Calculate **nominal GDP** from sets of **national income** data, using the expenditure method (HL).
- Calculate GNP/GNI from data (HL).
- Calculate real GDP, using a price deflator (HL).

Calculate nominal GDP from national income data using the expenditure method (HL)

Total expenditure is the sum of household spending on domestically produced goods (C), spending by firms on capital goods and services (I), spending by government (G), and spending on exports by foreigners minus spending on imports (X–M).

Data in Table 42.1 shows expenditure in all the categories stated above at current prices. Nominal GDP = C + I + G + (X–M) (US bureau of economic analysis).

Table 42.1 shows the breakdown of expenditure in the US in 2009.

Expenditure	$ Billion
Household expenditure on the consumption of domestically produced goods/services (C)	10,001
Expenditure by firms on domestically produced capital goods/services (I)	1590
Government expenditure (G)	2914
Expenditure on exported goods/services minus expenditure on imported goods/services (X–M)	−386
Gross domestic product: C + I + G + (X–M)	14,119

Source: US bureau of economic analysis

Table 42.1

The sum of all expenditure, C + I + G + (X–M), is $14,119 billion. This is a relatively easy calculation to make. You might be asked in paper 3 to calculate the contribution of each category to total GDP.

Calculation of the contribution of government expenditure (HL) – a step-by-step guide

> **Trouble shooter**
>
> The contribution of government expenditure as a percentage of GDP =
> $$\frac{\text{Government expenditure}}{\text{GDP}} \times 100$$
>
> $\frac{2914}{14,119} \times 100 = 0.2064 \times 100 = 20.64\%$
>
> Government expenditure accounted for 20.64% of GDP.

Calculate nominal GDP from national income data using the income method (HL)

The income method of calculating GDP is done by adding the payments made by firms to households for the use of the **factors of production**. In paper 3 you may be shown a table listing the income earned. Total income is the sum of wages, rents, interest, and profit. If asked to calculate the contribution of one category of income as a percentage of GDP calculate it by following, in principle, the example shown in the trouble shooter above.

Calculate real GDP, using a price deflator (HL)

Nominal GDP is the value of **final goods** produced in a given year at current prices. However, prices can increase each year. Therefore, increases in nominal GDP are caused, in part at least, by **inflation** (inflation will be covered in detail later). Governments and economists want to know the proportion of any increase in GDP that is not caused by inflation. Increases in **real output** might be the result of increases in **productivity**, international competitiveness, **foreign direct investment**, and more firms setting up in business in the country. In order to calculate real GDP over a given period of time the effects of inflation must be taken into account.

Subject vocabulary

nominal GDP gross domestic product that has not been adjusted to take into account the effect of inflation

national income the sum of all income earned in a country in a given period of time

factors of production the inputs into the production process (land, labour, capital and entrepreneurship)

final goods a finished good that does not require further processing

inflation an increase in the general level of prices of goods/services in an economy over a given time period, usually a year

real output the quantity of goods and services produced in a given time period

productivity the quantity of output per unit of input

foreign direct investment cross-border investment, usually by firms, that involves the acquisition of assets in a foreign country. FDI can be the purchase of a minimum of 10% of the shares of a foreign company but also includes the creation of productive capacity.

To calculate real GDP economists use a deflator to take into account the effect of inflation. The index deflates or reduces nominal GDP so that the stated GDP represents the value of actual output.

The formula used to calculate real GDP is: real GDP = nominal GDP/GDP deflator × 100

Calculate real GDP from the data using a deflator (HL) – a step-by-step guide

Trouble shooter

Country X's nominal GDP in 2011 was $980 billion.

Country X's nominal GDP in 2013 was $1,300 billion.

The rate of inflation between 2011 and 2013 was 11%.

GDP deflator = base year index 100 + rate of inflation = 100 + 11 = 111.

Nominal GDP in 2013 = $1300 billion and the GDP Deflator = 111.

Real GDP = nominal GDP/GDP deflator × 100.

Real GDP = $1300 /111 × 100 = 11.7117 × 100 = $1171.17 billion.

Real GDP has increased by $191.17 billion ($1171.17 – $980).

Calculate the rate of real economic growth (HL)

Real economic growth is an increase in real GDP over a given time period. **Negative economic growth** is a fall in real GDP over a given time period. It is measured as a percentage change.

A change in economic growth is calculated using the formula:

Percentage change in real GDP = $\dfrac{\text{the new real GDP – the original GDP}}{\text{the original GDP}} \times 100$

Carrying on with the example above between 2011 and 2013 there has been an increase in real GDP of $1171.17 billion – $980 billion = $191.17 billion.

Percentage change in real GDP = $\dfrac{\$1171.17 \text{ billion} – \$980 \text{ billion}}{\$980 \text{ billion}} \times 100 = \dfrac{\$191.17}{\$980} \times 100 = 0.1951 \times 100 = 19.51\%$

The rate of economic growth between 2011 and 2013 was 19.51%.

In HL paper 3 you might be tested on how to calculate real GDP, the GDP deflator and economic growth. Below are examples of types of questions you could be asked along with the answers.

1. Nominal GDP of a country was $12,100 billion in 2012. This increased to $13,200 billion in 2013. The rate of Inflation in 2013 was 5%.

Calculate real GDP for 2013 (HL) – a step-by-step guide

Trouble shooter

2012 is the base year and the index is 100.

Inflation rate in 2013 was 5%.

The index number for year 2, 2013 is 100 + 5 = 105.

GDP deflator = 105.

Nominal GDP in 2013 = $13,200 billion.

Real GDP = $\dfrac{\text{nominal GDP}}{\text{GDP deflator}} \times 100$

Real GDP = $\dfrac{\$13,200}{105} \times 100$ simplify by dividing 100 by 105.

Real GDP = $13,200 × 0.9524 = $12,571.43 billion.

The GDP deflator can be calculated using the formula: GDP deflator = $\dfrac{\text{nominal GDP}}{\text{real GDP}} \times 100$

To work out the deflator using this formula nominal and real GDP must be known.

2. Nominal GDP of a country in 2013 was $840 billion and the real GDP in 2013 was $720 billion.

Calculate the GDP deflator and inflation rate for 2013 (HL) – a step-by-step guide

Trouble shooter

Nominal GDP = $840.

Real GDP = $720.

GDP deflator = $\dfrac{\text{nominal GDP}}{\text{real GDP}} \times 100$

GDP deflator = $\dfrac{840}{720} \times 100$ simplify by dividing 840 by 720.

GDP deflator = $1.166 \times 100 = 116.67$.

Inflation rate = GDP deflator – base year index = $116.67 - 100 = 16.67$.

The rate of inflation in 2013 was 16.67%.

3. Real GDP of a country in 2012 was $960 billion. It increased in 2013 to $1000 billion.

Calculate the rate of economic growth in 2013 (HL) – a step-by-step guide

Trouble shooter

Economic growth is an increase in real GDP from one year to the next. It is the percentage change in real GDP from one year to the next.

A change in economic growth is calculated using the formula:

Percentage change in real GDP = $\dfrac{\text{the new real GDP – the original real GDP}}{\text{the original real GDP}} \times 100$

Percentage change in real GDP = $\dfrac{1000 - 960}{960} \times 100$ simplify by subtracting 960 from 1000.

Percentage change in real GDP = $\dfrac{40}{960} \times 100$ simplify by dividing 40 by 960.

Percentage change in real GDP = 0.04166×100.

Percentage change in real GDP = 4.167%.

The rate of economic growth in 2013 was 4.167%.

Test your understanding of this unit by answering the following questions

- Nominal GDP = $ in year 1 was $640 billion. In year 2 the rate of inflation was 6% and the nominal GDP was $700 billion. Calculate real GDP for year 2.
- Nominal GDP in 2013 was $740 billion and the real GDP in the same year was $780. Calculate the GDP deflator and the rate of inflation for 2013.
- Real GDP in a country in 2012 was $860 billion. It increased in 2013 to $940 billion. Calculate economic growth in percentage terms for 2013.

Learning Outcomes

- Explain, using a business cycle diagram, that economies typically tend to go through a cyclical pattern characterized by the phases of the business cycle.

- Explain the long-term growth trend in the business cycle diagram as the potential output of the economy.

- Distinguish between a decrease in GDP and a decrease in GDP growth.

Subject vocabulary

business cycle the fluctuations in economic activity over time. There are four stages of the business cycle: (1) recession, when economic activity slows down; (2) trough, when the recession is at its deepest; (3) recovery, when the economy begins to grow; and (4) peak/boom, when economic activity is high.

potential output the maximum output an economy can produce when all resources are efficiently employed

factors of production the inputs into the production process (land, labour, capital and entrepreneurship)

economic growth an increase in real GDP

recession two consecutive quarters of negative economic growth

inflation an increase in the general level of prices of goods/services in an economy over a given time period, usually a year

Glossary

fluctuation(s) frequent change(s) especially from a high to a low level and back again

slope the angle/gradient of the curve

made redundant being told by your employer that there is no longer a job for you

Synonyms

diminishing......becoming smaller

Using a business cycle diagram, explain that economic growth is not constant but cyclical

The **business cycle** (also called the economic cycle or the trade cycle) shows increases and falls in real GDP over a given period of time. Over time the economy expands and contracts. In a 50-year period, for example, real GDP increases. The capacity of the economy to produce goods and services increases. Over time the level of **potential output** increases. Potential output is the level of output that can be achieved when all the **factors of production** are employed. This is shown by the long-term growth trend in Figure 43.1. However, during this period of time there have been **fluctuations** in the rate at which the economy has grown. The change in real GDP over time in the short-term fluctuates, shown by the line that rises and falls above and below the long-term trend line. The fluctuating line shows changes in actual output in the short-term.

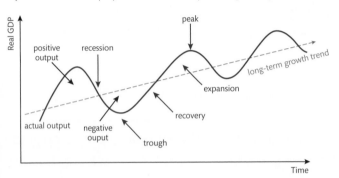

Figure 43.1

Initially in Figure 43.1 the rate at which the economy is growing is increasing as illustrated when the actual output line **slopes** upwards. Eventually the rate at which the economy grows begins to decrease. The economy is still growing but at a **diminishing** rate. For example, in a particular year the economy grows by 3%. The following year it grows by 2% and the year after by 1%. **Economic growth** is positive and increasing but it is increasing at a decreasing rate. It rises and then reaches a peak. As time moves on economic growth becomes negative; the economy contracts and real GDP falls. Therefore the actual output line slopes downwards. If the rate of economic growth is negative over two consecutive quarters of the year (6 months) it is called a **recession**. When real GDP has reached its lowest point it is called a recessionary trough. During this period of recession real output is falling. Firms are reducing output in response to falling levels of consumption and a lack of confidence in future levels of demand. Firms will go out of business, factories will close, and workers will be **made redundant**. Unemployment of labour and other factors rise.

When consumption rises and business confidence returns, firms respond by employing more factors of production in order to increase output. The economy, although at a low point, begins to grow. Economic growth is positive and the actual output line slopes upwards again. The economy is now in the recovery phase. As consumption and business confidence continues to grow firms employ more and more factors to boost output and real GDP begins to rise at an increasing rate. Unemployment of the factors of production begins to fall. The economy is expanding and does so until it reaches the peak. At this point demand for goods and services is very high and firms may not be able to increase supply enough to keep up with the very high levels of demand. This can lead to **inflation**. The government might introduce policies to reduce excess demand and thereby lower inflationary pressures (these policies are discussed in detail on pages 152–54). Such policies may cause the economy to move into a period of negative economic growth. The actual output line slopes downwards at this point as the economy potentially enters a recessionary phase of the business cycle.

One complete business cycle measured from one recession to the next can last a relatively long time. In 1990 the UK moved into recession. The economy entered the recovery phase in 1993 starting a long period of positive economic growth until the recession of 2008. This business cycle was 15 years long.

Distinguish between potential output and actual output

The long-term trend line shows a **uniform** increase in real output over time. It shows the potential output of an economy. The actual output line shows the fluctuations above and below the long-term potential level of output that occurs in the short-term over time. At times the economy is performing below its potential. Real GDP is less than the **potential GDP**. This is called a **negative output gap**. It is characterized by relatively high levels of unemployment of the factors of production and relatively low rates of inflation. When real GDP is above the long-term potential there is a **positive output gap**. Total demand in the economy exceeds potential output. This is characterized by low levels of unemployment and increasing rates of inflation as the economy 'overheats' as short-term output exceeds the capacity of the economy to supply goods and services. This **trade-off** between levels of employment and inflation is discussed in detail on pages 155–58.

Model sentence: When actual output is greater than potential output there is a positive output gap and the economy has no or little spare capacity. When actual output is less than potential output there is a negative output gap and the economy has at least some spare capacity.

Distinguish between a decrease in GDP and a decrease in GDP growth

Model sentence: A decrease in GDP growth occurs when the rate of economic growth is positive and increasing but at a diminishing rate. A decrease in GDP occurs when the rate of economic growth is negative.

Test your understanding of this unit by answering the following question

- Using a business cycle diagram, explain the terms positive output gap and negative output gap.

2.2 Aggregate demand and aggregate supply

Learning Outcomes

- Distinguish between the microeconomic concept of demand for a product and the macroeconomic concept of aggregate demand.

- Construct an aggregate demand curve.

- Explain why the AD curve has a negative slope.

- Describe consumption, investment, government spending, and net exports as the components of aggregate demand.

Distinguish between the concept of demand and the concept of aggregate demand

In microeconomics demand is a measure of the quantity of goods and services an individual consumer or all the consumers in a particular market are willing and able to buy at a range of prices. Aggregate demand (AD) is the sum of all demand for goods and services in a country at a given **price level** during a given time period. In other words AD is the sum of all expenditure in a country at a given price level usually measured over a period of one year. Total expenditure, which is the sum of all demand in a country (AD), is equal to GDP.

In microeconomics the demand curve diagram shows the price of a good on the y axis and quantity of that good on the × axis shows. The aggregate demand diagram shows the average price level on the y axis and the total quantity of all goods and services on the × axis. The total demand is national output. National output (real GDP) = national expenditure = national income.

Describe the components of aggregate demand

AD is the total expenditure on goods and services. Expenditure comes from four sources.

Consumption (C) by households of domestically produced goods and services. Consumer goods or **final goods** can be durables meaning the goods last a relatively long time, such as electronic goods or non-durables such as food and writing paper, which are consumed relatively quickly and are purchased again in the short term.

Investment (I) by firms on domestically produced **capital** goods and services. Investment is the addition to capital stock. Firms have to invest in new capital when current capital wears out. This is called replacement investment. The firm must buy new capital to continue to supply output at current levels. Firms usually replace old capital with more technologically advanced capital thereby potentially increasing **productivity**. A firm also buys capital in order to increase output in response to an increase in demand or when demand is expected to rise. Therefore as AD rises or if firms expect AD to increase in the future firms in the country increase investment. This is called induced investment.

Government expenditure (G) on goods and services. A recession is characterized by falling incomes and expenditure. Therefore **direct tax** and indirect tax revenues fall. Unless the government borrows from the financial markets government expenditure will fall. A booming economy is characterized by rising incomes and expenditure therefore **tax revenues** increase and the government is able to increase expenditure. Alternatively a government might decide to pay back some of the **national debt** rather than increase expenditure.

Net exports (X–M) is expenditure on exported goods and services minus expenditure on imported goods and services. When expenditure by foreigners on domestically produced goods and services rises, *ceteris paribus*, net exports will rise. Whereas when expenditure rises on imported goods net exports fall.

Model sentence: AD = C + I + G + (X–M)

Why does the aggregate demand curve have a negative slope?

The price level is the average price level of all the goods and services in a country. A positive **inflation rate**

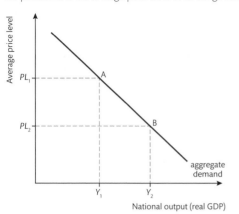

Figure 44.1

causes the average price level to increase. Inflation reduces the **purchasing power** of **nominal income** therefore consumers can buy fewer goods. A negative inflation rate, which is called deflation, causes the average price level to fall. Purchasing power increases and consumers can buy more goods. Therefore as the price level rises, *ceteris paribus*, the total demand for goods and services in the country falls. When the price level falls total demand for goods and services in a country increases. The AD curve **slopes** downwards because there is a negative or inverse relationship between the price level and **real GDP**. In Figure 44.1 as the price level falls from PL_1 to PL_2 national output increases from Y_1 to Y_2.

Model sentence: A change in the price level leads to a change in the purchasing power of consumer income causing a change in AD and a movement along the AD curve.

Test your understanding of this unit by answering the following questions

- What is aggregate demand?
- Explain the cause of a movement along the aggregate demand curve.
- Distinguish between durable and non-durable goods.
- Distinguish between replacement investment and induced investment.
- Explain the term 'net exports'.

Subject vocabulary

inflation rate the rate at which a weighted average price of a basket of goods and services is rising measured in percentage terms

purchasing power a measure of how many goods and services a given amount of money can buy

nominal income the numerical value of income which has not been adjusted to take into account the effect inflation has on the purchasing power of income

real GDP the value of all output of an economy produced in a given period of time, usually a year, adjusted to take into account the effect of inflation

interest rate the percentage amount charged by a lender for money borrowed

unemployment occurs when there are people actively looking for work at the equilibrium wage rate but are not able to find work

Learning Outcomes

- Explain how the AD curve can be shifted by changes in consumption due to factors including changes in consumer confidence, **interest rates**, wealth, personal income taxes (and hence disposable income), and level of household indebtedness.

- Explain how the AD curve can be shifted by changes in investment due to factors including interest rates, business confidence, technology, business taxes, and the level of corporate indebtedness. Explain how the AD

curve can be shifted by changes in government spending due to factors including political and economic priorities.

- Explain how the AD curve can be shifted by changes in net exports due to factors including the income of trading partners, exchange rates, and changes in the level of protectionism.

Explain the causes of changes in consumption

Discussed below are the determinants of aggregate demand. A change in a determinant of AD, *ceteris paribus*, changes the total amount of goods and services consumed at each price level in a country in a given period of time.

Changes in confidence affect consumers' willingness to buy goods and services

If the economy is entering a recession and firms begin to lay workers off some people will be worried that they might become unemployed. The threat of **unemployment** is enough to change the behaviour of consumers. Consumer expectations concerning future levels of income plays an important role in consumption decisions. Fear of unemployment and falling income in the future leads consumers to postpone consumption today, particularly consumption of luxury goods with relatively high **income elasticity of demand**. If consumers expect the economy to take a **downturn** the demand for goods and services such as foreign holidays and new cars falls. Consumers postpone consumption until expectations about future economic activity improve. If households feel optimistic about economic growth and believe employment is secure and that incomes

Subject vocabulary

income elasticity of demand a measure of how quantity demanded responds to a change in income in percentage terms

Glossary

slope the angle/gradient of the curve

Synonyms

downturn.......... decline/fall

loan repayment money paid back by the borrower of the loan to the lender

durable goods type of final good that is consumed over a relatively long period of time. It is not consumed in one use. The consumer gains benefit from its use over time.

financial capital the money used by firms and entrepreneurs to purchase the resources needed to produce goods or services

inverse relationship a change in the value of one variable leads to an opposite change in direction in the value of the other variable. For example an increase in price leads to a fall in quantity demanded.

mortgages loans that are secured against property

asset an item of value owned by an individual or firm, especially one that could be converted to cash

share a unit of ownership of a company's capital. The owner is entitled to a proportion of the company's profit.

government bonds issued by the government to investors in exchange for lending it money. The investor is entitled to interest payments on the loan as well as repayment of the loan when the bond matures

income tax a direct tax on individual earnings (wages, rent, profit, interest) and paid to the government

disposable income household income after direct taxation has been deducted

savings income that is not spent

interest rate the percentage amount charged by a lender for money borrowed or paid to a person for saving money

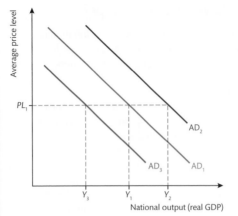

Figure 45.1

may rise in the future people are more likely to be willing to bring consumption of such goods forward. Consumers are more likely to borrow money from a bank to buy higher priced goods because they are confident that they can afford the **loan repayments**.

When expectations are positive, consumption at each price level increases leading to a **shift** up and to the right of the AD curve from AD_1 to AD_2 and when consumers have negative expectations about the future state of the economy consumption at each price level falls and the AD curve shifts down and to the left from AD_1 to AD_3 as shown in Figure 45.1.

Changes in the interest rate particularly affect the consumption of relatively high-priced durable goods

Consumers often borrow to buy **durable goods** such as cars, televisions, lap top computers, carpets, furniture, and so on. Consumers borrow in order to bring forward consumption. Consumers who borrow from a bank must pay back the **financial capital**, which is the actual amount of money borrowed, and the interest charged on the capital.

The interest is the price of money. It is the price the consumer pays in order to have the money now. The interest payable on a loan is calculated as a percentage of the amount of money borrowed. A consumer wants to buy a car and borrows $10,000 over a period of a year at an interest rate of 5%. She has to pay back to the bank by the end of the year the capital amount borrowed, which is $10,000 plus the interest which is $500, a total of $10,500. If the interest rate is 15% then interest payment on the loan would be $1500. An increase in the rate of interest, *ceteris paribus*, effectively increases the price the consumer pays for the car. Therefore there is an **inverse relationship** between interest rates and consumption. Also as the interest rate falls repayment on existing loans such as **mortgages** falls leaving households with more of their income to spend on goods and services.

Model sentence: As the interest rate increases, *ceteris paribus*, consumption at each price level falls and the AD curve shifts down and to the left. As the interest rate falls consumption at each price level rises and the AD curve shifts up and to the right.

Changes in wealth affects total consumption in a country

Wealth is the value of the **assets** or possessions owned by a household less household debt. Real or physical assets include houses, jewellery, gold, and works of art. Financial assets include **shares** in companies, **government bonds**, savings accounts, and pension funds. It is the value of houses and shares that has the greatest impact on consumption. When house prices fall the value of the consumers' main asset falls and this affects confidence. Consumers are likely to reduce consumption. If house prices rise consumers grow in confidence, they feel wealthier and are likely to increase consumption. As the price of shares held by a household increase the household feels wealthier and more confident. Again this will lead to increases in consumption.

Model sentence: *Ceteris paribus*, when the value of household assets change the total demand for goods and services in a country changes at each price level causing a shift of the AD curve.

Changes in income affects total consumption

As an economy grows national income increases and consumers can buy more goods and services at each price level and the AD curve shifts up and to the right. The extent to which increases in income affect consumption of domestically produced goods depends on a number of factors.

If **income tax** increases then households' **disposable income** falls leaving less to spend on goods. If income tax rates fall disposable income rises therefore consumption will increase and the AD curve shifts up and to the right.

If the interest paid by the banks on household **savings** increases the incentive to save increases. Households save more of their income and spend less on consumption. *Ceteris paribus*, consumption falls as the **interest rate** on savings increases and the AD curve shifts down and to the left.

If demand for **imported goods** increases then households have less income to spend on domestically produced goods therefore total consumption falls.

Model sentence: The amount of income households spend on goods and services in an economy is dependent upon the rate of tax, the interest rate, and the proportion of income spent on imports.

The level of household indebtedness affects total consumption in a country

Household indebtedness is a measure of the amount of money households owe lenders of money such as banks. It includes money owed on credit cards, and loans from a bank borrowed to finance expenditure on durable goods. As households borrow to buy, indebtedness increases and consumption rises. Debts must be repaid out of future income. Therefore increased indebtedness now reduces the amount of income in the future available for consumption. If a person expects future earnings to increase he is more likely to increase indebtedness now believing that the debt can be repaid in the future. If expectations concerning income in the future are less positive then households are less likely to build up personal debt thereby reducing current consumption. Also, when households are worried about future income, expecting it to fall, they will pay back more of their debt thereby reducing current consumption.

Explain the causes of changes in investment

Discussed below are factors that affect the level of investment in an economy.

National income

Investment is the addition to **capital stock**. It is an injection into the **circular flow of income**. Firms invest in order to replace worn out capital, to increase **productivity** and to expand production. As **national income** rises consumption increases. Firms work their capital harder and for longer periods in order to keep up with demand. Therefore capital wears out more quickly and will need replacing more often. This is called replacement investment. As AD continues to increase and expectations are that AD will rise further in the future firms buy more capital in order to increase future potential levels of output. This is called **induced investment**.

Business confidence

Business confidence concerning economic growth and future levels of AD affect the amount of induced investment in a country because in order to meet potential higher levels of demand and to earn the greater profits available the firms must be able to satisfy that demand. If the economy enters a recession and it is expected to be a long and deep one national income and consumption falls along with business confidence causing a fall in both replacement and induced investment.

Technological change

The use of **technologically advanced capital** increases productivity and reduces the average cost of production. When there is technological change in the state of capital firms must buy it in order to remain competitive both domestically and internationally. If a firm fails to invest in the technologically advanced capital while others do its average costs will be higher than its competitors and profits lower. It is likely that the firm would not survive in the long term because at some point **market price** will fall below the average cost.

The rate of interest

Investment comes from two sources. Either the firm uses some of its **retained profit** or it borrows. If the interest rate changes the cost of borrowing changes. As the cost of borrowing rises, *ceteris paribus*, investment falls. As costs fall investment rises. As the cost of an investment increases, *ceteris paribus*, the potential profit earned on the investment falls thereby reducing the incentive to invest. Also as interest rates rise the **opportunity cost** of the investment increases because the money could earn relatively higher **returns** simply deposited in the bank. There is a **negative relationship** between interest rates and investment as shown in Figure 45.2.

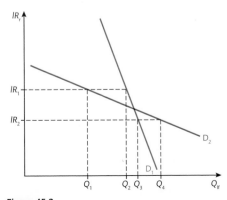

Figure 45.2

loanable funds the sum of money in an economy that is saved rather than used for consumption and made available to those wishing to borrow

corporation tax a tax levied in the UK on company profits

debt an amount of money that is owed

private sector the part of the economy that is regulated but not controlled by the state and concerns individuals and groups bringing together the factors of production normally with the aim of making a profit

public expenditure money spent by government

budget deficit occurs when government expenditure is greater than tax revenue

national debt the total amount of money a government has borrowed. When a government runs a budget deficit it must borrow the difference thereby adding to the national debt

fiscal policy government policy designed to achieve macroeconomic objectives through government expenditure and taxation

recession two consecutive quarters of negative economic growth

tax revenue the income the government receives through the levying and collection of taxes

The demand for **loanable funds** curve D_1 is relatively inelastic with respect to interest rates. This means quantity demanded of funds for investment is insensitive to changes in the rate of interest.

Whereas D_2 represents a situation where quantity demanded of investment funds is relatively elastic with respect to interest rates. This means quantity demanded of loanable funds is sensitive to changes in the rate of interest.

Model sentence: If firms expect future levels of aggregate demand to fall the effect on investment from a fall in interest rate will be minimal thus the demand for investment funds will be highly inelastic.

Firms pay tax on profits earned. Business taxes, such as **corporation tax** which is a tax on company profits, affect the quantity of investments. As tax rates fall, after-tax profits rise leaving the firm more retained profit to invest. Also lower taxes act as an incentive for firms to invest because firms can keep more of the profit thereby increasing the return on any investment. Relatively high taxes act as a disincentive to invest because high taxes reduce potential returns on any investment.

The level of corporate indebtedness

Firms' indebtedness is a measure of the amount of money firms owe lenders of investment funds such as banks. As firms borrow to invest, indebtedness increases and investment in the country rises. **Debt** and interest on the debt must be repaid out of future profit. Therefore increased indebtedness now reduces the amount of profit in the future available for investment. If firms expect future profits to rise they are more likely to increase indebtedness now believing that the debt can be repaid in the future. If expectations about profits in the future are low then firms are less likely to build up debt by borrowing to invest thereby reducing current levels of investment. Also, when firms expect profits to fall in the future they might pay back debt now thereby leaving less retained profit for current investment.

Explain the factors that affect government expenditure

According to the 2011 'Index of Economic Freedom' many European countries have relatively high levels of government expenditure as a percentage of GDP. In the UK government expenditure accounts for 47% of GDP. In Belgium, France, and Sweden government expenditure accounts for just over 50% of GDP. In countries such as these the governments provide many goods and services including healthcare and education for all the citizens, as well as spending on transport **infrastructure**, social housing, and national defence. Also government subsidizes industries in the **private sector** using taxpayers' money.

Through taxes on goods and services such as VAT, and taxes on income the government raises the government revenue needed to finance expenditure. Many countries where **public expenditure** is relatively high run a **budget deficit**. This occurs when government expenditure exceeds tax revenue therefore the government must borrow the difference from the financial institutions and doing so increases the **national debt**.

Citizens in many countries expect the government to provide lots of services while at the same time are not always happy to pay more tax to fund the expenditure. Political parties in countries have different views on the role of government in an economy and society and it is these views that can affect **fiscal policy** when in government. Nevertheless, whatever the political party that forms the government its expenditure makes a significant contribution to overall consumption.

Increasing government expenditure increases AD and national income. This can lead to increases in consumption by households and investment by firms. Unemployment falls leading to further increases in consumption. In this way government expenditure could bring an economy out of **recession**. However, in a recession **tax revenue** is low so the government will have to borrow to expand expenditure increasing the national debt. This debt, plus the interest paid on it, must be repaid in the future by the next generation of tax payers. Taxes will have to be higher in the future thereby reducing the disposable income of those households. However, it can be argued that when the economy grows tax revenues increase and the government should be able to pay off at least some of the national debt.

It can be seen that fiscal policy has a major impact on changes in aggregate demand. Increases in government expenditure shift the AD curve up and to the right and decreases shift the AD curve down and to the left. Reductions in tax increase disposable income and increase consumption causing a shift up and to the right of the AD curve.

Model sentence: The aim of **expansionary fiscal policy** is to increase aggregate demand by reducing the rate of tax and increasing government expenditure. The aim of **contractionary fiscal policy** is to reduce aggregate demand by increasing the rate of tax and reducing government expenditure.

Explain how changes in net exports affect aggregate demand

Increases in **international trade** means that most countries import and export both **consumer goods** and services and **capital** goods and services. A **current account deficit** occurs when expenditure on imports exceeds expenditure on exports and a current account surplus occurs when expenditure on exports exceeds expenditure on imports. A deficit reduces GDP and a surplus increases GDP.

Expenditure on imports is a leakage out of the circular flow of income and expenditure on exports is an injection. When consumers switch expenditure from domestically produced to imported goods the current account deficit increases or the surplus is reduced and AD falls. As expenditure on exports increases the deficit falls or the surplus increases and AD rises.

Ceteris paribus, when national income increases in a country expenditure on imports rises increasing the leakages from the circular flow of income, worsening the deficit or reducing the surplus on the current account. Demand for exports rises when the national income rises in a foreign country. Foreigners will buy more of another country's exports, increasing the flow of income injected into the economy and improving its current account balance.

The **exchange rate**, the price of one currency in terms of another currency, in a floating exchange rate system fluctuates over time and this affects the price foreigners pay for imports. For example, when the £ appreciates against the $ UK exports to the US become more expensive. The price in $ US citizens pay for UK goods increases therefore **quantity demanded** falls and the US consumers buy fewer UK goods; thus expenditure on UK exports to the US falls reducing aggregate demand in the UK. The opposite occurs when the £ falls in value against the $.

If a government wants to protect **domestic firms** from international competition it can for example give subsidies to domestic producers and place a **tariff** on imported goods. A tariff is a tax on goods coming from abroad. It increases the price of imports thereby reducing the quantity demanded. Consumers switch expenditure away from imported goods towards domestically produced goods thus increasing AD and improving the current account deficit. Of course other countries can retaliate by placing a tariff on goods imported in from the competitor country.

The inflation rate is a measure of the increase in prices over a given period of time. As prices rise in a country exports become less price competitive and quantity demanded falls leading to a fall in AD. If a country's inflation rate is relatively low then it will have an advantage in international trade as the relative price of imports increases and price of exports falls. Quantity demanded of exports increases and quantity demanded of imports falls improving the current account balance and boosting AD.

Model sentence: The exchange rate, inflation rate, **protectionism**, and levels of national income all affect the quantity demanded of imports and exports thereby affecting the value of **net exports** and aggregate demand.

Test your understanding of this unit by answering the following questions

- Explain why the quantity demanded of loanable funds might be insensitive to a change in the interest rate.
- Discuss the significance for economic growth of consumer and producer confidence.
- Using an AD diagram, explain the effect on a country's AD of an increase in its national income.
- Explain how indebtedness affects AD.
- Explain the effects on AD of an expansionary fiscal policy.

Subject vocabulary

expansionary fiscal policy policy involving the increase of government spending and/or the reduction of taxation

contractionary fiscal policy government policy designed to eliminate an inflationary gap through increasing taxes and/or reducing government expenditure

international trade the cross-border exchange of goods and services

consumer goods goods that are ultimately consumed by households rather than goods used by firms in the production of another good

capital (goods) manufactured goods that are used in the production of other goods

current account deficit occurs when the amount of money flowing out of a country from the trade in goods and services, investment income, and transfers is greater than the amount flowing in

exchange rate the price of a country's currency in terms of another currency

quantity demanded the amount of a good consumers are willing and able to buy at a given price over a given period of time

domestic firm a firm that produces its output in the home country

tariffs a tax placed on imported goods and services

protectionism government policies, including tariffs, quotas and subsidies, that restrict the extent of international trade and which are implemented in order to protect domestic industries from cheaper imports

net exports export revenue minus import expenditure

Learning Outcomes

- Describe the term aggregate supply.

- Explain, using a diagram, why the short-run aggregate supply curve (SRAS curve) is upward sloping.

- Explain, using a diagram, how the AS curve in the short run (SRAS) can shift due to factors including changes in resource prices, changes in business taxes, subsidies, and supply shocks.

- Explain, using a diagram, that the monetarist/new classical model of the long-run aggregate supply curve (LRAS) is vertical at the level of potential output (full employment output) because aggregate supply in the long run is independent of the price level.

- Explain, using a diagram, that the Keynesian model of the aggregate supply curve has three sections because of 'wage/price' downward inflexibility and different levels of spare capacity in the economy.

- Explain, using the two models above, how factors leading to changes in the quantity and/or quality of factors of production (including improvements in efficiency, new technology, reductions in unemployment, and institutional changes) can shift the aggregate supply curve over the long term.

Subject vocabulary

aggregate supply the total supply of goods and services produced in an economy at a given price level in a given time period

aggregate supply curve a graph that shows the relationship between the average price level and aggregate supply

supply curve a graph that shows the relationship between price and quantity supplied

price level the current weighted average price of a selected group of goods and services produced in a country over a period of time

real output the quantity of goods and services produced in a given time period

costs of production the amount the firm pays for the factors of production used to produce goods or services

overtime time spent working in addition to normal working hours

wage rate the amount of money paid to labour per unit of time or unit of output

total cost the sum of total fixed cost and total variable cost

average cost is equal to total cost divided by quantity of output

continued on page 125

Synonyms

shift(s) .... move(s)

What is aggregate supply (AS)?

Aggregate supply is the sum of the amount of goods and services all industries in a country are willing and able to supply at each price level. The **aggregate supply curve** is the addition of all the **supply curves** of all industries in a country. Aggregate supply is measured both in the short run and in the long run.

Why does the short-run aggregate supply curve (SRAS curve) slope upwards?

The SRAS curve is drawn showing the relationship between the **price level** and **real output** while holding all factor prices constant. When firms increase output they incur higher total **costs of production**. The firms, for example, have to employ more workers and pay workers **overtime** or some form of bonus payments in order to increase output in the short run. Although the **wage rate** has not increased firms' labour costs increase therefore **total cost** and **average cost** increase. (HL students see pages 65–66 for an explanation of how marginal cost and average cost increase because of the law of diminishing returns to the variable factor.) In order to maintain **profit margins** firms increase prices thereby passing the higher costs on to the consumers. Therefore as firms in the economy increase output the price level increases. There is a **positive relationship** between real output and the price level and to illustrate this relationship the SRAS curve slopes upwards as shown in Figure 46.1.

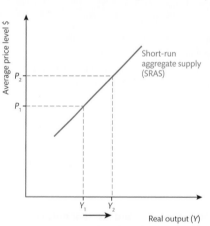

Figure 46.1

Explain the causes of a shift in the SRAS curve

Holding all other determinants of SRAS constant, when the price level of goods and services increases firms in the economy increase quantity supplied leading to a movement up and along the SRAS. A change in any of the determinants of SRAS other than the price level leads to a change in SRAS at each price level and a **shift** of the SRAS curve.

What are the effects on SRAS of a change in price of the factors of production?

If rents, the price of capital or the price of **raw materials** change costs of production change. The change in costs of production change the amount of profit earned at each price level thereby affecting the firms' willingness to supply. SRAS changes leading to a shift of the SRAS curve. When price of factors increase, firms reduce output at each price level and the SRAS curve shifts up and to the left. When price of factors fall firms increase output at each price level and the SRAS curve shifts down and to the right.

The effect of a change in the price of labour – a step-by-step guide

Trouble shooter

As the wage rate, which is the price of labour, rises the firms' costs of production increase.

Firms earn less profit at each price level and therefore reduce output.

The SRAS curve shifts up and to the left from $SRAS_1$ to $SRAS_3$ as shown in Figure 46.2.

A fall in the price of labour leads to a fall in the costs of production.

Firms earn more profit at each price level and therefore increase output.

The SRAS curve shifts down and to the right from $SRAS_1$ to $SRAS_2$.

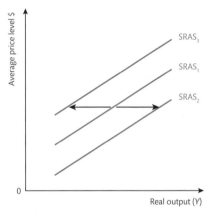

Model sentence: A change in the price of a factor of production changes the costs of production and affects firms' profitability at each price level. Therefore firms change output at each price level leading to a shift of the SRAS curve.

Figure 46.2

What are the effects on SRAS of an indirect tax and a subsidy?

In effect an indirect tax increases costs of production. Firms earn less profit at each price level and therefore reduce output and the SRAS curve shifts up and to the left.

In effect a subsidy reduces costs of production. Firms earn more profit at each price level and therefore increase output and the SRAS curve shifts down and to the right.

What is a supply-side shock?

A supply-side shock is a sudden event that affects the price of a factor of production thereby affecting costs of production. For example, in the early 1970s oil prices increased rapidly due to **conflict** in the Middle East and there was a **subsequent** restriction in the supply of oil on to the world market. Industries' costs of production rose sharply. Output of industries fell shifting the SRAS up and to the left leading to high levels of **inflation**.

A sudden fall in a country's **exchange rate** leads to an increase in the price of imports including the price of imported raw materials. As the exchange rate falls the price of imported raw materials increases thereby increasing costs of production. Firms reduce output at each price level and the SRAS curve shifts up and to the left.

The examples above are negative supply-side shocks. A positive supply-side shock leads to fall in costs of production. A sudden **technological advance** increases **productivity** and profit leading to an increase in output and a shift of the SRAS curve down and to the right.

Explain why the monetarist/new classical model of the long-run aggregate supply curve is vertical at the level of potential output

There are two **conflicting** views concerning **long-run aggregate supply**. One model is called the monetarist or new classical model; the other is called the Keynesian model named after the economist John Maynard Keynes. The differences between the **assumptions** of each model explain why the LRAS curves of each model are not the same.

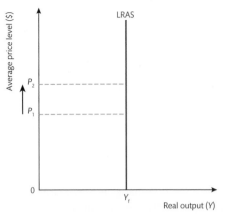

Figure 46.3

Followers of the new-classical model believe that government should not intervene in markets and that **the forces of demand and supply** operating in a **free market** should determine how **resources** are allocated.

LRAS is the level of output achieved when all factors of production are employed efficiently. This is the **full employment level of output**. The economy is operating at **full capacity**. The level of LRAS in a country is dependent on the total quantity of factors of production and the **productivity** (quality) of those factors. In this model LRAS is not dependent on the price level therefore the LRAS curve is perfectly inelastic in respect to the price level and is vertical at full employment levels of output as shown in Figure 46.3. An increase in LRAS can only be brought about through increases in the quantity and/or the productivity of the factors of production.

Model sentence: If the productivity of labour increases more output can be produced with the same quantity of factors. If the quantity of workers increases full employment levels of output increases. In both cases the LRAS curve shifts to the right.

Why does the Keynesian model of the aggregate supply curve have three sections? (see Figure 46.4)

No **distinction** is made between the short run and the long run under this model. Keynesians argue that there are three distinct sets of circumstances that the economy experiences as it moves through **business cycles** and that the shape of the AS curve is determined by the economy's position in the cycle.

In stage 1, output is a long way below full employment levels of output. This would occur in a **recession**. There is lots of **spare capacity**. Unemployment of all factors is high including labour and capital. It is relatively easy for firms to increase output. As the supply of the factors is high increasing demand for them does not push factor prices up. Firms are able to raise output while holding average costs constant. While this is the case the AS curve is perfectly elastic.

As output rises, in response to increases in **aggregate demand, the negative output gap**, which is the difference between actual output and full employment level of output, falls. As the economy enters stage 2 an increasing number of factors are employed by firms in order to increase output and the amount of spare capacity falls. Firms have to compete with each other for a smaller pool of available factors. In order to obtain them the firms must pay a higher price. This pushes up the costs of production. For example, as the demand for labour increases the price of labour, the wage rate, rises, thereby increasing costs of production. The price of raw materials rises as demand increases and rents also rise as demand for factory space increases. The price level begins to increase to cover the increasing costs of production.

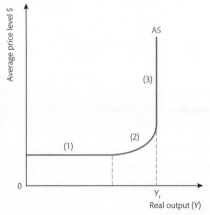

Figure 46.4

As AD increases firms want to raise output but find it increasingly difficult due to a lack of spare capacity. When the economy is operating at full capacity with constant productivity of the factors it is impossible to boost output beyond the full employment level of output, Y_f. At this point the AS curve is perfectly inelastic. Any increases in AD at this point results in higher price levels as AD exceeds AS. The Keynesian AS curve reflects the LRAS curve under the new classical model.

(Further analysis of the consequences of the shape of the Keynesian AS curve and of 'wage/price' **downward inflexibility** is covered on pages 128–31.)

Explain the causes of an increase in LRAS

The main causes of a change in LRAS are changes in the quantity and/or productivity (quality) of the factors of production. An increase in the quantity of land, which includes the **natural resources** found in land, leads to an increase in the potential level of output of a country. For example, if more land is taken into productive use, such as unused land put to use producing agricultural goods, then LRAS increases. If an oil field is discovered and exploited LRAS increases. Also if productivity of the land increases LRAS rises. For example, the use of new fertilizers increases output of agricultural goods from a fixed area of land.

If the quantity of labour increases through, for example, an increase in **net immigration**, an increase in the birth rate or an increase in the retirement age, LRAS increases. Increases in productivity of labour brought about by education and training also increase full employment levels of output because more output is produced by a fixed quantity of labour. Also as the population rises the number of **entrepreneurs** increase. There are more people willing to take a risk and set up business in pursuit of profit.

Investment increases the quantity of capital in the economy. More goods and services can be produced with more capital. Increases in productivity of capital comes about through advances in technology. As productivity of capital increases LRAS increases.

As the full employment level of output increases the LRAS curve in both models shifts to the right as shown in Figure 46.5.

If an economy suffers from high levels of long-term unemployment it is possible that a proportion of the potential workforce will lose their skills through lack of use. They become **deskilled** and there is a decrease in productivity leading to a shift to the left of the LRAS curve. If resources are destroyed by a natural disaster such as an earthquake or through war then LRAS falls and the LRAS curve shifts to the left. An increase in **net emigration**, particularly if those leaving the country are highly skilled, leads both to a fall in the quantity of labour and a fall in the productivity of labour causing full employment level of output to fall and the LRAS curve to shift to the left.

Subject vocabulary

natural resources assets, such as mineral deposits and timber, that occur in nature and can be used in production

net immigration/emigration the difference between the number of people entering an area to live (usually a country) and the people leaving an area, measured over a given period of time. When more people enter than leave, net immigration is positive and net emigration is negative.

entrepreneur an individual who, in pursuit of profit, brings together the other factors of production in order to produce a good or service

investment the addition to capital stock

deskilled describes labour that has lost skills due to lack of use. Also production is deskilled when skilled labour is replaced by unskilled labour due to the introduction of new technologies.

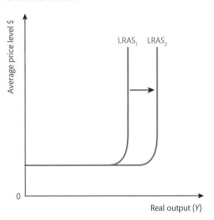
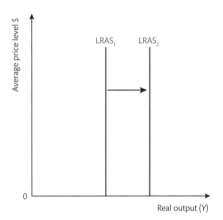

Figure 46.5

(Government plays an important role in encouraging increases in LRAS. Policies designed to affect LRAS are called supply-side polices. These are discussed in detail on pages 189–95.)

Model sentence: The quantity and quality of the factors of production are determinants of LRAS. Changes in the determinants causes a change in LRAS leading to a shift of the LRAS curve.

Test your understanding of this unit by answering the following questions

- Explain the causes of a shift of the LRAS curve.
- Explain the shape of the Keynesian AS curve.
- Why is the LRAS curve vertical at the full employment level of output?
- Explain the effect on SRAS of a supply-side shock.
- Explain the effects on SRAS of a change in price of factors of production.

Learning Outcomes

- Explain, using a diagram, the determination of short-run equilibrium, using the SRAS curve.
- Examine, using diagrams, the impacts of changes in short-run equilibrium.
- Explain, using a diagram, the determination of long-run equilibrium, indicating that long-run equilibrium occurs at the full employment level of output.
- Explain why, in the monetarist/new classical approach, while there may be short-term fluctuations in output, the economy will always return to the full employment level of output in the long run.
- Examine, using diagrams, the impacts of changes in the long-run equilibrium.

Explain the determination of short-run equilibrium and why equilibrium might change

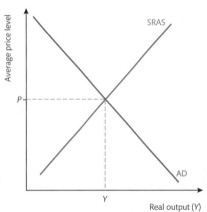

Figure 47.1

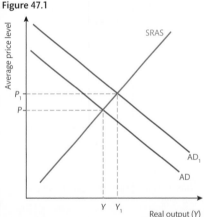

Figure 47.2

A country's economy is in equilibrium in the short run when **aggregate demand** equals **short-run aggregate supply**. This is where consumers' total demand for goods and services is equal to the total output produced by all industries in the country. There are no excesses: AD = SRAS.

This is shown in Figure 47.1. AD = SRAS with total level of output Y at the **price level** P. At current levels of consumption there is no incentive for firms in the economy to increase or reduce output. However, a change in any of the determinants of AD or determinants of AS causes a shift of the AD or SRAS curve leading to a change in the price level and a change in output.

As AD increases, say through an increase in consumer confidence, the AD curve shifts up and to the right as shown in Figure 47.2. Firms respond by increasing supply. As they do so their labour costs increase. Firms pass the increase in costs on to the consumer to pay causing an increase in the price level. Equilibrium price level and output increase to P_1, Y_1.

Explain why, in the new classical view, the long-run equilibrium is at the full employment level of output

Followers of the new classical model argue that, as long as the markets are free from any form of intervention, particularly government intervention the economy automatically adjusts to its long-run equilibrium level of output. In Figure 47.3 initially the economy is in long-run equilibrium at the full employment level of output at P_1, Y_f where AD = SRAS = LRAS. A change in a determinant of AD leads to a change in the price level but the economy returns automatically to the **full employment level of output**.

Say there is a fall in consumer confidence and aggregate demand falls. The AD curve shifts down and to the left from AD_1 to AD_2 and the price level falls. Firms in the economy respond to the fall in expenditure on goods and services and the price level by reducing quantity supplied. This leads to a movement down and along the SRAS curve, $SRAS_1$.

Demand for the **factors of production** is a **derived demand**. Firms demand factors because consumers demand goods and services. Therefore as AD falls the demand for factors falls leading to a fall in factor prices.

For example, demand for labour falls causing an excess supply of labour in the labour market. Therefore the wage rate falls to eliminate the excess. A fall in the price of all factors leads to a fall in the **costs of production**. Believers in the new classical model argue that if factor markets are free, if there is no form of intervention and the **forces of demand and supply** are allowed to operate freely the price of factors will instantly change when demand for them changes. Therefore costs of production immediately change.

In the example shown in Figure 47.3 the short-run equilibrium level of output, P_2, Y_1, which is below the full

Subject vocabulary

factors of production the inputs into the production process (land, labour, capital and entrepreneurship)

derived demand demand for a good, or factor of production, that is a consequence of the demand for something else

costs of production the amount the firm pays for the factors of production used to produce goods or services

forces of demand and supply changes in the determinants of demand and supply in a market that affect the market price and the allocation of resources

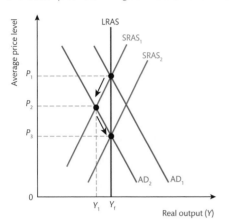

employment level of output, exists momentarily. Factor prices fall instantly therefore costs of production do the same. In response, firms increase output leading to a shift down and to the right of the SRAC curve, from SRAS$_1$ to SRAS$_2$.

As the price level falls expenditure increases and there is a movement down and along the AD curve AD$_2$. The economy automatically returns to the long-run equilibrium, P_3, Y_f, at the full employment level of output. The only changes brought about by the fall in aggregate demand are a fall in factor prices and a fall in the price level from P_1 to P_3.

Figure 47.3

Why does the economy return to the long-run equilibrium at the full employment level of output after an increase in AD? – a step-by-step guide (see Figure 47.4)

Trouble shooter

Initially the economy is in long-run equilibrium at the full employment level of output.

AD increases and the AD curve shifts up and to the right from AD$_1$ to AD$_2$.

As AD increases the price level rises.

Firms respond to the increase in AD and the higher price level, increasing quantity supplied by working the capital harder and paying workers overtime. There is a movement up and along the SRAS curve, SRAS$_1$.

The short-run equilibrium is P_2, Y_1. Actual output is higher than the long-run full employment level of output.

There are no spare factors. Competition between firms for the existing factors is intense leading to an increase in factor prices.

Costs of production rise. Any increase in profit from the higher prices no longer exists; therefore firms reduce output causing the SRAS curve to shift up and to the left from SRAS$_1$ to SRAS$_2$.

As PL rises expenditure falls leading to a movement up and along the AD curve, AD$_2$.

The economy automatically returns to the long-run equilibrium, P_3, Y_f, at the full employment level of output. The only change brought about by the initial increase in aggregate demand is an increase in factor prices and a rise in the price level from P_1 to P_3.

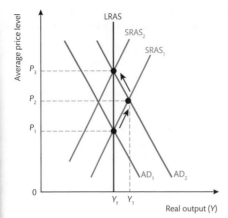

Figure 47.4

Examine the effects of changes in the long-run equilibrium

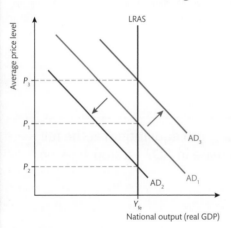

Figure 47.5

Followers of the new classical view assume that aggregate demand does not determine the level of output. They assume output and AD are unrelated. No matter what the level of total expenditure the economy always automatically returns to the long-run equilibrium at the full employment level of output. This assumption rests on the belief that factor prices are **perfectly flexible** and change immediately in response to changes in demand thereby affecting costs of production and in turn output decisions. As shown in Figure 47.5 a change in aggregate demand leads only to a change in the price of factors and a change in the price level.

Is the assumption that the economy automatically returns to the long-run equilibrium at full employment level of output realistic?

The economy only returns automatically to the long-run equilibrium at the full employment level of output after a fall in aggregate demand if factor prices are perfectly flexible. If prices are perfectly flexible when demand falls for the factors of production factor prices fall immediately to clear the markets. However, there are factors that restrict the drop in price.

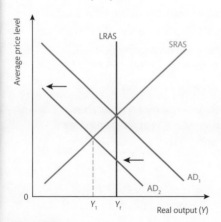

Figure 47.6

A firm hiring a workshop has a contract with the owner agreeing to pay a certain rent each month. Therefore rents will not fall straight away in response to a fall in demand for the workshops. Workers have contracts of employment. Firms cannot cut wages immediately. Some industries have come to an agreement on pay with the **trade unions** representing the workers. The threat of **industrial action** could **deter** firms from cutting pay. **Minimum wage** laws mean that the price of labour cannot fall below a certain amount even if the minimum wage is higher than the **clearing rate**. Firms have reached agreements on price with, for example, suppliers of **raw materials** and energy suppliers. The prices of these **resources** do not fall straight away.

Prices are **'sticky' downwards**. When aggregate demand falls, leading to a fall in the demand for the factors of production, prices do not immediately fall to clear the market. Prices are resistant to change. The **deflationary gap** (Y_f–Y_1) shown in Figure 47.6 occurs when total expenditure (AD) in the economy is not enough to purchase the total output produced if all of the factors of production are employed. Some economists believe that because of interventions in the factor markets factor prices will fall but only in the long run.

Model sentence: How long a deflationary gap lasts depends on how 'sticky' downwards factor prices are. The length of a recession is dependent on the flexibility of factor prices, particularly wages, over time.

If it is assumed that wages and other factor prices are flexible over time, eventually firms take on more workers and SRAS increases, price level falls and the economy will adjust to the long-run equilibrium at full employment level of output.

Test your understanding of this unit by answering the following questions

- Using a diagram, explain why in the new classical model, the economy automatically returns to the long-run equilibrium at the full employment level of output after a change in aggregate demand.
- Using a diagram, explain why the economy might not immediately return to the long-run equilibrium at the full employment level of output after a change in aggregate demand.

Learning Outcomes

- Explain, using the Keynesian AD/AS diagram, that the economy may be in equilibrium at any level of real output where AD intersects AS.

- Explain, using a diagram, that if the economy is in equilibrium at a level of real output below the full employment level of output, then there is a deflationary (recessionary) gap.

- Discuss why, in contrast to the monetarist/new classical model, the economy can remain stuck in a deflationary (recessionary) gap in the Keynesian model.

- Explain, using a diagram, that if AD increases in the vertical section of the AS curve, then there is an inflationary gap.

- Discuss why, in contrast to the monetarist/new classical model, increases in aggregate demand in the Keynesian AD/AS model need not be inflationary, unless the economy is operating close to, or at, the level of full employment.

Explain why, in the new classical view, a deflationary gap only occurs in the short run and that the economy will return to the long-run equilibrium at the full employment level of output

As **aggregate demand** falls firms reduce output and **lay off** workers. Economic theory suggests that when **unemployment** is high and demand for workers is relatively low the price of labour will fall to eliminate the **excess supply** in the **labour market**. Falling wages is an incentive for firms in the economy to employ more workers and as wages fall **costs of production** fall. In response to falling costs firms reduce prices leading to an increase in consumption of goods and services. Lower wages cures unemployment and lower prices increases consumption. The economy returns to the long-run equilibrium at the full employment level of output. **Demand-deficient unemployment** or Keynesian unemployment, caused by insufficient expenditure in the economy, occurs but only in the short run. As wages and prices fall, the economy returns to full employment. The new classical view is that unemployment and lack of aggregate demand only occur in the short run. In the long run as wages fall firms demand more workers **eliminating involuntary unemployment** occurs when a person is willing and able to work at the given wage rate but is unable to find workand the economy returns to the full employment level of output. The length of time this process takes depends on how long it takes the wage rate to adjust.

In the short run wages are 'sticky' downwards. For example, employment contracts, minimum wage legislation, and pay agreements between management and **trade unions** make it impossible to cut wages very quickly. Wages are not perfectly flexible, nor are other factor prices such as rent, so costs of production do not fall quickly. Firms are unable to lower prices so consumption does not increase. Low levels of consumption and high levels of unemployment will persist until factor prices have had sufficient time to adjust. Some economists argue that such agreements on wage should be **abolished** to make wages more flexible. They argue that intervention in the labour market is the cause of unemployment and the deflationary gap.

The return to the long-run equilibrium under the new classical model – a step-by-step guide (see Figure 48.1)

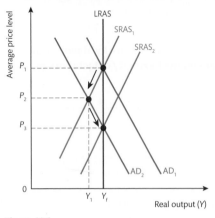

Figure 48.1

Explain why, in the Keynesian model, the actual macroeconomic equilibrium can be below full employment level of output and that the economy can be stuck in a deflationary gap

Model sentence: Keynesians argue that high levels of unemployment can persist for a long time because of the lack of aggregate demand. It is low levels of expenditure that causes unemployment not inflexible factor markets.

Even if wages fall, Keynesians argue, firms will not employ more workers in order to increase output because of insufficient demand for goods and services. **Recessions** are characterized by falling levels of expenditure. Consumer spending and business **investment** both fall. Unemployment increases, demand falls further, and firms go **bankrupt**. AD falls even further and a cycle of falling spending and investment follows leading to increasing levels of unemployment. Unemployment is caused by a lack of aggregate demand in the economy.

Model sentence: The solution to unemployment, Keynesians argue, is to boost aggregate demand leading to increases in supply and falls in unemployment. Output is determined by demand.

Keynesians believe that a recession, without government intervention, could be deep and long leading to high levels of long-term unemployment of labour and persistent low levels of expenditure. Keynesians argue that equilibrium levels of output are determined mainly by the strength of AD. Therefore the government should implement **demand-side policies** that increase AD. In response firms then employ more factors in order to increase output. Keynesians are interventionists, believing that the government has a key role to play in managing AD so that the macroeconomic objectives such as low unemployment and **economic growth** are achieved.

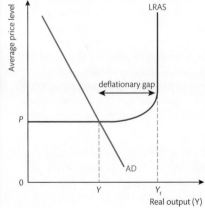

Figure 48.2

Figure 48.2 shows an economy where there is a deflationary gap $(Y_f - Y)$, which occurs when total expenditure (AD) in the economy is not enough to purchase the total output produced if all of the factors of production are employed. Keynesians argue that the deflationary gap can persist for many years unless consumption increases. Whereas **advocates** of the new classical model believe factor prices will adjust in the short run and the economy will return to the long-run equilibrium at the full employment level of output.

Explain why, in the new classical model, an increase in aggregate demand causes an inflationary gap and the price level to rise

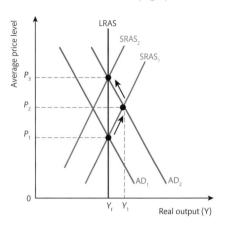

Figure 48.3

In Figure 48.3 initially the economy is in equilibrium at P_1, Y_f. Aggregate demand increases and the AD curve shifts up and to the right from AD_1 to AD_2. The **inflationary gap** is the difference between the full employment level of output, Y_f and actual real output Y_1. It occurs when total expenditure cannot be satisfied by the full employment level of output. The income available for expenditure at the current price level is greater than the number of goods and services the economy can produce at full employment levels of output. In other words aggregate demand exceeds **long-run aggregate supply**. Inflationary pressures build up and the price level rises from P_1 to P_2. This is called **demand-pull inflation**.

Firms want to increase output and demand more **factors of production** in order to do so. As demand rises in the factor markets, factor prices, including the wage rate, increase in order to eliminate the **shortages**. Costs of production therefore rise and **short-run aggregate supply** falls causing the SRAS curve to shift up and to the left from $SRAS_1$ to $SRAS_2$. Firms pass on the higher costs to the consumers to pay and the price level rises from P_2 to P_3. This is called **cost-push inflation**. The result of the increase in AD is that consumers pay higher prices for the same output of goods but workers now earn higher wages to compensate.

Model sentence: An increase in aggregate demand beyond the long-run equilibrium full employment level of output increases costs of production causing both demand-pull and cost-push inflation.

Explain why, in the Keynesian model, an increase in aggregate demand does not always cause inflation

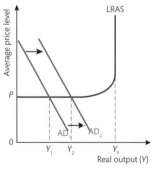

Figure 48.4

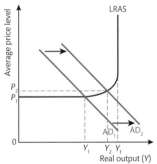

Figure 48.5

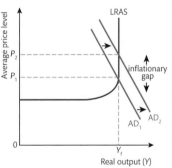

Figure 48.6

In Figure 48.4 the economy is in equilibrium at price level P and actual real output Y_1. There is a relatively large deflationary gap (Y_f-Y_1). This means that total expenditure is not sufficient to buy all of the full employment level of output Y_f. There are many unemployed factors so that in the factor markets supply exceeds demand. As expenditure rises and AD shifts from AD_1 to AD_2 firms respond by employing more factors, including labour, which are added to the fixed **capital** in order to increase output. **Real output** in the economy rises from Y_1 to Y_2. Although there is an increase in demand for the factors, the prices in the factor markets do not rise because there is so much **spare capacity**. Costs of production do not increase therefore inflationary pressure does not build up. Also firms are reluctant to raise prices because levels of AD are still relatively low and price competition is more intense.

As expenditure continues to increase, as shown in Figure 48.5, the AD curve shifts up and to the right from AD_1 to AD_2 and real output rises from Y_1 to Y_2 reducing the deflationary gap. The demand for factors continues to rise, including demand for labour, in order to increase output in response to higher expenditure. At this stage in the **business cycle** the economy has moved out of recession and is now experiencing rising levels of aggregate demand and increasing levels of real output. Demand for all factors continues to rise. There is now less spare capacity so as demand in the factor markets increases factor prices start to rise, including the price of labour. Firms' costs of production increase and they pass at least some of these higher costs on to the consumer to pay. The price level rises from P_1 to P_2.

In Figure 48.6 the economy is in long-run equilibrium (P_2, Y_f) at the full employment level of output. As expenditure increases the AD curve shifts up and to the right from AD_1 to AD_2. The economy enters the boom phase of the business cycle. With the given quantity and quality (**productivity**) of the factors of production it is not possible for the economy to raise output. All factors are employed. Therefore as AD rises real output remains constant. **Aggregate demand** exceeds aggregate supply. More expenditure is chasing the same quantity of goods and services therefore prices must rise to allocate them. There is an inflationary gap meaning the increasing level of expenditure cannot be satisfied by the existing factors of production.

Model sentence: In the Keynesian model the effect on the price level and real output of an increase in expenditure is dependent upon the amount of spare capacity in the economy. As AD continues to rise demand for factors increases and inflationary pressures build up.

Learning Outcomes

- Explain, with reference to the concepts of leakages (withdrawals) and injections, the nature and importance of the Keynesian multiplier. (HL)
- Calculate the multiplier using either of the following formulae: $\frac{1}{(1 - MPC)}$ or $\frac{1}{MPS + MPT + MPM}$ (HL)
- Use the multiplier to calculate the effect on GDP of a change in an injection in investment, government spending, or exports. (HL)
- Draw a Keynesian AD/AS diagram to show the impact of the multiplier. (HL)

Subject vocabulary

marginal propensity to consume is the proportion of additional income that an individual spends on goods and services. MPC = the change in consumption divided by the change in income.

average propensity to consume the percentage of income that is spent on goods and services. Calculated by dividing average household consumption by average income per head.

Synonyms

consumption......... use

What is the marginal propensity to consume (MPC)?

Aggregate demand = **consumption** + investment + government expenditure + net exports. Consumption is one of the components of AD. It signifies expenditure on domestically produced consumer goods and services in the economy in a given period of time. The factors that determine the level of aggregate demand are discussed on pages 119–23.

The amount of income is the most significant factor determining the level of consumption.

Model sentence: As income increases consumption increases. The extent of the increase in consumption is measured by the marginal propensity to consume. It is the proportion of an increase in income that is spent on domestically produced consumer goods and services.

$$MPC = \frac{\text{change in consumption}}{\text{change in income}}$$

A household's income rises from £2000 per month to £2500 leading to an increase in consumption of £300 per month the MPC = £300/£500 = 0.6. Each household has a different MPC. Some households will save all the extra income, some will spend all the extra income and others will spend only some of it.

The government calculates the **average propensity to consume** (APC) so that it is able to assess the effect on consumption of a rise or fall in national income.

$$APC = \frac{\text{consumption}}{\text{income}}$$

Say national income of a country is $120 billion and the APC = 0.7

$$0.7 = \frac{\text{consumption}}{\$120 \text{ billion}}$$

Consumption = 0.7 × $120 billion = $84 billion

Explain the terms the marginal propensity to tax (MPT), the marginal propensity to save (MPS), and the marginal propensity to import (MPM) and describe how they affect the marginal propensity to consume (MPC)

The proportion of any extra income available for consumption of domestically produced goods and services depends on the proportion of the extra income that is taxed, saved, or spent on imports. Income that is taxed, saved, or spent on imports is a leakage of income out of the **circular flow of income model** (see pages 107–109 for a detailed explanation of the circular flow of income model).

The **marginal propensity to tax** (MPT) is the proportion of additional household income which is taxed, by the government. The tax revenue goes to the government, some of which is injected back into the circular flow through government expenditure. Ceteris paribus, as MPT increases MPC falls.

The **marginal propensity to save** is the proportion of an increase in income that is saved by households. Savings, which includes income used to pay back existing debt, are leakages out of the circular flow of income model. Income flows from households to the **financial sector** and is injected back into the economy when firms borrow to **invest**. **Interest rate** is the reward for saving. The incentive to save increases as interest rate rises. Ceteris paribus, as the interest rate increases the MPS increases leading to a fall in the MPC.

The **marginal propensity to import** is the proportion of additional income that is spent on **imported goods** and services. Expenditure on imports is a leakage out of the circular flow of income. The income goes to firms abroad and then flows to the foreign households. As MPM increases, ceteris paribus, MPC falls.

All household income is either spent on domestically produced goods and services, saved, taxed, or spent on imports. Therefore MPC + MPS + MPT + MPM = 1. Savings, taxes, and expenditure on imports are leakages from the circular flow of income. Another term for leakages is withdrawals. The collective name for MPS + MPT + MPM is the **marginal propensity to withdraw** (MPW): MPW = MPS + MPT + MPM. As shown above MPC+ MPS + MPT + MPM = 1. Therefore MPW + MPC = 1. When MPW and MPC are added together they always equal 1 therefore an increase in MPW leads to a fall in MPC.

Model sentence: A change in the marginal propensity to withdraw leads to a change in the marginal propensity to consume.

What is the Keynesian multiplier and what is its impact on national income? (UL)

Investment by firms, government expenditure, and expenditure on **exports** are all injections into the circular flow. The following example highlights the overall effect on national income of an injection into the circular flow of income. A government invests €100 million building new hospitals. The money goes to firms in the economy. For example, the money flows to the many firms involved in the construction of the buildings, to firms who make the carpets, the blinds and curtains, the beds, the floor and wall tiles, the office desks and chairs, the computers, the medical capital equipment, and so on. There are lots of firms involved in the provision of hospitals and all get a share of the €100 million.

Government expenditure is a component of aggregate demand. In this case there is an initial increase in expenditure of €100 million. In order to produce output firms must hire the factors of production from households. They pay wages for labour, rent for land, interest for capital, and profit for entrepreneurship. Wage, rent, interest, and profit are the four components of income.

€100 million flows from the government to the firms. €100 million then flows from the firms to households as payment for the use of the factors. Household incomes rise by €100 million. The proportion of the extra €100 million of income that is spent on **domestically produced goods** and **services** is dependent on the MPC and the MPW. If the MPW in the country is 0.4 (the addition of MPS = 0.1, MPT = 0.1, MPM = 0.2) then MPC must be 0.6. Therefore, 0.4 of the additional income, which is €40 million, leaks out of the circular flow as savings, taxes, and expenditure on imports and 0.6 of the additional income, which is €60 million, is spent on domestically produced goods. €60 million flows from households to firms in the economy. It then flows back to households as payments for the use of the factors. Household incomes increase by €60 million. 0.4 of the €60 million, which is €24 million, leaks out, and 0.6 of the €60 million, which is €36 million, is spent on domestically produced goods and services. €36 million flows from households to firms and then back to households for payments of the factors. This process continues until the remains of the initial government expenditure available for consumption falls to zero.

National income initially increases by €100 million but further rounds of household expenditure brought about by the initial government expenditure means that eventually the total increase in income is greater

Subject vocabulary

circular flow of income an economic model that shows the flow of money between households and firms and, in more complex versions, the flows of money into and out of the financial sector, government sector, and the international sector

marginal propensity to tax the rate at which additional income is taxed

marginal propensity to save the proportion of additional income that an individual saves. MPS = the change in savings divided by the change in income.

financial sector the part of the economy which includes the financial institutions (banks, building societies, insurance companies, and stock market), which allow for the flow of financial capital and the extension of credit

invest to buy capital goods and services

interest rate the percentage amount charged by a lender for money borrowed

marginal propensity to import the proportion of additional income that an individual spends on imported goods and services. MPM = the change in expenditure on imports divided by the change in income.

imported goods goods sold into a country from another country

marginal propensity to withdraw is the proportion of additional household income that is taxed, saved and spent on imports. MPW = MPT + MPS + MPM

investment the addition to capital stock

exports goods produced in one country that are sold into another country

domestically produced goods goods produced within one's own or a specified country

services products that cannot be seen or touched, such as a train journey and car insurance

national income the sum of all income earned in a country in a given period of time

autonomous expenditure spending not affected by the level of income of the four macroeconomic sectors: households, government, business, and foreign.

the multiplier the number by which the value of the expenditure is multiplied to give the total increase in national income. The multiplier = 1/1-MPC

unemployment occurs when there are people actively looking for work at the equilibrium wage rate but are not able to find work

capital (goods) manufactured goods that are used in the production of other goods

induced investment investment by firms that is caused by increases in consumption. As aggregate demand increases, and is forecast to continue to rise, firms need to increase the quantity of capital in order to meet future levels of demand.

demand-pull inflation occurs when aggregate demand is greater than aggregate supply

aggregate demand the total demand for goods and services in the economy at a given price level in a given period of time

aggregate supply the total supply of goods and services produced in an economy at a given price level in a given time period

than the initial injection of €100 million. In this example MPC = 0.6 and the **autonomous expenditure** is €100 million. This causes further rounds of expenditure of €60 million + €36 million + €21.6 million + €12.96 million + €7.77 million + €4.67 million + €2.8 million, and so on. Income continues to leak out of the circular flow so eventually there is nothing left of the government expenditure of €100 million.

Explain how to calculate the multiplier (HL)

The **multiplier** is the number used to multiply the autonomous expenditure by in order to work out the overall change in national income from the injection into the circular flow. A government can assess the effect on national income of investments by firms, government expenditure, and expenditure on exports, by applying the multiplier. The following formulae are used to work out the multiplier.

$$\frac{1}{(1 - MPC)} \text{ or } \frac{1}{MPS + MPT + MPM}$$

In the previous example the initial or autonomous expenditure is €100 million. MPC = 0.6, MPS = 0.1, MPT = 0.1, MPM = 0.2. Therefore MPW = 0.4.

$$\frac{1}{(1 - MPC)} = \frac{1}{(1 - 0.6)} = \frac{1}{0.4} = 2.5$$

$$\text{Or } \frac{1}{MPS + MPT + MPM} = \frac{1}{0.1 + 0.1 + 0.2} = \frac{1}{0.4} = 2.5$$

The multiplier = 2.5

To calculate the overall effect on national income of an autonomous expenditure of €100 million, the autonomous expenditure is multiplied by the 'multiplier'.

€100 million × 2.5 = €250 million

The autonomous expenditure of €100 million leads to an increase in income not of €100 million but of €250 million.

The multiplier can be used to calculate the increase in national income from any injection in to the circular flow whether it is investment by firms, government expenditure, or expenditure on exports.

Model sentence: An increase in the marginal propensity to consume leads to an increase in the multiplier. Therefore the higher the MPC the greater will be the total increase in national income brought about by autonomous expenditure.

Using an AD/AS diagram show the impact on AD of the multiplier and discuss its significance (HL)

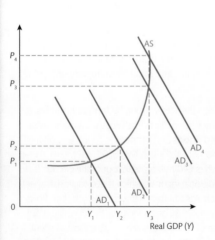

Figure 49.1

Keynesians believe the government should increase government expenditure in order to increase aggregate demand thereby increasing output and lowering **unemployment**. They argue that the impact on AD is significantly affected by the multiplier. AD will rise much further.

Increasing consumption induces firms to invest in more **capital** so that firms can increase supply and keep up with growing demand. **Induced investment** is an injection into the circular flow and is also subject to the multiplier. In this way AD continues to increase, output and incomes rise, and unemployment falls. As unemployment falls AD rises even further. Figure 49.1 shows AD increasing. The larger the multiplier the greater the impact on AD of injections into the economy and the larger the shift up and to the right of the AD curve.

However, this policy can cause **demand-pull inflation** when **aggregate demand** begins to exceed **aggregate supply**.

When the economy is in a **recession** with low levels of expenditure, income and output **tax revenues** are low. The government must borrow from the financial institutions in order to increase government expenditure. **Interest payments** on an increasing **national debt** will grow. Future tax-payers will have to pay back the debt from their income thereby affecting future levels of expenditure.

It is very hard for the government to work out the value of the multiplier. It is not certain that an accurate figure can be worked out given all the possible variables that affect its size. There are changes in the economy that occur that affect the size of the multiplier from one year to the next. For example, changes in expectations about the future state of the economy lead to changes in households' propensity to save and to consume. If households are pessimistic about future economic prospects they are likely to pay back more personal debt rather than consume more when incomes increase.

If the exchange rate increases the price of imports falls leading to an increase in quantity demanded. The marginal propensity to import increases leading to a fall in MPC and therefore a fall in the size of the multiplier.

The impact on national income of the multiplier is not immediate. It takes time for the further rounds of consumption to take place. There are significant **time lags** between the autonomous expenditure and increases in income and expenditure. And during these time lags economic conditions affecting MPC and the size of the multiplier change.

Test your understanding of this unit by answering the following questions

- What is MPC?
- Explain the factors that affect the size of the Keynesian multiplier.
- Explain the impact of the multiplier on the change in national income brought about by increases in government expenditure. Use an AD/AS diagram to illustrate your answer.
- How might changes in expectations, the exchange rate, interest rates, and the rate of tax affect the size of the multiplier?

Subject vocabulary

recession two consecutive quarters of negative economic growth

tax revenue the income the government receives through the levying and collection of taxes

interest payments the money paid at regular intervals on loans

national debt the total amount of money a government has borrowed. When a government runs a budget deficit it must borrow the difference thereby adding to the national debt

Glossary

time lag(s) period(s) of time between two linked events

2.3 Macroeconomic objectives – Low unemployment

Learning Outcomes

- Define the term unemployment.
- Explain how the unemployment rate is calculated.
- Explain the difficulties in measuring unemployment, including the existence of hidden unemployment, the existence of underemployment, and the fact that it is an average and therefore ignores regional, ethnic, age, and gender disparities.
- Calculate the unemployment rate from a set of data (HL).

- Discuss possible economic consequences of unemployment, including a loss of GDP, loss of tax revenue, increased cost of unemployment benefits, loss of income for individuals, and greater disparities in the distribution of income.
- Discuss possible personal and social consequences of unemployment, including increased crime rates, increased stress levels, increased indebtedness, homelessness, and family breakdown.

Subject vocabulary

unemployment occurs when there are people actively looking for work at the equilibrium wage rate but are not able to find work

labour force people who are working or who are actively seeking work

economically active describes people of working age who are employed or actively seeking employment

unemployment rate the percentage of people in the labour force who are unemployed

Define the term unemployment and explain how it is calculated

Low levels of **unemployment** is a key macroeconomic objective of most governments. Unemployment occurs when those who are actively seeking work are unable to find work. Therefore those who are not working are not necessarily counted as unemployed. People must be actively seeking work. For example housewives and househusbands, retired people, students, and those not legally allowed to work such as school children and prisoners are not working but are not looking for work and therefore are not counted as unemployed. People who are both not working and not actively seeking work are not part of the **labour force**. The labour force is made up of the employed and those actively seeking work and as such are described as being '**economically active**'.

The labour force participation rate is the percentage of the working-age population that is economically active. The meaning of working-age population varies from country to country because countries have different retirement ages and ages at which young people are legally allowed to leave school and look for full-time work.

The **unemployment rate** is calculated as a percentage using the following formulae.

$$\text{Unemployment rate (UR)} = \frac{\text{the total number of unemployed} \times 100}{\text{the labour force}}$$

Calculate the UR from data (HL)

A country has a labour force of 20 million people. This means that 20 million people are working or actively seeking work. The number of people unemployed is 4 million.

$$UR = \frac{4 \text{ million}}{20 \text{ million}} \times 100 = 0.2 \times 100 = 20\%$$

Calculate the size of the labour force when the unemployment rate is 15% and the number unemployed is 10 million.

$15 = \frac{10}{LF} \times 100$ simplify by multiplying both sides by LF

$15 \times LF = 1000$ simplify by dividing both sides by 15

$LF = 1000/15 = 66.67$

The labour force is 66.67 million.

Calculate the number unemployed when the UR rate is 5% and the labour force is 25 million.

$5 = \frac{\text{unemployed}}{25 \text{ million}} \times 100$ simplify by multiplying both sides by 25 million

$5 \times 25m = \text{unemployed} \times 100$ simplify by dividing both sides by 100

$125 \text{ million}/100 = \text{the number of unemployed} = 1,250,000$

Explain the difficulties associated with measuring unemployment

Government employment statistics are not always an accurate indicator of the true level of unemployment in an economy. Discussed below are the reasons for this.

The number of people working part-time in the UK has grown over the last few years. Many people who have taken on these part-time jobs did so because they were unable to find full-time jobs. Although they want to work longer hours and are underemployed they are not officially classified as unemployed because they are working. These people are not contributing as much as they would like to the output of the country.

Many people take jobs because they are unable to find the type of work that they are qualified to do. Some people who have been searching for work for a long period of time become very **frustrated** and eventually drop out of the labour force entirely because they believe they will never find suitable employment. As they are not actively looking for work they are not counted as unemployed and yet their potential contribution to economic growth is wasted. The type of unemployment discussed above is **hidden unemployment** and is not taken into account when calculating the UR. Therefore the UR is not necessarily a valid indicator of the true level of unemployment and the welfare of households. The UR underestimates the true level of unemployment.

A country's UR rate is calculated for the whole country. The rate however can vary dramatically across regions. Also the UR varies across different age groups. The UR rate of young adults in Spain in 2013, for example, is higher than the national average. Unemployment maybe higher amongst women, particularly when women find it hard to find full-time work and have to take part-time jobs. They are often underemployed. Some employers discriminate against particular ethnic groups. Therefore the unemployment rate of these groups is often higher than the national average. Also firms are reluctant to employ people if they do not speak the national language.

Model sentence: Distribution of unemployment is unequal due to geographical, age, ethnic, and gender disparities.

Discuss the costs of unemployment for the economy, society, and households

There are many costs to households, society, and the economy associated with unemployment. Unemployment is a waste of a scarce **resource**. Fewer goods and services are produced than is possible. Output is below the **full employment levels of output**. The higher the level of unemployment the bigger the **deflationary gap**. Aggregate demand is relatively low. Total expenditure in the economy is not sufficient to buy all the goods and services that could be made if all **factors of production** are fully utilized.

Discuss the private costs of unemployment

The costs borne by the people who are unemployed are called private costs. They suffer from low levels of income and have a lower **standard of living** than those employed. The amount of wants they can satisfy are limited by the **purchasing power** of their income. They suffer a fall in welfare.

In some countries the unemployed receive relatively generous unemployment benefit but in others no or very low benefit payments are provided by the government and therefore the unemployed struggle to satisfy their **basic needs**.

The children of those unemployed also are **adversely** affected. Statistically children of the long-term unemployed are less likely to enjoy a good standard of living in adulthood.

Cancer rates and obesity rates, for example, are higher amongst poorer members of the community. Mental health problems such as depression are also associated with low levels of income as is family breakdown.

Discuss the external costs of unemployment

Those who are unemployed for long periods of time become **deskilled** thereby reducing their chances of finding work. There is a connection between long-term unemployment and health problems. Those unemployed for long periods are statistically more likely to be involved in criminal activity such as theft and vandalism. Therefore there are costs associated with unemployment that must be borne by society. These are called **external costs**. They are the costs that are paid for by **third parties** such as the taxpayer. External costs include the cost to the taxpayer of police work associated with crime, the extra cost to the **judicial system** and the cost of keeping more people in prison. And there are the additional costs of medical treatment paid for by the taxpayer.

Subject vocabulary

hidden unemployment occurs when people have given up actively looking for work. They are not included in the official unemployment statistics despite being unemployed

resources the inputs into the production process, the factors of production

full employment level of output the potential quantity of output that can be produced in an economy when all factors of production are employed

deflationary (recessionary) gap the situation in which the actual output of an economy is less than its potential output

factors of production the inputs into the production process (land, labour, capital and entrepreneurship)

standard of living the level of well-being of a person or groups of people

purchasing power a measure of how many goods and services a given amount of money can buy

basic needs the elements required for survival such as water, food, and shelter

deskilled describes labour that has lost skills due to lack of use. Also production is deskilled when skilled labour is replaced by unskilled labour due to the introduction of new technologies.

external cost occurs when the production or consumption of a good creates a cost that must be paid by third parties

third parties people who are not directly involved in a transaction but are nevertheless affected by the transaction. People who are external to the market.

Synonyms

frustrated .... disturbed/ annoyed

disparities .... differences/ inequalities

adversely .... negatively

Glossary

judicial system relating to the law and the decisions that court judges make

Discuss the effect on the government of unemployment

National income and expenditure is at a relatively low level therefore the government collects less tax revenue. Income tax revenues fall as unemployment rises and indirect tax revenue, revenue raised from the tax charged on the sale of goods and services, also falls. As expenditure falls profit earned by firms falls leading to a fall in revenue from **corporation tax**.

As unemployment rises total benefit payments made by the government to the unemployed increase. Also government pays for the external costs associated with unemployment. This represents a significant opportunity cost. As revenues fall and **government expenditure** increases the country's budget position worsens. A **budget deficit** is likely to occur. The government must borrow from the financial markets in order to fund the shortfall. This increases the size of the **national debt** leading to an increase in **interest payment** on the debt.

Discuss the effect on business investment and international competitiveness of unemployment

With low levels of expenditure and increasing unemployment firms do not feel confident about future economic prospects and are less likely to invest in new **capital** thereby reducing AD even further. This lack of expenditure and investment means that the country does not remain competitive as average costs of production rise above those of its international competitors. Demand for the country's exports falls leading to a fall in **net exports**, a component of AD. As the incomes of those who lose their jobs falls there is an increase in **income inequality**. The distribution of income becomes more unequal. (Distribution of income is discussed in detail on pages 164–67.)

Model sentence: There are both the private costs and the external costs (negative externalities) caused by unemployment. Tax revenues fall and government expenditure rises leading to a budget deficit and increases in the national debt.

Test your understanding of this unit by answering the following questions

- A country has a labour force of 15 million people. The number of people unemployed is 3 million. Calculate the unemployment rate.
- Explain the costs of unemployment to individuals, society, and the economy.
- Explain the limitations of the unemployment rate.

Learning Outcomes

- Describe, using examples, the meaning of frictional, structural, seasonal, and cyclical (demand-deficient) unemployment.
- Distinguish between the causes of frictional, structural, seasonal, and cyclical (demand-deficient) unemployment.
- Explain, using a diagram, that cyclical unemployment is caused by a fall in aggregate demand.
- Explain, using a diagram, that structural unemployment is caused by changes in the demand for particular labour skills, changes in the geographical location of industries, and labour market rigidities.
- Evaluate government policies to deal with the different types of unemployment.

Explain the differences between, and causes of, the different types of unemployment

The two most important types of unemployment are **structural unemployment** and **cyclical unemployment**. Cyclical unemployment is also known as **demand-deficient unemployment** or **Keynesian unemployment**.

The demand for labour is a derived demand. Firms demand labour in order to produce output. Therefore the demand for labour is derived from the demand for goods and services. As aggregate demand increases firms respond by increasing output. In order to increase output firms employ more workers therefore unemployment falls. As aggregate demand falls firms respond by reducing output. Fewer workers are now required to produce fewer goods and services therefore unemployment rises. This is called cyclical unemployment because the numbers employed depends upon where the economy is in the **business cycle**. In a boom total expenditure (AD) is relatively high. Firms wish to produce more goods therefore unemployment falls. As AD falls the economy begins to slow down. Fewer workers are required and unemployment rises. This is why

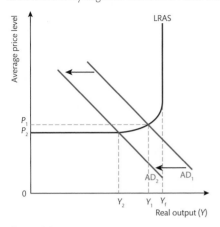

Figure 51.1

this type of unemployment is called demand-deficient unemployment. It is caused by a lack of aggregate demand. This type of unemployment changes with the business cycle and so is temporary. As an economy moves out of **recession** cyclical unemployment falls as firms employ more workers in order to raise output.

As total expenditure falls the aggregate demand curve shifts down and to the left from AD_1 to AD_2. In response firms reduce output from Y_1 to Y_2. The **deflationary gap** increases from $Y_f - Y_1$ to $Y_f - Y_2$ and the **price level** falls from P_1 to P_2. Total expenditure is not sufficient to buy all the goods and services that can be produced at the **full employment level of output,** Yf. Workers become unemployed due to a lack of aggregate demand.

Structural unemployment is caused by changes in the structure of industries in a country. In the UK, for example, over the last few decades there have been major changes in the types of industries. Heavy industry, such as mining and ship building, has all but disappeared. **Manufacturing industries** in general now contribute significantly less to **GDP**. There has been a move away from heavy industry and manufacturing towards the **tertiary sector** or service sector. The skills needed by industries have changed. Some workers' skills do not match those now in demand. Workers are **occupationally immobile**. They cannot obtain work in the emerging industries because they do not have the required skills. The skills they do have are now not in demand and therefore workers are unable to gain employment.

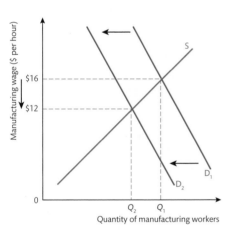

Figure 51.2

Figure 51.2 represents the labour market for manufacturing workers. Structural changes, caused by a move away from manufacturing towards the service sector leads to a fall in the demand for manufacturing workers. Fewer workers are demanded at each **wage rate** causing the demand for labour curve to shift down and to the left and leading to a **excess supply** of labour at the original equilibrium wage of $16 per hour. Wage falls to $12 per hour to eliminate the excess supply and equilibrium quantity of workers employed in manufacturing falls from Q_1 to Q_2. As time goes by demand falls even more leading to more structural unemployment in this sector.

Structural unemployment occurs in developing countries as the economy moves away from producing agricultural output to producing manufactured goods. The demand for those with farming skills falls and the workers become unemployed. As economies grow they move away from reliance on the agricultural sector and structural unemployment increases. This also occurs when a country moves away from manufacturing to the service sector.

A flexible labour market is one in which workers are willing and able to respond to changes in the pattern of demand for labour and to changes in the wage rate. If workers are occupationally mobile it means they have skills that are demanded by industry. The greater the number of skills the more occupationally flexible the labour force is and the quicker it is able to adapt to structural changes thus reducing levels of structural unemployment.

Industries sometimes relocate, normally in order to reduce costs. Workers are often unable to move to where the industry has relocated. They are **geographically immobile**. This can be because of the high cost of moving from one region to another or simply because they do not want to move because of family and social ties. The cost of commuting to and from work may also act as a barrier to mobility. People in this situation find themselves unemployed because their skills are no longer demanded in the region they live and they are unwilling or unable to relocate. Geographical immobility leads to excess supply of certain types of labour in

Subject vocabulary

continued from page 140

cyclical/demand-deficient unemployment/ Keynesian unemployment unemployment caused by a lack of aggregate demand. Unemployment changes as the economy goes through the business cycle, increasing when AD falls and decreasing when AD rises.

business cycle the fluctuations in economic activity over time. There are four stages of the business cycle: recession, trough, recovery, and peak/boom.

recession two consecutive quarters of negative economic growth

deflationary (recessionary) gap the situation in which the actual output of an economy is less than its potential output

price level the current weighted average price of a selected group of goods and services produced in a country over a period of time

full employment level of output the potential quantity of output that can be produced in an economy when all factors of production are employed

manufacturing industries industries that use labour and capital to turn raw materials and components into finished goods

GDP Gross Domestic Product is the monetary value of all the finished goods and services produced within a country in a given period of time, usually measured over a year

tertiary sector the part of the economy concerned with the provision of services

occupationally immobile occurs when workers do not have the necessary skills to change jobs

wage rate the amount of money paid to labour per unit of time or unit of output

excess supply occurs when quantity supplied is greater than quantity demanded

geographically immobile describes workers who are unable to relocate in order to find work, often because of the high costs of moving

one area and excess demand in others. The greater the degree of geographical flexibility the lower the level of unemployment.

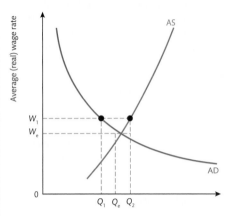

Figure 51.3

Government, industries, and **trade unions** intervene in the labour market. Governments in some countries have introduced **minimum wage** legislation and trade unions, which are organizations that negotiate with management on behalf of the workers, try to increase the wage rate of workers. Some industries are monopsonies. A monopsony is a sole demander of a certain type of labour and therefore has the market power to push wages down. All these economic agents intervene in the labour market pushing wage away from the **equilibrium wage** that is determined by the **forces of demand and supply**. In these circumstances there is **wage rigidity**.

The equilibrium wage in a **free labour market** is W_e and equilibrium employment is Q_e as shown in Figure 51.3. The government introduce a minimum wage set at W_1. At W_1 the quantity supplied of labour, Q_2, exceeds the quantity demanded, Q_1. Wage in a free market would fall in order to eliminate the excess supply of labour. However, this cannot happen because of the minimum wage. Q_2 is the number of workers willing to supply labour at the minimum wage and Q_1 is the number of workers demanded. The minimum wage has caused unemployment of Q_2 to Q_1. Inflexibility of the wage rate causes unemployment. This type of unemployment is called classical unemployment or real-wage unemployment caused by intervention that does not allow the market to clear.

The state of technology also changes over time. As capital becomes more technologically advanced it replaces the need for workers with certain skills. For example, in car manufacturing welding, the fusing of metal, was done by workers using welding machines. The use of automated welding equipment has left these workers without jobs. Unemployment caused by the introduction of such capital is called technological unemployment. The industry has become more **capital-intensive** and less **labour-intensive**.

Frictional unemployment is short-term unemployment caused by workers who have left one job to search for another. It is thought to be of benefit to an economy because workers are moving to jobs to which they are best suited and most productive. Workers often want to move to earn a higher wage and to develop careers. Frictional unemployment is a sign that this process is occurring. Seasonal unemployment occurs in industries when demand for labour changes depending on the time of year. When the weather is very wet, for example, less construction of buildings takes place and therefore demand for building workers falls. In the hospitality industry demand for hotel stays falls therefore demand for bar staff, waiters, and other hotel workers also falls causing unemployment.

Evaluate government policies to deal with the different types of unemployment

Demand-deficient unemployment

Demand-deficient unemployment is caused by low levels of aggregate demand therefore government could introduce policies with the aim of increasing aggregate demand. AD = C + I + G + (X – M). The government through changes in policy, can try to affect the components of AD. Policies that are aimed at changing AD are called demand-side policies. There are two types of demand-side policies: **fiscal policy** and **monetary policy**.

Fiscal policy involves taxation and government expenditure. If the government reduces the tax on household income the total amount of **disposable income** in the economy rises. Households will spend a proportion of the extra income on domestically produced goods and services thereby increasing AD.

Model sentence: The actual increase in AD depends on households' aggregate marginal propensity to consume. The higher the MPC the greater the increase in consumption and therefore the greater the fall in demand deficient unemployment. (See pages 134–37 for a detailed explanation of marginal propensity.)

If households save or spend most of the extra income on imports **marginal propensity to withdraw** would be relatively high and the increase in consumption on domestically produced goods will be less. If a country has a relatively high MPW then the increase in disposable income will have less impact on AD.

Model sentence: An increase in consumption increases AD and firms respond by employing more workers in order to increase output leading to a fall in demand-deficient unemployment.

If households expect the economy to grow in the future and think that their jobs are secure then the MPC will be relatively high leading to a greater fall in unemployment. If households are less **optimistic** then they are more likely to save the extra disposable income or pay back existing debt. Therefore the increase in consumption will not be as great and the effect of the fiscal policy on unemployment will not be as big. Increases in AD cause induced investment. Firms increase investment in order to increase output in response to higher levels of consumption. Investment is a component of AD therefore AD rises even further as firms invest.

The government could reduce the rate of **corporation tax** leaving firms with higher after-tax profit. *Ceteris paribus*, investment rises leading to an increase in AD. Investment is an injection into the circular flow of income model and is subject to the **Keynesian multiplier** (see pages 134–37). Higher levels of investment causes further increases in income and expenditure. Therefore AD increases by more than the initial investment leading to a greater fall in unemployment.

The government could reduce indirect taxes such as VAT and **duty** charged on the sale of goods and services. A reduction in indirect tax in effect reduces the costs of production causing the SRAS curve to shift down and to the right. The price level falls leading to an increase in **quantity demanded**. A fall in the price level increases households' **real income** therefore consumption rises and unemployment falls.

The government could increase government expenditure. It could invest in **transport infrastructure** for example. Government expenditure is a component of AD and an injection into the circular flow of income model. Like private investment by firms, government expenditure is subject to the multiplier causing increases in income and expenditure greater than that caused by the initial expenditure.

However, **expansionary fiscal policy** can lead to a worsening budget deficit (occurs when government expenditure > tax revenue) because tax revenue falls at the same time as government expenditure increases. The government must borrow more money from the financial sector leading to increases in the national debt. The debt and the interest charged on the debt must be repaid by the taxpayers in the future, thereby reducing the future taxpayers' disposable income and their levels of consumption.

The government could introduce an expansionary monetary policy by reducing the **interest rate**. As the cost of borrowing falls households are more likely to borrow money from banks in order to buy relatively more expensive goods, such as cars, leading to an increase in household consumption. The interest payment on existing loans also falls thereby increasing households' **discretionary incomes** leaving people with more money to spend on goods and services. AD rises and unemployment falls. Again, confidence about the future of the economy has a major effect on the amount of the extra income that households spend rather than save.

As interest rate falls, *ceteris paribus*, firms are more likely to borrow in order to invest because it reduces the cost of an **investment** and thereby increases potential returns. However, demand for **loanable funds** is not very sensitive to changes in interest. Far more important are the expectations firms have regarding future levels of AD. If firms are not optimistic about future levels of aggregate demand lower interest rates are unlikely to encourage them to borrow in order to invest.

Model sentence: Fiscal policy and monetary policy are called demand-side policies because their purpose is to change the components of aggregate demand.

Structural unemployment

Structural changes in the economy lead to **occupational immobility**. Demand for certain skills falls leading to a rise in unemployment. These workers are willing to work but do not possess the skills that industries now demand. Increasing AD will not affect this type of unemployment. The government could introduce policies that lead to an increase in the supply of labour that possess the skills that are in demand. Such policies are **supply-side policies** because the aim is to affect a factor of production that is used in order to supply goods and services.

Government can increase **occupational flexibility** through education and training. A good education in schools should give young people the necessary skills to be able to adapt to the demands of industry, enabling them to be able to learn new skills later in life. Post-16 and -18 colleges could offer courses that give students the necessary skills so that they can find jobs. In this way government directly intervenes by providing the training

Subject vocabulary

marginal propensity to withdraw is the proportion of additional household income that is taxed, saved and spent on imports. MPW = MPT + MPS + MPM

corporation tax a tax levied in the UK on company profits

Keynesian multiplier the number by which the value of the expenditure is multiplied to give the total increase in national income. The multiplier = 1/1-MPC

quantity demanded the amount of a good consumers are willing and able to buy at a given price over a given period of time

real income income after taking into account the effects of inflation on purchasing power

transport infrastructure the physical capital that supports a transport system

expansionary fiscal policy policy involving the increase of government spending and/or the reduction of taxation

interest rate the percentage amount charged by a lender for money borrowed

discretionary income income after tax and expenditure on basic necessities such as rent, heating, and food

investment the addition to capital stock

loanable funds sum of money in an economy that is saved and available to those wishing to borrow

structural change long-term shift in the fundamental industrial structure

occupational immobility occurs when workers do not have the necessary skills to change jobs

supply-side policies government policy designed to affect the level of aggregate supply in an economy by increasing the quantity and/or productivity of the factors of production

occupational flexibility describes a situation in which workers are able to perform a variety of tasks because they have the necessary skills

Synonyms

optimistic.............. positive

duty .... tax

needed to correct **market failure** caused by occupational immobility. This type of training is funded by **tax revenue**. There is a large **opportunity cost** of direct provision meaning that there will be less investment in other areas such as **transport infrastructure** and health services. The government can encourage private firms to offer training and **apprenticeships** through the provision of subsidies. A subsidy reduces the **private cost** of providing training and apprenticeships thereby increasing their supply. Again there is an opportunity cost of this policy. The firms might use the subsidy for purposes other than training and therefore not always provide sufficient training. The government must use scarce **resources** in order to make sure that training takes place.

The government can reduce the cost of moving from one area to another in order to reduce **geographical immobility**. For example, governments can provide relatively cheap social housing in areas where rents are relatively high or reduce households' **tax rates**. Increasing investment in transport infrastructure will reduce commuting times thereby making it possible for people to get to and from work efficiently without having to move house. The government could encourage firms to relocate to areas of high **structural unemployment** by, for example, reducing local business taxes and **corporation tax**.

Introduction of all these policies involves large opportunity costs. Less tax revenue is available for alternative investments. The policies are effective only in the long term. The supply of labour with the skills demanded by industry increases slowly over time. If the policies are to be effective government must also have accurate information about the type of skills not only needed now but those that will be needed by industry in the future.

Real wage/classical unemployment

Policies introduced to reduce the power of trade unions to negotiate with management a higher wage rate will reduce classical unemployment. The removal of the guaranteed minimum wage removes a barrier to wage flexibility. Such policies allow the wage rate to be flexible so that it can change in response to market forces. When there is **excess supply** of labour at the wage rate the wage then can fall until quantity of labour demanded and the quantity of labour supplied are equal and the market clears thereby curing classical unemployment.

The removal of the minimum wage would reduce the **standard of living** of low-paid workers making the **distribution of income** more unequal. The workers might be better off claiming unemployment benefits so they will leave the **labour force** entirely and perhaps start working in the **hidden economy**. This would reduce the **full employment level of output**.

Frictional unemployment

If the government reduced unemployment benefit it would act as an incentive for those between jobs to seek and take jobs more quickly. Government could improve the lines of communication between firms who demand labour and people who want to supply their labour by providing information about job vacancies through work agencies. School leavers and graduates who are looking for work are included in frictional unemployment statistics. Schools and universities could be instructed by government to provide career advice and information about job vacancies.

What is the natural rate of unemployment?

There is always some unemployment in a country even when the economy is producing at full employment levels of output. There will always be some people who are between jobs, those who are unemployed because demand for labour in some industries changes throughout the year or who are occupationally immobile. It is expected and even beneficial to the economy that workers will change jobs and that school leavers and graduates take time to find work. It is assumed that certain workers will be unemployed at certain times of the year due to a fall in demand for the output of certain industries. A developing and growing economy will go through structural changes so occupational immobility is a natural consequence of these changes and some occupational unemployment is in some ways a good thing because it is an inevitable result of **economic growth**.

Model sentence: Natural unemployment is the sum of frictional, seasonal, and structural unemployment. This sum expressed as a percentage of the labour force is the natural rate of unemployment.

Learning Outcomes

- Distinguish between inflation, disinflation, and deflation.

- Explain that inflation and deflation are typically measured by calculating a consumer price index (CPI), which measures the change in prices of a basket of goods and services consumed by the average household.

- Construct a weighted price index, using a set of data provided. (HL)

- Calculate the inflation rate from a set of data. (HL)

- Explain that different income earners may experience a different rate of inflation when their pattern of consumption is not accurately reflected by the CPI.

- Explain that inflation figures may not accurately reflect changes in consumption patterns and the quality of the products purchased.

- Explain that economists measure a core/underlying rate of inflation to eliminate the effect of sudden swings in the prices of food and oil, for example.

- Explain that a producer price index measuring changes in the prices of factors of production may be useful in predicting future inflation.

Explain the difference between inflation, disinflation, and deflation

Low and stable levels of inflation is a macroeconomic policy objective of government. Inflation is defined as a continuing or **sustained** increase in the average price level of goods and services in an economy over a given period of time. Deflation is a continuing fall in the average price level over a given period of time. A single increase or decrease in the price of a particular good is not inflation or deflation. During a year, the price of some goods and services increase while the price of others decrease. For example, the price of energy may increase and the price of clothes may decrease. Inflation or deflation is an increase or decrease in the *average* price level of goods and services. The rate of inflation is the rate at which prices increase over time. Disinflation is a fall in the rate of inflation. In other words, the average price level continues to increase but at a diminishing rate. Creeping inflation occurs when there is a relatively small increase in the average price level each year. Hyper-inflation occurs when there are sustained, very large increases in the average price level.

Model sentence: Inflation is a sustained increase in the average price level, deflation is a fall in the average price level, and disinflation is a fall in the rate of inflation.

Explain how inflation is measured

Inflation is a sustained increase in the average price level of goods and services. An index is used to measure the price level. If at the beginning of the year the **price index** was 100 and by the end of the year it rose to 104 this means that the rate of inflation was 4%. The consumer price index (CPI) is used by many governments to measure the changes in the price level of consumer goods and services. Prices of a large selection of goods and services (called the 'basket' of goods) are monitored by the government each month. Goods and services in this 'basket' include food and drinks, gas and electricity, rent, car insurance, clothes, electrical goods, mobile phones, petrol, train and bus fares, along with many others. Prices of some goods in the basket increase and some fall but when the price of the basket of goods shows an overall increase it means that there has been an increase in the average price level. Prices are taken from a number of suppliers and **retailers** across different regions of a country and an average of the change in price of each good is calculated and then **converted** into a price index.

The contents of the basket of goods changes over time. For example, a change in technology leads to changes in the consumption of goods. Now many people buy laptop computers and buy music by downloading it. These items are now included in the basket of goods. The goods selected to be in the basket changes with patterns of consumer consumption so that it is representative of the goods consumed by the average household. This means that the calculated inflation rate is one that is experienced by the average household.

Model sentence: When calculating the rate of inflation the base period is a specific point in time that is chosen by the government in order to be able to measure changes in the price of a basket of goods from the chosen point in time to a later point in time.

Calculate the CPI – a step-by-step guide

This method of calculating the rate of inflation is oversimplified and not very useful because it does not take into account the proportion of income spent by the average household on each type of good. Each good is assumed to be equally as important. But the **purchasing power** of an average household's income is affected more by changes in the price of petrol and rents than it is by changes in the price of a box of matches and the price of chocolate.

Construct a weighted price index, using a set of data provided, and calculate the rate of inflation (HL)

An average household spends a higher proportion of its **disposable income** on some goods than it does on others. For example, the average household might spend 30.8% of its disposable income on housing, 16.2% on food and non-alcoholic drinks, 15.5% on transport, and 13.5% on recreation and leisure, spending a much lower proportion on tobacco, alcohol, and education.

Model sentence: The government puts the goods and services included in the basket of goods into categories and calculates the proportion of the average household's income that it spends on each category.

Using this data the government gives a weight to each category. For example, the category of food and non-alcoholic drinks includes lots of items such as bread, butter, beef, potatoes, peas, milk, tea, coffee, as well as ready-prepared meals. The transport category includes petrol, new cars, bus fares, train fares, car insurance, and so on. The weight each category is given is a reflection of the proportion of income that the average household spends on the goods and services in each category. The sum of the weights given to each category equals 100. Shown in Table 52.1 is an example of the weighted categories for a country.

Also shown is the change in price in each category. The price of the goods and services included in the housing category has increased by an average of 5%. To calculate a 5% increase in the proportion of income spent on housing multiply 30.8 by 1.05: 30.8 × 1.05 = 32.34. The average price of goods in the health category has increased by an average of 10%. To calculate the 10% increase in the proportion of income spent on health, multiply 2.1 by 1.1: 2.1 × 1.1 = 2.31. The same is done for all categories and appear in the final column and are added to give the total.

Category	Weight/%age of income spent on each category Base time period	Change in price in each category after 1 year	New time period CPI time period 2
Housing	30.8	1.05	32.34
Food and non-alcoholic drinks	16.2	1.02	16.524
Transport	15.5	1.1	17.05
Recreation and leisure	13.5	1.02	13.77
Clothing	6.4	1.05	6.72
Furniture and household goods	5.6	1	5.6
Alcohol and tobacco	3.3	1.03	3.465
Communication	3.7	1.01	3.737
Education	2.9	1.04	3.016
Health	2.1	1.1	2.31
Total	100 (CPI Base index)		104.532 (CPI)

Table 52.1

The consumer price index can be used to calculate the rate of inflation (IR) between two periods of time by using the following formula:

$$IR = \frac{\text{CPI time period 2 – CPI base index}}{\text{CPI time period 1}} \times 100$$

Using the example in Table 52.1, $IR = \frac{(104.532 - 100)}{100} = 0.04532 \times 100 = 4.532\%$

If the CPI increases from 104.532 to 106.6 in the following year, the inflation rate over the two-year period is calculated in the following way:

$$IR = \frac{\text{CPI time period 3 – CPI time period 1}}{\text{CPI time period 1}} \times 100 = \frac{(106.6 - 100)}{100} = 0.066 \times 100 = 6.6\%$$

The rate of inflation between period 2 and 3 is calculated in the following way:

$$IR = \frac{\text{CPI time period 3 – CPI time period 2}}{\text{CPI time period 2}} \times 100 = \frac{(106.6 - 104.532)}{104.532} = 0.0978 \times 100 = 1.98\%$$

In Table 52.1, housing prices increased by 5% while the price of clothing did not change. In Table 52.2, the price of housing remains unchanged while the price of clothing increases by 5%. The calculations are done as before and are shown in the table.

Category	Weight/%age of income spent on each category Base time period	Change in price in each category after 1 year	New time period CPI time period 2
Housing	30.8	1	30.8
Food and non-alcoholic drinks	16.2	1.02	16.524
Transport	15.5	1.1	17.05
Recreation and leisure	13.5	1.02	13.77
Clothing	6.4	1.05	6.72
Furniture and household goods	5.6	1	5.6
Alcohol and tobacco	3.3	1.03	3.465
Communication	3.7	1.01	3.737
Education	2.9	1.04	3.016
Health	2.1	1.1	2.31
Total	100		102.992

Table 52.2

The index has risen from 100 to 102.992: $IR = \frac{102.992 - 100}{100} = 2.992\%$

A percentage change in the price of housing has a greater effect on the overall rate of inflation than the same percentage change in the price of clothing.

The rate of inflation over the year was just under 3%, compared with over 4% in the previous example. This highlights the importance of weighting the various categories. The rate of inflation is affected more by changes in the price of goods that the average consumer spends a relatively higher proportion of their income on and is affected least by changes in the price of goods that the average consumer spends a relatively lower proportion of their income on.

Model sentence: The proportion of income spent by each household on the categories of goods is different, therefore each household has a different rate of inflation.

Explain the limitations of the consumer price index as a measure of inflation

The CPI measures changes in the average price of goods and services that are bought by a typical household over a given period of time. The idea is that the rate of inflation should give a true reflection of how price changes affect most people living in a country. Households buy different baskets of goods and in varying proportions. A household on low income spends a higher than average proportion of its **disposable income** on food, rent, and other necessities, and a much lower than average proportion of income on luxuries such as holidays abroad than a household earning relatively high income. Therefore, when the price of necessities increases, it has a much greater impact on the **standard of living** of those on low incomes than it does on households earning a much higher income. The inflation rate for the low income household in this example is higher than the CPI average rate of inflation because very low income earners spend nearly all their income on necessities.

Price increases are sometimes caused by advances in technology and these are not taken into account when calculating the rate of inflation. The quality and efficiency of washing machines and computers for example has improved a lot over the years and these advances can lead to an increase in price but the new goods are in some ways not comparable with the older, less technologically advanced goods.

Patterns of consumption can change relatively quickly and the government must change the basket of goods so that it represents the purchasing habits of the average household. It takes a relatively long period of time to make the necessary changes to the basket of goods; therefore, at any one time the goods in the basket are not an accurate representation of the quantity and types of goods currently consumed. Therefore, the average rate of inflation is inaccurate.

Inflation is defined as a sustained increase in prices. However, the statistics gathered by the government do not take into account short-term changes in price caused by changes in supply-side factors. Food prices can rise steeply at certain times of the year due to shortages but can fall again quite quickly once supply rises. Petrol price increases can also change quickly due to supply-side factors but over the long term the trend in price increases is more stable. Such increases in price can give a misleading inflation rate. Governments try to take into account the effects of these changes in price by calculating a 'core' inflation rate by excluding the goods from the basket of goods.

CPI measures changes in the price of **consumer goods**. The price of **factors of production** is not taken into account. A **producer price index** (PPI) measures a basket of goods made up of **raw materials**, **capital**, and energy. PPI is a useful measure because it shows what is happening to **costs of production** and therefore can be used to predict what will happen to the price of consumer goods in the future. If costs of production increase, firms increase prices of the goods they produce in order to maintain their **profit margins**. Inflation caused by increases in the price of factors of production is called **cost-push inflation**.

Errors occur in the collection of the data affecting the accuracy of the calculated rate of inflation. Also only a small percentage of retailers and suppliers are used to collect the data on price changes. The government could extend the number of retailers and suppliers and increase the number of areas of the country where data is collected, but this increases the **resources** needed and adds to the costs of data collection.

The basket of goods and the ways data is collected varies across countries. This makes international comparisons of rates of inflation both difficult and misleading.

Test your understanding of this unit by answering the following questions

- Distinguish between inflation, disinflation, and deflation.
- Explain the term 'the basket of goods'.
- What are the limitations of CPI as a measure of inflation?
- What is the producer price index?
- Explain why individual households experience different rates of inflation.
- Answer the questions below by using the information in the table (HL).

CPI date for country 1; Q3 = third quarter (i.e. July–September); Q4 = foruth quarter (i.e. October–December) etc.

	Q3 2008	Q4 2008	Q1 2009	Q2 2009	Q3 2009	Q4 2009	Q1 2010
Country I's CPI	108.4	107.9	107.7	108.3	108.5	108.6	109.1

a Calculate Country I's inflation rates between each of the seven quarters.

b Between which quarters was the inflation rate hightest? Lowest?

c Between which quarters did Country I experience disinflation?

d Between which quarters did Country I experience deflation?

Learning Outcomes

- Discuss the possible consequences of a high inflation rate, including greater uncertainty, redistributive effects, less saving, and the damage to export competitiveness.

- Discuss the possible consequences of deflation, including high levels of cyclical unemployment and bankruptcies.

- Explain, using a diagram, that demand-pull inflation is caused by changes in the determinants of aggregate demand (AD), resulting in an increase in AD.

- Explain, using a diagram, that cost-push inflation is caused by an increase in the costs of factors of production, resulting in a decrease in short-run aggregate supply (SRAS).

- Evaluate government policies to deal with the different types of inflation.

Explain the effect inflation has on the purchasing power of money

Inflation causes **real incomes** to fall. This occurs when the rate of inflation is greater than the rate at which income grows. Changes in real income are calculated by subtracting the percentage change in **nominal income** from the rate of inflation. If the rate of inflation is 5% and nominal income increases by 2%, then real income falls by 3%. Inflation causes the **purchasing power** of money to fall. The amount of goods and services that can be bought with a set nominal income falls. Consumers cannot satisfy as many wants with their income, therefore **consumer welfare** falls.

Model sentence: If the percentage increase in nominal income is equal to the rate of inflation, then real income stays the same, leaving the purchasing power of income unchanged.

Explain the effect of inflation on the incentive to save

Some households save a proportion of their **disposable income** in a **savings account** at a bank. In return for the use of the money the bank pays the saver **interest** on the amount of money saved. For example a saver puts $10,000 in the bank at an **interest rate** of 5% per annum (each year). The interest paid to the saver is 5% of $10,000 which equals $500. At the end of the year, the saver has $10,500 in the bank (less any tax that must be paid on the interest earned). The purchasing power of the savings has increased. However, if the rate of inflation is greater than the rate of interest then the purchasing power of the saved money falls. If inflation is 6% and the **nominal rate of interest** is 5%, the **real value of the money** saved falls by 1%. Fewer goods and services can be bought with the savings than could have been bought at the start of the year. If inflation is 3% and the nominal rate of interest is 5% then the real value of the savings increases not by 5%, the nominal rate of interest, but by only 2%. Therefore, in order to calculate the increase in the real value of the savings, inflation must be taken into account.

Model sentence: The real interest rate takes into account the effects of inflation on the purchasing power of the saved money. The real rate of interest = the nominal rate of interest − the rate of inflation.

It is important to say that the formulae used above are simplified versions of the formulae actually used by economists when working out real income and the real interest rate for government and other institutions.

When the rate of inflation is greater than the nominal rate of interest, the real rate of interest is negative. The savings could buy more goods at the start of the year than at the end. Households bring forward consumption

Subject vocabulary

real income income after taking into account the effects of inflation on purchasing power

nominal income the numerical value of income which has not been adjusted to take into account the effect inflation has on the purchasing power of income

purchasing power a measure of how many goods and services a given amount of money can buy

consumer welfare a measure of the benefit obtained from the consumption of goods

disposable income household income after direct taxation has been deducted

savings account a bank account, which pays interest on deposits.

interest the price paid for the use of borrowed money/ the money earned from bank deposits

interest rate the percentage amount charged by a lender for money borrowed

nominal rate of interest the rate which has not been adjusted to take into account the effect of inflation

real value of money obtained by removing the effect of inflation on the nominal value of money

returns on investment
expressed as a percentage
it is calculated using the
formula: return on investment
= (gain from investment –
cost of investment) / cost
of investment × 100. It is
used by firms to evaluate the
effectiveness of an investment
project and to compare
the potential returns from
investment options.

asset an item of value owned
by an individual or firm,
especially one that could be
converted to cash

equilibrium price the price at
which the quantity consumers
are willing and able to buy is
equal to the quantity firms are
willing and able to produce

nominal rate of return the
amount of money earned on
money invested, expressed
as a percentage of the sum
invested, not adjusted for
inflation

positive real return when
the return on investment
is positive after it has been
adjusted to take into account
the effect inflation has on its
value

long-run economic growth
an increase in the productive
capacity of a country

productivity the quantity of
output per unit of input

**full-employment level
of output** the potential
quantity of output that can
be produced in an economy
when all factors of production
are employed

circular flow of income an
economic model that shows
the flow of money between
households and firms and,
in more complex versions,
the flows of money into and
out of the financial sector,
government sector, and the
international sector

cyclical unemployment
unemployment caused by a
lack of aggregate demand.
Unemployment changes as
the economy goes through
the business cycle, increasing
when AD falls and decreasing
when AD rises.

current account deficit
occurs when the amount
of money flowing out of a
country from the trade in
goods and services, investment
income, and transfers is greater
than the amount flowing in

when high levels of inflation are expected because the money spent now can buy more goods and services than in the future. Inflation encourages consumption now and discourages saving. This could lead to a fall in the supply of loanable funds available for firms to borrow and therefore to a fall in investment. Investment is needed for the economy to grow.

When the real interest rate is low, households try to find ways of earning higher **returns on investment**. So instead of putting income into a savings account, a household might buy **assets**, such as gold, property, shares, and art instead. When real interest rates are low, often the price of gold increases. This is because demand for gold increases as households try to increase their returns on savings thereby pushing up the **equilibrium price** of gold.

Model sentence: *Ceteris paribus*, the higher the rate of inflation, the lower the real rate of interest. High inflation encourages households to bring consumption forward and low real rates of interest reduce households' incentive to save.

Explain the redistributive effects of inflation

Inflation causes the real interest rate to fall causing a transfer of resources away from savers to borrowers. For savers, inflation leads to a fall in the real value of their savings but for borrowers, inflation reduces the real value of their debt. Inflation is bad for savers but benefits borrowers.

There are many people who live on a fixed income, such as income from a private pension or from a savings account. Many incomes from private pensions do not increase each year with inflation. The nominal income never increases. It is fixed. Inflation reduces the purchasing power of their income year by year but nominal income does not increase to offset the loss of real income caused by inflation. The standard of living of those on a low fixed income is affected more by inflation than those who work because workers occasionally receive increases in their nominal income.

Explain how inflation affects business certainty, economic growth, and employment

Unstable rates of high inflation lead to business uncertainty. Firms are uncertain about how much their costs of production will be and what the price of the good will be. This makes it difficult to assess potential returns on investment projects thereby reducing total investment in the economy. Firms want to earn a higher **nominal rate of return** on any investment to offset the effect of inflation. This means that less investment will take place because the risk of not making a **positive real return** increases when there are high rates of inflation. Investment is needed for **long-run economic growth** because increasing the quantity and **productivity** of capital leads to an increase in **full-employment levels of output**. Also investment is a component of aggregate demand (AD) and an injection into the **circular flow of income**. The initial investments cause further increases in expenditure and income. As AD increases, firms take on more workers in order to increase supply and **cyclical unemployment** falls. Therefore, as investment falls it will have a negative effect on employment.

Explain how inflation affects international competitiveness

If the rate of inflation is greater in Italy than in countries with which Italy trades, consumers in the other countries have to pay a higher price for Italian goods and the quantity demanded of Italian exports falls. Also Italians will buy fewer domestically produced goods as they switch expenditure away from the relatively more expensive Italian goods to the relatively lower priced imported goods. Expenditure on imports increases and expenditure on exports falls leading to an increase in an existing **current account deficit**. Relatively high rates of inflation lead to a fall in international price competitiveness.

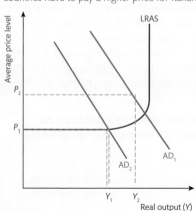

Figure 53.1

Explain the causes and consequences of deflation

Deflation occurs when there is a sustained fall in the average price level. The purchasing power of money increases. As the average price level continues to fall, more and more goods and services can be bought with the same nominal income.

Deflation can be caused by falling aggregate demand. The negative output gap or the deflationary gap, which is the difference between actual output and full-employment level of output, gets bigger as AD falls. This is the difference between Y_2 and Y_1 as shown in Figure 53.1. Falling AD, from AD_1 to AD_2 leads to an excess of **aggregate supply** over aggregate demand and the average price level falls from P_2 to P_1 in order to eliminate it. Total expenditure in the economy is not sufficient to buy all the goods and services produced when all factors of production are employed. Firms **lay off** workers as they reduce output in response to falling demand and **cyclical unemployment** or **demand-deficient unemployment** rises. Remember that the demand for labour is a **derived demand**. It is derived from the demand for goods and services.

Deflation can also be caused by an increase in the full potential level of output. This occurs when there is

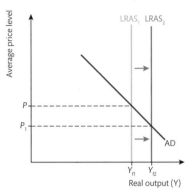

Figure 53.2

an increase in the quantity and/or quality (productivity) of the factors of production. The full-employment level of output is at Y_{f1} as shown in Figure 53.2. After an increase in the quantity and/or quality of one or more of the factors of full-employment, the level of output increases and the **long-run aggregate supply** (LRAS) curve shifts to the right. Full-employment levels of output increases from Y_{f1} to Y_{f2}. This causes an excess of aggregate supply at price level P and the average price level falls to P_1 in order to eliminate it. However, when firms invest in new capital, it increases aggregate demand. If AD increases at the same rate as LRAS, deflation will not occur. Deflation is much more likely to be caused by falls in AD.

As expenditure and prices fall, firms receive less **producer revenue** (price × quantity sold). Firms reduce output in response to falling consumption. Firms need fewer workers and reduce their labour force. Cyclical or demand-deficient unemployment increases and firms' profits fall. As profits fall, some firms make a **loss** or **negative profit**. Firms can make losses in the short run. Firms will keep trading in the hope that demand for their output will increase in the future. But if losses continue to be made in the long run, firms will close down owing money to their suppliers.

Unemployment rises, therefore **government expenditure** on **unemployment benefit** increases while at the same time government revenue received from income tax falls. A growing deflationary gap might lead to an increase in the **budget deficit** as the difference between government revenue and government expenditure grows.

Consumers delay or hold back consumption of non-necessities if it is expected that prices will continue to fall. A household might delay the purchase of a new car or television set until prices have fallen even more. Aggregate demand continues to fall, increasing levels of unemployment and **bankruptcy** rates.

Consumer confidence is very important in determining levels of aggregate demand. If households believe that they might lose their jobs then they will reduce present expenditure. Deflation reduces the value of assets such as houses and gold. A fall in **wealth** leads to a fall in confidence, which leads to a fall in expenditure.

Deflation leads to an increase in the value of debt because debt repayments are made with money that is increasing in value. Deflation causes the value of household and business debt to rise. Household and business debt repayments are usually fixed. Repayments made by households and firms do not fall as prices fall, therefore the value of the debt rises. Deflation leads to a fall in producer revenue but debt repayments do not fall, thereby the burden of debt increases.

Households continue to make the repayments on the debt. Increasing debt reduces consumer confidence, which in turn reduces expenditure. Deflation increases the real value of business debt. Business loans must be paid back at a time when profits are falling, leading to more bankruptcies. As aggregate demand, revenues, and profits fall firms lack the confidence to invest. Therefore, investment, a component of AD, falls.

Explain the causes of demand-pull inflation

Demand-pull inflation is caused by an excess of aggregate demand over aggregate supply. AD = consumer expenditure on domestically produced goods (C) + investment by firms (I) + government expenditure (G) + (expenditure on exports (X) – expenditure on imports (M)). For example, an increase in AD might be caused by growing confidence in the economy. Consumer expenditure (C) increases and firms respond to higher levels of consumption by increasing investment (I) and the AD curve shifts up and to the right as shown in Figure 53.3. The increase in AD can be caused by an increase in one or more of the components of AD.

Increasing levels of AD 'pull-up' prices in the economy. Aggregate demand (total expenditure) begins to exceed aggregate supply (total output). Firms increase supply in response to increases in consumption but when

cost-push inflation inflation caused by an increase in the costs of production, resulting in a decrease in aggregate supply

profit margin the percentage of producer revenue that ends up as profit for the firm. Profit margin = profit/producer revenue × 100. If a firm earns a profit of $20m from sales of $80m its profit margin is 25%.

factors of production the inputs into the production process (land, labour, capital and entrepreneurship)

supply-side shocks occurs when there is an unexpected change in the supply of a good resulting in a sudden change in its price

corporation tax a tax levied in the UK on company profits

minimum wage the minimum amount of money a firm is legally allowed to pay a worker for one hour's work

monetary policy the control of the supply of money by the central bank to affect the economy (e.g. changing interest rates)

fiscal policy government policy designed to achieve macroeconomic objectives through government expenditure and taxation

demand-side policies policies that are designed to influence aggregate demand

contractionary monetary policy policy involving the reduction of the money supply and the increase of interest rates

deflationary monetary policy a policy designed to eliminate an inflationary gap through reducing the money supply and increasing interest rates

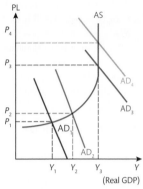

Figure 53.3

expenditure increases quickly it increases at a faster rate than the increase in output. Prices rise in order to eliminate the excess. In Figure 53.3, AD increases from AD$_1$ to AD$_2$. Firms are able to increase output from Y$_1$ to Y$_2$. The average price level rises from P$_1$ to P$_2$, a relatively small increase in prices. This is because aggregate supply increases at almost the same rate as aggregate demand. As AD rises from AD$_3$ to AD$_4$, firms are unable to increase output. The economy is at full-employment levels. It is not possible for firms to increase supply. Increases in AD are not matched by increases in aggregate supply (AS). AD exceeds AS. The average price level must increase by a relatively large amount in order to eliminate the excess.

Model sentence: When AD rises at a faster rate than AS, the price level rises to eliminate the excess AD.

Explain the causes of cost-push inflation

Model sentence: Cost-push inflation occurs when the costs of production increase, causing firms to increase price in order to maintain **profit margins.**

Cost-push inflation often occurs in a boom phase of the business cycle when demand for the **factors of production** is high. Increasing demand for raw materials or labour, for example, leads to an increase in their price, thereby causing an increase in the costs of production. Inflation is also caused by **supply-side shocks**. For example, when the price of oil in the early 1970s went up very quickly, the costs of production for industries all over the world went up, leading to cost-push inflation.

If the country's currency depreciates in value relative to other currencies, the price of all imported goods, including raw materials rises. This is called imported inflation. Firms have to pay a higher price for imported

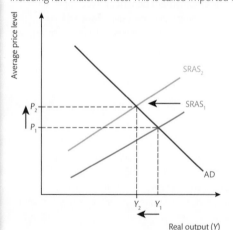

Figure 53.4

raw materials, leading to an increase in the costs of production and in turn to cost-push inflation.

Governments can cause inflation. An increase in **corporation tax** reduces company profits. Firms may increase the price of their goods. An increase in the **minimum wage** causes an increase in the costs of production and firms may increase the price of their goods in order to maintain profit margins.

This is shown in Figure 53.4 as a shift up and to the left of the short-run aggregate supply curve from SRAS$_1$ to SRAS$_2$. The average price level rises, causing aggregate demand to fall. Real output falls from Y$_1$ to Y$_2$ leading to a rise in unemployment.

Model sentence: Increases in the cost of production cause both inflation and demand-deficient unemployment.

Explain how an increase in interest rates reduces aggregate demand

Governments use both **monetary policy** and **fiscal policy** to control inflation. These policies are **demand-side policies** because the aim of the policies is to change the level of aggregate demand. Monetary policy is concerned with controlling the money supply in the economy and this is usually achieved by changing interest rates. **Contractionary monetary policy** or **deflationary monetary policy** is introduced by government to reduce the supply of money and thereby reduce spending in an economy. The main way the supply of money is reduced is by increasing interest rates.

Although in most countries the setting of interest rates is controlled by the central banks and not governments, the main objective of most central banks is to keep inflation low and stable, and they try to achieve this by managing interest rates.

Fiscal policy is concerned with government expenditure and government tax revenue. A contractionary or deflationary fiscal policy aims to reduce AD by reducing expenditure and increasing taxes. If inflation is caused by excess aggregate demand (demand-pull) then reducing expenditure in the economy should reduce the rate of inflation.

(Remember: AD = C + I + G + (X-M))

Government or central banks increase the interest rate in order to reduce inflationary pressures caused by high levels of expenditure. Households borrow money from banks in order to bring forward consumption of relatively higher priced durables such as TVs, washing machines, carpets, and cars. Increasing the interest rate increases the cost of borrowing and in effect increases the price the consumer pays for the good. As the cost of borrowing rises, expenditure (C) on these items falls, therefore AD falls.

Higher interest rates means higher interest payments on existing loans. Households with **mortgages** must pay more each month in interest payments on the loan thereby reducing **discretionary income** and in turn household expenditure (C). Some firms are **highly geared**. This means much of their investments have been financed by borrowing. Higher interest rates leads to higher interest payments on the loans and a fall in profit leaving firms with less profit to invest so investment (I) falls.

As interest rates rise, the cost of investment projects increase because interest payments on the loan increase. *Ceteris paribus*, as interest rates rise profit made on each investment falls therefore firms are less likely to make the investment. Higher interest rates leads to a fall in investment (I) therefore AD falls. As interest rates on savings accounts increase the minimum opportunity cost of any investment increases. Instead of investing in **productive capacity**, which comes with a relatively high risk, the firm may simply choose to place the money in a savings account and earn the interest payments at zero risk.

Model sentence: As interest rates rise the cost of borrowing increases reducing expenditure that is financed through loans.

Relatively high interest rates attract **financial capital** from abroad from individuals and **financial institutions** looking for higher returns on their money. Demand for the currency rises and it appreciates against other currencies. As the price of the currency rises, the price foreigners pay for the country's exports increases leading to a fall in quantity demanded of exports (X), therefore AD falls.

A high rate of interest leads to an increase in saving. More of households' disposable income is saved. If income is saved, it cannot be spent on goods and services.

Model sentence: *Ceteris paribus*, as interest rates rise the incentive to save increases. The more income that is saved by households, the less is spent. Therefore, as the interest rate rises, AD falls.

Explain how a fall in government expenditure and increases in taxes reduces aggregate demand.

Keynesians argue that the government should manage aggregate demand in order to achieve its macroeconomic objective of low and stable inflation. Taxes can be increased and government expenditure (G) reduced to reduce excess aggregate demand and bring the average price level down.

If the government increases income tax **disposable incomes** fall, leading to a fall in household expenditure on domestically produced goods (C). An increase in corporation tax reduces the incentive for firms to invest as less profit from each investment is made. Also after-tax profits fall leaving less profit available for investment (I), therefore AD falls. Government can reduce government expenditure (G) by spending less on **merit goods** and public goods and by reducing benefit payments, thereby reducing AD. Cuts in government expenditure and increases in tax lead to a fall in the **government's borrowing requirement** and the government might be able to achieve a **balanced budget**, where government expenditure equals tax revenue.

Model sentence: As tax rates increase, household disposable income and company profits fall, leading to a fall in household expenditure and business investment.

As aggregate demand falls, firms respond by reducing output. Therefore, demand for the factors of production fall leading to a fall in factor prices. This lowers the costs of production, thereby reducing inflationary cost-push pressures.

public sector the part of an economy that is controlled by the state. It concerns the provision of government services including national defence, education, and health.

private sector the part of the economy that is regulated but not controlled by the state and concerns individuals and groups bringing together the factors of production normally with the aim of making a profit

supply-side policies government policy designed to affect the level of aggregate supply in an economy by increasing the quantity and/or productivity of the factors of production

productivity the quantity of output per unit of input

state monopolies state-owned sole suppliers of goods and services

entrepreneur an individual who, in pursuit of profit, brings together the other factors of production in order to produce a good or service

international trade the cross-border exchange of goods and services

tariffs a tax placed on imported goods and services

quota a physical limit placed on the number of goods that can be traded or produced

open economy an economy in which firms engage in the international exchange of goods and services

external supply-side shock occurs when there is an unexpected change in the supply of a good produced abroad that results in a sudden change in its price

Governments can affect the inflation rate directly by controlling wages and prices in the **public sector**. If the state owns industries and services, it employs lots of workers such as nurses, teachers, railway workers, bus drivers, and post office workers. The government can minimize wage increases in the public sector. Reducing the real wage of the public sector workers reduces government expenditure and may persuade those in the **private sector** to accept cuts in their real wage. The government could minimize price increases of goods and services produced by state-owned industries. However, profits will fall and any losses must be subsidized by the taxpayer. The influence a government has is dependent on the number of industries under state control. The government can reduce indirect tax on goods, thereby reducing costs of production; for example, by reducing duty on petrol.

Explain how a fall in the rate of inflation can be achieved using supply-side policies

The objective of **supply-side policies** is to increase the quantity and quality (**productivity**) of the factors of production. This causes the aggregate supply curve to shift down and to the right pushing the average price level down. Increasing the full employment level of output of the economy leads to a shift to the right of the LRAS curve, which means that it is possible for excess aggregate demand to be eliminated by increases in aggregate supply, thereby holding the average price level down. The following are examples of supply-side policies: the provision of subsidies to firms to increase the amount of training of workers; making markets more price competitive by removing barriers to entry into industries; privatizing **state monopolies**; introducing strong laws on anti-competitive behaviour; and reducing tax on profits to encourage investment in new capital and to encourage potential **entrepreneurs** to set up businesses. **International trade** can be encouraged by removing **tariffs** and **quotas**. Domestic firms must become more productive if they are to compete with the most efficient firms in the world. By trading with other countries, consumers and producers can buy lower priced imported goods and services, reducing firms' costs of production and increasing the purchasing power of household income.

Evaluate government policies to deal with the different types of inflation

In the short run, government can try to keep inflation low and stable by managing aggregate demand through fiscal and monetary policy. The aim is to keep aggregate demand at a level that is enough to buy full- or nearly full-employment levels of output. When aggregate demand exceeds aggregate supply, causing demand-pull inflation, governments introduce deflationary policies to reduce aggregate demand and bring down the price level. Lowering aggregate demand reduces demand for the factors of production, including labour, lowering factor prices, and thereby reducing cost-push inflationary pressures. However, the fall in demand for labour leads to higher levels of demand-deficient unemployment. There is a **trade-off** between inflation and unemployment. Government tax revenue falls and government expenditure rises as benefit payments increase. This can cause a budget deficit and the government must borrow from the financial markets, thereby increasing the national debt.

Trade is becoming more globalized. Most countries have **open economies**. Inflation in one country can be caused by what happens in other countries. Controlling inflation by managing aggregate demand will not be successful if cost-push inflation is caused by **external supply-side shocks**, such as oil price increases caused by disruption of the world supply of oil.

Deflationary fiscal and monetary policies are unpopular with households and firms because higher taxes and interest rates reduce company profits and household income. Politicians do not want to upset the voters before an election for fear of losing votes.

Governments are not able to change fiscal policy quickly. There is a long legislative process that must be gone through before a deflationary fiscal policy can be introduced and after such a policy is introduced it takes time for households to change their patterns of consumption in response to a fall in disposable income. Therefore, it is not possible for government to use fiscal policy to quickly affect levels of aggregate demand. Governments find it very difficult to make real cuts in government expenditure. They have many commitments, such as the provision of state pensions, transport infrastructure, health services, and other merit and public goods. With growing demands and expectations, it is very difficult for governments to make cuts in public spending. Because of the limitations of fiscal policy, governments tend to favour the use of interest rates to manage levels of aggregate demand.

Relatively high taxes and interest rates discourage investment and entrepreneurship. The less income people keep for themselves, the less likely they are to risk their time and money starting a new business and there is less incentive for firms to make investments. The higher the cost of borrowing, the lower the return on any investment funded through borrowed money; therefore, the less likely firms are to borrow to invest. Deflationary policy therefore has a negative impact on the future potential levels of output of an economy. It is easier for a government to control inflation if the potential output of the economy is steadily growing. As stated before, this is achieved through supply-side policies aimed at increasing labour mobility, market competetiveness, innovation, and productivity. Aggregate demand can steadily increase without demand-pull and cost-push inflationary pressures building up.

A summary of the main points

Fiscal and monetary policies are used to reduce AD, thereby reducing demand-pull and cost-push inflation. However, doing so can cause unemployment, leading to a budget deficit and an increase in the national debt.

Imported inflation cannot be controlled by reducing AD.

Tax increases are unpopular so politicians may not be prepared to introduce this policy through fear of not being re-elected.

There is long time lag between an increase in tax and changes in aggregate demand.

Governments have spending commitments so it is very difficult to make real cuts in expenditure that will reduce aggregate demand.

Higher rates of tax discourage investment by firms and entrepreneurial activity leading to a reduction in long-run economic growth.

Fiscal policy has many disadvantages; therefore, some governments prefer to use interest rates as a method of controlling inflation and use supply-side policies to increase productivity and LRAS, thereby reducing demand-pull inflationary pressures.

Test your understanding of this unit by answering the following questions

- Using diagrams, distinguish between demand-pull and cost-push inflation.
- Explain the consequences of deflation.
- Discuss the effectiveness of deflationary demand-side policies as a cure for inflation.

Learning Outcomes

- Discuss, using a short-run Phillips curve diagram, the view that there is a possible trade-off between the unemployment rate and the inflation rate in the short run.

- Explain, using a diagram, that the short-run Phillips curve may shift outwards, resulting in stagflation (caused by a decrease in SRAS due to factors including supply shocks).

- Discuss, using a diagram, the view that there is a long-run Phillips curve that is vertical at the natural rate of unemployment and therefore there is no trade-off between the unemployment rate and the inflation rate in the long run.

- Explain that the natural rate of unemployment is the rate of unemployment that exists when the economy is producing at the full-employment level of output.

Discuss the possible trade-off between the unemployment rate and the inflation rate in the short run

The trade-off between **inflation** and **unemployment** is based on the assumption that there is a **negative causal relationship** between money **wages** and levels of unemployment.

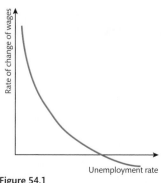

Figure 54.1

When **aggregate demand** (AD) increases from a very low level, firms increase their demand for labour but, because there is a relatively large supply of unemployed workers and because demand for workers is still relatively low, money wages do not increase. As AD continues to increase and the economy moves towards a boom and full-employment levels of output, the supply of unemployed workers falls. Firms must compete with each other to employ the falling number of unemployed workers thereby pushing up money wages. Also firms offer higher wages to attract workers already employed by other firms. So as unemployment falls, money wages increase. When the **business cycle** moves back towards a recession, with falling levels of AD, firms reduce output and **lay off** workers. Unemployment grows and workers might accept lower money

costs of production the amount the firm pays for the factors of production used to produce goods or services

cost-push inflation inflation caused by an increase in the costs of production, resulting in a decrease in aggregate supply

full-employment level of output the potential quantity of output that can be produced in an economy when all factors of production are employed

Phillips curve a graphic representation of the inverse relationship between unemployment and inflation

stagflation occurs when an economy experiences a period of increasing inflation, negative or zero economic growth, and rising unemployment

demand-deficient unemployment unemployment caused by a lack of aggregate demand. Unemployment changes as the economy goes through the business cycle, increasing when AD falls and decreasing when AD rises.

short-run aggregate supply SRAS shows the amount of total output firms are willing to produce and sell in an economy at each price level in a given period of time when factor productivity and factor prices are held constant

price level the current weighted average price of a selected group of goods and services produced in a country over a period of time

wages in order to keep their jobs. So as unemployment increases money wages fall. Figure 54.1 shows the relationship between the rate of change of money wages and the rate of change of unemployment.

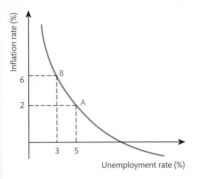

Wage is a **cost of production**. Changes in costs of production affect the rate of inflation. When demand for labour falls, wages fall, leading to a fall in the cost of production. A fall in the cost of production leads to a fall in the rate of inflation. As AD increases, firms increase output and to do so demand more workers. Wages increase leading to an increase in the cost of production. Increased costs lead to **cost-push inflation**. As shown in Figure 54.2, as the economy moves towards **full-employment levels of output**, unemployment rates fall from 5% to 3% and the rate of inflation increases from 2% to 6%.

Figure 54.2

The **Phillips curve**, named after Bill Phillips, an economist who in the 1950s researched the relationship between money wages and unemployment, shows the trade-off between the rate of inflation and the rate of unemployment.

Model sentence: As AD rises, firms increase their demand for labour in order to increase output; therefore, unemployment falls. But increases in AD lead to demand-pull and cost-push inflation. There is a trade-off between unemployment and inflation.

In the 1970s many countries experienced long periods of stagflation. **Stagflation** occurs when inflation is high but aggregate demand is 'stagnant' (low for a long period of time). There was no trade-off between unemployment and inflation. Countries had at the same time high levels of **demand-deficient unemployment** and high levels of inflation. This is not what the theory says should happen. The theory was criticized by many economists because there was no trade-off between unemployment and inflation happening in the real world.

Explain, using a diagram, that the short-run Phillips curve may shift outwards, resulting in stagflation

Supply-side shocks cause stagflation. For example, when the price of oil rose quickly during the early 1970s, costs of production for firms around the world increased quickly, leading to cost-push inflation.

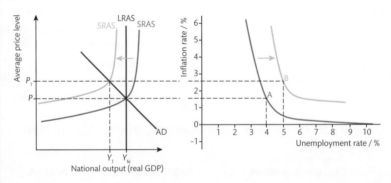

Figure 54.3

An increase in the cost of production leads to a shift up and to the left of the **short-run aggregate supply** curve from SRAS to SRAS₁ as shown in Figure 54.3. This causes a rise in the average **price level** from P to P₁ and a fall in output from Y_fe to Y₁. As firms reduce output, they lay off workers therefore unemployment increases. The country has at the same time rising prices and rising unemployment. At each rate of inflation the rate of unemployment is now higher. To show this new relationship between inflation and unemployment the Phillips curve shifts out to the right. Before the supply-side shock at the long-run equilibrium full-employment the economy is at point A on the Phillips curve. After the supply-side shock both the rate of unemployment and the rate of inflation are higher at point B. Stagflation can be caused by any changes in the economy that lead to a rise in the costs of production such as increases in taxes on businesses and increases in the price of factors of production. Increases in the cost of production cause cost-push inflation and the SRAS curve shifts up and to the left. Firms lay off workers as they reduce output leading to an increase in unemployment and the price level and the Phillips curve shifts up and to the right.

Model sentence: A supply-side shock causes an increase in the cost of production leading to cost-push inflation. Short-run aggregate supply falls causing an increase in the price level which leads to a fall in expenditure. Firms lay off workers to reduce supply and unemployment rises.

Discuss, using a diagram, the view that there is no trade-off between unemployment and inflation in the long run

New classical economists believe that the economy will always move towards the **long-run macroeconomic equilibrium** at full-employment levels of output.

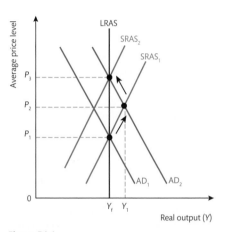

Figure 54.4

For example, an increase in AD leads to an increase in the demand for labour causing **excess demand** for labour in the labour market. Therefore, the wage rate rises to remove the excess demand. An increase in wages leads to an increase in the costs of production. Believers in the new classical model argue that, if there is no intervention in the labour market and wage rates are perfectly flexible, wages will rise immediately when demand for labour increases. Therefore, costs of production immediately increase. In Figure 54.3 the AD curve shifts up and to the right. The **short-run macroeconomic equilibrium** level of output, P_2, Y_1, which is greater than the full-employment level of output, exists only for a very short period of time. Wages increase leading to an increase in the costs of production and a shift up and to the right of the SRAS curve, from $SRAS_1$ to $SRAS_2$.

As the price level rises, total expenditure falls and there is a movement up and along the AD curve AD_2. The economy automatically returns to the long-run equilibrium, P_3, Y_f, at the full-employment level of output. The only changes brought about by the increase in aggregate demand from AD_1 to AD_2 are an increase in wages and an increase in the price level from P_1 to P_3. Employment increases above full-employment levels but only in the short run, quickly returning to the long-run equilibrium level. So new classical economists argue that there is no trade-off between inflation and unemployment.

Workers that get a wage increase may believe that they are now able to buy more goods and services and are therefore better off. However, inflation reduces the real value of the wage. If inflation rises at the same rate as wages the workers are in fact no better off. Real wage does not change. Workers who believe they are better off after an increase in the money wage but in fact are not because of the effect inflation has on the real wage are experiencing **money illusion**.

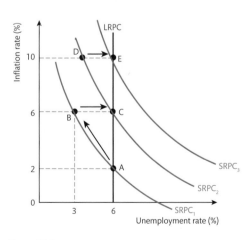

Figure 54.5

In Figure 54.4 at point A the rate of inflation is 2% and the rate of unemployment is 6%. The economy is at the long-run equilibrium level of output. Therefore, there is no demand-deficient unemployment. Unemployment is made up from **frictional unemployment** and **structural unemployment**. Together they make up **natural unemployment.** Therefore at point A the natural rate of unemployment is 6%. If the government, for example, introduced an **expansionary fiscal policy** to reduce unemployment below 6%, the increase in AD would lead to **demand-pull inflation** and cost-push inflation. At the same time there is an increase in the demand for labour as firms increase output. The increase in the competition for labour pushes wages up.

At the higher money wage, the rate of **voluntary unemployment** falls. Some people, who before the wage increase did not want to supply their labour, will now enter the labour market because of the increase in wages. Unemployment in the short run falls from 6% to 3%. The rise in inflation and the fall in unemployment caused

Subject vocabulary

long-run macroeconomic equilibrium occurs when total expenditure is sufficient to buy the potential output in a given period of time. It is represented by the intersection of the AD and LRAS curves.

excess demand occurs when quantity demanded is greater than quantity supplied

short-run macroeconomic equilibrium occurs where aggregate demand is equal to short-run aggregate supply

money illusion the idea that people consider the nominal value of money rather than its real value thus ignoring the purchasing power of their income. People therefore have an unrealistic picture of their income and wealth.

frictional unemployment occurs when people move from one job to another and when people leave voluntary unemployment to look for work

structural unemployment unemployment caused by a change in the type of labour firms demand. It is caused by a mismatch of the skills of those unemployed and the skills needed by firms.

natural unemployment the combination of frictional and structural unemployment a certain amount of which always occurs in an economy. Therefore natural unemployment exists when an economy is producing at full-employment levels of output.

expansionary fiscal policy policy involving the increase of government spending and/or the reduction of taxation

demand-pull inflation occurs when aggregate demand is greater than aggregate supply

voluntary unemployment occurs when people choose not to work at the equilibrium wage

by the increase in AD is shown as a movement up and along the short-run Phillips curve SRPC$_1$ from point A to point B.

At first those people who enter the labour market because of the higher money wage have money illusion. They did not take into account the effect of inflation on wages. As soon as they understand that inflation has reduced the value of the higher nominal wage they will stop working and leave the labour market.

Now that the rate of inflation has increased, workers will expect prices to continue to rise into the future. In Figure 54.4 (on page 157) workers expect prices to carry on increasing by 6% each year. Workers talk with the owners of firms to get a wage increase. Workers are likely to get a wage increase because demand for workers is high at point B. However, as wages increase, the demand for workers falls: firms lay off workers and unemployment rises. The economy is now at full-employment level of output at point C. The rate of unemployment has gone back to 6% but inflation is now higher at 6%. Government policy introduced to reduce unemployment by increasing AD has failed.

The government continues to use **demand-side policies** to increase aggregate demand in order to reduce unemployment. AD rises, leading to demand-pull inflation and cost-push inflation. The rate of inflation increases from 6% to 10%. At the same time, firms demand more workers in order to increase output, and unemployment falls from 6% to 3%. So in the short run there is a trade-off between unemployment and inflation and a movement up and along SRPC$_2$. With higher expected inflation, workers demand higher wages to offset the effects of expected inflation on the real value of the money wage. In the long run, as wages increase, firms lay off workers and unemployment moves back to its natural rate of 6% but inflation has now increased to 10% shown as point E.

When the economy is at full-employment levels of output, there are always some people unemployed. There will always be those people who are frictionally unemployed, meaning they are between jobs and searching for work, and school and university leavers looking for their first jobs. There are people who are **occupationally immobile**, meaning they do not have the skills demanded by industry and there are people who are **geographically immobile**, meaning even if they do have the skills demanded by industry they are unable to move to where the jobs are. The **natural rate of unemployment** is made up from these people. As explained above, the government can reduce unemployment below its natural rate by increasing levels of aggregate demand but only in the short run. In the long run, unemployment returns to its natural rate but with a higher rate of inflation. There is no trade-off between unemployment and inflation in the long run.

The **long-run Phillips curve** (LRPC in Figure 54.4 on page 157) is vertical at the natural rate of unemployment where the economy is at the long-run macroeconomic equilibrium at full-employment levels of output. When the government tries to reduce unemployment below the natural rate using demand-side policies it causes inflation without any effect, in the long run, on the rate of unemployment. Because of this, the natural rate of unemployment is also called the **non-accelerating inflation rate of unemployment** (NAIRU). It is the rate of unemployment required for a stable, 'non-accelerating' rate of inflation.

Model sentence: At the non-accelerating rate of unemployment the rate of inflation is constant because the demand for labour is not changing and therefore wages are stable. When the demand for labour rises because of increases in AD, wages are pushed up leading to cost-push inflation.

Subject vocabulary

demand-side policies policies that are designed to influence aggregate demand

occupational immobility occurs when workers do not have the necessary skills to change jobs

geographically immobile describes workers who are unable to relocate in order to find work, often because of the high costs of moving

natural rate of unemployment the rate of unemployment at which inflation stabilises. At the natural rate of unemployment, all who want to work at the market wage can find work therefore there is no involuntary unemployment.

long-run Phillips curve a vertical line at the natural rate of unemployment showing that in the long-run there is no relationship between unemployment and inflation

non-accelerating inflation rate of unemployment the rate of unemployment that occurs in an economy without causing a change in the rate of inflation. If unemployment increases above this level the rate of inflation falls if unemployment falls inflation increases.

Test your understanding of this unit by answering the following questions

- Discuss, using a short-run Phillips curve diagram, the view that there is a possible trade-off between the unemployment rate and the inflation rate in the short run.
- Explain, using a diagram, the possible causes of stagflation.
- Discuss, using a diagram, the view that there is no trade-off between the unemployment rate and the inflation rate in the long run.

Learning Outcomes

- Define economic growth as an increase in real GDP.
- Describe, using a production possibilities curve (PPC) diagram, economic growth as an increase in actual output resulting from factors such as the utilization of unemployed resources and increases in productive efficiency, leading to a movement of a point inside the PPC to a point closer to the PPC.
- Describe, using a PPC diagram, economic growth as an increase in production possibilities caused by factors including increases in the quantity and quality of resources, leading to outward PPC shifts.

- Describe, using an LRAS diagram, economic growth as an increase in potential output caused by factors including increases in the quantity and quality of resources, leading to a rightward shift of the LRAS curve.
- Evaluate the view that increased investment is essential to achieve economic growth.
- Evaluate the view that improved productivity is essential to achieve economic growth.
- Discuss the possible consequences of economic growth, including the possible impacts on living standards, unemployment, inflation, the distribution of income, the current account of the balance of payments, and sustainability.

What is economic growth?

Economic growth is a macroeconomic objective of most governments. The three ways in which economic growth can be measured and the distinction between **nominal GDP** and **real GDP** are discussed in detail in Section 2.1 – The level of economic activity.

There are three ways to calculate GDP. The output method is the monetary value added to the inputs in the production process by all firms in the economy. The cost of the **resources** used in the production are subtracted from the sales revenue (price × quantity sold) in order to calculate the monetary value added by the firm. This means that the resources are not double counted. The income method is the sum of all payments made by firms to households for the use of the **factors of production**. It is the sum of wages, rent, profit, and interest. The expenditure method is the monetary value of total spending on goods and services in a given year.

Calculation of GDP is achieved through the addition of the price of all final goods produced in a country in a given year. GDP that measures the value of output in current prices is called nominal GDP. Increases in GDP year on year can occur because prices have increased. In other words, increases in GDP can occur because of inflation rather than an increase in economic performance. Nominal GDP will overstate any increase in the value of output. To calculate the real value of the output from one time period to another, the effects of inflation on the value of GDP must be taken into account. Nominal GDP is adjusted to take into account the effects of inflation on the value of output in order to value output at constant prices. Real GDP = nominal GDP adjusted for inflation.

Model sentence: Economic growth is an increase in the monetary value of total income, total expenditure, or total output of a country taking into account the effects of inflation.

What is a production possibility curve (PPC)?

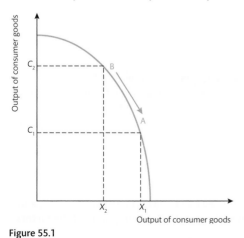

Figure 55.1

A PPC is a curve that shows the various combinations of goods that an economy is able to produce at a given time when the quantity of all factors of production and technology (quality/productivity of the factors) are fixed and all factors are employed efficiently.

The economy can produce two types of goods: **capital** goods and **consumer goods**. At point A on the PPC all factors are employed efficiently and quantity X_1 of consumer goods and C_1 of capital goods are produced. If the country wants to produce more capital goods it has to take away factors from the production of consumer goods and use the factors to make capital goods. As fewer factors are now used to produce consumer goods the quantity

Subject vocabulary

nominal GDP gross domestic product that has not been adjusted to take into account the effect of inflation

real GDP the value of all output of an economy produced in a given period of time, usually a year, adjusted to take into account the effect of inflation

resources the inputs into the production process, the factors of production

factors of production the inputs into the production process (land, labour, capital and entrepreneurship)

capital (goods) manufactured goods that are used in the production of other goods

consumer goods goods that are ultimately consumed by households rather than goods used by firms in the production of another good

that can now be made falls. As more factors are now used to produce capital goods it is possible to make more of them. This is shown in Figure 55.1 (on page 159) as the move from point A to point B. Output of capital goods increases from C_1 to C_2, and output of consumer goods falls from X_1 to X_2.

In order to increase the quantity of capital goods from C_1 to C_2, the country has to give up X_1-X_2 of consumer goods. The **opportunity cost** of the increase in the quantity of capital goods is the quantity of consumer goods foregone. If the economy is producing within the PPC it means that some factors are unemployed. It is not possible for the economy to produce at a point outside the PPC because it does not have enough factors or the factors are not productive enough to produce that quantity of goods.

Model sentence: When the economy is producing on the PPC, all factors are employed; therefore, the economy cannot increase the quantity of one good without reducing the quantity of the other.

Describe how economic growth can be shown on a PPC diagram and an AD/AS diagram

Short-run economic growth is an increase in real output caused by increases in **aggregate demand** or short-run **aggregate supply**. In the short run, a variable quantity of factors are added to a quantity of fixed factors to produce output. At real output Y_1, shown in Figure 55.2a, not all factors are employed. There is a deflationary gap, which is the difference between actual real output Y_1 and **full-employment level of output** Y. When AD increases from AD_1 to AD_2 (perhaps because the government has introduced an **expansionary fiscal policy**), firms increase output by employing more workers by using more of their existing fixed quantity of capital. Real output increases from Y_1 to $Y_2 = Y_f$. Unemployment of factors falls as more factors are employed to increase output in response to an increase in AD. This fall in unemployment and increase in real output is shown in the PPC diagram, Figure 55.2b, as a movement towards the PPC from point a to point b. The economy is producing more of both capital and consumer goods in response to increases in AD.

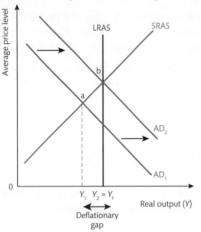

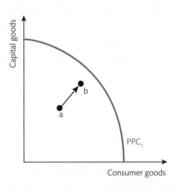

Figure 55.2a   **Figure 55.2b**

Short-run growth can also be caused by firms using existing factors more efficiently. If firms in the economy became more **technically efficient** with their given quantity of factors, they could increase output. The SRAS curve shifts down and to the right, the price level falls leading to an increase in the quantity of AD. This increase in technical efficiency and the resulting increase in real output is shown in Figure 55.2b as a movement from a to b.

In the long run, the quantity and quality (productivity) of all factors of production are variable. Long-run economic growth is an increase in potential GDP caused by increases in the quantity and quality of the factors of production. For example, an increase in the working population, increases in **investment** leading to an increase in the amount of **capital**, increases in the productivity of labour through training, and improvements in the technology that makes capital more productive are all factors that increase potential full-employment levels of output. The increase in **potential output** is shown in Figures 55.3a and 55.3b as a shift to the right of the **long-run aggregate supply** curve from $LRAS_1$ to $LRAS_2$ and a shift outwards of the production possibility curve from PPC_1 to PPC_2.

Model sentence: Short-run economic growth is caused by increases in AD and/or SRAS, and long-run economic growth is caused by increases in the quantity and/or quality of the factors of production.

Subject vocabulary

opportunity cost the next best alternative forgone

aggregate demand the total demand for goods and services in the economy at a given price level in a given period of time

aggregate supply the total supply of goods and services produced in an economy at a given price level in a given time period

full-employment level of output the potential quantity of output that can be produced in an economy when all factors of production are employed

expansionary fiscal policy policy involving the increase of government spending and/or the reduction of taxation

technically efficient describes a firm which maximises output with its given inputs

investment the addition to capital stock

capital (goods) manufactured goods that are used in the production of other goods

potential output the maximum output an economy can produce when all resources are efficiently employed

long-run aggregate supply the potential level of national output of a country determined by the quantity and productivity of the factors of production

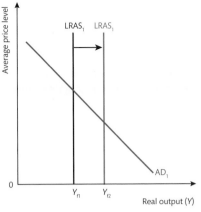

Figure 55.3a

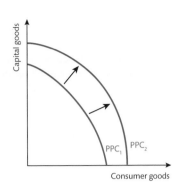

Figure 55.3b

Explain how investment and improved productivity causes economic growth

Human capital is a measure of the quality of labour in terms of labour's ability to produce goods and services. The better educated labour is and the more skills labour has, the greater the value of human capital. Investment in human capital comes mainly from education at schools, technical colleges and universities, training given by firms in the workplace, and the provision of healthcare services. Investment in human capital will increase **labour productivity**. **Output per head** increases, thereby increasing full-employment levels of output, shifting the LRAS curve to the right and the PPC outwards.

Increases in training will reduce **occupational immobility** caused by changing patterns of demand thereby reducing **structural unemployment** and the **natural rate of unemployment**. This increases the quantity of workers willing and able to work, thereby increasing potential output and shifting the LRAS curve to the right. It will also increase AD because the workers who are now employed earn an income, some of which will be spent. Better qualified, more highly skilled workers earn higher incomes leading to increases in AD.

The higher the value of human capital, the greater the ability to be inventive and innovative. For example, scientists and engineers make discoveries that lead to increases in the **state of technology**, which in turn lead to increases in the **productivity** of capital, which then leads to an increase in the full-employment level of output and a shift to the right of the LRAS curve.

Investment is expenditure by firms in the private sector and government on capital goods. It is a **component** of AD and, therefore, increases in investment lead to increases in AD, which in turn leads to increases in real output. Investment is the addition to the stock of capital; therefore, an increase in investment is an increase in the quantity of capital, which leads to an increase in full-employment level of output. Potential output increases leading to long-run economic growth and the LRAS curve shifts to the right and the PPC moves outwards.

When firms and the government invest it is likely that they will buy more technologically advanced capital that is more productive than the old capital. The increase in productivity means that potential output is greater, leading to long-run economic growth and the LRAS curve shifts to the right and the PPC moves outwards.

A country's **natural resources** might include **hydro-power**, mineral water, oil, natural gas, tin, iron **ore**, lead, and timber. Many natural resources are non-renewable. Some countries are dependent on their natural resources for their income. Economies in the Middle East have grown through the **extraction** and sale of oil. In the UK the discovery and extraction of North Sea oil led to an increase in the potential output of the UK. When a country finds new **reserves** of a natural resource potential output increases causing the LRAS curve to shift to the right and the PPC to shift outwards. Also as more income is earned in the industries extracting the natural resources AD increases leading to a rise in real output.

Discuss the importance of improved productivity and the consequences of economic growth

Growing **real incomes** leads to increases in AD causing **demand-pull inflation** due to excess AD. Increases in the productivity of the factors of production increases the potential output of a country and shifts the LRAS curve to the right. Aggregate supply meets the higher levels of aggregate demand, thereby reducing the inflationary pressures. The strength of the inflationary pressure is determined by the rate of change in AD and

productive capacity the maximum possible output of a firm, industry, or an economy

excess capacity occurs when actual output is less than the quantity of output that could be produced if all factors were employed

average total cost equal to total cost divided by quantity of output

quantity demanded the amount of a good consumers are willing and able to buy at a given price over a given period of time

current account balance the sum of the value of exported goods and services, minus the sum of the value of imported goods, plus net income from abroad and net current transfers

marginal propensity to import the proportion of additional income that an individual spends on imported goods and services. MPM = the change in expenditure on imports divided by the change in income.

negative externalities occur when the production or consumption of a good creates costs that must be paid by third parties. The existence of negative externalities means that social cost is greater than private cost.

market failure when resources are not allocated or used efficiently

tax revenue the income the government receives through the levying and collection of taxes

merit good a good/service that the government believes will be under consumed left to the free market

continued on page 163

the rate of change in LRAS. If they increase at the same rate, the price level would not change. Supply-side policies introduced to increase productivity, such as subsidies paid to firms to increase the value of human capital, help to keep inflation down when AD starts to exceed aggregate supply. However, if AD is not strong enough, increases in **productive capacity** lead to **excess capacity**, causing a fall in the price level.

Model sentence: Rising real incomes leads to increasing AD and demand-pull inflation. However, inflationary pressures can be reduced by increases in long-run aggregate supply.

As households' incomes rise, people are able to consume more goods and services. They are able to satisfy more wants. The standard of living and consumer welfare increase as the economy grows. As the economy grows it is possible for firms to increase investment in the research and development of new technologies and new goods. New goods create new demands that can be satisfied, thereby increasing consumer welfare.

Increases in the productivity of labour and capital lead to a fall in **average total cost**. Firms are able to sell at lower prices and still make a profit. This makes them more internationally competitive on price, leading to an increase in the **quantity demanded** of exports thereby increasing AD and improving the **current account balance**. However, increases in income can lead to increases in the demand for imports, thereby worsening the current account balance. The extent to which demand for imports increases after an increase in income is dependent on the nation's **marginal propensity to import**.

Model sentence: Increases in investment lead to increases in productivity and lower average total costs, thereby increasing international competitiveness.

However, increases in a country's output can lead to increases in the **negative externalities** created by production, such as higher carbon emissions, and may cause **market failure**. The quantity of natural resources, many of which are non-renewable, will fall as output increases leaving fewer resources available for future generations who will have to pay a higher price for them. As economies grow and output increases, natural resources might be reduced at such a rate that is not **sustainable**.

Higher incomes lead to an increase in **tax revenues**. Government has more tax revenue to spend on **merit goods** and **public goods** as well as investments in **infrastructure**, such as roads and telecommunications networks. Increased government spending on education and training, which are merit goods, may lead to increases in productivity. Improvements in transport infrastructure, for example, lead to increases in productivity because goods and workers can move more quickly, saving time and reducing transport costs.

Higher tax revenues may reduce the **budget deficit** and the government's borrowing requirements. Over time the government may be able to reduce the **national debt**. This would reduce the **interest payments** on the debt thereby reducing the amount of tax taxpayers in the future must pay for interest payments leaving them more income to spend on goods and services. In the UK in 2013 the average household paid £1,900 in tax just to cover the interest payments on the national debt.

If more of a country's factors are used for investment it is possible that there will be fewer factors available for the production of consumer goods. This is shown in Figure 55.1 (on page 159) as a movement from point a to point b. However, in the long run, greater investment leads to an increase in the productive capacity of the country and an outward shift in the PPC as shown in Figure 55.3b (on page 161). This means that the economy in the long run may be able to produce more of both capital and consumer goods and satisfy more wants, increasing society's welfare. However, greater investment in capital can lead to higher levels of **technological unemployment** as capital is used in production instead of labour. However, the demand for labour to produce the capital and build the factories increases.

As economies grow over time they can move away from producing mainly agricultural output towards the production of manufactured goods. And as economies continue to grow, factors may be reallocated away from the production of manufactured goods and **heavy industry** towards the production of services. As economies grow they go through structural changes and this causes structural unemployment, where people are unemployed because the skills they have are not demanded by the current industries.

Test your understanding of this unit by answering the following questions

- Using diagrams, explain the distinction between short-run economic growth and long-run economic growth.
- Using diagrams, explain how investment in both human capital and physical capital can cause economic growth.
- Discuss the consequences of economic growth.

Learning Outcome

● Calculate the rate of economic growth from a set of data. (HL)

The calculation

The rate of economic growth is the rate of change in a country's **real GDP** from one period of time to another expressed as a percentage. Usually the time period is one year but growth is regularly measured over quarters (3 months).

The formula used to calculate economic growth is set out below.

The rate of economic growth = $\frac{\text{(real GDP in time period 2 − real GDP in time period 1)}}{\text{real GDP in time period 1}} \times 100$

Below is listed real GDP from 2006 to 2009 for country 'X'.

Year	Country 'X' Real GDP (US$ millions)
2006	1 680 044
2007	1 710 488
2008	1 790 562
2009	1 728 212

Calculate the rate of economic growth for country 'X' between 2006 and 2007 – a step-by-step guide

Trouble shooter

The rate of economic growth = $\frac{\text{(real GDP in 2007 − real GDP in 2006)}}{\text{real GDP in 2006}} \times 100$

The rate of economic growth = $\frac{(1\,710\,488 − 1\,680\,044)}{1\,680\,044} \times 100$

The rate of economic growth = $\frac{(30\,444)}{1\,680\,044} \times 100$

The rate of economic growth = 0.01812×100

The rate of economic growth in country 'X' between 2006 and 2007 was 1.81%.

Calculate the rate of economic growth between 2008 and 2009

Growth rate = $\frac{(1\,728\,212 − 1\,790\,562)}{1\,790\,562} \times 100 = \frac{−62\,350}{1\,790\,562} \times 100 = −0.0348 \times 100 = −3.48\%$

The rate of economic growth in country 'X' between 2008 and 2009 was -3.48%.

Calculate the rate of economic growth between 2006 and 2009

Growth rate = $\frac{(1\,728\,212 − 1\,680\,044)}{1\,680\,044} \times 100 = \frac{48\,168}{1\,680\,044} \times 100 = 0.0287 = 2.87\%$

The rate of economic growth between 2006 and 2009 was 2.87%.

The economy grew year on year between 2006 and 2008. Real GDP reached its highest point in 2008. Between 2008 and 2009 the country entered a **recession** experiencing a negative rate of growth of −3.48%. However, overall between 2006 and 2009 the country's economy grew by 2.87%.

Test your understanding of this unit by answering the following questions

● Using the data set out in the table below, calculate the rate of economic growth for country 'Y' between each of the years and between 2010 and 2013.

● Describe the changes to economic growth between 2010 and 2013.

Year	Country 'Y' Real GDP (€ millions)
2010	2 420 488
2011	2 380 835
2012	2 340 903
2013	2 390 432

Learning Outcomes

- Explain the difference between equity in the distribution of income and equality in the distribution of income.

- Explain that due to unequal ownership of factors of production, the market system may not result in an equitable distribution of income.

- Analyze data on relative income shares of given percentages of the population, including deciles and quintiles.

- Draw a Lorenz curve and explain its significance.

- Explain how the Gini coefficient is derived and interpreted.

Distinguish between equality and equity in the distribution of income

Income is the payment made by firms to households for the use of the **factors of production**. Income is made up of wages, rent, profit, and interest. National income is the sum of all these payments made in a country over a given period of time, usually a year. The average income per head is calculated by dividing total national income by the population. The average income in the UK in 2013 was about £24,000. There are many people who earn much more than this amount and many who earn less. People do not earn the same amount of income; therefore, income is not distributed equally. There are many reasons for this, which will be discussed later in this unit. The amount of inequality of income can be studied, measured, and published. Equity means fairness or justice. What is fair to one person may not seem fair to another. Is income distribution equitable? This is a difficult question to answer. Answers may vary depending on personal opinions and circumstances.

Inequality of income is not always inequitable or unfair. It seems fair that a worker who does the same job in the same factory as another worker but works longer hours gets a greater wage. And if a worker saves some of his income it is fair that he receives **interest** payments from his **savings**. Another worker who spends all his income on satisfying present wants has no savings and therefore receives no interest payments. Again, income distribution is unequal but it is not necessarily unfair or inequitable.

Distinguish between horizontal equity and vertical equity

Horizontal equity occurs when people who are in the same situation are treated in the same way. For example, it is fair that two workers who earn $35,000 pay the same rate of **income tax**. If this does not happen it would be unfair. A woman applying for a job who has the same skills as the male applicant should have an equal chance of getting the job. The same is true of people of different ages, races, or religious beliefs. Any other outcome is unfair. Horizontal equity in a society means that people are not discriminated against in any situation on the basis of race, age, gender, or religion. Many countries have laws that make discrimination illegal in order to make society more equitable, although discrimination still occurs.

Vertical equity occurs when people earning different incomes are treated differently so as to make society more equitable. For example, those people that earn higher incomes pay a higher rate of tax. The government can then use the revenue to redistribute income more fairly and more equally.

Explain why the unequal ownership of factors may lead to an inequitable and unequal distribution of income

People receive different amounts of income in a **market**-based economic system because the ownership of the factors is not distributed equally. There are some people who can work, selling their labour to firms. There are some people who are not able to work and therefore cannot sell their labour in order to earn a wage. Some people own land and property, and receive rent. **Shareholders** receive a dividend payment each year which is a share of the company profits. Ownership of the resources can be built up over time. A person may inherit property and **shares**, and because these **assets** earn income that person may more easily be able to buy more property and shares, thereby increasing the amount of income earned. In time the accumulated assets can be passed on to the next generation. People who own assets earn more income and are therefore able to buy more assets that provide even more income. It can be argued that the distribution of income is becoming more unequal and inequitable. Those people on lower incomes are not given the same opportunity as others to buy assets and thereby increase their income. Often poorer people only own their labour and therefore can only earn a wage.

There is a high **supply of workers** who are unskilled or have few skills. Low skilled workers make relatively little extra **revenue** and profit for the firm. Because the wage firms are willing to pay for unskilled workers is low and the supply of unskilled workers is high, the **equilibrium wage** in this **labour market** is relatively low. There is a lower supply of skilled workers and, because they provide greater additional revenue and profit for a firm, demand is higher. Lower supply and higher demand for such workers means that the equilibrium wage in this labour market is higher. For example, a successful marketing manager is able to increase revenue and profits of a firm by a large amount but a cleaner is not. The marketing manager will therefore be paid a higher wage than the cleaner. Those who do not have the skills demanded by industries will not be able to find a job and will not receive a wage. Those who receive state benefits, such as a state pension or unemployment benefit, earn a fixed income. Their income is determined by government and because the unemployed and pensioners have no or very little power to gain an increase in their **nominal income**, the real value of their income can fall over time because of inflation. In many countries the proportion of the population that is in retirement has been growing and therefore the distribution of income has become relatively more unequal.

The price of shares is determined by the **forces of demand and supply** in the **stock market**. The dividend paid to the owner of shares is closely linked to its price. The price of property is determined by **market forces** in the property market. Demand for property, both commercial and residential, in central London is relatively high and supply is relatively low whereas in Sunderland, in the north of England, demand is much lower and supply higher. The excess demand in the property market in London pushes prices up and the excess supply in Sunderland pushes price down. Rents paid on property are linked to its price. Therefore, the income earned on property in London is relatively high and in Sunderland it is relatively low.

Firms in **uncompetitive industries** are able to reduce supply of the good and increase price thereby forcing the consumer to pay a higher price than the price that would be paid in a **competitive market**. The firm increases its profit at the expense of the consumers. Under **imperfect competition** there is a transfer of wealth from consumers to the shareholders. Some governments try to reduce monopoly power, by reducing or removing barriers to entry into industries and by making illegal anti-competitive behaviour such as **destroyer pricing**, so that new firms can enter the market and compete.

It is clear that the distribution of income is unequal. Governments in many countries are able to make the distribution more equitable. Taxing those on relatively high incomes more means the government is able to redistribute income to those on relatively low incomes. Income distribution will be more equal and more equitable. The government can encourage firms to give **employees** an opportunity to own shares in their business and by **privatizing state monopolies** can encourage people who would not normally buy shares to do so. The Conservative government in the UK during the 1980s tried to extend property and share ownership. Many state monopolies were privatized and many people bought shares. However, most of the shares were sold to **financial institutions** soon after they were bought. Many gained a quick profit on the sale but widespread share ownership did not last. People were encouraged to buy their council house (government-owned houses that were rented to people). The price was set below market price and many people did buy the houses they rented.

Most economists and politicians argue that an unequal distribution of income is a good thing because if every person earns the same income there would be little incentive to study hard at school and to work hard to learn new skills. The **value of human capital** would fall because there would be no opportunity to earn a higher income. All industries would become less productive and therefore less competitive. Real GDP would fall and most people would have less income. Economists and politicians often disagree about the optimum or best distribution of income.

Analyze data on relative income shares of given percentages of the population

Set out below in Table 57.1 are data on the distribution of income in four countries in 2010. The households are divided into **quintiles** ranging from the poorest to the richest. The percentage of the total national income they receive is calculated and listed under each of the quintiles. The distribution of income in the UK and Russia are similar. In the UK the poorest 20% of the population earns 6.14% of the total income and in Russia the poorest 20% earns 6.46% of the country's income. The UK's 2nd, 3rd, and 4th quintiles earn a little over 1% more of total income than in Russia. The poorest 20% in Argentina earn 4.48% of total income. This is less than in the UK and Russia. A much higher proportion of people in South Africa are poor. The poorest 20% earn less than 3% of the nation's total income and the poorest 40% earn less than 8% of total income. Argentina's richest 20% earn 49.36% of total income, just over 2% more than in Russia and just over 5% more than in the UK.

Country	Poorest 20%	2nd 20%	3rd 20%	4th 20%	Richest 20%
United Kingdom	6.14	11.41	15.96	22.47	44.02
Russia	6.46	10.35	14.77	21.29	47.13
Argentina	4.38	9.31	14.78	22.17	49.36
South Africa	2.7	4.63	8.16	16.3	68.21

Table 57.1 *Source: Index Mundi*

In South Africa, however, the richest 20% of the population earn almost 70% of the nation's income. The percentage of total income earned by the first four quintiles is much lower than in the other three countries. Income is distributed most equally in the UK and least equally in South Africa.

Table 57.2 sets out the poorest 20% and the richest 20% in the UK and South Africa once the data have been divided into **deciles**. The table shows clearly the differences in the distribution of income between the two countries. The second poorest 10% of households in the UK earn 4.08% of total national income whereas in South Africa the second poorest 10% earn only 1.53%. The richest 10% of households in the UK earn 28.49% of income; in South Africa the richest 10% earn a much greater 51.69% of income.

Country	Poorest 10%	2nd 10%	9th 10%	Richest 10%
United Kingdom	2.06	4.08	15.53	28.49
South Africa	1.17	1.53	16.52	51.69

Table 57.2

Explain the significance of a Lorenz curve

Economists use a **Lorenz curve** to measure inequalities in the distribution of income. In Figure 57.1 the cumulative percentage of the population of a country is plotted on the horizontal axis and is set out in order of income earned. The cumulative percentage of its income is plotted on the vertical axis. The 45 degree line is called the 'line of equality'. The 45 degree line shows each person earning the same percentage of income. The first 20% of the population earns 20% of the income, the next 20% of the population also earn 20% of the income and the top 20% of the population earn 20% of the income. Each person earns the same amount of income. Income is distributed perfectly equally.

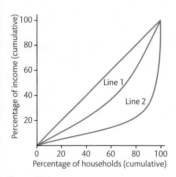

The Lorenz curves are the bowed or curved lines, line 1 and line 2. Line 1 shows the distribution of income in one country; line 2 shows the distribution of income in another country. Both lines are bowed and therefore show an unequal distribution of income. Line 1 shows the poorest 20% of the population earn 10% of the income and the richest 20% earn 40% of income. Line 2 shows the poorest 20% earn 2% of income and the richest 20% earn 70% of income. The distribution of income is more unequal in the country represented by line 2, than in the country represented by line 1. The further away the Lorenz curve is from the 45 degree line of equality, the more unequal is the distribution of income.

Figure 57.1

Explain how the Gini coefficient is derived and what it means

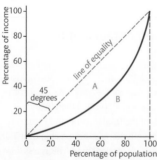

Figure 57.2

Inequality in the distribution of income can be measured by the Gini coefficient. It is the ratio of the area above the Lorenz curve and below the 45 degree line (area A) to the area of the triangle that is below the 45 degree line (area A + B). The value of the Gini coefficient is between 0 and 1. As the Lorenz curve moves further away from the 45 degree line the proportion of area A to the total area below the 45 degree line gets bigger. The value of A/A+B gets bigger when A gets bigger. Therefore, the higher the value of the Gini coefficient the more unequal the distribution of income.

If income is distributed perfectly equally the coefficient is equal to 0. And if income is distributed perfectly unequally, so that one person earns 100% of the income and all the others earn 0% of the income, the Gini coefficient is equal to 1.

The Gini coefficient can be written as an index out of 100. Gini coefficient = 0.4 is the same as Gini index = 40.

The Scandinavian counties have relatively low Gini indexes: Denmark's Gini index = 24 and Sweden's = 25. The governments of these countries redistribute income from the relatively high income earners to the relatively low income earners through taxation and government spending. In such countries the rate of tax is relatively high. In Southern African countries the Gini indexes are relatively high. For example, Botswana has an index of 61 and Namibia's Gini index is 63.9. In these countries the ruling **elite** often receive most of the income and the rest of the population live in relative poverty. Income inequality is very high. As can be seen in Table 57.1 (on page 165), in the UK the distribution of income is relatively more equal than in South Africa. The UK's Gini index is 34 while South Africa's is 63.1.

Test your understanding of this unit by answering the following questions

- Explain why the distribution of the ownership of factors of production affects the distribution of income.
- The Gini index of country X is 24 and the Gini index of country Y is 65. Using a diagram, explain the significance of these statistics.

Glossary

elite a group of people with a high level of power/influence because they have money/ knowledge/skills

Subject vocabulary

absolute poverty occurs when people do not have enough resources to satisfy their basic needs

Learning Outcomes

- Distinguish between absolute poverty and relative poverty.
- Explain possible causes of poverty, including low incomes, unemployment, and lack of human capital.
- Explain possible consequences of poverty, including low living standards, and lack of access to healthcare and education.
- Distinguish between direct and indirect taxes, providing examples of each, and explain that direct taxes may be used as a mechanism to redistribute income.
- Distinguish between progressive, regressive, and proportional taxation, providing examples of each.
- Calculate the marginal rate of tax and the average rate of tax from a set of data. (HL)

Explain the difference between absolute poverty and relative poverty

Absolute poverty occurs when people are not able to satisfy their basic needs. People who are homeless, who are unable to keep warm or who are underfed live in absolute poverty. Absolute poverty exists in all countries but there are more people living in absolute poverty in the less developed economies than in countries with relatively higher **GDP**. Given the size of national income in relatively wealthy countries, in theory the government could eliminate absolute poverty completely through the redistribution of income.

Relative poverty occurs when the standard of living of a person in society is low compared to the standard of living of others in society. When a person's income is less than a specified proportion of the average income, then that person is living in relative poverty.

Explain the causes of poverty

People who do not own any physical assets or financial assets and who are unskilled, who lack **human capital** are more likely to be poor. Those who do not own assets that provide income, such as savings accounts, shares, or property and whose labour is not demanded by firms cannot earn an income. Lack of human capital is caused by low educational achievement, such as the inability to read and write, and a lack of skills. Workers with these characteristics find it difficult to sell their labour to firms in the **labour market**. Supply of unskilled workers is high, which pushes down the wage. People who are well educated and have skills demanded by firms receive higher wages. In many countries there is an **excess supply** of unskilled workers so wages are low and many workers are unemployed. The amount of unemployment benefits varies from country to country, but in most cases those who are unemployed are relatively poorer than those who have jobs and are more likely to live in absolute poverty.

Explain the consequences of poverty

There are **private costs** and **external costs** created by poverty. People on very low incomes are much more likely to live in poor housing, have unhealthy diets, and are less likely to have access to high quality health services. Therefore, those living in poverty are more likely to suffer from poor physical and mental health, and die at a younger age.

Subject vocabulary

GDP gross domestic product is the monetary value of all the finished goods and services produced within a country in a given period of time, usually measured over a year

relative poverty a measure of poverty that relates to the average income earned in a country or region. Definitions vary but many governments define it as an income less than 50% of the median income.

human capital the store of knowledge and the set of skills that a worker possesses which can be used in the production process. The higher the value of human capital the more productive the worker is. Human capital can be improved through investment in education and training.

labour market a market in which firms demand labour and workers supply labour. The interaction of demand and supply of labour determines the equilibrium wage.

excess supply occurs when quantity supplied is greater than quantity demanded

continued on page 166

Some economists and sociologists say there is a link between poverty and crime. Some people who are unable to earn a sufficient income engage in criminal activities such as theft. High levels of unemployment and poverty can lead to **social unrest**, such as rioting and violent protest.

The external costs of poverty are high. Resources have to be used to police social unrest and crime. Bad diets and unhealthy living conditions lead to greater demands on health service providers. And those who are poor, unskilled, or uneducated are a wasted resource because they do not make a positive contribution to GDP. Many governments are aware of the private and external costs, and want to reduce these costs. A more equal distribution of income is therefore an objective of some governments.

Distinguish between direct tax and indirect tax

A tax is a direct tax when the tax paid goes directly from those who owe the tax to the government. Income tax is a direct tax because the amount of tax charged on the wage earned is paid directly to the government. Usually this is done by the employer on behalf of the worker. Corporation tax is a tax on company profits which is paid directly from the company to the government. **Dividend payments** and the **interest** paid on savings are taxed, and the tax is paid straight to the government by the income earner. Legally, these taxes are unavoidable because income earners must tell the government how much income they have earned.

Indirect tax does not go directly to the government. Indirect taxes are taxes on **expenditure**. Examples include 'value added tax' (VAT) in the UK and 'goods and services tax' (GST) in Australia. When the consumer buys a good or service, the tax charged on the sale is included in the price paid by the consumer. The seller of the good collects the tax and then sends the tax to the government. Households are able to avoid paying indirect tax by not buying the goods; however, basic necessities such as fuel and clothes are taxed so it is impossible to avoid paying taxes completely.

Distinguish between progressive, regressive, and proportional taxation

A progressive tax is a tax where the proportion or percentage of income that is taxed (the rate of tax) increases as income increases. For example, the Federal tax brackets in 2013 on taxable income for a single person in the US were as follows:

Income $	Tax bracket %
0–8 925	10
8 925–36 250	15
36 250–87 850	25
87 850–183 250	28
183 250–398 350	33
398 350–400 000	35
400 000 and above	39.6

Table 58.1

It can be seen in the data above that the rate at which income is taxed increases as income rises. For example a single person earning $40 000 pays 10% tax on $8 925, 15% on income earned between $8 925 and $36 250, and 25% on income between $36 250 and $87 850.

Model sentence: The marginal rate of tax is the rate of tax paid on the next unit of currency earned. In the case of a progressive income tax, the marginal rate of tax increases as income rises from one tax bracket to the next.

A regressive tax is a tax for which the proportion or percentage of income that is taxed decreases as income increases and increases as income falls. This type of tax does not take into account the amount of income a person earns. It does not take into account the 'ability to pay'. Indirect taxes are regressive taxes. Take two people: one earns $20 000 and the other earns $40 000. Each buys a car and each pays a sales tax of $1 000. The amount paid in tax is the same, but the percentage of tax paid is different: $1 000 is 2.5% of $40 000 ((1 000/40 000) × 100 = 2.5%), whereas $1 000 is 5% of $20 000 ((1 000/20 000) × 100). The tax is regressive because the percentage rate of tax is higher for the person on a lower income. As incomes fall, the rate of tax increases.

A proportional tax is a tax for which the proportion or percentage of tax that is paid does not change as income changes. For example a person earning an income of $20 000 pays the same rate of tax as a person earning $40 000. A 10% rate of tax on $20 000 = $2 000 tax paid. On $40 000 $4 000 is paid in tax. Although the rate of tax is the same, the higher the income, the higher the actual amount of tax paid. Some countries are moving towards a proportional or flat tax rate system. (An evaluation of this system appears on pages 171–73.)

Model sentence: For progressive taxes, the percentage of income paid in tax increases as income increases; for regressive tax, the percentage of income paid in tax falls as income increases; and for proportional tax, the percentage of income paid in tax stays the same as income increases.

Explain how direct taxes may be used to redistribute income

The tax system used by a government plays an important role in how income is distributed. A government can introduce a more progressive tax system in order to redistribute income away from richer people to poorer people. Taxes raised by government can be used to increase **transfer payments** from those on higher income to those on lower income. For example the **tax revenue** can be used to fund increases in unemployment benefit. The Scandinavian countries have the lowest Gini indexes, showing that income is distributed more equally in these countries than anywhere else in the world. These countries also have the highest marginal rates of tax in the world. Those countries with high Gini indexes tend to have low **marginal rates of tax**. Some politicians and economists argue that more tax revenue should be raised from progressive taxes on income and less from regressive taxes on expenditure because it is more equitable.

Model sentence: Progressive taxation takes into account the ability to pay the tax. A move away from a regressive tax system to a more progressive one is likely to lead to a more equal distribution of income.

(Government policy introduced in order to redistribute income is evaluated on pages 171–73.)

Calculate the marginal rate of tax and the average rate of tax from a set of data (HL)

The average rate of tax (ART) is the tax paid divided by gross income multiplied by 100. Gross income is income earned before deductions, such as income tax, are made. Net income is the actual amount received by the worker after all deductions have been made.

ART = (tax paid/gross income) × 100

The marginal rate of tax (MRT) is the change in tax divided by the change in gross income multiplied by 100.

MRT = (change in tax/change in gross income) × 100

Table 58.2 shows the marginal rates of tax on income earned in country X.

Gross income $	MRT %
10 000	10
10 001–20 000	20
20 001–30 000	30
30 001–50 000	40
50 000 and above	50

Table 58.2

continued from page 171

quasi-public goods goods that share some of the characteristics of public goods but are not fully non-excludable and non-rival. A road is an example. Most roads are free at the point of use but it is possible to make people pay through tolls and when traffic is heavy the amount available to others to use does begin to diminish so there can be rivalry in consumption.

private sector the part of the economy that is regulated but not controlled by the state and concerns individuals and groups bringing together the factors of production normally with the aim of making a profit

value of human capital a measure of the quantity and quality of the skills of the labour force that can be employed to produce goods and services. An increase in the value of human capital leads to an increase in labour productivity.

productivity the quantity of output per unit of input

cycle of poverty occurs in a country which has low income and therefore low levels of savings. Low levels of savings means little investment can take place and the economy is unable to grow, thus income remains low.

redundancy payment a sum of money paid by the employer to a former employee who has been made redundant (laid off work)

sick pay a sum of money paid by an employer to an employee who is not working due to illness

relative poverty a measure of poverty that relates to the average income earned in a country or region. Definitions vary but many governments define it as an income less than 50% of the median income.

real-wage unemployment occurs when the real wage is above the equilibrium wage thereby causing an excess supply of labour

classical/real-wage unemployment when wages are above the market clearing level leading to an excess supply of labour

excess supply occurs when quantity supplied is greater than quantity demanded

Using the data in Table 58.2, calculate the ART for a worker earning $25 000 and a worker earning $70 000 per year – a step-by-step guide (HL)

Trouble shooter

Worker earning $25 000 per year:

$10 000 taxed at 10% = $10 000 × 10% = $1 000

$10 000 taxed at 20% = $10 000 × 20% = $2 000

$5 000 taxed at 30% = $5 000 × 30% = $1 500
          = $25 000   = $4 500

ART = (tax paid/ total gross income) × 100 = ($4,500/$25 000) × 100 = 18%

Worker earning $70 000 per year:

$10 000 taxed at 10% = $10 000 × 10% = $1 000

$10 000 taxed at 20% = $10 000 × 20% = $2 000

$10 000 taxed at 30% = $10 000 × 30% = $3 000

$20 000 taxed at 40% = $20 000 × 40% = $8 000

$20 000 taxed at 50% = $20 000 × 50% = $10 000
          = $70 000   = $24 000

ART = (tax paid/ total gross income) × 100 = ($24 000/$70 000) × 100 = 34.29%

Using the data in Table 58.1, calculate the MRT for a worker who receives a pay increase from $30 000 to $45 000 (HL)

At $30 000 the worker was paying in tax:

($10 000 × 10%) = $1 000

($10 000 × 20%) = $2 000

($10 000 × 30%) = $3 000 +
                   $6 000

At $45 000 the worker is now paying:

($10 000 × 10%) = $1 000

($10 000 × 20%) = $2 000

($10 000 × 30%) = $3 000

($15 000 × 40%) = $6 000 +
                   $12 000

Tax paid increases from $6 000 to $12 000 as income increases from $30 000 to $45 000.

MRT = (change in tax/change in gross income) × 100 = ($6 000/$15 000) × 100 = 40%

Test your understanding of this unit by answering the following questions

- Distinguish between progressive, regressive, and proportional taxation.
- Explain possible causes of poverty.
- Explain possible consequences of poverty. Distinguish between the private costs and external costs.
- Using the data set out in the table below, calculate the average rate of tax for a worker earning £25 000 and the marginal rate of tax for a worker who receives a pay increase from £28 000 to £64 000.

Gross income $	MRT %
0–10 000	0
10 001–15 000	10
15 001–20 000	15
20 001–30 000	20
30 001–50 000	30
60 001 and above	50

Learning Outcomes

● Explain that governments undertake expenditures to provide directly, or to subsidize, a variety of socially desirable goods and services (including healthcare services, education, and infrastructure that includes **sanitation** and clean water supplies), thereby making them available to those on low incomes.

● Explain the term transfer payments, and provide examples, including old-age pensions, unemployment benefits, and **child allowances**.

● Evaluate government policies to promote equity (taxation, government expenditure, and transfer payments) in terms of their potential positive or negative effects on efficiency in the allocation of resources.

The government collects taxes and uses the tax revenue to provide many goods and services, particularly **merit goods** that are underprovided and under consumed if left to the **free market**, and **public goods** that would not be supplied at all. Governments provide such goods in order to correct **market failure**. The government in many countries provides education services and health services so that society benefits from the **positive externalities** and **private benefits** of consumption of them. Infrastructure, often **quasi-public goods**, such as water and **sewage** services, transport infrastructure, and social housing are provided by the government. The government either provides these goods or services directly or the government pays subsidies to firms in the **private sector** to provide them. (See pages 36–38 for a detailed explanation of how a subsidy increases supply and consumption of merit goods.) Governments provide these goods and services because if they were left to the free market people on low incomes would not have enough money to buy them.

For example, in countries where education is not provided by the government, many children do not go to school because their parents cannot afford to buy educational services in the private market. Governments in countries with low GDP often do not have enough tax revenue to pay for these goods and services. Therefore, it is very difficult to raise the **value of human capital** and improve the quality of life of the citizens. When the state provides education for all young people each person is given the same opportunity. Young people in low income families are not discriminated against thereby making society more equitable. An education gives them a greater opportunity to earn a higher income in the future, thereby possibly making the distribution of income more equal.

Model sentence: A country where the human capital is poor and where the infrastructure is basic will have very low productivity and will not be able to escape the cycle of poverty.

What are transfer payments?

A transfer payment is a payment made by the government to a person for which no good or service is provided. They are payments made in order to increase the income of certain people in the economy. Transfer payments are used to redistribute income from those on relatively high incomes to those on relatively low incomes. Examples include unemployment benefit and state pensions. Governments also subsidize university tuition fees, the cost of heating a home, and rents.

Comment on government policies to promote equity and to distribute income more equally

Governments introduce laws to promote equity. Discrimination based on age, sex, race, and religion is illegal in many countries. This is to ensure that in society all people are treated equally and have equal opportunities. Employers are made to provide more than just a wage. Workers who lose their jobs are given a **redundancy payment**; if workers are ill, firms provide **sick pay**. All firms must pay a minimum wage set by the government. A higher minimum wage may lift people out of absolute poverty and reduce **relative poverty**. A higher wage acts as an incentive for people to supply their labour. People are more likely to come off state benefits and find a job if the wage is greater than benefits. However, a high minimum wage can cause **real-wage unemployment** or **classical unemployment**. As wages rise, firms demand less labour but supply of labour increases, leading to an **excess supply** of labour and an increase in unemployment. If the cost to the firm of employing workers increases, *ceteris paribus*, fewer workers will be employed by the firm, leading to an increase in unemployment and perhaps an increase in income inequality.

Transfer payments affect behaviour. High welfare benefits introduced to reduce poverty and to make society more equitable discourage workers from seeking a job, thereby reducing economic activity and GDP.

Glossary

sanitation the removal/treatment of waste/water

child allowance money given by the government to families with children

sewage a mixture of human waste and used water

Subject vocabulary

merit good a good/service that the government believes will be under consumed left to the free market. Consumption of a merit good may generate positive externalities therefore the social benefit of consumption is greater than the private benefit.

free market a market where the forces of demand and supply are allowed to operate without any forms of intervention

public good a good that is non-excludable and non-rival. Once provided it is not possible to stop people benefitting from the consumption of it and therefore people free ride - they do not pay. The good will not be supplied left to the free market because no firm would be able to make a profit. Also, consumption of the good by one person does not diminish the amount available for others to consume.

market failure when resources are not allocated or used efficiently

positive externalities occur when the production or consumption of a good causes benefits to third parties. The existence of positive externalities means that social benefit is greater than private benefit.

private benefit the benefit firms or consumers receive from their own production or consumption of a good

continued on page 170

overtime time spent working in addition to normal working hours

marginal rates of tax the rate of tax paid on the next unit of income earned

corporation tax a tax-levied in the UK on company profits

retained profit after-tax profit that is not paid out to shareholders but is kept by the firm to be reinvested in the business or used to pay back debt

technologically advanced capital capital that incorporates new technology and is used in place of existing capital to produce goods and services thereby increasing productivity

average total cost is equal to total cost divided by quantity of output

exporting industries industries that produce output in one country and sell at least some of the output to buyers in other countries

economic growth an increase in real GDP

real output the quantity of goods and services produced in a given time period

foreign direct investment cross-border investment, usually by firms, that involves the acquisition of assets in a foreign country. FDI can be the purchase of a minimum of 10% of the shares of a foreign company but also includes the creation of productive capacity.

utility a term that refers to the benefit or satisfaction a person receives from the consumption of goods

market forces the forces of demand and supply that interact in a competitive market and determine equilibrium price

misallocation of resources occurs when the allocation of resources leads to welfare loss and therefore a reallocation of resources could increase society's welfare

continued on page 173

Increasing tax rates discourages workers from working longer hours because after-tax income falls. Workers are less likely to work **overtime** or come off benefits to start work. High **marginal rates of tax** discourage workers from developing new skills and seeking promotion. And some people may decide to work in another country where tax rates are lower. Overall this has a negative effect on GDP.

If the government increases the tax rate on profit it may lead to less economic activity. Entrepreneurs take a risk by investing resources into starting up businesses. They may lose a lot of money if the business is not successful and has to close. They are willing to take the risk because there is a chance a profit can be made. The greater the possible profit, the more likely they are to start a business and take that risk. As tax rates increase, the profit that is kept by the entrepreneur falls and therefore the incentive to take the risk and start a business falls. Fewer small businesses will be started. Small businesses can grow and make important contributions to employment and GDP.

Model sentence: Higher tax rates discourage entrepreneurial risk-taking and thereby negatively affect future levels of GDP.

Existing companies will be affected by increases in **corporation tax**. A higher tax rate reduces **retained profit** and therefore reduces the amount of profit available for investment. The lack of investment in more **technologically advanced capital** would mean that productivity does not increase. **Average total cost** would remain higher, possibly leading to higher prices and a fall in international competitiveness and a loss of jobs in **exporting industries**. Investment is essential for **economic growth**. Lower taxes lead to greater investment and an increase in **real output**. In the long run, all people will receive more income. *Ceteris paribus*, as tax increases fewer foreign firms will invest in a country, leading to a fall in the amount of inward investment, thereby reducing GDP.

Model sentence: High corporation tax discourages foreign direct investment and acts as an incentive for domestic firms to move abroad, thereby negatively affecting GDP.

Some economists say that redistributing income can increase society's benefit or **utility**. The benefit or utility gained from the consumption of a good diminishes as more of the good is consumed. This is the law of diminishing marginal utility. People on low incomes consume fewer goods than people on higher incomes. If $20 is taken from a rich person and given to a poor person then the utility the poor person gains from the consumption of a good bought with the $20 is greater than the utility the rich person would gain because the rich person will consume more anyway, and therefore the marginal utility is lower. Therefore, by redistributing income the sum of utility of the rich person and the poor person is increased. A poor person may not be able to satisfy his needs. If a relatively high income earner spent $100 on his tenth pair of jeans he gains utility from its consumption. However, if the $100 was given to a poor person to feed his hungry family, the utility gained would be greater than the utility the rich person gained from the consumption of the jeans. The $100 spent by the poor person gained more utility than if spent by the rich person. Therefore, redistributing the $100 increases society's total utility.

Model sentence: According to the law of diminishing marginal utility, total utility can be increased by redistributing income away from rich people to poor people.

However, it is impossible to compare the utility gained from the consumption of a good between individuals so it can be argued that redistributing income might not lead to an increase in society's total utility.

Governments intervene in markets in order to redistribute income because they believe that resources are not allocated in way that is fair by **market forces**. Government expenditure is used to correct a **misallocation of resources** when the existence of **positive externalities** leads to **market failure**. In these cases government intervention can lead to a greater **allocative efficiency**. Redistribution of income can lift people out of poverty and provide opportunities for people to make a positive contribution to economic growth. Also redistribution of income can increase society's overall utility. However, government intervention can lead to **allocative inefficiency**. A redistributive tax system affects the behaviour of **economic agents**. Higher transfer payments and higher taxes discourage people from working, and reduce the amount of investment and entrepreneurial activity. In the long run, economic activity falls, leading to higher levels of unemployment, lower **real incomes**, and an increase in poverty.

Model sentence: It is difficult for the government to create a tax system that promotes equity and, at the same time, provides the right set of incentives that will lead to higher economic growth.

The poor have a relatively high **marginal propensity to consume** and a relatively low **marginal propensity to save**. This means they spend a relatively high proportion of extra income received and save a relatively low proportion of extra income. Redistributing income away from relatively high income earners to those on relatively low incomes therefore leads to a greater level of consumption and a lower level of saving in the economy. Redistribution of income therefore can lead to higher levels of **aggregate demand**.

Explain why increasing the tax rate in order to redistribute income may lead to a fall in tax revenue

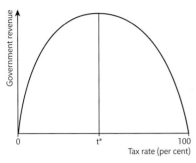

Figure 59.1

Tax rates on higher incomes may be increased by a government in order to raise more tax revenue so that income can be redistributed. However, increasing tax rates may lead to a fall in revenue not an increase.

As shown in the Laffer curve, Figure 59.1, at 0% tax rate no tax revenue is made. When tax rates are 100%, no tax revenue is made because nobody has an incentive to work if all income earned is taken by the government. Therefore, it must be the case that tax revenue is maximized at a tax rate between 0% and 100%.

As the tax rates increase from 0%, the government begins to collect tax revenue. However, when tax rates have increased to a certain level tax revenue begins to fall. In the diagram tax revenue is maximized at t*. An increase in the tax rate beyond t* leads to a fall in tax revenue. This occurs because high tax rates act as a disincentive to work and act as a disincentive to declare taxable income. For example, workers will do work for 'cash in hand' rather than telling the government about their earnings. If tax on profits is high, fewer entrepreneurs will start up businesses because the incentive to do so falls as tax rates increase. High tax rates reduce **entrepreneurial** activity and risk taking, thereby reducing **investment**. High tax rates can have a negative effect on **productivity** and potential output of an economy and may lead to a slower rate of economic growth. Therefore, it can be argued that increasing tax rates may lead to a fall in tax revenue and reducing tax rates may lead to an increase in tax revenue.

Test your understanding of this unit by answering the following questions

- Comment on the possible consequences of a tax system put in place in order to reduce income inequality and to promote equity.
- Using a diagram, explain why reducing the tax rate may increase tax revenue.

Subject vocabulary

continued from page 172

positive externalities occur when the production or consumption of a good causes benefits to third parties. The existence of positive externalities means that social benefit is greater than private benefit.

market failure when resources are not allocated or used efficiently

allocative efficiency the best or optimal allocation of resources from society's point of view. It occurs when the market is in equilibrium and social surplus is maximized (where P = MC).

allocative inefficiency occurs when a market is in disequilibrium, where price does not equal marginal cost leading to a suboptimal allocation of resources from society's point of view

economic agents individuals and organizations whose actions have an impact on the economy, such as households, firms, and the government

real income income after taking into account the effects of inflation on purchasing power

marginal propensity to consume is the proportion of additional income that an individual spends on goods and services. MPC = the change in consumption divided by the change in income.

marginal propensity to save the proportion of additional income that an individual saves. MPS = the change in savings divided by the change in income.

aggregate demand the total demand for goods and services in the economy at a given price level in a given period of time

entrepreneur an individual who, in pursuit of profit, brings together the other factors of production in order to produce a good or service

investment the addition to capital stock

productivity the quantity of output per unit of input

2.4 Fiscal policy: The government budget

Learning Outcomes

- Explain that the government earns revenue primarily from taxes (direct and indirect), as well as from the sale of goods and services and the sale of state-owned (government-owned) enterprises.

- Explain that government spending can be classified into current expenditures, capital expenditures, and transfer payments, providing examples of each.

- Distinguish between a budget deficit, a budget surplus, and a balanced budget.

- Explain the relationship between budget deficits/surpluses and the public (government) debt.

Distinguish between a budget deficit, a budget surplus, and a balanced budget, and explain how the budgetary position affects government debt

The government budget is a forecast of the amount of government expenditure and government revenue for the coming year.

Model sentence: A budget surplus occurs if government revenue is greater than government expenditure. A budget deficit occurs if government expenditure is greater than government revenue, and a balanced budget occurs if government expenditure equals government revenue.

When a deficit is expected the government must make arrangements to borrow money from **financial institutions** and the public to make up the difference between expenditure and revenue. Many countries have a budget deficit. Borrowed money contributes to government revenue. Government debt, often called the national debt, is the total amount of money that the government has borrowed over the years that has not been paid back. When a government expects a budget surplus, it can plan to pay back to the lenders some of the national debt. When the government expects a budget deficit, it must plan to borrow more money, thereby adding to the national debt.

Model sentence: When a government continues to run a budget deficit year after year the national debt and the interest payments on the debt will continue to rise.

What are the main sources of government revenue and the different types of government expenditure?

Government borrowing means that government expenditure can exceed revenue. The largest contribution to government revenue comes from **direct taxes** and indirect taxes. Another source of revenue comes from the sale by the government of state-owned businesses. For example, in 2013 the UK government sold Royal Mail, a **state-owned enterprise**, the main business of which was the delivery of residential and business letters and parcels. The government sold **shares** in Royal Mail to the public and to financial institutions. The shareholders then became the new owners. The money raised from the sale of the shares, in excess of £2 billion, went to the government, increasing government revenue. When a state-owned business makes a profit it is a source of revenue for the government while any loss is subsidized by the taxpayer. Since the privatization of Royal Mail, the profit goes to the shareholders who are now the owners of the business.

Total government expenditure is the sum of current expenditures, capital expenditures, and transfer payments. Transfer payments include state pensions and welfare payments such as unemployment benefits.

Current expenditure is spending on goods and services that only last a relatively short period of time and, therefore, it is expenditure that takes place continuously. They are goods that are used up quickly in the provision of a service: for example, medicines in the health service. The wages paid to people who work for the state are also part of current expenditure. For example, the wages of doctors and nurses, soldiers, and teachers are part of current expenditure. Capital expenditure is spending on durable **capital** goods: goods that last a long time. They are goods that can be used again and again, but that at some point will need repairing or replacing. Capital expenditure is spending on **infrastructure** such as new schools, hospitals, roads, and capital equipment such as computers.

Subject vocabulary

financial institution a business, such as a bank, that provides a service allowing firms and households to make deposits and take out loans and to make investments

interest payments the money paid at regular intervals on loans

direct taxes a tax that is paid directly by an individual or firm to the government. For example income tax on wages and company profits.

state-owned enterprise a business that is partially or fully owned by a government

share a unit of ownership of a company's capital. The owner is entitled to a proportion of the company's profit.

capital (goods) manufactured goods that are used in the production of other goods

Glossary

infrastructure the basic structure/systems of a country (e.g. roads/railways)

Model sentence: Capital expenditure has lasting positive effects on the economy. It increases productivity and GDP whereas current expenditure has only short-term benefits.

Test your understanding of this unit by answering the following questions

- Explain the relationship between total government debt and the budgetary position.
- Distinguish between government current expenditure and capital expenditure.

Learning Outcomes

- Explain how changes in the level of government expenditure and/or taxes can influence the level of aggregate demand in an economy.

- Explain the mechanism through which expansionary fiscal policy can help an economy close a deflationary (recessionary) gap.

- Construct a diagram to show the potential effects of expansionary fiscal policy, outlining the importance of the shape of the aggregate supply curve.

- Explain the mechanism through which contractionary fiscal policy can help an economy close an inflationary gap.

- Construct a diagram to show the potential effects of contractionary fiscal policy, outlining the importance of the shape of the aggregate supply curve.

Explain the relationship between fiscal policy and aggregate demand

Fiscal policy relates to the use of taxation and government expenditure to achieve macroeconomic objectives. Aggregate demand is the sum of all expenditure in the economy in a given period of time. Aggregate demand = household consumption of domestically produced goods + private sector investment + government expenditure + (export revenue – import revenue): AD = C + I + G + (X – M).

Model sentence: *Ceteris paribus*, **a change in government expenditure leads to a change in AD and a shift in the AD curve.**

Model sentence: *Ceteris paribus*, **a change in the rate of income tax changes the amount of disposable income received by households, leading to a change in household expenditure and a shift in the AD curve.**

A change in corporation tax changes the amount of **retained profit** received by firms. This affects the amount of investment leading to a shift in the AD curve. **Foreign direct investment** (FDI) is affected by changes in corporation tax. As corporation tax changes, it changes the level of **inward investment**, thereby affecting AD.

Model sentence: *Ceteris paribus*, **reducing taxes and/or increasing government expenditure increases aggregate demand, and increasing taxes and/or reducing government expenditure reduces aggregate demand.**

Reducing taxes and increasing government expenditure may lead to increases in the **budget deficit** thereby increasing the national debt. The debt and the interest payments on the debt have to be paid by the taxpayers. Therefore, taxes have to be relatively higher in the future leaving households with less disposable income to spend. Government borrowing can lead to lower AD in the future.

Model sentence: Expansionary fiscal policy increases aggregate demand and contractionary fiscal policy reduces aggregate demand.

Using diagrams, explain how fiscal policy can affect the deflationary/inflationary gap

When the economy enters a **recession** aggregate demand and output is falling, as shown in Figure 61.1 (on page 176) by a shift of the AD curve from AD_1 to AD_2 and a fall from the full-employment level of output Y_f to Y_1. The deflationary gap or the **recessionary gap** is the difference between Y_f and the actual level of output, Y_1. Aggregate demand is not high enough to buy all the goods and services that can be produced

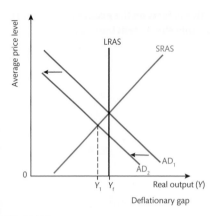

Figure 61.1

when all factors are being used. As AD falls, demand-deficient unemployment rises. The government can use expansionary fiscal policy in order to increase aggregate demand so that it is high enough to buy all goods and services produced at Y_f. Reducing taxes and/or increasing government expenditure increases aggregate demand and the AD curve shifts back to the right from AD_2 to AD_1 and firms increase output in response to higher levels of expenditure thereby closing the deflationary gap and reducing unemployment. However, increasing levels of aggregate demand causes **demand-pull inflation** and the price level increases.

At first the economy is in **long-run macroeconomic equilibrium** at the full employment level of output Y_f. At the present level of AD there are no pressures on the price level to change. However, an increase in

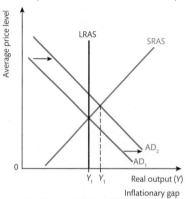

Figure 61.2

aggregate demand, from AD_1 to AD_2 opens up an inflationary gap where actual output, Y_1, is greater than the full-employment level of output, Y_f. Aggregate demand exceeds **aggregate supply**, pulling the price level up. This is called demand-pull inflation, which can lead to **cost-push inflation** as factor prices start to rise. Low and stable inflation is a government objective so the government may use contractionary fiscal policy of higher taxes and lower expenditure in order to reduce aggregate demand and output, shifting the AD curve back down and to the left from AD_2 to AD_1 until the economy is in long-run macroeconomic equilibrium.

Explain the significance of the shape of the short-run aggregate supply curve on the effects of fiscal policy

The effect on the change in output, **unemployment**, and **inflation** of fiscal policy depends on the size of the change in taxation and government spending and the slope of the SRAS curve. The size of the change in tax and government spending affects the size of the shift of AD and therefore its effect on the price level and output as shown in Figures 61.3 and 61.4. The significance of the slope of the SRAS can also be seen in the diagrams.

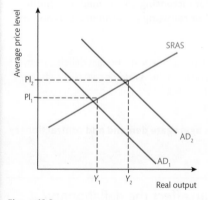

Figure 61.3

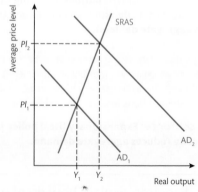

Figure 61.4

The SRAS curve is relatively shallower at lower levels of AD and output. There is lots of **spare capacity** in the economy. Unemployment of factors is relatively high. Demand for factors is low. As aggregate demand increases from AD_1 to AD_2, as shown in Figure 61.3, firms respond by increasing output from Y_1 to Y_2. Demand for factors increases but because supply of factors is high and demand still relatively low, factor prices rise only by a small amount leading to a relatively small increase in **costs of production**. Therefore, there is only a small increase in the price level. Also there is a relatively large deflationary gap so increases in AD do not cause demand-pull inflation. As there is lots of spare capacity and there are lots of factors available, firms are easily able to increase output in response to an increase in aggregate demand; therefore, there is a relatively large increase in output.

The SRAS curve is steeper in Figure 61.4 than in Figure 61.3. The deflationary gap is not as big. As there are fewer factors of production available and firms have very little spare capacity, firms are only able to increase supply by a relatively small amount in response to an increase in AD.

Model sentence: The effect on output and price level from a change in AD depends on the slope of the SRAS curve. The shallower the slope, the greater the change in output and the smaller the change in the price level.

Test your understanding of this unit by answering the following questions

- Using a diagram, explain how fiscal policy can be used to reduce the recessionary gap.
- Explain how the shape of the SRAS curve can affect changes in output and the price level caused by changes in AD.

Glossary

fluctuation(s) frequent change(s) especially from a high to a low level and back again

Learning Outcomes

- Explain how factors including the progressive tax system and unemployment benefits, which are influenced by the level of economic activity and national income, automatically help stabilize short-term **fluctuations**.

- Evaluate the view that fiscal policy can be used to promote long-term economic growth (increases in potential output) indirectly by creating an economic environment that is favourable to private investment, and directly through government spending on physical capital goods and human capital formation, as well as provision of incentives for firms to invest.

- Evaluate the effectiveness of fiscal policy through consideration of factors including the ability to target sectors of the economy, the direct impact on aggregate demand, the effectiveness of promoting economic activity in a recession, time lags, political constraints, crowding out, and the inability to deal with supply-side causes of instability.

Explain the term 'automatic stabilizer'

As the economy moves through the business cycle from **recession** to **boom** and back to recession, the amount of **tax revenue** the government receives and the amount the government spends changes automatically. When the economy is booming, there is lots of economic activity. Aggregate demand is high and the economy is producing at full potential levels of output so there are very low levels of unemployment. High levels of AD can lead to demand-pull inflation and cost-push inflation. Tax revenue from **direct taxes**, which are taxes on income, are high because employment is high and tax revenue from **corporation tax** is high because company profits are high. As the economy grows, incomes rise. In a **progressive tax system** the percentage rate of tax paid on extra income earned rises, thereby further increasing the amount of tax revenue. Tax revenue from indirect taxes, which are taxes on consumption, is high because household expenditure is high. When the economy is producing at the full-potential level of output, unemployment is low. Government expenditure on welfare benefits, such as unemployment benefit, is therefore relatively low. With higher taxes and lower government expenditure, the amount of money in the economy is reduced, thereby reducing aggregate demand.

Model sentence: As the economy continues to grow, government expenditure falls and tax revenue rises, thereby 'automatically' reducing aggregate demand, the rate of growth and inflationary pressures.

In this case the rate of economic growth is reduced by the 'automatic stabilizer' and not by government contractionary fiscal policy.

In a recession, **economic growth** is negative. GDP is falling. Aggregate demand falls to a low level and firms respond by reducing the size of their workforce. Incomes fall, therefore direct tax revenue falls. Corporation tax revenue falls as company profits fall. Indirect tax revenue falls as expenditure on goods and services fall. At the same time, government expenditure on unemployment benefits increases. With lower taxes and higher government expenditure, the amount of money in the economy is increased, thereby increasing aggregate

Subject vocabulary

recession two consecutive quarters of negative economic growth

boom a period of time during which an economy experiences sustained high levels of consumption and output often leading to increases in wages and inflation

tax revenue the income government receives through the levying and collection of taxes

direct taxes a tax that is paid directly by an individual or firm to the government. For example income tax on wages and company profits

corporation tax a tax levied in the UK on company profits

progressive tax system a system of taxation in which the rate of tax increases with income

economic growth an increase in real GDP

expansionary fiscal policy
policy involving the increase of
government spending and/or
the reduction of taxation

induced investment
investment by firms that
is caused by increases in
consumption. As aggregate
demand increases, and is
forecast to continue to rise,
firms need to increase the
quantity of capital in order to
meet future levels of demand.

**technologically advanced
capital** capital that
incorporates new technology
and is used in place of existing
capital to produce goods and
services thereby increasing
productivity

investment the addition to
capital stock

foreign direct investment
cross-border investment,
usually by firms, that involves
the acquisition of assets in a
foreign country. FDI can be
the purchase of a minimum of
10% of the shares of a foreign
company but also includes
the creation of productive
capacity.

value of human capital
a measure of the quantity
and quality of the skills of
the labour force that can be
employed to produce goods
and services. An increase in
the value of human capital
leads to an increase in labour
productivity.

labour productivity the
quantity of goods that a
worker produces in a given
period of time

fiscal policy government
policy designed to achieve
macroeconomic objectives
through government
expenditure and taxation

**sustainable economic
growth** economic growth that
meets the needs and wants of
the current generation in such
a way that does not prevent
future generations from
meeting their needs and wants

market failure when
resources are not allocated or
used efficiently

externalities consequences
of production or consumption
that affect third parties

continued on page 179

demand. The rate at which real output falls is reduced not by **expansionary fiscal policy** but by the 'automatic stabilizer'.

Explain how fiscal policy can promote long-run economic growth

As taxation falls as part of expansionary fiscal policy, households' disposable income increases, leading to an increase in expenditure. As AD increases, firms respond by increasing output. If firms expect demand to continue to increase they must invest in capital in order to be able to supply the higher future levels of demand. This is called **induced investment**. When firms buy more capital, they are likely to buy more **technologically advanced capital**. Higher levels of AD lead to an increase in **investment**, thereby increasing the quantity and quality (productivity) of capital in the economy. Full-employment level of output increases. To encourage growth, the government can cut corporation tax leaving firms with more profit to invest. Again the quantity and quality of capital in the economy rises leading to an increase in potential output. Lower corporation tax also encourages **foreign direct investment**. If foreign firms are allowed to keep more of their profits, they are more likely to set up business in the country. Increases in FDI increase the quantity and quality of capital in the economy, thereby increasing potential output. Lower tax rates encourage entrepreneurial activity, thereby increasing the number of small businesses in the economy. This contributes to increases in potential output.

As firms increase output, they employ more workers and buy new capital; therefore, more workers receive training and the **value of human capital** rises, increasing **labour productivity** contributing to increases in long-run economic growth.

Model sentence: Lower taxes lead to an increase in aggregate demand, causing an increase in induced investment and an increase in the quantity and quality of capital.

Infrastructure is the stock of fixed physical capital in an economy including roads, railways, airports, seaports, factories, communication networks, schools, and hospitals. The government in most countries provides much of the infrastructure directly through government expenditure or indirectly by setting policies that encourage private investment. Infrastructure contributes to potential output. With more factories it is possible to produce more goods; with more roads, railways, and airports, more goods and people can be transported more quickly and efficiently. With more schools and colleges of further education, it is possible to educate and train more workers thereby increasing the productivity of labour. Government spending on infrastructure is called government capital expenditure.

Model sentence: Increases in government capital expenditure on infrastructure increases the quantity and quality of physical and human capital leading to an increase in the full-employment level of output.

To show long-run economic growth on an AD/AS diagram, the long-run aggregate supply curve shifts to the right and on a production possibility diagram, the PPC moves outwards.

Evaluate the effectiveness of fiscal policy

Fiscal policy is used by government to achieve objectives. The main objective is to improve macroeconomic performance and the aims are to have low and stable inflation, low unemployment and **sustainable economic growth**. Fiscal policy is also used to achieve a more equal and **equitable** distribution of income and to correct **market failure** caused by **externalities** in production and consumption in the goods market, and market failure caused by **occupational immobility** and **geographical immobility** in the **labour market**. Set out below are ways fiscal policy can be evaluated.

Explain how government borrowing 'crowds out' private sector investment

One way to evaluate the effectiveness of fiscal policy is to examine the idea of 'crowding out'. An expansionary fiscal policy of low taxation and high government expenditure introduced to increase economic activity and reduce unemployment leads to an increase in the **budget deficit** and therefore an increase in government borrowing. In order to raise the money, the government sells **government bonds** to the public and **financial institutions**. The government has to compete with other borrowers for the limited supply of money available for lending (the supply of loanable funds). To encourage financial institutions and the public to lend to the government rather than to firms in the **private sector**, the government increases **interest rates** on the bonds. The public and financial institutions take some of their money out of the banks in order to buy government bonds, thereby reducing the amount of money banks have to lend to the private sector. Banks also lend more to the government, attracted by the higher rates of interest; therefore, the banks have less money to lend to firms in the private sector. Increases in government borrowing lead to a fall in the supply of loanable funds available for the private sector.

Model sentence: Government borrowing to fund the budget deficit 'crowds out' private sector borrowing and pushes up interest rates, leading to a fall in investment by firms in the economy.

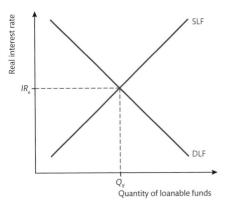

Figure 62.1

The supply of loanable funds curve (SLF) in Figure 62.1 shows the amount of savings in the economy available for lending at each interest rate. As interest rates rise, the incentive to save increases therefore the quantity supplied of loanable funds rises. The demand for loanable funds curve (DLF) shows the demand for loanable funds at each rate of interest. As interest rate rises, the cost of borrowing increases, therefore the quantity demanded of loanable funds falls. The equilibrium interest rate, IR, is the rate at which quantity supplied of loanable funds is equal to the quantity demanded.

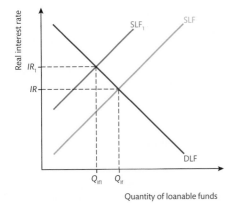

Figure 62.2

When the government borrows more money, the supply of loanable funds available for the private sector falls and the supply of loanable funds curve shifts up and to the left from SLF to SLF_1. At the original rate of interest, IR, quantity demanded of funds is greater than quantity supplied. In order to remove the excess demand the interest rate rises. As it rises, quantity demanded falls and quantity supplied increases until the new equilibrium IR_1 and Q_{lf1} is reached. The effect of government borrowing is to increase interest rates on private sector borrowing, thereby reducing the quantity of private sector investment.

Increased government expenditure does increase aggregate demand but to increase expenditure the government must borrow. This pushes up interest rates. Higher interest rates means that households increase the amount of income they save, thereby reducing household expenditure and aggregate demand. Higher interest rates also reduce investment by firms leading to a further fall in aggregate demand. This negative effect on aggregate demand may mean that the government might not achieve its macroeconomic objectives.

Explain why fiscal policy may lead to some macroeconomic objectives not being achieved

Another possible negative effect on AD of expansionary fiscal policy comes from higher levels of expenditure. The government reduces taxation and increases government spending in order to increase aggregate demand and economic growth and to reduce unemployment. If the economy grows too quickly, it can lead to demand-pull and cost-push inflation. If this happens the government might use contractionary fiscal policy to reduce aggregate demand in order to reduce inflation. However, this policy might put the economy back into recession. The government now has to reduce taxes and increase government expenditure in order to encourage economic growth. Economists call this the 'stop-go cycle' because fiscal policy is used to stop the economy growing and then the policy must be changed in order to get the economy going again.

How might expansionary fiscal policy affect the demand for imports and exports?

Higher interest rates brought about by increases in government borrowing will attract foreign investors looking for better returns on their savings. If, for example, demand for UK government bonds increases because of the

foreign exchange market a
decentralized global market
for the buying and selling of
currencies

current account deficit
occurs when the amount
of money flowing out of a
country from the trade in
goods and services, investment
income, and transfers is greater
than the amount flowing in

exchange rate the price of a
country's currency in terms of
another currency

**marginal propensity to
import** the proportion of
additional income that an
individual spends on imported
goods and services. MPM =
the change in expenditure on
imports divided by the change
in income.

**demand-deficient
unemployment**
unemployment caused by a
lack of aggregate demand.
Unemployment changes as
the economy goes through
the business cycle, increasing
when AD falls and decreasing
when AD rises.

structural unemployment
unemployment caused by a
change in the type of labour
firms demand. It is caused by a
mismatch of the skills of those
unemployed and the skills
needed by firms.

**natural rate of
unemployment** the rate
of unemployment at which
inflation stabilizes. At the
natural rate of unemployment,
all who want to work at
the market wage can find
work therefore there is no
involuntary unemployment.

external supply-side shock
occurs when there is an
unexpected change in the
supply of a good produced
abroad that results in a sudden
change in its price

productivity the quantity of
output per unit of input

infrastructure the basic
structure/systems of a country
(e.g. roads/railways)

time lag(s) period(s) of time
between two linked events

higher interest rate on UK bonds, foreigners who want to buy bonds must buy £s with their currency which they then use to buy the bonds. The demand for the £ increases on the **foreign exchange market**, pushing up the value of the £. As the £ goes up in value against other currencies, the price foreigners have to pay for UK exports goes up and the price UK consumers pay for imports falls, leading to a fall in consumption of exports and an increase in consumption of imports. Net exports (X – M) falls causing a fall in AD and an increase in the **current account deficit**. The size of the increase in aggregate demand brought about by expansionary policy might therefore not be as big as the government wanted.

When AD increases and incomes rise, households buy more goods including more imports. The quantity of extra imports that households buy depends on the **marginal propensity to import**. If the demand for imports rises at a greater rate than demand for exports, net exports falls leading to a fall in AD and an increase in the current account deficit.

Explain the effect time lags have on the success of fiscal policy decisions

The statistics on inflation, unemployment, and economic growth take a long time to research and gather. By the time policymakers have the information, it will be out of date. The statistics gathered may also be unreliable. Therefore, the decision to increase or decrease aggregate demand by changing fiscal policy may be the wrong decision and therefore will not help to achieve the macroeconomic objectives and may even make the situation worse.

It takes time for households to react to changes in policy. Households will not immediately increase expenditure when taxes are cut. It can take months before households change their patterns of consumption, therefore, aggregate demand will not be affected immediately. However, tax cuts are likely to affect aggregate demand more quickly than increases in capital expenditure. Government investment in **infrastructure** will take a long time to affect economic activity. Government decisions to build a new railway or new roads cannot be made quickly and it will be years before building starts and for the money to be injected into the circular flow of income. The long **time lags** and the possible inaccuracy of the national statistics means that using fiscal policy to achieve macroeconomic objectives may not work.

Why might political considerations affect fiscal policy?

Politicians decide on fiscal policy. Politicians and political parties want to be re-elected at the next election. Tax cuts are popular with the people. Politicians may decide to cut taxes and increase benefit payments before an election to gain votes even if the economy is near to full-employment level of output. An expansionary fiscal policy at this time may increase the chances of the political party being re-elected but would cause high levels of inflation in the months after the election. If aggregate demand is high and there are dangers of demand-pull and cost-push inflation, the government should increase taxes to reduce aggregate demand. However, if this occurred near an election the government may not cut taxes for fear of losing votes.

Are unemployment and inflation always caused by demand-side factors?

Demand-deficient unemployment can be reduced by increasing aggregate demand through expansionary fiscal policy. However, **structural unemployment** needs supply-side solutions. Fiscal policy will not directly affect levels of structural unemployment. If a government tried to reduce unemployment below the **natural rate of unemployment** it might lead to inflation. Inflation is not only caused by high levels of aggregate demand. Inflation can be caused by **external supply-side shocks**. If a currency falls in value against other currencies, the price of imports, including the price of raw materials, increases leading to inflation. In these cases, inflation cannot be reduced directly by changes in fiscal policy. Poor economic performance is not always due to demand-side factors. Low levels of **productivity** due to lack of investment in physical capital and human capital over time makes firms internationally uncompetitive. If competitiveness falls demand for imports will rise and demand for exports will fall leading to lower levels of economic activity. In this case, the productivity of the factors is the cause of the problem and supply-side policies are needed to increase productivity.

Test your understanding of this unit by answering the following questions

- Explain the term 'automatic stabilizer'.
- Evaluate the use of fiscal policy to achieve government macroeconomic objectives.

2.5 Monetary policy: Interest rates

Learning Outcomes

- Describe the role of central banks as regulators of commercial banks and bankers to governments.

- Explain that central banks are usually made responsible for interest rates and exchange rates in order to achieve macroeconomic objectives.

- Explain, using a demand and supply of money diagram, how equilibrium interest rates are determined, outlining the role of the central bank in influencing the supply of money.

What is the role of a central bank?

The main responsibilities of a central bank (for example, the Bank of England, the US Federal Reserve and the European Central Bank) are set out below.

The central bank acts as the banker to the government. It looks after the **national debt**, organizing the sale of **government bonds** so that the government can run a **budget deficit**. The bank organizes the repayment of the loans and the **interest payments** to the lenders. The central bank acts as the banker to the commercial banks. The central bank controls the supply of money and issues coins and notes (cash) that are sold to other banks in the banking system. The coins and notes are then passed onto the customers of the banks when they withdraw cash from their bank accounts. If there is a shortage of cash in the banking system (not enough **liquidity**), the central bank increases the supply of cash into the system to remove the **excess demand**. If a commercial bank needs more cash because it does not have enough to meet the demand of its customers the central bank lends cash to the bank so that it can continue to perform its function and not go out of business. The aim is to stabilize the banking system. The central bank will only do this if there are no other possible alternatives. That is why the central bank is 'the lender of last resort'.

Using diagrams, explain how the central bank can change the interest rate to achieve macroeconomic objective

The central bank sets the **monetary policy** of an economy. Many central banks are free from direct political control so that monetary policy is determined by the need to achieve economic objectives and not political objectives. Monetary policy involves controlling the supply of money in the economy in order to achieve **macroeconomic objectives**. The main objective central banks try to achieve through monetary policy is low and stable inflation. The main way in which the central bank achieves macroeconomic objectives is through the setting of interest rates. The interest rate is the price of money. The interest payment on a loan is the amount the borrower has to pay to have the money to spend now. If a person borrows $10000 for a year at an interest rate of 5%, by the end of the year the amount borrowed has to be repaid to the lender plus the interest on the loan, which in this example is $500 ($10000 × 5%). The price of $10000 is $500.

The interest rate is determined by the demand and supply of money. Households and firms 'demand' money to buy goods and services that are bought on a regular basis. Households and firms must hold enough money to be able to buy these goods and services. Those on higher incomes are likely to hold money because they buy more goods. Inflation reduces the **purchasing power** of money; therefore, inflation leads to an increase in the amount of money households and firms need to hold for spending on these goods.

Money (cash) is an **asset**. As the interest rate rises, the **opportunity cost** of holding money in the form of cash or a cash equivalent, such as money held in a non-interest bearing current account at a bank, increases. Households and firms who hold money are forgoing the interest paid on non-money assets such as savings accounts and government bonds. As the interest rate increases, the greater the amount of interest the households and firms **forgo**. The demand curve for money is also called the liquidity preference schedule. As seen in Figure 63.1 (on page 182), it slopes downwards. As the interest rate rises, households and firms 'prefer' to own non-money assets rather than hold money. Therefore, the quantity of money demanded falls as the interest rate increases. Households and firms hold more money in the form of cash when the interest rate is low because the returns available on non-money assets are not so attractive.

Model sentence: As the interest rate increases, the opportunity cost of holding money increases; therefore, the quantity of money demanded falls and the demand for interest-paying non-money assets rises.

The supply of money is controlled by the central bank and is not determined by the rate of interest. The money supply is constant at each interest rate; therefore, the supply of money curve is perfectly inelastic with respect to interest rates.

Subject vocabulary

national debt the total amount of money a government has borrowed. When a government runs a budget deficit it must borrow the difference thereby adding to the national debt

government bonds issued by the government to investors in exchange for lending it money. The investor is entitled to interest payments on the loan as well as repayment of the loan when the bond matures.

budget deficit occurs when government expenditure is greater than tax revenue

interest payments the money paid at regular intervals on loans

liquidity the degree to which an asset can be sold and converted into cash. A savings account is very liquid, property is less liquid.

excess demand occurs when quantity demanded is greater than quantity supplied

monetary policy the control of the supply of money by the government to affect the economy (e.g. changing interest rates)

macroeconomic objectives the main aims of government macroeconomic policy, such as low and stable inflation, low levels of unemployment and sustainable economic growth

purchasing power a measure of how many goods and services a given amount of money can buy

asset an item of value owned by an individual or firm, especially one that could be converted to cash

opportunity cost the next best alternative forgone

Synonyms

forgo .... sacrifice/give up

rate of interest the percentage amount charged by a lender for money borrowed or paid to a person for saving money

excess demand occurs when quantity demanded is greater than quantity supplied

government bonds issued by the government to investors in exchange for lending it money. The investor is entitled to interest payments on the loan as well as repayment of the loan when the bond matures.

budget deficit occurs when government expenditure is greater than tax revenue

excess supply occurs when quantity supplied is greater than quantity demanded

inflation an increase in the general level of prices of goods/services in an economy over a given time period, usually a year

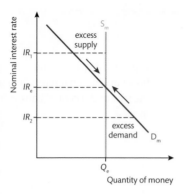

Figure 63.1

In Figure 63.1 the equilibrium **rate of interest** occurs at IRE where the quantity of money supplied by the central bank is equal to the quantity of money demanded by households and firms. If the interest rate is at IR₂ there is **excess demand** for money. Households and firms want to increase the amount of money they hold. In order to increase their money holdings they sell some of their non-money assets such as **government bonds** and withdraw money from saving accounts held at banks thereby turning non-money assets into money. Now the government has to increase the interest rates payable on bonds to attract enough buyers in order to be able to cover the **budget deficit**. Banks have to increase interest rates in order to attract more savers. In this way an excess demand for money pushes up the interest rate towards equilibrium.

At IR₁ quantity of money supplied by central government exceeds the quantity of money demanded by households and firms. There is an **excess supply** of money. Households and firms now hold more money than they want to hold. They deposit some of the money in saving accounts at banks and buy more government bonds, leading to a fall in the interest rate offered on savings account and bonds.

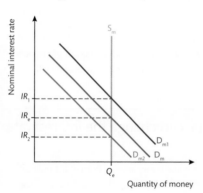

Figure 63.2

If incomes increase or **inflation** occurs demand for money at each rate of interest increases causing a shift up and to the right of the demand for money curve from Dₘ to Dₘ₁ as seen in Figure 63.2. There is now excess demand at the original equilibrium interest rate IRₑ so the interest rate increases to IR₁ as explained above. The reverse happens when incomes fall and deflation occurs. The demand for money curve shifts down to the left from Dₘ to Dₘ₂, causing excess supply. The interest rate falls to IR₂ to restore equilibrium.

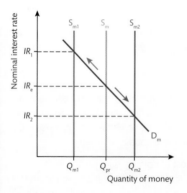

Figure 63.3

The central bank controls the money supply. Changing the money supply changes the equilibrium interest rate. Reducing the money supply shifts the supply of money curve to the left from Sₘ to Sₘ₁ as shown in Figure 63.3 causing excess demand for money at the original equilibrium interest rate IRE. As explained above, the interest rate rises to the new equilibrium rate IR₁ where quantity of money demanded equals the quantity of money supplied.

By changing the money supply, the central bank can change the rate of interest.

Explain how the central bank changes the money supply

Commercial banks lend money to firms who want to invest and to households who want a loan to buy goods and services. Banks do this because they charge interest on borrowed money. This is one way commercial banks earn revenue and profit. Commercial banks also buy government bonds. Commercial banks are paid interest by the government on these bonds. Bonds are tradable non-money assets issued initially by the government to raise money but which are then bought and sold on the bond market. Bonds pay an interest payment to the holder so therefore bonds have a value. When the central bank wants to increase the money supply it buys bonds from the commercial banks. This increases the supply of money because the money used to buy the bonds goes to the commercial banks. The public also sell their bonds and the money goes into their accounts at the banks. The banks now hold more money on which they are not earning interest. They want to lend the extra money they now have to households and firms in order to earn interest. To encourage firms and households to borrow the extra money banks reduce the rate of interest charged on loans. Demand for loans increases, firms and households borrow more to fund investment and consumer expenditure, thereby increasing **aggregate demand** in the economy. The purchase of government bonds by the central bank is therefore an **expansionary monetary policy**.

When people and banks buy bonds from the central bank, they take money out of their accounts in order to buy them thereby reducing the supply of money. The supply of money available for firms and households to borrow falls leading to an increase in the interest rate. Overall less money is borrowed by firms and households, reducing the amount of **investment** and consumer expenditure in the economy, leading to a fall in aggregate demand. The sale of government bonds by the central bank is therefore a **contractionary monetary policy**.

Model sentence: When the central bank buys government bonds, it increases the supply of money leading to a fall in the rate of interest and an increase in investment and household consumption.

Model sentence: When the central bank sells government bonds, it reduces the supply of money leading to an increase in the rate of interest and a fall in investment and household consumption.

Another way in which the central bank can control the supply of money is to change the **reserve requirement** for banks. When households deposit money in their accounts the banks use this money to create loans. The banks have to keep a percentage of the deposited money on reserve so that it can continue to make its daily transactions, for example, paying money back to its customers who wish to make cash withdrawals. If the central bank increases the percentage of any deposits that must be held in reserve the banks must reduce the supply of money available for loans. This increases the interest rate and reduces the amount of money firms and households borrow. Investment and household expenditure falls leading to a fall in aggregate demand. Increasing the reserve requirement is therefore a contractionary monetary policy.

If the central bank reduces the reserve requirement it increases the supply of money available for loans. This reduces the interest rate and increases the amount firms and households borrow. Investment and household expenditure increases, leading to an increase in aggregate demand. Reducing the reserve requirement is therefore an expansionary monetary policy.

The central bank can control the money supply by increasing the interest rate on the loans it makes to commercial banks. This is called the discount rate. When the discount rate increases, it increases the cost of borrowing for commercial banks. To avoid having to borrow from the central bank the banks reduce the supply of money available for loans leading to higher interest rates. This reduces the amount of money firms and households borrow. Investment and household expenditure falls leading to a fall in aggregate demand. Increasing the discount rate is therefore a contractionary monetary policy.

Lowering the discount rate makes it cheaper for banks to borrow from the central bank. Banks therefore increase the supply of money available for loans leading to a fall in the interest rate. This increases the amount firms and households borrow. Investment and household expenditure increases, leading to an increase in aggregate demand. Reducing the discount rate is therefore an expansionary monetary policy.

Test your understanding of this unit by answering the following questions

- Using a demand and supply of money diagram, explain how the equilibrium interest rate is determined.
- Explain how the central bank can use monetary policy to change the rate of interest.

Learning Outcomes

- Explain how changes in interest rates can influence the level of aggregate demand in an economy.
- Explain the mechanism through which easy (expansionary) monetary policy can help an economy close a deflationary (recessionary) gap.
- Construct a diagram to show the potential effects of easy (expansionary) monetary policy, outlining the importance of the shape of the aggregate supply curve.
- Explain the mechanism through which tight (contractionary) monetary policy can help an economy close an inflationary gap.
- Construct a diagram to show the potential effects of tight (contractionary) monetary policy, outlining the importance of the shape of the aggregate supply curve.

Explain how a fall in the interest rate affects aggregate demand and closes the deflationary gap

By increasing the **money supply** the central bank can reduce the interest rate (see the previous unit). A change in interest rates affects **aggregate demand** (AD). A fall in interest rates leads to an increase in AD as explained below.

Households borrow more money from banks in order to buy relatively more expensive goods and services such as cars and holidays because the cost of borrowing has fallen. Mortgage interest repayments fall leaving households with greater **discretionary income**, some of which they spend on goods and services. Firms borrow more in order to make **investments**. The lower interest repayments on loans increases the potential profit that can be made on each investment project, therefore more investment occurs. Lower interest payments on existing loans reduce the **costs of production**, thereby increasing **retained profit**. With more profit, firms may invest more.

Lower interest rates reduce the demand for the currency because fewer foreigners want to hold non-money assets in the country. As demand for the currency falls the currency depreciates, or falls in value, against other currencies. Its exports become less expensive for foreigners to buy, therefore quantity demanded increases, leading to an increase in AD. (Exchange rate determination is discussed in detail in a later unit.)

Model sentence: Increasing the money supply is an expansionary monetary policy because an increase in the supply of money causes interest rates to fall leading to an increase in aggregate demand.

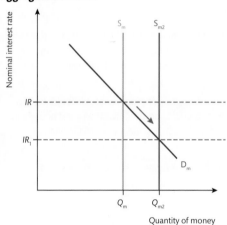

Figure 64.1a

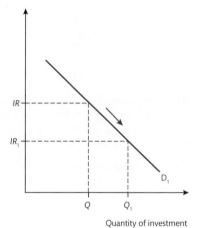

Figure 64.1b

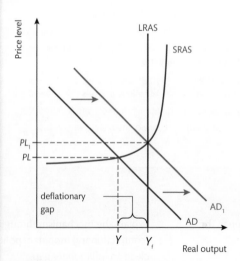

Figure 64.1c

As shown in Figure 64.1a, when the central bank increases the money supply, for example by buying government bonds, it reduces the equilibrium rate of interest from IR to IR_1. The fall in the interest rate increases the demand for loans increasing the quantity of investment demanded by firms from Q to Q_1 as shown in Figure 64.1b. Households also borrow more to buy goods and services. Investment and household expenditure are **components** of aggregate demand therefore aggregate demand increases and the AD curve shifts up and to the right as shown in Figure 64.1c. Firms respond by increasing output from Y to **full-employment level of output**, Y_f. The **price level** rises from PL to PL_1 and **demand-deficient unemployment** falls. The deflationary gap, which is the difference between actual output at Y and full employment level of output at Y_f, has been removed as AD has increased.

(For an explanation of the significance of the shape of the short-run aggregate supply curve, see page 176.)

Explain how an increase in the interest rate affects aggregate demand and closes the inflationary gap

By reducing the money supply the central bank can increase the interest rate (see the previous unit for a full explanation). An increase in **interest rates** leads to a fall in aggregate demand as explained below.

Households borrow less money from banks in order to buy goods and services because the cost of borrowing has increased. Mortgage interest repayments rise, leaving households with less discretionary income to spend on goods and services. As the cost of borrowing increases, firms reduce investments. The higher interest repayments on loans reduce the potential profit that can be made on each investment project, therefore firms make fewer investments. Higher interest payments on existing loans increase the cost of production, thereby reducing retained profit. With less profit, firms make fewer investments.

Higher interest rates increase the demand for the currency because more foreigners want to hold non-money assets in the country. As demand for the currency increases the currency appreciates or rises in value against other currencies. Its exports become more expensive for foreigners to buy, therefore demand for them falls leading to a fall in AD. (Exchange rate determination is discussed in detail in a later unit.) As the currency appreciates, the price of imports also falls causing firms and households to buy from abroad rather than from domestic producers, further reducing AD.

Model sentence: Reducing the money supply is a contractionary monetary policy because a reduction in the supply of money causes interest rates to rise, leading to a fall in aggregate demand.

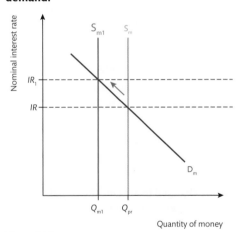

Figure 64.2a

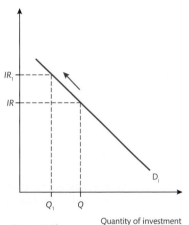

Figure 64.2b

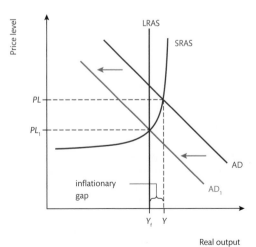

Figure 64.2c

As shown in Figure 64.2a, when the central bank reduces the money supply, for example by selling **government bonds**, it increases the equilibrium rate of interest from IR to IR_1. The increase in the interest rate reduces the demand for loans thereby reducing the quantity of investment demanded by firms from Q to Q_1 as shown in Figure 64.2b. Households also borrow less money to buy goods and services. Investment and household expenditure are components of aggregate demand therefore aggregate demand falls and the AD curve shifts down and to the left as shown in Figure 64.2c. Firms respond by reducing output from Y to full-employment level of output, Y_f. The price level falls from PL to PL_1 as the **excess demand** in the economy is reduced. The inflationary gap, which is the difference between actual output at Y and full employment level of output at Y_f, in Figure 64.2c has been removed as AD has fallen.

Test your understanding of this unit by answering the following question

- Using diagrams, explain how a central bank can reduce the deflationary gap by increasing the supply of money.

Learning Outcomes

- Explain that central banks of certain countries, rather than focusing on the **maintenance** of both full employment and a low rate of inflation, are guided in their monetary policy by the objective to achieve an **explicit** or **implicit** inflation rate target.

- Evaluate the effectiveness of monetary policy through consideration of factors including the independence of the central bank, the ability to adjust interest rates **incrementally**, the ability to implement changes in interest rates relatively quickly, **time lags**, limited effectiveness in increasing aggregate demand if the economy is in deep recession, and conflict among government economic objectives.

Evaluate the effectiveness of monetary policy

Why might monetary policy be more effective than fiscal policy?

Monetary policy aims to affect levels of aggregate demand in the economy in order to control inflation, unemployment, and economic growth. There are some advantages of using monetary policy rather than fiscal policy to achieve macroeconomic objectives.

Unlike **fiscal policy**, monetary policy can be put into action quickly. If the central bank believes that inflationary pressures are building up because of high levels of aggregate demand, it can make the decision to sell its **government bonds** in order to reduce the money supply and increase the **interest rate**. In the same way if the central bank is concerned about the economy moving into **recession** it can quickly buy bonds, thereby increasing the money supply and reducing the interest rate. It is relatively easy for the central bank to achieve its target interest rate, reducing it or increasing it by simply selling or buying government bonds.

Most central banks are independent from political control, therefore it is not necessary for them to consider the popularity of the policy. Central banks are free to consider only the economic objectives. They do not have to worry about political objectives unlike the politicians who decide on fiscal policy.

An **expansionary fiscal policy**, unlike expansionary monetary policy, normally causes an increase in the **budget deficit** forcing the government to sell more bonds. This reduces the money supply available for banks to lend to firms and households thereby increasing the rate of interest and crowding out private sector activity.

Model sentence: Monetary policy is easily and quickly changed to achieve the target rate of interest, it is free from political control and private sector investment is not crowded out by government borrowing.

Why might investment and consumer expenditure be unresponsive to changes in the rate of interest?

The interest rate is not the most important variable that firms and households consider when making investment and expenditure decisions. If firms and households expect aggregate demand to fall, firms are less likely to borrow. Households will wait to make purchases if they are worried that they may lose their jobs or if they believe their income will fall in the future. And firms will not buy new capital if they believe that higher potential output will not be met by higher levels of demand for the good they produce. If confidence is low, firms will not want to increase their **costs of production** by investing and households will not increase expenditure even if interest rates are reduced. When the aggregate demand is expected to increase, investment will be relatively responsive to a change in the interest rate and the demand for investment funds will be relatively elastic with respect to interest rates, in other words %ΔQ of investment >%ΔIR. When aggregate demand is expected to fall and confidence is low the demand for investment funds will be relatively inelastic with respect to interest rates as shown in Figure 65.1. In other words the %ΔIR>%ΔQ of investment. Because of the time it takes for firms and households to react to changes in the interest rate, the elasticity of demand of investment in respect to interest rates might stay inelastic for a long time, particularly if it is believed interest rates might rise again in the near future.

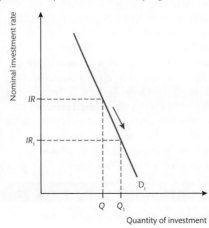

Figure 65.1

Why does monetary policy affect the exchange rate and how do changes in the exchange rate affect AD?

The exchange rate is the rate at which one currency can be exchanged for another. If a country has a **floating exchange rate** system, like the system in the UK, monetary policy can affect the exchange rate. An increase in the UK's interest rate, a contractionary monetary policy, means that returns on non-money assets increases. Foreigners looking for higher returns are attracted by the higher interest rate. In order to buy the non-money assets in the UK, foreigners must exchange their currency for the pound sterling (£). There is an increase in demand for the £ on the **foreign exchange market**. The increase in demand increases the price of the £.

As the interest rate rises, the £ rises in value therefore foreigners buying goods made in the UK (UK exports) must pay more of their currencies for UK goods. For example, a firm in the US buying UK goods must exchange more dollars to buy £s with which to pay the firm in the UK. The price in $s of all exports from the UK to the US increases, therefore quantity demanded of exports falls. A higher valued £ means that the price in £s for goods from the US (UK imports) falls thereby increasing quantity demanded of imports. A contractionary monetary policy therefore can lead to an increase in the **current account deficit** or a fall in the **current account surplus** as demand for exports falls and demand for imports rises. The leakage of income out of the **circular flow of income** to pay for the imports is greater than the **injection** of income into the circular flow from the sale of exports, leading to a fall in AD.

A lower interest rate reduces demand for the £ as returns on holding UK non-money assets falls. The supply of the £ in the foreign exchange (forex) market increases as some holding UK non-money assets sell them to buy non-money assets in other countries which pay higher interest rates. These investors supply £s onto the forex market and demand the currency of the country in which they are buying the assets. The increase in the supply of £s on the forex market pushes the price of the £ down. The price of UK exports abroad falls therefore quantity demanded of export increases while the price of imports for UK households and firms increases, leading to a fall in quantity demanded of imports. Net exports increase, thereby increasing the current account surplus or reducing the current account deficit, leading to an increase in AD.

Explain the conflicts between government macroeconomic objectives caused by monetary policy

Demand-pull inflation can be reduced by contractionary monetary policy. Reducing the money supply pushes up interest rates thereby reducing aggregate demand. However, as aggregate demand falls, firms reduce their output and lay off workers. The policy may reduce demand-pull inflation but at the same time increase unemployment. There is a trade-off between inflation and unemployment.

Contractionary monetary policy will not be effective at reducing inflation if inflation is caused by supply-side shocks that increase the costs of production.

In a recession the central bank may increase the money supply by buying government bonds in order to reduce the interest rates. At lower interest rates firms borrow more to invest and households borrow more to buy goods and services. The lower interest rate leads to a fall in the exchange rate causing an increase in demand for exports as the price of exports falls. Consumer expenditure, private investment, and expenditure on exports are parts of aggregate demand: AD = C + I + (X − M). As aggregate demand increases, firms employ more workers in order to increase output leading to a fall in unemployment. Higher levels of expenditure cause **induced investment** as firms want to increase their **capacity**. The country enters a period of economic growth.

Model sentence: Higher levels of aggregate demand can cause demand-pull inflation. The higher demand for factors pushes factor prices up, leading to cost-push inflation and the fall in the exchange rate causes the price of imports to increase, leading to imported inflation.

Also the price of imported resources used by firms pushes up costs of production contributing further to cost-push inflation.

Monetary policy can cause an increase in AD leading to a fall in unemployment. However, an increase in AD can also cause inflation. There is a trade-off between unemployment and inflation.

What is inflation targeting?

Inflation targeting is a policy set by central banks stating publicly their intention to use monetary policy to maintain inflation at the stated rate or between two rates. The banks also publicly state the measures to be taken to achieve and maintain the target inflation rate. The central bank forecasts changes in the rate of inflation and the difference between the target rate and the forecast rate determines monetary policy.

Subject vocabulary

floating exchange rate a situation where the value of a currency is determined by the demand for and the supply of the currency

foreign exchange market a decentralized global market for the buying and selling of currencies

current account deficit occurs when the amount of money flowing out of a country from the trade in goods and services, investment income, and transfers is greater than the amount flowing in

current account surplus occurs when the amount of money flowing out of a country from the trade in goods and services, investment income, and transfers is less than the amount flowing in

circular flow of income an economic model that shows the flow of money between households and firms and, in more complex versions, the flows of money into and out of the financial sector, government sector, and the international sector

demand-pull inflation occurs when aggregate demand is greater than aggregate supply

induced investment investment by firms that is caused by increases in consumption. As aggregate demand increases, and is forecast to continue to rise, firms need to increase the quantity of capital in order to meet future levels of demand.

cost-push inflation inflation caused by an increase in the costs of production, resulting in a decrease in aggregate supply

imported inflation inflation caused by an increase in the price of imported goods. For example as the price of imported raw materials increase, it leads to an increase in the price of domestically produced goods.

Glossary

injection putting money into a plan/organization

capacity the amount of something a firm is able to make

There are 28 countries that target inflation in this explicit way. A few are listed below.

Country	Inflation targeting adoption date	Inflation rate at adoption date (percent)	2010 end-of-year inflation (percent)	Target inflation rate (percent)
New Zealand	1990	3.30	4.03	1–3
Canada	1991	6.90	2.23	2 +/– 1
United Kingdom	1992	4.00	3.39	2
Australia	1993	2.00	2.65	2–3
Sweden	1993	1.80	2.10	2

Table 65.1 *Source: IMF*

Most countries aim to achieve the inflation target over the medium term (2 to 3 years) allowing for short-term **fluctuations** in the rate of inflation. In this way the bank can also focus on other macroeconomic objectives. For example the bank might allow inflation to rise above the target rate because increasing interest rates to reduce inflation might deepen and lengthen a recession or damage the chances of an economic recovery.

An advantage of inflation targeting is that firms have more confidence that government is taking inflation seriously and they know what the central bank will do to keep inflation under control. If firms believe inflation will be controlled at relatively low levels they are more likely to make investments.

There are many central banks that do not have explicit targets including the European Central Bank, the Federal Reserve, the Swiss national bank, and the Bank of Japan. However, the banks all have low and stable inflation as a main objective.

Test your understanding of this unit by answering the following questions

- Explain why it is difficult for an economy to achieve low inflation, low unemployment, and economic growth through the use of monetary policy.
- Explain the possible effect on the exchange rate of contractionary monetary policy.
- Evaluate the effectiveness of expansionary monetary policy on increasing investment and household expenditure.

2.6 Supply-side policies: The role of supply-side policies, interventionist supply-side policies

Learning Outcomes

- Explain that supply-side policies aim at positively affecting the production side of an economy by improving the institutional framework and the capacity to produce (that is, by changing the quantity and/or quality of factors of production).

- State that supply-side policies may be market-based or interventionist, and that in either case they aim to shift the LRAS curve to the right, achieving growth in potential output.

- Explain how investment in education and training will raise the levels of human capital and have a short-term impact on aggregate demand, but more importantly will increase LRAS.

- Explain how policies that encourage research and development will have a short-term impact on aggregate demand, but more importantly will result in new technologies and will increase LRAS.

- Explain how increased and improved infrastructure will have a short-term impact on aggregate demand, but more importantly will increase LRAS.

- Explain that targeting specific industries through policies including tax cuts, tax allowances, and subsidized lending promotes growth in key areas of the economy and will have a short-term impact on aggregate demand but, more importantly, will increase LRAS.

What is the general aim of supply-side policies?

The aim is to increase the quantity and quality (productivity) of the **factors of production** in order to increase the **potential output** of the economy. Supply-side policies affect the quantity and quality of the factors thereby affecting the amount of goods and services that can be produced. Increases in the productive potential of the economy are shown as a shift to the right of the long-run aggregate supply curve and an outward movement of the **production possibility curve**. Supply-side policies are either interventionist or market-based.

What are interventionist policies and why might they cause an increase in AD?

They are called interventionist supply-side policies because they require the government to take action in order to raise the quantity and quality of the factors. When a government intervenes it spends money, for example government expenditure on infrastructure is very high and it makes a big contribution to aggregate demand, shifting the AD curve to the right. The aim of supply-side policies is to shift the LRAS curve to the right. This might reduce the price level leading to an increase in expenditure. Increasing productivity can also lead to economic growth and a rise in national income leading to an increase in aggregate demand. Increasing factor productivity reduces average total cost thereby increasing international competiveness and increasing the demand for exports, a part of AD.

Explain how investment in education and training affects potential output

Education and training are merit goods. There are **positive externalities** created by consumption. Left to the **free market** the markets would fail. Not enough factors would be allocated to the provision of education and training and they would be underprovided and under consumed. Society would not enjoy all the benefits of a well-educated and well-trained population. The government therefore might intervene in the markets to ensure that more factors are allocated to the provision of education and training leading to an increase in the amount of education and training consumed. This increases the **value of human capital**. In all advanced countries the government provides education directly and it is available to all young people. Many governments subsidize further education to increase the number of young people who stay in education and training.

A modern successful economy requires a well-educated and skilled workforce. Giving workers the skills demanded by industries reduces **structural unemployment** thereby increasing the economy's potential output. Governments can help improve the skills of the workforce by giving subsidies to firms to provide training.

A well-educated and highly skilled workforce increases the productivity (quality) of labour. Therefore, potential levels of output increase, pushing the long-run aggregate supply curve to the right.

Model sentence: Increases in the value of human capital leads to a fall in occupational immobility and an increase in labour productivity, causing an increase in the potential output of the economy.

revenue the income a firm receives from consumers in exchange for goods (revenue = price × quantity sold)

capital (goods) manufactured goods that are used in the production of other goods

costs of production the amount the firm pays for the factors of production used to produce goods or services

private costs the cost incurred by firms or consumers from their own production or consumption of a good

property rights laws concerning how people can control, benefit from and transfer property

tax breaks a reduction in the amount of tax that must be paid by an entrepreneur, firm, or industry in order to encourage economic activity. For example a reduction in the rate of corporate tax in order to increase FDI.

quasi-public goods goods that share some of the characteristics of public goods but are not fully non-excludable and non-rival. A road is an example. Most roads are free at the point of use but it is possible to make people pay through tolls and when traffic is heavy the amount available to others to use does begin to diminish so there can be rivalry in consumption.

geographically immobile describes workers who are unable to relocate in order to find work, often because of the high costs of moving

infant industries a new industry which often is not able to compete against established foreign industries and therefore needs to be protected from the competition through subsidies and tariffs

tariff a tax placed on imported goods and services

economies of scale the cost advantages gained by a firm from increasing the scale of its production. Average cost falls in the long run as the size of a firm's operation increases.

Increases in labour productivity increases the amount of goods workers can produce in a given time period thereby increasing producer **revenue** from the sale of the goods. This increases the demand for the workers and pushes wages up. Higher wages lead to an increase in expenditure and an increase in aggregate demand.

Explain how policies that encourage research and development affect potential output

Increases in productivity can also be achieved through the introduction of new production methods. Advances in technology increase the productivity of **capital** but these advances can only be made through research and development (R&D) which adds to **costs of production**. Firms will not pay the **private costs** of R&D if they do not think that they will receive enough private benefit, which is the extra revenue and profit gained from the use of the new technology. The government can guarantee **property rights** of any new development which might encourage firms to pay the costs of R&D. The government can increase the amount of research and development into new, more technologically advanced, capital by giving subsidies to firms to carry it out. Or the government might provide **tax breaks** to firms by not charging tax on profit that is used for R&D. Governments might also pay for R&D directly by spending money on research at universities.

Model sentence: Advances in technology increase the productivity of capital leading to an increase in the potential output of the economy and a shift to the right of the LRAS curve.

Explain how investment in infrastructure can increase potential output

Infrastructure is the very large physical capital, such as schools, hospitals, airports, seaports railways, roads, communication networks, water and energy supply, and national defence and security. Economic growth is dependent on infrastructure. Poor countries find it difficult to grow because of the lack of good quality infrastructure. These capital goods are public goods, **quasi-public goods**, or merit goods, therefore the government is nearly always involved in providing them. An improved transport system will allow goods to be moved more quickly reducing transport costs for firms. People can get to work more quickly and in greater numbers. **Geographical immobility** would be reduced if people are able to get to where the jobs are. Hospitals and schools help to improve productivity of labour and a modern communications network is essential for business to operate effectively. Improved infrastructure can reduce costs of production and increase productivity leading to an increase in potential output and a shift to the right of the LRAS curve.

Explain how targeting specific industries can increase potential output

The government can target specific industries by giving subsidies and through the provision of tax breaks. Governments, particularly in developing economies, provide protection for **infant industries** by placing a **tariff** on imported goods in order to help the smaller domestic industries that do not benefit from large **economies of scale** to compete. The industries can then grow and in time will be able to compete globally. Some industries are given help by government to establish contact with international customers. This happens for example in the **arms industry**.

Test your understanding of this unit by answering the following questions

- Explain how government intervention in research and development can affect economic growth.
- Explain how and why the government might intervene to increase the value of human capital.

Learning Outcomes

● Explain how factors including deregulation, privatization, trade liberalization, and anti-monopoly regulation are used to encourage competition.

● Explain how factors including reducing the power of **labour unions**, reducing unemployment benefits, and abolishing minimum wages are used to make the labour market more flexible (more responsive to supply and demand).

● Explain how factors including personal income tax cuts are used to increase the incentive to work, and how cuts in business tax and capital gains tax are used to increase the incentive to invest.

● Evaluate the effectiveness of supply-side policies through consideration of factors including **time lags**, the ability to create employment, the ability to reduce inflationary pressure, the impact on economic growth, the impact on the government budget, the effect on **equity**, and the effect on the environment.

Explain government policies that might create a more competitive business environment

What are the possible effects of deregulation?

Deregulation is the act of removing or reducing government regulations to create more competitive markets. The government might remove regulations which stop firms from competing in the market thereby making the market more competitive. For example, the government could grant more licences giving new firms the right to enter a market. In the UK in the 1980s, the government deregulated the bus industry so that new firms could enter the bus industry. The aim of such government policy is to improve **productive efficiency** and lower prices by increasing the amount of competition.

Most government regulation increases costs of production. Firms have to obey health and safety laws, and environmental laws. These add to business costs. The labour market is heavily regulated. In the European Union there are laws regulating the number of hours a person can work. Firms have to contribute to workers' pensions and pay redundancy payments to workers they lay off. All regulations increase costs of production, therefore deregulation reduces industries' costs leading to an increase in supply and a fall in unemployment. The **short-run aggregate supply** curve shifts down and to the right. Average total costs fall increasing their competitiveness. It is possible that prices will fall leading to an increase in **real income**.

What are the possible effects of privatization?

Privatization is the act of transferring the ownership of state-owned industry or business from the public sector to the private sector. Over the last few decades there has been a massive increase in the number of privatizations. For example, most European airlines and telecom companies previously owned by the state are now in the private sector. And since the collapse of the Soviet Union much of Russia's state-owned industries are now privately owned.

State-owned industries are **X-inefficient.** They are often large businesses and have **monopoly power**. They have no incentive to produce at lowest average total cost and are productively inefficient. It is difficult for the government to control the management of the industries. Most of the workers are members of **trade unions**, therefore wages are above the equilibrium free market wage. If an industry makes losses, even in the long-run, it will not shut down. The government pays the losses with **tax revenue**. In effect the taxpayer subsidizes the industry. For political reasons the government might continue to give subsidies to loss-making state-owned industries for a long time in order to avoid higher levels of unemployment which would be unpopular. Governments privatize industries to increase competition, thereby increasing productivity and reducing the price. Also the government does not have to give subsidies to loss-making industries.

What are the effects of trade liberalization?

Governments can protect their domestic industries from international competition by putting a tariff on imported goods, by setting quotas and by subsidizing domestic industry. Domestic firms can be productively inefficient and still stay in business because they are protected from the more efficient foreign competition which can supply goods to consumers at lower prices.

Model sentence: Trade liberalization is the removal of barriers to trade in order to make markets more competitive thereby increasing productivity, lowering prices, and increasing the quantity of goods traded.

Glossary

labour union(s) organization(s) fomed by workers to protect their rights

time lag(s) period(s) of time between two linked events

equity fair treatment for everyone

deregulation the removal of government rules/controls from business activity

Subject vocabulary

productive efficiency occurs when a given quantity of output is produced at the minimum total cost per unit of output

short-run aggregate supply SRAS shows the amount of total output firms are willing to produce and sell in an economy at each price level in a given period of time when factor productivity and factor prices are held constant

real income income after taking into account the effects of inflation on purchasing power

X-inefficient a lack of technical and productive efficiency that exists in large firms

monopoly power the degree of control a firm has over the setting of price

trade unions an association of employees whose aim is to negotiate with employers over pay and working conditions using the collective power of the members of the trade union

tax revenue the income the government receives through the levying and collection of taxes

anti-trust laws laws to protect consumers from the consequences of monopolistic behaviour by firms, which ensure markets are competitive

market concentration a measure of the degree to which a relatively small number of firms control a relatively large percentage of market share

factors of production the inputs into the production process (land, labour, capital and entrepreneurship)

productivity the quantity of output per unit of input

working conditions a term that covers many aspects of the conditions of employment including pay, working hours, and holiday entitlement as well as the environment of the work-place including noise levels, health and safety, and employee facilities

bargaining power the extent to which workers can influence the decisions of firms, particularly over pay and conditions

industrial action collective action, such as strikes, taken by workers, usually members of a trade union, in order to gain increases in pay and/or improved working conditions

real-wage unemployment occurs when the real wage is above the equilibrium wage thereby causing an excess supply of labour

wage flexibility wages are flexible when the equilibrium wage changes quickly in response to changes in the supply of labour and/or the demand for labour

market forces the forces of demand and supply that interact in a competitive market and determine equilibrium price

excess supply occurs when quantity supplied is greater than quantity demanded

aggregate supply the total supply of goods and services produced in an economy at a given price level in a given time period

What are the effects of anti-monopoly regulation?

(HL students, see Section 1.5: Theory of the firm and market structures – Monopoly.)

Monopolies have the power to set price or restrict supply. They use their monopoly power to increase price thereby increasing their profits. Governments use **anti-trust laws** to reduce monopoly power by not allowing firms to join together to become one big firm and by breaking up existing monopolies.

Model sentence: The aim of anti-monopoly policy is to reduce market concentration and increase competition thereby increasing productive efficiency and consumer choice, and reducing the price consumers pay.

Give examples of anti-competitive business practices

Competition law does not allow some anti-competitive business practices. For example, predatory pricing is illegal in some countries. It occurs when a firm sets a very low price, sometimes below cost, with the intention of driving its competitors out of business and of creating a barrier to entry so that new firms cannot enter the market. However it is difficult to prove that a price cut is a deliberate attempt to drive the competition out of business rather than simply the result of price competition in a competitive market.

Other anti-competitive practices that are illegal in some countries include exclusive dealing where a retailer must only buy goods from a particular supplier, limit pricing where a monopolist sets prices at a level that is intended to stop new firms entering the industry, and dividing territories where two or more firms in the same industry agree not to compete with each other in particular areas.

What are market-based solutions?

A market economy is one in which prices of goods and services and **factors of production** are determined by the forces of demand and supply in markets free from intervention. Market-based solutions therefore focus on changing markets so that they can operate more freely. Some economists say that free markets lead to greater competition which increases **productivity** and efficiency. (HL students, see Section 1.5: Theory of the firm and market structures – Perfect competition.)

Model sentence: The aim of market-based solutions is to increase the incentives for workers to supply labour and firms to invest, thereby increasing long-run aggregate supply.

Explain how the government can make the labour market more flexible

Discussed below, under separate headings, are the ways in which government can increase labour market flexibility.

What are the effects of reducing trade union power?

A trade union is an organization that works to look after the interests of its members who are the workers in a particular industry. A representative of the union talks with management of the industry or firm to try to get higher pay and better **working conditions**. If all the workers in an industry are members of the union, the union representative has more **bargaining power**. The threat of **industrial action** by the workers if they are not given a higher wage means that they are more likely to be given a pay rise. Therefore, wages are higher in industries that are heavily unionized. The negotiated union wage is above the equilibrium wage causing **real-wage unemployment**. Policies introduced to reduce the power of trade unions will reduce unemployment. The reduction in trade union power reduces a barrier to **wage flexibility**. If the agreed union wage rate is removed the wage can then change in response to changes in **market forces**. When there is **excess supply** of labour at the wage rate, the wage then can fall until quantity of labour demanded and the quantity of labour supplied is equal and the market clears, thereby reducing real-wage unemployment.

Model sentence: Reducing trade union power reduces wages and real-wage unemployment. Firms' costs of production fall and aggregate supply increases.

What are the effects of abolishing the minimum wage?

A **minimum wage**, like an agreed trade union wage, is above the equilibrium wage determined by the **forces of the demand and supply** of labour. Removing the minimum wage increases labour market flexibility because the wage can change in response to changes in the demand and supply of labour. When the minimum wage is above equilibrium wage, quantity supplied of labour exceeds quantity demanded. Remove the guaranteed minimum wage and the forces of demand and supply push wages down. Firms' costs of production fall, therefore they increase supply and more workers are employed raising the potential output.

What are the effects of reducing unemployment benefits on the incentive to work?

When the unemployment benefit a person receives is more than the wage that can be earned from working it can be argued that it is in the interest of the person not to work. People in this situation have an incentive not to work. Therefore reducing unemployment benefit below the wage will give people the incentive to work. The higher the wage is above unemployment benefit, the greater the incentive to look for work.

Model sentence: When there are jobs available in the economy, reducing unemployment benefit increases the incentive to work and unemployment falls thereby increasing potential output.

What are the effects of cutting income tax on the incentive to work?

When **income tax** is reduced, **disposable income** increases: workers keep more of the money earned. Under a **progressive tax system** the rate of tax increases as income increases. Higher rates of tax discourage people who are in work from working harder and longer. The opportunity cost of leisure (not working) is the wage forgone. Reducing taxes increases the benefits of working and increases the opportunity cost of not working. Therefore as taxes fall the supply of labour onto the labour market increases.

Model sentence: When taxes are cut it encourages those already working to increase their supply of labour and it encourages those who are not working to supply their labour.

What are the effects of cutting corporate taxes on the incentive to work?

Corporate taxes are taxes on company profits. If corporate tax is cut, **retained profit** increases encouraging firms to increase supply leading to a fall in unemployment. Firms have more profit to invest in new capital, training, and research and development. More investment increases the stock of capital in the country and more training increases the value of human capital. An increase in research and development leads to advances in technology and the development of new products. All this leads to an increase in the potential output of the economy, shifting the **long-run aggregate supply** curve to the right.

Evaluate the effectiveness of supply-side policies

Set out below under separate headings is an evaluation of the effectiveness of supply-side policies.

Discuss the effect on inflation, unemployment, and growth of supply-side policies

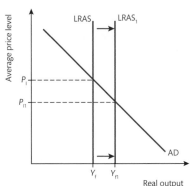

Figure 67.1

Supply-side policies are used to increase the rate of **economic growth**. They increase the potential level of output of the economy shifting the long-run aggregate supply curve out to the right as shown in Figure 67.1. Supply-side policies affect other macroeconomic variables such as inflation and unemployment. Potential output increases from Y_f to Y_{f1}. *Ceteris paribus*, this reduces the **price level** from P_1 to P_{f1}. **Inflation** caused by high levels of **aggregate demand** can be controlled by supply-side policies that keep the growth in aggregate supply in line with the growth in aggregate demand. As aggregate demand and aggregate supply increase, unemployment falls.

Unemployment is affected by supply-side policies. New more technologically advanced capital increases productivity. Fewer workers are needed to make the same number of goods. Without increases in demand some workers will lose their jobs. This is called **technological unemployment**.

If LRAS increases and AD at some point falls lots of firms will have spare capacity. Many factors will be unemployed. Firms that have invested in new capital now have higher costs. If **producer revenue** falls because of a lack of demand, firms' profits will fall and some will go out of business leading to a large **deflationary gap** and higher unemployment. However, if the economy is growing, and incomes and aggregate demand increase, new jobs are created and unemployment will fall. Also new goods come to market through increases in R&D, creating new demands and new jobs.

Supply-side policies lead to increases in supply and greater productivity. **Average total costs** fall and firms become more price competitive. More goods can be supplied at lower prices thereby increasing both

Subject vocabulary

current account deficit occurs when the amount of money flowing out of a country from the trade in goods and services, investment income, and transfers is greater than the amount flowing in

merit good a good/service that the government believes will be under consumed left to the free market. Consumption of a merit good may generate positive externalities therefore the social benefit of consumption is greater than the private benefit. Individuals do not take into account the positive externalities when deciding the amount to consume therefore the good is underprovided and under consumed.

budget deficit occurs when government expenditure is greater than tax revenue

private benefit the benefit firms or consumers receive from their own production or consumption of a good

external benefit occurs when the production or consumption of a good causes a benefit to third parties

free market a market where the forces of demand and supply are allowed to operate without any forms of intervention

cycle of poverty occurs in a country which has low income and therefore low levels of savings. Low levels of savings means little investment can take place and the economy is unable to grow, thus income remains low.

real income income after taking into account the effects of inflation on purchasing power

tariffs a tax placed on imported goods and services

quota a physical limit placed on the number of goods that can be traded or produced

continued on page 195

Glossary

infrastructure the basic structure/systems of a country (e.g. roads/railways)

reform(s) change(s)/ improvement(s) to a law/ system to make it fairer/more effective

---

domestic demand and demand for exports. Higher exports reduce the **current account deficit** and increase employment in the exporting industries.

Discuss the effects of investment in labour and infrastructure

Supply-side policies can increase economic growth, reduce unemployment and inflation, and can reduce the current account deficit. However, there are costs of supply-side policies. The cost to the government of increasing the value of human capital through training and education and the provision of healthcare are high.

Governments of countries with relatively high national income have large tax revenues and are more able than poorer countries to pay for the high costs of these **merit goods**. Public health services, public education, and training are available to almost everyone in developed countries. In poor countries with relatively low national income, many go without. Therefore the value of human capital of a country is dependent in part on the size of the tax revenues and the ability of governments to borrow in order to continue to fund the services when the country has a **budget deficit**.

Many people in richer countries gain the **private benefits** from the consumption of these merit goods, such as the ability to earn higher income and a longer life span, and the economy gains the **external benefits** including increases in productivity leading to economic growth. Left to the **free market** these services would be underprovided and under consumed. Governments in richer countries are able to increase production and consumption, but poorer countries that lack the necessary tax revenue are not.

The benefit from the investment in **infrastructure** is not gained straightaway. Large building projects, such as a new railway or motorway, take a long time to build but are essential for long-run economic growth. Such goods are quasi-public goods which would be underprovided or not provided at all by free markets. Again poorer countries are not able to fund the building of a network of transport infrastructure or develop an up-to-date communications system. Infrastructure is essential for economic development, high productivity and growth. Poor countries get left behind because they are unable to break out of the **cycle of poverty**, and the relative poverty gap between the rich countries and the poor countries gets bigger.

Discuss the effects of privatization and anti-monopoly laws

Consumers in many countries have benefited from privatization, and anti-monopoly laws have increased competition forcing firms to increase productivity and lower price. Prices have fallen for many goods and services, such as air flights, as competition and greater productivity have pushed prices down thereby increasing consumers' **real incomes**. Trade liberalization, the removal or reduction of **tariffs** and **quotas**, has increased competition in many industries. Domestic firms have had to increase productivity and product quality in order to survive against the foreign competition. However, those domestic firms unable to reduce their average total costs have gone out of business. Privatization and trade liberalization have led to more consumer choice, lower prices, higher real incomes, and greater consumption. However, many domestic industries did not survive leading to increases in **structural unemployment** and a fall in GDP. For example many firms in Europe in the textile industry have gone out of business because they were not able to compete against the lower priced imports from China. The increase in global trade has led to an increase in the current account deficit of many countries belonging to the European Union, including the UK, France, Spain, Portugal, and Greece.

Discuss the effects of deregulation and labour market reforms

Deregulation and labour market **reforms** are not popular with everybody. When the local government in Rome wanted to increase the number of taxi licences thereby increasing the number of taxis for hire the taxi drivers went on strike and violent protests broke out in the city as they tried to protect their '**market power**'. Industrial action is often taken by members of trade unions when a government tries to introduce reforms that reduce their power. In many countries governments have introduced or are trying to introduce **performance-related pay** in the public sector for teachers and to end **collective national bargaining**. The trade unions representing teachers are against these reforms and teachers have taken industrial action to protect their interests.

Health and safety legislation does increase costs of production but such laws have reduced work-related injuries and deaths by a large amount. However, even with the regulation, the total cost, including **private costs** and **external costs**, in 2010/11 in the UK of workplace illness, injury, and deaths was £5.4 billion. Just over half the costs were paid by the individual, with the rest paid for by employers and the government. These costs should be taken into account by the government when considering changing health and safety laws.

There are external costs of production, such as pollution, which regulation aims to reduce. Removing regulation that controls harmful emissions would reduce costs of production but would at the same time increase the external costs leading to greater environmental damage and non-sustainable economic growth.

Removing the minimum wage would reduce further the income of those already on relatively low pay. If unemployment benefit stayed the same many workers would leave work, thereby increasing government expenditure on benefits and reducing aggregate supply. Reduction in benefits and the removal of the minimum wage could increase **absolute poverty** and **relative poverty** and lead to a less equal and less **equitable** distribution of income.

Discuss the effects of a cut in tax

Reducing higher **marginal rate of taxes** does increase the incentive to work harder and might increase **potential output**. However, a greater tax burden would fall on those on lower incomes, thereby increasing income inequality as income is redistributed from the poor to the rich making the tax system less progressive and more inequitable. Some economists say that cutting tax leads to economic growth and higher GDP, and therefore everybody's income will be higher. Cutting taxes might increase consumer expenditure and firms' retained profit, thereby increasing aggregate demand, but at the same time tax revenue could fall increasing the government's budget deficit. The amount of the increase in consumer expenditure and investment by firms, depends on expectations concerning job security and the future levels of demand.

Discuss the limitation of supply-side policies caused by time lags

The time it takes for a supply-side policy to have an impact on the economy after it has been introduced is normally very long. For example, occupational immobility is a cause of long-term unemployment. Those who are unemployed because they do not have the skills demanded by industries need to be trained so that they gain the skills that firms need. To increase the level of skills of the labour force so that structural unemployment falls and the **productivity gap** is reduced takes a long time.

A country may need more and better transport infrastructure to improve efficiency. However, large investment projects such as airports and roads take a long time to build and the country will not benefit from the infrastructure for a number of years.

Test your understanding of this unit by answering the following questions

- Explain how cutting tax might increase potential output.
- Explain how reducing trade union power and abolishing the minimum wage might increase economic growth.
- Explain how deregulation and trade liberalization might increase productivity.
- Using a diagram, explain the possible effects on growth, inflation, and unemployment of supply-side policies.
- Discuss the impact of deregulation on the economy.

Subject vocabulary

continued from page 194

structural unemployment unemployment caused by a change in the type of labour firms demand. It is caused by a mismatch of the skills of those unemployed and the skills needed by firms.

current account deficit occurs when the amount of money flowing out of a country from the trade in goods and services, investment income, and transfers is greater than the amount flowing in

market power the ability of a firm to change the market price of a good or service

performance-related pay where some or all the payment for labour is determined by how the workers perform

collective national bargaining where bargaining between management of firms and the representatives of the workers over pay and conditions takes place at the national level

private costs the cost incurred by firms or consumers from their own production or consumption of a good

external cost occurs when the production or consumption of a good creates a cost that must be paid by third parties

absolute poverty occurs when people do not have enough resources to satisfy their basic needs

relative poverty a measure of poverty that relates to the average income earned in a country or region. Definitions vary but many governments define it as an income less than 50% of the median income.

marginal rates of tax the rate of tax paid on the next unit of income earned

potential output the maximum output an economy can produce when all resources are efficiently employed

productivity gap the difference between the output per worker in one country compared with the output per worker in another country

Synonyms

equitable .... fair/equal

3.1 International trade: Free trade

Learning Outcomes

- Explain that gains from trade include lower prices for consumers, greater choice for consumers, and the ability of producers to benefit from economies of scale, the ability to acquire needed resources, a more efficient allocation of resources, increased competition, and a source of foreign exchange.

- Describe the objectives and functions of the WTO.

Model sentence: The benefits from trade include an increase in competition and economies of scale that lead to improvements in efficiency, lower prices, and more consumer choice. The sale of exports provides foreign exchange with which countries can buy resources it does not have.

Explain the gains from trade

Trade allows countries to buy resources they do not have. Each country has different amounts of resources. Some countries have oil, some have none. Therefore a country without oil can buy it from an oil-producing country. The same is true for many other goods such as certain food products and **raw materials**, such as copper used in the production of other goods. Regions of some countries such as Italy specialize in the production of wine because the climate is favourable, the land is productive, and there is a large workforce that has the necessary skills. Other countries such as the UK can make wine but at a higher cost per unit because its factors are not as productive at making wine. The UK produces other goods and services that its factors of production can produce efficiently, such as financial services.

Japan and the US for example produce lots of computers and other technologically advanced goods. Other countries do not have the resources to be able to produce such goods so they must **import** them. South Korea has very few **natural resources**. It **exports** a variety of manufactured goods thereby earning the money it needs to import the natural resources its industries need.

Model sentence: A country's exports are a source of foreign exchange. The country can use the money it receives from the sale of its exports to buy the imported resources it needs.

International trade leads to an increase in consumer choice. Because countries trade, consumers are able to buy different goods from all around the world, goods which they would not be able to consume if countries did not trade with each other. More wants can be satisfied, increasing **consumer welfare**.

Industries that export have a global mass market. An industry producing for a large market can benefit from **economies of scale**. For example, mass production techniques can be used, employing expensive technologically advanced, highly **specialized capital**. Such production methods greatly increase productivity and reduce **long-run average total cost**.

Countries can specialize in the production of particular goods that they can produce most efficiently with their resources. It can then export these goods and import other goods from countries specializing in the production of goods that they are most efficient at producing. By specializing and **trading** it is possible to maximize the world output of goods and services from a given quantity of resources: maximizing output from a fixed quantity of **inputs**. It is possible that each good can be produced at lowest possible average total cost. Therefore, in competitive markets prices are pushed down. Lower prices and increasing **real income** is therefore a gain from trade.

A domestic monopoly in a **closed economy** has **market power**. It can set price or limit supply to drive up prices and profit. Because of high profits it can be **X-inefficient**. Average total cost will be above the minimum. In an **open economy** the domestic industry has to compete with foreign industries. If the domestic industry is to survive it must make sure the quality of the product is good and improve productivity, thereby reducing average cost so that it can sell its goods at a competitive price.

Model sentence: All industries that are competing internationally in a free market have to be productively efficient in order to be price competitive if they are to stay in business. Therefore international trade leads to improvements in efficiency and lower prices.

What are the aims and functions of the World Trade Organization (WTO)?

The WTO's main objective is the promotion of global **trade liberalization**. This means that it encourages trading countries or trading blocks to remove or reduce barriers to trade, such as **tariffs** and **quotas** on imported goods and services, and subsidies given by a government to its domestic industries. It also promotes **anti-dumping legislation**. The WTO provides a **forum** for the governments of countries to negotiate the taking down of the barriers to free trade and it witnesses the signing of agreements. The WTO acts as a mediator or referee when arguments and disputes occur over the negotiated signed agreements. The WTO tries to settle the arguments between countries and ensure that the agreements are not broken. It acts as a 'court' to which countries can bring their complaints and disputes, and the WTO can make a judgement for or against a country.

Learning Outcomes

- Explain the theory of absolute advantage. (HL)

- Explain, using a diagram, the gains from trade arising from a country's absolute advantage in the production of a good. (HL)

- Explain the theory of comparative advantage. (HL)

- Describe the sources of comparative advantage, including the differences between countries in factor endowments and the levels of technology. (HL)

- Draw a diagram to show comparative advantage. (HL)

- Calculate opportunity costs from a set of data in order to identify comparative advantage. (HL)

- Draw a diagram to illustrate comparative advantage from a set of data. (HL)

- Discuss the real-world relevance and limitations of the theory of comparative advantage, considering factors including the assumptions on which it rests, and the costs and benefits of **specialization**. (HL)

Explain the theory of absolute advantage (HL)

A country has absolute advantage in the production of a good if it can produce the good using fewer **resources** than another country. In other words, a country has absolute advantage in the production of a good if output of the good from a given amount of resources is greater than in another country.

	Wine	Cheese
Country X	10	15
Country Y	20	10

Table 69.1

Table 69.1 shows two countries, X and Y. Each country has the same amount of resources. Each country produces wine and cheese. If country X uses its resources to produce wine it can produce 10 units of wine in a given time period and if it uses them to produce cheese it can produce 15 units of cheese in a given time period.

If country Y uses its resources to produce wine it can produce 20 units of wine and if it uses them to produce cheese it can produce 10 units of cheese. Country X has an absolute advantage in the production of cheese and country Y has absolute advantage in the production of wine.

If the countries do not specialize and trade they can produce a combination of wine and cheese with their resources as shown in Figures 69.1a and 69.1b (both on page 198). The production possibility curve shows all possible combinations of outputs of two goods when all resources are employed. Country X is using its resources to produce 6 units of cheese and 6 units of wine which is at point A on its PPC. Country Y is using its resources to produce 6 units of cheese and 8 units of wine which is at point B on its PPC.

If the two countries specialize the total output of goods produced using all the resources of both countries increases. It is now possible to produce 20 units of wine and 15 units of cheese. If the two countries specialize and trade it is possible for both countries to consume a greater quantity of both wine and cheese. It is possible for both countries to consume a combination of the two goods at a point that is outside their PPCs. For example, if the countries trade it is possible for country X to consume 7 units of cheese and 10 units of wine, which is at point A1, outside its PPC, and for country Y to consume 8 units of cheese and 10 units of wine, which is at point B1, outside its PPC.

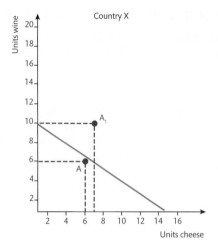

Figure 69.1a

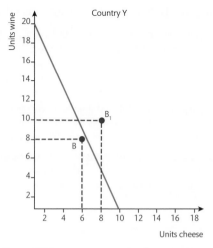

Figure 69.1b

Model sentence: With a fixed amount of resources total output can be increased and more wants can be satisfied when the two countries specialize in the production of the good in which they have an absolute advantage and then trade.

Explain the theory of comparative advantage (HL)

The theory of comparative advantage explains why it would be beneficial for both countries to trade even if one of the countries has an absolute advantage in the production of both goods.

Subject vocabulary

opportunity cost the next best alternative forgone

A country has a comparative advantage in the production of a good when it can produce the good at a lower **opportunity cost** than another country. If a country is using all its resources and wants to produce an additional unit of a good it must transfer resources away from the production of the other good. The opportunity cost of producing an additional unit of one good is the quantity of the other good forgone (given up).

	Wine	Cheese
Country X	200	100
Country Y	600	150

Table 69.2

Table 69.2 shows the output of wine and cheese in two countries, X and Y. Country Y has an absolute advantage in the production of both goods.

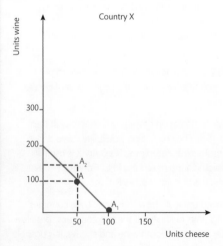

Figure 69.2a

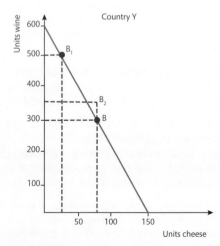

Figure 69.2b

To show that both countries can benefit from specializing and then trading it is necessary to calculate the relative opportunity costs of production. The information in Table 69.2 is used to draw the production possibility curves for each country shown in Figures 69.2a and 69.2b. The PPC for each country shows the possible combinations of output of the two goods when all resources are employed.

What is the opportunity cost of a unit of wine in country X? – a step-by-step guide

Trouble shooter

If country X uses all its resources to produce wine it can produce 200 units of wine and 0 units of cheese.

If country X uses all its resources to produce cheese it can produce 100 units of cheese and 0 units of wine.

If country X wants to produce wine instead of cheese it must give up 100 units of cheese in order to produce 200 units of wine.

100 units of cheese must be given up in order to produce 200 units of wine.

The opportunity cost of 1 unit of wine $= \frac{100}{200} = \frac{1}{2} = \frac{1}{2}$ a unit of cheese.

What is the opportunity cost of cheese in country X?

If country X uses all its resources to produce cheese it can make 100 units of cheese and 0 units of wine. If country X wants to produce cheese instead of wine it must give up 200 units of wine in order to produce 100 units of cheese. The opportunity cost of 1 unit of cheese $= \frac{200}{100} = \frac{2}{1} = 2$ units of wine.

What is the opportunity cost of a unit of wine in country Y?

If country Y uses all its resources to produce wine it can produce 600 units of wine and 0 units of cheese. If country Y wants to produce wine instead of cheese it must give up 150 units of cheese in order to produce 600 units of wine. The opportunity cost of 1 unit of wine $= \frac{150}{600} = \frac{1}{4}$ of a unit of cheese.

What is the opportunity cost of a unit of cheese in country Y?

If country Y uses all its resources to produce cheese it can make 150 units of cheese and 0 units of wine. If country Y wants to produce cheese instead of wine it must give up 600 units of wine in order to produce 150 units of cheese. The opportunity cost of 1 unit of cheese $= \frac{600}{150} = 4$ units of wine.

A country has a comparative advantage in the production of a good when it can produce the good at a lower opportunity cost than another country.

The opportunity cost of 1 unit of wine in country X is a $\frac{1}{2}$ unit of cheese.
The opportunity cost of 1 unit of wine in country Y is a $\frac{1}{4}$ unit of cheese.
Therefore, country Y has a comparative advantage in the production of wine.

The opportunity cost of 1 unit of cheese in country X is 2 units of wine.
The opportunity cost of 1 unit of cheese in country Y is 4 units of wine.
Therefore, country X has a comparative advantage in the production of cheese.

Using PPC diagrams, show what happens to total output and consumption if the two countries specialize

Total output from a given quantity of resources can be increased if countries specialize. Figures 69.2a and 69.2b show the production possibility curves for country X and country Y. The PPC for each country shows the possible combinations of output of the two goods when all resources are employed. The **slope** of the PPC shows the opportunity cost.

If country X uses half of its resources to produce wine and half to produce cheese it can produce 100 units of wine and 50 units of cheese, which is at point A on its PPC.

If country Y uses half of its resources to produce wine and half to produce cheese it can produce 300 units of wine and 75 units of cheese, which is at point B on its PPC.

Total output of country X and Y = 400 units of wine and 125 units of cheese.

Country X has a comparative advantage in the production of cheese and country Y has a comparative advantage in the production of wine. Country X specializes in the production of cheese at point A₁ on the PPC producing 100 units of cheese and 0 units of wine. Country Y specializes in the production of wine but wants to keep the combined output of cheese at 125 units. It produces 25 units of cheese and with its remaining resources is able to produce 500 units of wine, at point B₁ on its PPC.

Total output of country X and country Y after specializing = 500 units of wine and 125 units of cheese. Specializing leads to an increase in output of 100 units of wine.

If country X trades 50 units of cheese in exchange for 150 units of wine from country Y (an exchange rate of 1 unit of cheese for 3 units of wine) it is possible for both countries to consume a combination of the two goods at a point that is outside their PPCs. Country X is at point A_2 (150 units of wine and 50 units of cheese) and country Y is at point B_2 (350 units of wine and 75 units of cheese).

Explain why the countries should specialize and trade

If each country specializes in the production of the good in which it has a comparative advantage, it is possible to increase total output from the combined **resources** of both countries. Total output will be greater than if each country tried to be self-sufficient. There is an increase in output from a given quantity of resources thereby increasing economic welfare.

Model sentence: Specializing and trading allows countries to move to points outside their production possibility curves.

Model sentence: More goods are produced and consumed from a given quantity of resources if the two countries specialize in the production of goods in which they have a comparative advantage.

Model sentence: By specializing it is possible to increase the quantity of output from a given quantity of resources, thereby increasing economic welfare.

What are the sources of comparative advantage?

Factor endowment is an important source of comparative advantage. A country that has lots of productive farming land and a suitable climate will have a comparative advantage in the production of agricultural goods. For example, in parts of California in the US the land and climate are favourable for growing grapes; therefore, this region has a comparative advantage in the production of wine. The wine producers in this region also use technologically advanced **capital** thereby further reducing **costs of production**. A country that has many highly skilled engineers might have a comparative advantage in the production of technological goods. London has a comparative advantage in the production of financial services because there are many people there that have the necessary skills. A country that has lots of unskilled workers will have a comparative advantage in the production of basic manufactured goods. A country with lots of natural resources, such as natural gas and timber, has a comparative advantage in the supply of the resource.

Model sentence: If a country has a large quantity of a resource, such as timber, the labour with the necessary skills to exploit the resource, and technologically advanced capital to produce the good then the good can be produced at a relatively low average cost per unit.

Discuss the limitations of comparative advantage (HL)

The theory of comparative advantage is based on a number of **assumptions**. These assumptions cannot be applied to the real world of international trade thereby limiting the relevance and usefulness of the theory.

What are the assumptions of comparative advantage? – a step-by-step guide

> **Trouble shooter**
>
> *No transport costs*: Some countries have high transport costs when they specialize and trade. These countries may be worse off if they specialize because of the high costs of transporting the goods that they trade.
>
> *The goods traded are homogeneous*: Some goods such as copper and wheat are almost identical and are bought on price. Manufactured goods are not identical. Goods are **branded** and consumers have preferences. Consumers do not only consider price. For example, they consider quality, packaging, image and so on. Consumer preferences can change comparative advantage.
>
> *No barriers to trade*: For example if a **tariff** or **quota** is placed on imports the price consumers pay increases thereby reducing any comparative advantage.

Subject vocabulary

resources the inputs into the production process, the factors of production

economic welfare the standard of living of people in an economy, often measured in terms of income per capita

factor endowment the amount of land, labour, capital, and entrepreneurship that a country has that can be used to produce goods and services

capital (goods) manufactured goods that are used in the production of other goods

costs of production the amount the firm pays for the factors of production used to produce goods or services

branded goods that have been given an identifiable mark, logo or label in order to distinguish them from substitutes

tariffs a tax placed on imported goods and services

quota a physical limit placed on the number of goods that can be traded or produced

Glossary

assumption(s) something thought/believed to be true but without proof

Consumers and producers have perfect knowledge: Buyers and sellers do not have perfect knowledge. They do not always know where to buy goods at the lowest possible price.

Costs are constant: It is assumed that costs are constant. However, firms experience **increasing returns to scale** and **decreasing returns to scale** because of **economies of scale**. Economies of scale lead to increasing returns to scale and falling long-run average total costs, therefore any comparative advantage is increased. **Diseconomies of scale** lead to decreasing returns to scale and rising average costs, therefore any comparative advantage is reduced. When a country trades internationally it is producing for a very large market and is likely therefore to enjoy economies of scale that reduce costs and increase productive efficiency giving the country greater comparative advantage.

Factors are perfectly mobile: When calculating comparative advantage the assumption is made that all factors are employed. The production possibility curve shows all possible combinations of output of two goods when all factors are employed. In the real world there are always some factors that are unemployed because factors are not always mobile. For example, the UK lost its comparative advantage in ship building and the ship yards closed down; there were high levels of **structural unemployment** of labour and capital left unused. Workers and capital were unemployed. Specializing can be harmful if labour is not mobile. If workers cannot move to the industry in which the country is specializing, unemployment will increase.

There are only two economies: In the real world there are many countries all trading with each other. The assumption means that it is relatively easy to work out the comparative advantages and demonstrate the benefits of trade. However, it is possible to work out comparative advantage when studying lots of countries but the mathematical models required are much more difficult to create and understand.

Test your understanding of this unit by answering the following questions

- Explain the sources of absolute and comparative advantage.
- Explain why the assumptions of comparative advantage limit the usefulness of the theory of comparative advantage.
- Using a fixed quantity of resources, country X and country Y can produce the quantities of wine and cheese shown in the table.

	Units of Wine	Units of Cheese
Country X	60	15
Country Y	90	30

1. Draw the PPC diagrams for country X and country Y.
2. Calculate the opportunity cost of wine and cheese in country X.
3. Calculate the opportunity cost of wine and cheese in country Y.
4. State which country has the comparative advantage in the production of wine.
5. State which country has the comparative advantage in the production of cheese.
6. Explain how both countries can benefit from specializing and then trading.
7. Show on the PPC diagrams how both countries can increase consumption.

Learning Outcomes

- Explain, using a tariff diagram, the effects of **imposing** a tariff on imported goods on different stakeholders, including domestic producers, foreign producers, consumers, and the government.

- Explain, using a diagram, the effects of setting a quota on foreign producers on different stakeholders, including domestic producers, foreign producers, consumers, and the government.

- Explain, using a diagram, the effects of giving a subsidy to domestic producers on different stakeholders, including domestic producers, foreign producers, consumers, and the government.

- Describe administrative barriers that may be used as a means of protection.

- Evaluate the effect of different types of trade protection.

Discuss the effects of a tariff

A tariff is a tax placed on imports. Figure 70.1 shows the effect of a tariff charged on imported corn.

The demand curve shows the quantity demanded of corn by domestic consumers at each price. It slopes downwards showing as price rises **quantity demanded** falls. The domestic supply curve shows quantity supplied of corn by the domestic industry at each price. It slopes upwards showing that as price increases **quantity supplied** increases. The domestic equilibrium price, where quantity demanded by domestic consumers is equal to the quantity supplied by domestic producers is P_e.

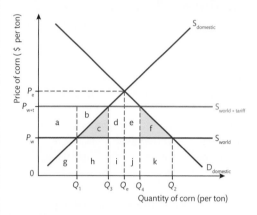

Figure 70.1

The world supply curve S_{world} is **perfectly elastic** with respect to price. The foreign producers of corn are willing and able to supply any quantity of corn at the world price shown as P_w. A tariff is placed on corn. It increases the world price from P_w to P_{w+t}. The tariff is not paid by domestic producers.

A tariff in effect increases the **costs of production** of foreign producers and therefore affects the world's supply of corn, shifting the supply curve up by the amount of the tax from S_{world} to $S_{world + tariff}$.

A tariff increases the price domestic consumers pay thereby reducing quantity demanded. Domestic producers do not pay the tariff so they keep all of the higher price. Because the price domestic producers receive increases they are willing to increase quantity supplied. Foreign producers do not receive the higher price because the tariff that consumers pay goes to the government not the foreign producers. They receive the same price as they did before the tariff.

After the tariff the price consumers pay increases and the quantity demanded falls. Domestic producers increase quantity supplied in response to the higher price. Domestic producers now supply a greater quantity than before the tariff and because quantity demanded has decreased the quantity supplied by foreign producers falls.

Model sentence: A tariff increases the price consumers pay leading to a fall in consumer surplus and a fall in the purchasing power of their income.

Describe the market for corn before the tariff

The world price of corn is P_w. At P_w the quantity of corn demanded by domestic consumers is Q_2 tons of corn. At P_w domestic producers are willing to supply Q_1 tons of corn. The rest of the corn, $Q_2 - Q_1$, is supplied by foreign producers.

Producer revenue = price × quantity sold. Domestic producer revenue = $P_w \times Q_1$ represented by the area marked g.

Foreign producer revenue = $P_w \times (Q_2 - Q_1)$ represented by the area h + i + j + k.

Describe the market for corn after the tariff

The tariff increases the world price of corn from P_w to P_{w+t}. The supply curve S_{world} shifts up to $S_{world + tariff}$. At P_{w+t} the quantity of corn demanded by domestic consumers falls from Q_2 to Q_4 tons of corn. At the higher price P_{w+t} domestic producers are willing to increase quantity supplied from Q_1 to Q_3 tons of corn. The rest of the corn, $Q_4 - Q_3$, is imported. The quantity of corn imported falls from $Q_2 - Q_1$ to $Q_4 - Q_3$.

Domestic producer revenue increases from $P_w \times Q_1$ to $P_{w+t} \times Q_3$. The area representing domestic producer revenue increases from g to g + a + b + c + h.

Foreign producers receive $P_{w+t} \times (Q_4 - Q_3)$ represented by the area i + d + e + j. However, the tariff on the sale of the imported corn must be paid to the government. The government tax revenue = $(P_{w+t} - P_w) \times (Q_4 - Q_3)$ represented by the area d + e. The rest of the revenue from the sale of the imported corn goes to the foreign producers. Foreign producer revenue is represented by the area i + j. Foreign producer revenue falls from area h + i + j + k to area i + j.

Discuss the effects on welfare of a tariff

The tariff leads to an increase in the quantity supplied of corn by domestic producers from Q_1 to Q_3. The minimum revenue domestic producers are willing to take to supply Q_1 to Q_3 of corn is represented by the area h + c, the area under the domestic supply curve and between Q_1 and Q_3. Before the tariff foreign suppliers were willing to supply Q_1 to Q_3 of corn for less revenue represented by area h, the area under the world supply curve and between Q_1 and Q_3. Before the tariff Q_1 to Q_3 of corn was supplied by the more efficient foreign producers of corn. They were willing to supply Q_1 to Q_3 of corn at P_w because their average total cost is low enough to make a profit on each unit sold at that price. Area c is the difference between the minimum revenue needed by domestic producers and the minimum needed by foreign producers.

The less efficient domestic producers use more of the world's scarce resources to produce Q_1 to Q_3 of corn than those used by the more productive foreign producers. Therefore fewer of the world's scarce resources could be used to produce corn. If domestic producers used their resources to produce goods that they are most efficient at producing then total output from a limited quantity of resources could be increased. Area c represents a loss of world efficiency caused by a tariff.

Before the tariff, consumer expenditure on $Q_2 - Q_4$ of corn at P_w was represented by the area k ($P_w \times (Q_2 - Q_4)$). Total consumer surplus was represented by the area above P_w and below the demand curve. The tariff leads to a fall in quantity demanded of corn by domestic consumers from Q_2 to Q_4 as the price of corn increases from P_w to P_{w+t}. $Q_2 - Q_4$ of corn is now not bought nor is it consumed. Therefore consumer expenditure falls. After the tariff there is a fall in consumer expenditure represented by the area k. Consumers no longer spend this amount. Area f represents the loss of consumer surplus that consumers used to receive on the consumption of $Q_2 - Q_4$ of corn when price was at P_w. The loss of consumer surplus, a **welfare loss**, is caused by the tariff.

Area c and area f in Figure 70.1 represent the welfare loss to society from the imposition of the tariff.

Model sentence: A tariff increases government tax revenue. Government can use this revenue to increase expenditure on public goods, quasi-public goods and merit goods increasing production and consumption of them and thereby correcting market failure.

Model sentence: A tariff increases the quantity supplied by domestic producers thereby protecting domestic jobs. This reduces the private costs and external costs of unemployment.

The government spends less on unemployment benefits and receives more **income tax** revenue thereby reducing the **budget deficit** or increasing the **budget surplus**.

What are the effects of a tariff on costs of production, price of consumer goods, and international competiveness?

Corn is used by firms in the production of other goods for example in animal feed and in the production of ethanol. An increase in the price of corn increases costs of production leading to **cost-push inflation**. Firms pass on the higher cost to the consumer to pay in the form of higher prices. Corn is used to feed chickens, therefore the tariff on corn leads to an increase in the price of chicken meat and other meat products. The increase in price reduces consumer surplus and reduces the purchasing power of income leading to a fall in **consumer welfare**. Higher prices lead to a fall in international competitiveness and a fall in quantity of exports demanded, causing unemployment in exporting industries.

Discuss the effects of a quota

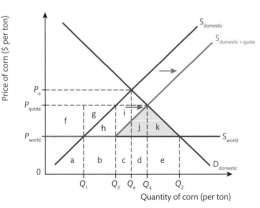

A quota is a physical limit on the quantity of an imported good. The quantity of an imported good allowed to enter a country is set by the government. The effects of a quota are shown in Figure 70.2.

Figure 70.2

Subject vocabulary

welfare loss the sum of the loss of consumer and producer surplus caused by market or government failure

quasi-public goods goods that share some of the characteristics of public goods but are not fully non-excludable and non-rival. A road is an example. Most roads are free at the point of use but it is possible to make people pay through tolls and when traffic is heavy the amount available to others to use does begin to diminish so there can be rivalry in consumption.

merit good a good/service that the government believes will be under consumed left to the free market. Consumption of a merit good may generate positive externalities therefore the social benefit of consumption is greater than the private benefit.

private costs the cost incurred by firms or consumers from their own production or consumption of a good

external cost occurs when the production or consumption of a good creates a cost that must be paid by third parties

income tax a direct tax on individual earnings (wages, rent, profit, interest) and paid to the government

budget deficit occurs when government expenditure is greater than tax revenue

budget surplus when tax revenue exceeds government expenditure

cost-push inflation inflation caused by an increase in the costs of production, resulting in a decrease in aggregate supply

consumer welfare a measure of the benefit obtained from the consumption of goods

Describe the market for corn before the quota

Before the quota the price per ton of corn is P_{world}. The world supply curve is perfectly elastic with respect to price. Foreign producers are willing to supply any quantity of corn at P_{world}. At P_{world} domestic producers are willing to supply Q_1 of corn. Their revenue is represented by the area a. Domestic demand at P_{world} is Q_2 of which Q_1 is supplied by domestic producers and the rest, $Q_2 - Q_1$ of corn is imported. The foreign producer's revenue is represented by the area b + c + d + e.

Describe the market for corn after the quota

The government sets a quota of $Q_3 - Q_1$. The quantity of corn imported falls from $Q_2 - Q_1$ to $Q_3 - Q_1$. Domestic producers continue to supply Q_1 of corn because the price has not changed. Total quantity supplied falls from Q_2 to Q_3. The quantity of corn demanded stays at Q_2 because the price has not changed.

After the quota at the price P_{world} quantity demanded is greater than quantity supplied. There is **excess demand** of $Q_2 - Q_3$ at the world price. In order to remove the excess demand the price rises. As price rises foreign producers would like to supply more corn but are not able to because they are already supplying $Q_3 - Q_1$ which is the physical limit allowed. Domestic suppliers, however, increase quantity supplied in response to the higher price.

Ceteris paribus, as price increases profit in the industry increases. The higher profit available to producers of corn attracts new firms into the industry. The number of firms in an industry is a **determinant of supply**. There are now more farmers producing corn; therefore, the supply of corn increases at each price and the domestic supply curve shifts down and to the right from $S_{domestic}$ to $S_{domestic + quota}$.

As price increases quantity demanded falls. The equilibrium price with a quota depends, in part, on the size of the shift of the domestic supply curve. In Figure 70.2 (on page 203) the equilibrium price with a quota is P_{quota} and the equilibrium quantity is Q_4.

At the price P_{quota} domestic producers supply $Q_1 + (Q_4 - Q_3)$ of corn. Their revenue increases from area a to area a + c + d + f + i + j.

Foreign producers supply $Q_3 - Q_1$. Their revenue changes from b + c + d + e to area b + g + h. It is possible for their revenue to rise or fall. This depends, in part, on the size of the quota and the size of the shift of the domestic supply curve.

Discuss the effects on welfare of a quota

After the quota domestic producers supply an additional quantity of corn, $Q_4 - Q_3$. In order to supply this quantity they need a minimum revenue represented by the area c + d + j. This is the area below the supply curve, $S_{domestic + quota}$ and between Q_3 and Q_4. The foreign producers are more efficient and produce each unit at a lower average total cost. Therefore, they needed less revenue to produce $Q_4 - Q_3$ of corn. They were willing to supply this quantity for the revenue represented by the area c + d. This is the area below the supply curve, S_{world} and between Q_3 and Q_4. Area j is the difference between the minimum revenue needed by domestic producers and the minimum needed by foreign producers.

After the quota more of the world's scarce resources are used to produce corn because the foreign producers are more efficient and are able to produce $Q_4 - Q_3$ of corn using fewer resources. A quota leads to a less efficient outcome and a **welfare loss** represented by the area j.

Before the quota the quantity demanded was Q_2. Total **consumer surplus** was represented by the area above P_w and below the demand curve. After the quota the price increased from P_w to P_{quota} leading to a fall in quantity demanded from Q_2 to Q_4. Consumer expenditure on $Q_2 - Q_4$ of corn was represented by the area e. After the quota consumers do not buy this quantity of corn. Area k represents the consumer surplus that consumers used to receive on the consumption of $Q_2 - Q_4$ of corn at the world price P_w. The loss of consumer surplus is a welfare loss caused by the introduction of a quota.

Using a tariff to protect domestic industry and domestic jobs does increase government tax revenue. Using a quota to reduce the quantity of imported goods does not directly increase tax revenue. However, the possible increase in revenue and profits of the domestic producers might lead to an increase in the amount of tax raised on company profits.

Discuss the effects of a subsidy

A subsidy per unit is a payment made by the government to domestic producers on each unit of output. In effect a subsidy reduces the domestic producers' costs of production, therefore the producers are willing to supply more at each price and the domestic supply curve shifts down and to the right as shown in Figure 70.3.

Subject vocabulary

excess demand occurs when quantity demanded is greater than quantity supplied

ceteris paribus latin phrase meaning 'all other things being equal' or 'all other things being held constant'

determinants of supply factors that affect quantity supplied at each price

welfare loss the sum of the loss of consumer and producer surplus caused by market or government failure

consumer surplus the difference between the price a consumer is willing and able to pay and the price the consumer actually pays

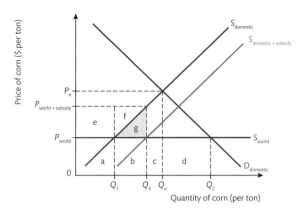

Figure 70.3

Describe the market for corn before the subsidy

Before the subsidy, at the world price P_{world}, the quantity demanded by domestic consumers was Q_2. At P_{world} domestic producers supply Q_1. The amount of revenue they received is $P_{world} \times Q_1$ represented by the area a. $Q_2 - Q_1$ was supplied by foreign producers. The amount of revenue they received is represented by the area b + c + d.

Describe the market for corn after the subsidy

The subsidy per unit causes the domestic supply curve to shift down and to the right from $S_{domestic}$ to $S_{domestic + subsidy}$. The vertical distance between the supply curves is equal to the subsidy per unit.

The price consumers pay does not change because the price is determined on the world market which is not affected by the subsidy. Domestic consumers therefore continue to demand the same quantity of corn, Q_2.

After the subsidy domestic producers are willing to increase supply because they now receive the world price plus the subsidy per unit. At $P_{world + subsidy}$ domestic supply increases from Q_1 to Q_3. The revenue they receive increases from the amount represented by area a to the amount represented by area a + b + e + f + g.

Area a + b is revenue domestic producers receive from the consumers and area e + f + g is the total subsidy paid by the government to the producers.

After the subsidy the quantity of corn supplied by foreign producers falls from $Q_2 - Q_1$ to $Q_2 - Q_3$. The revenue they receive falls from the amount represented by area b + c + d to the amount represented by area c + d.

Discuss the effects on welfare of a subsidy

After the subsidy domestic producers supply an additional quantity of corn, $Q_3 - Q_1$. The minimum amount of revenue they need to supply this additional quantity is represented by the area b + g. This is the area below the original supply curve $S_{domestic}$ and between Q_1 and Q_3. The foreign producers are more efficient and produce each unit at lower average total cost. Therefore they would be willing to supply this quantity for less revenue. The amount of revenue they would need is represented by area b. This is the area below the supply curve, S_{world} and between Q_1 and Q_3. Area g is the difference between the minimum revenue needed by domestic producers and the minimum needed by foreign producers.

After the subsidy more of the world's scarce resources are used to produce corn because the foreign producers are more efficient and are able to supply $Q_3 - Q_1$ of corn using fewer resources than the domestic producers. A subsidy leads to a less efficient outcome and loss of welfare represented by the area g.

The price paid by the consumer is not affected by the subsidy. Consumer surplus represented by the area above the world price and below the demand curve is not changed by the subsidy. Therefore a subsidy does not cause a loss of consumer surplus. Consumer expenditure on Q_2 of corn is represented by the area a + b + c + d before and after the subsidy. Consumers continue to spend the same amount. However, government expenditure increases by the amount of the subsidy represented by the area e + f + g. Therefore the government might have to increase taxes in order to pay the subsidy, which would reduce households' disposable income and consumer expenditure.

Model sentence: There is also an opportunity cost of a subsidy. The tax revenue spent on the subsidy cannot be spent on public goods and merit goods.

Subject vocabulary

opportunity cost the next best alternative forgone

public goods a good that is non-excludable and non-rivalrous. Once provided it is not possible to stop people benefitting from the consumption of it and therefore people free ride – they do not pay. The good will not be supplied left to the free market because no firm would be able to make a profit. Also, consumption of the good by one person does not diminish the amount available for others to consume.

merit goods goods that the government believes will be under consumed left to the free market. Consumption of a merit good may generate positive externalities therefore the social benefit of consumption is greater than the private benefit.

Explain how administrative barriers can be used to protect domestic producers

Model sentence: As more countries sign free trade agreements and remove tariffs and quotas, governments look for other ways to protect domestic producers including administrative barriers.

Some countries increase the amount of paperwork that it is necessary to complete before imported goods can enter a country. Imported goods must go through **customs** before entering a country. Lots of time is taken to check the goods and the necessary documents at the port. The people who do these jobs can do them very slowly if told to by the government. The procedures that exporters must follow are often unclear and the exporting firms must correctly fill in a very large quantity of documents. All this increases firms' costs of production leading to a fall in competitiveness and some firms give up trying to export their goods into that country.

Some countries put up barriers by making health and safety standards, environmental standards, and quality standards very difficult to meet. For example, drug companies exporting drugs find it more difficult to get the necessary **licence** from the importing country thereby protecting domestic drug producers from foreign competition.

Technical standards can be set that require the exporting firms to carry out long and difficult tests to show that the very high, and at times unreasonable, standards have been met. For example, there are technical standards that must be met on food, and the safety of toys and cars. Some goods must be a particular size or shape, and be packaged and labelled in a certain way. Goods are tested and checked to make sure they meet the required standards.

Model sentence: Meeting the technical standards of the importing country increases the firm's costs of production reducing its competitiveness, and thereby protecting the less efficient domestic firms from foreign competitors.

Test your understanding of this unit by answering the following questions

- Using a diagram, explain the effects of a tariff on producer and consumer revenue.
- Explain why a tariff reduces consumer surplus.
- Using a diagram, explain the effect of a subsidy per unit on the quantity of imports.
- Using a diagram, explain how a quota affects the use of the world's scarce resources.

Subject vocabulary

tariff a tax placed on imported goods and services

quotas a physical limit placed on the number of goods that can be traded or produced

Glossary

customs the place at a port, airport, or frontier where officials check incoming goods, travellers, or luggage

licence a permit from an authority to own or use something, do a particular thing, or carry on a trade

corruption illegal/immoral behaviour particularly by person(s) in power

Subject vocabulary

multinational corporations a corporation that operates in two or more countries

economies of scale the fall in average cost in the long run brought about by an increase in the size of a firm's operation

Learning Outcomes

- Discuss the arguments in favour of trade protection, including the protection of domestic jobs, national security, protection of infant industries, the maintenance of health, safety and environmental standards, anti-dumping and unfair competition, a means of overcoming a balance of payments deficit and a source of government revenue.

- Discuss the arguments against trade protection, including a misallocation of resources, the danger of retaliation and "trade wars", the potential for **corruption**, increased costs of production due to lack of competition, higher prices for domestic consumers, increased costs of imported factors of production, and reduced export competitiveness.

Discuss the arguments for and against protectionism

Discussed below are some of the advantages and disadvantages of protectionism.

Discuss the use of trade barriers to protect infant industries

Large **multinational corporations** produce goods on a very large scale and therefore benefit from **economies of scale**. The firms are able to produce output at relatively low average total cost. An **infant industry** that starts up in a country has a much smaller market and therefore produces fewer goods. It does not benefit from the economies of scale available to the much larger foreign producers. The average costs are therefore higher. The infant industry is unable to compete at the price set by the foreign producers. The new infant industry's average cost is likely to be higher than the price charged by the foreign producers, therefore the infant industry is unable to make a profit at that price.

Subject vocabulary

infant industry a new industry which often is not able to compete against established foreign industries and therefore needs to be protected from the competition through subsidies and tariffs

Restricting the number of imports, for example by a tariff, increases the price of the good and allows the infant industry to compete even though its average cost is higher than the foreign competition. Protected from the more efficient competition the infant industry has time to develop a skilled workforce and efficient methods of production and to build up market share. As output increases the infant industry can benefit from economies of scale. When its average costs have fallen enough, the tariff can be removed.

However, an infant industry that is protected from competition can become **productively inefficient**. It can stay in business even when producing goods at a relatively high average cost. Governments come under pressure from the industry to continue protecting it. In response foreign governments might protect their own industries which reduces the quantity of goods the infant industry exports, thereby limiting its growth.

Discuss the use of trade barriers to protect domestic jobs

Protectionist policies can protect domestic jobs. For example a US tariff on imported steel raises its price thereby increasing the sale of US steel to domestic buyers. Without protection there would be less domestic consumption of US steel and fewer steelworkers employed. A tariff might reduce the budget deficit as expenditure on unemployment benefits falls and tax revenue rises.

Steel is used by US firms in the production of lots of goods such as cars, trains, washing machines, fridges, and paperclips. After a tariff is introduced US firms have to pay a higher price for steel thereby increasing their **costs of production**. Firms put up prices to maintain their **profit margins** making them less competitive. **Quantity demanded** falls and firms reduce the number of workers they employ. Therefore protectionist policies might protect jobs in the protected industry but lead to higher prices and an increase in unemployment in other industries. In effect protectionist policies transfer resources away from domestic consumers to the protected industry.

The protection of industries leads to **cost-push inflation** as firms increase prices in response to higher costs of production. This reduces consumers' **real income** leading to a fall in **aggregate demand** and a rise in unemployment.

If the US government puts a tariff on imported goods, foreign governments may respond by placing a tariff on imports from the US leading to a fall in quantity demanded of US exports and a rise in unemployment in **exporting industries**.

Protectionist policies lead to a change in production away from countries producing at relatively low average total cost to countries producing at relatively high average total cost. More of the world's scarce resources are used to produce the goods than is necessary leading to a loss of social welfare.

Model sentence: Protectionism leads to a loss of the gains from international trade that come from the comparative advantage each country has in the production of particular goods.

Discuss the use of trade barriers to protect industries from cheap imports from low labour costs countries

Some countries have relatively low labour costs. Therefore their costs of production are lower and they are able to sell their goods in foreign markets at a lower price than domestic firms that have higher labour costs. To protect the industries from cheaper imports a country can put up **barriers to trade**. Some countries have a comparative advantage in the production of some goods because of their low labour costs. Domestic industries and jobs are protected by the barriers to trade but the less efficient firms continue to use resources to produce the goods when these goods could be produced by foreign firms using less of the world's scarce resources. Therefore there is a **misallocation of resources**. Domestic firms should use the resources to produce goods for which they have a comparative advantage in producing. In this way the world's scarce resources can be used to produce more output.

Model sentence: Free trade allows consumers to buy goods at a lower price increasing consumer surplus and increasing real income. As real income rises aggregate demand increases leading to a fall in unemployment.

Discuss the use of trade barriers to prevent dumping

Dumping occurs when goods are exported to a country and sold at a price that is below average total cost. Therefore each good is sold at a loss. Firms dump their goods into foreign markets for a number of reasons. Firms with **excess supply** that they are unable to sell can 'dump' the goods in order to earn at least some **producer revenue**. If the price the firm receives for the good is above its **average variable cost** the firm can use this revenue to pay some of its fixed costs.

Model sentence: A foreign firm can drive domestic firms out of business by dumping. The domestic firms are unable to compete at the low price and they leave the industry. The foreign firm can then increase its price and earn higher profits.

Protectionist policies can be used to increase the price of the imports thereby protecting domestic firms and jobs from dumping. Domestic firms continue to make **profit** and workers continue to earn a wage. The government receives tax revenue from income earned and pays out less in unemployment benefits. However, domestic consumers can benefit from dumping because they are able to buy goods at lower prices leading to an increase in **consumer surplus** and a rise in **real income**.

Discuss the use of trade barriers to protect standards

Countries have legal health and safety and environmental standards that goods must meet. If this is done to protect consumers from **private costs of consumption** then such standards are valid. Imported goods must also meet the standards set by the government. Increasingly countries are using the standards to stop the importing of goods that the government says will cause harm to the consumers. Domestic firms are protected from foreign competition. For example, some US beef producers inject cattle with hormones. Some countries have banned the importing of beef from the US because of the possible harmful effect on health. However, the evidence that the beef causes harm has not been proven. The US government believes that foreign countries have used the health and safety standards not to protect the health of its domestic consumers but to protect domestic producers.

Foreign producers must meet the standards set and this increases their costs of production. The **comparative advantage** in the production of these goods is lost and the less efficient domestic producers are protected from the more efficient foreign producers leading to a **welfare loss**.

Discuss the use of trade barriers to reduce a current account deficit and as a source of government revenue

A country has a current account deficit when expenditure on its imports by domestic consumers is greater than the expenditure on its exports by foreign consumers. The country spends more income on imports than it earns on exports. Protectionist policies reduce the demand for imports and increase demand for domestically produced goods thereby income spent on imports falls. As expenditure on imports falls the current account deficit falls. However, it is likely that foreign countries will put up barriers to trade in response. Therefore demand for exports falls leading to a fall in expenditure on exports. The fall in the current account deficit from a reduction in expenditure on imports is reversed by a fall in expenditure on exports. Therefore the use of trade barriers to reduce the current account deficit does not work. Instead the government should consider the introduction of **supply-side policies** that will improve the **productivity** of domestic industry thereby helping domestic industry to compete against more efficient foreign firms. In this way domestic firms become more competitive and some consumers will switch expenditure away from foreign firms to domestic firms, thereby reducing the current account deficit.

Tax revenue from **tariffs** is an important source of tax revenue for a government. In some countries the **black market** makes up a relatively high proportion of **GDP**; therefore, tax is avoided and tax revenue is relatively low. The tax raised on imported goods is very important to the governments of such countries.

What are the main arguments against trade protectionism?

Many of the arguments against **protectionism** have been discussed above. These arguments are summarized below.

It is likely that when a country seeks an advantage by raising barriers to trade against other countries these countries will respond by raising barriers to trade against that country. A trade war occurs between countries when each country keeps responding to the action of the other. In this way barriers continue to rise. A trade war is a possible outcome of protectionist policy and everyone loses out as explained below.

Barriers to trade lead to a loss of welfare. When barriers to trade are raised, consumers switch expenditure away from foreign firms that produce goods at relatively low average total cost to domestic firms producing at relatively high average total cost. There is a misallocation of resources because more of the resources are used to produce goods than is necessary.

Model sentence: When barriers to trade are raised, the potential gains from trade brought about by the comparative advantage countries have in the production of goods are lost. Fewer goods are produced with a given quantity of resources.

Subject vocabulary

profit the difference between total revenue (price × quantity sold) and economic costs (explicit costs + implicit costs)

consumer surplus the difference between the price a consumer is willing and able to pay and the price the consumer actually pays

real income income after taking into account the effects of inflation on purchasing power

private costs of consumption the cost incurred by consumers from their own consumption of a good

comparative advantage when a country, firm, or individual is able to produce a particular good or service at a lower opportunity cost than other countries, firms, or individuals

welfare loss the sum of the loss of consumer and producer surplus caused by market or government failure

supply-side policies government policy designed to affect the level of aggregate supply in an economy by increasing the quantity and/or productivity of the factors of production

productivity the quantity of output per unit of input

tariffs a tax placed on imported goods and services

black market an illegal market in goods or services

GDP gross domestic product is the monetary value of all the finished goods and services produced within a country in a given period of time, usually measured over a year

protectionism government policies, including tariffs, quotas, and subsidies, that restrict the extent of international trade and which are implemented in order to protect domestic industries from cheaper imports

Domestic firms become productively inefficient when protected from foreign competition leading to higher costs of production. The domestic firms are able to charge a higher price and earn higher profits.

Without access to cheaper imported goods, the price the consumers pay increases. Real incomes fall leading to a fall in **aggregate demand**.

Model sentence: When barriers to trade are raised, consumers pay a higher price for goods leading to a loss of consumer surplus and a fall in real incomes.

Barriers to trade on resources used in the production of other goods increase the price domestic firms pay for the resources, thereby increasing their costs of production. Firms put up the price of their goods in order to maintain **profit margins**. This leads to a fall in the quantity demanded by foreign consumers of the final goods. The expenditure spent on exports falls leading to an increase in the current account deficit.

Test your understanding of this unit by answering the following questions

- Outline the benefits of protectionism.
- Does the use of a tariff protect domestic jobs?
- Explain why consumers might not benefit from protectionism.
- Discuss the effects on welfare of protectionist policies.

Subject vocabulary

aggregate demand the total demand for goods and services in the economy at a given price level in a given period of time

profit margins the percentage of producer revenue that ends up as profit for the firm. Profit margin = profit/producer revenue × 100. If a firm earns a profit of $20m from sales of $80m its profit margin is 25%.

Learning Outcomes

- Calculate from diagrams the effects of imposing a tariff on imported goods on different stakeholders, including domestic producers, foreign producers, consumers, and the government. (HL)

- Calculate from diagrams the effects of setting a quota on foreign producers on different stakeholders, including domestic producers, foreign producers, consumers, and the government. (HL)

- Calculate from diagrams the effects of giving a subsidy to domestic producers on different stakeholders, including domestic producers, foreign producers, consumers, and the government. (HL)

Calculate the effects of a tariff on foreign and domestic producers, consumers, and the government using the information in Figure 72.1 (HL)

A tariff is a tax placed on imported goods by the government which increases the price of the good. The quantity of steel demanded at each price is shown by the **demand curve** $D_{domestic}$. It slopes downwards showing that as price rises **quantity demanded** falls. The **quantity supplied** at each price by domestic producers is shown by the **supply curve** $S_{domestic}$. The domestic supply curve slopes upwards showing that as price increases the quantity of steel domestic producers supply increases. The quantity supplied by foreign producers is shown by the supply curve S_{world}. World supply is **perfectly elastic** with respect to price. This means that foreign producers are willing to supply any quantity of steel at the world price.

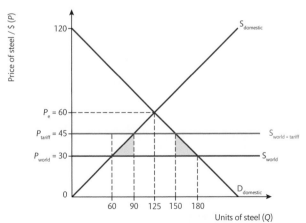

Figure 72.1

Subject vocabulary

demand curve a graph that shows the relationship between price and quantity demanded

quantity demanded the amount of a good consumers are willing and able to buy at a given price over a given period of time

quantity supplied the amount of a good that firms are willing and able to produce at a given price over a given period of time

supply curve a graph that shows the relationship between price and quantity supplied

perfectly elastic at a particular price quantity supplied is infinite but falls to nothing as price changes. The absolute value of PES is equal to infinity.

Calculate the foreign producer revenue, domestic producer revenue, and government revenue before the tariff – a step-by-step guide

Trouble shooter

Price = P_{world} = $30 per unit. Quantity demanded by domestic consumers at $30 per unit = 180 units.

Foreign producers are willing to supply an unlimited amount at $30 but there is only demand for 180 units.

Quantity supplied by domestic producers at $30 per unit = 60 units

Quantity supplied by foreign producers = 180 – 60 = 120 units

Domestic producer revenue = P_{world} × Quantity = $30 × 60 = $1800

Foreign Producer revenue = P_{world} × Quantity = $30 × 120 = $3600

Government revenue = tariff per unit × the quantity of imports = $0 × 120 = 0

Calculate the foreign producer revenue, domestic producer revenue, and government revenue after the tariff – a step-by-step guide

Trouble shooter

A tariff is a tax placed on imported goods by the government, which increases the price of the good by the amount of the tariff.

World price before tariff = $30. World price after the tariff = $45. Tariff =$45 – $30 = $15.

Quantity demanded by domestic consumers at $45 per unit = 150 units

Foreign producers are willing to supply an unlimited amount at $45 but there is only demand for 150 units.

Quantity supplied by domestic producers at $45 per unit = 90 units

Quantity supplied by foreign producers = 150 – 90 = 60 units

Domestic producer revenue = P_{tariff} × Quantity = $45 × 90 = $4050

World price + tariff = $30 +$15 = $45.

For each unit sold foreign producers get $30 and the government gets $15.

Foreign producer revenue = P_{world} × Quantity = $30 × 60 = $1800

Government revenue = tariff per unit × the quantity of imports = $15 × 60 = $900

Calculate the changes in foreign producer revenue, domestic producer revenue, and government revenue – a step-by-step guide

Trouble shooter

Foreign producer revenue after tariff =$1800, and revenue before the tariff = $3600

The change in foreign producer revenue = $1800 – $3600 = –$1800

Foreign producer revenue falls by $1800.

Domestic producer revenue after the tariff = $4050, and revenue before the tariff = $1800

The change in domestic producer revenue = $4050 – $1800 = $2250

Domestic producer revenue increases by $2250.

Government revenue after the tariff = $900, and revenue before the tariff = $0

Government tax revenue increases by $900.

Calculate the loss of consumer surplus caused by the tariff – a step-by-step guide

Trouble shooter

Consumer surplus is the total difference between the price consumers are willing to pay and the price consumers actually pay. It is represented by the area above price and below the demand curve. The formula to calculate the area of a triangle is $\frac{1}{2}$ × base × height).

Before the tariff the highest price the first consumer is willing to pay is $120. The price actually paid is $30.

The difference = $120 – $30 = $90. The height of the triangle = 90.

The quantity bought and sold at $30 per unit is 180 units. The base = 180.

Consumer surplus = $\frac{1}{2}$ (base × height) = $\frac{1}{2}$ (180 × 90) = $\frac{1}{2}$ × 16 200 = $8100.

Before the tariff consumer surplus, the total difference between the amount consumers were willing to pay for the 180 units of steel and the total amount consumers actually paid is $8100.

After the tariff the highest price the first consumer is willing to pay is $120. The price actually paid is $45.

The difference = $120 – $45 = $75. The height of the triangle = 75.

The quantity bought and sold at $45 per unit is 150 units. The base = 150.

Consumer surplus = $\frac{1}{2}$ (base × height) = $\frac{1}{2}$ (150 × 75) = $\frac{1}{2}$ × 11 250 = $5625.

The loss of consumer surplus = $8100 – $5625 = $2475

Calculate the net welfare loss caused by the tariff – a step-by-step guide

Trouble shooter

The two shaded triangles represent the net welfare loss.

The height of the triangle on the left = 45 – 30 = 15. The base = 90 – 60 = 30.

$\frac{1}{2}$ base × height = $\frac{1}{2}$ (30 × 15) = $\frac{1}{2}$ × $450 = $225

The height of the triangle on the right = 45 – 30 = 15. The base = 180 – 150 = 30.

$\frac{1}{2}$ base × height = $\frac{1}{2}$ (30 × 15) = $\frac{1}{2}$ × $450 = $225

Total net welfare loss = $225 + $225 = $450

Calculate the effects of a quota on foreign and domestic producers, consumers, and the government using the information in Figure 72.2 (HL)

A quota is a physical limit put on the number of goods that can be imported. The government sets a quota of 30 units of steel as shown in Figure 72.2 (on page 212).

Calculate domestic and foreign producer revenue before the quota

Before the quota, world price is $30 per unit and quantity demanded is 180 units of which 60 units (60 – 0) are supplied by domestic producers and 120 units (180 units – 60 units) are supplied by foreign producers.

Domestic producer revenue
(Price × Quantity) = $30 × 60 = $1800

Foreign producer revenue = $30 × 120 = $3600

Calculate domestic and foreign producer revenue after the quota

The government sets a quota of 30 units. The quantity demanded stays at 180 units because price has not changed and domestic producers continue to supply 60 units (60 – 0). Foreign producers can only supply 30 units (90 – 60), therefore total quantity supplied = 90 units (60 + 30). There is an **excess demand** of 90 units (180 – 90).

Subject vocabulary

excess demand occurs when quantity demanded is greater than quantity supplied

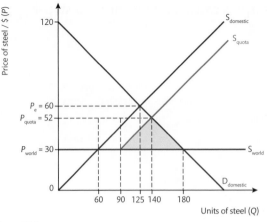

Figure 72.2

To remove the excess demand, price rises and **profits** earned by domestic producers increase, attracting new firms into the **market**. The number of firms in an **industry** is a **determinant of supply**. There are now more domestic producers and the domestic supply curve shifts down and to the right from $S_{domestic}$ to S_{quota}.

The **equilibrium price** rises from $30 ($P_{world}$) to $52 ($P_{quota}$). As price rises to $52 quantity demanded falls from 180 units to 140 units. The foreign producers would like to increase the quantities supplied but cannot because they are not allowed to supply more than 30 units. At $52 per unit of steel domestic producers increase quantity supplied from 60 units (60 – 0) to 110 units (60 – 0 + 140 – 90).

Price = $52. Quantity demanded =140 units. Total producer revenue = $52 × 140 = $7280. Domestic producer revenue after the quota = $52 × 110 = $5720 an increase of $3920 ($5720 – $1800). Foreign producer revenue after the quota = $52 × 30 = $1,560 a fall of $2040 ($1560 – $3600).

Calculate the loss of consumer surplus caused by the quota

Consumer surplus is the total difference between the price consumers are willing to pay and the price consumers actually pay. It is represented by the area above price and below the demand curve. The formula to calculate the area of a triangle is $\frac{1}{2}$ × base × height.

Before the quota the highest price the first consumer is willing to pay is $120. The price actually paid is $30. The difference = $120 – $ 30 = $90. The height of the triangle = 90.
The quantity bought and sold at $30 per unit is 180 units. The base = 180.
Consumer surplus = $\frac{1}{2}$ × base × height = $\frac{1}{2}$ × 180 × 90 = $\frac{1}{2}$ × 16,200 = $8100.

After the quota the highest price the first consumer is willing to pay is $120. The price actually paid is $52. The difference = $120 – $52 = $68. The height of the triangle = 68.
The quantity bought and sold at $52 is 140 units. The base = 140.
Consumer surplus = $\frac{1}{2}$ × base × height = $\frac{1}{2}$ × 140 × 68 = $\frac{1}{2}$ × 9520= $4760.

The loss of consumer surplus = $8100 – $4760 = $3340

Calculate the net welfare loss caused by the quota

The shaded triangle represents the area of net welfare loss.
The height of the triangle = $52 – $30 = 22. The base = 180 units – 90 units = 90.
Net welfare loss of quota = $\frac{1}{2}$ × base × height = $\frac{1}{2}$ × 90 × 22 = $\frac{1}{2}$ × 1980 = $990.
No government revenue is raised by a quota.

Calculate the effects of a subsidy on foreign and domestic producers, consumers, and the government using the information in Figure 72.3 (HL)

Calculate domestic and foreign producer revenue before the subsidy

Before the subsidy world price of steel is $30 per unit and quantity demanded by domestic consumers is 180 units as shown in Figure 72.3. At $30 domestic producers supply 60 units. Domestic producer revenue = $30 × 60 = $1800. Foreign producers supply 120 units (180 – 60). Foreign producer revenue = $30 × 120 = $3600.

Calculate domestic and foreign producer revenue after the subsidy

A subsidy per unit is a payment made by the government to domestic producers on each unit of output. In effect a subsidy reduces the domestic producers' costs of production so more profit is made at each price. The domestic producers are willing to supply more at each price and the domestic supply curve shifts down and to the right by the amount of the subsidy as shown in Figure 72.3. The vertical distance between the domestic supply curves is equal to the subsidy per unit. The subsidy in this example is $15. The subsidy is paid to domestic producers by the government so the price consumers pay does not change, therefore quantity demanded stays at 180 units.

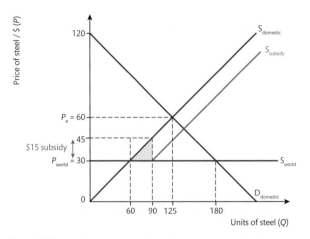

Figure 72.3

The price received by domestic producers increases from $30 to $45 ($30 from the consumer and $15 subsidy from the government). Domestic producers increase supply from 60 units to 90 units. Domestic producer revenue received from consumers = $30 × 90 = $2700 and the revenue received from the government = subsidy per unit × quantity = $15 × 90 = $1350. Total domestic revenue = $2,700 + $1350 = $4050. Domestic producer revenue increases by $2250 ($4050 − $1800) after the subsidy.

After the subsidy the quantity supplied by foreign producers falls from 120 units (180 − 60) to 90 units (180 − 90). The revenue they receive = $30 × 90 = $2700. Foreign producer revenue falls by $900 ($2700 − $3600) after the subsidy.

Calculate the loss of consumer surplus caused by the subsidy

Consumer surplus is the total difference between the price consumers are willing to pay and the price consumers actually pay. It is represented by the area above price and below the demand curve. The formula to calculate the area of a triangle is $\frac{1}{2}$ × base × height.

Before the subsidy the highest price the first consumer is willing to pay is $120. The price actually paid is $30.

The difference = $120 − $30 = $90. The height of the triangle = 90.

The quantity bought and sold at $30 per unit is 180 units. The base = 180.

Consumer surplus = $\frac{1}{2}$ × base × height = $\frac{1}{2}$ × 180 × 90 = $\frac{1}{2}$ × 16200 = $8100.

The subsidy does not change the price consumers pay; therefore, the subsidy does not cause a loss of consumer surplus.

Calculate the net welfare loss caused by the quota

The shaded triangle represents the area of net welfare loss.

The height of the triangle = $45 − $30 = 15. The base = 90 units − 60 units = 30.

Net welfare loss of the subsidy = $\frac{1}{2}$ × base × height = $\frac{1}{2}$ × 30 × 15 = $\frac{1}{2}$ × 450 = $225.

Calculate the government expenditure caused by the subsidy

Government expenditure = subsidy per unit × quantity of domestic units = $15 × 90 = $1350.

Test your understanding of this unit by answering the following questions

- Draw a diagram showing the effects of a tariff from the following information:
  - When price is $15 quantity demanded = 15 units, and quantity supplied = 45 units
  - When price is $10 quantity demanded = 30 units, and quantity supplied = 30 units
  - When price is $5 quantity demanded = 45 units, and quantity supplied = 15 units
  - The world price = $5, and the tariff = $3.
- Calculate producer and consumer revenue before and after the tariff, government revenue after the tariff and the level of welfare loss.

3.2 Exchange rates: Freely floating exchange rates

Learning Outcomes

- Explain that the value of an exchange rate in a floating system is determined by the demand for, and supply of, a currency.

- Draw a diagram to show determination of exchange rates in a floating exchange rate system.

- Describe the factors that lead to changes in currency demand and supply, including foreign demand for a country's exports, domestic demand for imports, relative interest rates, relative inflation rates, investment from overseas in a country's firms (foreign direct investment and portfolio investment), and speculation.

- Distinguish between a depreciation of the currency and an appreciation of the currency.

- Draw diagrams to show changes in the demand for, and supply of, a currency.

- Evaluate the possible economic consequences of a change in the value of a currency, including the effects on a country's inflation rate, employment, economic growth, and current account balance.

Explain why countries must exchange currencies in order to trade

Money is used to **facilitate** exchange. Money is used so that households can exchange their labour for money and in turn so that households can buy goods and services from firms. Buyers in the US earn dollars and firms in the US want to be paid in dollars. Firms in other countries have to be paid for their goods in their own currencies. For example, German firms want to be paid in euros for their goods. Importers of German goods in the US cannot pay the German firms in US dollars. Importers must exchange their dollars for euros so that they can pay the German firms in euros. German importers of US goods must exchange euros for dollars so that they can pay the US firms in dollars. The exchange of currencies allows money to be used to facilitate international exchanges. Currencies are exchanged on the foreign exchange market. This is a global market for the buying and selling of currencies.

What is the exchange rate?

The exchange rate is defined as the rate at which one currency is exchanged for another currency. The equilibrium exchange rate is the exchange rate at which the demand for a currency equals the supply of that currency in the forex market. For example on 5 January 2014 the US dollar for euro equilibrium exchange rate was $1 = €0.7357 or €1 = $1.359 (1/0.7357). This means that the price of $1 is €0.7357 and the price of €1 is $1.359. At $1 = €0.7357 the market for dollars is in equilibrium as shown in Figure 73.1.

A US firm imports **raw materials** from Germany. The price for the raw materials is €10000. The US firm must pay the German firm €10000, therefore the US firm must buy €10000 paying for it with US dollars. The exchange rate is $1 = €0.7357. To calculate the amount of dollars needed to buy €10000 divide 10000 by 0.7357: 10000/0.7357 = $13592.5. The US firm must exchange $13592.5 for €10000 so that they can pay the German firm for the raw materials.

What are the sources of the demand for, and supply of, currencies?

International trade leads to changes in the demand and supply of currencies. Buyers of imports must use their currency in order to buy another currency. For example, US importers of German goods supply US dollars to the foreign exchange market and demand euros. Therefore, when buyers in the US buy imported goods from Germany the supply of dollars increases and the demand for euros increases. When German buyers buy US goods the supply of euros increases and the demand for dollars increases.

Foreign direct investment leads to changes in the demand and supply of currencies. When US firms invest in Germany they supply dollars and demand euros. When German firms invest in the US they supply euros and demand dollars.

Portfolio investment, such as the buying of foreign company shares and depositing money in interest-earning saving accounts in a foreign bank, leads to changes in the demand and supply of currencies. When US institutions and individuals put their savings in German banks and other institutions they must exchange their US dollars for euros. They supply dollars and demand euros. When German savers put their money in US banks they must exchange their euros for US dollars. They supply euros and demand dollars. When US buyers purchase shares in German companies they supply dollars and demand euros. When German buyers purchase shares in US companies they supply euros and demand dollars. Note that if a buyer purchases more than 10% of the shares of a foreign company, it is classified as foreign direct investment not portfolio investment.

Speculation leads to changes in the demand and supply of currencies. Traders of currencies buy and sell currencies in the foreign exchange markets with the aim of making a gain. For example, if some traders believe that the US dollar will rise in value in the future they will buy dollars thereby increasing demand for the currency. If some traders believe the value of the dollar will fall, they will sell dollars thereby increasing the supply of dollars.

What is a floating exchange rate system?

In a floating exchange rate system the price of one currency in terms of another is determined by the demand for and supply of that currency in the foreign exchange market. When demand for the currency exceeds supply the currency rises in value against the other currency. This is called an appreciation of a currency. When supply exceeds demand, the currency falls in value against the other currency. This is called a depreciation of a currency. The government does not intervene in the market to increase or decrease the value of the currency. For example, the government will not sell its **foreign reserves** and buy its own currency in order to increase demand for the currency and thereby increase its value.

Why does the demand curve for a currency slope downwards?

Figure 73.1 shows the market for US dollars in terms of the euro. When the price of $1 = €0.7357 the market is in equilibrium. The quantity of dollars demanded and the quantity supplied are equal at Q_e.

The demand curve shows the quantity of dollars demanded at each quantity of euros. As the amount of euros needed to buy $1 falls the quantity demanded of dollars increases. If the price of dollars falls against the euro

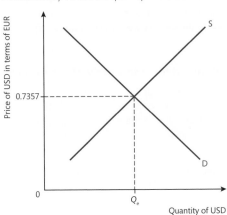

Figure 73.1

(fewer euros are needed to buy $1) the price of imported goods from the US falls in terms of the amount of euros needed to buy them. The quantity of US goods demanded by German buyers increases and therefore the quantity of dollars demanded increases in order to buy the additional goods. For example, in order to buy a good priced at $100 when the exchange rate is $1 = €0.7357 German buyers need to pay €73.57 (100 × €0.7357). If the dollar depreciates (falls in value) to $1 = €0.70 German buyers pay €70 (100 × €0.70) for the good. As the price of the good falls, the quantity of the goods demanded increases leading to an increase in the quantity of dollars demanded in order to buy the additional goods. A fall in the price of the dollar leads to an increase in quantity demanded of dollars, therefore the demand curve slopes downwards.

Why does the supply curve of a currency slope upwards?

A fall in the value of the US dollar increases the amount of dollars needed to buy a given quantity of euros. In order to buy a German good priced at €100 when the exchange rate is $1 = €0.7357, US buyers need to pay $135.92 (100/0.7357=135.92). If the price of the dollar falls to $1 = €0.70 (a dollar buys fewer euros) the price of German imports increases. A good priced at €100 now costs $142.86 (100/0.70=142.86). As the price US buyers must pay for the German good increases, quantity demanded falls, therefore the amount of dollars supplied to buy the goods falls. A fall in the price of the US dollar leads to a fall in the quantity of dollars supplied, therefore the supply curve slopes upwards.

Explain the causes of a shift of the demand and the supply curves

The various causes of a change in demand for, and supply of, a currency are discussed below.

How does international trade in goods and services affect the demand for, and supply of, a currency?

When **national income** rises in Germany demand for **normal goods** increases, including demand for US imported goods. German buyers must buy more US dollars with their euros to pay for the goods. An increase in

inflation an increase in the general level of prices of goods/services in an economy over a given time period, usually a year

interest rate the percentage amount charged by a lender for money borrowed

the quantity of US exports leads to an increase in the demand for dollars, causing the demand curve to shift up and to the right from D to D_1 as shown in Figure 73.2.

If US buyers demand more German goods because income in the US rises, they must buy more euros with their US dollars to pay for the goods. An increase in the quantity of US imports leads to an increase in the supply of dollars causing the supply curve to shift down and to the right from S to S_1 as shown in Figure 73.3.

If **inflation** in the US is higher than in Germany, then US goods become relatively more expensive than German goods. Demand for German goods therefore increases and US buyers will buy more German goods; therefore, the supply of US dollars increases causing the supply curve to shift down and to the right from S to S_1 as shown in Figure 73.3.

If inflation in Germany is higher than in the US, then German goods become relatively more expensive than US goods. Demand for US goods therefore increases and German buyers will buy more US goods; therefore, the demand for US dollars increases, causing the demand curve to shift up and to the right from D to D_1 as shown in Figure 73.2.

How does a change in the interest rate affect the demand for, and supply of, a currency?

If the **interest rate** in the US increases, savers in other countries including Germany will want to move some of their savings to the US. To do this, savers must exchange their currencies for dollars. German savers, for example, buy dollars and pay for them with euros. The demand for dollars increases and the demand curve shifts up and to the right as seen in Figure 73.2. The savings that are moved from one country's financial institutions to another country's financial institutions are called hot money. Hot money moves around the world, sometimes very quickly, in response to changes in the relative interest rates, as savers try to earn the highest returns.

If savers in the US move their savings to German financial institutions because the interest rate in Germany increases, the supply of dollars increases. Hot money flows out of the US into Germany. US savers buy euros with their dollars, therefore the supply of dollars increases causing the supply curve to shift down and to the right from S to S_1 as shown in Figure 73.3.

How does foreign direct investment affect the demand for, and supply of, a currency?

Long-term investment in a country by a foreign firm increases the demand for the currency of that country. For example, a German car manufacturer builds and manages a car factory in the US. To do this the German firm demands dollars and pays for them with euros. The demand for dollars increases and the supply of euros increases. The demand curve shifts up and to the right as shown in Figure 73.2.

Investment by US firms in Germany increases the supply of dollars because the firm must buy the euro with dollars. Demand for the euro increases and the supply of dollars increases causing the supply curve to shift down and to the right from S to S_1 as shown in Figure 73.3.

How does speculation affect the demand for, and supply of, a currency

If traders in currencies believe that the US dollar is going to rise in value against the euro they will sell euros and buy dollars. The supply of euros increases and the demand for dollars increases. The increase in demand for dollars causes the demand curve to shift up and to the right from D to D_1 as shown in Figure 73.2.

If traders in currencies believe the dollar is going to fall in value they will sell dollars for another currency. The supply of dollars increases causing the supply curve to shift down and to the right from S to S_1 as shown in Figure 73.3.

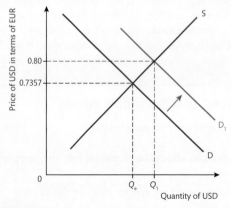

Figure 73.2   **Figure 73.3**

Explain how changes in the demand for a currency affect its exchange rate

The equilibrium exchange rate is $1 = €0.7357. Quantity of dollars demanded = quantity of dollars supplied at Q_e. Demand for the dollar increases, for example, when German buyers demand more US goods. The demand curve for dollars shifts up and to the right from D to D_1 as shown in Figure 73.2. The market for dollars is now in **disequilibrium** at the original equilibrium exchange rate. At $1 = €0.7357 demand for dollars exceeds supply. The price of the dollar rises or appreciates against the euro until the market is once again in equilibrium at $1 = €0.80. The price of a dollar rises from $1 = €0.7357 to $1 = €0.80.

Model sentence: An increase in demand for a country's exports increases demand for its currency, leading to a rise in the exchange rate of that currency.

When speculators believe the dollar is overvalued and will fall in value in the future, the supply of the dollar increases. Speculators sell dollars and the supply of dollars on the market increases causing the supply curve to shift down and to the right from S to S_1. The market for dollars is now in disequilibrium at the original equilibrium exchange rate. At $1 = €0.7357 the supply of dollars exceeds demand. The price of the dollar falls or depreciates against the euro until the market is in equilibrium at $1 = €0.65. The price of a dollar falls from €0.7357 to €0.65.

If traders of currencies believe a currency will fall in value, they sell the currency and therefore it does fall in value.

Model sentence: When speculators believe a currency is overvalued and will fall in value, they sell the currency, leading to an increase in supply of the currency and a fall in the value of that currency.

Model sentence: An increase in demand for imports increases the supply of the country's currency, leading to a fall in the value of that currency.

Evaluate the possible economic consequences of a change in the value of a currency

To answer this it is necessary to examine the advantages and disadvantages of changes in the exchange rate.

Discuss the advantages of an appreciating currency

As a currency appreciates in value the price of imported consumer goods falls. The fall in the price of these goods leads to an increase in the purchasing power of income. **Consumer surplus** increases and more wants can be satisfied with a given income. The price of imported **raw materials** also falls leading to a fall in the **costs of production** and possibly a shift of the **aggregate supply** curve down and to the right, thereby reducing the **price level**.

An appreciating currency might lead to lower prices of some domestically produced goods because domestic producers must compete against the relatively cheaper imports. They have to become more productively efficient in order to lower prices and survive in business. Therefore an appreciating currency in the long term can improve the **productivity** of domestic producers, lowering **average total costs** and increasing their international competitiveness.

Discuss the disadvantages of an appreciating currency

As a currency appreciates in value the price of imports falls and the price of exports rises. This could lead to an increase in the quantity of imports demanded and a fall in the quantity of exports demanded. The amount of income flowing out of the country to buy imports is greater than the flow of income coming into the country to buy exports, thereby increasing the **current account deficit** or reducing the **current account surplus**.

The increase in the price of exports leads to a fall in the quantity of exports demanded. In response, exporting producers reduce output. As output falls, **demand-deficient unemployment** increases. The fall in the price of imports leads to an increase in the quantity of imports demanded and a fall in demand for domestically produced goods. Domestic producers reduce output in response to a fall in demand and unemployment increases.

Therefore, a relatively high exchange rate can lead to a fall in **aggregate demand** and an increase in the **deflationary gap**. The price level falls but unemployment of labour and **capital** increases.

Model sentence: An appreciating currency reduces the price of imports leading to a fall in inflation. However, the price of exports increases, leading to fall in quantity of exports demanded and a rise in unemployment.

Discuss the advantages of a depreciating currency

As a country's currency depreciates in value, the price foreigners pay for its exports falls making exports more price competitive. This leads to an increase in the quantity of exports demanded. Exporting producers increase output in response to higher demand and unemployment falls. Exports are a component of aggregate demand and as aggregate demand increases, producers might have to invest in new capital in order to meet higher levels of demand. Investment is a component of aggregate demand, therefore aggregate demand increases further. At the same time the price of imports increases. Domestic **substitutes** become more price competitive leading to a fall in the quantity of imports demanded and a rise in the quantity of domestic goods demanded. Aggregate demand increases, firms respond by increasing output and unemployment falls. It is possible that a low exchange rate can help a country recover from a **recession**.

More income flows into the country to buy exports and less income flows out to buy imports, leading to a fall in the **current account deficit** or an increase in the **current account surplus**.

Discuss the disadvantages of a depreciating currency

As a currency falls in value the price of imported consumer goods increases. The price of imported **resources** also increases leading to an increase in the costs of production leading to **cost-push inflation**. Inflation caused by the increasing price of imported goods is called imported inflation. If there are few or no substitute domestic consumer goods or resources, demand for imported goods might be **price inelastic**. Therefore as price rises quantity demanded falls but at a lower rate. And because **expenditure** on imports increases, the current account deficit rises.

Imported inflation leads to a fall in the **purchasing power** of income. **Consumer surplus** falls and fewer wants can be satisfied with a given income.

Model sentence: A depreciating currency reduces the price of exports leading to an increase in the quantity of exports demanded and a fall in unemployment. However, the price of imported goods increases, leading to inflation.

Test your understanding of this unit by answering the following questions

- Describe the sources of demand and supply of a currency.
- Using a diagram, explain how changes in the interest rate can affect the exchange rate.
- Using a diagram, explain how changes in the international trade of goods can affect the exchange rate.
- Discuss possible consequences of a high exchange rate.
- Discuss possible consequences of a low exchange rate.

Learning Outcome

- Calculate the value of one currency in terms of another currency. (HL)
- Calculate the exchange rate for linear demand and supply functions. (HL)
- Plot demand and supply curves for a currency from linear functions and identify the equilibrium exchange rate. (HL)
- Using exchange rates, calculate the price of a good in different currencies. (HL)
- Calculate the changes in the value of a currency from a set of data. (HL)

Calculate the price of $1 in terms of the £ when the exchange rate is £1 = $1.65 (HL)

£1 = $1.65 therefore $1 = 1/1.65 = £0.606.

A firm in the UK buys raw materials from a firm in the US. The price of the raw materials is $12 500. The exchange rate is $1 = £0.606. Calculate the price of the raw materials in £s

If $1 = £0.606 then $12 500 = 12 500 × £0.606 = £7575.

A **linear function** is an equation that states how a **variable** is determined, the graph of which is a straight line. The **demand function** Qd = a – bP states how **quantity demanded** of a good is determined by the price of the good. The **supply function** Qs = c + dP is an equation that shows the relationship between price and **quantity supplied** of a good.

The linear equations for the demand and supply of a currency in the **foreign exchange market** are expressed in the same way as the linear equations for the **demand** and **supply** of a good in the goods market.

The linear demand equation for a currency is Qd = a – bP. It shows the relationship between the price of a currency in terms of another currency and the quantity demanded.
Qd is the quantity demanded of the currency.
P represents the exchange rate which is price of the currency in terms of another currency.
A change in the value of a changes demand for a currency.
The **coefficient** b determines the responsiveness of quantity demanded of the currency to a change in the exchange rate and therefore determines the slope of the demand curve.

The linear supply equation for a currency is Qs = c + dP. It shows the relationship between the price of a currency in terms of another currency and quantity supplied.

Qs is quantity supplied of the currency.
P represents the price of the currency in terms of another currency.
A change in the value of c changes the supply of a currency.
The coefficient d determines the responsiveness of quantity supplied of the currency to a change in the exchange rate and therefore determines the slope of the supply curve.

Using the linear functions calculate quantity demanded and quantity supplied of £s when the exchange rate is £1 = $1, £1 = $2 and £1 = $3 (HL)

The demand function for the £ is Qd = 50 – 5p and the supply function for the £ is Qs = 25 + 10p

Qd = 50 – (5 × 1) = 50 – 5 = 45   Qs = 25 + (10 × 1) = 25 + 10 = 35
Qd = 50 – (5 × 2) = 50 – 10 = 40   Qs = 25 + (10 × 2) = 25 + 20 = 45
Qd = 50 – (5 × 3) = 50 – 15 = 35   Qs = 25 + (10 × 3) = 25 + 30 = 55

Draw the demand schedule and supply schedule

Exchange rate	Qd of £s (billions)	Qs of £s (billions
£1 = $1	45	35
£1 = $2	40	45
£1 = $3	35	55

Using the functions calculate the equilibrium exchange rate – a step-by-step guide

Trouble shooter

The equilibrium exchange rate is the rate at which quantity of the currency demanded = quantity of the currency supplied.

Qd = Qs when 50 – 5p = 25 + 10p

50 – 5p = 25 + 10p   simplify by subtracting 25 from both sides

25 – 5p = 10p   simplify by adding 5p to both sides

25 = 15p   simplify by dividing both sides by 15

1.66 = p

The equilibrium exchange rate is £1 = $1.66.

Subject vocabulary

linear function an equation, the graph of which is a straight line

variable a value that can change

demand function an equation that shows how quantity demanded of a good is determined by the price of the good

quantity demanded the amount of a good consumers are willing and able to buy at a given price over a given period of time

supply function equation that shows how quantity supplied of a good is determined by the price of the good

quantity supplied the amount of a good that firms are willing and able to produce at a given price over a given period of time

foreign exchange market a decentralized global market for the buying and selling of currencies

demand the amount of a good that consumers are willing and able to buy at each price

supply the amount of a good that a firm is willing and able to produce at each price

coefficient a number used to multiply a variable by

Using the functions and the exchange rate, calculate the equilibrium quantity – a step-by-step guide

Trouble shooter

The demand function is Qd = 50 – 5p. The supply function is Qs = 25 +10p. p represents the exchange rate.

Substitute 1.66 for *p* in the functions.

Qd = 50 – (5 × 1.66) = 50 – 8.3 = 41.7

Qs = 25 + (10 × 1.66) = 25 + 16.7 = 41.7

The equilibrium quantity = £41.7 billion.

Using the information from the demand and supply schedule, plot the demand and supply curves for the £ (HL)

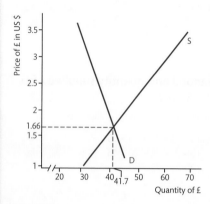

The equilibrium exchange rate where the quantity of £s demanded is equal to the quantity of £s supplied is £1 = $1.66. The equilibrium quantity of £s is £41.7 billion.

Figure 74.1

Calculate the new equilibrium exchange rate and equilibrium quantity after an increase in the demand for a currency. Illustrate your answer with a diagram (HL)

A change in the value of *a* in the demand function represents a change in demand for a currency. For example, if demand for a country's exports increases, demand for the country's currency increases, leading to an increase in the value of *a* and a shift of the demand curve up and to the right.

A change in the value of *c* in the supply function represents a change in the supply of a currency. For example, if speculators believe a currency will fall in value they will sell the currency, leading to an increase in its supply and an increase in the value of *c*. The supply curve shifts down and to the right.

When income rises in the US, for example, the demand for UK exports increases. The value of *a* in the linear demand function Qd = a – bP increases from 50 to 55. The new linear function is Qd = 55 – 5p. The supply function Qs = 25 +10p does not change.

Using the linear functions calculate Qd and Qs of £s when the exchange rate is £1 = $1, £1 = $2, and £1 = $3.

Qd = 55 – (5 × 1) = 55 – 5 = 50   Qs = 25 + (10 × 1) = 25 + 10 = 35

Qd = 55 – (5 × 2) = 55 – 10 = 45   Qs = 25 + (10 × 2) = 25 + 20 = 45

Qd = 55 – (5 × 3) = 55 – 15 = 40   Qs = 25 + (10 × 3) = 25 + 30 = 55

Draw the demand and supply schedule

Exchange rate	Qd of £s (billions)	Qs of £s (billions)
£1 = $1	50	35
£1 = $2	45	45
£1 = $3	40	55

Using the functions calculate the new equilibrium exchange rate after the change in the value of a in the linear demand function Qd = a + bP from 50 to 55

The demand function changes from Qd = 50 – 5p to Qd = 55 – 5p.

The equilibrium exchange rate is where quantity demanded = quantity supplied.

Qd = Qs when 55 – 5p = 25 + 10p

55 – 5p = 25 + 10p   simplify by subtracting 25 from both sides

30 – 5p = 10p   simplify by adding 5p to both sides

30 = 15p   simplify by dividing both sides by 15

2 = p

The new equilibrium exchange rate is £1 = $2.00.

Using the functions and the exchange rate, calculate the new equilibrium quantity

The demand function is Qd = 55 – 5p. The supply function is Qs = 25 +10p. p represents the exchange rate.

Substitute 2 for p in the functions.

Qd = 55 – (5 × 2) = 55 – 10 = 45

Qs = 25 + (10 × 2) = 25 + 20 = 45

The new equilibrium quantity = £45 billion.

Using a diagram, show the changes in demand, equilibrium exchange rate, and equilibrium quantity (HL)

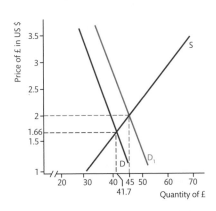

Figure 74.2

The increase in demand for UK exports from US buyers leads to an increase in demand for the £. The demand curve shifts up and to the right from D to D₁ causing **excess demand** at the exchange rate £1 = $1.66. The price of £s in terms of $s increases to remove the excess demand. The price of the £ continues to rise until the quantity of £s demanded = the quantity of £s supplied. The new equilibrium exchange rate is £1 = $2. The new equilibrium quantity is £45 billion.

The increase in demand for the £ causes the £ to appreciate in value against the dollar from £1 = $1.66 to £1 = $2.00 and equilibrium quantity increases from £41.7 billion to £45 billion.

Subject vocabulary

excess demand occurs when quantity demanded is greater than quantity supplied

Calculate the change in the exchange rate from a percentage change in price (HL)

A change in a country's exchange rate leads to a change in the price of imports and a change in the price of exports. When a country's exchange rate appreciates, the price of its imports falls and the price of its exports increases. When a country's exchange rate depreciates, the price of its imports increases and the price of its exports falls.

If the price of the £ rises by 5% then the price of the UK's exported goods increases by 5%. Therefore if the price of the UK's exports rises by 5% it can be assumed that the £ has appreciated by 5%. If the price of UK exports falls by 5% it can be assumed that the £ has depreciated by 5%. If the price of imports falls by 5% then it can be assumed that the £ has appreciated by 5%. If the price of imported goods into the UK increases by 5% it can be assumed that the £ has depreciated by 5%.

The price of the euro in terms of Australian dollars (AUD) is 1 euro = 1.5 AUD. Italy exports olive oil to Australia. The price per unit is 10 euro. Australian buyers of imported olive oil pay 15 AUD per unit (1.5 × 10 = 15). The price per unit of the imported olive oil then increases by 10%.

Calculate 10% of 15 AUD

(15/100) × 10 = 0.15 × 10 = 1.5. The price increases by 1.5 AUD. 1.5 AUD + 15 AUD = 16.5 AUD. The price of olive oil per unit rises from 15 AUD to 16.5 AUD.

The price paid by domestic buyers in Italy remains at 10 euro. The price of exported olive oil from Italy into Australia has increased by 10% therefore it can be assumed that that the euro has appreciated against AUD by 10%.

Calculate the percentage change in the value of the euro – a step-by-step guide

Trouble shooter

Before the price increase the price per unit of olive oil in Italy was 10 euros and the price in Australia was 15 AUD.

The formula to calculate the exchange rate for euros against AUD using these prices is:

Price of the good in AUD/price of the good in euros = the price of euros in terms of AUD

15 AUD/10 euro = 1.5. The exchange rate is 1 euro = 1.5 AUD.

After the 10% increase in price, Australian buyers of imported olive oil pay 16.5 AUD.

Price of the good in AUD/price of the good in euros = the price of euros in terms of AUD.

16.5 AUD/10 euro =1.65.

The exchange rate is 1 euro = 1.65 AUD.

The price of the euro in terms of the AUD has increased from 1 euro = 1.5 AUD to 1 euro = 1.65 AUD.

The formula used to calculate the percentage increase in the value of the euro is

(The new exchange rate – the original exchange rate) × 100

(1.65 AUD – 1.5 AUD) × 100 = **0.15** × 100 = **15** = 10%

The value of the euro has appreciated by 10%.

It now costs 10% more to buy the same quantity of euros. The value of AUD has depreciated by 10%.

Test your understanding of this unit by answering the following questions

- The price of Yen in terms of euros is 1 Yen = 0.0070 euro. Calculate the price of euros in terms of Yen.
- The price of a good produced in France is €80. How much is this good in Yen?
- The exchange rate changes from US$1= €0.70 to US$1 = €0.80. Calculate the percentage change in the value of the US$ against the euro. Explain the change in price in euros of a good that is exported from the US to Spain priced at $1,500.
- Given the linear functions Qd = 50 – 10p and Qs = 25 +15p, calculate the exchange rate for British pounds in terms of US dollars. The value of a in the demand function Qd = a – bP increases by 5. Calculate the new exchange rate.

Learning Outcomes

- Describe a fixed exchange rate system involving commitment to a single fixed rate.

- Distinguish between a devaluation of a currency and a revaluation of a currency.

- Explain, using a diagram, how a fixed exchange rate is maintained.

- Explain how a managed exchange rate operates, with reference to the fact that there is a periodic government intervention to influence the value of an exchange rate.

- Examine the possible consequences of overvalued and undervalued currencies.

- Compare and contrast a fixed exchange rate system with a floating exchange rate system, with reference to factors including the degree of certainty for stakeholders, ease of adjustment, the role of international reserves in the form of foreign currencies, and flexibility offered to policy makers.

Describe a fixed exchange rate system

A fixed exchange rate is an exchange rate that is set by the government and maintained by the central bank so that the value of the currency in terms of another currency does not change – it is fixed.

Explain how a fixed exchange rate is maintained

A floating exchange rate is determined by the demand and supply of a currency. A change in the demand for the currency and the supply of the currency leads to a change in the **exchange rate**.

Model sentence: When changes in the forces of demand and supply lead to a change in the exchange rate, the central bank must intervene in the foreign exchange market in order to keep the exchange rate at its fixed rate.

In this example, the Australian government wants to fix the price of the Australian dollar (AUD) against the euro at 1 AUD = 0.60 euros. When the equilibrium exchange rate determined by the demand and supply of the currency is 1 AUD = 0.60 euros the central bank does not have to intervene. However, if there is a fall in demand for the AUD, for example because the demand for Australian exports to Europe falls, the exchange rate will fall. In Figure 75.1 the demand curve shifts down and to the left from D to D_1. Without government intervention there would be **excess supply** of AUD at the fixed exchange rate. To remove the excess the exchange rate falls from 1 AUD = 0.60 euros to 1 AUD = 0.50 euro. In order to maintain the fixed rate of 1 AUD = 0.60 euros the Australian central bank must increase the demand for the AUD, thereby shifting the **demand curve** up and to the right from D_1 back to D.

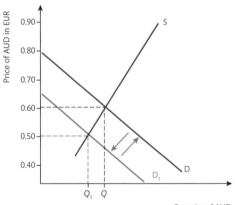

Figure 75.1

In this example, there is an increase in demand for Australian exports. The demand for its currency increases leading to a shift up and to the right of the demand curve from D to D_1 as shown in Figure 75.2. There would be **excess demand** for the AUD and the exchange rate would rise to 1 AUD = 0.70 euros if the Australian central bank does not intervene. To maintain the fixed exchange rate the central bank must increase the supply of AUD thereby removing the excess demand. The **supply curve** shifts down and to the right from S to S_1 and the exchange rate returns to the fixed rate 1 AUD = 0.60 euros.

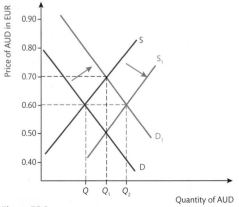

Figure 75.2

Subject vocabulary

foreign reserves the amount of foreign currency and gold that is held by the central bank of a country

interest rate the percentage amount charged by a lender for money borrowed

international trade the cross-border exchange of goods and services

quota a physical limit placed on the number of goods that can be traded or produced

tariffs a tax placed on imported goods and services

foreign direct investment cross-border investment, usually by firms, that involves the acquisition of assets in a foreign country. FDI can be the purchase of a minimum of 10% of the shares of a foreign company but also includes the creation of productive capacity

investment the addition to capital stock

How do governments and central banks change the demand for, and supply of, its currency?

Foreign reserves, usually US dollars and euros, are currencies held by central banks. When the demand for AUD falls the Australian central bank can use its reserves of euros to buy Australian dollars thereby increasing demand for the currency. The demand curve shifts back up and to the right from D_1 to D returning its value to the fixed exchange rate as shown in Figure 75.1 (on page 223). When demand for AUD increases leading to excess demand at the fixed exchange rate, the Australian central bank can sell its own currency on the foreign exchange market thereby increasing its supply and removing the excess demand. The supply curve shifts down and to the right from S to S_1 as shown in Figure 75.2 (on page 223) and the exchange rate returns to its fixed rate.

If there is excess supply of AUD at the fixed exchange, the central bank can increase **interest rates** thereby increasing the returns on money saved in Australian banks. In order to deposit money in Australian banks foreign savers exchange their currencies for AUD, thereby increasing demand for the AUD and removing the excess supply. The demand curve shifts up and to the right from D to D_1 and the exchange rate returns to the fixed rate 1 AUD = 0.60 euros.

When demand increases for the AUD the central bank can lower interest rates to push the value of the currency back down. Some savers will remove their deposits of AUD from Australian banks in order to earn higher returns in another country's bank. The depositors sell AUD and buy another currency thereby increasing the supply of AUD. The supply curve shifts down and to the right from S to S_1, as shown in Figure 75.2 (on page 223), thereby maintaining the exchange rate at 1 AUD = 0.60 euros.

If through **international trade** there is pressure pushing the value of the currency down from its fixed rate the government can reduce the number of imports to reduce the supply of its currency. Limiting imports leads to a fall in the supply of its currency used to buy the imported goods thereby putting upward pressure on the value of the currency. To achieve this objective the government raises barriers to trade by the use of **quotas** and **tariffs**. If there is downward pressure on a currency the government can encourage **foreign direct investment**, for example by reducing the amount of tax on company profits. This increases demand for its currency thereby pushing its value up.

Distinguish between appreciation and revaluation, and between depreciation and devaluation

The appreciation of a currency occurs when the value of the currency increases due to changes in the demand for, and supply of, a currency under a floating exchange rate system. Revaluation is when the rate at which a currency is fixed is raised.

The depreciation of a currency occurs when the value of the currency falls due to changes in the demand for, and supply of, a currency under a floating exchange rate system. Devaluation is when the rate at which a currency is fixed is reduced.

Subject vocabulary

continued from page 225

trade barriers restrictions put in place by government on international trade in order to protect domestic jobs and industries. Examples include subsidies and tariffs.

contractionary fiscal policy policy involving the reduction of government spending and/or the increase of taxation

current account a record of the amount of money flowing out of a country and into the country from the rest of the world from the trade in goods and services, investment income, and transfers in a given period of time

Explain how a managed exchange rate operates

Most countries intervene at some point in response to extreme pressure on their exchange rates even if they use the floating exchange rate system. Most countries do not have a fixed exchange rate but manage their currencies so that the value does not rise above or fall below acceptable levels. If the central bank believes that the value of its currency might be moving beyond the upper or lower values, the government intervenes by selling or buying reserve currencies and/or by changing interest rates. This affects the value of its currency as previously explained. A government does not want the value of its currency to rise or fall too much because it affects the price of imports and exports leading to business uncertainty. For example, if export prices go up and down it is difficult for exporting firms to estimate demand for their goods. This can lead to a fall in **investment**.

Compare and contrast a fixed exchange rate system with a floating exchange rate system

To answer this it is necessary to examine the advantages and disadvantages of both systems.

Discuss the advantages of a fixed exchange rate system

A fixed exchange rate system leads to greater business certainty than under a floating exchange rate. Importers and exporters are more certain of the prices of imports and exports. For example, wholesalers buying consumer goods from foreign producers know that the price they pay is not going to be affected by changes in the exchange rate and importers of **raw materials** can be more certain of their future costs of production. Business investment is less risky because the quantity of their goods demanded will not change when the exchange rate changes.

Model sentence: A fixed exchange rate does not vary. The price of exports is not affected by exchange rate changes, therefore demand for them is more stable making investment less risky.

If speculators (traders in currencies) believe that the fixed rate is appropriate a fixed rate should reduce speculation in the foreign exchange market. Stability of an exchange rate is hard to achieve under a floating system due to speculation. If speculators believe the central bank is determined to maintain a fixed rate, it reduces the opportunities to gain from the buying and selling of currencies.

Inflation increases the price of exports leading to a fall in international price competitiveness. Under a fixed exchange rate system, the exchange rate cannot depreciate to reduce the price of exports, therefore the government and the central bank must follow **fiscal policies** and **monetary policies** that keep inflation under control in order to maintain the competitiveness of the country's exports. If the government is successful in controlling inflation the central bank will be able to set lower interest rates, which will help to increase investment and thereby increase **productivity**.

Discuss the disadvantages of a fixed exchange rate system and the consequences of overvalued and undervalued currencies

In order to ensure that all **stakeholders** in the economy are confident that the fixed rate will be maintained the central bank must be prepared to act when market forces push the value of the currency up or down. The main way in which a central bank affects the value of its currency is by changing interest rates. For example, if the demand for the currency falls the exchange rate will fall unless the government increases demand for the currency by increasing interest rates.

Model sentence: If interest rates are set to affect the exchange rate they cannot at the same time be used to achieve other macroeconomic objectives such as economic growth and low unemployment.

A high interest rate set to attract foreign deposits at a time of recession will lead to a deeper and longer **recession** and higher levels of unemployment.

If the exchange rate is set at the wrong level, too high for example, exporters may not be able to compete on price leading to a fall in **aggregate demand**. And the demand for imports would be high leading to a growing **current account deficit**. If the exchange rate is set too low it could lead to **imported inflation**. If a country finds itself having to defend the exchange rate continuously by selling its **foreign reserves** and buying its own currency, eventually the reserves will begin to run out. If speculators believe that the central bank will not be able to continue defending the currency and that the government will eventually devalue its currency they will sell the currency increasing its supply and putting further downward pressure on its value.

Some countries use a low exchange rate as a form of **protectionism**. A low exchange rate lowers the price of exports increasing their consumption. This can lead to international arguments over trade and other countries can respond to a country that is deliberately keeping its exchange rate low by raising **trade barriers**.

Discuss the advantages of a floating exchange rate system

Interest rates do not have to be used to affect the exchange rate, therefore they can be used to achieve domestic macroeconomic objectives. A government does not have to depend on fiscal policy to achieve macroeconomic objectives. Controlling inflation, for example, is likely to be more successful when the government can increase interest rates along with **contractionary fiscal policies**. Governments do not need to hold large quantities of foreign reserves to defend the currency so, for example, the money can be used by the government for investment purposes.

A floating exchange rate in theory should self-adjust so as to keep the **current account** in balance. If the income spent on imports is greater than the income spent on exports the country has a current account deficit. With fewer exports being bought the demand for the currency is low and with more imports being bought the

Subject vocabulary

raw material the basic material from which a good is made

inflation an increase in the general level of prices of goods/services in an economy over a given time period, usually a year

fiscal policy government policy designed to achieve macroeconomic objectives through government expenditure and taxation

monetary policy the control of the supply of money by the central bank to affect the economy (e.g. changing interest rates)

productivity the quantity of output per unit of input

stakeholders people or groups who have an interest in, or are affected by, the activities of organisations, particularly businesses

economic growth an increase in real GDP

unemployment occurs when there are people actively looking for work at the equilibrium wage rate but are not able to find work

recession two consecutive quarters of negative economic growth

aggregate demand the total demand for goods and services in the economy at a given price level in a given period of time

current account deficit occurs when the amount of money flowing out of a country from the trade in goods and services, investment income, and transfers is greater than the amount flowing in

imported inflation inflation caused by an increase in the price of imported goods. For example as the price of imported raw materials increase it leads to an increase in the price of domestically produced goods.

foreign reserves the amount of foreign currency and gold that is held by the central bank of a country

protectionism government policies, including tariffs, quotas, and subsidies, that restrict the extent of international trade and which are implemented in order to protect domestic industries from cheaper imports

continued on page 224

forces of demand and supply changes in the determinants of demand and supply in a market that affect the market price and the allocation of resources

investment the addition to capital stock

resources the inputs into the production process, the factors of production

substitute a good that can be used in place of another good

price inelastic the percentage change in quantity demanded/supplied < the percentage change in price

cost-push inflation inflation caused by an increase in the costs of production, resulting in a decrease in aggregate supply

supply of the currency is high. The **forces of demand and supply** push down the value of the currency. As the currency depreciates exports become relatively cheaper and imports become relatively more expensive. Income spent on exports rises and income spent on imports falls leading to a reduction in the current account deficit.

A current account surplus is when income spent on exports is greater than income spent on imports. The demand for the currency is greater than the supply. The excess demand pushes up the exchange rate causing the price of exports to rise and the price of imports to fall. Income spent on export falls and income spent on imports increases leading to a fall in the current account surplus.

Model sentence: As the exchange rate rises the price of exports increases and the price of imports falls, leading to a fall in the quantity of exports demanded and an increase in the quantity of imports demanded.

Model sentence: As the exchange rate falls the price of exports falls and the price of imports rises, leading to an increase in the quantity of exports demanded and a fall in the quantity of imports demanded.

Discuss the disadvantages of a floating exchange rate system

Floating exchange rates can lead to business uncertainty. When the exchange rate changes the price of imports and exports changes. Businesses importing raw materials are unsure what their costs will be in the future. Demand for exports is in part determined by the exchange rate because changes in the exchange rate affect price. Uncertainty over future levels of demand and uncertainty over costs lead to an increase in the risk of **investment** and therefore a fall in investment. When prices are changing continuously it is difficult to work out potential returns on investment.

Model sentence: As the floating exchange rate goes up and down it leads to variable export prices and therefore variable demand for exports. This makes it difficult for exporters to plan future levels of production and makes investment more risky.

A country that has few or no **resources** must import them leading to a very high supply of its currency. The price of imported resources is high but firms have little choice but to carry on importing them as there are no domestic **substitutes** making demand for imports **price inelastic**. The exchange rate does not self-adjust because demand for imports and therefore supply of the currency remains high. The exchange rate remains low leading to higher business costs that can cause **cost-push inflation** making the goods less price competitive.

High inflation reduces a country's international price competitiveness leading to a fall in demand for its exports. The relative price of imports is lower thereby increasing demand for imports. Low demand for the currency due to low demand for exports and high supply of the currency due to high demand for imports lead to a low exchange rate. High demand for imports and low demand for exports will worsen the country's current account deficit. The exchange rate may self-adjust but this can take time.

A floating exchange rate encourages **speculation**. Speculation is arguably a waste of resources and can weaken an economy by reducing confidence in a currency even when the economy is doing well. Speculation can cause a sudden selling of a currency, increasing the supply of the currency and pushing the exchange rate down.

Test your understanding of this unit by answering the following questions

- Distinguish between a fixed exchange rate system and a floating exchange rate system.
- Explain how a fixed exchange rate is maintained.
- Discuss the advantages and disadvantages of a fixed exchange rate system and a floating exchange rate system.

3.3 The balance of payments

Learning Outcomes

- Outline the role of the balance of payments.
- Distinguish between debit items and credit items in the balance of payments.
- Explain the four components of the current account, specifically the balance of trade in goods and the balance of trade in services, income, and current transfers.
- Distinguish between a current account deficit and a current account surplus.
- Explain the two components of the capital account, specifically capital transfers and transaction in non-produced, non-financial assets.

- Explain the three main components of the financial account, specifically, direct investment, portfolio investment, and reserve assets.
- Explain that the current account balance is equal to the sum of the capital account and financial account balances.
- Examine how the current account and the financial account are interdependent.
- Calculate elements of the balance of payments from a set of data. (HL)

What is the balance of payments account?

It is a record of the financial transactions that occur between a country and the rest of the world. There are three separate accounts in the balance of payment account: The current account, the capital account, and the financial account.

Explain the components of the current account

The current account on the balance of payments is divided into four **components**. Trade in goods, trade in services, flows of income, and current transfers.

Trade in goods

The trade in goods is also called the trade in visibles (goods can be seen). The trade in services is also called the trade in invisibles (services cannot be seen).

Expenditure on goods exported from a country to other countries and expenditure on imported goods from other countries in to the country is recorded in the current account. Expenditure on all goods is recorded, including expenditure on consumer goods, **capital** goods, and **raw materials**.

Expenditure on imported goods flows out of the country from the domestic buyers in the country to foreign producers in other countries. Expenditure on imported goods is a leakage from the **circular flow of income** which reduces the country's **aggregate demand**. Expenditure on imported goods is recorded as a debit in the current account and is given a minus sign (–).

Expenditure on exported goods flows into the country from foreign buyers in other countries to domestic producers in the country. Expenditure on exported goods is an injection into the circular flow of income which increases the country's aggregate demand. Expenditure on exported goods is recorded as a credit in the current account and is given a plus sign (+).

The difference between expenditure on exported goods and expenditure on imported goods (measured in the country's currency) is called the balance of trade in goods.

Model sentence: A trade surplus in goods occurs when expenditure on exported goods is greater than expenditure on imported goods. A trade surplus in goods is a positive balance.

Model sentence: A trade deficit in goods occurs when expenditure on imported goods is greater than expenditure on exported goods. A trade deficit in goods is a negative balance.

Trade in services

Expenditure on services exported from a country to other countries, and expenditure on imported services from other countries in to the country, is recorded in the current account. Services include tourism, education, health services, banking, insurance, and transport services.

Expenditure on imported services flows out of the country from the domestic buyers in the country to foreign producers in other countries. Expenditure on imported services is a leakage from the circular flow of income

Synonyms

components .... parts

Subject vocabulary

capital (goods) manufactured goods that are used in the production of other goods

raw materials the basic material from which a good is made

circular flow of income an economic model that shows the flow of money between households and firms and, in more complex versions, the flows of money into and out of the financial sector, government sector, and the international sector

aggregate demand the total demand for goods and services in the economy at a given price level in a given period of time

which reduces the country's aggregate demand. Expenditure on imported services is recorded as a debit in the current account and is given a minus sign (–).

Expenditure on exported services flows into the country from foreign buyers in other countries to domestic producers in the country. Expenditure on exported services is an injection into the circular flow of income, which increases the country's aggregate demand. Expenditure on exported services is recorded as a credit in the current account and is given a plus sign (+).

The difference between expenditure on exported services and expenditure on imported services (measured in the country's currency) is called the balance of trade in services. A trade surplus in services occurs when expenditure on exported services is greater than expenditure on imported services. A trade surplus in services is a positive balance. A trade deficit in services occurs when expenditure on imported services is greater than expenditure on exported services. A trade deficit in services is a negative balance.

Model sentence: The balance of trade is the difference between expenditure on exported goods and services and expenditure on imported goods and services. This is called net exports (X – M).

Flows of income

Interest is earned on deposits in banks and on **government bonds**, **dividend payments** are earned on shares and rent is earned on property. Interest, dividends, and rent are types of income. Citizens and institutions of one country own assets in other countries. For example, some Americans have saving accounts in UK banks, own UK government bonds, shares in UK companies, and property in the UK. The income earned on these assets flows out of the UK and into the US. American workers working in the UK may send some of their wages back to the US. Wage is a type of income. Income flows out of the UK and into the US. In this example income flows out of the UK and is therefore recorded in the current account as a debit in the UK's current account and given a minus sign. The income flows into the US and is therefore recorded as a credit in the current account of the US and given a plus sign.

Model sentence: The balance of income is the difference between the amount of income flowing into a country and the amount of income flowing out. This is called net income (NY).

Current transfers

A transfer is a payment made for which no good or service is exchanged. For example a government of one country gives aid to the government of another country. Individuals also transfer money from one country to groups in another country for charitable purposes or to support certain causes. Transfers flowing out of a country are recorded in that country's current account as debits and given a minus sign. Transfers flowing in to a country record the transfers in their current account as credits and are given a plus sign.

Model sentence: The balance of current transfers is the difference between the current transfers flowing into a country and current transfers flowing out. This is called net current transfers (NCT).

Distinguish between a current account deficit and a current account surplus

The current account is the sum of the balance of trade + the balance of income + the balance of current transfers. It can be written as CA = (X – M) + NY + NCT. A country has a current account deficit when the amount of money flowing out of the country to other countries is greater than the money flowing into the country from other countries. There is a deficit on the current account when the sum of the debits is greater than the sum of the credits. This occurs when the sum of (X – M) + NY + NCT is negative. A country has a current account surplus when the amount of money flowing into the country from other countries is greater than the amount of money flowing out of the country to other countries. The sum of the credits is greater than the sum of the debits. This occurs when the sum of (X – M) + NY + NCT is positive.

Explain the two components of the capital account

The capital account is in two parts: capital transfers and exchanges of non-produced, non-financial assets.

What are capital transfers?

Some countries with relatively high **GDP**s provide finance to other countries that are relatively poor for the construction of fixed assets such as schools, hospitals, and roads. Countries may also give other countries

interest the price paid for the use of borrowed money/ the money earned from bank deposits

government bonds issued by the government to investors in exchange for lending it money. The investor is entitled to interest payments on the loan as well as repayment of the loan when the bond matures.

dividend payments payments made by companies to shareholders from the after-tax profits

GDP gross domestic product is the monetary value of all the finished goods and services produced within a country in a given period of time, usually measured over a year

capital goods such as computers and medical equipment. There is no payment made for these capital transfers. The country that receives money from another country records it in the capital account as a credit and it is given a plus sign because it is money flowing into the country. The country that gives the money records it in the capital account as a debit and it is given a minus sign because it is money flowing out of the country.

Countries loan money to other countries. There is an agreement that the loans are to be paid back. Sometimes the lender writes off the debt so that the borrower does not have to pay it back. This is called debt forgiveness. The country that is owed the money records the amount written off in the capital account as a debit and it is given a minus sign. The country that owes the money that is written off records the amount in the capital account as a credit and it is given a plus sign.

What are exchanges of non-produced, non-financial assets?

These assets include **patents**, **copyrights**, **trademarks**, the rights to **natural resources**, **acquisition** of **brands**, and **franchises**. Brands, for example are bought and sold internationally. When a company in one country buys a brand from a company in another country the transaction is recorded in the capital account. China has bought natural resources, for example forests with water rights from Japan and the rights to minerals, copper, and uranium in Africa. These exchanges are recorded as a debit in the capital account of China and a credit in the capital account of those countries selling the assets.

The purchase of the right to extract natural resources from the land of another country is different from the purchase of raw materials from another country. Raw materials are exported and imported and the payment for them is recorded as a debit in the current account of the importing country and as a credit in the current account of the exporting country.

Explain the three main components of the financial account: direct investment, portfolio investment, and reserve assets

The exchange between a country and other countries of **financial assets** and **real assets** is recorded in the financial account. Domestic owners of these assets can sell them to foreign buyers. Real assets include land and commercial property such as office buildings and factories. Financial assets include company shares and government bonds. China has bought a large proportion of US government bonds. The money flows from China to the US and is recorded in the financial account of China as a debit and a credit in the financial account of the US. Shares in companies are traded internationally. When shares in a company are bought or sold by a foreigner the transaction is recorded in the financial account.

What is direct investment?

When an investor buys a relatively large share of a foreign firm (at least 10% of the shares of the company) it is called foreign direct investment (FDI) and is classified as a direct investment.

The purchase of company shares in the domestic country by foreign investors is an example of direct investment. Direct investment also occurs when domestic investors buy shares and government bonds from foreign sellers. The way in which the transactions are recorded in the financial account is explained below.

When foreigners buy shares in a domestic firm money flows into the domestic economy and this is recorded as a credit in the financial account and is given a plus sign. When foreigners sell shares in a domestic firm to domestic buyers, money flows out from the domestic economy. This transaction is recorded in the financial account as a debit and is given a minus sign.

When **shareholders** in the domestic economy sell their shares in foreign firms to foreign buyers, money flows into the economy and is therefore recorded as a credit in the financial account and is given a plus sign. When domestic investors buy shares in foreign firms the money flows out from the domestic economy and the amount is recorded as a debit in the financial account and is given a minus sign.

What is portfolio investment?

This is investment in shares of foreign firms, foreign government bonds, and foreign company bonds by small investors. These are foreign financial assets. When relatively small domestic investors buy foreign financial assets money flows out from the domestic economy, therefore it is recorded as a debit in the financial account. When domestic investors sell financial assets the money flows into the domestic economy so it is recorded as a credit.

What are reserve assets?

Central banks hold foreign currencies, foreign government bonds and gold. These reserve assets are recorded in the reserve account of the financial account. The reserve assets are increased or reduced by the central banks to make sure the balance of payments always equals 0.

Model sentence: When there is an overall combined surplus on all of the accounts in a given year, that is the amount of money from international transactions flowing into the economy is greater than the money flowing out (credits > debits) the assets held in the reserve account increase by the difference.

Model sentence: When there is a combined deficit on all the accounts, that is the amount of money flowing out of the economy is greater than the amount flowing in (debits > credit) the assets held in the reserve account decrease by the difference.

Given the information above, it is true that the sum of all the accounts plus the change in reserve assets equals zero. A current account deficit is offset by an overall surplus in the capital and financial accounts. A current account surplus is offset by an overall deficit in the capital and financial accounts.

Calculate elements of the balance of payments from a set of data (HL)

Balance of payments figures for country X	Column1
Category	US $ billions
Imports of goods and services	–650
Exports of goods and services	+450
Net income	–90
Net current transfers	+60
Net capital transfers	+80
Net exchanges of non-produced, non financial assets	–35
Net direct investments	+30
Net portfolio investments	–70
Reserve assets	

How to calculate the current account balance

The current account has four components: the trade in goods and services, the flow of income, and current transfers.

Net exports = export revenue – import expenditure = $450 billion – $650 billion = –$200 billion.

Current account balance = net exports + net income + net current transfers: –200 –90 + 60 = –230.

The current account deficit = $230 billion (on the current account the money flowing out of the country is greater than the money flowing in by $230 billion).

How to calculate the capital account balance

The capital account has two components: capital transfers and exchanges of non-produced, non-financial assets.

Net capital transfers + net exchanges of non-produced, non-financial assets = 80 – 35 = $45 billion.

The capital account surplus = $45 billion.

How to calculate the financial account balance

The financial account has three components: direct investments, portfolio investments, and the reserve account which is used to eliminate a surplus or deficit on the balance of payments.

Net direct investments + net portfolio investments = 30 – 70 = –$40 billion.

The balance of payments = the current account balance + the capital account balance + the financial account balance + the reserve account.

The balance of payments = –230 + 45 – 40 = –$225 billion.

There is a deficit of $225 billion therefore the currency reserves held by the central bank falls by $225 in order to eliminate the deficit so that the balance of payments = 0: –230 + 45 – 40 + 225 = $0.

Test your understanding of this unit by answering the following questions

- Explain how a deficit on the balance of payment is eliminated.
- Describe the components of the current account.
- Distinguish between a current account deficit and a current account surplus.

Learning Outcomes

- Explain why a deficit in the current account of the balance of payments may result in downward pressure on the exchange rate of the currency.

- Explain why a surplus in the current account of the balance of payments may result in upward pressure on the exchange rate of the currency.

- Discuss the **implications** of a persistent current account deficit, referring to factors including foreign ownership of domestic assets, exchange rates, interest rates, indebtedness, international credit ratings, and demand management (HL).

- Discuss the possible consequences of a rising current account surplus, including lower domestic consumption and investment, as well as the appreciation of the domestic currency, and reduced export competitiveness.

- Explain the methods that a government can use to correct a persistent current account deficit, including expenditure switching policies, expenditure reducing policies, and supply-side policies, to increase competitiveness (HL).

- Evaluate the effectiveness of the policies to correct a persistent current account deficit (HL).

- State the Marshall-Lerner condition and apply it to explain the effects of depreciation/devaluation.

- Explain the J-curve effect, with reference to the Marshall-Lerner condition (HL).

Explain the effect of a current account deficit on the exchange rate

See pages 214–17 for a detailed explanation of how the exchange rate is determined in a floating exchange rate system.

The current account measures the balance of trade in goods and services and flows of income between a country and the rest of the world. A trade deficit can cause an overall current account deficit and a trade surplus can cause an overall current account surplus.

Model sentence: A balance of trade deficit occurs when import expenditure is greater than export revenue. In other words net exports (X – M) is negative.

The **exchange rate** of a currency is determined by the forces of demand for, and supply of, a currency. International trade makes an important contribution to the demand for, and supply of, a currency.

When domestic buyers in the US buy goods from foreign producers in the Eurozone the buyers must exchange US dollars for euros in order to pay the producers in euros. This leads to an increase in the supply of US dollars on the **foreign exchange market** and an increase in demand for euros. When domestic buyers in the Eurozone import goods from the US it leads to an increase in supply of euros and an increase in demand for the US dollar. If the US runs a current account deficit with the Eurozone it means that the value of imports from the Eurozone is greater than the value of its **exports** to the Eurozone. This means that the supply of dollars onto the foreign exchange markets is greater than the demand for dollars. As the exchange rate falls, the price of imports rises but the price of exports falls. The quantity of exports demanded rises therefore a low exchange rate leads to an increase in employment in exporting industries.

Synonyms

implications .... effects/outcomes

Subject vocabulary

devaluation the official lowering of the value of a country's currency in a fixed exchange rate system

net exports export revenue minus import expenditure

exchange rate the price of a country's currency in terms of another currency

foreign exchange market a decentralized global market for the buying and selling of currencies

exports goods produced in one country that are sold into another country

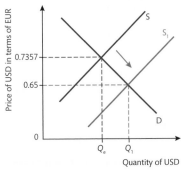

In Figure 77.1 at the equilibrium exchange rate $1 = 0.7357 euro the quantity of US dollars demanded = the quantity of US dollars supplied at Q_e. If the US current account deficit increases the supply of US dollars will put downward pressure on the exchange rate. There is now excess supply of US dollars and the price of the dollar against the euro must fall to eliminate the excess supply. The exchange rate falls from $1 = 0.7357 euros to $1 = 0.65 euros and the quantity of US dollars traded increase from Q_e to Q_1.

Figure 77.1

Explain the effect of a current account surplus on the exchange rate

Model sentence: A balance of trade surplus occurs when expenditure on export revenue is greater than import expenditure. In other words net exports (X – M) is positive.

When a country's export revenue is greater than its import expenditure, the demand for its currency is greater than the supply of its currency. There is an upward pressure on the price of the currency leading to an increase in the exchange rate. As the exchange rate increases, the price of imports falls but the price of exports rises. The quantity of imports demanded increases and the quantity of exports demanded falls. Therefore a high exchange rate can lead to unemployment in exporting industries.

How do changes in the exchange rate correct the current account imbalance?

As explained above, a current account surplus leads to an increase in the exchange rate, which in turn leads to an increase in import expenditure and a fall in export revenue. As import expenditure increases and export revenue falls the current account surplus is reduced. A current account deficit leads to a fall in the exchange rate, which in turn leads to a fall in import expenditure and an increase in export revenue. As import expenditure falls and export revenue increases the current account deficit is reduced.

Discuss the consequences of a current account surplus (HL)

When the exchange rate increases the price of imported consumer goods and imported raw materials falls. The purchasing power of households' income increases. **Consumer surplus** increases lead to an increase in consumer welfare. Consumers are able to satisfy more wants with their **nominal income**. Costs of production also fall for firms that import raw materials, leading to an increase in supply. Firms' average costs fall making the firms more price competitive.

When the exchange rate increases the price of exports increases, leading to a fall in international price competitiveness and a fall in the quantity of exports demanded. Therefore a high exchange rate can lead to high **demand-deficient unemployment** in exporting industries. Exports are also a component of **aggregate demand** and an injection into the **circular flow of income**. So a high exchange rate can have a negative effect on the economy as a whole.

A country has a very high current account surplus when the value of its exports is a lot greater than the value of imports. Some countries use lots of their **resources** to produce goods that are exported and consumed by foreigners and fewer resources are used to produce goods for domestic households to consume. Also, a country that has a high current account surplus might import fewer goods for domestic consumption. Therefore, domestic consumption of goods might be relatively low when the country has a very high current account surplus. The government must offset the surplus on the current account by purchasing reserve assets.

Discuss the consequenses of a persistent current account deficit (HL)

Set out below is a detailed discussion of the various effects of a persistent current account deficit.

What is the effect of a persistent current account deficit on the exchange rate?

When a country has a **persistent** current account deficit, the expenditure on imports is continuously greater than the revenue from exports. Supply of its currency in the forex market is persistenly greater than the demand for its currency, therefore there is continuous downward pressure on the **exchange rate**. There is a possibility that the balance on the current account self-adjusts because as the exchange rate falls the price of imports increases and the price of exports falls leading to an increase in demand for exports and a fall in demand for imports causing an improvement in the current account balance.

However, if demand for imports is **price inelastic** the quantity of imports demanded will fall when the exchange rate falls but the expenditure on them will increase, thereby possibly worsening the deficit (see the Marshall-Lerner condition discussed in detail on pages 236–37).

A fall in exchange rate increases the price of imports leading to **imported inflation**. The price of imported consumer goods increases and the price of **raw materials** increases leading to **cost-push inflation**.

Model sentence: A persistently low exchange rate caused by a current account deficit leads to higher import prices causing an increase in the rate of inflation.

What is the effect of a persistent current account deficit on interest rates?

When a country has a current account deficit it must make up for this deficit by having a surplus on the capital account and financial account. In order to increase flows of money into the country the Central Bank may raise interest rates. This acts as an incentive for foreigners to deposit money in the country's banks, therefore the flow of money into the country increases, creating a surplus to offset the current account deficit. The money that flows in and out of countries' financial markets as investors try to earn the highest rate of interest is called hot money.

However, the need for high interest rates means the central bank cannot lower interest rates as part of an **expansionary monetary policy**. A **recession** therefore, might be deeper and longer because high interest rates are needed to attract hot money in order to offset the current account deficit. Government is therefore forced to use **fiscal policy** to increase aggregate demand.

Model sentence: If high interest rates are needed to attract 'hot money' then the central bank is unable to reduce interest rates to encourage economic growth.

What is the effect of a persistent current account deficit on the interest paid on government bonds?

When a country has a current account deficit it must make up for this deficit by having a surplus on the capital account and financial account. Direct investment and portfolio investments are recorded in the financial account. This investment includes foreigners buying the country's **government bonds**. In order to increase demand for the bonds, and thereby increase demand for the currency of the country, the interest rate paid on the bonds must rise. The increase in the flow of money coming into the country will help to offset the deficit on the current account.

However, high interest rates increase the cost of borrowing, thereby reducing the demand for loans for **investment** and reducing the demand for household loans for the purchase of consumer goods, leading to a fall in aggregate demand and a lower rate of **productivity**. Also, high rates of interest paid on government bonds crowds out **private sector** investment because less investment funds are available for the private sector to borrow.

Model sentence: Low levels of investment leads to a fall in international competitiveness causing an increase in the current account deficit as the demand for the country's exports falls.

What is the effect of a persistent current account deficit on foreign ownership of domestic financial and real assets?

As explained above when a country has a current account deficit it must make up for this deficit by having a surplus on the capital account and financial account. The exchange between a country and other countries, of **financial assets** and **real assets**, is recorded in the financial account. A country can offset the current account deficit from the sale of domestic assets to foreigners. Money flows into the country from abroad, increasing the demand for the country's currency. Ownership of domestic assets is transferred to foreigners. However, if foreign owners of a country's assets believe that they will fall in value in the future they will sell them, thereby increasing the supply of the currency and causing the exchange rate to fall.

A surplus on the capital account may not be large enough to offset the current account deficit. In this situation the central bank runs down **foreign currency reserves** in order to increase the capital account and thereby offset the deficit. However, if the deficit is persistent the reserves at some point in the future will run out.

What is the effect of a persistent current account deficit on indebtedness?

When a country has a persistent deficit on the current account the financial account has to have a persistent surplus to offset the deficit. Financial assets include government bonds. A country can attract flows of money into the country by selling government bonds to foreign countries. This helps to offset the current account deficit, but at the same time it increases the country's **national debt**. The debt must be paid back at some time in the future along with the interest payments.

Continuously borrowing to offset a persistent current account deficit leads to a persistent growth in the national debt and the interest paid on the debt. Interest payments on the debt are paid by the taxpayers. **Tax revenue** is used by the government to pay the ever-growing interest. The national debt of the UK at the end of 2013 was about £1,300 billion. The interest payment on the debt was about £50 billion. This money flows out of the UK abroad, thereby reducing potential levels of aggregate demand as the tax revenue cannot be spent on goods and services produced in the UK. As the debt grows the government may have to increase taxes in order to pay the interest. This reduces households' **disposable income**, thereby reducing aggregate demand and restricting **economic growth**.

budget deficit occurs when government expenditure is greater than tax revenue

government borrowing requirements the amount of money a government needs to borrow in order to offset its budget deficit

barriers to trade restrictions imposed by a government on the free exchange of goods or services between countries

substitute goods a good that can be used in place of another good

price inelastic the percentage change in quantity demanded/ supplied < the percentage change in price

protectionism government policies, including tariffs, quotas, and subsidies, that restrict the extent of international trade and which are implemented in order to protect domestic industries from cheaper imports

quotas a physical limit placed on the number of goods that can be traded or produced

tariffs a tax placed on imported goods and services

productively efficient occurs when a given quantity of output is produced at the minimum total cost per unit of output

free trade the unrestricted buying and selling of goods and services between countries without the imposition of barriers to trade such as quotas and tariffs

What is the effect of a persistent current account deficit on international credit ratings and demand management?

A credit rating agency is a company that assesses a country's ability to repay its debt and its ability to pay the interest on the debt. When a persistent current account deficit is offset by the selling of government bonds national debt continues to grow. If the agency believes that the country will have difficulty in paying back the debt, and paying the interest on the debt, then it will reduce the creditworthiness of the country. Buyers of government debt will consider that lending to the government of the country is more risky and, in order to sell the bonds, the government will have to raise the interest rate to attract lenders. Higher interest payments on the national debt increase the amount of tax revenue that the government must pay to investors, thereby reducing the amount available for the government to spend in the domestic economy and causing a fall in levels of aggregate demand. Higher interest payments may increase the **budget deficit**, leading to an increase in the **government borrowing requirement**, further increases in the national debt, and further increases in interest payments.

Discuss the methods that a government can use to reduce a persistent current account deficit (HL)

Discussed below are government policies that can be used to correct a persistent current account deficit, including expenditure switching policies, expenditure reducing policies, and supply-side policies.

Discuss how expenditure switching policies might reduce a persistent current account deficit

These policies are aimed at reducing the consumption of imports and increasing the consumption of domestically produced goods, thereby reducing expenditure on imports and increasing revenue from domestically produced goods so that the flow of money leaving the country falls thereby reducing the current account deficit. There are two main ways in which the government and the central bank can achieve this objective: devaluing its currency and raising **barriers to trade**.

Discuss how a fall in the value of a currency might reduce a persistent current account deficit

There are two main ways in which the central bank can reduce the value of its currency. It can exchange its currency for foreign currencies on the foreign exchange market, thereby increasing the supply of its currency and lowering its price. As the exchange rate falls the price of imports increases. Domestically produced **substitute goods** become more price competitive. Domestic buyers switch expenditure away from imports to domestically produced goods, thereby reducing the money flowing out of the country and leading to a fall in the current account deficit. At the same time the price of exports falls as the exchange rate falls, leading to an increase in expenditure on exports. The success of this policy depends upon the availability of domestically produced substitutes. If few are available then buyers will have little choice and many will continue to buy the imports. When demand for imported goods is **price inelastic** the percentage increase in the price of imports is greater than the percentage fall in quantity demanded. Therefore, although the quantity demanded of imports falls, the expenditure on them increases. If the demand for exports is price inelastic then the percentage fall in price is greater than the percentage increase in quantity demanded. Quantity of exports demanded rises as price falls but expenditure on them falls. Therefore a fall in the exchange rate will not always reduce the current account deficit: it is dependent on the price elasticities of the demand for exports and imports (the relationship between PED of imports and exports and the deficit is discussed in detail on pages 236–37).

Discuss how protectionism might reduce a persistent current account deficit

The government can use **protectionism** to reduce the consumption of imports and increase the consumption of domestically produced substitutes by the use of **quotas** and **tariffs** (see pages 202–209 for a detailed explanation of the effects of protectionist policies). A tariff or a quota increases the price of imports, thereby making domestically produced goods more competitive. Consumers will switch expenditure away from imports to domestically produced goods, leading to a fall in the quantity of money flowing out of the country and a fall in the current account deficit.

However, many countries have signed trading agreements with other countries and when a country breaks the agreement the other countries are likely to raise barriers to trade against that country, thereby reducing the demand for its exports. This reduces the money flowing into the country, thereby increasing its current account deficit. Also, protected but relatively inefficient domestic firms are able to stay in business even though they are producing at a relatively high average cost. When they are protected the domestic firms do not need to be productively efficient. There is a misallocation of resources as more of the world's scarce resources are used to produce the goods than would be the case under **free trade** (see pages 202–209 for a detailed explanation of how protectionism affects efficiency).

Discuss how expenditure reducing policies might reduce a persistent current account deficit

If total expenditure falls then there will also be a fall in expenditure on imports. A fall in expenditure on imports reduces the amount of money flowing out of the country, thereby reducing the current account deficit. A government can achieve a fall in expenditure by introducing **contractionary fiscal policy** and/or **contractionary monetary policies**. The effects of these policies are discussed below.

Discuss how contractionary fiscal policy might reduce a persistent current account deficit

Increasing income tax, a **direct tax** and tax on goods and services, an indirect tax, and reducing government expenditure causes a fall in aggregate demand. Households have less disposable income to spend and firms have less after-tax profit to spend, leading to a fall in household expenditure and business **investment** on both domestically produced goods and imported goods. As AD falls, firms respond by reducing quantity supplied. Unemployment increases, and the rate of economic growth falls. This policy might lead to a reduction in the current account deficit but the government is unlikely to achieve its main macroeconomic objectives of low unemployment and economic growth.

However, lower levels of aggregate demand will put a downward pressure on prices, thereby slowing down the **rate of inflation**. This makes exports more price competitive, leading to an increase in the quantity of exports demanded which increases the amount of money flowing into the country. As more money flows in the current account deficit falls.

An increase in interest rates increases the cost of borrowing, leading to a fall in household and business borrowing and therefore a fall in household expenditure and business investment on both domestically produced goods and imported goods. So this policy will reduce the flow of money leaving the country. Like contractionary fiscal policy, contractionary monetary policy leads to higher unemployment and a fall in the **rate of economic growth**, but also leads to a lower rate of inflation which increases price competitiveness of exports, leading to increases in the flow of money into the country from abroad and a further fall in the current account deficit.

The relatively high interest rate attracts **hot money** flows as foreign investors try to earn high interest on their deposits. This increases money flows into the country helping to offset the current account deficit. The demand for the domestic currency also increases, leading to an increase in the exchange rate. The price of exports increases and the price of imports falls. This will not help to reduce the current account deficit because it might cause a fall in the amount of money flowing into the country from the sale of exports and an increase in the amount of money flowing out from the purchase of imports.

Discuss how supply-side policies might reduce a persistent current account deficit

As explained above there are negative effects on **macroeconomic objectives** of contractionary policies. Therefore, a government may look to **supply-side policies** to reduce the current account deficit.

Many countries of Western Europe and the US have experienced **structural changes**. There has been a fall in **heavy industry** and manufacturing and a rise in the **service sector**. Countries such as China now have the **comparative advantage** in manufacturing of some goods. Supply-side policies are needed to ensure that these countries gain a comparative advantage in the production of other goods and services so that they are able to export these goods and services to the rest of the world and thereby reduce the current account deficit. These policies are discussed below.

Discuss how investment might reduce a persistent current account deficit

A lack of investment in **human capital**, **physical capital**, and research and development leads to an increase in the **productivity gap**. Firms that produce at relatively high average cost are not able to compete on price internationally, leading to a fall in the demand for exports and an increase in demand for imports. Productivity can be increased by increasing investment in human and physical capital. Government could encourage firms to train workers by giving **subsidies** to firms or by providing it directly, for example, through colleges of further education. The government might encourage advances in technology by providing **grants** to universities and by subsidizing firms to carry out research and development. The government can provide incentives for firms to invest in technologically advanced capital by keeping interest rates low and by giving **tax breaks** on reinvested profit.

Subject vocabulary

contractionary fiscal policy policy involving the reduction of government spending and/or the increase of taxation

contractionary monetary policies policy involving the reduction of the money supply and the increase of interest rates

direct tax a tax that is paid directly by an individual or firm to the government. For example income tax on wages and company profits.

investment the addition to capital stock

rate of inflation the rate at which a weighted average price of a basket of goods and services is rising

rate of economic growth the percentage increase in a country's output in a given period of time

hot money money that flows internationally between financial markets as investors attempt to maximise returns on savings

macroeconomic objectives the main aims of government macroeconomic policy, such as low and stable inflation, low levels of unemployment and sustainable economic growth

supply-side policies government policy designed to affect the level of aggregate supply in an economy by increasing the quantity and/or productivity of the factors of production

structural changes a long-term shift in the fundamental industrial structure of economy (e.g. a change from the primary sector to the secondary sector)

heavy industry industries that use very large and expensive machinery and plant and produce large quantities of output such as car manufacturers and oil and steel producers

service sector the part of the economy that produces intangible goods such as banking, insurance, transport, and hospitality

comparative advantage when a country, firm, or individual is able to produce a particular good or service at a lower opportunity cost than other countries, firms or individuals

continued on page 236

human capital this relates to the store of knowledge and the set of skills that a worker possesses which can be used in the production process. The higher the value of human capital the more productive the worker is. Human capital can be improved through investment in education and training.

physical capital any manufactured good that is used in the production of other goods and services such as machinery and buildings

productivity gap the difference between the output per worker in one country compared with the output per worker in another country

subsidies payments made by government to firms per unit of output

grants an amount of money given by a government or other organization to an individual, firm, or industry for a particular purpose

tax breaks a reduction in the amount of tax that must be paid by an entrepreneur, firm, or industry in order to encourage economic activity. For example a reduction in the rate of corporate tax in order to increase FDI.

investment the addition to capital stock

technologically advanced capital capital that incorporates new technology and is used in place of existing capital to produce goods and services thereby increasing productivity

price elasticity of demand a measure of how quantity demanded responds to a change in price in percentage terms

Such policies might lead to a fall in average costs, thereby reducing the productivity gap and increasing international competitiveness. As industries in a country become more price competitive, expenditure on exports increases and expenditure on imports falls leading to a fall in the current account deficit. Non-price factors can also affect the demand for exports. Investment in product design and product reliability, for example, will help to increase demand for exports.

The decline of the UK motorbike industry can be used as an example of how lack of **investment** can lead to an increase in the current account deficit. Japanese manufacturers in the 1960s and 1970s invested heavily in **technologically advanced capital** and in the research and development of more reliable and efficient engines. They also invested heavily in design. In the UK investment in the motorbike industry was much less in all these areas. In time the average cost of Japanese bikes was much lower, and the bikes more reliable than bikes made in the UK. Japanese bikes became more competitive and imports into the UK of Japanese bikes increased while exports of British bikes to the rest of the world fell, contributing to the UK's current account deficit.

Explain the Marshall-Lerner condition and the J-curve effect (HL)

Model sentence: It is not the quantity of exports and the quantity of imports traded that determines the current account balance; it is determined by the levels of expenditure on them.

When the exchange rate changes it changes the price of exports and imports leading to a change in quantity demanded for them. Changes to the expenditure on exports and imports are dependent on the value of their **price elasticity of demand** (PED).

What is the effect of an increase in the price of imports on the money flowing out of a country?

An increase in the price of imports leads to a fall in quantity demanded. If demand for imported goods is price inelastic the percentage increase in price will be greater than the percentage fall in quantity demanded. Therefore, when the value of price elasticity of demand for imports is less than 1, the quantity of imported goods falls when price increases but the expenditure on them increases, thereby increasing the flow of money out of the country.

If demand for imported goods is price elastic the percentage increase in price will be less than the percentage fall in quantity demanded. Therefore, when the value of price elasticity of demand for imports is greater than 1, the quantity of imported goods falls when price increases and the expenditure on them also falls, reducing the amount of money flowing out of the country.

Model sentence: If PED for imports is less than 1, expenditure on them rises when the exchange rate depreciates. If PED for imports is greater than 1, expenditure on them falls when the exchange rate depreciates.

What is the effect of a fall in the price of exports on the money flowing out of a country?

A fall in the price of exports leads to an increase in quantity demanded. If demand for exported goods is price inelastic the percentage fall in price will be greater than the percentage increase in quantity demanded. Therefore, when price elasticity of demand for exports is less than 1 the quantity of exported goods increases when price falls but the expenditure on them falls, reducing the flow of money into the country.

If demand for exported goods is price elastic the percentage fall in price will be less than the percentage increase in quantity demanded. Therefore, when price elasticity of demand for exports is greater than 1, the quantity of exported goods increases when price falls and the expenditure on them increases, increasing the flow of money coming into the country.

Model sentence: If PED for exports is less than 1, expenditure on them falls when the exchange rate depreciates. If PED for exports is greater than 1, expenditure on them increases when the exchange rate depreciates.

Explain that the effect on the current account deficit from a change in the exchange rate is dependent on the sum of the values of the PED for imports and exports

It can be seen that the effect on money flows into and out of a country, from trade in imports and exports brought about by a change in the exchange rate, is determined by the value of the PED for imports and exports. Therefore, the effect on the current account deficit from a change in the exchange rate is dependent on the value of the PED for imports and exports.

The Marshall-Lerner condition states that if the sum of the values of the PED for exports and the PED for imports is greater than 1, then a fall in the exchange rate will cause the current account deficit to fall.

Model sentence: If PED X + PED M > 1 a fall in the exchange rate reduces the current account deficit.

If the sum of the values of the PED for exports and the PED for imports is less than 1, then a fall in the exchange rate will cause the current account deficit to increase.

Model sentence: If PED X + PED M < 1 a fall in the exchange rate increases the current account deficit. If PED X + PED M < 1 an increase in the exchange rate reduces the current account deficit.

Model sentence: If a government tries to reduce the current account deficit by reducing the value of the currency the policy will only be successful if PED X + PED M > 1. When PED X + PED M < 1 reducing the value of the currency will increase the current account deficit.

What is the J-curve effect?

The Marshall-Lerner condition states that if PED X + PED M > 1 a fall in the **exchange rate** reduces the current account deficit. But in the short term a depreciation of the exchange rate might not reduce the current account deficit because in the short term the value of PED for exports and the value of PED for imports are likely to be **price inelastic**.

When the price of imports increases due to a fall in the exchange rate the quantity of imports demanded will only fall by a relatively small amount. For example, firms importing **raw materials** cannot immediately find new suppliers after an increase in price. Firms might also be tied into contracts with suppliers for a given period of time and, therefore, cannot change suppliers immediately after an increase in price. Therefore, importers have to continue to buy the goods. The value of PED for imports immediately after an increase in the price of imports is very inelastic.

The same is true for exports. The price of exports falls after a fall in the exchange rate but firms in other countries are also tied into contracts and find it difficult to immediately find suppliers of cheaper **substitute goods**. Therefore, the value of PED for exports is inelastic in the short term.

When PED X + PED M < 1, as is the case in the short term, the deficit increases after a fall in the exchange rate. This is shown in Figure 77.2 by the line falling over time. In the long-term the buyers of imports have time to change suppliers, therefore the quantity of imports demanded falls further. In the long-term, the value of PED for imports becomes more elastic and the expenditure on them falls, leading to a fall in the flow of money out of the country. The value of PED for exports also becomes more elastic and expenditure on exports increases, leading to an increase in the flow of money into the country. When PED X + PED M > 1, the current account deficit falls. This is shown by the line rising over time.

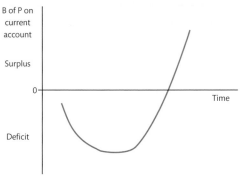

Figure 77.2

Model sentence: In the short run after a fall in the exchange rate PED X + PED M < 1 therefore the current account deficit increases. In the long term PED X + PED M > 1 therefore the current account deficit falls.

The deficit increases but in time will begin to fall leading to a J-shaped line shown in Figure 77.2. That is why it is called the 'J-curve effect' of a fall in the exchange rate.

Test your understanding of this unit by answering the following questions

- What is a current account deficit?
- Explain the relationship between the exchange rate and the current account deficit.
- Explain government policies designed to reduce the current account deficit.
- Explain why in the short term a fall in the exchange rate may worsen a current account deficit.

3.4 Economic integration

Learning Outcomes

- Distinguish between bilateral and multilateral (WTO) trade agreements.

- Explain that preferential trade agreements give preferential access to certain products from certain countries by reducing or eliminating tariffs, or by other agreements relating to trade.

- Distinguish between a free trade area, a customs union, and a common market.

- Explain that economic integration will increase competition among producers within the trading bloc.

- Compare and contrast the different types of trading blocs.

- Explain that a monetary union is a common market, with a common currency and a common central bank.

- Discuss the possible advantages and disadvantages of a monetary union for its members.

- Explain the concepts of trade creation and trade diversion in a customs union. (HL)

- Explain that different forms of economic integration allow member countries to gain from economies of scale. (HL)

What is economic integration?

Economic integration occurs when countries agree to remove barriers to the movement of goods and services, barriers to the movement of capital, and barriers to the movement of labour. The final stage of economic integration is the **unification** of the **fiscal policy** and **monetary policy** of the participating countries.

Distinguish between bilateral and multilateral trade agreements

An agreement on trade between two countries, usually concerning the removal of **trade barriers** such as of **quotas** and **tariffs**, is a bilateral agreement. A multilateral trade agreement is an agreement on trade involving more than two countries.

What is a trading bloc?

A trading bloc consists of a number of countries that come together to form an agreement to remove trade barriers that exist between them.

What is a preferential trade agreement (PTA)?

A preferential trade agreement is an agreement between two or more countries to reduce the barriers to trade on only certain goods and services. Tariffs could be reduced on certain imported goods but only on the named imported goods and only on those from the countries that have reached an agreement. The tariff is not reduced on these goods imported from all countries. These are called tariff preferences. A PTA is the first step towards economic integration.

Distinguish between a free trade area, a customs union, and a common market

A free trade area (FTA) is an extension of a preferential trade area. It is an agreement that allows free trade between participating countries. It can be a bilateral or multilateral agreement. Quotas and tariffs on all traded goods are removed. Each country in the FTA is able to come to their own agreement on trade with other countries outside of the FTA.

A customs union is a group of two or more countries that have agreed to remove trade barriers. Unlike an FTA a customs union puts up common barriers to trade, such as tariffs or quotas on some imported goods and services from countries that are not in the customs union. When the customs union has agreed a common tariff or quota it means that all participating countries must impose the same tariff or quota on imported goods. Goods move freely within the customs union but capital and labour do not.

A common market is a group of two or more countries that agree to remove barriers to trade and agree to put up common trade barriers against imported goods from non-member countries. Unlike a customs union a common market allows freedom of movement of capital and labour throughout the member countries. This is a further step towards full economic integration.

Model sentence: Customs unions and common markets, unlike free trade areas, erect common barriers to trade.

Model sentence: Common markets, unlike customs unions, allow the freedom of movement of capital and labour between member countries.

What are monetary unions?

A monetary union is another step toward full integration. Monetary unions have the same form of economic integration as common markets. The difference between a common market and a monetary union is that, in a monetary union, member countries agree to share the same currency. Member countries give up their own currency for the shared currency. The power to set the supply of the currency and interest rates are transferred from the central bank of each member country to a single central bank. The countries can no longer control their own monetary policy. The individual states of the USA do not control the money supply, or interest rates, these are set by the Federal Reserve. In 1999 some member countries of the European Union joined the **Euro-zone**. The countries gave up their currencies for the euro. Monetary policy in the Euro-zone is set by the European Central Bank. The countries in the Euro-zone still have tax-raising powers and control government expenditure. Therefore the Euro-zone is not fully integrated because fiscal policy is still determined by the governments of the individual countries in the Euro-zone.

Discuss the advantages and disadvantages of economic integration

Many of the advantages and disadvantages of economic integration come from the removal of barriers to trade and the promotion of free trade. These are discussed in detail in Section 3.1.

In summary the advantages gained by the removal of tariff and quotas are as follows.

The removal of tariffs and quotas reduces the price of imports thereby increasing the **purchasing power** of **nominal income**. **Real income** increases and consumers are able to satisfy more wants with their scarce income. As price falls consumer surplus increases and, therefore, **consumer welfare** increases. Firms that import raw materials benefit from lower costs of production, therefore, average costs fall and supply increases. Firms become more price competitive and demand for their exports increases. Consumers can also enjoy a greater choice and variety of goods and services, which also increases consumer welfare.

Free trade allows firms to export goods to a much larger market. Firms can gain cost advantages from **economies of scale** as output increases, thereby further reducing average costs. Growth in output of exporting industries increases investment in the industries. This brings benefits to the economy as a whole such as **economic growth**, greater levels of employment, and a reduction in the **current account deficit**.

Free trade allows for a more efficient allocation of **resources**. Industries that are no longer protected cannot hide inefficiencies behind tariffs and quotas. Goods and services are produced in countries that have a comparative advantage in their production. Fewer of the world's scarce **factors of production** are used to produce goods, therefore more goods can be produced with a given quantity and quality of factors.

Foreign direct investment may increase as firms outside of the trading bloc invest within the bloc in order to benefit from the large single market.

In summary the disadvantages of free trade are as follows.

The less efficient domestic firms will not be able to compete against lower priced imports. Firms shut down and unemployment rises.

Tax revenue from tariffs will no longer be available to governments, reducing the amount they have to spend on **public goods**, **merit goods**, and **infrastructure**.

When a country has few cost advantages, and its exporting industries are relatively inefficient, the demand for imports will be greater than the demand for its exports, leading to a persistent current account deficit. (The consequences of a high current account deficit are discussed in detail on pages 232–34.)

Countries no longer able to use tariffs and quotas to protect domestic industries may use other less **explicit** methods. Some countries put up barriers to trade by making health and safety standards, environmental standards, and quality standards very difficult to meet.

Discuss the advantages and disadvantages of monetary union

There are many advantages and disadvantages of monetary union. The main advantages are explained below:

Explain how the removal of transaction costs reduces business costs

When trade occurs between countries currencies must be exchanged on the **foreign exchange market**. Resources are used to do this. When countries within a monetary union trade they share one currency. Resources used to exchange currencies can be used for other purposes. So monetary union reduces business costs and frees up resources because currencies no longer need to be exchanged.

Explain how price transparency reduces business costs and improves efficiency

A single currency makes it a lot easier for buyers to see and compare the price of goods across many countries. Prices are more transparent, there is no need to calculate price in one currency from the many different exchange rates. Buyers have a much better knowledge about prices in the market. Over time firms can reduce their costs of production, and produce more efficiently, because they know where they can buy goods at the lowest price. In monetary unions, inefficient firms will not survive because governments can no longer devalue the currency to reduce the price of their exports. The firms either become more efficient or go out of business. The most efficient firms – able to produce at low **average total cost** and sell at low prices – will survive and grow.

Explain how the removal of exchange rate fluctuations increases investment

Fluctuations in the **exchange rate** change the earnings on foreign assets, because the returns on foreign investments are paid in the foreign currency and will need to be exchanged to the home currency of the owner of the assets. This increases the uncertainty and risk of cross-border investments including foreign direct investment. For example, when an investor in the UK invests in assets in Australia the British pound is exchanged for Australian dollars in order to buy the assets. The returns on the investment are paid in Australian dollars and must then be exchanged for British pounds. If the British pound increases in value against the Australian dollar it reduces the return paid on the investment. Therefore exchange rate fluctuations increase the risk and uncertainty of cross-border investment, leading to a fall in the level of investment. Cross-border investment within a monetary union is less risky because there is no exchange rate.

Explain how monetary union reduces currency speculation

Currency speculation occurs when investors buy a foreign currency in the hope of selling the currency at a higher price in the future. Currency speculation causes fluctuations in the exchange rate making the exchange rate unstable. This reduces confidence in the economy of the country and leads to a fall in investment. A single currency of a large monetary union, such as the Euro-zone, is less likely to come under attack by speculators and therefore the exchange rate will be more stable. A small country joining a monetary union might see this as a big advantage.

Explain how membership of a monetary union might reduce inflation

Relatively high **rates of inflation** reduce international competitiveness. A country can devalue its currency in order to make their exports more price competitive, offsetting the increase in price due to inflation. When a country joins a monetary union it loses the power to devalue its currency in order to reduce the price of its exports. Therefore it is more important for the government of the country to follow policies that keep inflation under control.

Model sentence: Membership of a monetary union increases the level of cross-border investments, reduces transaction costs, increases price transparency, and eliminates the disadvantages of exchange rate fluctuations.

The disadvantages of monetary union are explained below.

Explain the consequences of a single interest rate

Member countries belonging to the Euro-zone are in different stages of the **economic cycle**. A country that is experiencing high rates of inflation will need to set a relatively high interest rate to reduce inflationary pressures. A country in a **recession** will need to set a relatively low interest rate in order to increase **aggregate demand** and increase the **rate of economic growth**. The interest rate for the euro is set by the European Central Bank but the rate it sets might not be the right one for all the countries in the union. This means that recessions will be deeper and longer if the interest rate is high and inflation may not be brought under control if the interest rate is low. The central bank is not able to set the appropriate interest rate for all countries in the monetary union.

Model sentence: A single interest rate covering all countries in a monetary union means that individual countries lose the power to change monetary policy to suit their position in the business cycle.

Explain the consequences of losing control over the exchange rate

A country that wants to increase the competitiveness of its exports can devalue its currency in order to lower the price of its exports, thereby increasing the quantity of exports demanded. Countries in a monetary union are not able to do this so exporting industries may not survive, leading to a fall in **GDP** and an increase in unemployment.

Explain the consequences of losing control over fiscal policy

If fiscal policy is controlled centrally, countries may lose the power to reduce or increase their taxes in order to change aggregate demand. Governments also lose the power to be able to borrow in order to increase aggregate demand. Countries lose the power to introduce **contractionary fiscal policy** or **expansionary fiscal policy** to achieve their **macroeconomic objectives**.

Explain the costs of monetary conversion

There are costs of converting from one currency to another that are paid by the taxpayer and businesses. The old currency must be replaced with the new and distributed throughout the economy. All machines that take notes and coins have to be replaced or adjusted to accept the new currency. Businesses must re-price all goods and, for example, print new catalogues.

Explain the concept of trade creation (HL)

See pages 196–201 for a detailed explanation of how the theory of **comparative advantage** demonstrates that the removal of barriers to trade increases world output.

Trade creation occurs in a trading bloc when agreements are reached on reducing **trade barriers** that lead to an increase in production and consumption. When barriers to trade, such as **tariffs** and **quotas**, are reduced or removed the production of certain goods and services switch away from relatively high cost producers in one country to relatively low cost producers in another country. Buyers in countries in a common market now buy goods from firms producing at lower average total cost and selling at a lower price.

For example, a country outside of the European Union (EU) has placed a tariff on imported cars from the EU in order to protect the domestic producers of cars. The EU has placed a common tariff on cars entering the EU. The common tariff does not apply to cars produced and sold within the EU. The country now joins the EU, therefore the tariff on imported cars from member countries is removed. Buyers of cars in the country now switch expenditure away from the higher priced domestically produced cars to the lower priced imported cars. Expenditure moves away from high cost producers to low cost producers. Consumers in the country benefit because they are able buy cars at a lower price from more efficient producers. **Purchasing power** of income rises and consumers are able to buy more with their income, thereby increasing demand for other goods.

Firms in a country also benefit when the country joins a common market. They are able to buy **raw materials** from a supplier producing at low average total cost and selling at a low price, thereby reducing their costs of production. This might lead to an increase in supply and a fall in price of the goods they are producing.

Free trade agreements shift the production of some goods and services away from a high cost country to a low cost country that has the comparative advantage in the production of the good or service. Efficient firms increase their **market share** and increase output. Increases in the scale of production increase the cost advantages gained from **economies of scale** leading to lower average total costs.

In theory, when all firms in the common market specialize in the production of goods that they are able to produce most efficiently, the total output from a given quantity and quality of **factors of production** increases. Factors are allocated more efficiently leading to welfare gains.

Explain the concept of trade diversion (HL)

Trade diversion occurs when expenditure in a country switches away from low cost producers to high cost producers after the country joins a common market. The common market has in place common tariffs on certain imported goods coming into the common market from low cost countries outside the common market. Before the country joined the common market there were no tariffs placed on the goods coming from the low cost producers outside. Buyers enjoyed the advantages of paying a low price. After the country has joined the common market the common tariff placed on the goods increases the prices of the imported goods. It is now cheaper to buy the goods from high cost producers in countries that are members of the common market. Therefore expenditure in the country switches away from low cost countries to high cost countries.

Buyers now pay a higher price for certain goods which reduces the purchasing power of their income. More output is produced by less efficient firms and less is produced by the more efficient firms leading to a **misallocation of resources** and a reduction in society's **welfare**. However, the benefits gained from joining the common market may outweigh the disadvantages of not being a member.

Model sentence: Trade diversion occurs when a country joins a common market with common tariffs thereby shifting demand for goods away from low cost countries outside the common market to high cost countries within the common market.

Explain that economic integration allows member countries to gain from economies of scale (HL)

The size of a common market is greater than the size of a country's domestic market. As more countries join a common market the size of the market grows. The population of the EU, consisting of 28 member countries, is estimated to be 508 million. This is much higher than the most heavily populated member country, Germany, which has a population of about 81 million.

A firm producing within the EU, with no barriers to trade, that produces a good that is consumed by a large proportion of people living in the EU has the opportunity to increase sales by a very large amount. If a firm can take advantage of the size of the market it will be able to gain greater economies of scale. It is not easy for a firm to gain market share because tastes and preferences vary a lot across the 28 countries of the EU. There are many goods, however, produced by firms that are close substitutes, for example, food products and manufactured goods, such as office furniture and stationery and household durables such as washing machines, that can be sold to buyers throughout the EU. These firms, if they are able to produce at low average cost, may grow in size and be able to enjoy the economies of scale available from production on a large scale.

As the average cost of production on many goods falls throughout the common market it is possible that prices will fall leading to an increase in **consumer surplus** and **real income**.

Test your understanding of this unit by answering the following questions

- Distinguish between a customs union and a monetary union.
- Discuss the possible advantages and disadvantages of monetary union.
- Using the concepts of trade creation and trade diversion, explain the possible advantages for and disadvantages against a country joining a monetary union.

3.5 Terms of trade (HL)

Learning Outcomes

- Explain the meaning of the terms of trade. (HL)
- Explain how the terms of trade are measured. (HL)
- Distinguish between an improvement and deterioration in the terms of trade. (HL)
- Calculate the terms of trade using the equation: Index of average export prices/index of average import prices × 100. (HL)
- Explain that the terms of trade may change in the short term due to changes in demand conditions for exports and imports, changes in global supply of key inputs (such as oil), changes in relative inflation rates, and changes in relative exchange rates. (HL)
- Explain that the terms of trade may change in the long term due to changes in world income levels, changes in productivity within the country, and technological developments. (HL)

- Explain how changes in the terms of trade in the long term may result in a global redistribution of income. (HL)
- Examine the effects of changes in the terms of trade on a country's current account, using the concepts of price elasticity of demand for exports and imports. (HL)
- Explain the impacts of short-term fluctuations and long-term deterioration in the terms of trade of economically less developed countries that specialize in primary commodities, using the concepts of price elasticity of demand, supply for primary products, and income elasticity of demand. (HL)

What is the meaning of the terms of trade and how are they measured? (HL)

It is important not to confuse the terms of trade with the balance of trade. The trade balance is determined by the revenue earned from exports and the expenditure on imports. The terms of trade are the average price of exports relative to the average price of imports.

Improvement in the terms of trade occurs when the average price of exports increases relative to the average price of imports. If the average price of exports increases relative to the average price of imports, more imports can be bought with a given quantity of exports.

Deterioration in the terms of trade occurs when the average price of imports increases in relation to the average price of exports. If the average price of imports increases relatively to the average price of exports, fewer imports can be bought with a given quantity of exports.

If Australia's average price of exports increases by 5% relative to the average price of its imports from Singapore then Australia can buy 5% more imported goods from Singapore with the export revenue from a given quantity of its exports. Australia's terms of trade has improved. Singapore, on the other hand, must increase the quantity of exports sold to Australia in order to buy the same quantity of imports from Australia. Singapore's terms of trade have deteriorated.

The terms of trade is expressed as an index. It shows the value of the average export prices, relative to the value of its average import prices. The exported goods and imported goods are weighted. This is to take into account the importance of the contribution each exported good makes to total export revenue and the contribution each imported good makes to the total expenditure on imports. The equation used to calculate the terms of trade is:

The terms of trade = average export prices index/average import prices index × 100.

Synonyms

deterioration ...... weakening/ decline

Calculate the terms of trade using the data below and state for each year if the terms of trade improved or deteriorated – a step-by-step guide

Year	Index of average export prices	Index of average import prices	Calculation	Terms of trade
1	100	100	(100/100) × 100 = 100	100
2	103	100	(103/100) × 100 = 103	103
3	104	103	(104/103) × 100 = 100.97	100.97
4	109	110	(109/110) × 100 = 99.1	99.1
5	108	107	(108/107) × 100 = 101.83	100.93

Table 79.1

Year 1 is the base year. The index is given a value of 100 therefore the terms of trade = 100.

In year 2 the average price of exports increase and the average price of imports stay the same. The terms of trade increases to 103. A given quantity of exports can now buy 3% more imports than in year 1, therefore the terms of trade has improved.

In year 3 the average price of exports increase again but the relative increase in the average price of imports is greater. The terms of trade falls from 103 to 100.97. The terms of trade has deteriorated in year 3 because a given quantity of exports can buy fewer imports than in year 2.

In year 4, once again, the increase in the average price of imports is relatively greater than the increase in the average price of exports. The terms of trade falls from 100.97 to 99.1. The terms of trade has deteriorated in year 4 because a given quantity of exports can buy fewer imports than in year 3. Note that the same quantity of exports can buy fewer goods in year 4 than in year 1.

In year 5 the average price of exports and the average price of imports fall but the fall in the average price of imports is relatively bigger. The terms of trade increases from 99.1 to 100.93. The terms of trade has improved because a given quantity of exports can buy more imports than in year 4.

Model sentence: If the increase in the average price of exports is relatively greater than the increase in the average price of imports, the terms of trade improves and a given quantity of exports can buy more imports.

Model sentence: If the increase in the average price of imports is relatively greater than the increase in the average price of exports, the terms of trade deteriorates and a given quantity of exports can buy fewer imports.

Explain the short-run causes of a change in the terms of trade (HL)

There are four main short-run causes of changes in the terms of trade. They are explained below.

Explain how a change in the exchange rate affects the terms of trade

A **depreciation of the exchange rate** of a country leads to an increase in the average prices of its imports. For example, if the US dollar depreciates more dollars are needed to buy a given quantity of euros with which to buy imported goods from countries in the Euro-zone. Therefore, the average dollar-prices of US imports increase. Buyers of US goods need fewer euros to buy a given quantity of dollars but depreciation of the dollar does not change the dollar-price of US exports. US exporters continue to receive the same amount of dollars for their goods therefore the average dollar-price of exports does not change. However, because the dollar-price of imported goods has increased a given quantity of US exports can buy fewer imports therefore America's terms of trade deteriorates.

An **appreciation of the exchange rate** of the dollar against the euro leads to a fall in the average-dollar price of US imports from the Euro-zone. US importers need fewer dollars to buy a given quantity of euros with which to buy European goods. More euros are needed to buy a given quantity of dollars with which to buy US goods but the dollar-price of US exports does not change. US exporters continue to receive the same amount of dollars for their goods. The average dollar-price of US exports does not change but the average dollar-price of US imports falls therefore, a given quantity of US exports can buy more imports and America's terms of trade improves.

Model sentence: A change in the exchange rate changes the average price of imports and therefore changes the terms of trade.

Explain how changes in relative inflation rates affect the terms of trade

If prices in a country increase at a greater rate than in other countries the average prices of its exports will increase, relative to the average prices of its imports leading to an improvement in the terms of trade. A given quantity of the country's exports can buy more imports. However, inflation leads to a fall in the price competiveness of a country's exports.

Explain how changes in the determinants of demand for imports and exports affect the terms of trade

When a **determinant of demand**, such as income and consumer tastes and preferences, changes it causes a change in demand. The demand curve for the exported goods shifts leading to a change in equilibrium price.

Demand for a country's exports increases when income rises in other countries. This causes the average prices of the country's exports to increase, relative to the average prices of its imports. The country can buy more imports with a given quantity of exports leading to an improvement in the terms of trade.

A fall in income in other countries leads to a fall in demand for the country's exports. This causes the average prices of exports to fall, relative to the average prices of imports. The country can buy fewer imports with a given quantity of its exports, leading to deterioration in the terms of trade.

Model sentence: A change in a determinant of demand for exports leads to a change in the price of exports causing a change in the terms of trade.

Explain how changes in the world supply of primary goods affect the terms of trade

A country that supplies oil earns export revenue from selling the oil to other countries. And if it is heavily dependent on oil for its export revenues a change in its price can affect the country's terms of trade. An increase in the world supply of oil leads to a fall in the price of oil. The country can buy fewer imports, with a given quantity of exports leading to deterioration in the terms of trade. If the world supply of oil falls the price of oil increases. The country can buy more imports with a given quantity of exports leading to an improvement in the country's terms of trade.

Explain the long-term causes of a change in the terms of trade (HL)

The long-term causes are changes in income that lead to changes in the patterns of consumption, changes in productivity, and advances in technology.

Explain how changes in income affect the terms of trade of developed countries and less developed countries (LDCs)

An increase in income around the world leads to a change in the patterns of consumption. Increases in income lead to increases in demand for secondary goods and services mainly produced by **developed countries**. Demand for high tech goods and foreign holidays, for example, have a relatively high **income elasticity of demand**. As income increases, demand increases at a greater rate, leading to a relatively large increase in their price.

An increase in income leads to an increase in demand for **primary goods** mainly produced by LDCs. Price increases but income elasticity of demand is relatively low, therefore the increase in price, and the increase in export revenue, is relatively small compared to the increase in demand for, and price of, secondary goods. For an LDC the average import prices of secondary goods increase at a greater rate than the average prices of exported primary goods. The LDC can buy fewer imports with a given quantity of exports, leading to deterioration in the terms of trade. For a developed country, exporting secondary goods and importing primary goods, the terms of trade improve because the average export prices of secondary goods increase at a greater rate than the average prices of imported primary goods.

Model sentence: Increases in world income leads to an improvement in the terms of trade of advanced countries and a deterioration in the terms of trade of LDCs.

Explain how changes in technology and productivity affect the terms of trade

Increases in **productivity** lead to a fall in **average total costs** of production. There are many causes of an increase in productivity, including an increase in the **value of human capital** and the use of more **technologically advanced capital** in production. Increases in productivity in a country lead to a fall in the average price of its exports. *Ceteris paribus*, a given quantity of exports now buys fewer imports leading to deterioration in the terms of trade.

Subject vocabulary

determinant of demand factors that affect quantity demanded at each price

developed countries countries that have relatively high income per head and a relatively high Human Development Index

income elasticity of demand a measure of how quantity demanded responds to a change in income in percentage terms

primary goods a good that has not been processed and is in a raw state (e.g. fruit/wheat)

productivity the quantity of output per unit of input

average total costs equal to total cost divided by quantity of output

value of human capital a measure of the quantity and quality of the skills of the labour force that can be employed to produce goods and services. An increase in the value of human capital leads to an increase in labour productivity

technologically advanced capital capital that incorporates new technology and is used in place of existing capital to produce goods and services thereby increasing productivity

Explain how the effects of changes in the terms of trade on a country's current account is dependent upon the price elasticity of demand of exports and imports (HL)

See pages 227–37 for a detailed explanation of the current account

If **inflation** is increasing in a country at a greater rate than in the countries with which it trades, the average price of its exports will increase at a greater rate than the increase in the average price of imports. The country can buy more imports with a given quantity of its exports leading to an improvement in the terms of trade.

If inflation is increasing in a country at a lower rate than in the countries with which it trades, the average price of imports will increase at a greater rate than the average price of exports. A given quantity of exports can buy fewer imports leading to deterioration in the terms of trade. However, how the **current account** is affected by a change in the average price of exports and the average price of imports is determined by the price elasticity of demand for exports (PED X) and the price elasticity of demand for imports (PED M).

The value of PED X is a measure of the responsiveness of the quantity of exports demanded to a change in the average price of exports.

PED X = percentage change in the quantity of exports demanded/percentage change in the average price of exports.

PED X is inelastic when the percentage change in the average price of exports > the percentage change in the quantity of exports demanded.

When PED X is inelastic a percentage increase in the average price of exports is greater than the percentage fall in quantity demanded. Therefore an increase in the average price of exports (an improvement in the terms of trade) will lead to an increase in export revenue and an improvement in the current account balance. A fall in the average price of exports (a deterioration in the terms of trade) leads to a fall in export revenue because the percentage fall in price is greater than the percentage increase in quantity of exports demanded. In this case a fall in price leads to deterioration in the current account balance.

PED X is elastic when the percentage change in the quantity of exports demanded is greater than the percentage change in the average price of exports. When the average price of exports increases (an improvement in the terms of trade) the quantity demanded for them falls at a greater rate leading to a fall in export revenue and deterioration in the current account balance. When the average price of exports falls (deterioration in the terms of trade) the quantity of exports demanded increases at a greater rate, leading to an increase in export revenue and an improvement in the current account balance.

PED M is a measure of the responsiveness of the quantity of imports demanded to a change in the average-price of imports.

PED M = percentage change in the quantity of imports demanded/percentage change in the average price of imports. When PED M is inelastic a percentage increase in the average price of imports is greater than the percentage fall in quantity demanded. Therefore, an increase in the average price of imports (deterioration in the terms of trade) will lead to an increase in the expenditure on imports and deterioration in the current account balance. However, a fall in the average price of imports (an improvement in the terms of trade) will lead to a fall in import expenditure and an improvement in the current account balance.

When PED M is elastic a percentage increase in the average price of imports is less than the fall in quantity demanded. An increase in the average price of imports (a deterioration in the terms of trade) leads to a fall in import expenditure and an improvement in the current account balance. When PED is elastic, a fall in average import prices (an improvement in the terms of trade) leads to an increase in import expenditure and deterioration in the current account balance.

Explain the effects of short-term fluctuations and long-term deterioration in the terms of trade of LDCs (HL)

Many LDCs earn most of their export revenue from the sale of primary goods and less export revenue from manufactured goods. Primary goods are the raw materials used to produce other goods, such as agricultural goods, metals, and minerals.

Explain why, in the long term, the price of primary goods has fallen

Why has demand for primary goods increased?

Relatively fast economic growth in countries such as China and India, and an increasing world population, has led to an increase in demand for many primary goods – causing their prices to rise in the short term and increasing the revenue earned by those countries that export them. Earning more export revenue could lead to an increase in the number of goods that can be consumed, thereby increasing **consumer welfare**. Increases in the price of primary goods also give LDCs an opportunity to reduce international debt.

Why has the supply of primary goods increased?

World economic growth and population growth increases the demand for primary goods but there are supply-side factors that have pushed the long-term prices down.

Advances in technology have increased **productivity**, leading to increases in the world supply of primary goods. More efficient mining techniques have led to an increase in the world supply of minerals and the use of advanced **capital** in farming and the use of more effective fertilizers has led to an increase in the world supply of agricultural goods. In the long term, supply is increasing at a faster rate than the increase in demand putting downward pressure on prices.

Many developed countries protect their farming industries through the provision of **subsidies** giving farmers the incentive to increase supply, thereby causing a **surplus** of agricultural goods which increases the world supply and pushes the price down. If the average price of exports of LDCs is falling at a greater rate than the average price of imports, a given quantity of exports can buy fewer imports leading to deterioration in the terms of trade.

Model sentence: Demand for primary goods is increasing but supply increases at a greater rate leading to a long-term fall in the average price of exports of LDCs and a deterioration in their terms of trade.

What is the effect of income elasticity of demand on the demand for primary goods and the demand for manufactured goods and services (YED)? (HL)

- YED measures the responsiveness of demand for a good to a change in income.

- YED = the percentage change in demand for a good/the percentage change in income.

- When the percentage change in demand > the percentage change in income YED is elastic and YED > 1.

- When the percentage change in income > the percentage change in demand YED is inelastic and YED < 1.

Real income in the developed world has risen. But YED for primary goods is inelastic. This means that incomes have increased at a greater rate than increases in demand. However, YED for manufactured goods and services is elastic. This means that demand for them increases at a greater rate than the rate of increase in income. Therefore, as world income rises the demand for manufactured goods and services increases at a greater rate than the demand for primary goods.

What is the effect on the terms of trade of long-term increases in supply and of YED? (HL)

Increases in world income and population lead to an increase in demand for primary goods. However, supply over time is increasing at a greater rate than demand pushing down the price of primary goods in the long term.

YED is relatively more elastic for manufactured goods and services than for primary goods. Therefore, as incomes rises throughout the world the demand for manufactured goods and services produced increases at a greater rate than the demand for primary goods.

Prices of manufactured goods and services may fall over time as productivity increases but the price of primary goods will fall at a greater rate.

Subject vocabulary

consumer welfare a measure of the benefit obtained from the consumption of goods

productivity the quantity of output per unit of input

capital (goods) manufactured goods that are used in the production of other goods

subsidies payments made by government to firms per unit of output

surplus occurs when quantity supplied is greater than quantity demanded, another term for excess supply

real income income after taking into account the effects of inflation on purchasing power

Subject vocabulary

primary goods a good that has not been processed and is in a raw state (e.g. fruit/wheat)

current account deficit occurs when the amount of money flowing out of a country from the trade in goods and services, investment income, and transfers is greater than the amount flowing in

negative externalities occur when the production or consumption of a good creates costs that must be paid by third parties. The existence of negative externalities means that social cost is greater than private cost.

Glossary

degradation becoming worse in condition

Because of these differences in the conditions of supply and YED in the long term, the rate at which the price of **primary goods**, produced and exported by LDCs, falls is greater than the rate at which manufactured goods and services, produced and exported by developed countries, may fall.

Over time, developed countries can buy an increasing quantity of imports from LDCs with a given quantity of their exports leading to an improvement in the terms of trade of developed countries in the long term.

Over time LDCs can buy increasingly fewer imports from developed countries with a given quantity of their exports leading to a deterioration in the terms of trade of LDCs in the long term.

How might the current account of LDCs be affected by the PED of imports and exports?

The PED of primary goods is inelastic. The percentage increase in demand is less than the percentage fall in price. As the average price of primary goods falls in the long term, quantity demanded increases but at a lower rate.

Export revenue from primary goods = average price of primary goods × quantity sold. Therefore, when the average price of primary goods falls export revenue earned falls.

Many LDCs produce relatively few manufactured goods. In order to reduce their dependence on the revenue from primary goods LDCs must move away from primary production to secondary production. Many LDCs must import goods needed to produce other goods (capital) because they are not produced domestically. The PED of capital goods is inelastic and therefore as their price increases due to increases in demand expenditure on them increases. Expenditure on imports increases.

A fall in export revenue and an increase in import expenditure lead to a deterioration of the current account balance.

What are the consequences of the deterioration in the terms of trade for LDCs? (HL)

When the average price of an LDC's exports falls relative to the average price of its imports the terms of trade deteriorates. LDCs can buy fewer imports with a given quantity of exports leading to deterioration in the terms of trade. They have to sell more exports in order to buy a given quantity of imports. This puts pressure on them to increase supply. Increasing supply reduces price further, thereby increasing consumption of primary goods. However, because PED for exports is inelastic, the fall in price leads to a further fall in export revenue, possibly leading to an increase in the **current account deficit**.

LDCs' attempts to increase the supply of primary goods increase **negative externalities**. For example, land used for growing crops is over used, leading to soil **degradation**, thereby reducing future potential levels of output, income, and export revenues. Deforestation occurs when forests are cut down so that land can be used for farming. Deforestation has negative impacts on the environment. Many species of animals lose their habitats and become extinct and most scientists believe deforestation leads to climate change.

Many LDCs have large international debts. As export revenue falls countries find it very difficult to pay the interest on the debt. This leads to further borrowing and once again supply of primary goods is increased to try to increase export revenue.

Test your understanding of this unit by answering the following questions

- Explain the factors that determine the terms of trade of LDCs exporting primary goods.
- Using the concept of PED, explain why an increase in the average prices of primary goods leads to a deterioration in the current account balance of countries that export primary goods.
- Using the concept of income elasticity of demand, explain the effect of increases in world income on the demand for primary goods.

4.1 Economic development

Learning Outcomes

- Distinguish between economic growth and economic development.

- Explain the multidimensional nature of economic development in terms of reducing widespread poverty, raising living standards, reducing income inequalities, and increasing employment opportunities.

- Explain that the most important sources of economic growth in economically less developed countries include increases in quantities of physical capital and human capital, the development and use of new technologies that are appropriate to the conditions of the economically less developed countries, and institutional changes.

- Explain the relationship between economic growth and economic development, noting that some limited economic development is possible in the absence of economic growth but that, over the long term, economic growth is usually necessary for economic development (however, it should be understood that under certain circumstances economic growth may not lead to economic development).

- Explain, using examples, that economically less developed countries share certain common characteristics (noting that it is dangerous to generalize as there are many exceptions in each case), including low levels of GDP per capita, high levels of poverty, relatively large agricultural sectors, large urban informal sectors, and high birth rates.

- Explain that in some countries there may be communities caught in a poverty trap (poverty cycle), where poor communities are unable to invest in physical, human, and natural capital due to low or no savings; poverty is therefore transmitted from generation to generation, and there is a need for intervention to break out of the cycle.

- Explain, using examples, that economically less developed countries differ enormously from each other in terms of a variety of factors, including resource endowments, climate, history (colonial or otherwise), political systems, and degree of political stability.

- Outline the current status of international development goals, including the Millennium Development Goals.

Distinguish between economic growth and economic development

Economic growth is an increase in the real market value of goods and services produced by a country in a given period of time. Economic development, on the other hand, is not an easy term to define. It covers many areas of life. It is concerned with how economic growth can benefit people's living conditions through, for example, the provision of health-care services, housing, health and safety at work, and education and training. It is concerned with promoting a more equal distribution of income and wealth, and a more equitable society that provides equal opportunities for all, along with the promotion of human rights and freedoms and the elimination of absolute poverty and hunger. Economic development is concerned with increasing the welfare of humans and welfare is measured in many ways. The idea that a judgment can be made about individual welfare and society's welfare based only on a measurement of the real market value of goods and services is rejected.

What are the sources of economic growth in least developed countries (LDCs)?

Long-term economic growth is an increase in the productive capacity of a country. The level of potential output is determined by the quantity and quality (**productivity**) of the factors of production. Welfare and growth in most LDCs will not necessarily be increased by increasing the quantity of human capital. Increasing the size of the population might not lead to economic growth and even if it does it is more likely to reduce **income** per head. Many economists believe that the focus should be on improving the quality of human capital and **physical capital** in order to increase productivity. This is achieved through education to raise literacy and numeracy rates and training to give people the skills they need to earn an income. The provision of healthcare, good housing, and clean water also increases the quality of human capital leading to an increase in potential output.

Increasing the quantity and quality of physical capital leads to an increase in potential output. Physical capital includes the infrastructure such as transport networks, schools, hospitals, housing, factories, and commercial property. It also includes machines that are combined with labour to produce goods.

Investment in capital comes from **savings**. A relatively poor country has a high **marginal propensity to consume** and therefore a low **marginal propensity to save**. There are only limited funds available for investment in new capital and, without the necessary funds, research and development into new technologies

foreign direct investment cross-border investment, usually by firms, that involves the acquisition of assets in a foreign country. FDI can be the purchase of a minimum of 10% of the shares of a foreign company but also includes the creation of productive capacity.

tax revenue the income the government receives through the levying and collection of taxes

national income the sum of all income (wages, profits, rents, and interest) earned in a country in a given period of time

distribution of income how a country's total GDP is shared amongst its population

relative poverty a measure of poverty that relates to the average income earned in a country or region. Definitions vary but many governments define it as an income less than 50% of the median income.

external costs occurs when the production or consumption of a good creates a cost that must be paid by third parties

negative externalities occur when the production or consumption of a good creates costs that must be paid by third parties. The existence of negative externalities means that social cost is greater than private cost.

market failure when resources are not allocated or used efficiently

welfare loss the sum of the loss of consumer and producer surplus caused by market or government failure

gross domestic income the sum of all income earned by a country from the production of goods and services that occurs within its borders

continued on page 251

is very limited. Attracting **foreign direct investment** is seen by some LDCs as a way of increasing the quantity and quality of capital thereby increasing economic growth.

And LDCs have limited funds available to invest in the infrastructure that would increase the potential output of the economy. Governments in low income countries receive relatively small amounts of **tax revenue**, limiting the amount that can be invested in transport systems, schools, and hospitals.

Certain institutions are necessary for economic growth. Political stability provides greater certainty and can increase business investment, including foreign direct investment. Banking services must be available to provide interest on savings and a source of funds for investment. A legal system must be in place so that contracts and rights of ownership can be enforced so that businesses can invest with confidence.

Model sentence: An increase in economic growth is dependent on the quantity and quality of the factors of production and the existence of institutions that reduce business uncertainty and increase the potential for investment.

Is economic development dependent on economic growth?

As the economy grows **national income** increases. How this improves welfare in the country depends in part on how the income is distributed. If the **distribution of income** is very unequal **relative poverty** will increase and only a very small percentage of the population will benefit. The lives of most people will remain the same.

Increases in income should increase tax revenue but increases in the welfare of individuals are dependent upon how the government uses the extra revenue. If it invests in better infrastructure – such as health services, education, and transport systems – it will help to encourage economic development, improve the welfare of the people and increase productivity leading to economic growth. Making health services and education available to more people will also lead to a fairer, more equitable society. If the government is corrupt and politicians steal lots of the money or if it is invested in the military, for example, the extra tax revenue will have much less impact on welfare, development, and long-term growth. Tax revenue could also be used to redistribute income more equally, thereby ensuring everybody benefits from the increase in national income.

There are **external costs** created by economic growth. There are **negative externalities** of production and consumption leading to **market failure** and **welfare loss** such as global warming caused by the burning of fossil fuels and **degradation** of land caused by excessive farming. Growth also leads to the reduction of non-renewable natural resources. Such growth is not sustainable because it negatively affects the ability of future generations to maintain an acceptable standard of living.

Explain the common characteristics of LDCs

The characteristics (in bold) shared by most LDCs are set out below.

LDCs have **low levels of gross domestic product** (GDP) per head. GDP is the market value of all goods and services produced in a country in a given period of time. GDP per head of a country is calculated by dividing GDP by the number of people living in the country. GDP per head equals **gross domestic income** per head (see page 41 for a full explanation of GDP). Low levels of GDP per head means that most of the population are relatively poor, often with many living in **absolute poverty**. Because income is distributed unequally there will be some people who earn much more than the GDP per head and those that earn much less. The income per head per year in the UK and France is about $39,000 but in many countries such as Somalia and Ethiopia income per head is below $500.

Low incomes mean many parents cannot afford to pay for an education for their children, pay for health services, or afford good housing. Many individuals are **malnourished** and suffer from ill health. LDCs tend to have relatively high child mortality rates and low literacy rates. With low levels of GDP in some LDCs the government does not have enough tax revenue to invest in infrastructure in order to increase the availability of health services, education, and good social housing.

Most LDCs have relatively **low levels of productivity**. Productivity is the measure of output per unit of inputs. Inputs are the factors of production. Labour productivity, therefore, measures the amount of output from a unit of labour (a worker). An increase in labour productivity occurs when more output is achieved from a unit of labour in a given period of time. Output per worker = total output / number of workers. Output per worker is relatively low in LDCs. The low level of productivity is caused by a lack of investment in **human capital** and **physical capital**. LDCs often lack the quantity and quality of capital necessary for sustained economic growth.

Many LDCs have **high birth rates** and **low life expectancy rates**. In the UK and France per year there are about 13 babies born per 1,000 of the population. Most developed countries have similar birth rates. In Somalia and Ethiopia the birth rate is over 3 times as high at about 42 babies born per 1,000 of the population. High birth rates mean that there are a very large number of people under the age of 15. These children have to be supported by the working population. This task is made more difficult because of the low life expectancy rates in most LDCs. In most developed countries the life expectancy rate is about 80 years. In LDCs it is much lower – in many, life expectancy is below 60 years.

Many LDCs have many **large informal markets**. The lack of government control and legal systems, and a lack of financial institutions such as banks, are some of the reasons why there are larger informal markets in LDCs than in developed countries. The informal sector is hidden from the government. Trade takes place unofficially. No tax is paid to the government either on income earned or goods bought. Transactions are not recorded and therefore are not included in GDP statistics. Official GDP statistics, therefore, do not reflect the true level of output.

In Africa the informal sector is an important source of employment and income. With such a high birth rate many counties do not create enough jobs in the **formal sector**, so unemployment and levels of poverty would be higher without the informal markets. In Nigeria it is estimated that about 15% of cross-border trade is in the informal sector.

Many LDCs have relatively **large agricultural and primary sectors** that provide a large proportion of export revenue. This is discussed in detail in on pages 243–48.

Explain how LDCs can differ

It is true that LDCs share many characteristics, but they are not all the same. Discussed below are the main areas in which they can differ.

A country's factor endowment is the quantity of land, labour, capital, and **entrepreneurship** that it can use to produce goods and services. Some LDCs have lots of factors but still remain relatively poor. In these cases countries have failed to exploit their factor endowments to their full potential. The reasons for this are varied.

Angola in southern Africa is a country with very large endowments of oil, diamonds, copper, and gold. Between 1975 and 2002 there was a civil war. Much of the infrastructure was destroyed and many 100s of thousands of people died. Without political stability and infrastructure the country was unable to exploit its resources. This highlights the impact that religious and ethnic conflict has on economic development and growth.

After 2002 the economy began to grow. In 2013 the economy grew by 8%. It has attracted much foreign direct investment in the past few years, which brings with it new more efficient technologies. This highlights the importance of the roles of political stability and business confidence for economic growth. Recent fast economic growth has increased GDP per head to $6,000 per year, a lot less than in developed countries but a lot more than in other LDCs such as Burundi with GDP per head of about $250. Burundi is a useful country to investigate as its circumstances highlight the reasons why some countries are very poor. The greater the religious and ethnic conflict the more difficult it is for the economy to grow. In many LDCs, such as Rwanda and Ethiopia, conflict has hindered economic development. This is of course not the case for all LDCs.

LDCs have a variety of political systems. Some are more stable than others and therefore they attract more investment. China is a one-party state which attracts a great deal of investment because it is regarded as stable, and this gives confidence to investors. The legal system governing business contracts also protects investment further, increasing business confidence. The Chinese government encourages inward investment and the economy has grown quickly over the last few decades. North Korea is a military dictatorship which operates a mainly **closed economy**. Very little international trade occurs. The state owns all enterprises, unlike China that has introduced **market reforms**. North Korea's economy has a very low growth rate and GDP per head is estimated to be about $1,200. In China the GDP per capita is estimated to be about $6,500.

The agricultural sector of LDCs is usually large and makes a big contribution to the GDP of the countries. Of course, some countries' climates are more favourable for the production of agricultural goods than others giving them a **comparative advantage** in the production of such goods. However, the agricultural share of GDP in LDCs is much greater than in developed countries.

For example, in 2012, the agricultural share of GDP in Sierra Leone was 57% and in Rwanda it was 33%. In the UK it was 0.8% and in the USA it was 1.2%. However, it is not always the case that LDCs have a large agricultural sector (Botswana's agricultural share of GDP is under 3%). It is important not to underestimate the importance of this sector for LDCs. The average agricultural share in LDCs is 28% of GDP. The average agricultural share of GDP of developed countries is under 2%.

Subject vocabulary

continued from page 250

absolute poverty occurs when people do not have enough resources to satisfy their basic needs

human capital this relates to the store of knowledge and the set of skills that a worker possesses which can be used in the production process. The higher the value of human capital the more productive the worker is. Human capital can be improved through investment in education and training.

physical capital any manufactured good that is used in the production of other goods and services such as machinery and buildings

formal sector employment and expenditure that occurs in legal markets where income and expenditure are a source of tax revenue

entrepreneurship the process of bringing together factors of production in order to produce goods or services with the aim of making a profit

closed economy an economy that is self-sufficient and does not trade with the rest of the world

market reforms changes made to the way in which markets operate that reduce or increase the level of competition

comparative advantage when a country, firm or individual is able to produce a particular good or service at a lower opportunity cost than other countries, firms or individuals

GDP per head in Bangladesh in 2012 was about $750. It is one of the world's poorest countries. In 1950 agricultural share of GDP was 70% and manufacturing contribution was 4%. Over the years this changed and, in 2011, agricultural share of GDP was only 18% and manufacturing share increased to 30% of GDP.

A number of LDCs export tourism. For example, in 2011, the tourist sector accounted for 17% of GDP in Tanzania and 5.7% of the GDP in Kenya. Tourism is becoming a very important source of export and tax revenue for some LDCs.

Why are some countries caught in the poverty trap (poverty cycle)?

When incomes are very low households spend all of their income. Poor households must spend nearly all their income on satisfying their needs. Poor countries have a very high **marginal propensity to consume** and, therefore, a very low **marginal propensity to save**. A country that is very poor is not able to save and, therefore, there are few funds available for investment in **human capital** and **physical capital** – because there is little investment **productivity** changes very slowly. Investment is needed for economic growth, without it the economy cannot grow and incomes remain low. Income and expenditure are low, therefore **direct tax** and indirect tax revenue is low. The government has very little money to invest in **infrastructure** and with low levels of investment in infrastructure productivity remains low. The poverty cycle continues over generations unless it is broken by investment coming from outside of the country.

Model sentence: Low national income means that savings for investment are not accumulated and, therefore, productivity remains low leading to very slow rates of economic growth and low national income. This cycle of poverty has to be broken by inward investment.

Outline the Millennium Development Goals

In 2000, the United Nations agreed to a programme to achieve what are called the Millennium Development Goals by 2015. As discussed above, the economic development needs of LDCs are different, however the goals apply to all countries and are outlined in the illustration on page 253.

Source: World Family Organization.

The main goals are broken down into separate quantifiable targets. Progress towards these goals can be found on a number of websites. This information can be researched to gain an up-to-date assessment of progress so far.

Test your understanding of this unit by answering the following questions

- Describe the sources of economic growth in LDCs.
- Explain why economic development is dependent on economic growth.
- What are the common characteristics of LDCs?
- Explain why some countries cannot escape from the poverty cycle.

Subject vocabulary

marginal propensity to consume the proportion of additional income that an individual spends on goods and services. MPC = the change in consumption divided by the change in income.

marginal propensity to save the proportion of additional income that an individual saves. MPS = the change in savings divided by the change in income.

human capital this relates to the store of knowledge and the set of skills that a worker possesses which can be used in the production process. The higher the value of human capital the more productive the worker is. Human capital can be improved through investment in education and training.

physical capital any manufactured good that is used in the production of other goods and services such as machinery and buildings

productivity the quantity of output per unit of input

direct tax a tax that is paid directly by an individual or firm to the government. For example income tax on wages and company profits.

infrastructure the physical systems of a country that includes transport and communication networks and sewage, water, and energy supply systems

Millennium Development Goals - MDMs

Working the Millennium Development Goals at the Local Level and in the Family

MDGs - Local Authorities - Family. The Perfect Combination.

ERADICATE EXTREME POVERTY AND HUNGER

Reduce by half the proportion of people living on less than a dollar a day and suffering from hunger.

ACHIEVE UNIVERSAL PRIMARY EDUCATION

Ensure that all boys and girls complete a full course of primary schooling.

PROMOTE GENDER EQUALITY AND EMPOWER WOMEN

Eliminate gender disparity in primary and secondary education preferably by 2005, and at all levels by 2015.

REDUCE CHILD MORTALITY

Reduce by two thirds the mortality rate among children under five.

IMPROVE MATERNAL HEALTH

Reduce by three quarters the maternal mortality ratio.

COMBAT HIV/AIDS, MALARIA AND OTHER DISEASES

Halt and begin to reverse the spread and incidence of HIV/AIDS, malaria and other major diseases.

ENSURE ENVIRONMENTAL SUSTAINABILITY

Reduce by half the proportion of people without sustainable access to safe drinking water, achieve significant improvement in lives of at least 100 million slum dwellers, by 2020, and integrate the principles of sustainable development to reverse loss of environmental resources.

DEVELOP A GLOBAL PARTNERSHIP FOR DEVELOPMENT

Develop a comprehensive commitment between the International, National and Local Level to develop partnerships to achieve the Millennium Development Goals.

Figure 80.1 *Source: World Family Organization*

4.2 Measuring development

Learning Outcomes

- Distinguish between GDP per capita figures and GNI per capita figures.

- Compare and contrast the GDP per capita figures and the GNI per capita figures for economically more developed countries and economically less developed countries.

- Distinguish between GDP per capita figures and GDP per capita figures at purchasing power parity (PPP) exchange rates.

- Compare and contrast GDP per capita figures and GDP per capita figures at purchasing power parity (PPP) exchange rates for economically more developed countries and economically less developed countries.

- Compare and contrast two health indicators for economically more developed countries and economically less developed countries.

- Compare and contrast two education indicators for economically more developed countries and economically less developed countries.

- Explain that composite indicators include more than one measure and so are considered to be better indicators of economic development.

- Explain the measures that make up the Human Development Index (HDI).

- Compare and contrast the HDI figures for economically more developed countries and economically less developed countries.

- Explain why a country's GDP/GNI per capita global ranking may be lower, or higher, than its HDI global ranking.

The distinction between GDP per capita and GNI per capita is explained in detail on pages 110–112.

Distinguish between Gross Domestic Product (GDP) per capita and Gross National Income (GNI) per capita

GDP is a measure of the value of all final goods and services produced in a country in a given year. No account is taken of the ownership of the **factors of production**. As long as the goods and services are produced in the country the value of them is included in GDP. GDP per capita (per person) = GDP/population. *Ceteris paribus*, the greater the size of the population the lower is GDP per capita and the smaller the size of the population the greater is GDP per capita.

GNI includes the income generated by a country's factors wherever in the world the country's factors are located. GNI is a measure of income that is earned based on the ownership of the factors. In order to calculate GNI income paid to foreign factors (such as profit made by the foreign firms) is subtracted from GDP. Then the income earned by domestically owned factors operating in foreign countries is added. The difference between them is called net property income from abroad. Therefore GNI = GDP + net property income from abroad. GNI per capita = GNI/population.

Many developing countries try to encourage **foreign direct investment** to raise GDP. In such a country where many foreign firms own productive capacity its GDP is greater than GNP. Income earned is included in the GDP but does not often stay in the country, some of the income flows back abroad. For example, profits flow out of the country to the firms' countries of origin and foreign workers often send wages back home. This again is a loss of income. Because the income is not spent in the country it does not contribute to **economic growth**.

Compare GDP per capita figures and the GNI per capita figures for developed countries and LDCs

Model sentence: GNI = GDP + net property income from abroad. Therefore a country's GNI is greater than GDP when the income earned by the country's factors employed abroad is greater than the income earned by the foreign-owned factors employed in the country.

In 2013 Germany's GDP per capita and GNI per capita were both about $42,000. This means that income earned by German factors in other countries was almost the same as income earned by foreign factors employed in Germany.

The difference between GDP per capita figures and GNI per capita figures of developed countries is usually small. For example, the figures for Singapore, Japan, the UK, France, and the US show relatively small differences. Any difference represents a relatively small percentage of GDP and, over the years, the difference

Subject vocabulary

factors of production the inputs into the production process (land, labour, capital and entrepreneurship)

foreign direct investment cross-border investment, usually by firms, that involves the acquisition of assets in a foreign country. FDI can be the purchase of a minimum of 10% of the shares of a foreign company but also includes the creation of productive capacity.

economic growth an increase in real GDP

between them changes but not by very much. Income earned by domestically owned factors abroad is similar to income earned by the foreign factors in the domestic country.

Nigeria's GDP per capita is $1,600 and GNI per capita is $1,400, indicating that much economic activity in Nigeria is from foreign-owned factors. A proportion of the income earned by the foreign-owned factors is not spent in Nigeria but instead flows out of Nigeria to the owners of the factors. For example oil production makes an important contribution to Nigeria's GDP but most of the factors used in the production of oil are foreign owned, therefore lots of the income leaves Nigeria as payments for the factors. For example, profits flow out of Nigeria to the owners of the foreign firms.

In China, GDP per capita in 2013 was about $3,700 and GNI per capita was $3,600. There has been an increase in foreign direct investment (FDI) into China in recent years but at the same time the Chinese have increased their foreign investments. Income flowing out of China as payment for foreign-owned factors is only slightly higher than income flowing in to China as payments for Chinese factors employed abroad.

Model sentence: If an LDC attracted a lot of FDI it would lead to negative net property income from abroad because the income flowing out of the country as payment for the foreign owned factors would be greater than the income flowing in to the country from domestically owned factors employed abroad.

Distinguish between GDP per capita figures and GDP per capita figures at purchasing power parity (PPP) exchange rates

In order to make comparisons of income between countries, one currency is used. The US dollar is usually used to make comparisons of national statistics. However, the **exchange rate** between two countries does not reflect the relative prices in the two countries. The purchasing power of income in one country is different to the purchasing power of income in other countries. The price of a given selection of goods and services in one country is not the same as in other countries. In order to correctly reflect the purchasing power of income, purchasing power parity is used so that the purchasing power exchange rate reflects differences in purchasing power.

For example, at the time of writing, the exchange rate between the US $ and the UK £ was $1 = £0.6. The exchange rate between the US $ and the Algerian Dinar (DZD) was $1 = 79 DZD. If the exchange rates accurately reflect the purchasing power of the currencies a basket of basic food products costing the equivalent of $10 should cost £6 in the UK and 790 DZD in Algeria. However, 790 DZD buys more food in Algeria than £6 buys in the UK. In other words, each US dollar of income earned in Algeria can buy more goods than a dollar of income earned in the UK. If the difference in purchasing power of income is taken into account when calculating GDP per capita the result will give a more realistic comparison of the relative **standard of living** between countries.

Listed below are the IMF's figures from 2012 for GDP per capita and GDP per capita at purchasing power parity for four countries: two developed countries, the UK and Denmark, and two LDCs, Algeria and Indonesia.

Country	GDP per capita	PPP adjusted GDP per capita
Denmark	$46,160	$32,214
The UK	$37,707	$32,805
Indonesia	$1,812	$4,470
Algeria	$1,191	$3,202

Table 81.1 *Source: IMF*

The cost of living is very high in Denmark, therefore when this is taken into account the GDP per capita falls from $46,160 to $32,214, a fall of $13,946. In the UK it falls by $4,902. The figures tell us that the cost of living in Denmark is higher than in the UK. Developed countries have a relatively high cost of living therefore PPP adjusted GDP per capita is lower than GDP per capita.

The cost of living is relatively low in Indonesia and Algeria, therefore PPP adjusted GDP per capita is higher than GDP per capita. GDP per capita figures undervalue the standard of living in Indonesia and Algeria. PPP adjusted GDP per capita figures are more useful because it allows economists to judge the real level of poverty in LDCs.

Model sentence: LDCs have a relatively low cost of living therefore PPP adjusted GDP per capita is higher than GDP per capita.

Subject vocabulary

LDC least developed country

exchange rate the price of a country's currency in terms of another currency

standard of living the level of well-being of a person or groups of people

Compare two health and education indicators for economically developed countries and LDCs

Set out below are the statistics from 2011/2012 on GDP per capita PPP, life expectancy, infant **mortality**, literacy rate, and teacher concentration. Infant mortality rate is measured in deaths per 1,000 for babies under the age of one. The literacy rate is the percentage of the population over the age of 15 who are able to write a short story about their lives and able to read basic texts, and teacher concentration is the number of teachers per 1,000 people.

Country	GDP per capita PPP	Life expectancy	Infant mortality	Literacy rate	Teacher concentration
Australia	$41,954	83 years	4.49	96%	5.6
Japan	$35,855	84.6 years	2.17	99.91%	5
Italy	$29,813	83.1 years	3.33	99%	7.2
Angola	$6,092	52 years	81.75	70.4%	1.28
India	$3,843	70 years	42	74%	2.4
Kenya	$1,781	60 years	42	87%	3.5

Table 81.2 *Source: CIA The World Factbook*

The PPP adjusted GDP per capita is included in the statistics in order to show the relationship between income and the health and educational attainment of the citizens. Life expectancy and infant mortality rates are determined by a number of factors. Governments in high income countries have more resources than governments in LDCs.

A developed country usually has clean water supply, treatment of **sewage**, food supplies, health and education services, and political stability. LDCs do not have as much income to invest in these services. Availability of food supplies, health services, and clean water is not as widespread in LDCs as in developed countries and because of this infant mortality rates are higher and life expectancy lower. Many LDCs are affected by religious conflict and civil war, resulting in many deaths and the disruption of food supplies, thereby lowering life expectancy.

Literacy rates are directly related to the number of children and young people who are able to go to school. In developed countries the law states all people must go to school up to a certain age usually 16 or 18. In LDCs the proportion of young people going to school regularly is much less. The number of teachers per 1,000 people is an indication of the wealth of a country because most teachers are employed by the government. The LDCs have a much higher birth rate than developed countries so have a greater proportion of the population at school age. LDCs have a relatively low proportion of teachers. Therefore class sizes are usually much bigger in LDCs than in developed countries. With a smaller proportion of children attending school along with bigger class sizes it is not surprising that literacy rates are relatively low. The educational opportunities available are directly related to the wealth of the country as can be seen in the statistics above.

Model sentence: PPP adjusted GDP per capita of a country is the most important determinant of the state of the health and educational attainment of its population.

Although GDP per capita PPP is an important determinant it is not a perfect indication of welfare. For example, Angola's GDP per capita PPP is much higher than India's and Kenya's, but Angola's life expectancy and literacy rates are lower and infant mortality is much higher than in India and Kenya.

Compare and contrast the HDI figures for developed countries and LDCs

The Human Development Index (HDI) is a measure of economic development. It provides an index of economic development based on three variables: life expectancy at birth, educational attainment (which includes the adult literacy rate and the ratio of children and young people who attend primary, secondary and tertiary school), and PPP adjusted GDP per capita.

The performance of a country for each variable is given a value between 0 and 1 and then the scores are put together to produce one index value. Countries are placed in one of four groups:

Group	HDI
Very high human development	0.9 and over
High human development	0.8 – 0.899
Medium human development	0.5 – 0.799
Low human development	< 0.5

Table 81.3 *Source: UN Development Report 2013*

Listed in Table 81.4 are the four countries in 2013 with the highest HDI and the four countries with the lowest HDI.

Country	HDI 2013
Norway	0.955
Australia	0.938
United States	0.937
Netherlands	0.921
Chad	0.340
Mozambique	0.327
Congo	0.304
Niger	0.304

Table 81.4 *Source: UN Development Report 2013*

Country	GNI per capita	HDI	World ranking
UAE	$59,993	0.846	30
Singapore	$52,569	0.866	26
Australia	$34,431	0.921	2
Czech Republic	$21,405	0.866	26

Table 81.5 *Source: UN Development Report 2013*

The relationship between economic development and PPP adjusted GDP per capita is clearly shown. The countries with the highest HDI have high PPP adjusted GDP per capita. Those countries that have the lowest HDI have very low PPP adjusted GDP per capita. This is because developed countries have used their factors to earn relatively high incomes and have been able to save. **Savings** can be used for **investment** in **physical capital** and **human capital** increasing **productivity** and **economic growth**. Governments of these countries have the resources to invest in education and health services, thereby improving life expectancy, educational attainment, and school enrolment.

GDP per capita is only one measure of **economic development**. On its own it does not give an accurate picture of the well-being of the citizens of a country. GDP per capita = GDP/population. But income in the country might be distributed very unequally, therefore a relatively few number of people might be very rich whilst most of the population are relatively poor. HDI measures more than one indicator of economic development and may give a more accurate picture of the well-being of a country's citizens.

The United Nations Human Development Report 2011 set out the GNI per capita and HDI for all countries. Listed above in Table 81.5 are the figures for four countries.

These statistics show that GNI per capita is not always a valid indicator of human development and well-being. Australia has a much lower GNI per capita than UAE and Singapore but its HDI is a lot higher. And UAE's GNI per capita is more than double that of the Czech Republic but it has a lower HDI.

Explain why a country's GDP per capita global ranking may be lower, or higher, than its HDI global ranking

There is a strong relationship between a country's GDP per capita and its HDI. A country with a relatively high GDP per capita is more likely to have a relatively high HDI than a country with a low GDP per capita. This is because GDP per capita is one of the variables used to calculate HDI. Therefore a country with high GDP per capita is likely to have a higher HDI global ranking than a country with low GDP.

If a country's GDP per capita is relatively high and its HDI is relatively low, as is the case for the United Arab Emirates and Singapore (see Table 81.5), it is an indication that the countries are not using national income effectively to improve the health and educational attainment of the citizens. It is also an indication that income is distributed very unequally. The **Gini-coefficient** in 2011 of both the United Arab Emirates and Singapore is relatively high but for Australia and the Czech Republic it is relatively low. For example Singapore's Gini-coefficient is 0.48 and the Czech Republic's is 0.26 which indicates that income is much more equally distributed in the Czech Republic than in Singapore (see pages 164–73 for a detailed explanation of the Gini-coefficient and distribution of income and equity).

If income is distributed very unequally it limits the number of people who can afford to buy education and health services. Most countries with relatively low Gini-coefficients use **progressive taxes** to redistribute income. Government tax revenue is used to provide education and health services to all people leading to higher literacy rates and school attendance rates and therefore a higher HDI.

Test your understanding of this unit by answering the following questions

- Is GDP per capita a valid indicator of the well-being of the citizens of a country?
- Distinguish between GDP per capita and PPP adjusted GDP per capita.
- Why might HDI be considered a better indicator of economic development than GDP per capita?

Subject vocabulary

savings income that is not spent or paid in tax

investment the addition to capital stock

physical capital any manufactured good that is used in the production of other goods and services such as machinery and buildings

human capital this relates to the store of knowledge and the set of skills that a worker possesses which can be used in the production process. The higher the value of human capital the more productive the worker is. Human capital can be improved through investment in education and training.

productivity the quantity of output per unit of input

economic growth an increase in real GDP

economic development the sustained increase in the standard of living and well-being of the population of a country

Gini-coefficient the ratio of the area under the Lorenz curve to the area under the 45 degree diagonal (line of perfect equality) on a graph of the Lorenz curve. It is a number between zero and one. Zero corresponds to perfect equality and one to perfect inequality.

progressive taxes a system of taxation in which the rate of tax increases with income

4.3 The role of domestic factors

Learning Outcomes

- With reference to a specific developing economy, and using appropriate diagrams where relevant, examine how the following factors contribute to economic development:

  a) Education and health.

  b) The use of appropriate technology.

  c) Access to credit and micro-credit.

  d) The empowerment of women.

  e) Income distribution.

Discussed below are some of the factors that contribute to economic development.

Subject vocabulary

private benefits the benefit firms or consumers receive from their own production or consumption of a good

external benefits occurs when the production or consumption of a good causes a benefit to third parties

civil society the sum of all non-governmental organizations and institutions

economically active describes people of working age who are employed or actively seeking employment

human capital this relates to the store of knowledge and the set of skills that a worker possesses which can be used in the production process. The higher the value of human capital the more productive the worker is. Human capital can be improved through investment in education and training.

productivity of labour the quantity of goods that a worker produces in a given period of time

long-run economic growth an increase in the productive capacity of a country

national income the sum of all income (wages, profits, rents, and interest) earned in a country in a given period of time

economic growth an increase in real GDP

GDP gross domestic product is the monetary value of all the finished goods and services produced within a country in a given period of time, usually measured over a year

How does education and health contribute to economic development?

There are **private benefits** and **external benefits** of education and health. The private benefits of education enjoyed by individuals include the ability to read and write, and therefore the ability to earn a higher income from their labour. There is a strong relationship between educational attainment and income earned. People also benefit from the enjoyment that comes from reading and writing. People can communicate effectively with one another leading to an expansion of **civil society**. There is also a strong relationship between the educational attainment of women and birth rates. Educated women tend to have fewer children and are therefore more likely to be **economically active**.

External benefits are the benefits enjoyed by society from having a well educated population. A country needs people with skills – such as mechanics, engineers, teachers, and doctors – if it is to develop and grow. Investment in **human capital** through education and training increases the **productivity of labour**, which is an important determinant of **long-run economic growth**. Countries with relatively high **national income** invest heavily in the provision of educational services.

There is a strong relationship between **economic growth** and educational attainment. In Pakistan literacy rates have steadily increased. In 1951 the adult literacy rate was 16.4% and by 2012 it had increased to 69.66%. Pakistan has experienced economic growth over these years, some of which was caused by increases in educational attainment. The graph in Figure 82.1 shows GDP in Pakistan from 2004 to 2012.

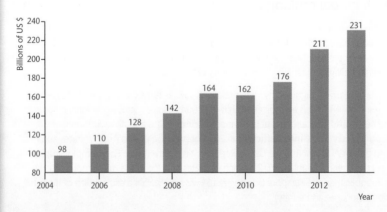

Figure 82.1 *Source: www.tradingeconomics.com*

Although there have been increases in literacy rates they have been slow and are now increasing at a decreasing rate. Female literacy rates are relatively low at 55% which harms prospects of development and growth. Less developed countries spend a relatively smaller proportion of **GDP** on education than do more developed countries. For example, Pakistan spends 2.7% of its GDP on education while Norway spends 6.8% of its GDP on education.

There are private benefits enjoyed by healthy people. They can live more of their lives free from pain and disease and they are able to continue to work for longer, thereby earning higher income. There are also external benefits enjoyed by society. The quality of human capital is an important determinant of economic development and growth.

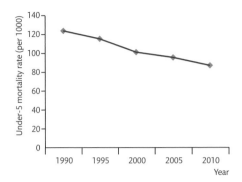

This graph shows that the under 5 years old mortality rate per 1,000 births fell from over 120 in 1990 to about 80 in 2010 and has continued to fall. Despite the fall in rates Pakistan has one of the highest child mortality rates in South Asia.

Life expectancy during this time has steadily increased and in 2013 it was 65 years. Increases in life expectancy, literacy rates, GDP per capita, and falls in the child mortality rate have led to an increase in Pakistan's HDI.

Figure 82.2 *Source: Index Mundi*

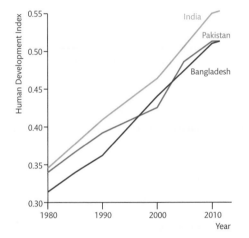

It can be seen in this graph that Pakistan's HDI has increased from under 0.35 in 1980 to over 0.5 in 2010. Its neighbouring countries' HDI have increased in similar ways.

Unsurprisingly, LDCs spend a smaller proportion of GDP on health services than developed countries. Pakistan spends 2.2% of its GDP on health services and has 0.8 doctors per 1,000 people. In Norway there are 4.2 doctors per 1,000 people and it spends 9.2% of its GDP on health services.

Model sentence: An increase in investment in education and health leads to an increase in productivity and higher income per capita.

Figure 82.3 *Source: UN Human Development Report 2013*

Why is the availability of credit and appropriate technology important for economic development?

The availability of **credit** is the most important determinant of entrepreneurial activity. An individual might have a good idea for a business but the idea cannot be turned into a real business without **start-up capital**.

In developed countries national income is relatively high. Higher income earners are able to put money into **saving accounts**. Banks therefore are able to lend to potential **entrepreneurs**. In low income countries households spend nearly all their income on satisfying needs, therefore, not very much money is saved and not much money is available for lending. In many regions of poor countries there are no banks. Credit is also needed by existing businesses to buy **capital** that will increase their **productivity**.

Productivity in agricultural output in developing countries such as Pakistan is relatively low. This is because farms in Pakistan are small and farmers are unable to benefit from technical **economies of scale**. Farmers do not have the money to invest in more **technologically advanced capital**. Agricultural output therefore earns farmers a low income from which they are unable to save. Availability of credit is needed if farmers are to break out of this cycle of low income and low productivity. A productive agricultural sector is needed to meet the higher demands of a growing industrial, urbanized, developing economy.

Model sentence: Businesses in LDCs have high average fixed costs due to low productivity. Without higher income or access to credit they are unable to invest in new capital therefore labour productivity and income remains low.

Micro-credit refers to relatively small loans, of a few hundred dollars, offered to groups or individuals by international financial institutions. Many women, who are unable to obtain credit in other ways, make use of micro-credit. The money is usually used to start up small businesses.

Subject vocabulary

credit an agreement in which a person or business borrows money, usually from a bank, and agrees to pay back the lender the sum borrowed plus the interest within an agreed period of time

start-up capital money that is needed to set up a new business

saving accounts a bank account which pays interest on deposits

entrepreneurs an individual who, in pursuit of profit, brings together the other factors of production in order to produce a good or service

capital (goods) manufactured goods that are used in the production of other goods

productivity the quantity of output per unit of input

economies of scale the fall in average cost in the long run brought about by an increase in the size of a firm's operation

technologically advanced capital capital that incorporates new technology and is used in place of existing capital to produce goods and services thereby increasing productivity

average fixed costs equal to total fixed cost divided by quantity of output

interest rate the percentage amount charged by a lender for money borrowed or paid to a person for saving money

unemployment occurs when there are people actively looking for work at the equilibrium wage rate but are not able to find work

labour market a market in which firms demand labour and workers supply labour. The interaction of demand and supply of labour determines the equilibrium wage.

technological unemployment unemployment caused by technological changes. It occurs when capital replaces labour in the production of goods.

intermediate technology technology that is appropriate for use in less developed countries that allows making use of the country's available resources and skills

labour-intensive describes production that requires a large amount of labour relative to the amount of capital

labour participation rate the percentage of the working-age population who are employed or actively seeking employment

GDP per capita equals gross domestic product of a country divided by the population

resources the inputs into the production process, the factors of production

progressive tax system a system of taxation in which the rate of tax increases with income

The loans require very little paperwork to organize but are sometimes time consuming and costly to administer because the loans go to people who live over a large geographical area, often in remote places, and because of this a relatively high **interest rate** is charged on micro-credit loans. Most are short-term loans due for repayment within the year.

Once a business has started to grow, and is profitable, entrepreneurs are able to borrow more money to enable the business to expand. The lenders in most countries are regulated by government and, although relatively high interest rates are charged on loans, borrowers do not have to borrow from unregulated money lenders who charge very high day lending rates and who sometimes use violence and other threats to ensure repayment of loans.

Model sentence: Micro-credit allows ideas to become small businesses which can grow to make a valuable contribution to a developing country's GDP.

Many developing countries have high levels of **unemployment**. Supply of labour onto the **labour market** exceeds demand for labour. Some economists believe that the introduction of technologically advanced capital at this stage of development is not appropriate because workers do not have the skills necessary to effectively use modern capital and workers currently employed would be replaced with capital, leading to **technological unemployment**. It has been argued that developing countries should employ **intermediate technology** that is more suited to the needs of LDCs. Capital employed should not require a high level of skill to operate it or maintain it.

Model sentence: Developing countries have a surplus of low skilled workers therefore intermediate technology appropriate for labour-intensive production should be used by businesses to ensure higher levels of employment.

Why would increasing gender equality contribute to economic development?

In the developing world many more women than men are not in the labour market. The female **labour participation rate** in Pakistan was 28% in 2013. The female participation rate in the US was 60%. The World Development Report by the World Bank, published in 2013, stated that 80% of Pakistani women believed family household duties and a lack of education were the causes of their non-participation in the labour market. Pakistan has the world's second-highest number of children not attending school, more than 5 million. More than 3 million of those not attending school are girls. Religious groups in some developing countries discourage girls from going to school, often threatening violence against those who try to attend.

Societies in many LDCs are very inequitable. Women are discriminated against in many ways. About 52% of the population in Africa are women and in 2013 it is estimated that on average women did about 75 percent of the agricultural work but earned only 10% of income. Most land is owned by older men, women own about 1% of the continent's assets. In most developed countries women have equal access to education and health services; this is not the case in LDCs. There is a strong relationship between education and birth rates. The more educated tend to have fewer children, and this means they are more likely to enter the labour market. The quantity and productivity of women in the labour market over the years in developed countries has led to an increase in **GDP per capita**.

Model sentence: Educating women leads to a fall in the birth rate and an increase in the labour participation rate.

The United Nations monitors gender equity in developing countries and, through discussion with politicians, encourages them to introduce policies that will reduce gender discrimination.

Model sentence: Low educational attainment and a low labour participation rate amongst women is a waste of the world's scarce resources. Empowering women in developing countries would lead to increases in GDP per capita and a reduction in poverty.

Why would reducing income inequality contribute to economic development?

A **progressive tax system** is used in developed countries in order to redistribute income. For example, by increasing the tax rate as income increases Norway has redistributed income away from those on high income to those on low income, making the distribution of income more equal. GDP is relatively high, therefore the government can collect and spend **tax revenue** to provide all citizens with education and health services, making society more equitable. Spending on education and health improves the **productivity of labour**, leading to increases in **GDP** and economic development.

Governments in developing countries are unable to distribute income more equally for a number of reasons. In developing countries GDP is low, limiting the amount of tax revenue governments can raise. A high proportion of economic activity takes place in informal markets. Income earned in these markets is not taxed. And because there are relatively few companies operating in developing countries taxes raised from company profits is low.

The **bureaucratic** infrastructure necessary to effectively collect taxes does not exist in many LDCs. Without an effective system of collecting taxes backed up with a legal structure to ensure payment, **tax avoidance** is high.

In many developing countries **wealth**, land, and **capital** are owned by a very small proportion of the population and there is a large gap between the educational attainment of the rich and the poor. Along with the absence of effective progressive taxation it is not surprising that the distribution of income is very unequal.

Many East Asian countries have experienced high levels of economic growth, along with increasing income equality. Governments have introduced progressive taxation and have invested in **human capital** and **physical capital**, including **transport infrastructure**.

Economic growth and the continued redistribution of income has provided an opportunity for more people to save leading to a more equal distribution of wealth and increases in **investment**.

A more equal distribution of income leads to greater political stability. Many developing countries have a very unequal distribution of income. A large proportion of the population do not have the opportunity to raise their **standard of living**. There are no **transfer payments** from government to households to help support poor and unemployed families. This can lead to social and political unrest.

Model sentence: A more equal distribution of income leads to greater social stability and increases in the rate of savings and investment.

4.4 The role of international trade

Learning Outcomes

- With reference to specific examples, explain how the following factors are barriers to development for economically less developed countries:

  a) Over-specialization on a narrow range of products.

  b) Price **volatility** of primary products.

  c) Inability to access international markets.

- With reference to specific examples, explain how long-term changes in the terms of trade is a barrier to development for economically less developed countries. (HL)

- With reference to specific examples, evaluate each of the following as a means of achieving economic growth and economic development:

  a) Import substitution.

  b) Export promotion.

  c) Trade liberalization.

  d) The role of the WTO.

  e) Bilateral and regional preferential trade agreements.

Discussed below are some of the factors that act as barriers to economic development in LDCs.

Why does over-specialization act as a barrier to economic development?

Model sentence: An LDC is dependent on the production of primary goods, making the country dependent on a limited number of goods for its export revenue, with which it can buy the imports it needs.

Over-specialization on a narrow range of goods means a country can be badly affected by changes in the relative prices of exports and imports. If the world price of the main export falls the **terms of trade** deteriorate. As industries become more productive, world supply increases – pushing long-term prices down – therefore the terms of trade of primary goods falls over time. Fewer imports can be bought with the revenue earned from a given quantity of exports.

Model sentence: As the world supply of primary goods increases and their price falls, an increasing quantity of agricultural or mineral output will be needed to pay for imported manufactured goods.

If a country does not increase the range of goods it produces the falling price of primary goods will lead to increases in poverty.

In order to increase export revenues, by meeting the increasing demand for primary goods in the developed world, LDCs use up their non-renewable resources, thereby reducing the opportunities for future generations to earn income. Some primary products will eventually run out, so economic development will be negatively affected if it does not increase the variety of goods produced. A country that is over-dependent on a narrow range of goods tends to concentrate most of its investment in those industries, leaving very little left for investment in industrialization, education, and health which would improve economic development in the long term.

Agricultural output, unlike manufactured goods produced in developed countries, is affected by changes in weather conditions. Supply, and therefore revenue earned, varies over short time periods. Developed countries also **dump** their **excess supply** at below cost prices, leaving the domestic suppliers in LDCs unable to compete.

Why does the price volatility of primary goods affect economic development?

As explained above, over-dependence on a primary good leads to **deterioration** in the terms of trade thereby limiting a county's ability to raise its standard of living. Another problem is that the world price of primary goods fluctuates in the short-term. Prices of primary goods are mainly determined by the world supply of them. Producers are price takers with very little influence over price.

The quantity of primary goods supplied is not very responsive to changes in price. For example, a farmer decides which crops to grow a long time before the goods come to market. It takes a long time to move **resources** away from the production of one crop to the production of another. It is not possible to change the quantity supplied in the short term, therefore supply of agricultural goods is **price inelastic**. Supply of manufactured goods are likely to be more **price elastic** than agricultural goods because it is easier for firms producing manufactured goods to reallocate their factors to different production processes and thereby increase output. And because there are few, if any, **substitutes** for some primary goods **price elasticity of demand** tends to be inelastic.

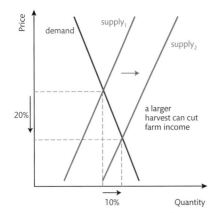

Figure 82.4

Changes in the world demand for, or supply of, primary goods lead to relatively large changes in the world price. Figure 82.4 shows an increase in supply of an agricultural good, perhaps through increases in productivity. As world output increases consumption rises by 10% but price falls by 20%. **Producer revenue** earned from the sale of the good falls. If a country is dependent on the export revenue from the sale of the agricultural good the fall in income flowing into the country will be large. The terms of trade will deteriorate and the **balance of trade** will worsen. Rwanda, for example, earns a high proportion of export revenue from the farming of coffee beans. A fluctuation in the world supply of coffee beans has a big effect on Rwanda's export earnings.

As incomes fall, farmers in developing countries try to increase supply in order to increase income. This can have the effect of reducing price even further. Land becomes over used, leading to soil **degradation** and negatively affecting **productivity**, harming the opportunities of future generations to earn income from the land.

Model sentence: Increases in productivity in the agricultural industry lead to increases in the world supply of agricultural products and a fall in price.

Why is the inability to access international markets a barrier to economic development?

The World Bank's 2009 World Development Report highlighted how important market access is to a country's economic development. Countries that are **landlocked** have a major disadvantage. It is more difficult for them to access overseas markets. For example, landlocked African countries have particularly low levels of economic development. Niger, Chad, Mali, and the Central African Republic are landlocked African countries and have amongst the lowest HDI in the world, all being under 0.36. Poor countries lack the investment needed to improve cross-border **transport infrastructure** making it costly and very difficult to get their goods to foreign markets. And lack of cooperation between neighbouring countries makes it more difficult for landlocked countries to gain access to international markets.

Governments throughout the world protect their domestic producers of primary goods from international trade restricting developing countries, access to foreign markets. **Protectionist policies** include **tariffs**, **quotas**, and **subsidies** to domestic producers along with non-price restrictions such as **technical trade barriers**. For example, the EU subsidizes the production of some agricultural output which acts as an incentive for European farmers to increase supply, pushing down the world price, thereby reducing the income of producers in developing countries. Some of the excess supply is dumped in developing countries at below cost prices, harming domestic producers. Such policies stop farmers in developing countries from benefiting from the **comparative advantage** they have in the production of such goods and reduce income earned from export revenues. Lack of income leads to low levels of investment leaving farmers in developing countries unable to raise productivity. (See pages 201–209 for a detailed discussion on the effects of trade protection on international trade.)

Discussed below are various ways by which economic growth and development can be achieved:

How might import substitution industrialization (ISI) affect economic growth and development?

Model sentence: The aim of ISI is to encourage domestic producers to make goods that are currently being imported so that domestic consumers switch expenditure away from imports to domestically produced goods.

Subject vocabulary

price elastic the percentage change in quantity demanded/supplied > the percentage change in price

substitutes a good that can be used in place of another good

price elasticity of demand a measure of how quantity demanded responds to a change in price in percentage terms

producer revenue the income a firm receives from consumers in exchange for goods (revenue = price × quantity sold)

balance of trade the difference between the monetary value of a country's exports and the monetary value of its imports

productivity the quantity of output per unit of input

transport infrastructure the physical capital that supports a transport system such as roads, railways, ports, airports

protectionist policies policies, such as tariffs and quotas, aimed at protecting domestic firms and industries from foreign competition

tariffs a tax placed on imported goods and services

quotas a physical limit placed on the number of goods that can be traded or produced

subsidies payments made by government to firms per unit of output

technical trade barriers things that may stop firms being able to export their goods into a country, e.g. technical regulations, minimum standards, certification for health and safety

comparative advantage when a country, firm, or individual is able to produce a particular good or service at a lower opportunity cost than other countries, firms, or individuals

Glossary

degradation becoming worse in condition

landlocked a country that is surrounded by other countries

average costs is equal to total cost divided by quantity of output

labour-intensive describes production that requires a large amount of labour relative to the amount of capital

infant industries a new industry which often is not able to compete against established foreign industries and therefore needs to be protected from the competition through subsidies and tariffs

technologically advanced capital capital that incorporates new technology and is used in place of existing capital to produce goods and services thereby increasing productivity

economies of scale the fall in average cost in the long run brought about by an increase in the size of a firm's operation

barriers to trade restrictions imposed by a government on the free exchange of goods or services between countries

raw materials the basic material from which a good is made

capital (goods) manufactured goods that are used in the production of other goods

export subsidies payments made by a government to its exporting firms or industries per unit of the good exported

exchange rate controls restrictions imposed by the government of a country on the buying and selling of its currency for another

comparative advantage when a country, firm, or individual is able to produce a particular good or service at a lower opportunity cost than other countries, firms, or individuals

GDP gross domestic product is the monetary value of all the finished goods and services produced within a country in a given period of time, usually measured over a year

human capital this relates to the store of knowledge and the set of skills that a worker possesses which can be used in the production process. The higher the value of human capital the more productive the worker is. Human capital can be improved through investment in education and training.

continued on page 265

Infant domestic industries would find it difficult to compete against the large existing foreign firms who produce at relatively low **average costs**. Therefore, the government of a developing country protects its emerging manufacturing industries through tariffs and quotas placed on imported manufactured goods and through subsidies paid by the government to domestic producers.

Developing countries have a large surplus of low skilled labour and should therefore focus on developing industries that are **labour-intensive**. Such industries include the textile industry (clothes and shoes) and the drinks industry. These goods are in high demand in developing and developed countries.

However, the new emerging **infant industries** must compete against foreign firms that have been in business a long time producing for a very large market. Existing large firms are able to invest in **technologically advanced capital** and they benefit from **economies of scale**, leading to low average costs. Infant industries in developing countries are not able to compete on price against the more productive foreign firms, the government must therefore put up protectionist barriers against cheaper imports.

Given time the emerging industries can increase the size of their market and gain economies of scale and the skills necessary to compete internationally, so that the barriers to trade can be reduced or removed. However, owners of the protected industries put pressure on the government to keep the tariffs and, because the government gains tax revenue from tariffs, the **barriers to trade** often remain in place for the long term. Without competitive pressure, domestic producers have little incentive to become more productive.

Other countries may raise trade barriers against imports coming from the developing country in response to tariffs placed on their goods. This will reduce the export revenues earned from the developing country's existing exporting industries.

The domestic market in developing countries is relatively small and incomes are low, thereby restricting the level of demand for the goods. Therefore potential revenue and profit is limited. Domestic producers must try to sell their output on the international market. But to do this, firms must use the time that they are protected to increase productivity so they are able to compete internationally. It is possible that, even if productivity was increased, foreign countries in the developed world would raise barriers to trade against the developing country.

Developing countries hoped that ISI would reduce dependency on imported goods. However, industrialization increased the quantity of imported **raw materials** and **capital** goods needed for production in the newly created industries.

Model sentence: ISI led to increases in the amount of export revenue needed to buy the imports necessary for production but the output was for domestic consumption and therefore earned no export revenue.

How might export promotion affect economic growth and development?

Export promotion is a policy aimed at increasing a country's export revenue through introducing protectionist policies, such as **export subsidies** and **exchange rate controls**. The aim is to take full advantage of the **comparative advantage** a country has in the production of particular goods and to encourage domestic production of the goods for export, thereby increasing export revenue, domestic incomes, and economic growth. Government can also help firms in the export market by providing advice on which goods to produce and on identifying potential international markets in which to sell the goods.

The government of a developing country can make its exports more competitive by paying subsidies to domestic exporting industries. In effect this reduces costs of production, allowing the exporters to sell at a lower price. Government can also devalue the domestic currency, thereby making the exports more price competitive.

During the 1960s, Korea put in place a policy of export-led growth. At first the aim was to promote the export of goods from industries that were labour-intensive in order to take advantage of Korea's surplus of low cost and low skilled labour. Export growth mainly came from the clothes and footwear industries. Taiwan and Malaysia followed a similar policy. **GDP** increased, leading to an increase in savings and investment. Over time, through investment in **human capital** and **physical capital**, the countries experienced **long-run economic growth**. Exporting industries no longer needed to rely on low-cost, labour-intensive production methods. Through economic growth and investment the countries' exporters moved towards **capital-intensive** production and produced a greater variety of manufactured goods for the export market.

Governments of developing countries must achieve certain **macroeconomic objectives** in order to ensure international competitiveness. Most importantly, governments must keep inflation low and stable. High rates of inflation reduce price competitiveness, harming the export industries. The government must also ensure that the **exchange rate** is kept at a rate that makes exports price competitive.

When a high proportion of income in a country comes from the sale of exports the country's economy can become over-dependent on demand for their goods from the rest of the world. **Recessions** in other countries lead to a fall in demand for all goods in those countries, including the demand for imports. In a global recession demand for the developing country's exports falls, leading to a big fall in the flow of income into the country and a fall in GDP.

The developed countries also want to protect their domestic industries from foreign competition. Barriers to trade such as tariffs are put up in response to cheaper imports from developing countries, thereby reducing the export revenues of developing countries.

The success of decades of export-led growth in improving economic development in South Korea and Taiwan can be judged by the value of the countries' HDI. In 2013, South Korea's HDI was 0.909 and Taiwan's was 0.890. These are very similar to the HDIs of older developed countries such as the UK, France, and Italy.

How might trade liberalization affect economic growth and development?

Trade liberalization is the reduction or removal of barriers to trade. Each developing country has a comparative advantage in the production of particular goods. That is, each country can produce a particular good at a lower opportunity cost than can other countries. If each country produces goods in which they have a comparative advantage, and then trades, more goods can be produced with the world's scarce resources thereby increasing economic welfare (see pages 196–201 for a detailed discussion on the benefits of free trade).

However, many developing countries have a comparative advantage in the production of **primary goods**. As explained earlier in this unit the prices of these goods fluctuate and are falling in the long term, leading to falling incomes. The advantage developing countries have in the production of manufactured goods comes from the surplus of low skilled workers that pushes labour costs down. In order to maintain this advantage wages in exporting industries must be kept low, leading to a low **standard of living** and high levels of poverty. Some economists argue that trade liberalization is encouraged by developed countries so that they can import cheap goods and thereby enjoy a higher standard of living at the expense of the low paid workers in developing countries. **Multi-national corporations** (MNCs) operating in developing countries also benefit from keeping wages low because it leads to higher profit. Some economists argue that trade liberalization benefits MNCs and buyers in developed countries but leads to increases in **relative poverty**, low wages, unequal distribution of income, and very poor working conditions in LDCs.

If a developing country removed its barriers to trade on imported goods the price of imports would fall, increasing buyers' **purchasing power**. But at the same time domestic producers would not be able to compete against cheaper imports, leading to a fall in demand for their goods and a rise in **demand-deficient unemployment**. The theory of comparative advantage says that developing countries should reallocate resources to the production of goods it can produce most efficiently. In the real world this is often not possible because factors of production are not perfectly mobile. In other words, it is often the case that factors used in one industry cannot be used in other industries. However, even if this is done, other countries can put up barriers to trade effectively eliminating the advantage.

The World Trade Organization encourages all countries to agree to the removal of barriers to trade whilst at the same time asking the developed world to consider the particular needs of developing countries. In particular, it encourages developed countries to remove agricultural subsidies and to stop **dumping**, and to allow imports of manufactured goods from LDCs free of tax and quotas in order to encourage industrialization and economic growth in LDCs.

Model sentence: The WTO's long-term aim is to encourage developed countries to put in place a set of agreements over trade that take into account the particular circumstances of developing countries, so that they are able to increase the size of their industrial sectors and reduce their dependence on the export revenue earned from the production of primary goods.

In the short term the WTO encourages regional trade agreements to increase economic integration. The WTO puts forward the view that free trade with neighbouring countries allows developing countries to gain from the benefits of trade liberalization (such as economies of scale) on a regional level amongst countries which have similar economic conditions without having to deal with the potential costs of trade liberalization with developed countries. See pages 238–42 for a detailed explanation of trade agreements and economic integration.

Subject vocabulary

physical capital any manufactured good that is used in the production of other goods and services such as machinery and buildings

long-run economic growth an increase in the productive capacity of a country

capital-intensive describes production that requires a large amount of capital relative to the amount of labour

macroeconomic objectives the main aims of government macroeconomic policy, such as low and stable inflation, low levels of unemployment, and sustainable economic growth

exchange rate the price of a country's currency in terms of another currency

recessions two consecutive quarters of negative economic growth

primary goods a good that has not been processed and is in a raw state (e.g. fruit/wheat)

standard of living the level of well-being of a person or groups of people

multi-national corporations a corporation that operates in two or more countries

relative poverty a measure of poverty that relates to the average income earned in a country or region. Definitions vary but many governments define it as an income less than 50% of the median income.

purchasing power a measure of how many goods and services a given amount of money can buy

demand-deficient unemployment unemployment caused by a lack of aggregate demand. Unemployment changes as the economy goes through the business cycle, increasing when AD falls and decreasing when AD rises.

dumping the export by a country or firms of goods at a price that is lower than the cost of production

terms of trade the amount of imported goods a country can buy per unit of its exported goods

price elasticity of supply a measure of how quantity supplied responds to a change in price in percentage terms

natural resources assets, such as mineral deposits and timber, that occur in nature and can be used in production

foreign direct investment cross-border investment, usually by firms, that involves the acquisition of assets in a foreign country. FDI can be the purchase of a minimum of 10% of the shares of a foreign company but also includes the creation of productive capacity.

corporation taxes a tax levied in the UK on company profits

fiscal policy government policy designed to achieve macroeconomic objectives through government expenditure and taxation

inflation an increase in the general level of prices of goods/services in an economy over a given time period, usually a year

exchange rates the price of a country's currency in terms of another currency

productivity the quantity of output per unit of input

national output the value of all goods and services produced in a country in a given period of time

cycle of poverty occurs in a country which has low income and therefore low levels of savings. Low levels of savings means little investment can take place and the economy is unable to grow, thus income remains low.

How might diversification affect economic growth and development?

The disadvantages of over-specialization have already been explained in this unit along with the advantages and disadvantages of export promotion and import substitution.

The global economic crisis and recession which began in 2008 has highlighted the structural weaknesses of many LDCs, particularly in Africa, which are dependent on export revenue from the sale of primary goods. Income flowing into an LDC is affected by world demand for primary goods. Global demand for primary goods decreased during the global recession, leading to a fall in price and deterioration in the **terms of trade**. Lower prices led to a fall in the export revenue of many LDCs and the fall in price from a fall in demand is relatively large because **price elasticity of supply** is inelastic. Also, extreme weather conditions in LDCs affect the supply of agricultural output leading to changes in supply and fluctuations in price.

Good governance is needed to create the economic conditions necessary for **diversification**. Government needs to ensure that **natural resources** are managed effectively and not over used. Investment in human capital will increase the skills and health of the labour force and thereby attract **foreign direct investment**. Further incentives, such as relatively low **corporation taxes** and a large surplus of low cost labour will also help to attract inward investment.

Governments can encourage trade on a regional basis by reaching trade agreements with neighbouring countries so that local producers can benefit from access to new, bigger markets and benefit from greater economies of scale.

Fiscal policy must be used to keep **inflation** at a low and stable level so that exports remain price competitive. **Exchange rates** must be low enough to ensure emerging exporting industries are competitive and the government must direct investment into improving the country's **infrastructure**, in particular transport and communication infrastructure, so that industries are able to access markets efficiently.

Diversification means that a country becomes less dependent on the sale of its primary goods for its income. Over time, through industrialization, GDP rises allowing more income to be saved. Increases in investment in human and physical capital lead to increases in **productivity** and **national output**. Government gains more tax revenue and can target spending on improving educational attainment and health services thereby increasing economic development and the country's HDI. In this way a country can break the **cycle of poverty**.

For some countries, particularly African landlocked countries such as Chad, Mali, and Niger, the prospects for diversification and economic development are not good. Many countries do not have the legal infrastructure or good governance necessary for economic development. Many politicians are only interested in gaining and holding onto power in order to make themselves and their friends and families rich. Many do not have to be re-elected and even when there are elections the outcome is fixed. Focus must be on responsible governance, creating the legal and financial infrastructure necessary for long-run economic growth and development.

Test your understanding of this unit by answering the following questions

- Distinguish between import substitution and export promotion.
- Explain why the price of primary goods is volatile.
- Explain how over-specialization on the production of primary goods affects a developing country's economic development.

4.5 The role of foreign direct investment (FDI)

Learning Outcomes

- Describe the nature of foreign direct investment (FDI) and multinational corporations (MNCs).

- Explain the reasons why MNCs expand into economically less developed countries.

- Describe the characteristics of economically less developed countries that attract FDI, including low cost factor inputs, a regulatory framework that favours profit repatriation, and favourable tax rules.

- Evaluate the impact of foreign direct investment (FDI) for economically less developed countries

What is foreign direct investment (FDI)?

FDI is investment by a company in other countries. FDI occurs when a foreign company builds new factories in a country. This is called greenfield inward investment, and when a company buys or leases existing productive assets it is called brownfield inward investment. For example, *Coca Cola* has invested in an existing factory in Uganda where the drinks are produced and bottled. The purchase by a foreign buyer of 10% or more of the shares of a company is also an example of FDI. When a company invests in productive assets in more than one country, by definition, they are multinational corporations (MNCs). Most FDI is investment by MNCs in productive assets in developing countries. FDI leads to an increase in the flows of **financial capital** into a country.

Why do MNCs locate in developing countries?

A MNC is looking for (or seeking) benefits that are unavailable in their home country. Most of these benefits have the effect of reducing **average costs**. Discussed below are the reasons why an MNC chooses to locate in a country.

Resource seeking

An MNC may locate in a country that has the **resources** it wants for the production of its good, such as **raw materials**, natural resources (e.g. oil and minerals), and a large supply of low skilled labour, all of which maybe unavailable where it is currently located.

Market seeking

An MNC may locate in a country in order to increase the size of its market thereby increasing sales. The MNC may want to take advantage of growing demand for its good in a particular country or region.

Efficiency/lower cost seeking

This reason for FDI is closely linked to the previous reasons. MNCs want to reduce **costs of production**. Locally available resources means that transport costs fall and production is unlikely to be affected by problems in the supply chain.

Where there is a **surplus** of low skilled workers wages will be low thereby reducing costs of production.

MNCs can increase the size of their market by locating in a country. With greater **demand** for its output it can expand production. The MNC can then benefit from greater **economies of scale** thereby reducing average costs. The cost of getting the goods to the market is also reduced.

By locating production in a country an MNC can avoid **barriers to trade** put up by that country. Instead of exporting goods into the country the MNC produces goods in the country, thereby avoiding the **tariffs** or **quotas** placed on imports. The avoidance of tariffs gives the MNC a competitive advantage.

Developed countries have strict health and safety regulations that firms must obey. The costs of complying with the regulations are high. In developing countries regulations are not as strict, therefore an MNC can avoid these costs by locating production in the developing country.

A developing country's government will reduce the **corporation tax** rate and other business taxes in order to attract investment from an MNC. This has the effect of reducing the MNC's costs of production.

Model sentence: MNCs locate in LDCs in order to lower average costs and thereby increase competitiveness and company profits.

Other factors that MNCs consider

The developing country must be able to provide at least some of the advantages to MNCs described above. The developing country must be politically stable. Civil war and religious conflict can seriously disrupt production and increase costs. MNCs want there to be an effective legal structure that protects property and **property rights** and enforces business contracts. **Transport infrastructure** must be good enough for the firm to be able to transport its goods efficiently to its markets.

An MNC wants to be able to repatriate profit so that profit can flow easily from the developing country to the MNC's home country. The MNC wants to exchange the foreign currency for their domestic currency when repatriating profits. If the developing country's government has put in place limits on the amount of capital that can flow out from the country the MNC may choose not to invest in that country. Some developing countries charge a 0% tax rate on all reinvested profit in order to reduce the amount of income leaving the country.

An MNC considers the macroeconomic conditions in a country. For example, an MNC will be put off investing in a country that has high rates of **inflation**.

Evaluate the effects of FDI on developing countries

Discussed below are the possible benefits gained by developing countries that attract FDI.

Explain the effects on employment, income, and tax revenues of FDI

FDI is an injection of capital into the economy of the developing country. An MNC uses some of a developing country's factors of production in order to make goods. In particular, FDI has a direct impact on employment and income. An MNC employs labour for which it pays a wage. Unemployment falls and income increases.

FDI also has an indirect impact on employment and income. A proportion of the extra income earned by those employed by the MNC is spent by households on goods and services, thereby increasing the amount of money flowing to other firms in the economy which in turn flows to households as income. As incomes rise **aggregate demand** increases, leading to an increase in **aggregate supply** and a fall in unemployment. FDI is an injection into the circular flow of income of the developing country and injections create a **multiplier effect** (see pages 134–37 for a detailed explanation of the multiplier effect).

FDI directly increases demand for goods and services from domestic businesses that can supply the MNC with raw materials, capital goods, and services.

Indirect tax is tax on expenditure. As wages increase spending increases, therefore **tax revenue** increases. **Direct tax** is a tax on income. As unemployment falls and more people are earning a wage, tax revenue increases.

The MNC's profit is also taxed therefore, tax revenue increases. The extra tax revenue may be spent by the government on education and health services thereby increasing the value of the country's **Human Development Index**.

Model sentence: FDI reduces unemployment, increases income and raises tax revenue.

Explain the effects on skills, technology, and productivity of FDI

Developing countries look to FDI from an MNC to provide training, expertise, and **technologically advanced capital**. New skills are learned, increasing the productivity of the workers. Managers in the developing country learn about efficient management techniques. These benefits will eventually reach other industries.

An MNC employs the most productive, up-to-date, capital which the developing county would not be able to afford. This provides an incentive for domestic firms to use more advanced capital. Domestic producers in the same industry will need to increase **productivity** if they are to compete successfully with the MNC. FDI creates a competitive environment and in order to survive firms must increase productivity leading to a more efficient use of scarce resources.

Model sentence: FDI is seen by governments of developing countries as a way to speed up the process of industrialization thereby reducing the country's dependency on the production of primary goods.

Explain the effects on the national accounts of FDI

FDI is an inward flow of money used for the purchase of a country's assets which is recorded on the capital account of the balance of payments. This increase of money flowing in to a developing country is a valuable source of foreign currency, allowing for the purchase of a greater quantity of imported consumer goods and **capital** goods.

However, there are other effects. An MNC's repatriated profits and money spent by the MNC on imported goods, such as raw materials, leads to an increase in the flow of money out of the country and is recorded as a negative value on the **current account**. If the MNC exports goods then money flows into the country from abroad and is recorded as a positive value on the current account. Many buyers in the country buy the good produced by the MNC in that country instead of imported goods. Therefore the money flowing out of the country for the purchase of imports falls.

Model sentence: The overall effect of FDI on the current account balance is determined by the relative size of the changes to the inflows of money from the sale of exports and the outflows of money from the purchase of imports.

The possible disadvantages of FDI

Discussed below are some of the drawbacks associated with FDI.

Explain the effects of political instability in developing countries

FDI is risky because the political conditions in some developing countries can change very quickly. Agreements made with one government may not be kept by a new government. MNC's assets might be seized by the government or tax advantages withdrawn.

Explain the effects of MNCs' influence on the governments of developing countries

MNCs sometimes put pressure on governments of developing countries to pass laws and introduce policies that are in their own interests but against the interests of the citizens and workers of the country. For example, health and safety regulations may be reduced or not enforced. **Natural resources** may be allowed to be overused and **negative externalities** caused by emissions ignored.

Explain how MNCs exploit the resources in developing countries

As stated above, an MNC may overuse the host country's natural resources in order to make gains in the short-term. The MNC's profits increase at the expense of **sustainable economic development** of the host country.

If an MNC is a **monopsonist**, wages can be pushed down. If the MNC is the largest employer or the only employer of low skilled workers in an area of the country it has the power in the **labour market** to push wages down. An MNC may also have **monopoly power** and can use this power to increase profits paid to the owners at the expense of payments paid to the other **factors of production** and restrict supply to increase prices and profit.

Explain why an increase in tax revenue from FDI is limited

In order to attract FDI the government of the developing country must charge low rates of corporate and business taxes, limiting any increase in tax revenue. When the government eventually increases the tax rate the MNC deliberately reduces its tax burden through the use of certain accounting practices. MNCs have branches in many countries. In effect the MNC transfers some of the profit made in the country where the tax rate is higher to a branch where the tax rate is lower.

Explain what happens to MCNs' profit

Not all income earned by the factors of production employed by an MNC stays in the developing country. Profit, which represents a large proportion of total income earned, is sent back to the MNC's home country.

The income that is spent in developing countries comes from the wages paid to the workers and the income spent on domestically produced inputs such as locally produced capital and raw materials.

Profit repatriation is a flow of money out of the economy. It is not spent in the economy and therefore does not contribute to economic growth and development.

Subject vocabulary

capital (goods) manufactured goods that are used in the production of other goods

current account a record of the amount of money flowing out of a country and into the country from the rest of the world from the trade in goods and services, investment income, and transfers in a given period of time

natural resources assets, such as mineral deposits and timber, that occur in nature and can be used in production

negative externalities occur when the production or consumption of a good creates costs that must be paid by third parties. The existence of negative externalities means that social cost is greater than private cost.

sustainable economic development economic growth that meets the needs and wants of the current generation in such a way that does not prevent future generations from meeting their needs and wants

monopsonist a firm or industry that is a single buyer of the product or service of many sellers

labour market a market in which firms demand labour and workers supply labour. The interaction of demand and supply of labour determines the equilibrium wage.

monopoly power the degree of control a firm has over the setting of price.

factors of production the inputs into the production process (land, labour, capital and entrepreneurship)

profit repatriation occurs when the profits earned on assets in one country go to the owners of the assets in another country

loanable funds the sum of
money in an economy that
is saved rather than used
for consumption and made
available to those wishing to
borrow

interest rates the percentage
amount charged by a lender
for money borrowed or paid
to a person for saving money

capital manufactured goods
that are used in the production
of other goods

economies of scale the cost
advantages gained by a firm
from increasing the scale of its
production. Average cost falls
in the long run as the size of a
firm's operation increases.

average costs is equal to total
cost divided by quantity of
output

barriers to entry factors that
prevent/make difficult the
entry of new firms into an
industry or market

labour-intensive describes
production that requires a
large amount of labour relative
to the amount of capital

intermediate technology
technology that is appropriate
for use in less developed
countries that allows making
use of the country's available
resources and skills

Some MNCs do not always use their own money for investment. Sometimes an MNC borrows from the local financial institutions. The increase in demand for **loanable funds** pushes up the **interest rates** and crowds out domestic firms that want to borrow.

Explain the effects of monopoly power on local businesses in developing countries

An MNC uses technologically advanced **capital** and benefits from **economies of scale** which pushes down **average costs**. Existing local firms find it very hard to compete. They lose customers to the MNC and are forced to lower their prices thereby reducing profits. Those that are unable to reduce average cost enough go out of business and workers lose their jobs. This increases the monopoly power of the MNC and it can dominate the market. **Barriers to entry** into the industry will be very high restricting entrepreneurial activity in the area.

Explain the effects of using inappropriate technology in developing countries

Developing countries have a surplus of low skilled workers and therefore it would be appropriate to use **labour-intensive** methods of production using **intermediate technology**. An MNC uses capital-intensive methods of production therefore the demand for low skilled workers is low, limiting the number of local people employed and the amount of extra income spent in the local economy.

Test your understanding of this unit by answering the following questions

- Explain how FDI might affect the current account balance.
- How might the levels of employment and income in a developing country be affected by FDI?
- Why do MNCs locate in developing countries?
- Evaluate the effects of FDI for developing countries.

4.6 The roles of foreign aid and multilateral development assistance

Learning Outcomes

- Explain that aid is extended to economically less developed countries, either by governments of donor countries, in which case it is called official development assistance (ODA), or by nongovernmental organizations (NGOs).

- Explain that humanitarian aid consists of food aid, medical aid, and emergency relief aid.

- Explain that development aid consists of grants, concessional long-term loans, project aid that includes support for schools and hospitals, and programme aid that includes support for sectors such as the education sector and the financial sector.

- Explain that, for the most part, the priority of NGOs is to provide aid on a small scale to achieve development objectives.

- Explain that aid might also come in the form of tied aid.

- Explain the motivations of economically more developed countries giving aid.

- Compare and contrast the extent, nature, and sources of ODA to two economically less developed countries.

- Evaluate the effectiveness of foreign aid in contributing to economic development.

- Compare and contrast the roles of aid and trade in economic development.

- Examine the current roles of the IMF and the World Bank in promoting economic development.

What is foreign aid?

FDI is a source of foreign currencies that helps developing countries close the **savings gap**. It can provide the investment funds necessary for countries to increase **productivity** and break free from the **cycle of poverty**. Foreign aid is also a source of investment funds. Foreign aid provided by governments is called official development assistance (ODA). Aid is also provided by non-governmental organizations (NGOs).

Distinguish between bilateral and multilateral aid

Bilateral aid is aid given by one country to another country. The aid is given directly to the country. Aid is called multilateral aid when countries give money to international organizations such as the World Bank, the IMF, and UNICEF (United Nations children's fund). The international organization is then responsible for delivering the aid.

Distinguish between loans and grants

Aid can be money loaned to a country. The receiver of the loan must pay back the money along with **interest payments**. A low **rate of interest** is charged on the loan and the country is given a long time to pay back the loan. A grant is money given to a country that does not have to be repaid.

Distinguish between tied aid and untied aid

Tied aid is aid given to a country that must be used for a specific purpose. For example, aid can be given to a country only if the country agrees to use the money to buy food or other goods such as **capital** goods from the **donor country**. Untied aid is given to a country which it can then use to buy goods and services from any approved country.

Distinguish between project assistance, technical assistance, and commodity assistance

Project assistance is a type of tied aid. It must be used to build infrastructure, such as schools, to increase educational attainment and the infrastructure required to provide fresh water supplies in order to improve health.

Technical assistance is a type of tied aid. For example, the IMF, through multilateral aid, provides technical assistance to governments concerning **macroeconomic policy** so that the government can create a stable and effective financial and banking sector. Other agencies provide training relating to the installation, operation,

Subject vocabulary

savings gap occurs when low incomes earned in a country are not high enough to provide savings for those who wish to borrow for investment purposes

productivity the quantity of output per unit of input

cycle of poverty occurs in a country which has low income and therefore low levels of savings. Low levels of savings means little investment can take place and the economy is unable to grow, thus income remains low.

interest payments the money paid at regular intervals on loans

rate of interest the percentage amount charged by a lender for money borrowed or paid to a person for saving money

capital (goods) manufactured goods that are used in the production of other goods

donor country a country that provides aid to another country

macroeconomic policy government policy aimed at affecting aggregate indicators such as unemployment, inflation, and GDP

and maintenance of modern capital equipment. The aim is to raise the productivity of **human capital** and **physical capital** so that developing countries can industrialize more quickly. The quantity and productivity of labour and capital are important determinants of **economic growth** and **economic development**.

Commodity assistance comes in the form of a grant for the purchase of **commodities** and **intermediate goods**, which are used in the production process. Examples include fertilizer, cement and other building materials, and wheat.

Distinguish between humanitarian aid and development aid

Humanitarian aid is short-term aid and is given in response to human suffering caused by natural disasters, such as earthquakes and droughts, and to relieve suffering caused by conflict. The aid comes in the form of grants from a number of sources. Some will be ODA, some will come from NGOs.

After a natural disaster emergency aid is initially provided to pay for what is needed immediately such as tents and blankets, water, food, fuel, and medicines. Some of the food is paid for and distributed by NGOs such as Oxfam and some medicines are paid for and distributed by NGOs, such as Médecins Sans Frontières, who also send doctors and nurses to disaster regions.

Official Development Aid is given to help a country improve the long-term welfare of its people by promoting the economic development of a region or country. Development aid is multilateral or bilateral official development assistance. This means that the aid comes from governments. It comes in the form of a long-term loan at favourable interest rates and can be tied or untied.

Many developed countries budget for ODA when planning **fiscal policy**. Listed below in Table 84.1 are the six countries which provide the most assistance as measured by percentage of GDP. Figures are for 2013.

Country	Percentage of GDP
Luxembourg	1%
Sweden	0.99%
Norway	0.93%
Denmark	0.84%
Netherlands	0.71%
UK	0.56%

Table 84.1 *Source: OECD*

The United Nations came to an agreement in 1970 that developed countries should aim to put aside 0.7% of GDP for ODA. By 2013 only 5 countries have achieved this target.

Non-official development aid is provided by NGOs and individual citizens. This aid is on a smaller scale than ODA. Oxfam, for example, place workers and materials in areas of poverty to provide direct help. They are involved with activities that promote health through the improvement of **sanitation** infrastructure and they provide support to improve crops. Wateraid is an NGO that promotes health by providing assistance in the provision of clean fresh water supplies in order to reduce disease.

One Cause is an NGO with a specific aim. This is their mission statement: 'We passionately believe that education is the answer to fighting poverty. We are committed to raising awareness and funds for the provision and advancement of education to those communities around the world that have little or no access to education. Our aim is to provide a socially, financially, and environmentally self-sustaining model so that local communities are empowered and equipped to pursue a more prosperous and sustainable future.

Why do developed countries give aid?

Humanitarian aid is given to reduce the suffering caused by manmade disasters, such as civil war, and natural disasters, such as a tsunami, by providing food, water, shelter, and medical services.

Longer-term aid is given to promote economic development and growth. LDCs are in the **cycle of poverty** with high levels of **unemployment** and low income leading to low **savings** and **investment**. The quantity and quality of capital is low and they are unable to industrialize and increase **productivity** in order to break free from the cycle of poverty. Aid is the inward investment LDCs need in order to increase the quality of human capital and physical capital and increase income, savings, and investment and thereby improve the well-being of their citizens. Many LDCs lack the basic **infrastructure** needed for economic growth and development.

Clean water supplies, sanitation, health and education services, transport, and communication networks are all necessary to improve economic development and increase the value of the **Human Development Index**. Because of low levels of income, countries are unable to build the infrastructure.

Model sentence: Project aid has an important role to play in the provision of the infrastructure required for economic growth and development.

Aid is sometimes given for political reasons. For example, during the Cold War, the Western bloc and the Soviet bloc gave aid to countries in Africa, Southeast Asia, and South America in an attempt to win **allies**. Aid has been used by Russia, China, and the US to influence the internal politics and the struggle for power in a country. For example, in 1979 and 1980 the US and the UK gave aid to, amongst other things, assist the Afghan forces fighting against the Soviet-led forces. In 2014 Russia is providing aid to support the Syrian government's fight against anti-government Syrian groups.

Economists, researching the motivations for aid giving, estimate that China has given $75 billion for development projects in Africa in the last decade to try to gain political and economic influence. Some economists and politicians argue that the aid is given so that China can secure the supply of **natural resources** found in many African countries that are needed for economic growth.

Developed countries give aid to increase the size of their own markets. Bilateral tied aid is given on the basis that the developing country buys goods and technical expertise from the donor country thereby increasing the size of the donor country's market and the sale of its exports.

Compare and contrast the extent, nature, and sources of ODA to two economically less developed countries

The Organization for Economic Co-operation and Development (OECD) is an international organization of 34 countries. Its aim is to promote democratic practices and a free market economy. The OECD website is a useful source of statistical information concerning aid and economic development. Information from the OECD has been used to answer this question, some of which is shown in tables 84.2 and 84.3, the statistics used are from 2012 and the two countries investigated are Mali in East Africa and Bangladesh in South Asia.

Mali's population of 14.9 million is much smaller than the population of Bangladesh, which has a population of over 150 million. Both have low **GNI** per capita. Mali's is $660 and Bangladesh's is $770. Income is very unequally distributed in both countries. The **Gini-coefficient** of both Mali and Bangladesh are under 0.34 and are amongst the lowest in the world. This means that a very high percentage of the population earn a very small percentage of total **national income**. HDI is 0.344 and Bangladesh's is 0.515 indicating that literacy rates, life expectancy, and **GDP** per capita are higher in Bangladesh than in Mali.

Mali received $1,001 million in ODA, whilst Bangladesh received $1,498 million. Bangladesh receives more ODA in total but receives much less ODA per capita. Mali's ODA per capita = $1,001 million/14.9 million people = $67.18. Bangladesh's ODA per capita = $1,498 million/150.5 million people = $9.95.

In Mali 73% of ODA is bilateral therefore 27% is multilateral. In Bangladesh ODA is more evenly split, 55% is bilateral therefore 45% is multilateral aid. It can be assumed that most of Mali's bilateral aid came from the US, because the US gave $311 million in ODA which represents 31% (311/1001 × 100) of the total ODA given to Mali by the top ten donors.

Bangladesh received $359 million from the International Development Association (IDA) which is the World's Bank fund for poor countries. This means that 24% of all ODA given to Bangladesh from the top ten donors was multilateral aid from the World Bank.

In Mali 40% of ODA is spent on health and other social sectors, which includes water and sanitation, so we might expect to see increases in life expectancy. Between 2002 and 2012 life expectancy has increased by 5 years from 47 years to 52 years, a relatively large increase. However, life expectancy in Mali is still one of the lowest in the world. Only 13% of ODA was spent on education and literacy rates have improved very little over the years. It was 31% in 2012, the fourth lowest in the world. Only 2% of ODA was spent on economic infrastructure. Mali is dependent for most of its GDP on the production of **primary goods** and has made little progress towards industrialization.

Bangladesh, on the other hand, spent 36% of ODA on economic infrastructure. Industrialization is one of the government's main aims. The government has recently invested heavily in transport infrastructure including high speed trains, more airports, and the road network. The country's ship building industry is growing steadily. By 2012, more than 75% of Bangladesh's **export revenue** came from the garment industry. Bangladesh is no longer dependent on the sale of primary goods for its export revenue. Industrialization has led to a fall of 25% in the poverty rate since 1990 and GDP per capita has doubled since 1975.

Bangladesh spends a much smaller proportion of ODA on health and other social sectors than Mali but its life expectancy rate is nearly 70 years. This represents an increase of 5 years since 2002. Literacy rates have increased quickly as well. In 2002 the adult literacy rate was 50%, by 2012 it was 60%.

Model sentence: Industrialization reduces dependency on the production of primary goods and can increase the rate of economic growth and economic development, leading to increases in the value of HDI in a country.

Mali

Receipts	2010	2011	2012
Net ODA (USD million)	1,089	1,217	1,001
Billateral share (gross ODA)	63%	62%	73%
Net ODA/GNI	12.1%	12.6%	10.2%
Net private flows (USD million)	-39	-15	-23

For reference	2010	2011	2012
Population (million)	14.0	14.4	14.9
GNI per capita (Atlas USD)	660	670	660

Top Ten Donors of gross ODA (2011–12 average)	(USD m)
1 United States	311
2 IDA	114
3 EU Institutions	113
4 Canada	105
5 France	79
6 Netherlands	53
7 AfDF	51
8 Germany	46
9 Sweden	31
10 IMF (Concessional Trust Funds)	27

Bilateral ODA by Sector (2011–12)

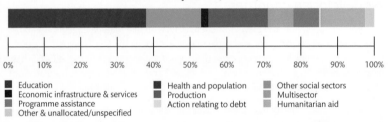

- Education
- Economic infrastructure & services
- Programme assistance
- Other & unallocated/unspecified
- Health and population
- Production
- Action relating to debt
- Other social sectors
- Multisector
- Humanitarian aid

Table 84.2 *Source: OECD*

Bangladesh

Receipts	2009	2010	2011
Net ODA (USD million)	1,226	1,415	1,498
Billateral share (gross ODA)	48%	50%	55%
Net ODA/GNI	1.3%	1.3%	1.3%
Net private flows (USD million)	182	-82	369

For reference	2009	2010	2011
Population (million)	147.0	148.7	150.5
GNI per capita (Atlas USD)	640	700	770

Top Ten Donors of gross ODA (2010–11 average)	(USD m)
1 IDA	359
2 United Kingdom	299
3 AsDB Special Funds	287
4 EU Institutions	174
5 Japan	172
6 United States	147
7 Netherlands	78
8 Canada	74
9 Denmark	72
10 Germany	71

Bilateral ODA by Sector (2010–11)

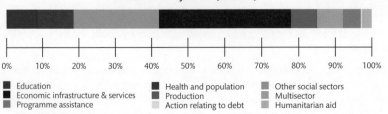

- Education
- Economic infrastructure & services
- Programme assistance
- Health and population
- Production
- Action relating to debt
- Other social sectors
- Multisector
- Humanitarian aid

Table 84.3 *Source: OECD*

Subject vocabulary

continued from page 275

recession two consecutive quarters of negative economic growth

indebtedness occurs when a household, firm, or organization owes money

Does aid promote economic development?

The purposes and benefits of aid have already been discussed in detail in this section. Some of the possible disadvantages of aid are discussed below.

Why is corruption a disadvantage?

Corruption in LDCs is widespread. Aid money is stolen by political leaders to use for their own benefit. For example, aid money is stolen and sent out of the country into personal bank accounts of politicians and their families. Aid is stolen and used to build large and luxurious homes for those in power. Those in power steal humanitarian aid, such as food and medicine and sell it for profit.

Why is tied aid a disadvantage?

An LDC that receives tied aid must accept specific conditions before a donor country gives aid. The aid might have to be spent on a particular project or the LDC must agree to use the aid to buy the donor country's goods. This means that the LDC cannot buy its imports at lowest cost, therefore not minimizing the **costs of production** of firms in the LDC. Aid is sometimes tied to the purchase of **capital** from the donor country. This can cause an increase in **technological unemployment**, particularly in a country with a large **surplus** of low skilled labour.

Why are a high degree of dependency on aid and the volatility of aid disadvantages?

When a country is very dependent on aid, measured as a percentage of **GNI**, the government's revenue goes up and down as the aid flowing into the country changes, making it difficult for the government to plan its expenditure effectively.

The proportion of income earned in LDCs that is taxed is relatively low. This is because there are large informal markets. LDCs lack the infrastructure needed to collect **tax revenue** effectively and enforce the payment of taxes. Aid acts as a disincentive for governments to improve the effectiveness of raising tax revenue.

The well-being of people living in a very poor country that needs aid to pay for basic health and education services is very badly affected by fluctuations in aid.

Why is procyclical aid a disadvantage?

Aid is **procyclical** when aid is given as the economy is growing and is on the upward slope of the **business cycle**. Procyclical aid can worsen the negative impacts on the economy when **GDP** falls and the economy is on the downward slope of the business cycle. **Countercyclical** aid, given when the economy is slowing and unemployment is rising, lessens the negative economic consequences of a **recession**.

Why is the ineffectiveness of aid agencies a disadvantage?

While there have been increases in ODA in the last decade lots of research has found that a relatively small proportion of all aid given by the donor countries reaches the LDCs. Some researchers found that many of the agencies involved in the distribution of aid are ineffective and wasteful. Much of the aid given is not used to increase the well-being of the poor in LDCs.

Why is aid in the form of loans a disadvantage?

Grants do not have to be repaid. They represent a transfer of currency from relatively rich developed countries to LDCs. Loans have to be repaid as do the interest payments on the loans. Over time the total **indebtedness** of LDCs increase. Debts must be paid back in the future, reducing the amount of income in the economy available for spending on other things such as education and health.

continued on page 274

terms of trade the amount of imported goods a country can buy per unit of its exported goods

subsidies payments made by government to firms per unit of output

excess supply occurs when quantity supplied is greater than quantity demanded

savings gap occurs when low incomes earned in a country are not high enough to provide savings for those who wish to borrow for investment purposes

productivity gap the difference between the output per worker in one country compared with the output per worker in another country

foreign direct investment cross-border investment, usually by firms, that involves the acquisition of assets in a foreign country. FDI can be the purchase of a minimum of 10% of the shares of a foreign company but also includes the creation of productive capacity.

economies of scale the cost advantages gained by a firm from increasing the scale of its production. Average cost falls in the long run as the size of a firm's operation increases.

export revenue income that flows into a country from the rest of the world from the sale of its goods and services to foreign buyers

barriers to trade restrictions imposed by a government on the free exchange of goods or services between countries

import substitution the promotion by government of domestic industries by protecting domestic producers

infant industries a new industry which often is not able to compete against established foreign industries and therefore needs to be protected from the competition through subsidies and tariffs

poverty cycle occurs in a country which has low income and therefore low levels of savings. Low levels of savings means little investment can take place and the economy is unable to grow, thus income remains low.

loanable funds the sum of money in an economy that is saved rather than used for consumption and made available to those wishing to borrow

Compare and contrast the roles of aid and trade in economic development

LDCs are over-dependent on the production of primary goods in which they have a comparative advantage. However, as explained on pages 262–63, the world prices of such goods are falling in the long term, leading to a deterioration in the **terms of trade** and a fall in export revenues.

Many LDCs are dependent on agricultural output for export revenues. World productivity in this industry is increasing, pushing up supply and pushing world prices down. Governments in developed countries give **subsidies** to farmers producing particular agricultural goods, leading to increases in output and **excess supply**. The excess is often dumped in LDCs at below cost price, a price at which the LDCs are unable to compete, thereby harming their ability to raise export revenue with which they can buy much needed imports, such as capital goods and manufactured consumer goods.

Income earned over time falls, leaving less available for saving and investment. A large **savings gap** and investment gap leads to an increase in the **productivity gap** because LDCs are unable to buy the capital goods needed to increase productivity. With low income, LDCs are unable to save in order to invest in the production of manufactured goods, thereby reinforcing their dependency on a narrow range of primary goods. The cycle of low levels of savings, low investment, and low income continues and LDCs are unable to break out of the poverty cycle.

As discussed previously in this unit, aid, along with **foreign direct investment**, can be used to provide LDCs with the investment needed to improve the productivity of existing industries and to help them on the road to industrialization, thereby reducing their dependency on the production of primary goods. If the developed countries also removed the subsidies on agricultural output, farmers in LDCs could expand their markets into the developed world and thereby benefit from greater **economies of scale** and lower average costs. An increase in income could lead to an increase in savings and investment and reduce aid dependency.

However, the removal of subsidies on agricultural goods would harm the LDCs that are net-importers of food. The world price of food would increase as subsidies are removed. More of the LDCs' **export revenue** would be needed to buy imported food leading to deterioration in their terms of trade. A food shortage causes human suffering, leading to social unrest and political instability.

Developed countries that reduce or remove **barriers to trade** might only do so if LDCs do the same. **Import substitution** would be ineffective if the **infant industries** are not protected from the developed countries' cheaper imports. This reduces the LDCs' chances of industrializing and breaking their dependency on the production of primary goods.

Economists disagree over the role trade and aid plays in the economic development of LDCs. Many argue that LDCs are so poor that in order to break free from the **poverty cycle** the developed world must provide aid as well as agree to a system of trade barriers that favours LDCs, allowing LDCs to export their goods free of tariffs whilst at the same time being able to protect their infant manufacturing industries.

Examine the current roles of the IMF and the World Bank in promoting economic development

What is the World Bank and what are its aims?

The World Bank is an agency that provides advice and loans. It is owned by 180 countries. It raises **loanable funds** in the world financial markets and from the governments of the 180 countries. Therefore, the World Bank provides multilateral funds. The interest rate the World Bank charges is determined by a number of factors including the rate at which the World Bank has to borrow and the creditworthiness of the country that is borrowing. But it does provide low-interest loans and grants to poor countries for education and health.

The World Bank is made up of two main institutions:

The International Bank for Reconstruction and Development (IBRD) focuses on providing loans and advice to middle income countries.

The International Development Association (IDA) focuses on providing loans and advice to LDCs.

Its stated aims are listed below:

1. Investing in people through health and education.

2. Protecting the environment.

3. Supporting private sector development.

4. Helping governments provide good quality services.

5. Promoting reforms to create a stable macroeconomic economy that is required for long-term investment.

Its mission statement is: 'to reduce poverty and improve living standards through sustainable growth and investment in people'.

Like the IMF the World Bank believes that relatively **free markets** work best.

The World Bank focuses on relatively small-scale projects aimed at improving the basic needs of the people. The environmental impact of each project is assessed. Each project should promote **sustainable economic development**.

The World Bank focuses on providing advice and loans in the following areas of the world:

Africa, East Asia and the Pacific, Europe and Central and South Asia, Latin America and the Caribbean, and North Africa.

Most of the World Bank's work is done in the following development areas: agriculture, transport, rural and urban development, water and sanitation, health, nutrition, population control, gender equality, and macroeconomic policy.

What are some of the criticisms of the World Bank?

Some economists believe that government plays a very important role in managing demand through **fiscal policy** and **monetary policy**. They argue that the World Bank's free market, non-interventionist approach has a negative impact on the success of the World Bank's aims and can lead to a worsening of economic development.

Such economists argue that firms and households in LDCs do not have enough income to invest, or spend, and therefore the economy cannot grow. They argue that when this is the case the government should increase **aggregate demand** through **expansionary fiscal policy** and **expansionary monetary policy**.

However, the World Bank often makes it a condition of its help that governments must put in place **contractionary fiscal policy** and **contractionary monetary policy**. Higher interest rates, higher taxes, and a reduction in government expenditure should help to keep the **budget deficit** under control and reduce inflationary pressures. However, increasing interest rates and taxes and reducing government expenditure reduces the possibility of **economic growth** because of the likely fall in consumption and investment. Cuts in government expenditure also lead to a fall in spending on education and health, thereby restricting economic development.

Model sentence: Contractionary fiscal and monetary policy leads to a fall in aggregate demand and low rates of economic growth leaving households with less income to satisfy basic needs and wants.

The World Bank promotes **trade liberalization** and can make it a condition of a loan that **barriers to trade** be removed, thereby leaving domestic industries unprotected. Some domestic industries will go out of business because of the price competitive foreign imports, leading to an increase in unemployment and a fall in income thereby limiting the benefit the loan may bring. Some economists argue that in some cases the value of the HDI has fallen because of loans from the World Bank.

When an LDC accepts a loan or grant from the World Bank the LDC loses control of its fiscal policy and monetary policy. The government is unable to set policy in response to changes in economic conditions. Instead it must follow policies that are controlled by an institution that has not been elected by the citizens of the LDC.

Loans and the interest must be repaid by the borrowing country. Borrowing increases the **indebtedness** of a country. Debts build up over time. Repayments must be made in the future, thereby reducing the income available to spend on much needed services. More **tax revenue** is needed to pay these debts leaving consumers with less to spend on satisfying their basic needs. High levels of debt reduce future levels of income leading to falls in future levels of aggregate demand.

Model sentence: Trade liberalization leaves infant industrial industries unprotected, therefore many will close down leading to higher unemployment, lower incomes, and an increase in poverty.

exchange rate the price of a country's currency in terms of another currency

foreign currency reserves the amount of foreign currency and gold that is held by the central bank of a country

foreign direct investment cross-border investment, usually by firms, that involves the acquisition of assets in a foreign country. FDI can be the purchase of a minimum of 10% of the shares of a foreign company but also includes the creation of productive capacity.

portfolio investment the purchase of a variety of financial assets such as shares and bonds

current account deficit occurs when the amount of money flowing out of a country from the trade in goods and services, investment income, and transfers is greater than the amount flowing in

fixed exchange rate an exchange rate system in which the value of a currency in respect to another currency is set and maintained

inflation an increase in the general level of prices of goods/services in an economy over a given time period, usually a year

export revenue income that flows into a country from the rest of the world from the sale of its goods and services to foreign buyers

investment the addition to capital stock

raw materials the basic material from which a good is made

capital (goods) manufactured goods that are used in the production of other goods

devaluation the official lowering of the value of a country's currency in a fixed exchange rate system

current account a record of the amount of money flowing out of a country and into the country from the rest of the world from the trade in goods and services, investment income, and transfers in a given period of time

Model sentence: An increase in a LDC's debt increases the amount of future income needed to pay off the debt, leaving less income to spend on health and education thereby harming economic development.

What is the International Monetary Fund (IMF) and what are its aims?

The IMF is an organization of 188 countries. The funds the IMF needs in order to operate come from the member countries. The contribution of money is called a quota. Voting power of each country in the decision-making process of the IMF is in proportion with the amount of each country's quota. Large countries, such as the US, have a great influence over IMF policy decisions because the US pays the biggest quota.

The IMF's goal is to promote international economic cooperation in order to increase international trade, economic stability, and sustainable economic growth and thereby reduce global unemployment and poverty.

One of its aims is to achieve global **exchange rate** stability. A country goes to the IMF for financial help when it has a shortage of **foreign currency reserves**. The shortage might be caused by a lack of **foreign direct investment** or **portfolio investment**. A country may need more foreign reserves to maintain its exchange rate or to finance its **current account deficit**.

For example, a country with a large current account deficit might reduce the value of its currency in order to reduce the price of its exports and increase the price of its imports and thereby reduce the current account deficit. But this leads to exchange rate instability. Therefore, the IMF loans money to the country which is a current transfer that increases the flow of money in to the country's current account, thereby reducing its current account deficit. The country no longer needs to reduce the value of its currency and exchange rate stability is maintained.

IMF funds might be needed by a country that has agreed to fix the value of its currency against another currency. For example, a country wanting to join the EU must maintain a **fixed exchange rate** between its currency and the euro for a given period of time before it is allowed to join. If there is downward pressure on the fixed exchange rate the country must increase demand for its currency by selling its foreign reserves and buying its own currency, thereby increasing demand for its own currency and pushing the exchange rate up. If the country does not have the reserves of foreign currency to do this the exchange rate will fall and the country will not be able to join the EU. The IMF is keen that countries keep to these agreements and therefore will provide the foreign reserves so that the exchange rate can be maintained.

Many LDCs have large debts that they are unable to finance because of low levels of income. The IMF steps in to renegotiate the terms under which the debt has to be repaid and provides funding for the repayment of debt. But there are conditions put in place before the IMF will agree to help.

The IMF usually insists that the LDC introduce contractionary (deflationary) fiscal policy and contractionary (deflationary) monetary policy, these policies lead to a fall in aggregate demand which includes the demand for imports thereby reducing the amount of foreign reserves needed to buy them. A fall in aggregate demand helps to keep **inflation** at low levels, thereby increasing the LDCs, international competitiveness and increasing the amount of income flowing into the LDC from **export revenue**. A contractionary (deflationary) monetary policy requires a high interest rate on borrowing which reduces aggregate demand. High interest rates also act as an incentive to save, thereby providing more funds available for **investment**.

Model sentence: Contractionary fiscal and monetary policy cause a fall in aggregate demand which includes a fall in the demand for imports. The fall in AD reduces inflation leading to increases in the demand for exports and an improvement of the current account balance.

The IMF may also require an LDC to devalue its currency. An LDC might over-value its currency in order to reduce the price of imported goods, such as **raw materials** and **capital** goods. Also, an over-valued currency reduces the repayments on debt that must be paid back in a foreign currency. **Devaluation** reduces the LDC's dependence on imports, encourages consumption of domestically produced goods, and makes exports more price competitive. The flow of income leaving the country falls and the flow of income into the country increases. This leads to a reduction in the current account deficit and a fall in the amount of foreign reserves necessary to balance the **current account**.

Model sentence: Devaluation reduces the demand for imports and increases demand for exports leading to a reduction in the current account deficit.

What are the criticisms of the IMF?

Discussed below are some of the disadvantages for LDCs associated with dealing with the IMF.

What are the costs of contractionary fiscal policy and monetary policy?

Some economists argue that the conditions laid down by the IMF lead to an increase in poverty and hardship for citizens of LDCs. Contractionary fiscal policy and contractionary monetary policy that must be introduced as a condition for financial help reduces aggregate demand leading to a **recession**. Unemployment increases and household incomes and **tax revenue** falls. **Absolute poverty** increases and governments do not have the revenue to pay for basic services.

Part of contractionary fiscal policy is a reduction in government expenditure. The government of the LDC must reduce spending on the provision of basic services. This has a negative impact on **economic development** and the welfare of its citizens.

Part of contractionary monetary policy is high interest rates. A high **interest rate** does increase the incentive to save but it also reduces the incentive to borrow for investment purposes. A fall in investment leads to an increase in the **productivity gap**, an increase in relative **average costs** and a fall in international competitiveness.

Model sentence: A fall in government spending leads to a fall in expenditure on education and health and a fall in the value of HDI.

What are the costs of devaluation?

Model sentence: Devaluation of a currency of an LDC leads to an increase in the price of imported necessities leaving some people unable to satisfy basic needs thereby increasing absolute poverty.

Domestic firms have to pay more for imported raw materials which increases **costs of production** leading to higher prices and a fall in international competitiveness and more job losses.

What are the costs of trade liberalization?

A condition of help from the IMF is the removal of **barriers to trade**. In order to get financial help an LDC must remove trade barriers that protect its domestic industries. The domestic industries may go out of business because they are not able to compete against lower priced imports. This condition means that import substitution industrialization will be difficult to achieve because the country cannot protect its **infant industries** thereby leaving the LDC dependent on the production of **primary goods**.

The IMF decision making is dominated by rich developed countries. These countries, therefore, decide on the conditions that LDCs must agree to. The conditions on **trade liberalization** are likely to benefit the developed countries and not the LDCs.

Test your understanding of this unit by answering the following questions

- Distinguish between bilateral aid and multilateral aid.
- Distinguish between official development assistance and humanitarian aid?
- Discuss whether or not aid promotes economic development.
- Why do developed countries give aid?
- Explain the possible disadvantages to economic development of assistance from the IMF.
- Evaluate the World Bank's impact on economic development in LDCs.

Subject vocabulary

recession two consecutive quarters of negative economic growth

tax revenue the income the government receives through the levying and collection of taxes

absolute poverty occurs when people do not have enough resources to satisfy their basic needs

economic development the sustained increase in the standard of living and well-being of the population of a country

interest rate the percentage amount charged by a lender for money borrowed or paid to a person for saving money

productivity gap the difference between the output per worker in one country compared with the output per worker in another country

average cost is equal to total cost divided by quantity of output

costs of production the amount the firm pays for the factors of production used to produce goods or services

barriers to trade restrictions imposed by a government on the free exchange of goods or services between countries

infant industries a new industry which often is not able to compete against established foreign industries and therefore needs to be protected from the competition through subsidies and tariffs

primary goods a good that has not been processed and is in a raw state (e.g. fruit/wheat)

trade liberalization the removal of, or reduction in, the international barriers to trade, such as tariffs and quotas

4.7 The role of international debt

Learning Outcomes

- Outline the meaning of foreign debt and explain why countries borrow from foreign creditors.
- Explain that in some cases countries have become heavily indebted, requiring rescheduling of the debt payments and/or conditional assistance from international organizations, including the IMF and the World Bank.
- Explain why the servicing of international debt causes balance of payments problems and has an opportunity cost in terms of **forgone** spending on development objectives.
- Explain that the burden of debt has led to pressure to cancel the debt of heavily indebted countries.

Synonyms

forgone .. sacrificed/given up

Subject vocabulary

interest the price paid for the use of borrowed money/ the money earned from bank deposits

current account deficit occurs when the amount of money flowing out of a country from the trade in goods and services, investment income, and transfers is greater than the amount flowing in

foreign direct investment cross-border investment, usually by firms, that involves the acquisition of assets in a foreign country. FDI can be the purchase of a minimum of 10% of the shares of a foreign company but also includes the creation of productive capacity.

primary goods a good that has not been processed and is in a raw state (e.g. fruit/wheat)

consumer goods goods that are ultimately consumed by households rather than goods used by firms in the production of another good

capital (goods) manufactured goods that are used in the production of other goods

physical capital any manufactured good that is used in the production of other goods and services such as machinery and buildings

productivity the quantity of output per unit of input

recessions two consecutive quarters of negative economic growth

continued on page 281

Glossary

persistent continues to exist/ happen for a long time

What is foreign debt?

International or external debt is the total amount of money that has been borrowed from foreign financial institutions, such as the World Bank and foreign commercial banks, and foreign governments that has not been repaid. International debt includes the total amount of **interest** that must be paid on the money borrowed.

The reasons why a country must borrow from foreign creditors are discussed below. The main reason a country borrows is because it has a **persistent current account deficit**. Therefore it is important to examine the causes of a current account deficit. (See pages 227–30 for a detailed explanation of the balance of payments.)

What are the causes of international debt?

A persistent current account deficit must be financed by flows of money onto the capital account. The flow of money on to the capital account comes from inward investment, such as **foreign direct investment** and borrowing from other countries.

Model sentence: A country borrows from foreign creditors in order to pay for the deficit on the current account.

Why do countries have persistent current account deficits?

Some of the causes of a current account deficit in LDCs are discussed below.

Why does over-dependence on primary goods worsen the current account deficit?

LDCs are over-dependent on export revenue from **primary goods** and the import of manufactured **consumer goods** and **capital** goods. The long-term price of primary goods is falling therefore export revenue falls over time leading to a worsening of the current account deficit.

Why does using borrowed money to finance current consumption worsen the current account deficit?

LDCs use much of the flows of money onto the capital account, including borrowed money, to buy imported consumer goods to satisfy current needs and wants. It is not all used to invest in **physical capital** and therefore foreign borrowing does not lead to an increase in the future level of **productivity** of the economy. Increases in productivity would lead to an increase in export revenue that is needed to pay back debt. Using borrowed money to finance current expenditure does nothing to help the country earn more income in the future to pay back the debt and the interest on the debt.

Why does economic growth abroad affect the current account deficit?

During global **recessions** and economic downturns, world income and consumption falls, including consumption of goods produced for export in developing countries. This leads to a fall in export revenues of developing countries and an increase in the current account deficit

Why does the price of oil affect the current account deficit and the level of indebtedness?

Some LDCs are dependent on oil for **industrialization**. The price of oil fluctuates. When the price of oil is high more export revenue is needed to buy the oil, thereby worsening the current account deficit and increasing the amount of money LDCs have to borrow. An LDC could choose to reduce the consumption of oil but this would restrict industrialization and slow the **rate of economic growth**. When oil prices are high oil producers deposit the high profits in financial institutions which then have more money to lend. Some of which is lent to developing countries. When financial institutions have lots of money available for lending, and there are countries wanting to borrow, international debt can get out of control.

Some of the consequences of high levels of indebtedness are discussed below.

The large debts of LDCs are repaid over time from current income, leaving less income available for much needed **investment**. Debt therefore restricts industrialization and economic growth leaving LDCs dependent on the production of primary goods. The countries are unable to break free from the **poverty cycle**.

When an LDC finds it difficult to repay debt it increases the risk of non-debt repayment, therefore lenders charge a higher rate of interest on new debt to compensate for the greater risk and sometimes foreign financial institutions will refuse to lend money because it is too risky. Higher interest rates increase the burden of debt, making it more difficult for the country to make its repayments, and without the borrowed money the private sector is not able to get loans to invest, thereby restricting economic growth.

Model sentence: There is an opportunity cost of borrowing and increased indebtedness. In order to make the repayments on debt the government must reduce spending on infrastructure, education, and health services, negatively affecting economic growth and development.

Explain the causes of the debt crisis during the 1980s and 1990s

Large quantities of debt in US dollars were built up by developing countries in the 1970s and 1980s. In 1982 the Mexican government defaulted on its debt. This means that Mexico stopped paying back its debt. The country did not have enough US dollars to pay back its debt.

Some LDCs were finding it very difficult to repay their loans. The situation was made worse when, in the early 1980s, the price of the US dollar increased. Countries needed more of their own currency to buy dollars in order to repay the loans, while at the same time interest rates increased. Countries borrowed more money in order to be able to pay the additional interest payments. Some existing loans were at variable interest rates. This meant that when the interest rates increased the repayments on existing loans also increased.

In the 1980s and 1990s for some LDCs the debt repayments were greater than the inward flow of money onto the capital account leaving countries unable to invest in new industries, infrastructure, health and educational services. Poor countries became poorer as the effects of high levels of **indebtedness** had a negative impact on economic growth and development.

How might the debt crisis be solved?

Some of the ways in which the debt crisis has been dealt with are discussed below.

What is debt forgiveness?

Much of the debt of LDCs must be paid back to the governments of developed countries, the IMF, and the World Bank. LDCs, and some economists and politicians, argued that the debts should be **written off** or partially written off. If this happened LDCs could use more export revenue to buy more capital goods leading to increases in the rate of industrialization, productivity, and **economic growth**.

However, some economists argued that if debts were forgiven it would provide an incentive for LDCs to borrow greater amounts of money because they would believe that, if necessary, these debts would also be forgiven. This is an example of the **moral hazard** argument. However, some debts of very poor countries were forgiven.

What role does the IMF play in debt rescheduling?

Financial institutions and governments, as an alternative to debt forgiveness, have renegotiated with the LDCs the terms of the repayments of loans. This is called debt rescheduling. For example, the IMF has encouraged lenders to increase the length of time over which LDCs have to make the repayments and to reduce the rate of interest on existing and new loans.

The IMF has offered help to resolve the debt crisis but only if a set of conditions are met by the LDC. These conditions are discussed below.

Devaluation of the currency

A country needs to increase its export revenues and reduce its expenditure on imports in order to have enough foreign currency to pay back its debts. **Devaluation** reduces the price of exports and increases the price of

Subject vocabulary

continued from page 280

industrialization the process in which a country changes its economy from one based primarily on agricultural output into one based on the manufacture of goods

rate of economic growth the percentage increase in a country's output in a given period of time

investment the addition to capital stock

poverty cycle occurs in a country which has low income and therefore low levels of savings. Low levels of savings means little investment can take place and the economy is unable to grow, thus income remains low.

indebtedness occurs when a household, firm, or organization owes money

economic growth an increase in real GDP

moral hazard a situation in which an individual or organization acts knowing that it is protected from the risks of such an action

devaluation the official lowering of the value of a country's currency in a fixed exchange rate system

Glossary

written off cancelled

inflation an increase in the general level of prices of goods/services in an economy over a given time period, usually a year

export revenue income that flows into a country from the rest of the world from the sale of its goods and services to foreign buyers

contractionary (deflationary) fiscal policy policy involving the reduction of government spending and/or the increase of taxation

aggregate demand the total demand for goods and services in the economy at a given price level in a given period of time

disposable income household income after direct taxation has been deducted

trade liberalization the removal of, or reduction in, the international barriers to trade, such as tariffs and quotas

subsidies payments made by government to firms per unit of output

tariffs a tax placed on imported goods and services

privatization the process of transferring the ownership of an enterprise or industry from the public sector to the private sector

deregulation removal of government legislation and laws governing particular markets

capital (goods) manufactured goods that are used in the production of other goods

long-term economic growth an increase in the potential output of an economy

imports. More exports are sold, thereby increasing export revenue and fewer imports are bought reducing the flow of money leaving the country.

Contractionary fiscal policy

Inflation reduces the burden of debt repayments so some countries print money and create **inflation**. There are many costs of inflation discussed in detail on pages 149–51. One of the costs of inflation is a fall in the price competitiveness of exports. Inflation increases the price of exports leading to a fall in demand for exports and a fall in **export revenue**. The country must agree to reducing inflation. **Contractionary (deflationary) fiscal policy** requires increases in taxes and reductions in government expenditure which reduces **aggregate demand** and thereby reduces the rate of inflation. Low inflation increases the competitiveness of exports leading to increases in export revenue. Domestically produced goods also become more price competitive, leading to a fall in demand for imports and a fall in the money flowing out of the country for the purchase of imports.

Increasing taxes and reducing government expenditure may increase the amount of money available to repay debt. Increasing taxes means that the citizens make a greater contribution to the repayment of debt but leaves them less **disposable income** with which to satisfy basic needs. Falls in disposable income and reductions in spending on health and education can lead to a fall in economic development.

Trade liberalization

One of the conditions for loans is **trade liberalization**. LDCs must reduce or remove **subsidies** given to domestic industries and **tariffs** on imported goods. A programme of **privatization** and **deregulation** must also be introduced.

Encouragement of foreign direct investment (FDI)

The advantages and disadvantages of FDI are discussed in detail on pages 267–69.

FDI is an inward flow of money used for the purchase of a country's assets which is recorded on the capital account of the balance of payments. This increase of money flowing into a developing country is a valuable source of foreign currency, allowing for the purchase of a greater quantity of imported consumer goods and **capital** goods as well as the repayment of debt. The IMF believes that FDI promotes **long-term economic growth** thereby reducing the county's dependency on loans in the future.

Why does debt repayment cause balance of payments problems?

(See pages 227–37 for a detailed explanation of the balance of payments and a breakdown of the national accounts.)

A persistent current account deficit occurs when a country continues to spend more income than it is earning. In other words, the country is consuming more than it is producing. In order to do this a country uses its reserves of foreign currency to make up the difference between income spent and income earned. If this is not enough the country must borrow from other countries. Savings used and money borrowed are recorded as a positive on the capital account because they balance out the deficit on the current account.

However, a country cannot **offset** the current account deficit forever. At some point the foreign reserves will run out. The country cannot borrow forever because as debt continues to build up the country will not be able to pay the interest on the debt. The interest on the debt is recorded on the current account as a negative.

Model sentence: *Ceteris paribus*, as interest repayments increase, the current account deficit worsens and the country will need to borrow more money in order to offset the increase in the current account deficit.

An LDC in this situation will not be able to borrow more money because lenders will think that the country will not be able to finance the interest payments on the debt. If this happens the country will be **bankrupt**. When this is likely to occur the IMF can provide assistance by, for example, rescheduling debt.

Test your understanding of this unit by answering the following questions

- Why do developing counties need to borrow from foreign countries?
- Explain why borrowing has an opportunity cost.
- Explain why the current account + the capital account = 0.
- Discuss the causes of high indebtedness in LDCs.

4.8 The balance between markets and intervention

Learning Outcomes

- Discuss the positive outcomes of market-oriented policies (such as liberalized trade and capital flows, privatization, and deregulation), including a more efficient allocation of resources and economic growth.

- Discuss the negative outcomes of market-oriented strategies, including market failure, the development of a dual economy, and income inequalities.

- Discuss the strengths of interventionist policies, including the provision of infrastructure, investment in human capital, the provision of a stable macroeconomic economy, and the provision of a social safety net.

- Discuss the limitations of interventionist policies, including excessive bureaucracy, poor planning, and corruption.

- Explain the importance of good governance in the development process.

- Discuss the view that economic development may best be achieved through a complementary approach, involving a balance of market-oriented policies and government intervention.

Some economists argue free markets are necessary for economic growth and development and that government intervention in markets is a barrier to growth and development.

What are the implicit assumptions of the theory of free markets?

Consumers and producers are self-interested and they are maximizers. Producers aim to maximize profit and consumers aim to maximize **utility** from their scarce income. Some economists argue that when consumers and producers pursue their own self-interest, social welfare will be maximized.

Explain how social welfare is maximized when consumers and producers pursue their own interests

Price plays an important role in a free market economy. If utility from the consumption of a good increases **quantity demanded** of the good increases at each price. When demand increases for a good **equilibrium price** must increase in order to remove the excess demand. As price rises, *ceteris paribus*, profit at each price increases therefore firms allocate more resources to the production of the good, thereby increasing output in order to increase profit. Demand and supply is in equilibrium, therefore **consumer surplus** and **producer surplus** is maximized. In other words, **consumer welfare** and **producer welfare** is maximized. The sum of producer and consumer welfare is called social welfare. If price changes in response to changes in demand and supply then resources will be allocated to the production of goods and services that maximize social welfare.

In competitive markets firms compete with other firms in the industry, leading to price competition. Firms must keep their **costs of production** as low as possible so that they can compete at the market price. This means that firms in a competitive industry must be **productively efficient** in order to survive in business. That is, they must produce at the lowest possible average total cost. Therefore, each good is produced using the minimum amount of resources. This leaves more resources available to produce other goods, increasing the number of goods that can be produced from a given quantity of resources thereby increasing social welfare.

Does trade liberalization increase social welfare and economic development?

Governments intervene in markets in order to protect domestic firms. Governments of developing countries that are trying to industrialize pay subsidies to domestic manufacturing industries and place tariffs on imported manufactured goods. This policy is called import substitution. Governments can also devalue their currency in order to make their exports more price competitive. This policy is called export promotion. (See pages 201–206 for a detailed explanation of the welfare loss caused by protectionist policies such as subsidies and tariffs.)

Free market economists believe that when governments put up barriers to trade it causes welfare loss. More of the world's scarce resources are used to produce a given quantity of goods than is necessary. If each country produced goods in which they had a **comparative advantage** total world output would increase. If the countries traded then the citizens of each country could consume more goods thereby increasing welfare. (See pages 196–201 for a detailed explanation of the gains from trade arising from absolute and comparative advantage.)

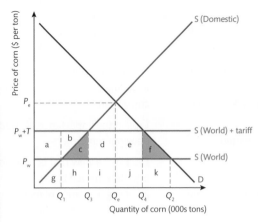

Figure 86.1

A developing country puts a tariff on corn in order to protect its domestic producers increasing the firms' welfare and the welfare of those employed in the industry. The world price of corn is P_w as shown Figure 86.1. Foreign countries are able to produce corn at a lower average total cost than many domestic producers and are therefore able to sell at a lower price. Domestic consumers pay P_w. The government sets a tariff and price increase to P_w +T. Domestic producers increase output from Q_1 to Q_3. Quantity demanded falls from Q_2 to Q_4. The quantity supplied by foreign producers falls from Q_2–Q_1 to Q_4–Q_3.

The less efficient domestic producers now supply more corn and the more efficient foreign producers supply less corn. More of the world's scarce resources are being used to produce a given output of corn than is necessary.

Consumers pay a higher price for corn thereby making them worse off. Areas c and f represent overall welfare loss. **Protectionism** may lead to a net fall in the welfare of the people of the developing country.

However, with more people working in the domestic industry, and the tariff on imports, the government collects more tax revenue, which can be spent on education and health thereby improving economic development.

Model sentence: Removing a tariff reduces the price consumers pay for goods increasing consumer surplus and the purchasing power of their given income. Consumers can buy more goods and therefore satisfy more wants thereby increasing their welfare.

The aim of import substitution is to protect infant manufacturing industries. Subsidies are paid to the manufacturing industry that in effect reduces the industry's costs of production and increases supply. Domestic producers now produce more goods and fewer goods are imported. Less efficient firms produce more goods and more efficient firms produce less. More of the world's scarce resources are used to produce a given output of goods than is necessary.

The price the consumer pays does not change, so there is no loss of consumer surplus, but the subsidies are paid from tax revenue. Taxes might have to increase to pay for the subsidies leaving consumers with less **disposable income**.

Model sentence: There is an opportunity cost of a subsidy. The tax revenue spent on the subsidy cannot be spent on education and health thereby harming economic development.

However, if the industry is protected it can grow. Unemployment falls and incomes increase over time. Once big enough the industry benefits from **economies of scale** lowering average total costs. The domestic industry is now able to compete with foreign producers on price. Then the subsidies can be removed.

Model sentence: In the long-term import substitution leads to an increase in domestic industry profits and employment and therefore an increase in tax revenue. The developing country can end its dependence on the production of primary goods thereby increasing export revenue.

Economic development might be improved by **trade liberalization** but this depends on the relative strengths in the long-term of the advantages and disadvantages of import substitution and export promotion.

Does privatization and deregulation lead to an increase in social welfare and economic development?

Privatization is denationalization. It occurs when the ownership of an industry or firm is changed from state ownership to private ownership.

State-owned industries often make a loss. Government subsidies, paid out of tax revenue or government borrowing, are required to pay for the loss leaving less revenue to spend on education and health thereby harming economic development and possibly increasing the national debt of the developing country.

Private businesses that are inefficient and produce at relatively high average total costs go out of business in the long term. However, loss-making, state-owned industries are subsidized because the government wants to protect jobs. The management of state-owned industries know that the government will continue to pay the losses so there is little incentive to use factors more efficiently and become more productive in order to lower average total cost.

Model sentence: Loss-making private firms will not survive in the long term if average total cost is not reduced. Privatization of loss-making state-owned firms therefore leads to improvements in productivity.

After privatization fewer resources are needed to produce a given quantity of goods and tax revenue will increase when profits are made, adding to total tax revenue. The additional revenue can be used to improve educational and health services thereby increasing economic development.

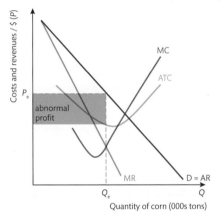

Figure 86.2

However, state monopolies have been brought into private ownership. With no competition and high **barriers to entry** the private monopolist reduces supply in order to increase price and earn **abnormal profit** as shown in Figure 86.2. This causes a misallocation of resources and a loss of welfare.

Model sentence: Privatization of an industry can lead to a more efficient use of resources, increases in productivity and a reduction in tax revenue used to pay subsidies. However, if the industry gains monopoly power privatization can lead to higher prices and welfare loss.

Deregulation occurs when barriers to entry into an industry are removed or reduced, making the industry more contestable. New firms can enter the industry, thereby increasing competition and industry supply. An increase in supply drives price down, thereby increasing consumer surplus. With increased price competition firms have the incentive to increase **productivity** in order to lower average total cost. In this way fewer resources are required to produce a given quantity of goods.

What are the effects of capital flows on economic growth and development?

Long-run economic growth is an increase in the potential output of an economy. It is caused by an increase in the quantity and quality (productivity) of the **factors of production**. In order to be able to grow, a country must save in order to invest. Fewer consumer goods need to be consumed today in order that resources can be used to increase the quantity and quality of **capital** so that more goods can be produced in the future. In other words, less consumption today means more can be consumed in the future.

The **opportunity cost** of investment is the benefit forgone from the present consumption of consumer goods. However, levels of income are very low in LDCs. Most people are poor and must spend 100% of their income in order to satisfy basic needs. It is not possible to raise enough funds for investment because savings are very low. People with higher incomes in LDCs often invest in foreign developed countries because of the higher rates of return and lower risks. Investment funds flowing out of a country is called capital flight.

LDCs are over-dependent on the production of primary goods, the price of which is falling in the long-term. Export revenue needed to buy imported capital is therefore falling, making progress towards industrialization very slow.

Model sentence: LDCs are stuck in the poverty cycle of low income, low savings, low investment, low growth, and low income and so on. To break free from the cycle, LDCs need inward investment.

Foreign direct investment (FDI) is an injection of investment capital from one country into the economy of another country (see pages 267–69 for a detailed evaluation of FDI). FDI can increase the rate of industrialization, reduce unemployment, increase income and tax revenue, and break the LDC's dependency on primary goods.

Subject vocabulary

negative externalities occur when the production or consumption of a good creates costs that must be paid by third parties. The existence of negative externalities means that social cost is greater than private cost.

natural resources assets, such as mineral deposits and timber, that occur in nature and can be used in production

economic growth an increase in real GDP

allocatively efficient the best or optimal allocation of resources from society's point of view. It occurs when the market is in equilibrium and social surplus is maximized (where P = MC).

external benefits occurs when the production or consumption of a good causes a benefit to third parties

external costs occurs when the production or consumption of a good creates a cost that must be paid by third parties

free rider problem occurs when people are able to benefit from the consumption of a good or service without paying the full price or without paying any money at all. The good will be under-provided or, in the case of a pure public good, not provided at all.

monopoly power the degree of control a firm has over the setting of price

marginal cost the change in total cost resulting from a change in output of one unit

profit/economic profit the difference between total revenue (price × quantity sold) and economic costs (explicit costs + implicit costs)

utility a term that refers to the benefit or satisfaction a person receives from the consumption of goods

private costs the cost incurred by firms or consumers from their own production or consumption of a good

continued on page 287

Synonyms

implied....... suggest/indicate

Glossary

respiratory related to breathing/the lungs

However, workers in the new industries are often paid very low wages. Most of the income earned is in the form of profit, and much of this flows out of the country to the foreign owners.

Industrial output creates **negative externalities** and the country's **natural resources** can be overused harming the future potential levels of output and income.

Capital-intensive methods of production are often used by foreign firms in LDCs. LDCs have a large surplus of low skilled workers. The use of capital-intensive methods limits the positive effects that FDI has on employment, wages, and **economic growth**.

A large firm investing in a LDC benefits from economies of scale and can produce at low average total cost. Small domestic firms are unable to compete and go out of business. The economies of scale are a barrier to entry which has the effect of reducing entrepreneurial activity.

The negative outcomes of free markets are discussed below.

Explain why free markets can lead to market failure

A free market is not necessarily **allocatively efficient**. Sometimes governments must intervene in markets in order to increase market efficiency. Left to the free market some goods are under produced and some are over produced. A market can fail when producers have monopoly power, when production creates **external benefits** or **external costs** and when the market does not exist because of the **free rider problem**. (See section 1.4 for a detailed explanation of market failure.)

Why does monopoly power lead to market failure?

(See pages 85–93 for a detailed explanation of the effects of monopoly power.)

Large multinational companies (MNCs) benefit from economies of scale and have strong brands. When an MNC invests in a developing country it has **monopoly power** in the market. New domestic firms cannot compete in the industry because of the high barriers to entry and existing domestic firms are driven out of the industry because their average total costs are too high.

The MNC restricts output to Q_e, as shown in Figure 86.2 (page 285), in order to increase revenue and profit. At this level of output the price is greater than **marginal cost**. That is, the value that consumers in society place on the consumption of the next unit is greater than the value of the resources used to produce it. There is a misallocation of resources and a loss of welfare due to monopoly power. Society's welfare would be increased if more factors were allocated to the production of the good.

Why does the existence of externalities lead to market failure?

(See the units on market failure for a full explanation of the effects of externalities.)

The **implied** assumptions in economics are that humans are self-interested and they aim to maximize their benefit. Producers want to maximize **profit** and consumers want to maximize their **utility** from their scarce income. When producers make decisions concerning the level of output they only consider their **private costs** and **private benefits**. When consumers decide on how much to consume they only consider their private costs and private benefits. Producers and consumers do not take into account the external benefits and external costs when deciding upon levels of production and consumption.

There are external benefits that arise from the consumption of education and healthcare. These are benefits that are enjoyed by third parties. An external benefit of these two **merit goods** is the increase in national income caused by an increase in the **value of human capital**. If left to the free market education would be under produced and under consumed and society would not gain the external benefits that arise from a well educated labour force. Those on low income would not be able to afford to buy an education for their children, therefore many children would also not gain the private benefits from education, leading to an inequitable society. Parents do not take into account the external benefits when deciding how much education to buy for their children, therefore the amount of resources allocated to education is not at the social optimum level and the market fails.

Industrialization can cause a market to fail. Firms, for example, do not take into account the external costs caused by pollution, particularly if laws governing emissions from factories are not strong. In China industrialization has led to an increase in air pollution leading to a rise in **respiratory** diseases. The external costs are high – many people are ill and cannot work reducing potential output of the economy and there are costs of healthcare that must be paid – output is therefore above the **social optimum level of output** and the market fails.

Why does the free rider problem lead to market failure?

Left to the free market, supply of some goods will be zero. Some goods are non-excludable and non-rivalrous. A good is non-excludable when once supplied by a firm people cannot be stopped or excluded from gaining the benefits available from consuming it. A good is non-rivalrous when consumption of it by one person does not reduce the amount of goods available for others to consume. In this situation there is no incentive for the consumer to pay so they will free ride, in the hope that others will pay. Because people will not pay, firms are unable to make a profit and therefore do not produce the good. Goods that are non-excludable and non-rivalrous are called pure public goods. National defence and street lights are examples of public goods.

Transport infrastructure is an example of a **quasi-public good**. It shares similar characteristics of pure public goods. Although it is possible to exclude people from using roads once provided there is no doubt that left to the free market the resources allocated to the construction of roads would not be enough to build a social optimum number of roads. Government expenditure is needed to increase output to the social optimum level thereby correcting market failure.

Why might free markets lead to market failure and an inequitable society in LDCs?

The level of skills and education in an LDC are low. The quantity and quality of the infrastructure, including transport systems, communication networks, schools, and health services are also low. There are many external benefits gained from these goods but left to free markets they would be under supplied thereby limiting economic growth and development.

It is argued by most economists that the government must intervene and make the investments necessary to increase economic growth and development. Society would also be less equitable without government intervention. For example only those who can afford education, training, and health services will be able to earn higher incomes, particularly in LDCs where highly skilled workers are in short supply.

Labour is the only asset owned by most people living in a LDC. There is a **surplus** of low skilled workers which pushes down the wage (income) that is earned from the asset. Left to the free market, without government investment in education and training, many people will continue to live in poverty while those few who are highly skilled, and those who own capital, earn higher incomes. The higher income can be used to purchase assets such as property, **saving accounts**, and **shares** which also generate income streams. In this way income distribution becomes more unequal and society becomes more inequitable.

Model sentence: Education, training, and health services generate external benefits that lead to an increase in economic growth and economic development. Left to free markets the market for these services would fail therefore the government must intervene.

What is a dual economy?

A dual economy occurs when two separate economic sectors exist in one country. For example, it occurs within a country which has a large rural agricultural sector and an urban industrial sector. A dual economy can come about through the introduction of import substitution and export promotion.

In time the demand for labour in the industrializing urban sector pushes up wages, leading to a poor rural population and a relatively richer urban population. Income distribution becomes more unequal. By focusing on industrialization most investment is centred on the expanding industrial sector, so little is left for investment in the agricultural sector leading to unbalanced economic growth.

A dual economy can also exist within one sector. For example when part of the agricultural sector uses **advanced technological capital** and the other part uses old, traditional farming methods.

What is unbalanced growth?

Unbalanced growth occurs when a country focuses investment in one sector. Some economists argue that governments of LDCs should follow an unbalanced growth strategy. For example an LDC does not have enough investment funds to invest in all sectors, therefore should focus investment on expanding the industrial sector. The industrial sector will therefore grow at a faster rate than the other areas of the economy.

As the sector expands, and supply increases, it creates demand for other goods and services. Firms that supply the growing industrialized centres will benefit from increased demand and the growing industrial centres will

Subject vocabulary

continued from page 286

private benefits the benefit firms or consumers receive from their own production or consumption of a good

merit goods goods that the government believes will be under consumed left to the free market. Consumption of a merit good may generate positive externalities therefore the social benefit of consumption is greater than the private benefit.

value of human capital a measure of the quantity and quality of the skills of the labour force that can be employed to produce goods and services. An increase in the value of human capital leads to an increase in labour productivity.

social optimum level of output the level of production or consumption where marginal social benefit is equal to marginal social cost

transport infrastructure the physical capital that supports a transport system such as roads, railways, ports, airports

quasi-public good goods that share some of the characteristics of public goods but are not fully non-excludable and non-rivalrous. A road is an example. Most roads are free at the point of use but it is possible to make people pay through tolls and when traffic is heavy the amount available to others to use does begin to diminish so there can be rivalry in consumption.

surplus occurs when quantity supplied is greater than quantity demanded, another term for excess supply

saving accounts a bank account which pays interest on deposits

shares a unit of ownership of a company's capital. The owner is entitled to a proportion of the company's profit.

advanced technological capital capital that incorporates new technology and is used in place of existing capital to produce goods and services, thereby increasing productivity

import substitution the promotion by government of domestic industries by protecting domestic producers

infant industries a new industry which often is not able to compete against established foreign industries and therefore needs to be protected from the competition through subsidies and tariffs

current account balance the sum of the value of exported goods and services, minus the sum of the value of imported goods, plus net income from abroad and net current transfers

comparative advantage when a country, firm, or individual is able to produce a particular good or service at a lower opportunity cost than other countries, firms, or individuals

labour-intensive industries industries that in production require a large amount of labour relative to the amount of capital

subsidies payments made by government to firms per unit of output

nationalization the process by which a government takes ownership of a private firm or industry

fiscal policy government policy designed to achieve macroeconomic objectives through government expenditure and taxation

monetary policy the control of the supply of money by the central bank to affect the economy (e.g. changing interest rates)

contractionary fiscal policy policy involving the reduction of government spending and/or the increase of taxation

contractionary monetary policy policy involving the reduction of the money supply and the increase of interest rates

aggregate demand the total demand for goods and services in the economy at a given price level in a given period of time

devaluation the official lowering of the value of a country's currency in a fixed exchange rate system

demand infrastructure, such as transport and communication networks. As demand rises, prices and profits increase, leading to an increase in entrepreneurial activity and an increase in new firms entering the market.

Through investment in a few industrializing centres and a policy of **import substitution** the developing country can protect the **infant industries** from foreign competition, thereby replacing the consumption of imports with the consumption of domestically produced goods thereby improving the **current account balance**.

Economists who support unbalanced growth argue that the government must intervene in free markets. Governments should direct investment into industries in which the country has a **comparative advantage**. LDCs have a surplus of low skilled workers, therefore investment should be focused on **labour-intensive industries**, such as the textile industry, and the government should protect the industry using **subsidies** until the industry has grown and the subsidies can be removed.

State intervention is limited to encouraging the growth of a particular sector, after which free market forces are allowed to operate so that as demand increases higher prices and profits attract further investment, leading to an increase in the allocation of resources and economic growth.

What is balanced growth?

Balanced growth occurs when different sectors of the economy grow at similar rates. The government of an LDC must intervene if balanced economic growth and development is to be achieved. The government increases taxes to provide investment funds for the **nationalization** of industries, subsidies to firms, and the provision of infrastructure necessary for growth. By spreading investment across different sectors the benefits of growth are not focused on just one sector. Balanced growth requires much greater government intervention. The government centrally coordinates and allocates the country's scarce resources so that the economy can achieve balanced growth.

What are the strengths of interventionist policies?

The strengths and weaknesses of interventionist policies are discussed below.

As demand increases for a good price, and profits rise, this leads to an increase in the quantity of resources allocated to the production of the good in order to increase output. When demand falls price and profits fall leading to a fall in the quantity of resources used to produce the good. It is the price mechanism that determines how resources are allocated in a free market.

The government may intervene in the market to achieve a different allocation of resources. Government may intervene in order to correct market failure caused by externalities or to create a more equal distribution of income or to achieve its macroeconomic objectives.

As discussed previously, without government intervention education, training, and healthcare would be under provided and under consumed. Left to the free market many people would go without these essential services thereby limiting economic growth and development and causing a very unequal distribution of income.

Transport and **sanitation** infrastructure, for example, are quasi-public goods. Without government investment infrastructure would be very basic limiting economic growth and development. People would suffer from more diseases and industry would be very inefficient without government investment in infrastructure.

Government must intervene to achieve its macroeconomic objectives such as stable and low inflation, low levels of unemployment, and sustainable economic growth. Government **fiscal policy** and **monetary policy** should promote the economic environment necessary for the achievement of these objectives. For example the government may need **contractionary fiscal policy** and **contractionary monetary policy** to reduce inflation in order to increase international competitiveness. To increase **aggregate demand**, investment, employment, and economic growth government may cut taxes and reduce interest rates.

Government intervention in a developing country is necessary to protect infant manufacturing industries in order for them to grow, thereby reducing the country's dependency on the production of primary goods for its export revenue. The government might need to devalue its currency in order to reduce the price of its exports, thereby making them more competitive. **Devaluation**, therefore, may lead to an increase in the country's export revenue.

Through a **progressive taxation** system the government can redistribute income more equally. Tax revenue can be used to provide **transfer payments** to households who are unemployed or unable to work because of disability or ill health thereby reducing **absolute poverty** and **relative poverty**.

What are the weaknesses of interventionist polices?

Resources must be allocated to the administration and carrying out of government policy. The more a government intervenes the more resources must be given over to the administrative process. For example, protectionist policies such as **quotas**, **tariffs**, and subsidies require many resources if the policy is to be carried out effectively. For example, a firm receiving subsidies must be overseen by government officials to ensure the subsidies are being used for the correct purpose and the government must allocate resources to the administration of nationalized industries. High levels of intervention require the use of many resources. There is a large **opportunity cost** of intervention. The resources are not available to the **private sector**. They cannot be used to produce goods and services. Labour, land, and capital used to carry out and administer government interventionist policies is unproductive, thereby reducing the potential output of the economy.

Import substitution and the supply of **merit goods** such as education, health services, and **quasi-public goods** such as transport infrastructure, require lots of planning and detailed knowledge. Central planners do not necessarily have the skills necessary to effectively carry out policies. They may not know the health needs of particular regions of the country. Planners may not have accurate information about the needs of industry. Lots of resources can be wasted on unnecessary investment projects. Badly needed basic health services may not be provided if the government does not have the correct information. Without accurate information and technical knowledge many of the country's scarce resources will be wasted.

How does corruption affect efficiency?

Corruption occurs when politicians and bureaucrats working for the government use their official public positions to make private gains. Corruption comes in many forms including the acceptance of bribes, fraud, and the theft of public money.

The firm which is employed to build infrastructure is often the one that is prepared to pay the government officials the most money and not the most efficient firm producing at lowest average total cost. Because of corruption, more of the country's scarce resources are used to produce the good than is necessary.

If firms have to bribe officials it increases their costs of production. Average total cost is higher leading to higher prices and a fall in competitiveness.

Public officials can ignore environmental concerns of an investment leading to market failure caused by **negative externalities** in the construction of infrastructure and the production of output.

Well educated and highly skilled people might be attracted to work as public officials because of the benefits available from the power of holding public office. People are maximizers, therefore many will work as public officials instead of working in the private sector. Scarce resources are allocated away from the productive sector to the unproductive sector. It is an inefficient use of labour.

How does corruption affect investment?

High levels of corruption reduce trust. If international and domestic firms fear that contracts will not be enforced it increases the risk of investment, thereby reducing the amount of external and internal investment in the country.

How does corruption affect human capital?

Public officials are more likely to allocate resources to the production of large-scale projects than into education and healthcare, because public officials can benefit from the payments large construction firms are prepared to make in order to get the job. Fewer funds are available for investment in education and health.

People have to bribe officials to receive education and healthcare. It acts as a tax on these services, reducing **disposable income** and aggregate demand. Some people on very low income cannot afford to pay the bribe and therefore do not gain the benefits the services provide.

How does corruption reduce tax revenue?

Lower investment and increases in business costs, because of corruption, limits profits and economic growth and thereby reduces the amount of tax raised by the government. Households and firms can also avoid taxes by bribing tax officials.

Subject vocabulary

progressive taxation a system of taxation in which the rate of tax increases with income

transfer payments a payment of money for which nothing is received in exchange

absolute poverty occurs when people do not have enough resources to satisfy their basic needs

relative poverty a measure of poverty that relates to the average income earned in a country or region. Definitions vary but many governments define it as an income less than 50% of the median income.

quotas a physical limit placed on the number of goods that can be traded or produced

tariffs a tax placed on imported goods and services

opportunity cost the next best alternative forgone

private sector the part of the economy that is regulated but not controlled by the state and concerns individuals and groups bringing together the factors of production normally with the aim of making a profit

merit goods goods that the government believes will be under consumed left to the free market. Consumption of a merit good may generate positive externalities therefore the social benefit of consumption is greater than the private benefit.

quasi-public good goods that share some of the characteristics of public goods but are not fully non-excludable and non-rivalrous. A road is an example. Most roads are free at the point of use but it is possible to make people pay through tolls and when traffic is heavy the amount available to others to use does begin to diminish so there can be rivalry in consumption.

negative externalities occur when the production or consumption of a good creates costs that must be paid by third parties. The existence of negative externalities means that social cost is greater than private cost.

disposable income household income after direct taxation has been deducted

Glossary

corruption illegal/immoral behaviour particularly by person(s) in power

Why is good governance a determinant of economic development?

Set out below are some of the characteristics of good governance.

Political legitimacy

The electoral process must be open for all to participate so that the government can act with the consent of the people that it governs. This will help to increase political stability, thereby promoting internal investment and inward investment that leads to increases in economic growth and development.

The rule of law

No individual or groups should be above the law. The law must apply equally to everybody in society. All people and all groups must be treated equally and everybody should know what the rules of law are.

Enforcement of property rights

If foreign and domestic firms do not believe that their property rights will be safeguarded by the government they are much less likely to invest in the country. Doubts concerning the enforcement of property rights increase business uncertainty, making investment much more risky. This leads to less investment taking place. In other words when property rights are not enforced it discourages economic activity. Investment is the most important determinant of economic growth therefore good governance must include the enforcement of property rights.

Accountability and transparency

Politicians and public officials must be accountable for their actions and decisions. All transactions between the government and the private sector and other institutions must be open and information on transactions should be freely available. This will reduce the level of bribery, thereby reducing firms' costs of production and lowering prices. Opening up contracts to fair competition between firms should ensure resources are allocated more efficiently. Fewer factors would be needed to produce a given quantity of goods.

The role of the state

The state should provide the opportunity for all to be involved in the political process and the state should work to maximize the benefits of all members of society. The state must create laws that enforce contracts and that allow for fair competition. This will promote FDI and internal investment and the efficient allocation of resources.

Correction of market failure

The state should correct market failure, caused by negative externalities of production. Public goods and quasi-public goods that are not provided by free markets should be provided by the government, including transport and communication infrastructure and national defence and security. Merit goods such as education and healthcare should be provided by the state so that all members of society can gain the **private benefits** from the consumption of these services and society can gain from the **external benefits**. The state funding of education and healthcare increases the **value of human capital** leading to increases in economic growth and development. State provision of infrastructure is essential for improvements in **productivity** and the promotion of industrialization.

Human rights

The government should protect the citizens from harm and suffering and ensure weak and vulnerable people in society are not **exploited** by the more powerful. Income should be redistributed so that no one is in **absolute poverty** and **relative poverty** is reduced.

There is a positive relationship between good governance and economic growth and development. Although no country meets all these standards, developed countries are much closer to meeting them than LDCs. Some economists argue that bad governance is the biggest barrier to economic growth and development.

Why might economic development be best achieved through a mixture of government intervention and market-orientated policies?

Most economists and politicians agree that all countries, including developing countries, need a mix of interventionist and market-orientated policies to promote economic development. The reasons for this are set out below.

1. Governments must intervene through fiscal and monetary policy to achieve macroeconomic objectives.

2. Protectionist policies are needed to protect infant manufacturing industries so that LDCs can break their dependency on the production of primary goods for export revenues. Free competition is likely to result in developing countries being unable to break free from the **poverty cycle**.

3. Governments may have to devalue the currency in order to make exports more price competitive.

4. A free market in which everyone pursues their own interest does not lead to an efficient allocation of resources. Governments must intervene to correct market failure caused by **positive externalities** and **negative externalities** and the **free rider problem**. A free market will not provide the infrastructure needed for sanitation and clean water, nor will it provide the transport and communications infrastructure. A free market would lead to under consumption of education and healthcare and under production of infrastructure. Intervention is therefore necessary for economic growth and development.

5. A free market leads to unsustainable economic growth. Without government intervention natural resources would run out and over production of the land would lead to a decline in soil quality (soil degradation). Industrialization would lead to increases in harmful emissions and poor air quality, increasing the external costs of production and the private costs of individuals.

6. A free market leads to a very unequal distribution of income. Governments must use the tax system to redistribute income more equally in order to reduce absolute and relative poverty.

7. Tax rates can be reduced by government to encourage much needed **foreign direct investment**.

However, a balance must be achieved because there are many benefits to be gained from competitive markets.

1. Privatization of state monopolies can reduce the waste of resources. If a firm must make a profit to survive it will try to reduce its average total cost by using resources efficiently.

2. **Deregulation** makes markets more contestable as it opens up markets to competition. This leads to increases in productivity, lower average costs, and greater supply thereby lowering prices and increasing the **purchasing power** of income.

3. The price mechanism leads to **consumer sovereignty**. As demand for goods increase, prices and profits increase, leading to an increase in the supply of the goods consumers want.

4. **Trade liberalization** leads to a fall in prices and increases in efficiency. Consumer welfare increases as consumers pay a lower price and the world's scare resources are allocated more efficiently because supply comes from the firms that are able to produce at lowest average costs.

5. If countries produce the goods in which they have a **comparative advantage** and then trade, the output from a given quantity of resources will increase and more wants can be satisfied.

Test your understanding of this unit by answering the following questions

- Explain the inefficiencies caused by corruption and bureaucracy.
- Why is good governance important for economic growth and development?
- Discuss the advantages of trade liberalization, privatization, and deregulation.
- Explain why government intervention is necessary for economic development.

Subject vocabulary

poverty cycle occurs in a country which has low income and therefore low levels of savings. Low levels of savings means little investment can take place and the economy is unable to grow, thus income remains low.

positive externalities occur when the production or consumption of a good causes benefits to third parties. The existence of positive externalities means that social benefit is greater than private benefit.

negative externalities occur when the production or consumption of a good creates costs that must be paid by third parties. The existence of negative externalities means that social cost is greater than private cost.

free rider problem occurs when people are able to benefit from the consumption of a good or service without paying the full price or without paying any money at all. The good will be under-provided or, in the case of a pure public good, not provided at all.

foreign direct investment cross-border investment, usually by firms, that involves the acquisition of assets in a foreign country. FDI can be the purchase of a minimum of 10% of the shares of a foreign company but also includes the creation of productive capacity.

deregulation removal of government legislation and laws governing particular markets

trade liberalization the removal of, or reduction in, the international barriers to trade, such as tariffs and quotas

comparative advantage when a country, firm, or individual is able to produce a particular good or service at a lower opportunity cost than other countries, firms, or individuals

Glossary

purchasing power the amount of goods or services that can be bought with a unit of currency

consumer sovereignty occurs when firms allocate resources to the production of goods in accordance with the wants of consumers

Internal Assessment

The idea of Internal Assessment (IA) is to give students the opportunity to demonstrate their understanding and application of economic theory to current real-world events.

Outline

The portfolio contains three separate pieces of work called commentaries. Each commentary, no longer than 750 words (see the IB Guide for details of what is not included in the word count), is based on a published news article. Each commentary must come from a different section of the IB Economics Course: Microeconomics, Macroeconomics, and International Economics and Development Economics. The whole portfolio is worth 20% of the final mark.

Ask your teacher for the section on Internal Assessment found in the IB Economics Guide and read it carefully.

Advice on writing the commentary

1. Choosing the article

- Each of the three articles must come from a newspaper, journal, or Internet news site (not from TV or radio broadcasts) and must be chosen by you, the student.
- Select articles that allow you to apply and explain economic concepts and theories that you have studied in class. Make sure that the article allows you to analyze using at least two diagrams. The article must not include economic analysis. It is for you to do this based on the general news story you have selected.
- Do not use long articles. Shorter articles are best. If you choose a long article you must highlight the parts of the article that your commentary focuses on.
- Articles should be topical. They must have been published no earlier than one year before you write your commentary.
- Each commentary must be based on articles from different sources. For example, you should not use two articles from the BBC news website.
- Consider using articles from local news media as well as from national and international news media.
- When writing your commentary you should use the same language as that used in the article. If not you must translate the original article and attach it to your commentary.
- You must not work with others on your commentaries. They must be your own work and it is advisable to pick an article that is not being used by other students.

2. Independent work

- The help your teacher is able to give you is limited.
- Your teacher can only advise you on the selection of articles – they are not allowed to search for an article for you. You must look for the article yourself and decide which one to use for your commentary.
- You can discuss with your teacher about which diagrams, concepts, and theories might be applied, based on the information in the article.
- Your teacher can read the first draft of your commentaries and feedback to you how you could make improvements; however the teacher is only allowed to give basic feedback and will not write down any suggested changes to the commentary.

3. Gaining high marks for your commentary

- Set out below are the criteria used by your teacher to mark your commentaries. The article should allow you to be able to score full marks for each criterion shown in the table below.

Criterion	Skill area	Marks	Top level descriptor
A	Diagrams	3	Relevant, accurate, and correctly labelled diagrams are included, with a full explanation.
B	Terminology	2	Terminology relevant to the article is used appropriately throughout the commentary.
C	Application	2	Relevant economic concepts and/or theories are applied to the article appropriately throughout the commentary.
D	Analysis	3	There is effective economic analysis relating to the article.
E	Evaluation	4	Judgements are made that are supported by effective and balanced reasoning.
	Total	14	

- When reading through the article write down the concepts, areas of analysis, and a list of economic terminology from the course specification that you could apply, ensuring that they come from the appropriate section of the course.
- Draw the diagrams (at least two) that could be used to improve economic analysis. If you find it difficult to apply diagrams and concepts then do not use the article and search for another.
- Write up a basic commentary structure. Set out an outline of each part of the commentary, highlighting the concepts and diagrams that can be applied along with evaluative points that can be made.

Writing your first draft

1. The opening paragraph

- This should include a very short outline of the article along with the key theories to be discussed. For example, the opening paragraph of your commentary based on a news story about a survey of air quality in Chinese cities might read as follows:

*Environmental officers reported that only three of the 74 major cities surveyed in China met national air quality standards in 2013. Rising industrial output has led to increases in **external costs** and **welfare loss**. Some politicians and environmentalists are considering policies that might reduce the external costs, thereby correcting **market failure**.*

- Study the IB criteria ensuring you understand how to gain marks. There are six criteria listed below along with advice on gaining the marks in each of them.

2. IB criteria

Criterion A: Diagrams

The diagram must relate to the news story. Each diagram should be given a title and be correctly labelled. You should:

- Write a brief introduction to each diagram along with a detailed written explanation.
- Remember to explicitly relate the diagram to the news story. A full, accurate, and relevant explanation of the diagram will help you gain top marks for criterion D. For example, if the article is about rent control you should draw a price ceiling diagram in order to help analyze the effects of a maximum rent on the market for rented accommodation, explicitly relating the analysis to the news story.

Criterion B: Terminology

Remember that you are writing as an economist.

- Use lots of economic terminology that relates to the article and define the words and terms that are central to your economic analysis.
- Terms should be defined only once within your portfolio of three commentaries, for example: *The economy moved into recession, which is two consecutive quarters of negative economic growth.*

Criterion C: Application and Criterion D: Analysis

- You should apply economic concepts that relate to the article. For example, if your article is about pollution caused by production, you would draw the **negative externalities** in production diagram and apply the concept of external costs and welfare loss, explaining clearly what they mean.
- Your analysis should relate to the events discussed in the news story. Say you have chosen an article that highlights air pollution caused by industrial output in China: the following passage shows how you might apply and explain concepts and write analysis that relates to the news story.

Subject vocabulary

third parties people who are not directly involved in a transaction but are nevertheless affected by the transaction. People who are external to the market

minimum wage the minimum amount of money a firm is legally allowed to pay a worker for one hours work.

relative poverty a measure of poverty that relates to the average income earned in a country or region. Definitions vary but many governments define it as an income less than 50 per cent of the median income.

stakeholders people or groups who have an interest in, or are affected by, the activities of organisations, particularly businesses

black market an illegal market in goods or services

As explained in the article, increases in industrial output in China have caused an increase in air pollution. This has led to negative externalities, such as the cost to **third parties** *of treating people with respiratory diseases. Producers do not take into account such external costs when setting levels of output.*

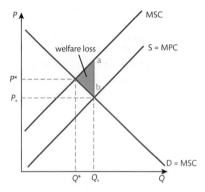

As illustrated in the diagram above, at the private optimum level of output QE, the marginal social cost of production, which is the addition to private costs plus the addition to external costs caused by producing the next unit of output, is greater than the marginal social benefit leading to welfare loss.

Criterion E: Evaluation

There are a number of ways you can make evaluative points.

- Say you are discussing real wage unemployment. Your analysis, along with a diagram, should show how the government **minimum wage** causes unemployment, and that by reducing the minimum wage unemployment falls. You can evaluate the extent to which this policy would be successful and how it might affect stakeholders. Evaluative points might include:
  i.   If the minimum wage is not below the equilibrium wage, removing or reducing it will not affect employment.
  ii. Reducing the minimum wage may provide an incentive for workers to reduce the number of hours they work or to leave the workforce altogether.
  iii. Reducing the minimum wage might lead to an increase in income inequality and **relative poverty** and cause an increase in the negative externalities associated with poverty.
  iv. Reducing the minimum wage might lead to the exploitation of vulnerable members of society.

- Say you are discussing the use of tax to correct market failure caused by negative externalities in the consumption of tobacco. Your analysis, along with the diagram, should explain how a tax can lead to the correction of market failure. You can evaluate the extent to which this policy would be successful and how it might affect certain **stakeholders**. Evaluative points might include:
  i.   Success of the policy depends on an accurate assessment of the external costs.
  ii. Tobacco is addictive therefore PED is inelastic. A relatively high tax would be needed to affect consumption and might lead to the formation of a **black market**. Government revenue from taxation falls but the external costs are not significantly reduced.
  iii. The tax per unit is a regressive tax. The tax might be described as inequitable. Those on low incomes are the most affected. They pay a higher proportion of their income in tax than those who are better off.
  iv. The extra tax raised by the government can be used to further reduce consumption. For example, the government might increase expenditure on negative advertising.

Criterion F: Rubric requirements

- To make sure you gain all 3 marks available in this section you must meet all five rubric requirements:
  i.   Each commentary must not exceed 750 words.
  ii. Each of the three articles in your portfolio must be based on a different section of the syllabus, e.g. one from the microeconomics section, one from macroeconomics, and one from international trade.
  iii. Each of the articles must come from different sources.
  iv. Each of the articles must have been published no earlier than one year before your writing of the commentary.
  v.   The completed coversheet for each of the commentaries, plus the summary portfolio coversheet, must be included.

Internal Assessment Economics	
Name	
Extract title	
Extract source (including hyperlink)	
Date accessed (if website)	
Date of extract	
Word count	
Date of commentary	
Section of syllabus	

3. Final checks

Once you have completed the first draft, hand it in to your teacher. They will give you feedback on how to improve the work and gain more marks. Before handing in a final draft, check that you have done the following:

- Met all five rubric requirements.
- Accurately defined the key economic terms.
- Included at least two diagrams that are correctly labelled and titled.
- Analyzed the diagrams using lots of economic terminology, with explicit reference made to events in the article – simply writing out a 'textbook' explanation of the diagrams is not sufficient.
- Included the main relevant economic concepts that can be related to the article in your analysis. Again, analysis should not simply be copied from the textbook – it must be related directly to the article.
- Included evaluative points concerning, for example, the effects of policy on various stakeholders, a discussion on the effectiveness of policy, and an examination of the validity of the economic concepts applied.

IA commentary – Example

Set out below is a news article concerning the Irish government's plans to reduce the costs caused by the consumption of alcohol. Read the article and consider the economic concepts that might be applied and the diagrams that might be used in the commentary.

According to the NHS, alcohol misuse means drinking excessively, that is drinking more than the recommended limits of alcohol consumption: 21 units of alcohol a week or less for adult men, and 14 units a week or less for adult women. Staying within the limits is known as 'sensible' or 'responsible' drinking.

The Irish Cabinet over the past few months has been discussing the issue of alcohol misuse and the measures it might take to encourage 'responsible' drinking. It was announced last week by the Minister of State at the Department of Health, Alex White, that the Cabinet has agreed to implement a range of policies designed to reduce the negative effects of the excessive consumption of alcohol, which include injuries, premature deaths, violence, vandalism, absenteeism from work and family breakdown.

The Minister of State said that the Cabinet was concerned about the wide availability through off-licences of low price, super-strength cider and lager, and cheap vodka, which has serious short- and long-term consequences, particularly for young consumers but also for the community at large. The Cabinet recognises that underage drinking establishes a pattern of consumption for life and that tackling this problem is a priority.

By establishing a minimum price per gram of alcohol, placing further restrictions on the advertising and marketing of alcohol, and extending the enforcement powers of Environmental Health Officers the Cabinet believes the negative effects created by the consumption of alcohol will be reduced.

The Minister of State sought to reassure the many publicans who voiced concerns, insisting that their businesses would not be affected by the proposed legislation because the price of drinks in pubs would be considerably higher than the minimum price. A source close to the Minister has suggested that the Cabinet is considering increasing the duty levied on alcohol. The drinks industry will be keeping a close eye on developments.

Adding his support for these policy measures, Health Minister Dr Reilly pointed to the burden on the taxpayer and on health service resources of alcohol consumption, referring specifically in his statement to

Subject vocabulary

private costs the cost incurred by firms or consumers from their own production or consumption of a good

external costs occurs when the production or consumption of a good creates a cost that must be paid by third parties

free market a market where the forces of demand and supply are allowed to operate without any forms of intervention

resources the inputs into the production process, the factors of production

market failure when resources are not allocated or used efficiently.

In the article the writer highlights a number of consequences of the consumption of alcohol, including both **private costs** and **external costs**, and he reports on the possible action that might be taken to reduce the costs. It is clear that you are able to apply economic terminology, theory and concepts, and use relevant economic diagrams in your commentary based on this article. Below are examples of how to meet the demands of the criteria – the intention is to give you a guide to writing a successful commentary:

- As stated earlier, your opening paragraph should include a brief outline of the article along with the main economic concepts that you intend to apply. Below is an example of an opening paragraph that sums up the information and the concepts. Remember that you are an economist and therefore must write as one. Note the use of lots of economic terminology. Do this right from the start and throughout your commentary. It will catch the eye of the examiner and help you earn full marks for criterion B: Terminology.

*The Irish Cabinet agreed to introduce policies designed to reduce the consumption of alcohol. As reported in the article, there are many private and external costs caused by drinking alcohol. Alcohol is a demerit good, meaning it is over-consumed and over-produced left to the **free market**. The negative externalities associated with its consumption cause a misallocation of **resources**, so the market fails. The Irish Government hopes that its policies will lead to a fall in both the private and external costs of alcohol and an efficient allocation of resources.*

- You must relate the economic concepts to the article. In this case you need to define private and external costs and give examples of them from the report. This meets the demands of criteria B: Terminology and C: Application. For example:

The consumption of alcohol generates private costs (costs borne by the individual consumer) and external costs or negative externalities (the negative spillover effects caused by the consumption of alcohol – the costs are borne by third parties). As stated in the report, the Irish Government recognizes some of the private and external costs caused by the consumption of alcohol 'which include injuries, premature deaths, violence, vandalism, absenteeism from work and family breakdown' as well as the cost to the taxpayer of treating the many patients in hospital 'with injuries and illnesses caused by drinking alcohol'.

- It is important to use at least two relevant diagrams in your commentary, which are clearly and fully explained within the context of the article. Using a diagram, you must explain how the consumption of alcohol causes the market to fail. In this case you need the diagram illustrating **market failure** caused by negative externalities in consumption. Remember to label the diagram appropriately. Set out on the right is the diagram and an explanation of it. Note how the explanation relates to the subject of the article. Doing this well will help you meet criteria A: Diagrams, B: Terminology, C: Application and D: Analysis.

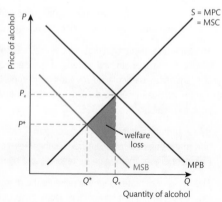

The consumption of alcohol creates social costs (private costs plus external costs). The consumer does not consider the external costs when deciding how much alcohol to consume. Only the marginal private costs (the addition to private costs from the consumption of the next unit of alcohol) and the marginal private benefits (the addition to private benefit from the consumption of the next unit) are taken into account. The consumer will consume up to the point where marginal private cost equals marginal private benefit. That is where the cost to the consumer of the additional

unit (which is mainly the price paid but also includes ill health and loss of income) is equal to the value of the benefit gained from the consumption of the additional unit. The private optimum level of consumption is at Q_e, as shown in the diagram above. However, the benefit gained by the consumer is greater than the benefit enjoyed by society as a whole. Therefore marginal social benefit is less than marginal private benefit and the marginal social benefit curve is lies below and to the left of the marginal private benefit curve.

At the private optimum level of consumption Q_e, marginal social cost (the addition to social costs from the consumption of the next unit) exceeds marginal social benefit (the addition to social benefit from the consumption of the next unit). This means the cost to society from the consumption of the next unit of the good is greater than the benefit society gains from the consumption of it. The social optimum level of consumption is at Q^*, where marginal social costs (MSC) equals marginal social benefit (MSB). For all consumption of alcohol between Q^* and Q_e, MSC > MSB therefore on each of these units of alcohol consumed there is a welfare loss. The total welfare loss is the shaded area in the diagram. There is a misallocation of resources (too many resources are allocated to the production of alcohol) and the market fails to produce an allocatively efficient outcome (where the social cost of the next unit of alcohol consumed equals the benefit society enjoys from the consumption of it).

- You might then address the issue of how the government intends to reduce the consumption of alcohol and thereby reduce the social costs and correct market failure. An effective explanation of how the policies of the Irish Government may correct market failure will help to meet criteria B: Terminology, C: Application and D: Analysis. For example:

The Irish Cabinet has approved an extensive package of measures to deal with alcohol misuse. These polices include minimum pricing (a price below which it is illegal to sell a unit of alcohol) and restrictions on the advertisement of alcohol. Some health specialists believe more resources should be devoted to negative advertising and educational programmes aimed at correcting information failure (which occurs in this case because buyers in the market do not have perfect knowledge of the social costs created by the consumption of alcohol) by informing people about the true costs of alcohol consumption. People weigh up the costs and benefits when deciding how much alcohol to consume. When in possession of all the information regarding the social costs consumers perceive there to be less benefit from the consumption of the marginal unit at each price and therefore demand falls. The marginal private benefit curve shifts down and to the left until the private optimum level of consumption, where MPC = MPB, is now equal to the social optimum level, where MSC = MSB at Q^* in the diagram. The government, by informing people of the full costs of alcohol consumption, corrects information failure and thereby reduces the quantity of alcohol consumed. Resources are reallocated away from the production of the good, thereby reducing the negative externalities and correcting market failure.

- To meet criterion E: Evaluation you must make evaluative points and judgments. You can do this throughout the commentary, not just at the end. Judgments must, however, be based on comprehensive and accurate economic analysis. In this case you might evaluate the extent to which the Irish Government's policies will succeed in correcting market failure. For example, in your commentary you might examine the following points:

Introduction of the policies may lead to government failure (occurs when government intervention causes a more inefficient allocation of goods and resources than would occur without that intervention). The reduction of consumption will lead to unemployment and an increase in benefit payments and a fall in income tax revenue. Taxes collected on the sale of alcohol, such as duty (tax charged per unit of a good), will fall. This will cause an increase in the budget deficit (occurs when government expenditure > tax revenue) and an increase in the Irish Government's borrowing requirement (the amount of money government must borrow from the financial markets in order to cover the budget deficit).

Success of the policies depends upon an accurate assessment of the **negative externalities** associated with the consumption of alcohol. If costs are underestimated, government action may not reduce consumption enough to correct **market failure**. If overestimated, then consumption may be reduced to a level where **marginal social benefit** exceeds **marginal social cost**.

There is an opportunity cost (the next best alternative forgone) of government action. For example, the **resources** used by government to correct information failure are then not available for the provision of additional public services.

Increasing the price through higher taxes or through the introduction of a minimum price might lead to an increase in informal market or black market activity. Consumption switches from the regulated, legal and taxed market to the unregulated, illegal and untaxed market. Consumption does not fall, so the **external costs** remain unchanged while the government collects less tax revenue.

demerit goods goods that
are overprovided and over
consumed if left to the
free market. Consumption
sometimes produces negative
externalities, in which cases
marginal social costs are
greater than marginal private
costs.

external costs occurs
when the production or
consumption of a good
creates a cost that must be
paid by third parties

external benefits occurs
when the production or
consumption of a good causes
a benefit to third parties

economic growth an increase
in real GDP

tradable permits an
allowance issued by the
government that allows a
firm to emit pollution up to
a specified limit. There is a
market for permits where firms
who have reached their limit
can buy permits from firms
who have not used up their
allowance.

positive externalities
occur when the production
or consumption of a good
causes benefits to third parties.
The existence of positive
externalities means that social
benefit is greater than private
benefit.

free market a market
where the forces of demand
and supply are allowed to
operate without any forms
of intervention

resources the inputs into the
production process, the factors
of production

merit good goods that the
government believes will be
under consumed left to the
free market. Consumption
of a merit good may
generate positive externalities
therefore the social benefit of
consumption is greater than
the private benefit.

subsidies payments made by
government to firms per unit
of output

fiscal policy government
policy designed to achieve
macroeconomic objectives
through government
expenditure and taxation

monetary policy the control
of the supply of money by
the central bank to affect
the economy (e.g. changing
interest rates).

continued on page 299

General advice for completing your commentaries

- Make sure you select a news report or article that allows you to apply economic concepts and theories and use economic diagrams. When reading the article, it should be clear which concepts, theories and diagrams could be applied.

- Write an opening paragraph that summarizes the content of the article, being sure to state the key theories and concepts to be applied. Remember you should, if necessary, rewrite the introduction when you have completed the commentary, ensuring that it reflects all the key concepts and theories that you actually applied.

- Remember that you are an economist so you must write like an economist. Use lots of economic terminology throughout remembering to define those important words and phrases.

- Throughout your commentary ensure that you always relate the economic concepts, theories and analysis to the subject matter of the article.

- Use appropriate diagrams and write out a detailed explanation of them using precise economic terminology, and remember to relate your explanation to the article.

- Evaluative points can be made throughout the commentary. Judgments must be based on and supported by accurate and comprehensive economic analysis.

- Make sure you meet all rubric requirements.

If you follow all of the advice and ask your teacher for help (your teacher is your most important resource), you should meet all of the criteria and gain high marks for your commentary portfolio.

The basis of a good commentary is an appropriate report or article that allows you to apply economic concepts and theories. Listed below are just a few suggestions regarding the type of subject matter that you might consider searching for, along with a few concepts and theories that it might be appropriate to apply – **it is not a comprehensive list**.

Section 1: Microeconomics

Look for articles that discuss the costs of the consumption of alcohol, cigarettes or fatty foods and measures that can be taken to reduce demand for them. These are **demerit goods**. They have negative externalities associated with their consumption, leading to a misallocation of resources and market failure. You can discuss why the market fails using the negative externalities in consumption diagram to illustrate your explanation. You can also explain, using further diagrams, how the market failure can be corrected along with an evaluation of each method.

Articles discussing the **external costs** and **external benefits** of **economic growth** lend themselves to the application of economic terminology, concepts, theories and diagrams. You can discuss why the market fails using the negative externalities in production diagram to illustrate your explanation. You can also explain, using further diagrams, how market failure might be corrected, along with an evaluation of each method. For example, it might be appropriate to discuss the use of **tradable permits**, regulation and taxes.

Articles discussing the external benefits of goods lend themselves to economic analysis. Articles on the benefits of education and training or provision of health care are ones to look out for. You can explain, using the **positive externalities** in consumption diagram, why the **free market** might fail, and discuss the relevant policies that might increase the allocation of **resources** to the production of the **merit good**, such as the provision of **subsidies** and the correction of information failure.

Section 2: Macroeconomics

Articles concerning government **fiscal policy** and **monetary policy** aimed at increasing economic growth and employment or at reducing **inflation** allow for the application of economic concepts and analysis. AD/AS diagrams can be used to illustrate your explanations. Evaluation might include the consequences of **contractionary fiscal and monetary policy** and **expansionary fiscal policy and monetary policy**. For example, you can discuss the impact of higher **interest rates**, introduced to reduce **aggregate demand**, on other economic variables such as employment, economic growth and the **exchange rate**. You might discuss the tradeoff between inflation and unemployment. A change in the rate of tax has many consequences. For example, you could, using the Laffer curve diagram, examine the impact the change has on the incentive to supply labour and the incentive to invest, and therefore the effect of a change in the rate of tax on the amount of tax revenue raised. Appropriate articles on macroeconomic policy give you the opportunity to do lots of economic analysis and evaluation.

Section 3: International trade

Articles concerning the introduction or removal of protectionist policies such as **tariffs**, **quotas** and subsidies allow you to apply economic concepts and theories, and to use diagrams in your commentary. For example, the many consequences of the introduction/removal of a tariff/quota/subsidy can be discussed using the appropriate diagram to illustrate your explanation. There are many advantages and disadvantages of protectionist policies, so such an article will allow you to make a number of evaluative points.

Some articles concerning exchange rates lend themselves to economic analysis. The causes of an increase/decrease in the value of a currency (such as demand for imports/exports, interest rates, inward investment and speculation) can be discussed within the context of the article, with currency demand and supply diagrams used to illustrate your explanations. The various effects of a currency appreciation/depreciation can be explored, including the impact on the relative prices of imports and exports, the **balance of trade** and the **current account**. Evaluation might include a discussion on the Marshall-Lerner condition and the J-curve effect.

Subject vocabulary

continued from page 298

inflation an increase in the general level of prices of goods/services in an economy over a given time period, usually a year

contractionary fiscal policy policy involving the reduction of government spending and/or the increase of taxation

contractionary monetary policy policy involving the reduction of the money supply and the increase of interest rates

expansionary fiscal policy policy involving the increase of government spending and/or the reduction of taxation

expansionary monetary policy expansion of the money supply and a decrease in interest rates to encourage consumption, investment and economic growth

interest rates the percentage amount charged by a lender for money borrowed or paid to a person for saving money

aggregate demand the total demand for goods and services in the economy at a given price level in a given period of time

exchange rate the price of a country's currency in terms of another currency

tariffs a tax placed on imported goods and services

quotas a physical limit placed on the number of goods that can be traded or produced

balance of trade the difference between the monetary value of a country's exports and the monetary value of its imports

current account a record of the amount of money flowing out of a country and into the country from the rest of the world from the trade in goods and services, investment income, and transfers in a given period of time

Extended Essay

Introduction

The Extended Essay is an in-depth study of a focused topic that promotes intellectual discovery, creativity, and writing skills. It provides you with an opportunity to explore and engage with an academic idea or problem in your favourite IB diploma subject. A successful essay will help you develop high-level research skills that will be invaluable at university. The final result will be a major piece of formally presented, structured writing, of which you can be immensely proud. Many students find the Extended Essay a valuable stimulus for discussion in interviews for university or employment.

The Extended Essay should be written in a correct and formal academic style. You are required to use the following format: 12-point readable font; double spacing, page numbering; no candidate name or school name on the title page or page headers.

The upper limit is 4,000 words. Any information that appears after the limit has been reached will not be read by the examiner, and will therefore not be rewarded. The following items are not included in the word count: contents page, diagrams, tables and charts, equations, formulas and calculations, footnote or end note references (if information is contained in footnotes or end notes other than for referencing purposes, this will be included in the word count), bibliography, and the 'Reflections on planning and progress form'.

Diagrams, charts, graphs, and tables must be clearly labelled and easily interpreted. They must relate directly to your research, and titles and labels must relate to the area under investigation; they must not be generic in nature.

Appendices are not required and will not be read by the examiner. Therefore you must include all relevant analysis, discussion and evaluation in the main body text. Avoid appendices other than for an example of a questionnaire or interview questions, and an example of permission letters.

There are six required parts of the final work that will be submitted to the examiner.

These are: the title page, the contents page, the introduction, the body of the essay, the conclusion, and the references and bibliography.

Title page

The title page must include only the following information: the title of your essay, the research question, the subject for which the essay is registered, and the word count.

You must not include your name or the name of your school.

The title of your essay must be clear and give the reader an indication of your research topic. It must not be a question. For example:

Title: *The externalities caused by the oil industry in Nigeria*

The research question associated with this title might be: *How does the exploration and extraction of oil in the Niger Delta affect the wellbeing of farmers in this region?*

Contents page

The contents page appears at the beginning of your essay. All pages must be numbered. An index is not required.

Introduction

In your introduction you should make it clear what the focus of your essay is. You should lay out how you intend to answer the question by commenting on the scope of your research and on the economic theory to be applied. You should indicate your line of inquiry and the line of argument you will take.

It is common practise to rewrite your introduction after you have completed your essay.

Body of the essay

Your essay should be presented in the form of a logically structured, cohesive, and reasoned argument. All conclusions should be based on appropriate and relevant analysis, and not merely your own personal opinions. It should be clear to the reader that your arguments are developed and based on evidence you have gathered and analysed.

Conclusion

In your conclusion you should lay out what you have achieved. You should comment on questions that have not be fully answered or resolved, and on any limitations of your: research, sources (both primary and secondary), and economic theory. Your conclusion should not be a list of all the conclusions drawn throughout your essay, but a final summative conclusion that directly relates to your research question.

References and bibliography

An Extended Essay must reflect intellectual honesty in research practices and provide the reader with exact sources of quotations, ideas, and points of view, through accurate references and bibliographies. Documenting your research allows the reader to evaluate the evidence for themselves, and shows your understanding of the significance of the sources used.

You should agree with your supervisor before you start your essay on the style of academic referencing. You should add references or footnotes as you go. Keep a list of all sources, including page numbers, as you may wish to use them at some point.

Marking criteria

The mark you receive for your essay is based on the extent to which your work meets the assessment criteria. Set out below are the IB criteria and how they relate to an Economics Extended Essay.

Criterion A: Focus and method (6 marks) - Topic, research question, and methodology

Your topic under investigation must be related to a specific event, issue, or policy that dates from no longer than five years ago. The topic must not be based on possible future, or hypothetical, events.

The research question must be appropriate for the subject in which the essay is registered. Therefore you must be able to apply economic theory to help you to answer the question.

The title of your essay must be written as a question. The question must not be double-barrelled; in other words it should not be more than one question.

The question must be focused. For example: 'What has been the impact of the oil industry on Nigeria?' is far too broad. A focused question might be 'How does the exploration and extraction of oil in the Niger Delta affect the wellbeing of the farmers in this region?' The question is now focused on a region, not a whole country, and on a specific community, not the whole population.

You must be able to apply economic theory in order to answer the question. For example the question 'How does the exploration and extraction of oil in the Niger Delta affect the wellbeing of the farmers in this region?' allows you to apply many economic concepts (e.g. market failure).

At the beginning of the essay you must explain why the topic is important, and why it is worthy of investigation. Your question must allow you to conduct meaningful research in order to answer it. The answer should not be immediately obvious.

At the beginning of the essay you must explain clearly the economic theory that you intend to relate to the essay, demonstrating why it is appropriate.

Throughout the essay you must show that you have chosen an appropriate range of sources, including: relevant secondary research, relevant economic concepts and models, and recent academic analysis.

You do not have to conduct primary research. However if you do, it might include an interview with a person who has expertise in the area under investigation. Surveys and questionnaires can be used if the results will give information that can help answer the question. The number of people surveyed must be sufficient enough to ensure that the results are statistically significant.

Towards the beginning of the essay you must outline the type of research conducted and the nature of the data collected.

Criterion B: Knowledge and understanding (6 marks) - Context, subject specific terminology, and concepts

In your essay you must show that you understand the economic theory that you apply. Your economic analysis must be accurate and detailed, and it must be clear that it addresses the question. You must also define the key terms that you have used in the body of the text, not in the footnotes.

All data used must be relevant to the research question. Knowledge and understanding should be demonstrated through the appropriate application of economic models. Where possible, the models should be based on information gathered regarding the topic.

All diagrams should relate to the topic of your essay; do not use generic diagrams from a secondary source. They should have relevant labels, numbers, and titles. Explanations of diagrams must be clear and detailed, and should relate directly to your topic; explanations should not be generic. Do not include diagrams if you are unable to demonstrate that they are relevant to the research question.

Remember that if your analysis is not relevant to the research question, you can only be awarded a maximum of 4 marks for this criterion. If your essay breaks the five year rule, you can also only be awarded a maximum of 4 marks for this criterion.

Criterion C: Critical thinking (12 marks) - Research, analysis, discussion, and evaluation

Research includes information gathered concerning your topic and research into relevant economic theory. If you include information that is not clearly relevant to the research question, marks awarded for analysis will be taken away- and you will not be able to gain a high mark for this criterion.

Economic theory should directly relate to where you are in your discussion and you must demonstrate that the theory relates to the real world evidence you are using. Your analysis must be supported by specific and relevant information from your research. You can demonstrate that your arguments are logical and relevant by linking them to the research question. You will be unable to gain high marks for this criterion if your essay is descriptive; it must include lots of analysis.

Analysis of all data in the form of diagrams, charts, tables, graphs and images must be close to where the data appears in your essay. You must clearly demonstrate that all the data you use helps to answer the research question.

To gain high marks for this criterion you must demonstrate that you understand the limitations of your own research and the limitations of the economic theory you have used. For example, you can assess whether or not the economic theory supports the real-world outcomes under investigation. If the economic theory suggests a different outcome, you should offer an explanation of why this might be the case. Your evaluation should not appear under a separate heading, in a separate section of the essay, or only in the conclusion; you must evaluate as you go along.

At the end of your essay you should then give a summative conclusion to the research question. Do not simply list all the previous conclusions that have appeared throughout your essay. Questions that have arisen as a result of your research may be included at the end of your essay.

If your research question breaks the five year rule, you can only gain a maximum of 6 marks for this criterion.

If the research question is not appropriate for the subject in which the essay has been registered, you can only gain a maximum of 3 marks for this criterion.

Criterion D: Formal presentation (4 marks) - Structure and layout

It is not a requirement to use subheadings, but you may use them if they serve a purpose. They should give your essay a logical structure, and they should always relate to what is written beneath them. However avoid using too many subheadings.

Only processed data should be included in the body of your essay. Any diagrams, graphs, charts, tables, and images used must be directly relevant to your research question and must clearly help in the development of your arguments. Your essay should not include an excessive number of graphs, charts, and tables, as too many will disrupt the flow of your arguments. They must all be of a good visual quality. Tables containing lots of raw data should be included in an appendix, not in the main body of the essay. Tables should not include excessive amounts of text; if they do, the words will be included in the word count.

Examiners are not required to read your appendices, therefore all information that relates directly to your analysis and evaluation should be included in the essay.

You must formally acknowledge any data, ideas, comments or arguments that are not your own. These must be referenced and must include the name of the author, the date of publication, the title of the source and the page number (where applicable). You must present your bibliography in a standard format.

Your essay should be no longer than 4,000 words. Diagrams, graphs, calculations, formulas and equations are not included in the word count. Examiners will not read more than 4,000 words, and any writing or processed data beyond 4,000 words will not be marked.

Criterion E: Engagement (6 marks) - Process and research focus

After assessing your essay, the examiner will then mark this criterion.

Marks awarded for this criterion are based on your reflections in the 'Reflections on planning and progress' form. Your reflections on the form should be no more than 500 words. The examiner will also take into account your supervisor's comments.

You must write your reflections on the decision making and planning process you undertook whilst completing your essay.

This should include a description of the process you went through when choosing your topic. You should include a comment on how and why you decided upon the final research question. If you changed your topic during the planning of your essay, or refocused your research question, explain why.

You can reflect on the methods and approach you finally used. Reflect on the decisions you took regarding your research and the economic theory you applied.

You might reflect on the relative success of your approach, including possible weaknesses. You might reflect on problems that arose with your primary and secondary research, and what you did to overcome these problems- or what you would do differently if you were to do the research again.

You might consider how and why your understanding of the topic has changed since researching and writing your essay.

You might also reflect on the success or otherwise of the economic theory applied and suggest possible alternatives that might have been appropriate.

In your reflections you must demonstrate that you have been on a journey of discovery throughout the process of researching and writing your essay. Your reflections must not solely be descriptive. You must show the examiner that you have thought critically throughout the process of researching and writing your essay, and that you have questioned the approach you have taken.

Reflections on planning and progress form

Make sure you get a copy of this form from your supervisor at the beginning of the process. You must complete this form whilst you are researching and writing your essay.

You will have three formal reflection sessions with your supervisor, each lasting about 30 minutes.

In the first session you should focus on your initial ideas and the type of research that needs to be undertaken.

The interim session takes place after you have completed a significant amount of research.

The final reflection session is an interview (*viva voce*) with your supervisor that takes place after you have handed in your Extended Essay. Your supervisor might ask you questions concerning your approach and methods. The supervisor may ask you about the suitability of the economic theory you applied, your analysis and conclusions, and what you have learned throughout the process.

After each session you must record your reflections on the form, and these must be signed and dated by your supervisor.

Your three reflections combined must be no more than 500 words.

The form is submitted along with your essay and is used by the examiner to assess Criterion E.

Check-in sessions

Outside of your formal reflection sessions you may meet up with your supervisor. The number and duration of these meetings will depend upon your needs. For example, you can meet up briefly if you wish to clarify the application of a concept or are confused over a piece of economic analysis. Alternatively, you may want to meet up for a longer period of time to discuss possible changes to your topic or question. You might also want to discuss access to resources. These meetings are not part of the formal reflection process and do not need to be formally recorded.

How to write an email requesting help

You may wish to contact an academic directly to ask for further details of a paper they have published or for other information. In some cases, you may wish to arrange to meet them to discuss a particular matter.

General tips

Being a young person carrying our challenging research, you will probably find that people are very willing to help you, providing you approach them politely and respectfully.

- Keep it **brief**. Show that you respect the fact that they are busy.
- Make a **request**; do not demand. You are asking a favour.
- Be **polite**, not sycophantic. It is a good idea to show an interest in their work, but flattery will just make you look naïve (e.g. say you are 'interested', not 'enthralled' or 'intrigued').
- Be as **specific** as possible. Do not make vague requests for assistance and certainly don't make it sound as if you want them to do the project for you!

Example:

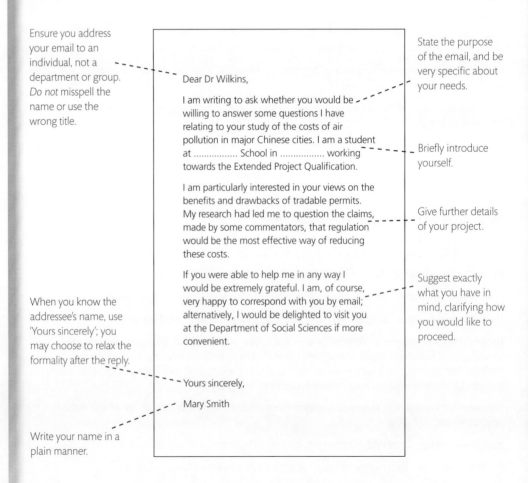

Ensure you address your email to an individual, not a department or group. *Do not* misspell the name or use the wrong title.

State the purpose of the email, and be very specific about your needs.

Dear Dr Wilkins,

I am writing to ask whether you would be willing to answer some questions I have relating to your study of the costs of air pollution in major Chinese cities. I am a student at .... School in .... working towards the Extended Project Qualification.

Briefly introduce yourself.

I am particularly interested in your views on the benefits and drawbacks of tradable permits. My research had led me to question the claims, made by some commentators, that regulation would be the most effective way of reducing these costs.

Give further details of your project.

If you were able to help me in any way I would be extremely grateful. I am, of course, very happy to correspond with you by email; alternatively, I would be delighted to visit you at the Department of Social Sciences if more convenient.

Suggest exactly what you have in mind, clarifying how you would like to proceed.

When you know the addressee's name, use 'Yours sincerely'; you may choose to relax the formality after the reply.

Yours sincerely,

Mary Smith

Write your name in a plain manner.

Bibliography

- You must provide an alphabetical list of all of the works you use at the end of your essay. (Works which you have read but found to be irrelevant or unhelpful can be omitted.)
- In the academic world there are various systems, all with specific rules on how to cite. You might choose to follow the 'Notes and Bibliography' version of the **Chicago** system. Discuss this with your teacher.
- Set out below are examples of how you should write up the bibliography for various types of publications using the Chicago system:

Book	Wolf, M. *Why Globalization Works*. Yale University Press: New Haven and London, 2004
Introduction or preface	Hawken, P. Introduction to *Small is Beautiful: a Study of Economics as if People Mattered*, by E.F. Schumacher. Hartley and Marks Publishers Inc., 1999
Article in a journal	Akitomi, H. 'The British Trade Policy Plan During the First World War: a Modified "Imperialism of Free Trade"?' *The Journal of European Economic History*, Volume 35, Number 3, (Winter 2006): 617–643
Article in newspaper	Ford, R. 'UKIP Have Torn up the Map.' *The Daily Telegraph*, May 27, 2014
Websites, web page	BBC News UK. 'Air Pollution: High Levels to Spread across England.' BBC. http://www.bbc.co.uk/news/uk-26844425 (accessed May 27, 2014)
Film & TV documentaries, interviews, etc.	*The World at War*. 1973. [Television series] Directed by Ted Childs and Martin Smith. England: Thames Television

- For a type of text (or other source) not outlined above, please refer to *The Chicago Manual of Style* for guidance: http://www.chicagomanualofstyle.org/tools_citationguide.html

Generating a bibliography in Word

Formatting a bibliography correctly can be a time-consuming and laborious business. Thankfully, Word has a feature which does all of the formatting for you – though you do still have to enter all of the publication data yourself.

- First, select 'Chicago' from the drop-down menu under 'Citations and Bibliography' on the 'References' tab (this refers to the referencing style):

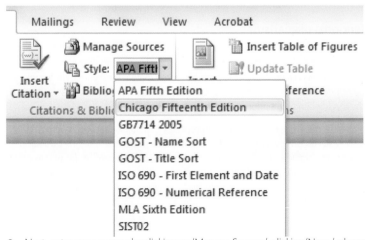

- Next, enter your sources by clicking on 'Manage Sources', clicking 'New...', choosing the type of source, and then entering information into the fields. For a book, the default fields that appear are:

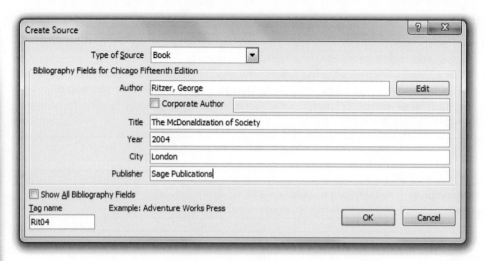

- Once all of your various sources have been entered, select them in the 'Master List' box (on the left) and click 'Copy' to add them to the 'Current List' (on the right).
- Generating the bibliography is now only a matter of choosing 'Bibliography' and then 'Insert Bibliography'. This will sort all of the entries by author, present them with a professional-looking hanging indent, place the publishing details for each in the right order, and format them correctly (using brackets, italics etc.).
- The information in the example above results in the following line being generated:

  Ritzer, George. *The McDonaldization of Society*. London: Sage Publications, 2006.

- Consult your teacher regarding using the Chicago footnoting method.

A note on plagiarism

What is plagiarism?

When you present someone else's ideas as your own, whether orally or on paper, you are plagiarizing that person's work. Plagiarism is therefore a form of cheating. Learning to take on other people's ideas and to use them as a way of framing your own understanding is an important skill, however, and it is the responsibility of your school to make sure you understand the line between this kind of proper scholarship and plagiarism.

Some plagiarism is deliberate: for example, when pupils cut and paste material from a website, copy coursework from other pupils, or reproduce passages from a book and pretend it is their own original work. More commonly, plagiarism comes about as a result of inexperience or ignorance of the rules of scholarship. This can be avoided if pupils listen very carefully to the advice and guidelines given by teachers when setting up coursework tasks, or other projects that involve analysis or research.

How can I avoid unintentional plagiarism?

Whenever you take notes from a book you are reading, or material from a website, you must discipline yourself to make a note of the source, which should include the title of the book and its author, and the number of the page from which the information has been taken. This is true both of quoted material and your own summary of what a writer says. If you do not do this, it is sometimes hard to remember which were your ideas and which were from another source, and this is when unintentional plagiarism can happen.

When you write your essay, you must make clear when you are using ideas or material that you have noted down from someone else's work. You can do this by putting the source details in brackets after the quotation or summary of the idea, or by means of a footnote. You must also include any of these references (as well as other texts you have consulted but not quoted from) in a bibliography, which is a list of those books that you have consulted and used in your essay. This is part of good scholarship, and you will get marks for acknowledging your sources in this way.

Glossary: Command terms

Analyze Break down in order to bring out the essential elements or structure.

Apply Use an idea, equation, principle, theory, or law in relation to a given problem or issue.

Calculate Obtain a numerical answer showing the relevant stages in the working.

Comment Give a judgment based on a given statement or result of a calculation.

Compare Give an account of the similarities between two (or more) items or situations, referring to both (all) of them throughout.

Compare and contrast Give an account of similarities and differences between two (or more) items or situations, referring to both (all) of them throughout.

Construct Display information in a diagrammatic or logical form.

Contrast Give an account of the differences between two (or more) items or situations, referring to both (all) of them throughout.

Define Give the precise meaning of a word, phrase, concept, or physical quantity.

Derive Manipulate a mathematical relationship to give a new equation or relationship.

Describe Give a detailed account.

Determine Obtain the only possible answer.

Discuss Offer a considered and balanced review that includes a range of arguments, factors, or hypotheses. Opinions or conclusions should be presented clearly and supported by appropriate evidence.

Distinguish Make clear the differences between two or more concepts or items.

Draw Represent by means of a labelled, accurate diagram or graph, using a pencil. A ruler (straight edge) should be used for straight lines. Diagrams should be drawn to scale. Graphs should have points correctly plotted (if appropriate) and joined in a straight line or smooth curve.

Evaluate Make an appraisal by weighing up the strengths and limitations.

Examine Consider an argument or concept in a way that uncovers the assumptions and interrelationships of the issue.

Explain Give a detailed account including reasons or causes.

Identify Provide an answer from a number of possibilities.

Justify Give valid reasons or evidence to support an answer or conclusion.

Label Add labels to a diagram.

List Give a sequence of brief answers with no explanation.

Measure Obtain a value for a quantity.

Outline Give a brief account or summary.

Plot Mark the position of points on a diagram.

Show Give the steps in a calculation or derivation.

Show that Obtain the required result (possibly using information given) without the formality of proof. "Show that" questions do not generally require the use of a calculator.

Sketch Represent by means of a diagram or graph (labelled as appropriate). The sketch should give a general idea of the required shape or relationship, and should include relevant features.

Solve Obtain the answer(s) using algebraic and/or numerical and/or graphical methods.

State Give a specific name, value, or other brief answer without explanation or calculation.

Suggest Propose a solution, hypothesis, or other possible answer.

To what extent Consider the merits or otherwise of an argument or concept. Opinions and conclusions should be presented clearly and supported with appropriate evidence and sound argument.

Index

Improve your learning

Take a look at some of the interactive tools on your eText.

Note that the examples below may be from a different title, but you will find topic-appropriate resources on your eText.

Vocabulary lists

Complete vocabulary lists help support you to understand any unusual terms.

Theory of Knowledge

Supporting every learner across the IB continuum

Aboriginal people the people who have been in a region since ancient times

abstract existing in thought as an idea without an actual existence

abstract ideas existing in thought as an idea without actual existence

abstractions things reduced to their most basic characteristics

acquired to have taken possession or ownership of

adopted legally made part of a family that someone was not born into

agnostics people who doubt that there is a God

agricultural purposes related to farming

algebra the part of mathematics that uses letters and other general symbols to represent numbers, and quantities in formulae and equations

Allah the Muslim name for God

altruistic unselfish, willing to make sacrifices

ambiguity confusion because words or sentences have more than one meaning

Amish a Christian group living in old-fashioned ways in Pennsylvania and Ohio

...ysing engaging in a detailed examination
  ... detailed examination

...metry the branch of algebra that
  ...tric objects such as points, lines,

atheists people who do not believe... deities

atom the smallest component of an... living thing

audience participation the ability of t... to take part, ask questions

authoritarian governments governme... concentrate power in the hands of ... small group; people are not given fr... rights

authority figures people in a position ... over someone else

authority right to be believed or hav...

autism a mental condition that begi... childhood and which causes diffi... human communication and lan...

awakening reaching a higher lev...

axioms basic rules in mathema... considered to be absolute...

Babylon Noah's city in Ir... was the capital of a...

Behaviourists psy... observable, s...

biases opi... ide...

Audio

Audio versions of definitions and articulation sentences help you to understand and unlock key information.

...gy

1.1 Introduction to cells

Main idea

In many celled organisms, individual cells take on specific tasks. Individual cells may replace damaged or diseased cells when needed.

Understanding: According to the cell theory, living organisms are composed of cells.

Model sentence: The cell theory **states that** organisms **are made up of one or more cells.**

- Some living organisms are composed of only one cell, such as *Paramecium*. These organisms are referred to as unicellular.
- Multicellular organisms, such as trees and birds, are composed of many cells.

Hints for success: Whenever the term organism is used, think of cells and life.

Nature of science: In biology, there are often exceptions to theories and belief... There are exceptions to the cell theory statement that says all organisms ar... made up of cells.

...ntists recognize that exceptions to the cell theory include giant fun... ...ot have walls separating cells, and striated muscle cells in...

...ulary

...rtant cellular
...that all
...of one or
...e smallest
...ome from
...exist

...ng the

Interactive glossary

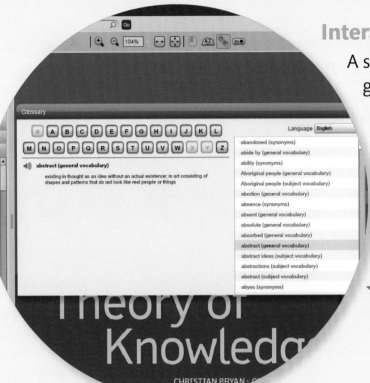

A searchable audio glossary gives you a handy reference tool for any difficult words, with audio to support your learning. Select highlighted words in the text to hear the audio version of the term and definition.

Notes

Add and save handy notes to help aid your revision.

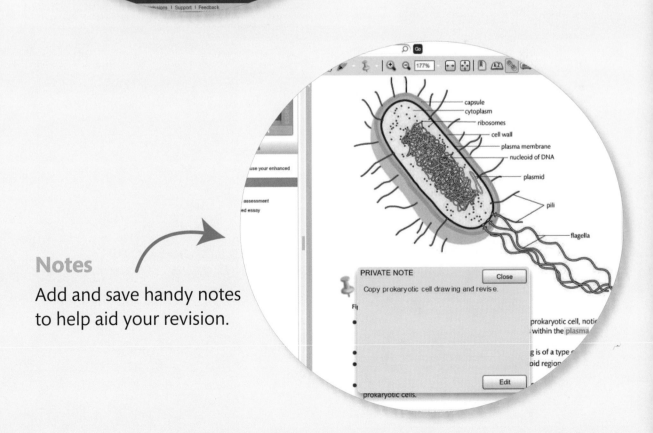